1415

Ian Mortimer has BA and PhD degrees in history from Exeter University and an MA in archive studies from University College London. He was elected a Fellow of the Royal Historical Society in 1998, and was awarded the Alexander Prize (2004) by the Royal Historical Society for his work on the social history of medicine. He is the author of three other medieval biographies, *The Greatest Traitor: The Life of Sir Roger Mortimer* (2003), *The Perfect King: The Life of Edward III* (2006) and *The Fears of Henry IV: The Life of England's Self-Made King* (2007) as well as the bestselling *The Time Traveller's Guide to Medieval England* (2008). He lives with his wife and three children on the edge of Dartmoor.

ALSO BY IAN MORTIMER

The Greatest Traitor:
The Life of Sir Roger Mortimer,
1st Earl of March,
Ruler of England, 1327–1330

The Perfect King:
The Life of Edward III,
Father of the English Nation

The Fears of Henry IV:
The Life of England's Self-made King

The Time Traveller's Guide to
Medieval England:
A Handbook for Visitors to the
Fourteenth Century

IAN MORTIMER

1415

Henry V's Year of Glory

VINTAGE BOOKS
London

Published by Vintage 2010

2 4 6 8 10 9 7 5 3 1

First published in Great Britain in 2009 by The Bodley Head

Vintage
Random House, 20 Vauxhall Bridge Road,
London SW1V 2SA

www.vintage-books.co.uk

Addresses for companies within The Random House Group Limited
can be found at: www.randomhouse.co.uk/offices.htm

The Random House Group Limited Reg. No. 954009

A CIP catalogue record for this book
is available from the British Library

ISBN 9781845950972

The Random House Group Limited supports The Forest Stewardship
Council (FSC), the leading international forest certification organisation.
All our titles that are printed on Greenpeace approved FSC certified
paper carry the FSC logo. Our paper procurement policy can
be found at www.rbooks.co.uk/environment

Mixed Sources
Product group from well-managed
forests and other controlled sources
www.fsc.org Cert no. TT-COC-2139
© 1996 Forest Stewardship Council
FSC

Typeset by Palimpsest Book Production Ltd,
Falkirk, Stirlingshire
Printed and bound in Great Britain by
CPI Cox & Wyman, Reading, RG1 8EX

This book is dedicated to my brother
Robert Mortimer,
a fire-fighter, a saver of lives
– a real hero –
and the kindest of men.

Contents

Appendices

Author's Note

Foreign names have been treated in two ways. Members of the French royal family, including royal cousins (e.g. John the Fearless; Philip, count of Vertus) have been given in English. French individuals who were not members of the royal family have been named in French (e.g. Jean Petit, Jehanne de Lesparre) with the exception of the one reference to Joan of Arc, whose name is well known in the English-speaking world. Other foreign names have normally been given in the usual spelling in the original language – e.g. Duarte of Portugal, João of Portugal, Juan of Castile, Pedro de Luna, Giovanni Dominici – where possible. However, some Eastern European names have been given in English, e.g. Lord John of Chlum, Wenceslas of Dubá and Peter of Mladoňovice.

With regard to currencies, readers might like to bear in mind that the pound sterling (£) was just one of two units of account in England. The other was the mark, which was the equivalent of two-thirds of a pound, or 13 shillings and 4 pence (13s 4d). Thus the gold coin called a noble – 6s 8d – was one third of £1 and one half of a mark,

French money has usually been quantified in terms of crowns (*écus à la couronne*). The usual conversion rate has been taken as 6 crowns to £1 (so one French gold crown = one English gold half-noble). The discussion concerning the dowry of the Princess Katherine in early June 1415 touched upon treating the matter in terms of francs; as explained in the text, the franc was worth very slightly less, there being about 10.5 francs to 10 crowns.

The term 'Gascony' in this book should be taken to mean all the territory under English rule in the southwest of France, as in my previous books.

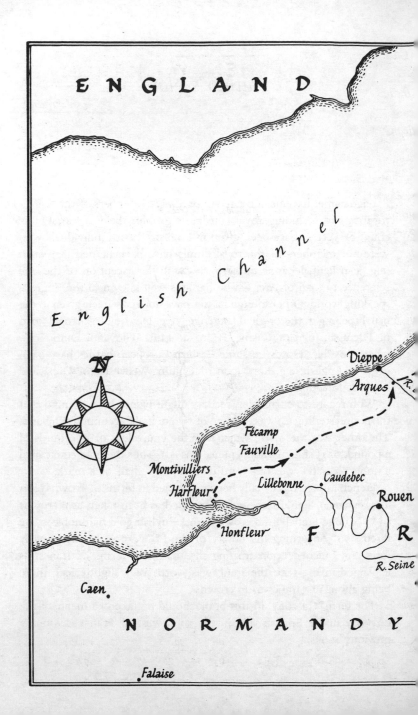

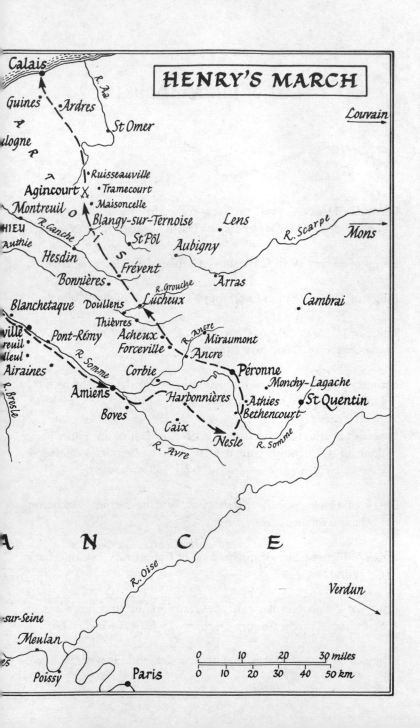

HENRY'S MARCH

List of Illustrations

Portrait of Henry V, *c.* 1523, probably copied from a lost original (*The Royal Collection © 2009 Her Majesty Queen Elizabeth II, RCIN 403443*).

Effigy of Henry IV in Canterbury Cathedral (*author's collection*).

Effigy of Queen Joan in Canterbury Cathedral (*author's collection*).

Effigy of Thomas, duke of Clarence, in Canterbury Cathedral (*Dean and Chapter of Canterbury Cathedral*).

Manuscript illumination of John, duke of Bedford, from the Bedford Hours (*British Library, Add MS 18850 fol. 256v.*).

Sixteenth-century crayon drawing by J. le Boucq of Humphrey, duke of Gloucester, copied from a lost portrait (*Médiathèque d'Arras, bibliothèque municipale d'Arras, MS Arras 266*).

Effigy of Henry Beaufort, bishop of Winchester, in Winchester Cathedral (*author's collection*).

Effigy of Henry Chichele, archbishop of Canterbury, in Canterbury Cathedral (*Ric Horner*).

Effigy of Ralph Neville, earl of Westmorland, and his wives in Staindrop Church, County Durham (*Dr John Banham*).

Effigy of Thomas Fitzalan, earl of Arundel, and his wife, Beatrice,

Portchester Castle, Hampshire (*author's collection*).

St Martin's Church, Harfleur (*Vigneron, http://upload.wikimedia.org/wikipedia/commons/2/21/Harfleur_pont-Gorand.JPG*).

Château d'Arques, Arques-la-Bataille (*AD, http://fr.wikipedia.org/wiki/Fichier:Chateau_alb_1.jpg*).

Memorial brass of Lord and Lady Camoys, Trotton Church, Sussex (*courtesy of H. Martin Stuchfield*).

Sculpture of Sir Thomas Erpingham, from the Erpingham Gate, Norwich (*Anglia Images/Alamy*).

Effigy of Michael de la Pole, earl of Suffolk, from Wingfield Church, Suffolk (*author's collection*).

The battlefield of Agincourt: looking southeast from the French position (*author's collection; edited by Stephen Read*).

The battlefield of Agincourt: looking northwest from the English position (*author's collection; edited by Stephen Read*).

Drawing of the town and harbour of Calais, *c.* 1535–40 (*British Library, Cotton Augustus I ii fol. 70*).

Original letter said to have been written by Henry V in his own hand (*British Library, Cotton Vespasian F iii fol. 9*).

Acknowledgements

In the course of researching and writing this book I have been assisted by many people and several organisations. In particular I would like to thank my editors, Will Sulkin and Jörg Hensgen at Random House, and my agent, Jim Gill, at United Agents. The Royal Literary Fund was extremely generous in supporting me financially during a very difficult period. Grants from two funds managed by the Society of Authors – the Frances Head Bequest and the Author's Foundation – were similarly crucial to my continuing to work on this book. I am very grateful to all those who showed such faith in this project that they kept me and the family from penury.

I am very grateful to Stephen Read for his assistance in editing my multiple images of the battlefield at Agincourt in seamless files. Ric Horner kindly provided me with the image of Archbishop Chichele's tomb – thanks Ric. I also owe a big thank you to the novelist Hayden Gabriel for several meaningful discussions about the objective correlative as we trudged over Dartmoor. More thanks to Kay Peddle for assistance with picture research. And thanks to my brother David Mortimer for the advice about blacksmiths and smithying.

More formally, I am grateful to the University of Exeter for continuing to have me as an Honorary Research Fellow and to grant access to a number of research resources and library facilities. I acknowledge the generosity of Professor Anne Curry and her publishers, Boydell and Brewer, in granting permission to quote from her translations in *The Battle of Agincourt: Sources and Interpretations* (Woodbridge, 2000).

With respect to accommodation on research trips, I would like to say a special thank you to both sides of the Gavrilenko family – both in Moretonhampstead (Liz and Laurent) and in Paris (Marie-Thérèse, François and Marie-Pierre). Thanks also to Jay Hammond, Zak

Reddan and Mary Fawcett for accommodating me on visits to London.

Last and most of all, I am very grateful to my wife Sophie for continuing to live with me while I have worked on this book. Living with a historian isn't always easy. Constantly tumbling through a galaxy of facts, day and night, is extremely disorientating; and writing experimental history is never conducive to a relaxed way of life. But I'm very glad that she has put up with everything – from being burnt at the stake at the Council of Constance, murdered in Paris, beheaded at Southampton, besieged at Harfleur and shot to ribbons at Agincourt. Greater love hath no author's wife than this.

Prologue

This book is not about a battle. It is about a man and his time. I have tried to show what he was and what he achieved over the course of one year: what he believed in, what he destroyed and what he became.

The subject was not an ordinary man. Indeed, Henry V was not an 'ordinary' king. He was a hero in his own lifetime. Following his early death in France in 1422, he was given a semi-legendary status. In the 1590s he was already established as an English national icon; Shakespeare simply took that icon and gave it an enduring value, even to less warlike generations, by putting his most patriotic speeches into Henry's mouth. Shakespeare also gave Henry a more rounded, likeable personality: he gave him a cheeriness that the real Henry never had. When presented with the good looks and dramatic flair of Lawrence Olivier, in his film of Shakespeare's *Henry V*, delivered in an appropriately patriotic style for English and American audiences during the Second World War, Henry became the archetypal English champion. His negative traits were forgotten, all the failures of the age were blamed on other men, and all the successes attributed to him.

As a result of this extreme adulation even the most scholarly historians have found it difficult to maintain their historical objectivity. The most famous example is the declaration by the English historian K. B. McFarlane that Henry V was, 'the greatest man that ever ruled England'.[1] Many other writers have presented Henry as the typical medieval warrior-hero, regardless of his solemnity and profoundly religious nature. So, although this book is about a man and his time, it is also about challenging certain assumptions that we make about him. I do think he was an extraordinary man, in that he demonstrated phenomenal organisational skills, focus, determination, resilience, leadership and – above all else – religious conviction; but I also feel he was a deeply flawed individual. He lacked the simpler qualities of compassion, warmth, and the understanding of human frailty that one naturally looks for in all men – yeomen and paupers as well as kings. McFarlane, preaching from a pulpit of academic prejudice against historical biography, failed to draw attention to these shortcomings of his character.[2] Thus my verdict on Henry's supposed 'greatness' is very different from Mr McFarlane's.

There are already dozens of books on Henry V and dozens more on Agincourt – many of them by academic specialists who have devoted decades to the study of Henry and his battles. So it is fair to ask: what can I hope to do historically, over and above their collective efforts? What are the aims of this book?

First, it is a continuation of my examination of the nature of personality and political ambition in the middle ages, continuing these themes from my earlier books about Roger Mortimer, Edward III and Henry IV. It is thus the fourth volume of my 'biographical history' of later medieval England. Second, I have tried to give a fuller and more representative view of Henry's non-military activities in this year, especially his religious deeds, which tend to be very briefly noted as examples of his spirituality in full-length biographies and books about Agincourt. Third, I have paid much more attention than usual to the characters and social movements that formed the backdrop to Henry's ambitions in 1415, especially with regard to the papal conflicts and the burning of Jan Hus at the council of Constance. It is important to remember that, at the same time as Henry was trying to reunite the 'kingdom of England and France', many people were trying to reunite the Church, and Henry himself drew parallels between the two unifying movements. Fourth, I have tried to show how Henry's activities were part of a wider attempt to unite religious and political authority at the time – a European-wide movement towards establishing the divine right of kings, and in many ways the basis for the shift towards absolutism in the following century.

The most significant innovation in this book is its calendar structure. One might call this an experiment in historical form. I have asked whether we can arrive at a different view of a historical subject through presenting well-known historical facts in a radically different way. As will be seen, a calendar-based form does permit many new insights.

It forces a greater degree of accuracy with regard to dates and developmental processes. Repetition of key aspects of Henry's behaviour appear in proportion to the evidence, and juxtapositions of important events go a long way to explaining some of his decisions. Above all else, the integration of all the various aspects of his life – the religious and the social, the judicial and the political – allow a vision of Henry that is very different from the patriotic stories with which we grew up. The book therefore is a demonstration of how a different framework may be used to see the past differently, and how we may obtain a new 'projection' (to borrow a term from geography) of the past by presenting historical events in a more chronologically precise way.

Having said that, the calendar form has its complications. Describing a whole year in a man's life, day by day, is a huge literary challenge. I do not think that it has been attempted previously for a medieval or early modern individual. This is a very different book from 1599 by James Shapiro, for example, which is not a day-to-day study of Shakespeare. It is impossible to avoid the fact that the calendar is a non-literary structure, like the Periodic Table of the Elements, and creating a literary work out of the Periodic Table *in atomic order* would be a challenge for anyone (even Tom Lehrer had to change the order of the elements in his famous song). The author has to maintain a balance between the facts on the one hand and readability on the other. This balance pivots around the question: which details should be included in their proper place, and which might be safely excluded or mentioned elsewhere? Normally historians resolve this question silently, through excising anything that is not relevant to their thesis or theme, and this process of selection is concealed within the structure of their books. However, in this study, which has no structure except the days of the year, *everything* relating to the king and his challenges is relevant. To exclude or change the position of anything would partially distort the picture of Henry V in 1415. Moreover, it is only by including everything that we can start to go beyond the evidence and to remark on aspects of normal medieval behaviour that do *not* feature in Henry's life – his lack of relationships with women, for example, or the lack of references to jousting. Herein lies the problem: to include every fact in its proper place would result in a massive book, full of repetitive lists of apparently inconsequential details; yet to cut or remove anything would distort our image of the man in this year, and ruin the experiment.

In trying to reconcile these problems of information, chronology and readability I have tended towards fullness and precision. I have included almost everything I can find relating to the king's decision-making, even such routine things as the confirmation of episcopal elections, warrants for arrest, commissions of inquiry, and the granting of royal pensions. In most cases these have been included under the heading of the day specified in the document. I have not included everything known for the year, however; I have excluded regular appointments and payments that were routinely made by the bureau-crats at Westminster (unless the nature of the grant suggests that Henry was personally involved). Some matters of accounting detail from May to August have been relegated to the notes section, to avoid tedious repetition. I have ignored administrative clarifications, such as confirmations of earlier royal grants by chancery officials, which would distract from the main purpose of the book. On the whole, I have tried to use as many facts as possible to give a full and multi-dimensional view of Henry – as a warrior, organiser, devoted Christian, patron, statesman and king – and I have sought to show how he behaved in relation to priests, subjects, women, diplomats, brothers and friends, as well as those who fought for him and those who fought against him.

At the heart of this book – at the heart of all historical endeavour – there is one overarching purpose: to satisfy an instinctive desire to understand our race in other ages and in different circumstances, with regard to both individuals and communities, and to see how we have changed over the intervening centuries. For this reason I make no apology for wanting to go beyond patriotic hagiography and to look for the 'real' Henry V, as opposed to the charismatic Shakespearian hero or McFarlane's 'greatest man'. I have tried to draw attention to the complexities within Henry as an individual as well as the complexities of generally understanding men in a violent, God-fearing age. As I stressed at the end of my study of Edward III, it is in the inconsisten-cies of a character that one gets close to knowing the man. It is not in the bland generalisations that we find truth, but in the apparent irregularities that demand explanation. If I have alerted people to the fact that a man may be a hero and yet a monster, that he can be seen as blessed by God and yet be a wanton destroyer of lives, and that even a king might set himself on the path to his own self-destruction and the negation of his humanity in order to win recognition as something that people associate with 'greatness', then I will have succeeded.

This book is, therefore, not just a book about a man and his time, and not just about the significance of this year in his life. Nor is it just about reversing any assumptions made about him. It is about the way we understand people in the past and, by implication, the way we understand ourselves.

Introduction

It was about eight o'clock in the evening of 23 November 1407. In her rented rooms upstairs in the rue Vieille du Temple in Paris, the thirty-four-year-old Jacquette Griffart was putting her young child to bed. She was anxious because her husband, Jean, a shoemaker, had not returned home. She went to the window to see if he was coming but the narrow street outside was too dark. Some of her child's clean bedclothes had been drying on a pole outside the window, so she lifted the pole and began to draw it back into the room. In the darkness she noticed two or three torches coming down the narrow street, carried by footmen; and by their light she briefly saw their master. He was playing with his gloves as he rode, singing to himself. With him were three or four other men on horseback. Thinking nothing more about it, she turned back into the room, crossed over to the cot, and lifted her child.

'Kill him!' shouted a voice in the street; 'kill him!'.

Jacquette stepped back anxiously to the window, holding her child in her arms. She saw the singing nobleman on the ground below, on his knees, desperately holding on to his saddle. He had been dragged from his horse by seven or eight armed men. His companions had fled. The attackers were gathered around him, some of them holding torches while others brought their swords down on his shoulders. He tried to fend them off with a flailing arm. 'What is this?' he yelled, clinging with one hand to the saddle of his horse. 'Who does it come from?' Not one of his assailants spoke. An axe severed the hand holding the saddle and he fell. The horse bolted. The men immediately stepped forward to beat down on his body with their weapons, stabbing him repeatedly.

To Jacquette it looked as if they were beating a mattress, so hard were their blows. Shocked, she found the word 'Murder!' and screamed it across the dark street.

'Shut up, you damned woman,' shouted back one of the men, just below her. 'Shut up!'

One of the assailants lifted his axe and cleaved the head of the dying lord in two. His brains spilled out on to the ground. Seeing this, a large man wearing a red hood stepped out from the shadows of the house opposite.

'Put out the lights,' he ordered, looking down. 'He's dead. Let's go. Take heart.' The men immediately followed him around the corner into the rue des Blancs-Manteaux.

When they had gone Jacquette noticed another man on the ground beside the dead lord, one of the man's valets. He too had been attacked. Dying, he crawled to his master's corpse. 'My master!' he called out before he too succumbed to his wounds.

Then there was quiet. A single torch burnt on the ground near the corner of the street, one of the attackers having failed to extinguish it in his haste.

Jacquette yelled out 'Murder!' again, several times. Another woman who lived in the rue des Rosiers arrived on the scene and took up the cry. It was not long before people gathered to view the appalling spectacle, and to see who was lying in the pool of blood.

It was Louis, duke of Orléans, the only brother of Charles VI, king of France. The king himself was suffering from an illness that left him often deranged. To all intents and purposes, the man who lay dead in the street was the ruler of France.

*

The late duke of Orléans was no saint. He had assumed control of his brother's government shortly after the death of their uncle, Philip the Bold, duke of Burgundy, in 1404. His taxes were unpopular with the people of Paris. So too were his morals. Not only was he believed to have fathered several children by the queen, had also seduced or raped several knights' wives, humiliating their husbands in the process. It was said he had a gallery of pictures of all the wives he had slept with. One cuckold, Albert de Chauny, not only had to suffer the indignity of all Paris knowing his wife had lain beneath the duke, but was rumoured also to have been forced to describe the beauty of her body when the duke had paraded her naked before an assembly, with her face covered. For this reason suspicions fell upon de Chauny as the murderer. But it soon emerged that he had not been in Paris for many months.

Other lines of enquiry were pursued. One of the Parisian water-carriers told the investigators that a man who had supplied water to the house where the killers had been waiting was being sheltered by John the Fearless, duke of Burgundy, the son of Philip the Bold. The investigators could not arrest him without the duke's permission. So on 26 November they sent word to John the Fearless, who was at the duke of Berry's house, the *hôtel de Nesle*.

When he was asked for, John's guilt showed in his face.

Seeing his expression, the duke of Anjou asked him directly what he knew of the murder. John confessed. He had paid the man in the red hood, Raoul d'Anquetonville, to organise the assassination of the duke of Orléans.

The duke of Anjou was astonished. John was a member of the royal family. He was the king's first cousin, and thus the dead man's first cousin. He had attended the memorial service the very day after the murder. How could he have done such a thing? The duke of Berry, who was also present, wept at the enormity of the deed. Both men were left speechless, unable to act. John the Fearless simply got up, left the room, went downstairs, and rode out of Paris with a handful of retainers.[1]

The realisation that John the Fearless had murdered his cousin came as a profound shock to the whole kingdom of France. When the king of England, Henry IV, had secretly murdered his cousin and rival Richard II seven years earlier, the French had condemned him in the most uncompromising language. Now they had seen a member of their own royal family commit the same crime. But the repercussions of the French royal murder were far more serious. The English one had been perpetrated by the anointed and crowned monarch, who was technically above the law. In contrast, the duke of Burgundy was a vassal of the king of France, and in no way above the law. Richard II's murder had largely been a precaution, in case he was restored to his throne as the result of a treasonable plot. The greater purpose was the stability of the kingdom. There was no comparable 'greater purpose' with regard to the killing of the duke of Orléans; it could only destabilise the kingdom. From its brazen manner to its political implications, the assassination of the duke of Orléans was more horrifying to contemporaries than any other murder in living memory.

There is another reason why the French royal murder was more serious than the English one, and it is the reason why a book about Henry V in the year 1415 has to begin with a description of this event. England was a kingdom in which the king reigned supreme: it was, in many respects, like a modern nation. Only at the margins of his realm – in Wales, Ireland, and the Marches of Scotland – could the king's authority be questioned with impunity. If a great lord committed a crime, then the king summoned an army and punished him. Edward II had done so several times in the early fourteenth century and Henry IV had done likewise several times in the early fifteenth. But the kingdom of France was different. A far larger and richer country, the principle members of the French royal family ruled semi-autonomous dukedoms that were primarily loyal to their duke, not the king. Hence, when John the Fearless fled from Paris after being found out, he went to Burgundy and then to Flanders. Here he met his brothers, Anthony, duke of Brabant, and Philip, count of Nevers, and his brother-in-law, William, duke of Holland. This coalition was very strong – no king of France could have simply marched an army into Burgundy or Flanders and brought the duke to heel. It would have resulted in a civil war. In addition, King Charles VI was mentally unstable and incapable of leading an army against anyone, let alone John the Fearless, who was an experienced battlefield commander. The king and his council had no option but to negotiate with John. This they did, reluctantly, at Amiens in January 1408.

If both sides had genuinely wanted peace, things might have ended there. But high-profile murders tend to be the start of things, not the end, and this was no exception. Having secured his position at the end of February 1408, John the Fearless rode back into Paris in triumph. He was feted as a hero by the Parisians, who had despised the interfering, philandering, high-taxing duke of Orléans. On 8 March a manifesto commissioned by John the Fearless was read out by its author, Jean Petit, declaring that the duke of Orléans had been a tyrant and that, because it was 'permissible and meritorious to kill a tyrant', John had done a good deed in butchering him. Jean Petit read this in the presence of King Charles himself – the dead man's brother – and the rest of the assembled royal family. This was shocking, distressing, unforgettable and unforgivable.

Petit outlined the basis of the late duke's tyranny. The duke had resorted to black magic to try to kill the king, having his sword, dagger and a ring consecrated by two devils. He had 'acquired a cherry branch that had been dipped in the blood of a red cockerel and a white chicken, which possessed such magic powers that no woman could resist the advances of its owner'. He had plotted with the duke of Milan to kill the king, and had tried to poison the late dauphin, Charles, with an apple thrown into the chamber where he had been playing. He had wilfully set fire to the king's clothes at a fancy-dress ball in 1393. He had made a pact with Henry of Lancaster – before he became Henry IV of England – that they should help each other usurp their respective thrones. He had tried to persuade the queen to leave France with him in order to control her. He had plotted with Pope Benedict XIII to declare the king and his children unfit to hold the throne, so he might become king himself. Finally he had taken control of the government by stationing his men in strategic castles, and had levied punitive taxes – supposedly to defend the kingdom against England but in reality to further his own ambitions. In his final summing-up, Jean Petit declared that 'my lord of Burgundy is not deserving of any blame whatever for what has happened to the criminal duke of Orléans. Nor ought the king our lord to be dissatisfied with him but, on the contrary, he should be pleased with what he has done, and requite him for it in three ways: in love, honour and riches.'[2]

European politics has rarely seen such a great insult thrust on to such a devastating injury. If the assassination itself had strained relations between the lords, Jean Petit's *Justification of the duke of Burgundy* gave further attempts at peaceable dialogue the character of a series of diplomatic manoeuvres prior to an outright declaration of war. The widowed duchess of Orléans looked on in disgust as her brother-in-law the French king absolved John the Fearless of any blame and forgave him the assassination of her husband. It was more than she or her sons could bear. Lawyers were summoned to refute Jean Petit's *Justification*. A defence was drawn up against the charges of treason and necromancy, and a long list of demands was read out before the court in September 1408. A meeting and reconciliation between John the Fearless and the new duke of Orléans, Charles, took place at Chartres in March 1409, but this was merely a plaster over a very deep wound. It only allowed John the Fearless to secure his position and to make the rest of the French royal family resent him even more bitterly.

John's own tyranny soon followed. A key officer of the royal court, Jean de Montagu, Grand Master of the king's household, was arrested, condemned to death and executed. His brother the archbishop of Sens was forced to flee for his life. Other royalists were thrown into prison or ousted from court. John the Fearless drew up a treaty with the king of Navarre, in which they agreed to support each other in the event of war with the duke of Orléans. John further secured his position by taking possession of the eleven-year-old dauphin, and establishing himself firmly in Paris, where his popularity could not be challenged. He built a strong tower for himself in his town house, the *hôtel d'Artois*, in which his strongly defended bedroom and a bathroom were at the very top, with nothing but huge stone supports beneath, so he could not be killed by the house being burnt.[3] He took every precaution he could to ensure that the brutal assassination of his cousin would not be visited back on him.

The young duke of Orléans was not alone in hating his father's killer. The duke of Berry, the king's uncle, was of the same opinion. So too was the king's maternal uncle, the duke of Bourbon. But both these men were old. The real political force supporting the young duke of Orléans was Bernard, count of Armagnac. When on 15 April 1410 the League of Gien came into existence, it consisted of all these lords, plus the counts of Alençon and Clermont, and the younger sons of the late duke of Orléans: Philip, count of Vertus, and John, count of Angoulême. The count of Armagnac and the duke of Orléans, in confirmation of their wholehearted support for the League, sealed the agreement with a marriage. The duke took as his wife Bonne, the count's daughter. Thus the League collectively came to be known as the Armagnacs. Against them stood the Burgundians: John the Fearless, his two brothers, his brother-in-law who ruled the Low Countries, and the king of Navarre.

France stood on the very brink of civil war.

*

Any sensible leader, when facing the prospect of war, reaches out for allies. This is true of civil wars too, not only international conflicts.

Thus it is meaningless to speculate on whether the events of 1415 would have turned out differently if neither the Burgundians nor the Armagnacs had sent ambassadors to England – there was never any doubt that one or both of them would do so. Technically speaking, England was still at war with France over the sovereignty of Gascony – as it had been for the last seventy years – and no peace was likely to prove acceptable in England until the French honoured the Treaty of Brétigny (1360), by which the whole of the ancient Angevin Empire was to return to English control. Thus both Burgundians and Armagnacs had to negotiate with the king of England just to ensure they were not attacked while settling their own domestic dispute. Obviously, if the English were a potential third force in the ensuing conflict, it made sense for both the Burgundians and the Armagnacs to try to secure the support – not the neutrality – of the English.

French ambassadors were regularly in negotiation with their English counterparts at this time, renewing the truce between the two countries for a year or so at each meeting. Burgundian negotiators also often dealt with English ambassadors to continue a separate truce operating in Flanders, England's principal trading partner, which fell within the domains of John the Fearless. However, with civil war looming, John realised that any advantageous offer he elicited from the English could be wrested from him – if he were to lose his influence over the king, then he would lose his English alliance. There could be no ambiguity as to which side the English were supporting. So, in the summer of 1411 he sent his own Burgundian ambassadors to England.[4] They were empowered to hand over four Flemish towns, as well as to agree for the duke's daughter to marry the eldest son of Henry IV. This was Henry of Monmouth, prince of Wales, duke of Cornwall and earl of Chester – the future Henry V.

For Henry IV the news of the arrival of the Burgundian ambassadors and the prospect of civil war in France was sadly ironic. Once he would have jumped at the opportunity of involving himself personally in a French war. It would have allowed him to pursue his dream of re-enacting the chivalric kingship of Edward III, his grandfather – the most successful form of kingship that anyone could remember. Edward III had demonstrated that, through successful overseas campaigning, a king could guarantee his kingdom domestic peace, national unity, strong government and foreign glory. Thus Henry IV had proclaimed his intention of leading an army into France on numerous occasions. But he had never done so. Within a few months of his coronation he had come under attack from friends of the late King Richard. From then on he was forced to confront a unique and hugely challenging series of political disasters which he endured magnificently but which cost him his health. The very nature of his accession meant that, far from Edward III's glorious kingship, his reign had become a period of domestic unrest, national disunity, financial insecurity and foreign antipathy. Now he was a spent force – suffering from a disease that resulted in his baldness, festering of his flesh, dehydration of the eyes, and the rupture of his internal organs.[5] He had fallen into a coma on at least one occasion. He was barely able to stand, let alone ride a horse. However much he might have longed to lead an army into France, he did not have the strength.

The irony did not end there, however. Such had been the decline in Henry IV's health that even this political decision was not wholly within his control. In many respects he was king in name alone. Since the end of 1409 real power had lain with his eldest son, Prince Henry, and the royal council. Moreover, relations between the king and his son's council were strained. The prince had assumed certain royal prerogatives that the king felt were prejudicial to his dignity. These included the enactment of a certain article in a statute that severely curtailed the king's power. The prince's council had also suspended the payment of annuities to the king's supporters – a measure that smacked of failure in the king's eyes. Another cause of the strained relations was the rivalry between Prince Henry and his brother, Thomas of Lancaster, the king's favourite son. Prince Henry ruled the council with the close advice of his uncle, Henry Beaufort, who was a rival of both Thomas of Lancaster and the king's closest confidant, Thomas Arundel, archbishop of Canterbury. So when the Burgundian messengers arrived, there were two sources of royal authority in England. On one hand there was the king, supported by his son Thomas of Lancaster and Archbishop Arundel; and on the other there was the prince of Wales, supported by Henry Beaufort and the rest of the council.

The Burgundian ambassadors initially approached the king but he refused to entertain them.[6] Henry IV did not like John the Fearless. Nor did he trust him. In 1399 he had sealed a mutual defence agreement with the murdered duke of Orléans, which could have entailed him taking action against John the Fearless.[7] Although Orléans turned against Henry IV in 1402, it seems the king of England was no fonder of the duke of Burgundy after this date than he had been before. John had attacked Calais on more than one occasion. Also, the duchess of Orléans was the daughter of the duke of Milan, a personal friend of Henry IV's from the 1390s.[8] And Henry IV had always been much closer to the old duke of Berry, now one of the Armagnac lords, than to the Burgundians.

Prince Henry had several reasons to listen to the Burgundians. The most obvious was that the safekeeping of Calais was his responsibility, and in that capacity his men already had experience of negotiating with John's ambassadors. Indeed, they were engaged in negotiations regarding infractions of the truce throughout the first half of 1411.[9] Henry could not easily agree to talk to them about a truce in one arena and refuse to entertain the idea of a truce in another. But he probably also had the long-term strategic implications in mind. To refuse to deal with the Burgundians over intervention in the French civil war meant having to deal with the Armagnacs (or losing the opportunity to capitalise on the civil war altogether). If he wanted to play one off against the other – in the hope of encouraging them to bid competitively for his friendship – then he had to parley with both sides.[10] And if a full-scale civil war were to break out in France, then an alliance with John the Fearless was an effective way of destabilising the kingdom, forcing the French king to agree to his demands. The ultimate target was the implementation of a peace treaty favourable to England, along the lines of the Treaty of Brétigny, 'The Great Peace', agreed between the kings of England and France in 1360, but which the French had torn up in 1369.

The king's and the prince's respective points of view resulted in a compromise. The king would not deal with the Burgundians himself, but he authorised Prince Henry to do so. This was good enough for John the Fearless, who could see outright hostilities coming ever closer, following the capture and torture of one of his officers by the duke of Orléans in January 1411. Orléans wrote to the University of Paris in March that year demanding that Jean Petit's *Justification of the duke of Burgundy* should be formally condemned.[11] Finally, at the end of July, Orléans sent John a letter in which he declared he would do everything in his power to harm him. With that, the negotiations between the ambassadors of John the Fearless and Prince Henry shifted from being merely precautionary to preparations for war against the Armagnacs.

The year 1411 saw the nadir of Henry V's relationship with his father. The exact nature of their mutual suspicions remains unclear, as the English royal family understandably did not want to publicise its own internal divisions. It is possible that problems arose from the prince's favour to Burgundy. It is also possible that their differences were purely related to the royal finances. It is likely that there was a personality clash between the two men, for they were similar in character in many respects, not the least of which was a distinctly overwhelming pride. Whatever the cause, the plans for armed intervention on behalf of Burgundy were affected. Although the king announced on 14 August 1411 that he would be sailing to Calais on 23 September, and although he issued instructions to the ambassadors going to John the Fearless on 1 September, offering him military aid against the duke of Orléans, he opted out of the expedition with a couple of days to spare.[12] On 21 September the king declared he would not be going to France. Instead he summoned a parliament to meet as soon as possible, in early November. So the fleet that sailed in late September was a private one, hired by the Burgundians from the prince of Wales as a mercenary force. It was led by Thomas Fitzalan, earl of Arundel, one of the prince's closest friends.[13]

The reason for the king's change of mind was not just because he supported the Armagnacs and Prince Henry supported the Burgundians. The king had been happy to issue orders for an army to sail to Calais in support of the Burgundian faction in August and early September, even though he had been in negotiations with the duke of Berry earlier that summer.[14] The reason was the relationship between him and his son. The fundamental issue was whether the sick king or the healthy prince should exercise royal power in England. This went far beyond mere foreign policy; there was talk of the prince and Henry Beaufort forcing the king to abdicate.[15] So, when Henry IV summoned parliament that autumn, his main objective was the resumption of royal power. This he effected on 30 November with a polite dismissal of the prince's council.

In the meantime the earl of Arundel was demonstrating that English archers could still determine the outcome of battles on French soil, just as they had done in the reign of Edward III. On 9 November 1411 a thousand English archers helped John the Fearless win a battle for the bridge at St-Cloud, near Paris, some of them serving in John's own bodyguard.[16] In early 1412 both Armagnacs and Burgundians again sent ambassadors to secure the support of Henry IV, now wholly in charge of the government. John the Fearless's ambassadors received their safe conducts on 11 January and arrived in England on 1 February. The Armagnac ambassadors were not far behind them, receiving their safe conducts on 6 February. But in reality the king's resumption of power meant that John the Fearless's representatives were always going to have a difficult job securing an agreement. In effect they were being used by Henry IV to encourage the Armagnacs to offer greater and greater concessions. The Armagnacs were now officially rebels, so they were in a desperate position. They agreed in principle to the main English objective in France: sovereignty over Gascony. They even agreed that they would fight their fellow Frenchmen to help Henry IV regain his inheritance. John the Fearless's men realised they could not compete and withdrew from negotiations on 4 March.

One month later, on 6 April 1412, the agreement between Henry IV and the Armagnac lords was finalised in the Treaty of Bourges. Later that same month the king ordered the enlistment of mariners, again announcing his intention to sail to France in person. On 18 May the treaty was ratified by the Armagnac lords. The English intervention in France was on course once more, but this time it was to march in support of the duke of Orléans, not the duke of Burgundy. Henry IV eventually decided against leading the expedition himself, and passed command to his second son, Thomas of Lancaster, whom he now created duke of Clarence. Thomas would be supported by Edward, duke of York, and Thomas Beaufort, earl of Dorset, together with 1,500 men-at-arms and 4,500 archers.

The only problem was Prince Henry. A year earlier he had been the master of England, exercising royal power in his father's name, presiding over the royal council and deciding on foreign policy. Now he had lost power, and with it he had lost face. He continued to oppose his father's policy of intervention on the side of the Armagnacs, and was forced into swearing an oath with his three brothers to accept and abide by the terms of the Treaty of Bourges on 20 May. The retinue allocated to the prince to proceed into France under his father's command was small – too small, he felt, for a man of his status and experience. When the king had decided not to lead the expedition in person, the prince had been passed over altogether, in favour of his younger brother. The message was clear: Prince Henry was not trusted by his father.

The prince was bitterly angry, and left court shortly afterwards. On 17 June he sent a letter listing his grievances. He repeated accusations that he had tried to usurp his father's throne, denying them outright but thereby drawing attention to their seriousness. Similarly he denied trying to obstruct his father's campaign in France. That he had to deny such things publicly alerts us to the fact that they were already common knowledge. The rift between him and his father was not closed until a tender reconciliation at Westminster at the end of June 1412, during which the prince begged his father to kill him if he believed him disloyal, holding out a dagger whereby his father might perform the deed.[17] The king, in tears, simply flung the dagger to one side and embraced his son. But even though their personal relationship was thereby restored, the prince remained in the political wilderness for the rest of his father's life. His only role in government was that of standing by and waiting for the king to die.

*

The Treaty of Bourges was illegal. The Armagnac lords had no right to recognise English sovereignty in Gascony or anywhere else; far less could they agree to fight Frenchmen to secure that sovereignty. It amounted to treason on their part, and resulted in the genuine hostility of the king of France. It is hugely ironic that the cause for which they were fighting – revenge for the murder of King Charles's brother – now led them into conflict with King Charles himself, and actually forced the king and his brother's murderer into a closer compact.

John the Fearless acted extraordinarily swiftly. Within a month of the treaty being ratified, he had raised a royal army and led it to Bourges, taking the king with him. On 15 July the duke of Berry surrendered the city to King Charles in person, and on 21 July a royal letter was issued in the king's name nullifying the treaty that the Armagnac lords had agreed with the king of England. The following day, at Auxerre, the dukes of Berry, Orléans and Bourbon all sealed a copy of this letter, which was sent to Henry IV. John the Fearless also affixed his seal to it. All the great lords promised to abide by the peace of Chartres of 1409.[18] The French were again united – at least for the time being.

Thomas, duke of Clarence, had no way of knowing this before he set sail. He landed at St-Vaast-la-Hougue on 10 August, expecting to be greeted as the leader of an auxiliary force bringing relief to the Armagnacs. Instead he found himself in charge of an invading army. Undaunted, he chose to take on the mantle of aggressor, destroying Armagnac lands in Maine and Anjou as he made his way to Blois. There on 16 September he issued a letter to the French that was tantamount to a refusal to accept the peace. Only a humiliating and costly offer from the Armagnac lords prevented him from continuing to ravage the country. In November, with a safe conduct from the king of France in his possession, he ordered his army to march across France to Gascony. There he would wait, keeping his troops ready for the 'defence' of the English province.

A murder had given way to a civil war, which had resulted in English mercenaries fighting in France. Now a substantial English royal army was established on the borders of France. It was in every way an unstable situation. All it needed was the political will to attack the French, and the two kingdoms would once again be at war.

Henry IV no longer possessed that political will. On 20 November 1412, probably in accordance with a prophecy that he would die in the Holy Land, he ordered three galleys to be constructed to bear him to his deathbed. He summoned his last parliament, and spent his last Christmas at Eltham, his favourite palace, with his beloved wife, Queen Joan. In January the faithful William Loveney, who had served him since at least 1386, undertook to cut down sufficient trees to make the said galleys.[19] But Henry IV never embarked. Parliament assembled in early February, and waited for the king to take the throne, but he was too sick to attend. At the end of the month he lapsed into unconsciousness in Westminster Abbey and was carried through to the Jerusalem Chamber, and laid on a bed in the abbot's lodging. On waking and being told where he was, he realised that he was now in the place where it had been prophesied he would die. The end came on 20 March, with Queen Joan and his sons Henry and Humphrey at his bedside.

In France it was said that the prince took the crown from his father's chamber before the king was dead, and tried it on, only to be told that he should not touch it until it was rightfully his. In a metaphorical sense this was correct; that is what Prince Henry had done in exercising royal power in 1410–11. But now the crown really had passed to him. In Gascony, on hearing the news, his brother Thomas immediately prepared to return to England. In the north of England, his brother John prepared to come south. In Henry V and his three brothers, the political will to fulfil their father's ambitions – to see a king of England once more lead an English army into France – had arrived.

Christmas Day 1414

It was the second Christmas since his father's death. Henry V, wearing his full royal robes and his golden crown, was seated on a marble chair beneath a tall silk canopy. He looked along the full length of the palace hall, beyond the gilt-silver goblets and golden plates before him.[1] Servants bustled around in their short tunics and coloured hose, serving the hundreds of knights and gentlemen seated on benches at the lower tables. The previous evening they had decked the hall with evergreens: ivy around the doors, and holly within, and they had prepared thousands of candles to burn through Christmas morning. Dozens of silver chandeliers hung from the rafters, adding a golden glow to the winter light of the windows on either side. Now, as the king began to eat, minstrels were playing: the notes of their harps, pipes and tambourines drifted over the hum of the assembly. Faces were bright, looking forward to courses of roast beef, pork and goose in rich sauces – so welcome after the long fast of Advent.[2]

Twelve days of festivity lay ahead of them. There would be music, carolling, dancing, play-acting and jokes. One servant would be appointed the Lord of Misrule, to oversee the household games. William, the king's fool, would perform for the select few. There would be serious events too: the re-enactment of the Nativity, the dole of pennies to paupers, and many more religious services in the king's presence, in the royal chapel of St Stephen, just a few steps from the hall. Outside the palace, in the cold streets of Westminster and London, people were preparing to carry antlers, carved animal heads and masks in their processions. Later the king would watch mummers dress in outlandish costumes and perform 'disguising games'. With such celebration and excitement in the air, one might almost say that men's cares had been laid aside.

Almost, but not quite. Henry knew his father's legacy still cast a shadow over many of those present. Men might have said that England now had a young, strong and pious king – but they had said the same about his father fifteen years ago. Everyone in that hall knew what Henry IV had achieved. He had been the greatest tournament fighter the English royal family had ever produced; he had fought a crusade with the Teutonic Knights in Lithuania; he had been on a pilgrimage to Jerusalem; he had three times led an army to victory in battle and had taken control of England when Richard II was threatening to become a tyrant. And yet even he had found it impossible to control the kingdom. He had suffered vicious political attacks in almost every parliament he had held. He had survived at least three assassination attempts, three armed insurrections, three other seditious plots, a decade of Welsh revolt, and continual piratical attacks by the French. His reign had been synonymous with rebellion, unease, heresy and doubt. No one could be certain that his son's reign would be any different.

Everything came down to the means whereby Henry IV had taken the throne. Whichever way you looked at it, to *take* the throne was not legally defensible. In 1376, the ageing Edward III had drawn up a settlement in which he made his grandson, Richard II, his heir. According to this document, if Richard died without sons, then John of Gaunt and his son, Henry of Lancaster (the future Henry IV) would become kings in turn. Thus Henry IV had grown up believing he had a right to succeed to the throne. But in 1399 he had deposed Richard – the rightful, anointed king. This was not inheritance; many men held that it was against God's law. Worse still, Richard apparently drew up his own settlement of the throne prior to his deposition, making not Henry but the duke of York and his sons his rightful heirs.[3] Although the old duke had no wish to become king, Richard's settlement automatically nullified that of Edward III. So Henry IV had been forced to find an arcane and highly dubious legal basis to justify his succession. He took the throne as the male heir of Henry III, who had died more than a century earlier.[4] In reality, his succession was due to overwhelming political support and an election in parliament. When that popular support sharply declined in early 1401, and parliament started to oppose him, the real basis of his kingship was undermined.

The great problem for Henry IV was that any sign of divine dis-approval of his rule could be attributed to his illegal occupation of the throne. In this respect, he was doubly compromised. Not only had he removed the previous king in an unlawful move, he had put forward his own claim to be Richard's successor in defiance of the dynastic rights of another family descended from Edward III, the Mortimer earls of March. Edmund Mortimer was the great-great-grandson of Edward III through Philippa, only daughter of Lionel, Edward III's *second* son. Henry IV was descended from Edward III's *fourth* son. Edmund therefore had a claim to the throne which was arguably stronger than that of the Lancastrians. Even though he was descended from Edward III through a woman (Philippa), the common law of England held that a woman could transfer her father's prop-erty and titles to her own heirs if she had no brothers – and Philippa had no siblings at all. So, if the crown of England was a 'property', then Henry's father had broken the law in taking it in 1399, for it should have descended to Edmund. All the opposition that Henry IV had suffered during his reign – from piratical attacks and the harvest failures to rebellions and bad weather – could be blamed on God's displeasure that the Lancastrians and not the Mortimers were occu-pying the throne.

Of course, we do not know what Henry V was thinking at that moment, as he ate, looking at his household over the great gold eagle-topped spice-plate.[5] But we can be certain his father's legacy had not been forgotten. His family's claim to the throne was tainted – twice over. In fact, one may say it was tainted thrice over, for it was tainted in respect to France too.

When Henry IV had claimed to be king of England as the male heir of Henry III he had claimed the throne of France also, even though Henry III had never been king of France. The English claim to the French crown had been inherited in 1328 by Edward III through his mother, Isabella, last surviving child of Philip the Fair. It was thus demonstrably the case that it could be inherited through a female, and so legally it should have passed to the heir general of Edward III (not the heir male). This was Edmund Mortimer again. Regardless of the merits of Edmund's claim on the throne of England, his claim on that of France was immeasurably stronger than Henry's. In reality there would have been little or no value in the Mortimer family laying claim to the throne of France – they could not have enforced it – but the right of inheritance should have passed from Edward III to his second son, Lionel; and then to Lionel's only child, Philippa; and then to her children, the Mortimers. It was a double embarrassment that many men saw Henry's claim to the throne of England as based on a half-truth, and his claim to that of France as based on an outright lie.

On such things did men brood, and think, and whisper darkly, even at Christmas, with holly around the hall and the bright chandeliers burning above them.

*

If you could have been there that day, standing before Henry V as he ate, what would you have seen? A thoughtful-looking man of twenty-eight, seated at a linen-covered table, with his brothers, other great lords, and bishops dining on either side of him. He had a long face, a straight nose, and a broad forehead. The scar of an old arrow wound disfigured his right cheek. Despite this, there was a certain innocence about his expression, a vestige of the earnestness of boyhood.[6] He had thick brown hair, cut short at the sides and the back, and hazel eyes. His ears were small, his neck thick and manly, his lips full and red, and his chin modest with a slight cleft. As for his physique, he was above average height, slim and athletic. He loved hunting and was an excellent shot with a crossbow. To his contemporaries he was tireless, his energy and determination being sufficient to power his lithe figure longer than his fellow huntsmen.[7]

He was conscious of his appearance. In his household you would have found several mirrors, as well as golden musk balls and a pomander – the former to hold perfume and the latter to sweeten the air and help prevent him breathing in noxious vapours.[8] Unlike most of his royal predecessors he was clean-shaven, like a priest. In this he took after the king whom his father had deposed – Richard II – who had knighted him at the age of thirteen. He wore several rings, and a Lancastrian livery collar over his shoulders, and a golden crown. His clothing was, of course, every bit as splendid as you would expect: kings had to dress the part in rich velvet cloth and ermine-trimmed robes. Whether wearing a high-collared, loose-sleeved long gown, or a gold-embroidered *hanseline* (very short tunic), his clothes were elegant and rich. Sleeves were slashed to reveal golden linings, or hugely extended to show elaborate embroideries within the cuffs.[9]

As you continued to look at Henry, you would have seen that this careful outward display had nothing to do with boyish showing-off. The man was not a fop. He spoke very little, although always paying close attention to the speaker. There was nothing about him that was easy-going or even particularly joyful; there was no frivolity in his personality. When he did say something, his words were succinct and well chosen, and he tended to deliver them in 'a low tone of voice'.[10] A monk of Westminster Abbey described him as 'devout, abstemious, liberal to the poor, sparing of promises – but true to his word, once given; a quick, wide-awake man, though at times reserved and moody, intolerant of laxity in priests, chivalrous towards women and rigid in repressing riot and crime'.[11] His closest friends claimed that he never took a mistress or slept with a woman after becoming king.[12] According to a chronicler who was personally acquainted with his youngest brother, Humphrey, Henry's youthful experimentation with the fair sex was renounced as sinful upon his accession.[13] The chronicler Thomas Walsingham, who attended court at this time, wrote that Henry was suddenly transformed at his coronation into a new man in gravity, honesty and moderation.[14] Adam Usk described him as 'upright . . . full of wisdom and virtue'.[15] Indeed, the words that most accurately reflect the man's character are 'circumspect', 'fastidious', 'solemn', 'conscientious', 'firm' and – apart from a deep pride – 'virtuous'.

His pride was probably his greatest weakness. When his honour was impinged he could suddenly become very angry. He allowed no one to look him in the eye – even though it was normal behaviour for men to look at their lords directly – and he could be roused to anger by anyone who dared to do so, even to the point of sacking an officer for looking at him in a manner that he found disrespectful.[16] Such pride inevitably affected his judgment. Pride had contributed to the volatility of his relationship with his father, especially after his father had overlooked him for the command of the expedition to France in 1412. Another example of pride getting the better of him was his determination to obtain a French bride. In 1400 the French royal family had refused to allow Henry's father to arrange a marriage between Henry and Isabella of France, the young widow of Richard II. Henry himself never seriously entertained any marriage other than with a French princess. After being rebuffed with regard to Isabella's hand, he sent ambassadors to negotiate his marriage with first one of her sisters, and then another.[17] When he declared he would marry no one but Katherine of France, in June 1414, she was twelve, less than half his age, and he had never seen her or spoken to her.[18] In all his negotiations, union with a daughter of the king of France – any daughter, it did not matter which – was a key objective. It was as if he was determined to reverse that original slight to his dignity. To him, marriage was not a matter of love. It was a matter of pride.

Henry was a sophisticated, educated man. He had had only a limited opportunity to benefit from his highly educated mother, Mary Bohun, who had died when he was not quite eight. But his father, who could read and write in English, Latin and French, intended that all his children should be similarly literate.[19] So young Henry had been brought up to be a polymath, and taught grammar, logic and rhetoric – perhaps under the tutelage of his uncle, Henry Beaufort, chancellor of the University of Oxford.[20] He also learnt music, just as his father and mother had done, playing the harp and singing. From the age of seven or eight he had a military tutor, and learnt to emulate his progenitors in jousting, horsemanship and wielding a sword. He was keen to use English as well as French in daily conversation, writing letters in English and commissioning translations of French and Latin books. Although it is often said that Henry was not born to be king, by the time of his birth – on 16 September 1386 – his father deemed his chances of succession very good indeed, and gave him an education fitting for a prince.[21]

The older men at that feast would have left you in no doubt that Henry V was every inch his father's son – intellectually, linguistically and musically. Father and son had much in common spiritually, too. Both were fervent in their beliefs and sufficiently confident in their personal religion that they could challenge church leaders when necessary.[22] Both men were ardent supporters of the Trinity: the mystical union of the Father, Son and Holy Ghost that bound many of the senior members of European nobility into a spiritual compact. In this they followed the by-now legendary eldest son of Edward III – Edward of Woodstock, known today as the Black Prince – who had died on Trinity Sunday 1376 and had been buried in the Trinity Chapel in

Canterbury Cathedral. Henry IV had been buried alongside him. Henry V was keen also to publicise his devotion to the English saints, St Edmund and St Edward the Confessor, as well as St George and the Virgin Mary – all of whom had been the subjects of Edward III's devotion in his wars against the Scots.[23] He was also inspired by St Bridget, St John of Bridlington (his special patron), and St John of Beverley, under whose banner English kings had often marched against the Scots.[24] It was said that he heard Mass three times a day, and conducted no other business when in his oratory.[25] One could say that Henry's religion was traditional and nationalistic, but, if so, then the tradition in question was that of the most serious personal commitment to the Catholic saints, and the nationalistic aspect was not just a means to a secular end but a spiritual one, too.

The scar on Henry's face was a legacy from the battle of Shrewsbury twelve years earlier. That was arguably Henry's true education – armed campaigning and military leadership. From 1400, when he was just fourteen, the responsibility of putting down the revolt of the Welshman, Owen Glendower, was partly delegated to him. In this he was assisted by Henry Percy, known as 'Hotspur'. But in 1403, Hotspur and his uncle, the earl of Worcester, rebelled. They raised an army in the hope of joining forces with Glendower, and marched to Shrewsbury. Young Henry held the town while his father led a hastily gathered army to relieve him and to attack the rebels on the English side of the River Severn. It was the first time on English soil that two armies of English longbowmen had faced each other. The battle was terrifying. Three thousand men ran away at the start. Many others were torn to pieces by the clouds of arrows in the first few minutes. The king's vanguard was destroyed, the earl of Stafford was killed. Henry and his father both put themselves into the thick of the fighting, and Henry himself was struck by an arrow in the face. It penetrated to a depth of six inches below his right eye, but he refused to leave the field of battle. His father eventually prevailed, leading his army to victory, killing Hotspur in the course of the battle, and capturing and beheading Worcester.

After his recovery from his arrow wound, Henry increasingly assumed responsibility for the defence of Wales. It was a testing period. Glendower's successes meant that more men deserted the English cause. Henry's own chamberlain at Chester, John Trevor, bishop of

St Asaph, joined the revolt. Although the king led annual expeditions
into Wales, normally in conjunction with Prince Henry, the Welsh
were too manoeuvrable, and evaded battle each time by retreating
into the mountains. After the English had withdrawn, they would
emerge again and devastate the borders and lands of English loyal-
ists. Thus fewer and fewer Welshmen contributed to Henry's income
and more and more Englishmen were in need of protection. There
was a financial strain as well as a military one; and this led to a shortage
of men to garrison the Welsh castles as well as a lack of soldiers in
the field. The castles of Harlech and Aberystwyth fell to the Welsh
in 1404. Henry's first victory, at Grosmont, in March 1405, was a rare
English success. Only with the battle of Usk later that year did the
tide turn: Glendower's brother was killed and one of his sons was
captured. By 1407, when Henry laid siege to Aberystwyth, the Welsh
revolt was losing strength. The following year Aberystwyth was recaptured, and the year after that Harlech was retaken.

What had the conflict taught Henry? Obviously he had acquired
certain leadership skills, and had come to understand an army's needs
in the field. Equally obviously there were the military and strategic
lessons of fighting a protracted campaign. But there were more subtle
lessons too. Henry saw for himself that, while *battles* might be won
by courageous men and teams of well-organised archers, *wars* required
high finance. He had lost Aberystwyth and Harlech in 1404 because
he had not been able to maintain large enough garrisons. Even more
importantly, in Wales he discovered his own fallibility. At Aberystwyth
in 1407 he had been on the point of re-taking the castle when he made
a serious mistake. He agreed to allow the Welsh to have free entry
and exit from the castle for a full month in return for bringing Owen
Glendower and a Welsh army to do battle with him at the end of
October.[26] But he did not allow sufficient time for an English army
to be gathered. Glendower appeared, found no army to fight, and was
able to reinforce the castle. Henry achieved nothing except to cast
doubt upon his own judgment. Aberystwyth was recaptured the
following year by men acting in Henry's name, not by Henry himself.

There were two further lessons that the Welsh wars had taught
him, and they are both essential to an understanding of him as a man.
The first was an awareness of his position in relation to God. The
battle of Shrewsbury was not just a fight between a king and a rebel

lord; it was a battle to determine in the eyes of God whether Henry's father had been right to depose Richard II and take the throne. If it was not God's will, then it would have been Henry IV's death that would have been commemorated by the church built on the battle-field. As it was, Hotspur was killed, and the king had given thanks to God for the victory. But the divine judgment had also contained a warning – in the arrow that found its way deep into Henry's face – and Henry himself was unlikely to forget it. Every time he saw men looking at his scar he must have been conscious of it. When his men won the battle of Grosmont in March 1405, he was quick to attribute the victory to God's will, not his own leadership. In 1408, after his failure at Aberystwyth, he set off on a pilgrimage to the shrines of St John of Beverley and St John of Bridlington. In Henry's mind there was no difference between the pursuit of military objectives and the enactment of God's will. If religion was a way to attain a military advantage, then victory was a means of demonstrating God's blessing.

This combination of nationalistic pursuits and the enactment of divine will, wrapped together in the person of the king, was hugely powerful. It permitted Henry and his father to justify their claim to the throne of France even though it had no basis in law. They could claim the French title on the basis that it was God's will – for God could over-ride and overrule the law. The only problem was that one had to take risks to invoke the approbation of the Almighty – to put oneself to the test, to show that God really did favour those who claimed to be acting in His name. No coward could claim to be exer-cising the will of God.

The other important lesson from the decade of conflict in Wales was that of the importance of loyalty. As far as medieval kings were concerned, loyalty was *the* cardinal virtue. One chronicler noted that Henry, when trying to reassure his father that he would protect and love his brothers, stated that he would not fail to execute justice on them, as if they were 'the worst and simplest persons', if they were not loyal to him.[27] He had good reason to place a high value on loyalty. In January 1400 he had experienced the treason of the Epiphany Rising, when certain lords loyal to Richard II had attempted to kill Henry's father as well as Henry himself and his three brothers. The subsequent rebellions against his father merely confirmed Henry's perceptions of his vulnerability. Hotspur had been Henry's lieutenant prior to his revolt in 1403, and the earl of Worcester had been his governor. How could men such as these take arms against him? How could men like Bishop Trevor, his chamberlain at Chester, desert him for Glendower? His closest friends became more important to him than ever. Those with whom he served in Wales – men such as the duke of York, the earls of Arundel and Warwick and Richard Courtenay – became the closest and most trusted friends he ever had.

For these reasons, had you been looking into the eyes of Henry V on Christmas Day, 1414, you would have added another word to that list. In addition to 'circumspect', 'fastidious', 'conscientious', 'solemn', 'firm', 'proud' and 'virtuous', you would have added 'intense'. The man was vulnerable, and had repeatedly been made conscious of the fact – from the arrow in his face in 1403 to the tactical blunder of 1407, his sacking as regent in 1411, and the public questioning of his trust-worthiness in 1412. His succession to the throne did not make him any less vulnerable, quite the reverse. His safety now rested upon his ability to command his friends and his continued enjoyment of God's blessing. At any moment he could be betrayed, or even murdered, or fall from God's grace through some unfortunate turn of events, as his father had done in his protracted sickness. It is not surprising, therefore, to find signs of worry and superstition at his court. Among his possessions we find such things as a triacle (a container for an oint-ment to protect against poison), and rings and crosses containing relics of saints. He took astrology very seriously – he possessed several astro-labes for charting the position of the stars. The idea of sorcery haunted him, as it did many of those in and around the late medieval court.[28] In the prince's palace at Westminster was a seat hanging worked with the inscription, *Je vous ayme loialment* (I love you loyally), as if the emphasis on *loyalty* somehow made it more substantial.[29] At his court there was a sense that everything good, noble, virtuous and worth loving hung by a slender thread, and might vanish in an instant.

*

As Henry sat dining at the high table in Westminster Hall, he would have been surrounded by family, friends, lords, bishops, servants and other members of the royal household. On his left would have been his three brothers.[30] First of these was Thomas, duke of Clarence, the next-in-line to the throne. He was only a year younger than Henry, having been born in the autumn of 1387. The two boys had grown up together, staying with their mother in childhood and, following their mother's death in 1394, with their grandfather, John of Gaunt. By 1398 Thomas had been singled out as his father's favourite son, his name appearing high on the list of recipients of Henry IV's New Year presents (while Prince Henry's name does not appear at all).[31] It is possible that their rivalry developed at this time, and perhaps was even caused by their father's favouritism. When their father was exiled by Richard II in October 1398, the two boys were separated: Richard II took Henry with him to Ireland, and knighted him there. Thomas was left behind in England – and had to wait until his father's coronation in 1399 for his own knighthood.

In 1401, the fourteen-year-old Thomas was appointed King's Lieutenant of Ireland. The intention was that he should be educated in the tough environment of a war zone, like his older brother at the same age. Although restricted to Dublin for much of the time, Thomas soon developed as a military commander of remarkable courage and ferocity. Four years later – and now an admiral – he ravaged the coast of France. In 1408 he returned to Ireland to fight in Leinster. By this time his martial career was beginning to outshine that of his elder brother, and their rivalry resurfaced. After Thomas returned to England in 1409, Prince Henry accused him of neglecting his Irish duties, and urged him to give up his Irish position. Thomas refused, and further irritated his brother and Henry Beaufort when, in 1410, he obtained papal permission to marry the widow of his uncle, John Beaufort (Henry Beaufort's elder brother). The king further compounded the breach between his rival sons in 1412, when he created Thomas duke of Clarence and appointed him commander of the expeditionary army to aid the Armagnacs, passing over Prince Henry in the process.

This rivalry continued after the death of their father. Henry held his coronation quickly, before Thomas could return from Gascony; in so doing he deprived Thomas of the chance to officiate at the coronation in his capacity as steward of England. Later Henry stripped Thomas of the stewardship altogether. He also sacked him as King's Lieutenant of Ireland. He gave him no other position of responsibility or important command. Henry's antipathy to his brother might have been exacerbated by the knowledge that Thomas had sealed important and binding treaties of support with many of the Armagnac lords while in France in 1412, including the duke of Orléans, the count of Armagnac, and Charles d'Albret, in direct opposition to Henry's own policy of favouring the Burgundians.[32] Alternatively it might have been because Henry suspected Thomas of being a closet heretic – a sympathiser of the Lollards, the followers of John Wycliffe, who denied transubstantiation in the Mass, who sought to strip the church of its wealth, and promoted the use of a vernacular Bible (a copy of which Thomas owned).[33] Whatever the true explanation, the rivalry challenged Henry's pride. Whether it went so far as to prevent Thomas attending the Christmas feast in 1414, it is not possible to say. If Thomas was there, then he would have been seated near to the king. His status as next-in-line to the throne would have demanded it.

John, duke of Bedford, was perhaps the most gifted of all four of Henry IV's sons. Aged twenty-five, he was just as solemn, religious, conscientious and circumspect as Henry himself; and yet he was also as brave as Thomas (although he did not have Thomas's hot-headedness). He also displayed many of the intellectual characteristics of their younger brother, Humphrey. The warrior, the thinker, the cultural patron and the man of God were most evenly balanced in John; one might even say that all these attributes were more evident in him than in any other individual of the age.

John was a large, strong man; one chronicler referred to him having 'powerful limbs'.[34] He had a round head with a beaked nose, and wore his hair cut short around the sides and back of his head, like the king. He could read and write in English, French and Latin, like his brothers. His practical education from the age of fourteen had been the control of the north of England, as one of the two wardens of the Scottish Marches. In 1414 Henry raised John to a dukedom, making him duke of Bedford, earl of Kendal and earl of Richmond. Henry valued him greatly, and trusted him absolutely.

The youngest of Henry's brothers was the twenty-four-year-old Humphrey, duke of Gloucester. Although he had been knighted along with his brothers Thomas and John in 1399, and nominated to the Order of the Garter the following year, he was nowhere near as gifted in military affairs as his three older brothers. Probably because of this, he alone of the four sons of Henry IV was not given a military command at the age of fourteen. Nor did he receive a title from his father; it was Henry V who created him duke of Gloucester. The talents Humphrey had inherited rather lay in the intellectual side of life: in argument and learning. In later years he would establish great collections of classical texts; the oldest part of the Bodleian Library at Oxford is still called Duke Humfrey's Library in his memory. He became an early patron of Italian humanism in England. His patronage of writers was extensive, and his own court came to include poets, astrologers, doctors and musicians, as well as those who simply engaged with his ideas. Like many intellectuals, he was not actually given over to intense scholarship himself, perhaps lacking the patience required to master ancient works. He is suspected of reading his classical texts in French, not Latin or Greek. But his failure to master foreign tongues should not detract from the fact that his intellectual abilities were of the highest order, for his engagement with contemporary writers and thinkers was genuine, ambitious, enthusiastic, impressive and important in the cultural development of the nation.

Humphrey's logic, confidence and clear-sightedness impressed his contemporaries. Yet men did not rush to follow him into battle. He was opinionated, fervent in his beliefs, and judgmental – but he was not reliable or particularly courageous. On this basis one might agree with a later pope who declared that Humphrey was 'more given to pleasure and letters than to arms, and valued his life more than his honour'.[35] But this would be a little misleading, for it would suggest that he harboured no martial ambitions. This was not the case. Like a true Renaissance man, Humphrey saw no end to his abilities. When in later years he encouraged an Italian poet in his service, Titus Livius Frulovisi, to write the history of the reign of Henry V, he was very keen to see his own military roles given prominence. So, although he lacked his older brothers' leadership skills, his ambitions also extended to commanding armies and winning chivalric glory. This fact was not lost on his eldest brother, the king, whom he idolised. If ever Humphrey was going to prove himself in battle, it was in the service of Henry V.

Before turning to the other people in the hall that day, it is worth considering the collective force of all four of these royal brothers. Past studies of Henry V have described him in terms of individual greatness, as a man isolated in his genius – quiet and circumspect in his speech because no one could match him for political and spiritual insight. Contemporary chroniclers presented the king as an individual, a saviour. Shakespeare played this up, for the sake of heroic drama. But Henry was far from being alone in his royalty. He certainly was his father's son, and displayed many of his father's talents; but so did his brothers. Never before or since has so much brilliance, energy, courage and intellectual understanding been packed into one generation of the royal family. Henry V's brothers might have looked up to him – idolised him – but that was because they expected so much of him. And in return he had to show that there was more to his kingship than royal blood. The respect of these intelligent, high-born men counted, and it was not something that he could simply have claimed as an inheritance.

*

Given that Westminster Hall was the largest medieval hall in England – 67ft 6ins wide and 240ft long – and given that there were more than five hundred men in the royal household, it hardly needs saying that there were many other people present. The width suggests that between twenty and thirty people were seated on the daïs. Among them would have been Henry's first cousin once-removed, Edward, duke of York – a great huntsman, and one of Henry's closest companions since the days of his youth. Edmund Mortimer, earl of March, may have been there too, having spent much of the year 1414 with Henry.[36] No doubt both Henry's uncles, Henry and Thomas Beaufort, were seated at the high table. They were the two surviving sons of John of Gaunt and Katherine Swynford, and so half-brothers of Henry's late father. The elder of the two, Henry Beaufort, was now in his early forties. He was bishop of Winchester, chancellor of England, and one of the most ambitious men of the age. Not satisfied with being born great, he wanted to achieve great things as well. Not much happened that did not come to his attention – whether as chancellor, bishop, or a member of the royal family. Thomas Beaufort, a year or two younger than his brother, was the earl of Dorset and admiral of England. He too was eminently capable, and had himself been chancellor of England in the past. Henry was close to them both.

Also at the high table would have been several high-ranking churchmen. Picture them, clean-shaven and tonsured (the tops of their heads shaved), and dressed in their ceremonial robes, seated directly on the king's right hand. Closest to Henry would have been Henry Chichele, the archbishop of Canterbury, aged about fifty-three. The slightly older bishop of Durham, Thomas Langley, would have been close by. Another priest, Stephen Patrington, deserves particular mention. He was in his mid sixties, and from Yorkshire: a friar who had been head of the Carmelite Order in England from 1399 until his appointment as Henry's personal confessor on his accession. To say he was delicately positioned – confessor to a warrior king – is an understatement.

Among the hundreds of men seated at the lower tables were lords, knights, esquires, gentlemen, sergeants-at-arms, priests, singers, minstrels, clerks, heralds and many other sorts of men. Most of the officers of the royal household would have been present. Old Sir Thomas Erpingham – the steward and the most senior officer of the royal household – would certainly have been standing with his staff of office somewhere near the king. So would the second most senior officer, Sir Roger Leche, the treasurer of the household (also known as the keeper of the king's wardrobe). Somewhere in the hall would have been William the king's fool, and Hugh Mortimer, who had served Henry as both a chamberlain and an ambassador.[37] Thomas Chaucer, the king's chief butler (and son of the great poet, Geoffrey Chaucer), may have been supervising the wine. The sixty-year-old John Prophet, keeper of the privy seal, would also have been in attendance on the king.

It is with respect to the women who may have been present that we start to encounter a problem. There is very little evidence of Henry having much to do with women at this time in his life. This was certainly due in part to the nature of the court of an unmarried king, and it is undoubtedly a consequence of the sorts of evidence that have survived. But it also seems to be due in part to the king himself. He did not sleep with women, and he seems to have spent little time in their company. He did not tolerate prostitutes in the royal household (unlike some of his forebears).[38] His petite stepmother, Queen Joan, might have been seated near him on the daïs that Christmas, but if so she was there as a guest; she was not a member of the royal household.[39] It is possible that Henry's aunt, Elizabeth, wife of Sir John Cornwaille, was present. The dowager duchess of York, now married to Henry's friend Lord Scrope, might also have been in the hall. But it is difficult to identify many other women who might have been there as guests. Henry was *chivalrous* towards women, but he was not *close* to them. He mentioned more than forty people in his will by name, but only two were women – his grandmother and his step-mother – and the reference to his stepmother, Queen Joan, was more out of duty than affection. He was single, celibate, facially disfigured, somewhat aloof and obsessed with religion, justice and war. In this respect it is interesting to see how determined he was to marry a French princess whom he had never met, and who was still sexually immature, rather than a woman of his own age to whom he was already close. Most of his predecessors had married for love – including his father, grandfather (John of Gaunt) and great-grandfather (Edward III) – but Henry was not so inclined.

*

On the night of 20 March 1413, after his father had breathed his last in the Jerusalem Chamber at Westminster, Henry had left his brother Humphrey and his stepmother, and gone into the abbey alone. Although he was king, the actual first day of his reign would be the following day, in accordance with tradition. He would take no royal actions on the day of his father's death, other than to issue the trad-itional order for the ports to be closed, to stop the enemies of England taking advantage of a transition in their government.

In the abbey he walked by candlelight among the silent tombs of his ancestors. Here was the jewel-encrusted shrine of Saint Edward the Confessor, founder of the abbey. There was the tomb of Henry III, the king who had rebuilt the abbey on a lavish scale. Under a plain black slab beside him was his son, Edward I, the most formidable warrior of his age. Opposite Edward I was the tomb of Richard II and his wife, Anne, although at that point Richard's body was still at Langley and had yet to be placed in the tomb. And next to Richard, surrounded by figures of all twelve of his children, there was the great Edward III, the king who had been prophesied to be a new King Arthur: who had defeated the Scots and French in battle repeat-edly, who had reclaimed his French inheritance, and built such magnif-icent palaces as Queenborough Castle and the royal apartments of

Windsor Castle. He had introduced a considerable programme of new legislation, delivered justice for his people, and created a sense that England was a kingdom of the first importance. Men sang songs about him, and based their stories of King Arthur on him. He had become the very epitome of great kingship.

Henry walked through to the south transept of the abbey church. Here in a cell near St Benet's chapel, there lived a hermit, called William Alnwick.[40] Henry sat down and began talking to him. He remained there all night. The personal qualities of a king, especially the king's morality, may well have entered the conversation. The duty of a king to prevent conflict among the nobles – the principal exhortation to kings for at least the last century – perhaps also entered the debate. Perhaps Henry's father had mentioned the same matter to him on his deathbed, having been worried that Henry and his brother Thomas would end up fighting for the crown.[41] There were certainly nobles who thought that the earl of March should be king. Even at that moment there was a protester, John Whytlock, taking sanctuary in the precincts of that same church. He had raised the old cry 'King Richard is alive!' This was tantamount to declaring that the Lancastrians had no right to the throne. Such a declaration on the eve of the new reign was not a good sign.[42]

Worse portents were to follow. A blizzard struck as Henry made the traditional procession from the Tower of London to Westminster before his coronation in early April, and the snows continued to fall in some counties for two days, covering men and animals. The chronicler John Strecche declared the heavy hail that day as exceeding anything since the days of the legendary ancient British king, King Lear![43] The interpretation of some contemporaries was that this reign would be cold and stern. Henry ate nothing through the whole feast that followed his coronation. If that was a penitential fast, it did no good. The summer of 1413 was one of excessive heat and widespread sicknesses. Terrible fires broke out at Norwich, Tewkesbury and Robertsbridge. The autumn saw another destructive hailstorm, and the winter was no better. Three days after Christmas the church of St Giles at Winchelsea was struck by lightning.

The ill portents heralded evil events. Early in January 1414 two men had come to the king with news of a Lollard rising planned by Sir John Oldcastle. He had already been sentenced to death for his heresy, but had escaped from the Tower of London. Now he was planning to assassinate Henry and his brothers. This was not just treason, it was personal disloyalty – for Oldcastle had fought alongside Henry in Wales. He had been captain of Hay Castle, and attended the siege of Aberystwyth with Henry. He had been a commissioner of the peace in Herefordshire and sheriff of the county. He had even fought with the earl of Arundel in France in 1411, in Henry's mercenary army. If anyone should have been trustworthy, it was Oldcastle. But on the night of 9–10 January 1414 he gathered a crowd of several hundred of his fellow Lollards at St Giles' Fields. Henry, having inside information from his two informants, had no difficulty rounding them up. Sixty-nine were accused of treason and condemned to death. Thirty-one were hanged, and a further seven burnt at the stake for heresy.[44] Oldcastle himself escaped. It was deeply worrying for Henry that the Lollards gathered there in St Giles' Fields came from all over southern England, from as far as Bristol in the west and Essex in the east.

Oldcastle's plot was never likely to succeed, but ironically for that very fact it was symbolically dangerous. It was a sign of desperation. Men like him could hardly change the customs of the Church by carrying out acts of treason against their king. Oldcastle was a peer of the realm – being also Lord Cobham in right of his wife – so he had the king's ear. If he had harboured a grudge against the king he could have come to see him personally. Instead he had given this influence up in order to stage a coup. When he could have recanted and saved his life, he had declared that 'the pope is [the] very Antichrist, that is, the head; that the archbishops, bishops and other prelates be his members, and that the friars be his tail'.[45] The worrying truth was that Oldcastle and his friends were as committed, sincere and fervent in their heresy as Henry himself was in his religious orthodoxy. If heretics as fervent as this were to be found right across the realm, from Bristol to Essex, then Henry had many potential enemies.

Henry's reaction to Oldcastle's plot – burning seven men alive – marked a profound change in his attitude to heresy. In 1410, when John Badby had been sentenced to the flames for his heretical utterances, Henry had tried all he could to persuade him to recant, dragging the fire away and offering him a pension. Badby had refused, preferring to suffer the agony of the flames. In 1414 Henry did not try to save any of the men similarly destined for the stake. Shortly afterwards he declared in parliament that the intent of Lollardy was not only 'to adnull and subvert the Christian faith and the law of God' but also 'to destroy our sovereign lord the king himself'.[46] For an anointed king, who believed he reigned by divine right, heresy and treason were now intertwined, and deviation in matters of faith was synonymous with political rebellion. Those who saw their faith as a justification for treason could expect no mercy.

*

Henry's problems at Christmas 1414 were far from insignificant. Oldcastle was still on the run. Lollardy was growing in strength. And Glendower was still a free man. Although the Welsh rebel no longer had command over an emergent independent nation, as he had briefly in 1404–5, he still attracted enough support for parliament to describe Wales as 'a country at war' in May 1414. There had been no knockout blow. Despite nine years in the field, in person, Henry had failed to secure the land of which he was nominally the prince.

Much the same could be said for Ireland and the Marches of Scotland. Henry had sacked his brother Thomas as King's Lieutenant of Ireland, and replaced him with Sir John Stanley soon after his accession. This had been a bad move. Whereas Thomas had commanded respect and support, Stanley had been a selfish failure. The English lords in Ireland claimed he had enriched himself through extortion. Unfortunately for him – but fortunately for Henry – Stanley died within six months. The Irish lords established their own interim government under Thomas Cranley, archbishop of Dublin, and sent the treasurer of Ireland back to England to give the king a full report of their calamitous position. A veteran of the Welsh wars, Sir John Talbot of Hallamshire (also known as Lord Furnival), was appointed as the next King's Lieutenant of Ireland in February 1414. However, he did not actually set sail until November.

As for the Scottish Marches, Henry's brother, John, had written to him about the state of the north in May 1414. Men loyal to Henry were suffering, John declared, because there had been a 'lack of good governance' for many years. Even though the king of the Scots was still a prisoner in the Tower, the Scottish lords had made frequent incursions into their lands. The gates, walls and drawbridges of Berwick, the border town, were in ruins. No gunpowder or cannon were available for its defence. The finances of the East March were more than £13,000 in arrears. John had had to melt down some of his plate to pay his men. He had also pawned his jewels and borrowed heavily from his friends to try to make ends meet. As with Ireland, this was a situation bordering on desperation, similar to the circumstances that had lost Henry possession of the castles of Harlech and Aberystwyth in 1404.

The situation in Gascony was similar. There were too many enemies and not enough men or supplies to guarantee the safety of the region. The financial situation there was chaotic, with taxes not agreed, let alone paid.[47] The only help that Henry's Gascon subjects had received since his accession was his authorisation of a campaign into the Saintonge area in 1413 under his uncle, Thomas Beaufort. Thomas had captured a number of small places quickly, and did manage to control access to the Charente for a few months, but ultimately he succeeded only in attracting more French troops and cannon to the area. A truce was agreed at the end of January 1414, which was to last until 2 February 1415. After that, war could be expected again. On 15 October 1414 Henry wrote to the Jurade – the mayor and jurats – of Bordeaux apologising for having done so little for them, and promising he would soon send them some artillery and a master gunner. The letter did not arrive for another eight months. Soon he was writing to the Jurade asking them to send *him* siege engines and cannon. His policy towards the defence of Gascony was chaotic – in fact, he seems to have had no policy at all.[48]

On top of all this, there was the situation in France.

Henry's alliance with John the Fearless, duke of Burgundy, had proved to be problematic. He had pursued it firmly, believing that it not only represented the best way to destabilise the French kingdom but also justified involving England in the French civil war. However, following the Cabochien revolt in Paris in late April 1413, the Armagnacs had gradually seized the initiative. On 23 August that year John the Fearless had fled from the city.[49] It left him in a desperate condition, prepared to enter any agreement to bolster his position, even entertaining the idea of swearing allegiance to Henry as king of France.[50] At the same time he had no qualms about agreeing with Henry's enemies that he would send troops to fight in Scotland against the English. Partly because of this duplicity, Henry's alliance with Burgundy was unstable. But Charles VI of France was no more reliable. He refused even to recognise Henry as the rightful king of England, describing him as 'our adversary of England'. From Henry's point of view, a more decisive intervention was necessary.

Henry sent an embassy to France in July 1414. Through his spokesmen he issued outrageous demands for the settlement of the war. He demanded the restitution of all the lands settled on Edward III by the Treaty of Brétigny in 1360, sovereignty over the duchies of Aquitaine, Normandy, Brittany and Flanders, and over the counties of Touraine, Maine and Anjou, half the county of Provence, and the repayment of 1.6 million crowns (£266,666) still owing from the ransom of John II of France (who had died in England in 1364). As if that were not enough, they also demanded the hand in marriage of the French king's daughter, plus a further two million crowns as a dowry.

Obviously the French could not have agreed to such demands. But they did not simply reject them. They offered to restore the whole of the duchy of Aquitaine to English control, in line with the illegal Treaty of Bourges in 1412.[51] They declared that a marriage between Henry and a French princess was acceptable in principle, and that her dowry might be as much as 600,000 crowns (£100,000). Provence was not a French lordship, but part of the kingdom of Sicily; so that was not within their gift. As for the outstanding portion of King John II's ransom, they declared that payments should be deferred, but it was not out of the question.

It was, on the face of it, a huge step towards what Henry wanted. But still he was not happy. He demanded satisfaction of his terms in full, even though they were so far beyond reasonableness that many people scoffed at them. The reality was that he wanted the French to fail. He wanted to restart the war.

There is no doubt about Henry's willingness to renew hostilities. He had been amassing money, armour, munitions and weapons ever since his accession. In June 1413 he had written to the people of Salisbury asking for money to aid his 'forthcoming expedition'.[52] In September that same year he had hired oxen and horses to bring heavy guns from Bristol to London. Smiths were commissioned to help make cannon in the Tower in February 1414.[53] In September 1414 he had commissioned Nicholas Merbury, master of the ordnance, to enlist stonemasons, carpenters and other workers to provide necessaries for the king's guns.[54] The same month he had prohibited the export of gunpowder. According to a contemporary chronicler, Thomas Walsingham, royal agents were scouring the country, looking for guns.[55] Another contemporary chronicler, John Strecche, noted that Henry was accumulating 'hauberks, helmets, shields, corslets, bucklers, lance-heads, gauntlets, plate-armour, swords, bows, many thousands of arrows, casks full of bowstrings, axes, saws, wedges, hammers, forks, mattocks, hoes, spades, caltrops and other tools for felling and splitting wood and mining walls'.[56] In October 1414 he had paid the expenses of those who had gathered and shaped 10,000 stone cannonballs.[57] It is very difficult to avoid the conclusion that the reason why Henry had issued such outrageous demands in 1414 was precisely so they *would* be rejected. He did not want terms; he wanted the French to break off negotiations and to appear unreasonable.

However, Henry could not just dismiss the generosity of the French ambassadors; he had to acknowledge their diplomatic readiness to compromise. So he summoned a council of lords and knights within days of hearing the news from France. The council recommended that he send ambassadors to 'every party' to state his case, stipulating that he wanted the terms of the Treaty of Brétigny satisfied in full. In the meantime, they said, he should continue preparations for his voyage, and take measures for the safety of the realm.[58] Henry took this as a sign to summon a parliament to arrange a grant of taxation to cover the expenses of the forthcoming war.

There was no ambiguity about the purpose of the parliament that followed in November 1414. In his opening speech the chancellor, Henry Beaufort, declared

> our most sovereign lord the king desires especially that good and wise action should be taken against his enemies outside the realm, and furthermore he will strive for the recovery of the inheritance and right of his crown outside the realm, which has for a long time been withheld and wrongfully retained, since the time of his progenitors and predecessors kings of England, in accordance with the authorities who wish that 'unto death shalt thou strive for justice'.[59]

Obviously Henry had no wish to await the outcome of further - negotiations. There was no provision to return any of the tax if war did not ensue. Members of Parliament thus knew that they were

being asked to decide whether England should go to war or not.
Although many were reluctant, and the Speaker, Thomas Chaucer,
had considerable difficulty in persuading those present to voice
support for the war, there were sufficient lords and knights who
were convinced of the need to defend the realm for Henry to be
granted his tax. If the ambassadors whom Henry had sent to 'every
party' failed in their mission, as Henry knew they would, then he
could take military action.

This determination to go to war explains why he rejected the most
generous terms he could have possibly expected from the French –
something which has long confused historians. It had always been his
intention to go to war, even before he became king. His father had
intended to lead an army into France and had failed to do so. Invading
France was a chance for Henry to go a step further than his father.
This ambition did not change with his accession; in fact it seems to
have grown more profound, becoming more of a religious responsibility to complete the work that Edward III had left unfinished, which
God had clearly blessed through delivering so many English victories.
Hence Henry's military preparations did not slow down. Eight days
after the parliament in which he declared that he was going to war
in France he commissioned William Woodward, founder, and Gerard
Sprong, to take 'copper, brass, bronze and iron and all other kinds of
metals for making certain guns of the king' as well as pots, bowls and
other vessels relating to the king's kitchen; and timber, saltpetre, stone
for the guns, and coals for making the guns, and workmen.[60]

It was not a situation that boded well for peace.

*

This was the state of the realm that Christmas Day. Not only was
Henry's kingdom being frayed at the edges, and fractured by internal
religious dissent, it was on the very brink of a full-scale war with
France, a kingdom with a population of about sixteen million people
– more than five times as many as in England. The security of the
realm was precarious, to say the least, and the fault for that lay partly
with the king.

What did Henry have to show for his reign by Christmas 1414? He
had started rebuilding Sheen, the palace on the Thames that Richard

II had destroyed after the death of his first wife there.[61] He had reburied Richard II's body at Westminster, in his proper tomb, and had commissioned the completion of the unfinished nave of the abbey church.[62] He had begun a process of reconciliation with the heirs of lords who had rebelled against his father's rule.[63] He had opened negotiations with Scotland for the return of their captive king, James I. He had issued commissions to try and restore law and order in Wales.[64] These were all positive moves, but none was especially impressive. His French diplomacy had been dramatic and dangerous, but had yielded no positive results.

To date his most significant achievement had been the passing of three statutes in the Leicester parliament of April 1414. These were the Statute of Lollards, which placed responsibility for revealing religious dissenters and heretics upon all royal officers; the Statute of Riots, which increased the powers of the chancellor to enquire into the causes of riots and to fine those involved; and the Statute of Truces, which sought to eradicate piracy against ships of kingdoms whose sovereign lord had a truce with the king of England. This hardly amounted to greatness. Henry commanded huge respect amongst the peers of the realm for his conscientiousness and virtuous character, and he had begun to show that he was keen to maintain law and order, and to uphold the dignity of the Church, but that was all.

However, had you been present at the feast, you would have realised that the situation on the ground and the situation in the king's mind did not match. For Henry was motivated by the most powerful vision. It amounted to a sort of compact with God to deliver a perfect religious kingship. He would eradicate heresy, as God surely wished, and reform the Church in conjunction with the Holy Roman Emperor. He would end the civil war in France and the war between France and England by subjecting both kingdoms to the rule of one spiritually enlightened monarch – himself. He would end the string of disasters that had befallen France by challenging something which he felt was displeasing to God: namely the refusal of the French to accept the divinely sanctioned, 'rightful heir', Edward III, as king of France. In setting about this he would himself emulate King Edward, his great-grandfather. Men were talking about that reign as a golden age; but he did not aspire to become a second Edward III just for the benefit of the English nation; it was more for the purpose of doing God's work.

If he could combine military endeavour with the exercise of God's will, and be seen to win divine approval as the saviour of both England and France, then he would achieve more even than his semi-legendary great-grandfather. Then Scotland, Gascony, Wales, Ireland and Lollardy would all appear like trivial issues, quibbles that he could silence with a word.

This was the true state of the realm at Christmas 1414. It was not the unsatisfactory small-scale conflicts around the periphery that mattered so much as the awe-inspiring spiritual vision of the man at the centre. It was not the long shadow of the last reign but the new king's intensity and commitment, and the support he enjoyed in the men around him. It was not Henry's sense of vulnerability that would direct policy but his means of overcoming it. But at that moment, as he lifted the wassail cup and saluted all the lords, bishops, knights, men-at-arms, officers and servants with the traditional shout of 'Wassail!', very few men inside or outside that hall understood what his vision really meant. And no one – not even Henry himself – could have predicted the outcome.

January

Tuesday 1st

The landscape was bleak in winter. Every tree stood with its branches stark against the sky. No evergreens lifted the colour except here and there a sparse Scots pine, and the occasional holly or yew tree, and the ivy found growing around leafless oaks. There were few trees at all near Westminster; there was little impression of natural renewal. The long roads approaching the abbey and palace were muddy and rutted with the wheels of carts and wagons, and the hooves of pack-horses. The wide fields were frozen hard, or flooded after the heavy rains. Piles of logs stacked outside houses were crested with snow. So too were barrels, their wooden sides icy to the touch. Long icicles hung from the eaves of houses, especially where the roofs were thatched.

Even before dawn there had been activity. In the choir of the church of the abbey, just a hundred yards from the palace, the monks had been singing in the early hours. The clock in the palace yard chimed the hours with a deep, resonant *dong* on the great bell called 'the Edward'. In the privy palace – the king's private quarters within the palace of Westminster – the marshal of the hall had made sure the servants were up and about their duties. Fires were lit, servants removed their mattresses from the hall floors; fresh rushes were strewn.

The silent flame of a cresset lamp illuminated the gold and red tapestries of Arras work which lined the royal bedchamber.[1] Figures of royal and biblical history looked down on the sleeping king: mottoes spoke to the silence. 'I am Nature,' declared one of the tapestries in the privy palace – a piece of Arras work 66ft long and 16ft high showing the seven ages of Man.[2] 'Here begins a tournament', declared another,

showing knights jousting. Another, 45ft long, depicted the lives of the
Roman emperors. Others showed scenes from hunting and tourna-
ments. Below his chamber windows, the water of the Thames lapped
at the stonework, sighing with the tide.

The king himself lay in a large feather bed surrounded with curtains,
his head resting on feather-filled pillows. Perhaps it was the 'bed of
the cherries', enclosed by a canopy embroidered with shepherds.[3] Or
maybe it was his black satin bed, enclosed within three curtains of
black tartarin which were stamped with gold and silver lions. Some
of his pillows were scented with lavender. Elsewhere in the room,
apart from the tapestries and a flickering lamp, were a silver ewer and
a basin full of rosewater on a wooden stand, and chests of the king's
possessions. These held the clothes which his chamber ushers had put
away carefully the night before. They also held items of treasure, faith
and superstition, such as his astrolabes, relics, jewels, books of devotion and his rock-crystal and jasper bowls and cups. Perhaps his clock
– in the shape of a ship – ticked slowly and quietly in the corner of
the chamber.[4]

The king would have been woken by the ushers before dawn, when
they came into his chamber to light the fire. According to John Russell,
who was an usher to Henry's youngest brother, the king would have
expected them to hold the basin and water while he washed his face
and hands. They should have had a clean and warm linen shirt ready
for him, and clean underwear, and well-brushed hose. Seated on a
cushioned chair, he would have had his hair combed and, when all
his dressing was finished, his shoes put on.[5]

Putting on the king's shoes was an important moment today, 1
January. It was the signal for the trumpets to sound outside the king's
chamber. With that loud, brass sound, a line of servants entered
bearing New Year's gifts from the king's closest companions and family
members.[6] All of the important men who had been at the Christmas
feast would have sent a present – an item of costly jewellery or similar
goldsmith's work.

Having received his presents, and thanked their bearers, the king
left his chamber. He might have had a small breakfast of bread and
cheese or cold meat before going into the royal chapel to hear Mass.
This would have been either in the royal chapel adjacent to his
chamber in the privy palace, which had been altered and extended

by his father, or in the great chapel of St Stephen, next to Westminster Hall. After that, his time was his own until dinner; perhaps to look over his falcons and hunting dogs at Charing, or to receive guests and important dignitaries, or to watch a mumming or a play. As 1 January was part of the feast of Christmas – the eighth day – the mood about the palace would still have been relatively relaxed. Henry probably feasted in the White Hall, or Lesser Hall, which was directly south of Westminster Hall itself. The amount spent on food for the household was around £90 – a little more than the other days of the twelve-day feast, except Christmas Day itself, which could easily see expenditure of more than £220.[7]

Henry liked Westminster. The privy palace, the Queen's Palace nearby (where his stepmother spent some of her time), the Prince's Palace (where he had lived before his accession), Westminster Hall, the White Hall, the Painted Chamber, the great bell tower, the king's chapel, St Stephen's Chapel – these all added up to a suitable base for a king. To the west there was the immense structure of the abbey church, with scaffolding around its still-incomplete west end. From the palace he could directly oversee the offices of government: the chancery and the exchequer. He could call an audience of the most important Londoners at the Guildhall, and be there within half an hour by taking the royal barge down the river. Similarly, he could be rowed to any one of a number of manors up or down the Thames: Windsor Castle, the Tower of London, Queenborough Castle, and the houses of the archbishop of Canterbury at Lambeth and Merton. Earlier in his reign he employed William Godeman and his bargemen to row him from Westminster to Sutton, Lambeth, and the royal hunting lodge at Rotherhithe.[8] His hunting dogs and birds were not far away, nor were the London markets, where there were goldsmiths, armourers and spicerers. Swans swam up and down the Thames. His tapestries and treasures were around him. He would spend most of the next six months here.

*

In Paris it was raining. It had been raining since November. According to the official chronicler at the abbey of St Denis, just to the north of Paris, the four winds did not cease to blow one way or the other from autumn 1414 to spring 1415. It rained consistently and heavily, so that the rivers were flooded. River transportation of merchandise became impossible – the harbour quays and cranes were under water. The rivers were too swollen and fast-flowing, and many roads were impassable. The necessities of life started to disappear from the markets. And the fields were inundated. Wheat stored in granaries became wet and started to rot, or became infested with insects. Even the vines which normally produced good wines started to produce an undrinkable vintage.[9]

In such disheartening weather, the duke of Bourbon founded a new military order: the Order of the Prisoner's Shackle. This consisted of the duke himself and sixteen other men – thirteen knights and three esquires – each of whom undertook to wear the symbol of a prisoner's chain on his left leg every Sunday for two years. Among the knights were Clignet de Brabant (the admiral of France) and Raoul de Gaucourt. The knights' shackles were to be made of gold, the esquires' made of silver. The purpose was to bind them into a fraternity which would meet an equivalent number of knights and esquires who would fight them all on foot with lances, axes, swords and daggers. Although it was not specified that the opposing knights should be English, that was clearly the assumption. A number of multiple fights of the sort envisaged had taken place between the knights of England and France over the years.

As with all orders of knighthood, there were strict rules. Members of the Order agreed that they would have a painted image of the Virgin Mary in their chapel in Paris. A shackle similar to the one they each wore was to serve as a candle holder; and a candle was to burn in it before the painting of the Virgin all day and night for two years. A sung Mass and a low Mass were to be performed every day. The arms of all the knights were to be displayed in the chapel; if they were successful in meeting an equivalent number of knights in battle, and defeating them, then each man was to have his portrait painted in armour, to hang in the chapel. And, as with all chivalric vows, the knights undertook to maintain the honour of all ladies and women of good birth, and to offer aid to women wherever they found them in need of it.[10]

*

In the moated and high-walled city of Constance, six hundred miles to the south, men were arguing about the price of fish, meat, bread and beds – and almost everything else. Bishops, priests, lords and their servants were gathering in large numbers for the church council that was beginning to get underway there. King Sigismund of Hungary, the Holy Roman Emperor, and his entourage had arrived. So too had Pope John XXIII attended by six hundred men. John had also brought thirty-three cardinals, each of whom had brought dozens of priests, lawyers and servants – a total of 3,056 men.[11] The pope's vice-chancellor, the cardinal bishop of Ostia, had entered the city with eighty-five horses in his train alone, and these all needed stabling, and the riders all needed accommodation.[12] Eventually there would be forty-seven archbishops, 145 bishops (with a total of six thousand servants), ninety-three suffragan bishops, and many other secular lords. One burgher of Constance, Ulrich Richental, exuberantly estimated that 72,460 people came to the city.[13]

The council had been summoned by Pope John XXIII at the emperor's request. It had two main objectives: the re-unification of the church and ecclesiastical reformation. The first objective arose from the split between the French papacy, based at Avignon, and the Roman papacy, based at Rome. This had divided the Church since 1378. A previous attempt to heal the schism – the council of Pisa in 1409 – had resulted only in the election of a third pope, Alexander V, who had swiftly died and been replaced by John XXIII, one of the worst possible candidates for the post. So now there were three popes – the Pisan pope, John XXIII; the Roman pope, Gregory XII; and the Avignon pope, Benedict XIII. None of them would acknowledge the others. None wanted to give up his own papal title. It had been a diplomatic triumph for the Holy Roman Emperor, Sigismund, to persuade John XXIII to summon the council in the first place.

On 1 January men were arriving in their hundreds. Sigismund had arrived a week earlier, on Christmas Day, and the townspeople had flocked to see him enter the cathedral in the company of his empress and Duke Rudolph of Saxony. Two days later Duke Ludwig of Bavaria-Heidelberg had arrived. The citizens of Constance marvelled at what was happening; their city was being transformed into the greatest retail centre of the Christian world. Merchants from other towns set up their stalls in courtyards and slept under makeshift shelters or huts.

Ulrich Richental estimated that 1,400 traders had come, including shop-keepers, furriers, farriers, shoemakers and spicerers. 1,700 musicians were either present already or on their way. So were seventy-two goldsmiths, sixteen master apothecaries, and seven hundred prostitutes, 'who hired their own houses or who lay in stables'.[14]

Pope John's advisers were worried about the freedom to speak and to come and go to and from the council. Just yesterday they had heard how Sigismund himself had threatened an agent of the duke of Milan, with whom he was at war. Sigismund had had the agent deported from the city and then yelled at him as he crossed the bridge, 'You are a spy, here in the service of that rebel against me. If it were not for my reverence for the pope, I would have you hanged! See to it that I do not find you here again!' On account of this the papal advisers decided that they should ask Sigismund to guarantee their safety, and the safety of all those who attended the council, in case they too incurred his anger for making statements which were not to his satis-faction. They also decided that action should be taken to limit the rapid increases in prices, as more and more men arrived in the city. They wanted to bring charges as quickly as possible against the supposed heretic, Jan Hus, who had been arrested on 28 November 'for the pernicious doctrine that he professed'. However, they were worried in case some of those who might testify against him would be put off if they feared the actions of the emperor.[15]

Fifteen prelates were elected to be a delegation to take these demands to the emperor. They met him today, 1 January, in the town hall of Constance, and expressed their concerns. Sigismund was humbled. He answered that, ever since he had decided on the city of Constance as the venue for the council, it had been his ardent wish to do all he could to facilitate the unification and reform of the Church. He assented that all people could come and go freely, without excep-tion, even those in rebellion against the Holy Roman Empire. With regard to the problem of prices, he decreed that four clergymen and four burghers would be appointed to regulate accommodation in the city. Prices would be set, controlling how much the innkeepers and other burghers of Constance could charge; and ordinances would be drawn up, stipulating (amongst other things) that innkeepers should make sure all bedding was washed once a month.[16] As to the third issue, Jan Hus, the emperor ordered that placards in support of him should be torn down. He added that formal accusations of heresy against individuals like Hus could be made at the council, as long as they were made in public.

*

The huge gathering at Constance may seem to have had little to do with Henry V, who was at Westminster, six hundred miles away. But it mattered a very great deal to him, for five reasons. Sigismund had written to Henry at the start of his reign, asking that he do all he could to work towards the re-unification of the Church. As a religious man, Henry was keen to be involved.[17] He was also no doubt aware that the emperor had written to Henry IV, asking the same thing, and so this represented another opportunity to outdo his father as king.[18] Also, the outcome would be of crucial importance for England, as his learned advisers would have told him. In 1046 a similar confusion of three popes (Gregory VI, Benedict IX and Sylvester III) had been sorted out by the then Holy Roman Emperor at the council of Sutri. The council deposed all three popes and elected a new man in their place. If the council of Constance managed to emulate the council of Sutri, then one man would eventually exercise spiritual authority over the whole of Christendom – and with an exceptionally strong mandate. It would be essential for every Christian king to establish a good relationship with such a man as soon after his election as possible.

The third reason why the council of Constance was of concern to Henry was the question of what 'reform' of the church would actually involve. Henry had his own programme of religious reform: a list of forty-six points drawn up at his request by the University of Oxford.[19] Among other things, he was concerned with the appoint-ment of bishops, the revocation of illegal appropriations of rectories, the control of lax clergymen who evaded punishment after they had been granted exemption by the pope, and control of the sale of local indulgences. The fourth reason for his interest lay in the question of international prestige. Would England be regarded as a nation on its own, alongside France, Italy, Spain and Germany, as it had been at Pisa in 1409? Or would it be subsumed within the mass of 'German' states?

Finally, there was the problem of imposing religious authority, especially with regard to heresy. Jan Hus had been in correspondence with Sir John Oldcastle, Richard Wyche and other English Lollards.[20] Religious thinkers in England continued to circulate the teachings of England's own pre-eminent religious reformer, the late John Wycliffe. Radical ideas such as the pre-eminence of Christ, the unchanged nature of bread and wine in the communion, and the limitations of papal authority were circulated in the form of Wycliffe's writings across the whole of Christendom. And these ideas continued to be hugely divisive, causing fear in those who saw lords, knights and clerics taking them up in Bohemia and Hungary as well as in England. Henry's own confessor, Stephen Patrington – who must have had a spiritual outlook in accord with Henry's own – had bitterly argued against Wycliffe at Oxford. The decisions made at Constance concerning Wycliffe, Hus and other anti-papal reformers would determine whether Henry was justified in burning such men as heretics, or whether he should tolerate them, and perhaps even listen to them.

As a result of these issues, Henry had appointed a prestigious embassy to the council. They had not yet all arrived at Constance. Thomas Polton had already addressed the council on Henry's behalf in December, but the majority were still strung out across Northern Europe in their various small travelling groups.[21] As it took a month for news to travel from Constance to England, it would be a long time before he knew how his ambassadors were advancing his religious and nationalistic ambitions.

Wednesday 2nd

Picture the great lords of France on this day riding through the rain, or being carried in their sedan chairs, in the narrow muddy streets of old Paris. They were due to attend a meeting of the royal council. The king would not be there, but the duke of Orléans would, with his younger brother the count of Vertus. Their great uncle, the seventy-four-year-old duke of Berry, would also be present. So would the dukes of Bourbon and Alençon, and the counts of Eu, La Marche and Vendôme. Other members of the French council included the duke of Berry's chancellor, Guillaume Boisratier, archbishop of Bourges, and Pierre Fresnel, bishop of Noyon.[22]

As can be seen from both the membership of the council and its agenda, it was the Armagnacs who were in control of the government, not Henry's ally, John the Fearless. Despite John's best efforts to regain the initiative – including bringing an army to the gates of Paris in February 1414 – he had failed to reassert himself. In the meantime the Armagnacs had enlisted the support of the University of Paris in the formal burning of Jean Petit's *Justification of the duke of Burgundy* outside the gates of Notre Dame. They had attacked John's city of Arras, and had come to an uneasy peace agreement with him there. John had not yet ratified the Peace of Arras, and it was beginning to look as if he had no intention of doing so. So the Armagnacs had declared six days ago that he was an enemy of the king and a traitor to France. All those who supported him were to leave Paris, together with their wives and families – on pain of being pilloried, losing a hand, or having a hole bored in their tongue.[23]

In these circumstances, the council's decision today to agree in principle to an extension of the truce with England was a minor issue. Perhaps the only councillor agitating for war was the belligerent duke of Bourbon. Not only had he founded the Order of the Prisoner's Shackle the previous day, he was about to lead an expedition against the English in Gascony.

Thursday 3rd

At Westminster, just as in Paris, those in government had to work. It might have been one of the twelve days of Christmas but a king could not ignore all his business for that long. Yesterday Henry had ordered the mayor and sheriffs of London to release all the ships of the county of Holland which had been arrested by royal command in December in reprisal for the arrest in Holland of John de Waghen of Beverley.[24] Today he sent orders to his lieutenant in Ireland, John Talbot, to sort out an argument over the inheritance of an estate which had been going on for the last thirty years. The petitioner, John Cruys, had been in wardship and deprived of his inheritance by his guardians. Henry also gave judgment today concerning the denization of a man who had been born in Calais to a Flemish woman and an English father. The man wished to be recognised as an Englishman from now on. Unsurprisingly, Henry agreed. [25]

Saturday 5th

In the cathedral of Notre Dame, in Paris, King Charles sat quietly in an oratory beside the altar, listening to the sermon preached by the chancellor of the cathedral, Jean Gerson. The service was in memory of the late duke of Orléans, and all the council was present. So too were many members of the University of Paris, where Dr Gerson was held in high esteem. Two cardinals were in attendance, and many bishops, priests and knights, as well as a crowd of Parisians. What Gerson said, according to the Burgundian chronicler Enguerrand de Monstrelet, was 'so strong and bold that many doctors [of theology] and others were astonished thereat'.[26] Gerson praised the manners of the deceased duke (despite his many seductions) and his government of the realm (despite his high taxes), and declared that it had been 'by far better administered than it had ever been since his death'. Monstrelet commented that

> he seemed in this discourse, more desirous of exciting a war against the duke of Burgundy than of appeasing it; for he said he did not recommend the death of the duke of Burgundy, or his destruction, but that he ought to be humiliated, to make him sensible of the wickedness he had committed, and that by a sufficient atonement he might save his soul.

Gerson went on to say that the burning of Jean Petit's *Justification* before the gates of Notre Dame had been a good first step, but more needed to be done. Knowing how controversial this was, he declared he would defend what he had just said about the duke of Burgundy before the whole world. Later that year, he would do just that, at Constance, where he would have to preach to the English and Burgundians, not just the converted Armagnacs.

Sunday 6th: the Feast of the Epiphany

The feast of the Epiphany was the commemoration of the moment when the three Magi came to worship the infant Christ. This was one of the most important days in the Christian calendar. Richard II – who had been born on Epiphany – had always been especially keen to see it celebrated. As Henry had spent some time in Richard's household, he may well have recalled his unfortunate cousin on this day. If so, he could reflect that he had now reburied Richard in his rightful place, in his tomb in Westminster Abbey. And he had done so with great respect; he had even reused some of the funeral trappings from his own father's funeral at Richard's reburial.

For Henry, as for his subjects, Epiphany started with a special Mass. In many places a gold star of Bethlehem was suspended in the body of the chapel. After the service the king feasted in state again, wearing his royal robes and crown, just as he had on Christmas Day (although the level of expenditure on food and drink was more moderate). Later he would watch 'disguising games' or mummings. Epiphany was the most popular occasion for watching such masked plays in the whole year.[27]

Tuesday 8th

The parliament of April 1414 had seen various petitions put forward by the commons. One had concerned the state of the kingdom's hospitals. These were not medical establishments so much as almshouses: places of refuge for the poor, sick and needy. As the petition stated, the noble kings of England and other lords and ladies

> have founded and built various hospitals in cities, boroughs and various other places in your said kingdom, to which they have given generously of their moveable goods for building them, and generously of their lands and tenements for maintaining there old men and women, leprous men and women, those who have lost their senses and memory, poor pregnant women, and men who have lost their goods and have fallen on hard times, in order to nourish, relieve and refresh them there. Now, however, most gracious lord, a great number of the hospitals within your said kingdom have collapsed, and the goods and profits of the same have been taken away and put to other uses by spiritual men as well as temporal, because of which many men and women have died in great misery through lack of help, livelihood and succour, to the displeasure of God.[28]

The petition went on to request that every hospital – whether of royal foundation or not – might be 'visited, inspected and administered in the manner and form which seems most appropriate and beneficial to you, in accordance with the intention and purpose of the donors and founders of the same'.

Henry had assented at the time to this petition, promising that ordinaries would inspect those hospitals which were of royal foundation, and ensure their correct administration, and that they would bear royal commissions to assist them in this work. Eight months had now gone by. So today he commissioned Richard Clifford, bishop of London, 'to enquire about the foundation, governance and estate of the hospitals within his diocese, and to certify in Chancery those being of royal foundation and patronage, and to make reform of others'.[29]

Thursday 10th

The convocations of Canterbury and York were gatherings of all the higher clergy of the two provinces. Like parliaments, they had the ability to grant or deny the king extra taxation. Also like parliaments, they were loath to be bullied into granting money. Repeated refusals by the convocation of York to grant subsidies to Henry IV in the early years of his reign had led to a crisis in 1405.[30] Today, the convocation of York was meeting to discuss granting the king's request for a further two subsidies.

It was much the same request as had been put to the convocation of Canterbury the previous October and to parliament in November. However, when the clergy of Canterbury had been asked to grant a subsidy of two tenths and two fifteenths (the equivalent of a 20% tax on the goods and chattels of townsmen and a 13.3% tax on those of country dwellers), the purpose was to facilitate sending an embassy to the council of Constance, to aid the reunification of the Church. Since then, parliament had been asked for a similar subsidy, and had been told that the reason for the taxation was to enable the king to lead an army into France.

Many of the prelates at York had been at that parliament, so they knew that they were being asked to fund a war of aggression. It was inevitable that there would be some dissent, just as there had been in parliament. They argued for some while in the presence of the archbishop of York, Henry Bowet (who was now in his seventies and confined to a litter). But Bowet was a loyal Lancastrian. He was aware of the reformers outside the Church who in 1404 had called for the confiscation of Church property.[31] He was also a firm supporter of Henry's anti-Lollard legislation, taking a positive stance with regard to the burning of heretics. These were probably crucial factors: Bowet and the other bishops could take the view that they needed to help the king in his military ambitions if they were to continue to look to him to preserve the income and authority of the church.

Eventually, after 'much altercation', the northern prelates agreed.[32] They opted to pay the tax, and thereby effectively voted to support Henry's war.

*

Jan Hus of Bohemia was about forty-three years old: a philosopher and a theological lecturer at the University of Prague. A man of deep religious conviction, he had come to lament the idle days of his youth, when he wasted too much time enjoying himself. As he himself admitted, he had played far too much chess and spent too much money on expensive clothes. The catalyst in his life had been the teachings of the great English church reformer John Wycliffe, the inspiration of the Lollards. Like Wycliffe, Hus was appalled at the sale of indulgences – grants of absolution for one's sins – by the Church. Following Wycliffe, he argued that forgiveness should be sought through repentance and atonement, not through the payment of money. He was also appalled by the idea that the pope could command what men should believe, and what they should say they believed, regardless of how God moved their hearts. Like Luther in the next century, the driving force behind his calls for religious reform was his own personal reformation: his conviction that the orthodox religion of the Church had strayed from the true path, and that he had a duty to set it right again.

Hus attracted a considerable following in his native Bohemia and in Hungary. He also attracted a number of opponents within the Church. By 1410 the divisions between him and the orthodox theologians at the University of Prague had become deep and verged on hostility. King Wenceslas of Bohemia – Sigismund's brother – had tried to reconcile Hus and the orthodox lecturers at Prague, but the religious authority of the pope remained a fundamental problem. Orthodox Catholics could not tolerate any challenge to the pope's position as head of the Church (even though there were three popes at the time). Hus refused to acknowledge that any man, including the pope, was in a greater position of authority than Christ himself, and asserted that a Christian soul might make an appeal directly to Jesus over the pope's head.

Hus knew how controversial his recitation and development of Wycliffe's writings were. In the margin of one of Wycliffe's works he had written 'Wycliffe, Wycliffe, you will unsettle many a man's mind!'[33] Pope Alexander V had excommunicated him in 1410, and in 1412 a council summoned by John XXIII placed him under the major excommunication.[34] This meant that the whole of Prague would suffer an interdict unless the city officials arrested him. So he had gone into voluntary exile, and taken shelter in the various castles of lords who were moved by his words. He looked on his sufferings as like those of Jonah in the whale, or Daniel in the lion's den – and repeatedly mentioned such necessary trials in his letters. He continued to celebrate Mass as before, and to preach and write letters outlining his views on religion and Wycliffe's teachings. His sermons were carried across the Holy Roman Empire, and also into England.

Hus could not bring about a reformation of the whole Church simply by writing and preaching. But he genuinely wanted the Church to discuss its future path with respect to the individual's direct relationship with Jesus Christ. So when Sigismund promised him a safe conduct if he would come to Constance to discuss his ideas with the council, he decided to accept. In October 1414 he bravely set out in the company of the Bohemian lords, Lord Wenceslas of Dubá and Lord Henry Lacembok, and the latter's nephew, Lord John of Chlum. With them travelled many of his friends and fervent supporters from Prague. At each city they came to Hus sent out letters declaring that all who opposed his views should come to Constance to discuss them with him.[35]

Hus arrived at Constance on 3 November 1414 and lodged with a widow in St Paul's Street. The next day Henry Lacembok and John of Chlum went to John XXIII to announce that Hus had come willingly to Constance under the emperor's safe conduct, and to ask that the pope be intolerant of any attempt to molest or interfere with Jan Hus during his stay. The pope gave this assurance, stating that Hus would be safe 'even if he killed the pope's own brother'.[36] However, Hus's enemies from Bohemia, especially Stephen Páleč and Michael de Causis, had also arrived. They set about drawing up indictments against him. While they showed their indictments to the cardinals and bishops attending the council, fomenting ill-will towards the Bohemian reformer, Hus was said to have preached to the people and attracted many followers. After three and a half weeks, two bishops were sent by the cardinals of the council to him, at the insistence of Páleč and de Causis. They demanded that he come before the cardinals. John of Chlum was angry at this interference, contrary to the pope's promise; but Hus willingly agreed to be examined by the cardinals as to any error in his theology. So he attended the convocation at the bishop's palace.

The meeting was a trap. The cardinals soon departed, praising Hus's honest intentions, but leaving him in the palace, which was surrounded by armed guards. John of Chlum left Hus and went to Pope John to accuse him of breaking his oath not to permit any interference with Hus in Constance. But in so doing he achieved nothing but to separate himself physically from Hus, who remained under guard in the palace. A supporter, Peter of Mladoňovice, was able to take Hus his fur coat and breviary that evening – 28 November 1414 – but that same night Hus was moved to a cardinal's house, and after eight days he was sent to the Dominican monastery situated on an island in the Rhine, and chained up in a round tower there, 'in a murky and dark dungeon in the immediate vicinity of a latrine'.[37]

Although John of Chlum petitioned the emperor for Hus's release, in line with the imperial safe conduct he had been granted, Hus remained in his dungeon.[38] But over the course of December 1414, the fumes from the latrine did their work, and he fell ill. He ended up vomiting repeatedly and violently, and suffering from a fever. So grave did his situation appear that his gaoler feared for his life. Worried about accusations of murder if he should die, the pope ordered that he be removed from the dungeon. Today, 10 January, he was moved elsewhere within the monastery – to a cell near the refectory.[39]

Thursday 17th

In trying to ascertain what actually happened in the distant past, account books can be hugely valuable. Chroniclers were often ill-informed, distant, biased, or writing years after the events, sometimes on the basis of misinformation. Similarly, letters from lords are often written in such a way as to conceal intentions rather than reveal them. Even royal letters can be unhelpful; important information was frequently conveyed by word of mouth. But account books were normally drawn up without bias. They were also subject to verification at the time, and often contain lengthy explanations of what the money was used for.

Sadly, 1415 is one of the most poorly represented years in all late medieval English royal accounting. No regular household accounts survive. Nor do any chamberlain's accounts. Even the great wardrobe accounts are short on entries for 1415 (with the notable exception of expenses for the Agincourt campaign). We are left with a very few series of documents from which to determine what the king spent his money on in the early months of 1415. The Issue Rolls are one of our best extant sources.

The first series of payments recorded on the Issue Rolls for 1415 are those dated 17 January.[40] Henry paid his almoner £100 for this term (a period of six months) to make donations on feast days and to distribute 4s per day among the poor. This was a traditional engagement of every monarch, and did not necessarily indicate remarkable piety or generosity.[41] Other spiritual and charitable donations included the payment of 25 marks (£16 13s 4d) to the house of Dominican friars at Canterbury, 25 marks to the Franciscan house at Canterbury, £20 to the Dominicans at London, and 25 marks to the Dominicans at Oxford.

There was a payment of £312 10s made to Sir John Neville, custodian of Carlisle, so he could pay the wages of the men defending the West March against the incursions of the Scots. The duke of York was paid for keeping the town and castle of Berwick and paying the wages of the men guarding the East March (£423 0s 6d). Similar payments were made for the sustenance of Calais. Other payments were of an administrative nature – sending out messengers and letters, for example, to the earl of Arundel (the treasurer), and to the sheriffs of the various counties. The poet Thomas Hoccleve, who worked as an exchequer clerk by day, was reimbursed 26s 8d for red wax obtained by him for the use of the privy seal. A payment was made to Henry's chamber of 2,000 marks (£1,333 6s 8d), and another of £100; these sums were effectively his personal spending money.

The most interesting items concern Henry's military preparations. A payment of £460 was made for a barge from Brittany called the *Katherine of Guérande*. There was a part payment of £28 owing to a Master William the Gunner for a cannon, paid by agreement with the king himself. Henry also paid £5 13s 4d to William Woodward, the founder, for gunpowder. Although these sums are not large, they alert us to what Henry was doing in the days which are otherwise not recorded above. He was building up his military supplies, as he had been doing since his accession.

*

This same day, in the city of Constance, a papal notary in the service of John XXIII drew up two documents in favour of Edmund Mortimer, earl of March. One of them was relatively innocuous: written permission for Mortimer to separate the alien priory of Stoke Clare from its Norman mother church and to turn it into a secular college under his direct patronage, thereby saving its estates from being confiscated by the king. The second document was anything but innocuous. It gave him official permission to marry one of his second cousins. Although it did not name her, the woman in question was Anne Stafford, daughter of the earl of Stafford.[42]

As mentioned above, Edmund Mortimer was the great-great-grandson of Edward III through Lionel, Edward III's second son (whereas Henry V was descended from Edward III's fourth son). Edmund therefore had a claim to the throne of England which was arguably stronger than Henry's own. He was also the rightful English claimant to the title of 'King of France'. Far from benefiting from his illustrious birth, however, Edmund had spent over half his lifetime in prison, confined and guarded by order of Henry's father. Edmund thus had both the reason and the dynastic right to be a thorn in Henry's side.

It goes without saying that Edmund was likely to be unhappy at the way his family had been treated by the Lancastrians. But the reality was even worse, for Edmund's maternal uncle had been the duke of Surrey, who had lost his life during the Epiphany Rising. Edmund and his younger brother, Roger, had subsequently been kept in close custody at Windsor Castle. After an unsuccessful attempt by Lady Despenser to free them in 1405, the Mortimer boys were guarded even more closely by Sir John Pelham at Pevensey Castle. Things improved for them in 1409 – after ten years of custody – when Henry IV transferred them to Prince Henry's own protection. This was an inspired move, for it made the eighteen-year-old Edmund dependent on his future king. When Henry succeeded to the throne he released the Mortimer boys, and knighted them.[43] But was this enough to secure Edmund's loyalty? Henry was not sure. In November 1413 he had forced Edmund to seal a recognisance that he would remain loyal, or forfeit the huge sum of 10,000 marks (£6,666 13s 4d).

As the Mortimer claimant to the throne of England, and the rightful heir to the English claim on the throne of France, Edmund's marriage had always been of great interest to Henry. At the time of his release, when he had still been underage, it was clearly stipulated that Edmund should not marry without the king's permission. Even though he had now reached adulthood, he must have known that his marriage to Anne Stafford, another descendant of Edward III, would make the king angry. But for the moment no one knew about it. It was just a piece of routine business being conducted by a stranger on the far side of Europe.

Saturday 19th

In his cell near the refectory of the monastery, Jan Hus wrote letters to his supporters and friends in Bohemia:

> I entreat you, lying in prison – of which I am not ashamed, for I suffer in hope for the Lord God's sake – to beseech the Lord God for me that He may remain with me. He has mercifully visited me with a grave illness and again healed me. He has permitted my very determined enemies to attack me – men to whom I had done much good and whom I had loved sincerely. In Him alone I hope and in your prayer, that He will grant me to remain steadfast in His grace unto death.

Should He be pleased to take me to Himself now, let His holy will be done; but should He be pleased to return me, likewise let His holy will be done. Surely I have need of great help; yet I know that He will not allow me to bear any suffering or temptation except for my and your benefit, so that being tested and remaining steadfast, we may obtain our great reward.[44]

In writing this, Hus revealed that, even though he had come voluntarily to Constance, he knew he might die there. At the same time he clung to the idea that he might yet return to Prague. But things were changing rapidly. Very shortly after writing this letter he sent another to John of Chlum saying that, if the above letter had not yet been sent, 'hide it and do not send it, for it may cause harm'. He went on to say in the same letter

I also pray, noble and gracious Lord John, if a hearing is granted me, that the emperor be present and that I am assigned a place near him, so that he may hear and understand me well. I also particularly beg you that you, and Lord Henry Lacembok and Lord Wenceslas of Dubá, and others if possible, be present, so you may hear what the Lord Jesus Christ, my procurator, advocate and most gracious judge, will have me say – so that whether I live or die, you may be true and proper witnesses, and the liars will not be able to say that I denied the truth that I preached.[45]

At the end of the letter he added the forlorn plea that, if he was allowed a hearing, he hoped the emperor would prevent him being returned to prison afterwards, so he could take counsel with his friends. He clearly had no idea how much trouble he was in.

Sunday 20th

At Westminster, Henry was attending to his invasion plans. Today he commissioned Henry Beaufort, and the duke of York, Sir Thomas Skelton, Sir John Berkeley and William Brocas to make an enquiry into the loss of income and rights from the royal castle of Southampton. Not all of these men would head off to the south coast; the reason for including the names of the chancellor and the duke was to give greater authority to the others. It was an emphatic way of ensuring that local officials complied.

Southampton was the location where Henry was concentrating his shipbuilding activities. His great ship the *Holy Ghost* was being refitted there at that moment. Then there was the value of Southampton as a port. There were several places on the south coast from which an army might be transported to France, but none was as convenient as Southampton. Plymouth was the major port for sailing to Gascony, but it was far too remote for most people. London was the most convenient port for the transportation of the stores held at the Tower, but it was not at all suitable to muster a large army in and around the city. Southampton on the other hand was conveniently in the middle of southern England. It had served as the port of embarkation for Edward III's great expedition of 1346, which Henry seems to have settled on as the blueprint for what he wanted to achieve this year in France. Even better, it was a well-defended, walled town, its defences having been rebuilt by the citizens over the last thirty years. Henry was even planning a gun tower to guard the entrance to the port.[46] The adjacent manors were suitable for the encampment of large numbers of men. Royal agents had an established presence in the town. And its mariners were experienced in Channel navigation. It was thus the obvious point from which to launch an invasion. Henry could not allow it to be subject to corrupt officials.

Today also Henry commissioned an esquire in his service, Roger Salvayn, to take 'two or three ships for the king's service in the port of Kingston upon Hull, and to equip them with master seamen and mariners'.[47] Salvayn was not just an esquire; he was also treasurer of Calais. Ever since the start of his reign Henry had been improving the defences of Calais, repairing the defences, renewing the thatch and shingle roofs of houses with slates and tiles.[48] As with Southampton, a commission of enquiry had been set up to eradicate any possibility of fraud in the port. Henry had himself appointed Sir William Lisle to be the military governor of the town as deputy to the earl of Warwick while the latter was away at Constance, and to maintain a strong force of men-at-arms and archers there.[49] Henry was already planning to use the town for his forthcoming expedition – as a bolt-hole, at least, if everything went wrong.

Monday 21st

Jacob Cerretano, a papal notary, wrote in his journal for today that, 'the solemn ambassadors of the king and realm of England . . . entered Constance with a large and handsome escort'. They were met by Bishop Challant of Lausanne, who was temporarily acting as the bishop of Terouanne; Nicholas of Robertis, master of Pope John's household; and many other members of the pope's and the cardinals' households, who rode out to greet them. Cerretano added, 'the next day the said ambassadors waited in fine array on our lord Pope John XXIII; and the lord bishop of Salisbury made an eloquent speech on church union, which was praised by all present'.[50]

Cerretano was not the only observer who was impressed with the English delegation. Ulrich Richental also noted their arrival, although somewhat less accurately than the papal notary.

> Two archbishops [sic] and one bishop from England rode in, with seven wagons and twenty-two sumpter horses carrying apparel and other things; and forty-two learned clerics, twelve of whom were doctors of theology, and the rest licentiates and doctors of canon law. With them came a princely earl, Richard of Warwick, with three trumpeters and four fifers. The first archbishop [sic], Lord Robert of Salisbury, had sixty-four horses and many men, and he went to the Hof behind the steps, where a gate leads into the cloister, and remained there until his death. The other archbishop [sic] . . . came with sixty-seven horses and many men. He went to the house or inn near St Lawrence, called The House of the Golden Sword, by the city gate, and remained there until he took his departure . . . The earl of Warwick rode with thirty-eight horses and many men to the house in the upper market called The Painted House, where he remained until he rode out of Constance.[51]

Henry's embassy had been travelling for about ten weeks – very slowly, perhaps on account of snow blocking the roads, or floods comparable to those in Northern France. The leader was Henry's great friend Richard Beauchamp, earl of Warwick. Now thirty-three years of age, he had a wealth of experience, including fighting along-side Henry in Wales, travelling to Rome and the Holy Land, fighting in Prussia, and serving on Henry's council. With him were Henry's chamberlain, Lord Fitzhugh, and Sir Walter Hungerford and Sir Ralph Rochford. These three men had also been crusaders with the Teutonic Knights in Prussia; all three had been to Jerusalem. In addition, they were marked out by personal demonstrations of piety. Lord Fitzhugh had become acquainted with the ideas of St Bridget in Denmark, and was also familiar with the teachings of English mystics. Hungerford had been educated for the church, was a collector of books on theology, and had founded several chantry chapels.

The clerical leader of Henry's embassy was Robert Hallum, bishop of Salisbury. He had been chancellor of the University of Oxford, had spent time at the papal curia of Gregory XII, in Rome, and had represented the English church at the council of Pisa in 1409. He had degrees in both civil and canon law, and was famous for his oratorical skill. He was accompanied by Nicholas Bubwith, bishop of Bath and Wells, John Catterick, bishop of St David's, and the abbots of Westminster and St Mary's, York, the prior of Worcester, and a small army of lawyers and theologians, headed by the king's protonotary, Dr John Hovingham.[52] The abbots of Fountains, Jervaulx, Selby and Beaulieu were also in attendance, as Cerretano noted.[53] Although these men were representing their monasteries, their presence must have made the English delegation seem all the more impressive.

Why did a delegation to a religious council include laymen like the earl of Warwick? The main reason was that Henry sought an alliance with Sigismund against the French, and looked at Constance as an opportunity to achieve it.[54] Henry's council in the autumn of 1414 had recommended that he send ambassadors to 'every party'. All these leading delegates to Constance were given a second commission expressly empowering them to treat with Sigismund. One of them, Sir Walter Hungerford, had already been in negotiations with Sigismund's ambassadors the previous year, when Henry had proposed a three-way agreement between the empire, France and England.[55] It is possible that Henry now sought to revive the idea of the three-way treaty. Almost certainly he sought to justify the war he was about to launch, and hoped for the emperor's acquiescence. All we can be certain of is Sigismund's response – the emperor was not convinced that Henry had done all he could to avoid a conflict with France.[56]

Tuesday 22nd

Henry issued a commission to two royal judges to investigate cases of counterfeiting money in the county of Essex.[57] This crime, although it does not sound of the greatest seriousness to us, was regarded as high treason, punishable by hanging, drawing and quartering. It was a particular concern of Henry's in this year, as further commissions of enquiry reveal.

Wednesday 23rd

On days when Henry was not sitting in state, or otherwise engaged with important council business, he would have a large cushion set up on a sideboard in his great chamber – a large but private audience chamber – and there he would spend an hour after dinner listening to petitions brought to him by his subjects.[58] It was a custom of engaging directly with the administration of justice which he had inherited from his father, who had also listened to petitions in this way. After the petitioner or his representative had been admitted by the king's chamberlain – or, during Lord Fitzhugh's absence at Constance, his underchamberlain – Henry would decide whether he would act or not in line with the petitioner's wishes. If he agreed, the bill would be endorsed by the acting chamberlain, and the bureaucratic machinery of government would do the rest.

Gerard Sprong came to see Henry today. He asked humbly to be discharged of accountability for the two tons of metal in a great cannon called the Messenger, which had blown up at the siege of Aberystwyth in 1407. He also wished to be discharged of his liability for a great gun called the King's Daughter, which had exploded at the siege of Harlech. Another gun which could not be salvaged was one which had shattered at Worcester, when being tested by Anthony the gunner. He also wished to be discharged of a number of other things he had delivered, including large quantities of gunpowder and smaller iron guns taken by Helman Leget to Bordeaux, or sent with Sir John Stanley to Ireland, as well as 1,500 quarrels used at the sieges of Aberystwyth and Harlech.[59]

Henry gave his assent. Sprong was simply guarding his back against the king's auditors questioning how he could have lost so many tons of bronze and iron. Besides, if Henry wished to have sufficient guns to conduct a siege of a major town or city, he would need every gun he could get, and Sprong was a key agent in amassing and organising his artillery.

Thursday 24th

Although the French council had decided in principle to prolong the truce with England on 2 January, official confirmation had yet to be drawn up. Today, Guillaume Boisratier, archbishop of Bourges, and Pierre Fresnel, bishop of Noyon, together with Charles, count of Eu, and Guillaume Martel, lord of Bacqueville, the king's chamberlain, authorised the extension of the truce in King Charles's name.

Not all of Henry's chief ambassadors were in France for the occasion. Bishop Langley and Thomas Beaufort were still in England, for they are recorded in the minutes of a privy council meeting in early February 1415.[60] It seems rather that Henry's ambassadors travelled separately or in small groups. Sir William Bourchier was the first to set out, on 10 December, travelling down to Southampton and from there to Harfleur.[61] Richard Courtenay, bishop of Norwich, was next: he left London on 12 December 1414 and sailed from Dover to Calais.[62] Sir John Phelip and William Porter set out two days later, following Bourchier down to Southampton and from there across to Harfleur. Richard Holme, Henry's secretary, set out the same day, but went via Winchelsea and Calais. Philip Morgan, a lawyer commissioned to attend the embassy, might have been with him. The other members – Bishop Langley, Thomas Beaufort, and Lord Grey of Codnor – followed afterwards, sailing from Dover to Calais.[63] Thus it seems that Courtenay, Holme and Morgan were the principal ambassadors in France in January, and it was these men who actually agreed the extension of the truce.

The chief of these three was Bishop Courtenay. Six feet tall, with golden brown hair, and strikingly handsome, he was about thirty-three years of age – four or five years older than Henry himself. He was a grandson of the earl of Devon, intelligent, studious and pious. In Wales he had served Henry as a royal clerk, and was responsible for administering the oath to the Welsh garrison of Aberystwyth which resulted in Henry's greatest military mistake to date. He therefore shared his moment of shame: a bonding experience every bit as significant as sharing a moment of glory. When Henry had succeeded to the throne, Courtenay found himself elected bishop of Norwich and appointed to the sensitive position of keeper of the king's jewels and treasurer of the chamber. The king was as close to him as he was to any man.

Courtenay had seen all the dealings with the French since Henry's succession. He knew that his current mission was, on the face of it, a futile one. He was only in Paris so Henry could be seen to have done what his council had advised. He knew that the French were never going to negotiate on Henry's terms. From their point of view, the forthcoming peace negotiations were not about war so much as the terms under which Henry V would marry Katherine of France. To them, the continuation of the war was just a negotiating tactic; no one really wanted to resume hostilities – or so they thought. Once the marriage was agreed, Henry would not threaten France for want of King John's ransom, surely? Nor would he jeopardise the restored parts of Gascony for a few more towns of dubious loyalty.

In the official documents for the truce, sealed today, the English referred to the French king as 'our adversary of France' and the French referred to Henry as 'our adversary of England'. The French wrote their documents in French, and Courtenay responded on Henry's behalf in Latin. All the formal insults and marks of honour were preserved on each side.[64] But Henry's vision of future Anglo-French relations involved his domination of the French, not a negotiated settlement. It involved revenge for wounded pride. Just yesterday he had written to the Jurade of Bordeaux stating that he expected that the throne of France would soon be restored to him.[65] And he was not referring to the likely success of the forthcoming embassy.

Saturday 26th

Henry ordered Nicholas Calton, clerk, and Richard Clitherowe, esquire, to muster 150 men-at-arms, three hundred archers and three hundred mariners. They were 'going on the king's service to sea in the company of Sir Gilbert Talbot and Sir Hugh Standish, and John Burgh esquire, in ships in the port of London and ports and places adjacent.'[66]

This was a significant move to ensure the safety of the south coast. Sir Gilbert Talbot was one of Henry's most capable enforcers – another one of those men who had served with him in the Welsh wars. He had been a captain in Henry's victorious army at the battle of Grosmont in March 1405, and had been nominated a Knight of the Garter in about 1408. When the great fortress of Harlech finally fell to Henry's army, it was Sir Gilbert Talbot who was in charge. He had subsequently continued to patrol Wales with three hundred men-at-arms and six hundred archers. If anyone was capable of protecting the south coast ports from a French naval attack, it was him.

Monday 28th

Among the royal grants recorded at Westminster for today we find one made to Henry, Lord Scrope of Masham, and his wife Joan.[67] Scrope was about forty, eleven years older than the king. He had fought on a crusade in his youth, and this chivalric status had served him well when Henry's crusading father became king. He was made constable of Laugharne Castle in South Wales, and fought alongside Henry and his father at the battle of Shrewsbury. Like so many men of the court, his relationship with Henry blossomed in Wales. When Henry became regent at the end of 1409, Scrope was appointed treasurer of England and admitted to the Order of the Garter. After Henry's accession he became a regular member of English embassies to France, dealing with the Burgundians as well as the French. He was a man whom Henry both respected and trusted greatly.

The previous December, Henry had forgiven Scrope and his wife, the dowager duchess of York, all their debts to him. Today's new grant of £46 15s annually was just one of a number of payments he settled on the couple, and a sign of his continued affection for them both.

Also today Henry confirmed the alien priory of Appuldurcombe (on the Isle of Wight) on the abbess and convent of Franciscan nuns outside Aldgate (otherwise known as the Minoresses). Alien priories were monasteries dependent on a foreign religious house – Appuldurcombe being a daughter of Montébourg in France. They supplied revenue back to their foreign parent monasteries, and these in turn supplied taxation to the French government in wartime. Therefore there was a long tradition of English kings confiscating the incomes of alien priories during periods of conflict. At the Leicester parliament of 1414, Henry had been petitioned by the commons to declare that, even if there were to be peace, he would never return the alien priories but would dissolve them all. He had already taken about fifty-four into his own hands: a precursor to the complete dissolution of all the English monasteries by Henry VIII in the 1530s. In many cases he had granted the estates to friends, family and supporters, thereby relieving himself of some of the financial pressure which his father had suffered. But in this case, Appuldurcombe was handed over to supplement the income of the Minoresses. Henry Kays, keeper of the hanaper in chancery, was ordered to deliver letters patent to them at the same time, freeing them forever from having to pay any taxes levied on these lands.[68]

Finally, Henry was petitioned in his capacity as the highest justice in the land concerning John Elynden of Hawkhurst, who had been taken to court by a creditor and ordered to pay 28 marks and 10 marks compensation. He had been unable to pay, and subsequently surrendered himself to the Fleet Prison as a debtor. Unfortunately, while in prison he had failed to appear before a royal judge commissioned to hear legal cases in Kent, and had been outlawed. Technically, this meant he could be killed on sight – he had no protection in the eyes of the law. However, as he could show that he had in fact paid 10 marks of the 38 marks he owed, and as the creditor had now died, and as he obviously could not have attended the court due to being in prison, Henry wiped the slate clean, pardoned his outlawry and ordered the debt to be cancelled.[69]

Wednesday 30th

There were three distinct themes to Henry's vision of kingship: military leadership, piety and justice. All three featured throughout this month, for example: in the expedition to Constance, in his continued gathering of munitions and weapons for an expedition to France, and in the answering of petitions from his subjects. Today, all three featured on the same day.

With regard to his spiritual welfare, Henry made a grant of pavage to the burgesses of Beverley, 'because of the devotion which the king bears to the glorious confessor St John of Beverley, whose body rests in the church of Beverley'.[70] Pavage was the right to levy a tax on those coming to and going from a town so that the streets could be paved. As most towns in medieval England were unpaved, Beverley was hoping not only to elevate itself in cleanliness and appearance above its neighbours but also to attract more visitors. This meant more pilgrims coming to the church, and a greater wealth and dignity being attached to the saint's shrine.

As for the defence of the realm, Henry gave orders for another three ships to be made ready with mariners and soldiers – the *Katherine of the Tower, Gabriel of the Tower*, and *Paul of the Tower*.[71] These were all royal ships – the *Katherine of the Tower* being the recently paid-for *Katherine de Guérande*. They are also identifiable in two naval surveys made in 1417: the *Katherine* was a *nef* or ship, but not a great ship, so it probably had a carrying capacity of about 100 tuns (a tun being a large barrel containing 252 wine gallons). The *Gabriel* was a balinger, a smaller vessel; and the *Paul* was the largest of the three, a carrack. They were all harboured at the Tower of London, the military base where Henry also assembled and stored all his munitions. Henry's determination to go to war required a large navy to be assembled. Edward III had commanded a navy in the region of forty or fifty royal ships; but all of those vessels had long since gone, and few had been replaced.[72] As the few ships which did remain in the royal navy were relatively small – not many were longer than 100ft from stem to stern – he would need several hundred more to transport a large army. These initial commissions were probably issued now for one of two purposes: either to assemble the necessary stores, weapons, munitions and provisions at the Tower, or to defend the coast against French attack.

The most memorable information we have about Henry on this day relates to his exercising of justice. Edmund Cornhill was a servant of Bishop Courtenay. On his way to Paris, Courtenay and his household had passed through Calais. The bishop had noticed a decaying corpse hanging from a gallows. On enquiry it turned out to be one William Cole, who had been found guilty of murdering a man from Calais. The judgment of the court had been that he should hang there until the rope around his neck broke. Moved by pity for the dead man, the bishop had asked the mayor and aldermen of Calais to allow the corpse to be cut down, and he gave Edmund Cornhill the task of removing the body and burying it. Cornhill did as he was ordered. But he was then arrested on the orders of the mayor and aldermen, who had decreed that anyone cutting down William Cole's corpse would himself be hanged. Poor Cornhill was thus detained in Calais and sentenced to death for a work of charity ordered by his lord, the bishop. His only hope was a royal pardon.

A petition was drawn up on his behalf and rushed to the king at Westminster. Leaning on his cushion in his great chamber, Henry listened and nodded his assent. And, with that gesture, he saved Cornhill's life.[73]

February

Friday 1st

It was the eve of Candlemas, the formal end of winter – or as contemporaries thought of it, the retreat of the dark. Good Christians were expected to fast on this day, in order to heighten the sense of anticipation for the feast itself.[1] As a deeply religious man, Henry may well have followed this exhortation. But it is unlikely that he forced the rest of his household to do likewise – accounts from the previous reign show that the royal household was accustomed to eat normally on 1 February.[2]

The king's fast is perhaps the reason why we find few orders dated today. John Melksop, the master of a London ship called *Cob John*, was commissioned to make his vessel ready and to have it manned for action.[3] Similarly Nicholas Dalton, master of the *Trinity of London*, and Perin de Fargh, master of a balinger called the *Petre de Bayonne*, were both ordered to prepare their vessels and to take on mariners and servants.[4]

*

The great bells of Constance Cathedral were rung early today, first at dawn, and then twice more, summoning all the prelates to assemble.[5] There was excitement in the air. The cardinal of St Mark, Guillaume Fillastre, had written a memorandum which had sparked great interest. In his words, 'it is a mark of a good shepherd that he lays down his life for his sheep. If he does not lay it down, he is not a good shepherd. And if he is bound to lay down his life, how much more [readily] should he lay down the accidents of life – honour, power, dominion!'

Cardinal Fillastre went further. If John XXIII or either of the other popes failed to resign, the council could compel any or all of them to do so. In a staggeringly direct assault on his own superior, he declared

> In view of the condition of the Church . . . the supreme pontiff and shepherd of the Church may be compelled for the peace and the unity of the church to offer to abdicate, on condition that the others agree to cease their usurpation of office and carry out their abdications honestly and freely . . . For since he is bound to abdicate, he may be compelled to do so . . . For when a man is commanded to make restitution and fails to obey the command, his property may be taken from him by armed force, or other means may be used to oblige him to perform his duty. If the pope does not obey, he may be deposed as bringing scandal on the Church of God, which he is bound to protect and cherish . . .[6]

That was not the end of it. It was not just *this* pope who was subject to such judgment by such a council, it was all popes.

> Many other reasons might be adduced from the laws of God, of nature and of Man, to prove that a general council is superior to a pope in matters which concern the universal state of the Church, such as the present case and numerous others. Nevertheless, although these conclusions are correct, we recognise the propriety of proceeding mildly at the outset.

No one in authority had had the courage to say these things before, but once they were written down and circulated, they were widely applauded. Pope John XXIII was horrified, and felt betrayed, but there was nothing he could do but play for time. He asked for fourteen days to consider the memorandum.[7]

A delegation of prelates and scholars from the kingdom of Sweden, Denmark and Norway, who had just arrived, were present at this session. They agreed that the pope ought to be deposed if he should refuse to resign. However, the future of the papacy was not the main purpose of their visit. Their mission was to request that St Bridget of Sweden be recognised as a saint by all those at Constance.

St Bridget had been the founder of a religious order, the Order of St Saviour, in the 1340s. After giving birth to eight children (one of whom, Catherine, became a saint herself) and going on a pilgrimage to Santiago de Compostela, she went on many more pilgrimages, spreading the word about the way to live a moral life, and distributing the rule of her Bridgettine nuns. She urged the pope to leave Avignon and return the holy see to Rome. Through this and other such spiritual interventions, and her own moral lifestyle, her advocation of peace, and her long-distance pilgrimages, she became an internationally renowned figure. She had finally obtained papal confirmation of the Rule of her Order in 1370, three years before she died. According to her representatives at Constance, many miracles were due to her sanctity. She had, in fact, been beatified once already, in 1391, but that act had been carried out by the Roman pope alone. The French pope did not recognise the beatifications of his rival. So now her followers and countrymen wanted the Church universally to recognise her as a saint.[8]

The council deliberated. They decided that nine doctors of theology among the scholars should swear to St Bridget's sanctity and miracles, and then she should be recognised as a saint. This was done: the nine doctors swore on the Holy Gospels. Then a figure representing St Bridget was set up on the altar, an archbishop from Denmark began to sing *Te Deum Laudamus*, and bells rang throughout the city, both after dinner and at night.

At some point in the day – whether before or after these events is unclear – Pope John XXIII provided the pious and hard-working John Catterick to the see of Lichfield, in line with Henry's wishes. No doubt Catterick took the lead in requesting that Henry's confessor, Stephen Patrington, be provided to the see of St David's (which Catterick had previously held). The pope agreed to this also.[9] Perhaps there was some genuine friendship between him and Catterick? Or maybe the pope felt he needed all the friends at Constance he could get, and gave in to Catterick in order to win his support? Either way, he was in for a shock.

Saturday 2nd: Candlemas

The feast of Candlemas had come, one of the principal feasts of the Christian calendar. It was more formally known as the feast of the Purification of the Blessed Virgin Mary. For Christians it was the day of Mary's purification or 'churching' – the fortieth day after the birth, when new mothers of male babies were welcomed back into the community, and thanks given for their safe delivery. It was also a celebration of Simeon's recognition of the Messiah. As the story appears in St Luke's gospel, Simeon was an old man in Jerusalem who had been promised by the Holy Ghost that he would not die before he had seen Christ. The Holy Ghost led him into the Temple at the same time as Joseph and Mary brought in the baby Jesus. Simeon understood the significance, and took up the child in his arms, and said:

Lord now let your servant depart in peace, according to your word,
for my eyes have seen your salvation,
which you have prepared before the face of all people:
a light to lighten the Gentiles, and the glory of your people Israel.[10]

This phrase, 'a light to lighten the Gentiles', accorded perfectly with the medieval view of the retreat of winter. The chapel royal at Westminster was thronged with candles – as many as possible for the celebration of this morning's Mass. Henry processed into the chapel with his acting chamberlain carrying his candles before him. There he was surrounded by the incense of the church, members of his household in prayer, and the paintings of scenes from the Bible. At the east end were the portraits of Edward III and all his family, including his sons Edward the Black Prince and Henry's own grandfather, John of Gaunt.

Fittingly Henry's business today included giving permission for Geoffrey Colville and several of his fellows to endow a religious fraternity or gild in a chapel of Holy Trinity church, Walsoken, near Wisbech. The usual fee of £5 was paid into the royal coffers.[11]

*

In Constance there were celebrations, too. Pope John celebrated Mass in the cathedral. The candles were blessed in his presence, and he himself sprinkled holy water over them, and read five collects. After Mass he went into the bishop's palace and stood on the balcony with four cardinals, overlooking the crowds in the square. He gave the people his blessing, and passed down huge candles, each weighing 6olbs, according to Ulrich Richental. As wax candles were expensive – far dearer than ordinary tallow ones – this was a mark of great generosity. Then his chaplains threw down smaller candles, and 'among the people there was a great scramble, one falling over another, and loud laughter'.[12] After

dinner the pope sent out candles to all the great lords present, both spiritual and temporal, so they might share the light with their households.

*

In Paris, the king's council had come to a decision regarding John
the Fearless and his untrustworthiness in relation to the Peace of
Arras. They presented the king with an *ordonnance* drawn up for his
approval. Anticipating the arrival of proctors from John the Fearless
who would agree to the terms of the *ordonnance* – namely John's
brother, the duke of Brabant, and his sister the duchess of Holland
– they proposed that a general pardon would be proclaimed for all
the followers of John the Fearless except five hundred named persons.
Lands taken in war would be restored. The peace agreed at Chartres
in 1409 would be renewed, and all treaties between French princes
and the English would be torn up.

> We strictly enjoin upon all those of our blood and lineage that they
> do not, on any pretence whatsoever, form any alliances with the English,
> or with others, to our prejudice, or to the prejudice of this peace; and
> should any such alliances have been formed, we positively command
> that all treaties be returned and annulled.[13]

Having drawn up this *ordonnance*, permission was sent to the proctors of John the Fearless to enter Paris, so they could also seal it and
swear the necessary oaths to maintain it. A letter was sent to the
ambassadors from the king of England, that they might enter the
capital in their official capacity.[14]

*

At about this time a council meeting was held at the London house
of the Dominican friars, or the Blackfriars as they were also known.
This was the council's usual meeting place in the king's absence.
Unfortunately the minutes are simply dated 'February' – but the pres-
ence of at least one councillor, Thomas Beaufort, in Paris by 21
February (at the latest) points to a meeting early in the month.[15]
Thomas Langley, bishop of Durham, who travelled to France with

Thomas Beaufort, was also present. The other councillors there were Henry Beaufort (the chancellor), the archbishop of Canterbury, the duke of York, Lord Scrope, Sir Thomas Erpingham (the steward of the royal household), and John Prophet (keeper of the privy seal). The purpose of their meeting was to decide what measures were necessary to safeguard the realm during the king's expedition abroad, presuming the ambassadors failed to arrange peace.[16]

The first striking thing about this council meeting is that there was no doubt in these men's minds that war was inevitable. There was no discussion of what would happen if the ambassadors to France were successful, even though two of them were present. Already it was a foregone conclusion that they would fail to secure a suitable peace.

The measures the council recommended for the safety of the seas 'during the voyage of the king' required a small force of two great ships (defined as capable of carrying a load of 120 tuns in peacetime), five barges (100 tuns) and five balingers. Each great ship and each barge was to be manned by forty-eight mariners, twenty-six men-at-arms, and twenty-six archers. Each balinger was to be manned by forty mariners, ten men-at-arms and ten archers. The council directed that the coast from Plymouth to the Isle of Wight should be guarded by the two ships, two of the barges and one balinger. Two barges and two balingers should patrol the sea from the Isle of Wight to Orfordness, in Norfolk. The remaining two balingers and one barge should guard the coast from Orfordness all the way north to Berwick. It sounds a paltry force to cover nearly a thousand miles of coastline, but even that thin coverage required a thousand men. The men-at-arms would expect to be paid 1s per day each, the archers 6d per day, the master mariners 6d per day, and the mariners 3d per day.[17] This amounted to £732 per month in wages alone for the twelve ships.

Guarding against a substantial Welsh or Scottish raid during the king's absence was council's next task. For the whole of Wales they allotted only one hundred men-at-arms and two hundred archers. Forty of the men-at-arms and eighty of the archers were to be stationed at Strata Florida, and the rest in the north. As for the Scottish Marches, the provision was even smaller. Just one hundred men-at-arms were allocated to guard the East March, stationed at Berwick – the council added that it was necessary to speak to the king about repairing Berwick Castle. The West March received no extra troops at all. Calais was relatively well provisioned by comparison, with an extra one hundred men-at-arms and two hundred archers.

This is the second striking thing about the council meeting. It recommended that very few men be stationed at the most dangerous places in the realm. The reason for this sparse allocation was hinted at in the next paragraph of the minutes. Councillors agreed that no final decision about payment should be made until the treasurer of England had made a full report of the finances of the kingdom. They urged the king to make a full enquiry into the state of the finances of his household, the income from the royal estates, and all the debts he had incurred since his coronation, including the annuities paid out. Only after these things had been seen to could the king make his expedition like a good Christian prince, they said, with God's approval, to accomplish the object of his voyage.

Sunday 3rd

With Candlemas over, Henry's representatives at Constance set about the serious business of their mission. The first objective was to secure the recognition of England as a 'nation'.

In the fourteenth century, the idea of a 'nation state' as we know it did not exist. Europe was made up of kingdoms (such as England and France), independent princedoms, duchies and counties (such as the palatine county of the Rhine, the duchy of Milan, and the duchy of Holland) and, in Italy especially, a number of independent city states, such as Venice and Florence. Some duchies, counties and city states – especially in Austria, Germany, Eastern Europe and the Low Countries – were part of the Holy Roman Empire, governed by the emperor, an elected overlord. The idea of a political 'nation', in which the people participated in one single financial, legal and defensive sovereign government, which supposedly ruled in the interests of the entire nation, was only just beginning to develop. The furthest along this line of development was England, which had seen a nationalist programme of reform under Edward III. This extended to parliamentary representation, the promotion of a national language, the adoption of a common law, and nationwide taxation for national defence. Even so, England would not yet have been described as a political 'nation' in the language of the time.

The word 'nation' did, however, have meaning in ecclesiastical circles. The Italian peninsula might have been made up of many city states, papal states, and the kingdom of Naples and the duchy of Milan, with no single over-arching government, but it was a 'nation' in the sense that all its prelates were regarded in the eyes of the Church as being part of the Italian nation. Likewise Spain was regarded as a nation, for the separate kingdoms of Portugal, Castile, Aragon and Navarre all fell geographically within Spain in the eyes of the Church. France – with all its semi-autonomous duchies and counties – constituted a third ecclesiastical nation. And the united kingdom of Sweden, Norway and Denmark, and all the states under the titular authority of the Holy Roman Emperor, were regarded as forming the German nation.

The anomaly was the British Isles. Traditionally the kingdoms of England and Scotland were regarded as part of the German nation, and their bishops and abbots sat with their German counterparts. But at the council of Pisa, England had been recognised as a nation in its own right.[18] The question was this: did the decision at Pisa constitute an aberration? Or should England be considered a fifth nation?

This was not just a matter of national pride. If England was an ecclesiastical nation, and if voting was to be done by nations, then there were four national votes to be cast at Constance – those of Germany, Italy, France and England. (No delegation from any part of the Spanish nation had yet arrived.) In such circumstances England's prelates would constitute one whole quarter of the electorate. Henry's ambassadors would find it much easier to carry out their king's wishes than those from all the German, Italian and French realms and states, who would first have to persuade the representatives of rival governments before securing the vote of their nation. On the other hand, if England was simply part of the German nation, then Henry's handful of ambassadors would simply be swallowed up. Henry's programme of ecclesiastical reform would be very unlikely even to be heard, let alone agreed.

Jacob Cerretano, the Italian papal notary, was clearly bored by the English insistence that England should be recognised as a nation in its own right. He described the discussions on this day as 'some difficulties raised by the English nation'.[19] However, in using that very term, 'nation', Cerretano reflected an important point. The English had already taken the matter into their own hands by sitting independently. While the Germans sat in the chapter house of the Franciscan monastery in Constance, the English had established themselves in the refectory. They had thus resolved the issue *de facto*. Furthermore, as they were soliciting Sigismund for a treaty, and likely to be amenable to his own programme of reform, the emperor saw possible advantages in recognising the English nation as an independent body. No doubt he thought that the English would act as a sidekick to his German prelates, and a counterbalance to the French and Italians present.

Monday 4th

The Issue Rolls record various payments under today's date.[20] There were the usual administrative payments, such as money paid by Sir Roger Leche, treasurer of the royal household, for 'mercery wares'. Two men were paid for auditing the chamberlain's accounts from South Wales. And there was a payment of 100 marks to the duke of York which had been owing since the reign of Edward III. This was originally part of a sum granted by the crown to the duke's father; it therefore marks a form of dynastic settling-up. It also included a sum of £94 8s 9½d paid to the late duke's widow, now the wife of Lord Scrope, in respect of her dower.

There are just three payments relating to the defence of the realm. Like the January entries, they reveal a concentration on the two ports: Calais and Southampton. Roger Salvayn, treasurer of Calais – whom Henry had commissioned to requisition ships the previous month – was paid 16 marks (£10 13s 4d) for his wages and for employing six men at Calais to shape stones for the guns to defend the town. The victualler of Calais, Richard Threll, was paid simply for 'stuff'.

At Southampton Henry was building up his navy. The ships he had inherited from his father were being refitted under the clerk of the king's ships, William Catton. Two of the largest, the *Trinity Royal* and the *Holy Ghost* – each requiring a crew of two hundred men – were being made ready for the forthcoming expedition. With only twenty or twenty-five vessels in his possession, all the ships had to be ready, seaworthy and defensible.[21] The reconditioning of the *Holy Ghost* was nearing completion. On this day William Soper was paid £4 13s 4d 'for timber and making a swan and an antelope for the king's new great ship, called the *Holy Ghost*, built at Southampton', these animals being the royal heraldic insignia with which it would set sail.[22]

By far the most important entries on this roll are two payments concerning the king's diplomatic activities. John Chamberlain, a clerk of the admiralty, was paid for a mission to the duke of Brittany for 'certain causes considered necessary by the king'.[23] Brittany – one of the most independent of the semi-autonomous duchies owing allegiance to the king of France – was home to many of the pirates who harassed English shipping in the Channel. Although the duke was the son of the dowager queen of England (Henry's stepmother, Queen Joan), piratical raids repeatedly took place. Henry's own ship, the *Gabriel of the Tower*, was a captured and reconditioned Breton vessel. Because of this, Henry had sought an agreement with the duke even before his accession. A ten-year truce had been agreed on 3 January 1414 and confirmed on 18 April that year. It specifically bound the duke not to assist Henry's enemies.[24] That was why Henry had been so keen in the subsequent parliament to pass the Statute of Truces. Any damage to the truce by continued piracy could threaten his invasion plans. In the light of the king of France's newly drafted *ordonnance*, which required all treaties between his subjects and Henry to be annulled, the duke of Brittany had to make a choice. Would he observe his ten-year truce with Henry? Or his oath of loyalty to the king of France?

Even more significant is another entry on this roll. It begins:

To various messengers sent with letters under the privy seal of the king to various archbishops, bishops, dukes, earls and other lords directing them to be at Westminster for a council of the said lord king there being held the 15th [day] after Easter next [15 April], for certain causes and necessary matters of the said lord our king.[25]

This was to be the great council at which Henry declared openly his plans for invading France. His peace negotiators had only just set out – and already Henry was preparing to announce that England was going to war. As the council minutes of early February made clear, and as this payment shows, peace was not an option.

It is typical, however, to note that on the same day as the above message was first circulated, relating to a bellicose act, Henry made a grant of a charitable nature. He ordered that the warden and scholars of King's Hall in the University of Cambridge be paid the sum of 50 marks yearly, in lieu of a grant originally made to them by Richard II.[26]

Tuesday 5th

John Conyn, the king's tent-maker, was today commissioned to employ workmen to make the tents necessary for the king's household and retinue on the forthcoming expedition, and to arrange the carriage of the said tents.[27]

Other minor issues dealt with today include the king's personal order to Henry Kays, the keeper of the hanaper in chancery, to deliver to the master of the king's minstrels, John Clyffe, and one Thomas Trompenell, letters patent granting them both royal pardons against any crime they might have committed, including treason, rape and murder.[28] Pardons of a different sort were granted to Sir Thomas Pomeroy and William Cheney for failing to deliver the requisite amounts due at the exchequer when they had each been sheriff of Devon.[29] Losses by Pomeroy in his time in office led to the king letting him off £30; and Cheney was forgiven £60 of his debt. Sir Lewis Robesart, one of the king's most trusted household knights, received a grant of £40, payable by the sheriffs of London, for his good service to the king.[30]

Wednesday 6th

At Constance, English interests were under attack. The French were proposing that all decisions should be decided by a ballot – one prelate, one vote. In this they were supported by the Italians, who heavily outnumbered the other nations at Constance.

If matters were to be decided by one prelate one vote, and if only cardinals, bishops and abbots were to be able to vote, as some prelates argued, then the three English bishops and five abbots would be lost amidst the hundreds of prelates in attendance. Not for the last time did a matter of religious protocol descend into a war of words between the English and the French. The English and Germans went so far as to state categorically that, if voting was to be conducted by heads, then they would not take any further part in the council. They demanded that an equal number of representatives from each nation should be deputed to discuss resolutions. That was not good enough for the French. The meeting broke up in disagreement.

The following morning, however, the French gave in. Voting would be conducted by nations. Perhaps they realised that they would never be able to force John XXIII to resign if every Italian prelate present had a vote on whether to depose him or not. No further objections were raised as to the English being a nation in their own right. The first of Henry's objectives had been achieved.[31]

Friday 8th

Henry issued a commission to Master John Eymere, doctor in law, to hear an appeal by Sir Edward Hastings against Reginald, Lord Grey, in the court of chivalry concerning a case of the right to bear a coat of arms.[32] It is perhaps worth noting that this is the last piece of business for several days which places the king at Westminster. All other recorded entries for the next week were either routine chancery business or orders under the authority of the office of the privy seal, which did not require the king to be present.

Saturday 9th

The chronicler Enguerrand de Monstrelet noted that 'around this time' the English ambassadors arrived in Paris, and that their arrival was followed on the morrow with feasting and tourneying, which they attended.[33] The date seems to be supported by the chronicler of St Denis, who notes their arrival on a Saturday after Thursday 7 February.[34] However, although this evidence seems unambiguous, it is difficult to accept it for the arrival of *all* the English ambassadors. Two of them had been at the council meeting at Blackfriars, which took place on or after 1 February; so they and their entourages would have still been several days' away from Paris.[35] They could hardly have hurried along at forty miles a day – twice the usual travelling speed – for one of the ambassadors was in his fifties, they had a huge entourage, daylight was limited, there was little moon (it had last been full on 25 January), and the roads were still very muddy.[36] Thus the reference to the arrival of the English ambassadors probably relates to the arrival of *some* English ambassadors – probably those who travelled via Harfleur, or Richard Courtenay, Richard Holme and Philip Morgan, who were already in France. As we have seen, the ambassadors all set off on different days and several of them took different routes.[37]

Courtenay probably arrived in Paris earlier than the others, and took up residence initially in the *hôtel de Navarre*.[38] There he met Master Jean Fusoris, an elderly gentleman, knowledgeable in astrology and mathematics. He had made clocks, spheres and astrolabes for the kings of France and Aragon, amongst others. Courtenay, who had been chancellor of the University of Oxford three times (although still only thirty-three), had been drawn to him on account of his astrological knowledge. The two men had talked at length, and Courtenay had bought seven astronomical instruments from the savant on his previous trip to Paris. However, he had not paid for them in full, and had left France owing 200 crowns. Having argued at the end of their first meeting about the rights and wrongs of Jean Petit's *Justification of the duke of Burgundy*, there may have been a personal reason in Courtenay's failure to pay what he owed.

When Fusoris called on Bishop Courtenay at the *hôtel de Navarre*, any past animosity had apparently vanished. They discussed King Henry's demands for peace, and Fusoris consulted his charts and determined that the English would probably be successful in obtaining what they desired. Courtenay told Fusoris that he wished he could introduce him to the king, for Henry was very interested in astrology. This was true; Henry owned several astrolabes of his own and had had his birth date and time subjected to astrological prognostication.[39] In the early fifteenth century it was supposed that the planets affected everything – from the origin of plagues to the outcome of wars, and even such small matters as the most propitious time to draw blood. Courtenay therefore pressed Fusoris on whether the proposed marriage between the king and Katherine of France would be a good one. Fusoris again consulted his charts and declared that it would.

Would it be accomplished in this embassy? Courtenay asked – and
with that question we can see he was stringing the poor old Frenchman
along. No, Fusoris declared. Courtenay, pushing disinformation out
all the time, then declared to Fusoris that he knew that Henry was
not in good health, and he was worried whether he would die. What
did the king's birth chart hold for the future? Fusoris refused to be
drawn on this question, however. Instead he asked for his 200 crowns.
Courtenay dismissed this and promised Fusoris that, if the Frenchman
could arrange to come over to England with the next diplomatic
embassy, he would arrange for him to be appointed physician to the
dowager queen of England, as Fusoris held a master's degree in physic.
Poor Fusoris seems to have been completely outwitted by the sly
Englishman, and left not quite knowing what he had to do to get his
money back.

*

At Westminster, a commission was drawn up for four more ships to
be made ready, with mariners and servants. These were all from the
fleet harboured in 'the pool of the Thames', beside the Tower (now
known as London Dock). Three of the four can be identified as barges
on the surveys of 1417: the *Thomas of the Tower*, captained by William
Hore; the *Trinity of the Tower*, captained by John Kingston; and the
Mary of the Tower, captained by Richard Walsh.[40] The fourth ship was
the *Philip of the Tower*, commanded by Robert Schedde.

Sunday 10th

The seventh Sunday before Easter was the first day of a three-day-
long period of communal over-eating, collectively known as Shrovetide.
The following Wednesday would be the first day of Lent, and a six-
week-long fast, so all the meat, soft cheeses and eggs had to be
consumed before then. The eating and drinking was accompanied by
dances, music, wrestling and games of football or camp-ball.

In Paris the courts were closed, flags were up in the streets, the
taverns were open, and people were living it up. Most spectacular of
all, a royal tournament was held in the rue St Antoine. Even the weak-

minded king took part. Dressed in armour, he rode against the duke of Alençon, who carefully and sportingly allowed the king to split a lance against him, for the delight of the spectators. John the Fearless's brother, the duke of Brabant, jousted cordially with the duke of Orléans in a show of dynastic reconciliation. The dauphin, who had just turned eighteen, indulged himself to excess in all his various pleasures, as he was increasingly wont to do. The queen of France and the dauphin's wife dressed in their finest clothes, and waited on the noblemen, ambassadors and proctors.[41]

Enjoyable as this might have been for those Englishmen who had already arrived, their negotiations were not due to begin for some days. First, the terms of the *ordonnance* had to be discussed. Peace between France and England would have to wait until peace between France and Burgundy had been achieved.

Tuesday 12th: Shrove Tuesday

The third and final day of Shrovetide was the day of the greatest excess. Yesterday had been 'Collop Monday' when slices of meat were traditionally consumed. Today was 'Fasting's Eve', or 'Shrove Tuesday' (the word 'shrove' coming from 'shriving', or absolution for the confession of one's sins).[42] Everything that was not eaten by the end of the day would be wasted, so gluttony – and generosity – prevailed. Cockfighting was conducted by boys, pestering the adults to bet on their birds. Towns and villages held games of football. Cockthreshing contests were held too. This was the game of trying to kill a tethered cock by throwing stones at it. The winner was rewarded with the carcass of the victim.

Wednesday 13th: Ash Wednesday

Today Henry would have washed his face and hands, dressed, and left his chamber to go into a private chapel. The crucifix would have been veiled before he entered. He would have made his confession to Stephen Patrington. A priest would have blessed ashes and sprinkled them with holy water, and then pressed some of the mixture on the king's forehead, saying 'Remember O Man that thou art dust and to dust thou shalt return'.[43]

From now until Easter there would be no feasting, no meat-eating, no eggs and no cheese. Popular dishes such as *leche Lombard*, stewed beef pottage, and bacon collops, were off the menu, as were flans and suet-based puddings.[44] Henry's diet would have been reduced to one of bread, fish, seafood, peas, onions, beans, raisins and nuts. Preserved fruit, such as quinces, and carefully kept apples and pears would have been available, as well as the occasional imported orange. His cooks and sauciers would have done their best to produce dishes fit for his high table, using almond milk instead of cows' milk, and flavouring food and sauces with sugar, garlic, mustard and spices. Some exotica slipped through the legal definition of 'fish', such as porpoise, beaver and whale, but these were rarities. On the whole, all men of substance looked forward to the end of Lent, and the return of roast meats and dairy products.

Thursday 14th

The feast of St Valentine was not a major feast in the medieval calendar; its social significance was rather that this was the day when birds were supposed to begin their courtship flights (thus St Valentine was the patron saint of birds). The poet Geoffrey Chaucer remarked upon the belief that birds chose their mates upon St Valentine's Day. However, he did not remark on any amorous connotations for men and women. In the later fifteenth century, Valentine's Day gifts would be sent to friends, without any attempt at anonymity, and apparently without carnal or amorous connotations.[45] Whether or not such presents indicated affection, it is highly unlikely that Henry regarded the day as having anything to do with love. Certainly he did not despatch any presents to Katherine – the third of the king of France's daughters to be the focus of his plans for a diplomatic marriage.

If the day had any wider meaning for Henry, it was in relation to Richard II, the man who had knighted him. On this day, fifteen years earlier, Richard had died in prison, murdered on the orders of Henry's father, probably by enforced starvation.[46] The *Brut* chronicle, written in the 1430s, records how the pope had enjoined upon Henry IV the penance of burning four candles around the dead king's tomb, and having Masses sung for his soul, and distributing alms on the anniversary of his death.[47] Henry IV had done none of these things, and had even temporarily buried him elsewhere, at Langley; but Henry V made good the things which his father had refused to do. Thus it was Henry V who made sure that the pennies were doled out to the paupers at Westminster, in remembrance of the murdered king, on this day.[48]

Friday 15th

As remarked above, hardly any royal business was conducted over Shrovetide this year. Henry may have taken a small band of friends with him and gone on pilgrimage. An absence of a week may suggest a pilgrimage to Canterbury, where his father and the Black Prince were both buried in the Trinity Chapel. There too was the point of the sword which had killed St Thomas Becket, and English kings had for generations made pilgrimages to it, to atone for the crime of their murderous ancestor, also called Henry. Alternatively, Henry may have taken a barge up the river to the royal manor of Sheen, where he had started rebuilding the manor house on a grand scale, around a large central courtyard, and where he was to begin work on a series of three new monasteries on both sides of the Thames.

If he had gone anywhere over Shrovetide, it is likely he was back by today. Or at least had finished his pilgrimage. A letter bearing this date was sent to the treasurer and barons of the exchequer ordering them not to trouble Lord Scrope, Henry's close friend, for his homage as the king had already taken homage from him for all his lands at the time of his coronation.[49]

*

At Constance, the English, German and French delegations met together. For once they had a common cause. They had decided that the best way to reunite the papacy was to secure the abdication of Pope John XXIII, and if not his abdication then his deposition, in line with Cardinal Fillastre's memorandum. Knowing that many members of the numerous Italian nation were against the deposition of the Pisan pope in principle, this meeting was to establish who was best qualified to tackle the Italians. They decided that the bishop of Toulon should act as their collective spokesman.

The bishop must have felt some sense of trepidation as he entered the refectory of the Dominican monastery, where the Italian nation sat, and looked at all the solemn faces. But he did not fail. According to Cerretano, he spoke with such elegance and persuasiveness that he 'charmed the ears of everyone in the congregation, moving many of them to tears of pleasure, and won them all to unanimous agreement with his proposal'.[50]

In reality, the decision had already been made. Pope Gregory XII had recently sent word to Sigismund that he was prepared to resign his papal title if his rivals would resign theirs. Only yesterday Cardinal Fillastre had urged John XXIII to travel to Nice so he could resign alongside Benedict XIII. Any Italians who still might have spoken up for Pope John XXIII were informed that a list of his crimes was quietly being circulated, to be used against him. If he was not made to resign, he would undoubtedly be deposed. And then he would not only lose his papal title but his good name too, dragging many Italians down with him. Although it is highly unlikely that there were any 'tears of pleasure' among the prelates who heard the bishop of Toulon's speech, there is little doubt that most of them accepted the decision without protest.

Saturday 16th

No medieval king achieved renown for paying his bills on time, and Henry was no exception. His uncle, Thomas Beaufort, was still owed a large proportion of the £5,397 he had spent on his soldiers' wages in Gascony the previous year. Medieval service required the captain in charge of an army to pay such bills himself and seek repayment from the king. Hence Henry's brother John had been forced to break up his silverware to pay the troops on the Scottish March in 1414. Only now did the king and council decide to reimburse Beaufort for his expenditure, with a payment of £2,000 'in full satisfaction' of the sum owed to him.[51]

The above grant, being made by the 'king in council', indicates that Henry was back at Westminster (if he had ever gone away). He spent part of the afternoon leaning on his cushion in the great chamber, listening to petitions presented by his chamberlain's office. Sir Hugh

Standish petitioned him today for a suit of armour from the Tower of London. Henry assented.[52]

*

At Constance, the two weeks which John XXIII had requested to think over his resignation were up. He called the whole council to meet after supper in the cathedral. In the candlelight he sadly declared that he had decided to resign. He then let the the cardinal of Florence, Francesco Zabarella, outline the resignation process, as he and his cardinals saw it taking place:

> Our most holy lord pope here present, although bound by no vows, oaths or promises whatever to this pledge, yet for the repose of the people of Christ proposes and agrees willingly and freely to give peace to the Church, even by the method of abdication, on condition that, and in as far as Pedro de Luna [Pope Benedict XIII] and Angelo Corrario [Pope Gregory XII], condemned by the holy council of Pisa for schism and heresy, and deposed from the papacy, make a sufficient renunciation of the rights they claim to the papal office. The abdication is to take place by methods and under circumstances to be named forthwith, and confirmed in negotiations to be held immediately hereafter between our lord or his deputies and your deputies.[53]

For those present, including the emperor, this was a great relief. The decision had been made, and made publicly. But this was not an appropriate way forward. It was too vague. Referring to the other pontiffs as schismatics and heretics was hardly the best way to encourage them also to resign. And it made John XXIII's own resignation conditional. Clearly it would not do. As they had learnt the hard way, after the council of Pisa: if you are going to get rid of a pope, you need to do it properly.

Sunday 17th

The most important act Henry performed today was undoubtedly the confirmation of the truce which had been arranged on 24 January.[54] The documents containing the French ambassadors' authority and the terms of the truce itself – to last until 1 May – had been received and checked by Henry's chancery staff for the king's approval. The king simply directed the chancellor to apply the great seal.

Henry's confirmation of this short truce was a foregone conclusion. More interesting are the grants he issued, many of which were endorsed 'by the king'. They included rewards for faithful service, such as the 100 marks yearly granted to Sir Richard Arundel, and the grant of the chancellorship of the collegiate church of St John of Beverley to the chaplain Robert Bryde.[55] However, some were clearly political. For example, he granted to 'Richard Beauchamp of Bergavenny, king's kinsman, and Isabel his wife, sister of Richard, son and heir of Thomas, late Lord Despenser . . . the reversion of all the castles, towns, lordships, manors . . . late of the said Thomas, which the king's kinsman Edward, duke of York, has for life.'[56] Thomas Despenser had been one of the lords who had tried to kill Henry and his father and brothers during the Epiphany Rising in 1400. All his lands had been confiscated and the reversion of them had been granted to the informant who had betrayed the conspiracy, the present duke of York. This grant was therefore part of a scheme of reconciliation with the families of Henry's attempted murderers. Further elements of this scheme were his grants to Constance of York, widow of Lord Despenser, and Eleanor Despenser, widow of Lord Despenser's son, allowing them to receive the rest of the Despenser estates.[57] This was reconciliation on a major scale, for not only had Constance been married to Despenser, but had herself committed treason when she had released Edmund Mortimer and his brother from prison in February 1405. Henry wanted there to be no residual animosity or any threat to his position while at war in France.

There were other grants, commissions and pardons made today, but only one other need be specified.[58] At the request of William, duke of Holland, Henry granted a pardon to one 'Nelle, Bartholomew's daughter' for all felonies, receipts of felons, concealments and trespasses. Henry also undertook to restore to her all her possessions in the town of Calais, and to allow her to live and trade there as before.[59] It is not known what Nelle did to get into trouble, but that is not the point. Her pardon raises a question about the relations between Henry and the duke of Holland at this time, for the granting of a pardon at the duke's request suggests a cordial relationship.

In exploring this relationship, it is worth noting that the English ambassadors sent in June 1414 to John the Fearless – the duke of Holland's brother-in-law and ally – had included Thomas Chaucer, Lord Scrope, Hugh Mortimer, Philip Morgan and John Hovingham.[60] Before they set out, Philip Morgan was given a safe conduct to treat with the duke of Holland, and he did indeed go to Holland after he had seen the duke of Burgundy.[61] What he said in Holland we do not know, but in a rarely consulted set of documents, the Teller's Rolls, we find that Thomas Chaucer also went to see the duke of Holland at about the same time. The entry reads 'to Thomas Chaucer sent to the duke of Holland and other lords in foreign parts for the king's secret negotiations'.[62] It looks very much as if there was a secret agreement with Holland. And, as later events proved, what had been promised went far further than merely restoring the goods and good name of 'Nelle, Bartholomew's daughter'.

Monday 18th

From a historical point of view, one of the most frustrating things about a medieval king's 'secret business' is that it tends to remain secret even today. When we declare that 'there is no evidence' for something, the line is a little disingenuous, as most of the king's really important business was never written down. Evidence and reality do not always match up. What are we to make of an order, issued today, for Sir Bernard Montferrat to speed to the king's presence 'for particular causes moving the king', stating that he should arrive by 1 May at the latest?[63] Maybe this was more of the king's secret business. Maybe he was planning to send this man – who has a Gascon-sounding name – to Gascony, to reveal to certain lords there what he was planning to declare at his great council on 15 April? Perhaps the man just owed the king some money?

Less uncertainty surrounds the formal appointment today of Sir Thomas Carew and Sir Gilbert Talbot as captains of the royal fleet, charged with resisting an invasion during the king's voyage abroad.[64] Henry placed 110 men-at-arms and no fewer than 520 archers at their command, thereby contradicting the advice of his council earlier in the month (which had recommended 232 men-at-arms and 232 archers).[65] The saving in wages was relatively slight – a daily cost of £17 8s as opposed to £18 10s – but the demonstration of faith in the archers is striking.

Also today Henry issued a warning to his estranged friend, Sir John Oldcastle. The offer of a free pardon to all the Lollards, offered on 9 December 1414, would be withdrawn if Oldcastle did not give himself up before the great council on 15 April.[66] In line with his reconciliation with the Despenser family and Constance of York, Henry wanted no trouble from Lollards while he was in France.

Tuesday 19th

By this time all the English ambassadors had arrived in Paris and taken up their lodgings at the *hôtel de Clisson*. According to the French chroniclers, they rode into the city with a cavalcade of six hundred mounted men. This number sounds like an exaggeration but it might not be: later in the year a French embassy received safe conducts for almost as many men. Either way, it suggests that the English embassy was impressive. The Parisians thronged the streets to see the glamorous display. The English leaders wore cloth of gold and silk.[67] The counts of Eu, Vertus and Vendôme went out to receive them with honour, and conducted them to the *hôtel de St Pol* where the king was residing. The dauphin entertained them in royal style at dinner; and there they saw the thirteen-year-old Princess Katherine, and accepted a portrait of her to take back to Henry. According to Monstrelet, the Englishmen 'carried themselves so magnificently . . . that the French, and particularly the Parisians were very much astonished'.[68]

Why did Henry send such an impressive peace mission if he was so determined on war? Surely the money would have been better spent on more armour or wages? The answer is not difficult to establish. Henry needed his war to be considered a *just* one – the shedding of Christian blood could not be condoned unless it was seen in that light. So he had to be seen to give the French a genuine chance to meet his demands. We might say that this was extremely cynical, and that he was only looking for the appearance of a just war; for we know he had already issued the summons for his lords to come to hear the declaration of war on 15 April. But that is precisely why the embassy was so prestigious. Its purpose was symbolic – to give the *impression* of seeking peace. It had to be magnificent to be convincing.

Wednesday 20th

On the Issue Rolls for today we find payments for mercery stuff by Sir Roger Leche, treasurer of the royal household, and Richard Clitherowe, formerly victualler of Calais.[69] Old debts were paid: John Horn, fishmonger of London, was reimbursed 100 marks for his losses when his ships had been requisitioned by the king for the siege of Harlech – in 1409, six years earlier. The sum of £300 was sent to pay the wages of the English men-at-arms and archers in Wales. Various messengers were paid for taking letters 'to all and singular the counties of England' summoning lords to the great council on 15 April, and now Henry added that they were to be informed that the meeting was to last three days, until the 17th. Frustratingly, we also find another of Henry's secretive payments. 'To William Bolton and Nicholas Auncell, messengers, sent with all speed with seven letters under the great seal directed to various sheriffs of various counties for making proclamations within their counties and for certain causes convenient to the king and especially touching his kingdom . . .'

With regard to preparations for his invasion, the clerk of the royal ships, William Catton, was paid for cables. Richard Porter was paid for iron spades and shovels for the royal stores, and Nicholas Frost of London, bowyer, was paid £57 3s 4d for making bows from the start of the reign up until 29 May 1414.

Far more intriguing are three payments on this roll to Henry Scrope. 'To Henry Lord Scrope of Masham sent on the king's embassy to the duke of Burgundy to discuss with the duke certain negotiations and secret matters moving our king . . . £111'. This included repayment of his passage across the sea each way. In itself there is nothing odd about this; we know that Scrope was absent on the king's business from 26 June to 28 October 1414, during which time he saw John the Fearless in person and sealed an agreement with the duke on Henry's behalf. In this agreement John the Fearless agreed to offer no opposition to Henry's attempt to wrest the crown of France from Charles VI but rather to support him and even to supply him with troops.[70] But that was just one voyage. Immediately after this entry, there is another, stating that Scrope had crossed the sea a second time on the same secret business with the duke of Burgundy, for which he was paid £180.[71] There had been another secret communication. What is important about these pieces of evidence is not what they say, it is what they do not say – their secretive nature. We cannot be certain, but the likelihood is that this second communication built on that earlier one, and confirmed John the Fearless's promise that he would not hinder Henry in his quarrel with the French king.

It is among the payments for the king's ships that we find the most astonishing detail. William Soper was today paid for painting swans and antelopes and various coats of arms on the king's great ship, the *Holy Ghost* at Southampton. He was also paid for painting a royal motto on this ship: *une sanz pluis* (one and no more). The fact that the motto was in French is significant – most royal mottoes had been in English since the 1340s, the one notable exception being the motto of the Order of the Garter. So this particular motto may have been directed at the French. However, the source is significant, for it almost certainly comes from a medieval French version of Homer's *Iliad* (which Henry would only have heard in French). The arrogance of the message is quite breathtaking: *'d'avoir plusieurs seigneurs aucun bien je n'y vois / qu'un sans plus soit le maistre et qu'un seul soit le roi* ('As for having several lords, I see no good therein / let one and no more be the master, and that one alone be the king'). It is difficult to read this as anything other than Henry's determination to exercise complete authority – over France as well as England, and over his religious subjects as well as his secular ones.[72]

Thursday 21st

In Constance John XXIII met the emperor and presented a new form of words whereby he proposed to resign. He added a clause requiring Sigismund to take arms against his rival popes if they refused to resign. As Fillastre noted, 'while the first declaration had been unsatisfactory, this second one was still more unsatisfactory'.[73] John had misunderstood why his first offer had been unacceptable. In terms of the unity of Christendom, he had no special rights or privileges over the other two popes. Pressure began to build against him, as it was suspected that he was trying to squirm out of his promise.

*

In Paris, another tournament was due to take place. A band of Portuguese knights had arrived in the city and challenged any Frenchmen who dared fight them to a joust of war. This contest would be a fight with steel lances and sharpened swords, axes and knives.

Jousts of war were relatively rare events, and so this one was bound to draw a huge crowd. As Portugal was an ally of England – Queen Philippa of Portugal being Henry V's aunt – it was decided that Thomas Beaufort, her half-brother, should lead three Portuguese knights out into the lists. With much pageantry and fanfares of trumpets, the seigneur d'Alenton, Sir Jean Cousaille and his brother Sir Peter Cousaille followed Thomas Beaufort and the other English lords into the rue St Antoine. Beaufort was the admiral of England, so it was deemed fitting that his opposite number, Clignet de Brabant, admiral of France, should lead out the three French knights. Then followed the various proclamations and oaths, determining the identity of the knights, and ensuring that they did not use concealed weapons or necromancy in their struggle. Thomas Beaufort and the English lords withdrew to the stands to watch the fight.[71]

The ensuing battle was hard. Eventually the Portuguese yielded, and begged for mercy – much to the indignation and embarrassment of Thomas Beaufort and the other English lords, which they made no effort to hide. The French were delighted, and their champions were given an honourable escort through the streets of Paris.

Friday 22nd

How do you keep a king prisoner? How do you ensure he remains a prisoner when you leave the country, taking most of the fighting men with you? Henry's solution to this was to follow his father's example and use the safest prison in the kingdom, Pevensey Castle, in Sussex. It was far more secure than the Tower of London, from which people did escape from time to time. King James of Scotland had now been in prison for nearly nine years, and Henry had every intention of keeping him in custody – at least until he could negotiate his return to Scotland on favourable terms. It was also vitally important that he keep James alive, for only a living king of Scotland could act as a check on the authority of the Scottish regent, the duke of Albany.

King James was quietly transferred from the Tower of London to Pevensey Castle, which had been guarded for many years by the redoubtable Sir John Pelham. If James strayed from his tower chamber, he was still confined within the enormously strong walls of the castle and the moat. Even if he were to escape from the castle he would find himself within the outer ward – the vast encircling walls which had been built by the Romans and which were still kept in a good state of repair. And if he managed to climb over those outer walls, he faced miles of marshland. The castle even had an *oubliette* – an underground dungeon which could not be accessed except by a trapdoor. There was no point in James even thinking of trying to escape. More importantly, there was no easy way for his fellow Scotsmen to spring him from this castle, one of the furthest from Scotland.

To be doubly sure, Henry allocated £700 today to be paid to Sir John Pelham, to guard his captive safely.[75]

*

Having given orders for the payment in respect of the king of Scotland, Henry took a barge up the River Thames. Here he had decided to found three new monasteries, two on the north side of the river, in the royal manor of Isleworth, and one on the opposite bank, at Sheen. Why, we might ask? Especially at this juncture, within a month of his council declaring that he did not have enough money to safeguard the realm? And even more so when Henry was closing down many monasteries – the alien priories – and sequestering their lands. Why did he not simply keep three of those priories open and save on the building costs?

There are two possible explanations, and perhaps both are correct. One is that Henry was seeking to do something which his father had failed to do. It is said that, because Henry IV had judicially murdered an archbishop, Richard Scrope, in 1405, Pope Gregory XII had enjoined upon him in 1408 the task of building three new monasteries.[76] Henry IV had not built one, let alone three; and even if he had been willing to make such foundations he could not have afforded to endow them. Henry V was keen to remedy all his father's failings. If this was indeed the reason why Henry now founded these monasteries, it was the fourth instance of him making good what his father had left undone. He had reburied Richard II in his proper grave in Westminster Abbey; he had commissioned a bronze effigy of his mother to be placed on her tomb; and he had renewed the building of the Lancastrian church in Leicester. If Pope Gregory really had instructed Henry IV to found three monasteries, then this work may certainly be seen in this light.

The other explanation for these foundations lies in their specific character. Each of the three was to follow the rule of one of the most respected and austere monastic orders. Today, for example, he had come to lay the foundation stone of one of the new monasteries on the north side of the river, which was to be a house of Bridgettine nuns – followers of the rule of St Bridget, 'a lover of peace and tranquillity'.[77] What Henry was about to do in France amounted to the very opposite of peace and tranquillity, so these foundations may well have represented a form of atonement for his forthcoming invasion – a reconciliation with God – in much the same way he was reconciling himself with rebel families through the restitution of their estates. In these monasteries, as with everything else, Henry was putting his own standing with God first.

Presumably Henry chose a day when the weather was not too inclement for his trip up the river. When he reached what is now known as the Old Deer Park, near Richmond, he would have seen the building site of Sheen Manor, which was one year into its five-year rebuilding programme. The hall, chapel and chambers were being constructed around a great square courtyard. Men were busying themselves about the scaffolding and carts, following the directions of the royal master mason, Stephen Lote. Stone for the building was being brought in from all parts of the kingdom – from Yorkshire, Devon, Kent, Surrey and Oxfordshire – and timber was arriving on wagons from Surrey. Bricks had been imported from Calais. Salvaged stone and timber from a royal house, Byfleet, which Henry had recently had demolished, were piled up and ready to be used in the new buildings.[78] Carved swans and antelopes were being prepared, to adorn the buildings when finished.

The monastery which Henry planned to build here was to be a Charterhouse, for Carthusian monks.[79] The Order had been founded in France in the tenth century and had spread to England in the late twelfth; but its strictness had deterred many Englishmen from joining it until the late fourteenth century. After the Black Death, very few monasteries were founded in England at all, apart from those whose rules were very strict and devout. Carthusians, who lived independently in cells arranged around the cloister of their monasteries, and who were not allowed to speak except for meetings in the chapter house, were one of the strictest orders of all. They had seen a spate of foundations – at London in 1371, Kingston upon Hull in 1377, Coventry in 1381, Axholme in 1397 and Mount Grace in 1398. Henry's Charterhouse at Sheen was thus one of the most fashionably severe examples of religious patronage which he could set – a mark of respectable austerity.

On the other side of the river, the north side, where his barge docked today, he planned the two other monasteries. One was for Celestine monks, an order of vegetarian hermits founded by Pope Celestine V who followed the Rule of St Benedict very closely. No Celestine houses had yet been founded in England. The idea had come from Bishop Courtenay, who had visited several Celestine monasteries in France the previous year and had returned to England with three French Celestine monks to make a start on the foundation.[80]

The third monastery Henry planned was the one already mentioned for which he had come to lay the foundation stone. Henry had no way of knowing that St Bridget had just been canonised at Constance for a second time. His association with the saint rather came from his sister, Philippa, queen of Sweden, Norway and Denmark. In 1406 several of Henry's friends had accompanied her on her journey to meet her husband, King Eric, and thus had come into contact with the Bridgettines at Vadstena, St Bridget's original foundation. Among the wedding party were Lord Fitzhugh and Sir Walter Hungerford (both currently at Constance) and Henry Lord Scrope. The devout Lord Fitzhugh in particular recommended the contemplative and peaceful Bridgettines. Henry's sister, Queen Philippa (who was a regular visitor to Vadstena), also sent word about St Bridget's foundation. That Henry was genuinely fervent about St Bridget's order is clear in that he managed to acquire a relic of St Bridget herself in a gold cross. He decided he would copy Vadstena on the north bank of the Thames. There would be thirteen monks (corresponding to the number of apostles, including St Peter), sixty nuns under the charge of an abbess, as well as four deacons, four lay brothers and four lay sisters. There would be separate chapels beneath the same roof where the monks and nuns could pray together, the nuns' chapel built on the floor above the monks' one. The name of the abbey – a point on which Henry was most particular – was to be 'the Monastery of St Saviour and St Bridget of Syon'.[81]

The foundation stone was laid on ground within the king's rabbit warren in the manor of Isleworth, in the parish of Twickenham. The space he measured out was marked with boundary stones. From the northern stone to a more southerly one it measured 646 yards, along the edge of Twickenham field; from this second stone to a stone by the river Thames 320 yards; from this stone to another back along the river bank 340 yards and from this stone back to the northern marker 327 yards – in all just over thirty acres. The river-side location made it somewhat damp, however. So Henry ordered a ditch to be dug, to drain the ground more effectively. Somewhat surprisingly, the buildings were built mostly of brick: Henry brought brickmakers over from Holland especially.[82] English readers auto-matically associate monasteries with stone ruins; but on the banks of the Thames there once stood a brick monastery, where prayers were said and Masses sung for the benefit of the souls of Henry V and Lord Fitzhugh.

*

In Paris, John the Fearless's proctors had finally agreed to the king's terms. Although John was at that moment some way from Paris – at Rouvres – he and all his supporters were pardoned by the king 'out of reverence for God, wishing to prefer mercy to rigorous justice'. Still the five hundred exceptions remained, mostly Parisians who had been caught up in the Cabochien revolt in 1413. These men were not to be allowed closer than 'four or five leagues' from the city; other-wise there would be a free pardon for all, and no prosecutions for loyalty to John. All castles were to be restored, and all parties were to swear to uphold the Peace of Arras, whether Burgundian or Armagnac.[83]

In the eyes of the English, it was a second public humiliation in as many days. A third awaited them. That same day the diplomatic representatives of Owen Glendower received a gift of £100 from the French king. They had been there since late the previous year, negotiating with the French how best to proceed together against the English.[84] Not long afterwards one of the English ambassadors, Sir William Bourchier, set out to return to England, to inform Henry of how his intentionally doomed embassy was being received. No doubt Henry's fierce pride was dented. But in reality, this public disrespect was exactly what he wanted.

Sunday 24th

A proclamation went out today to the sheriffs of London and all the sheriffs of coastal counties and county towns – from Newcastle upon Tyne and Yorkshire on the east coast, all the way round the south-eastern coast to Devon, Cornwall and Bristol – reiterating that an inviolable truce was in force between England and the Spanish kingdom of Castile and Léon. That the proclamation went out only to maritime counties suggests it was a pre-emptive announcement to any piratically minded master of an English ship who may have been waiting for the old year-long truce, agreed in February 1414, to run out. Henry's ambassador, Dr Jean Bordiu, archdeacon of Médoc, had now returned from the court of Castile with news that the truce had been prolonged for another year, to last until February 1416, at a formal meeting at Fuenterrabia on 27 November 1414.

Although this truce only applied to one of the Spanish kingdoms, Castile and Léon, the regent of that kingdom was Ferdinand, king of Aragon. Hence Aragon and Castile were bound as one political unit. On top of this, the dowager queen of Castile was Henry's aunt, Catalina, and the young king of Castile was his cousin. King Ferdinand of Aragon had himself sought a league with Henry from the start of the reign. So the interweaving of Spanish and English dynasties and diplomatic agreements meant that, as long as he could prevent English pirates from ransacking the Spanish ships, Henry had nothing to fear from the kingdoms of the Iberian peninsula. Not only would they not attack England, they would not fight for France.[85]

Tuesday 26th

By now readers will have become familiar with the sorts of payments one finds on the Issue Rolls. Payments fall more or less into the categories of administration, reimbursement of messengers' and ambassadors' expenses, rewards for good service, measures for the defence of Wales, the north and Calais, money handed over to the king's chamber, and, to a limited extent, gathering supplies for the forthcoming expedition. Today's payments touch on most of these areas. Robert Thresk and three other exchequer clerks were given 35 marks in recognition of their recent work and expenses in the exchequer. The sum handed over to the officers of the king's chamber for the king's personal use amounted to £1,331 18s 9d. Robert Umphraville, custodian of the castle of Roxburgh, was paid 100 marks for the wages of his men-at-arms and archers remaining there. Various messengers were sent to the sheriffs to collect the first instalment of the tax granted at the last parliament, which was due at Candlemas (2 February). Messengers were similarly sent out with letters under the great seal to the archbishop of York, the bishop of Durham and the bishop of Carlisle to ask, on behalf of the exchequer, who would be collecting the two tenths granted by the convocation of York in January.

While the king of Scotland was a prisoner in England, the kingdom of Scotland was ruled by a regent, the duke of Albany. It so happened that the duke's son, Mordach, earl of Fife, was also in an English prison. While the elderly duke did not particularly want to see King James return to Scotland, he was very anxious that his son should be returned to him. Henry was wisely biding his time on the prospect of returning the earl. Today's payments include one of 10 marks towards his upkeep in the Tower of London.

Finally, and at long last, we come to a payment which is a rare sign of human warmth in Henry. It states that Roger Castle esquire was paid for carriage of 250 wainscotes and regale to make doors, windows and other works to 'a chamber in the water under Kenilworth Castle'.[86] This was the 'Pleasance in the Marsh', a timber house about half a mile from Kenilworth Castle, on the other side of the lake there. Most kings had some form of retreat from the world at one or other of their palaces: a place where they could be alone with their friends.

Edward II had used a cottage and garden in the grounds of the abbey of Westminster which he called *Burgoyne* (Burgundy).[87] Richard II had a summer house built on an island in the Thames near Sheen Manor which he called *La Neyte*.[88] Like Richard II's house, Henry's *Pleasance* was surrounded by water and intended for small parties on hot days in summer.[89] Apart from the extravagant goldsmith's work under tomorrow's date, it is one of the very few personal indulgences of a relaxed or luxurious nature to be found in connection with Henry V throughout the whole of the year.

Wednesday 27th

The penultimate day of the month saw further payments recorded on the Issue Rolls.[90] Thomas Chaucer, the king's butler, paid £31 to Sir Roger Leche for wines imported from Bordeaux which had been intended for the king's household. Somewhat extravagantly, Henry's officers paid the huge sum of £976 to William Randolph of London, goldsmith, 'for making 12 dishes of pure gold, four dozen chargers of silver and eight dozen silver dishes for the king's use'.[91] Sadly the gold dishes did not long survive; they had been pawned or sold off by the time of the king's inventory in 1422, probably to pay the wages of soldiers.

There were, of course, more payments towards the war. Richard Porter was paid for more iron spades. Henry Bower and his staff were paid another £5 for making bows 'for the king's work'. And a messenger was sent with a letter under the privy seal to the mayor of Bristol for 'certain necessary reasons contained in the letter'.

Far more important – and much more helpful in determining what was going on in terms of Henry's secret diplomacy – is this entry:

> To Richard Clitherowe and Reginald Curteis esquires ordered by the lord the King to go to Zeeland and Holland to treat as well with the duke of Holland and other persons of those parts to provide ships for the king's present voyage in person, to accompany him abroad . . . £2,000.[92]

This, it must be remembered, is not an instruction to negotiate but a *payment*. And it is a huge one. Although the actual commissions for these men to obtain the ships were not issued until April, the handing over of so much cash at this stage implies that Henry already knew where he could obtain sufficient ships for his voyage. It also implies that he knew the duke of Holland would accede to his request. And that in turn implies that the duke of Holland knew that his brother-in-law and ally, John the Fearless, would not try to stop Henry.

Now we can see what Thomas Chaucer had been doing on the king's secret business to the duke of Holland the previous year; and Philip Morgan on his mission, too. And Lord Scrope on his various missions to Burgundy. Henry had been working on the lords of Burgundy and Holland so that they would help him transport his army to France, and not impede his progress against the French king when he got there.

Viewed in the wider perspective of Henry's diplomacy and dynastic links, these secret negotiations were even more significant. Henry now had a long-standing alliance with Portugal. He had in place a truce with Castile – and by implication Aragon. He had both the king of Scotland and the regent's son in his prisons. The kingdom of Sweden, Denmark and Norway was ruled by the husband of his deeply religious sister, Philippa, whom he had just flattered by asking to send some Bridgettine nuns for his new monastery at Syon. His embassy at Constance was at that moment negotiating with Sigismund for a treaty. As for his French and Low Countries alliances: the dukes of Brittany and Burgundy had both agreed they would not intervene in a struggle between Henry and the king of France. And the duke of Holland was planning actually to assist Henry in his expedition.

The French king and his Armagnac advisers had no way of knowing it, but even as they rejoiced in the proclamation of the Peace of Arras, two of the French dukes had secret alliances with the king of England. The French king's insistence that any such alliances should be torn up was futile. It remained to be seen what the other members of the Burgundian alliance would do. But in every other diplomatic respect, Henry had outmanoeuvred the French.

March

Friday 1st

At Dijon, Martin Porée, bishop of Arras, was about to set out on his journey to Constance. His mission was to represent John the Fearless at the council. As was becoming clear to all, the council had teeth; it was prepared to tackle difficult questions. In particular, it was prepared to discuss the boundaries of heresy. This had important implications for rulers who claimed to reign by divine right, for it touched upon the nature of treason. Dr Jean Gerson had just arrived (yesterday) at Constance, and his forthcoming speeches were bound to favour the Armagnacs. What might he say about the late Jean Petit's *Justification of the duke of Burgundy*? Did that document amount to heresy, as Dr Gerson had stated in Paris? If so, was John the Fearless guilty of supporting heresy? What was to stop the king of France ordering a crusade against him?

Martin Porée was not John the Fearless's only representative. Pierre Cauchon had already set out for Constance. A Burgundian nobleman called Gautier de Ruppes was also about to set out. All three of these men were eloquent speakers and highly respected for their judgment. Porée was especially noted for his deep, loud voice; when he spoke, people listened. John carefully briefed each of them. They were not permitted to accept gifts from anyone at the council. Nor were they to dine or sup with any member of the council outside their own lodgings. They were sworn to the secrecy of their mission. And they were empowered to bribe cardinals, archbishops and bishops in order to protect the good name of the late Jean Petit and the legal standing of his *Justification*.[1]

John the Fearless could withstand being accused of treason. Being condemned as a heretic was quite another matter.

*

This same day, Pope John XXIII came before the council with a third form of his resignation. This had been drawn up by representatives of the English, French and German nations, and was now deemed suitable for publication. John read it aloud himself in person, as he had been instructed.

> I, Pope John XXIII, for the repose of the whole people of Christ do offer, promise and pledge myself, swear and vow to God and the Church and this holy council willingly and freely to give peace to the Church by way of my own simple abdication and to do this and to put it into effect according to the decision of this present council, if and when Pedro de Luna and Angelo Corrario, known in their obedience as Benedict XIII and Gregory XII, likewise renounce in person or by their legal proctors their pretension to the papal office; the same promise to hold in case of either one's resignation or death or other event, whenever unity might be bestowed on the Church of God and the present schism terminated by my abdication.[2]

This version omitted the antagonistic statements about John XXIII's rival popes being schismatics and heretics and cut all reference to the Holy Roman Emperor taking force against them unless they abdicated. Dr Gerson and the other newly-arrived delegates from the University of Paris had spent their first night at Constance deliberating it. Gerson's advice was given special weight – at the council of Pisa he had foreseen the problems that would arise from electing a replacement pope before the other two had been forced to resign. Now he declared the form of words to be acceptable.

So it was that the pope who had summoned the council of Constance together was forced to agree to his own abdication. There could have been no stronger message to the rest of Christendom that this council meant business. Combined with the knowledge that Pope Gregory too would resign shortly, and that Sigismund would himself travel to France to seek the resignation of Benedict XIII, it seemed that the Almighty had intervened in men's hearts to bring about the re-unification of the Church under one pope.

All eyes now looked to Constance. Some looked to it for the reformation of the Church, others for the future course of the papacy, and still more for the eradication of heresy and the divine signal to exterminate the Lollards. A few lords looked in that direction to fight their own political battles on a holy platform. Others, including the Lollards, just looked on in fear.

Sunday 3rd

At Westminster, the great charter for the endowment of Henry's Bridgettine foundation at Syon was sealed today. It began with an exemplification of the spiritual virtues of founding monasteries, in order to please God, following the example of Henry's distinguished ancestors. These sentiments were predictable, wholly in line with Henry's extreme religiosity. One line in the preamble, however, does stand out. It states that Henry was inspired to found this abbey having been 'moved by the grace of the Almighty, in whose hands are the hearts of kings, and according to the scripture "he will turn where He wills"'.[3] These words (*ubi voluerit inclinabit*) were a biblical quotation (from Proverbs 21: 1) but they were also to be found in the first law of the first book of the *Codex Justinianus*, a key text in civil law, and so would have been well known to Henry's advisers. This particular law was entitled 'About the Trinity of the Holy Catholic faith, so that no one may dispute it publicly'. It was effectively a justification for stamping out heresy. As the same law said, 'kings rule by their tongues' (Proverbs 16: 102), so the justification for no one disobeying kings lay in the fact that what kings said was moved by God. This was absolute kingship writ in divine logic: Henry was not just *king* by divine right, his very rule was divinely inspired because his heart was in God's hands.

If any one aspect of Henry as a historical individual has not been fully appreciated down the centuries, it is his position as an absolutist monarch: a king sanctioned by God to wield complete power over all his subjects. We can see elements of this in his motto *une sanz pluis* and the philosophy that the king should be the master of all his peers.

In the phrase 'he will turn where He wills' we can see it more fully formed: Henry saw himself as a ruler who was above the law, answerable only to God. This is not to say he could do no wrong – he could still lose a battle or fall ill, which would demonstrate that he had offended God in some way – but Henry was less answerable to his people than even his predecessors as kings. Most significantly, his absolutism was largely of his own making. His father had preferred to debate the merits of his legitimacy and rule with rebellious friars, Members of Parliament and his confessor. It was perhaps the most profound debate of the later middle ages. Society was changing – religiously and socially – and people were asking whether the agents of change were acting in accordance with the will of God or against it. Henry was not alone in seeking to equate all questioning of ecclesiastical and secular authority as contrary to the will of God.

*

Across London, in St Martin's Lane, John Claydon was sitting in the chamber above his shop. His servant, John Fuller, had been copying out the text of a book called *The Lantern of Light*, in accordance with Claydon's instructions. As he finished each section he would read it back to Claydon. Today they had been working since eight in the morning on the last section, and had just about finished their work by dusk. Claydon was so pleased with the results that he declared he would happily have paid three times as much for copying the book than not have had possession of such a valuable treasure.

The Lantern of Light was a recent work, written by John Grime, a Lollard. It contained the text of a sermon preached at Horsleydown on the other side of London, which Claydon had witnessed being delivered.[4] The whole book was full of passionate, heartfelt rhetoric against the authority of the pope. For example, it said: 'that wicked antichrist the pope hath sowed among the laws of Christ his popish and corrupt decrees, which are of no authority, strength, nor value'. And on indulgences, 'the pope's and the bishop's indulgences be unprofitable, neither can they profit them to whom they be given by any means'. With regard to transubstantiation it denied that the bread and wine turned to the body and blood of Christ. Herein we also find the signal line: 'in the court of Rome is the head of Antichrist, and in archbishops and bishops is the body of Antichrist, but in these patched and clouted sects as monks and canons and friars is the venomous tail of Antichrist'.[5]

These were the very words used by Sir John Oldcastle in his defiance of the king's promulgation of orthodoxy. Claydon can have had no illusions that copying this book was anything other than heresy in the eyes of the Church. For him, however, it was the one way to salvation. It was the truth, no matter what the king or the prelates said. As the *Lantern* declared, followers of its light 'must needs suffer travail, if we will come to rest – and pain, if we come to bliss. He is a false coward knight that fleeth and hideth his head when his master is in the field beaten among his enemies . . .' Claydon was no 'coward knight'. He had already been imprisoned for two years in Conway Castle for heresy, and for another year in the Fleet Prison – in appalling conditions. When a heretical priest, William Sawtre, had been burnt alive in London in 1401, Claydon had recanted; but still he could not alter or set aside what he truly believed – not now, after twenty years of seeking his own spiritual path.

No doubt Claydon thought he was safe with his cherished heretical books behind locked doors. But it so happened that one of his apprentices, a fifteen-year-old boy called Alexander Philip, whom he had looked after for nearly three years, heard John Fuller reading parts of the *Lantern* to his master. And when Alexander Philip was dismissed from his apprenticeship with Claydon, he found another employer. This was none other than Thomas Falconer, the mayor of London.[6] Claydon was suddenly on very dangerous ground.

Tuesday 5th

If Jan Hus had seen a copy of *The Lantern of Light*, he would have been shocked at the outrageous and inflammatory language but he would have agreed with many of Grime's theological statements. Hus also followed Wycliffe in questioning both transubstantiation and the authority of the pope. His rhetoric was more restrained but his purpose was the same: to release Christians from the tyranny of the Church. He was far more dangerous than Grime, however, for two reasons. The first was that he preached a questioning of religious

authority from within – not so much a movement against the Church
as the need for the Church itself to change. The second was that he
was not an obscure English Lollard in hiding but a well-known theologian who was bold enough to argue his case at Constance itself.
Hence his incarceration in the Dominican monastery.

Today, from his prison cell near the monastic refectory, Hus wrote
to his loyal friend Lord John of Chlum. He thanked him for his steadfast support, and expressed his wish that 'by the mercy of God, you
await the conclusion of my trial like a soldier of Jesus Christ'. In his
letter he stated that he had been without news of his friends for a
considerable time – to the extent that he had been led to believe Lord
John of Chlum had packed up and gone home. Only some Polish
knights had been to see him, apart from one or two of his countrymen. He had been suffering terribly from kidney stones, as well as
vomiting and fevers. When an old friend came to see him, Master
Christian of Prachatice, Hus could not help himself and burst into
uncontrolled sobs and tears.

Hus knew that his physical weaknesses and social estrangement
were nothing compared to the sinister powers now being lined up
against him. Jean Gerson himself had issued a series of articles
condemning him, and other enemies were falsifying evidence against
him. Hus was too frightened to put his answers to religious questions
on paper, for fear his letters would be intercepted by the guards. The
letters that came to him he destroyed immediately after reading them,
so they could not be used against him. He seems to have placed all
his hope in the emperor: as he wrote,

> I would be glad if the emperor were to command that a copy of my
> responses to Wycliffe be given to him. Oh, that God would inspire
> his lips so that he would declare himself one of the princes for the
> truth![7]

Wednesday 6th

There are very few indicators of Henry's activity at Westminster in
late February and early March. Even the sealing of the charter of Syon
on the 3rd 'by the king himself' does not necessarily indicate that he

was at Westminster. After all, the same document states that it was witnessed by the earl of Warwick and Lord Fitzhugh, both of whom were still at Constance. Similarly a letter to the bishop of Salisbury, dated today at Westminster, recording Henry's assent to the election of John Brunyng as abbot of Sherborne, could have been drawn up by the keeper of the privy seal in the king's absence.[8] It is possible that the king left the palace at this time, perhaps to spend time with his closest companions away from the household, or maybe going on pilgrimage. One chronicle records that he went to several towns in person, demanding money – and the next we know of him for certain, he was doing just that, in London.

The reason for this line of speculation is not simply because of the absence of evidence locating the king at Westminster at this time. It is also because it is likely that Henry paid a visit to Southampton. Two months after this date a royal sergeant-at-arms was reimbursed for arresting one Christopher Rys and bringing him by royal command 'to the king's presence at Southampton'.[9] This is of course a retrospective payment, like most reimbursements of expenses on the Issue Rolls. But it seems Henry may have made a short visit to his port of embarkation between the last week of February and early March, to make preparations for the embarkation in the summer and perhaps to survey the area where the troops were to be billeted.

Sunday 10th

Henry was certainly back in the city before today. He went to the Tower of London, and commanded several of the most important men of the city to join him there. Among them were the mayor, Thomas Falconer, and all the aldermen. When they were all gathered in the hall, Henry entered and addressed them:

> Well-beloved. We do desire that it shall not be concealed from the knowledge of your faithfulness, how that, God our rewarder, we do intend with no small army to visit the parts beyond the sea, that so we may duly re-conquer the lands pertaining to the inheritance and crown of our realm, which have for long, in the time of our predecessors,

by enormous wrong been withheld. But, seeing that we cannot speedily attain to everything that is necessary in this behalf for the perfecting of our wishes, in order that we may make provision for borrowing a competent sum of money from all the prelates, nobles, lords, cities, boroughs and substantial men of our realm, knowing that you will be the more ready to incline to our wishes the sooner that the purpose of our intention, as aforesaid, redounds to the manifest advantage of the whole realm, have therefore not long since come to the determination to send certain lords of our council to the city aforesaid, to treat with you as to promoting the business above mentioned.[10]

Although this record of his speech falls someway short of Shakespearian oratory, the message was clear. Henry wanted money. He intended to obtain it from the leading London citizens. And he was not going to lower himself so far as to ask them for it in person; he would send others to tell them how much he required.

Monday 11th

A great session of all the prelates was held in the cathedral of Constance in order to decide how they might elect a new pope for the whole of Christendom. Various prelates spoke. Eventually Johan von Nassau, archbishop of Mainz, stood up. He was of the opinion that they were all beholden to Pope John XXIII and should re-elect him as supreme pontiff of the reunited Church. If they did not, the archbishop declared, he himself would not sit there with them any longer, for he would never pay obedience to another man.

After all the difficulties they had faced in getting John XXIII to agree to resign, the reaction was predictable – complete uproar. Pope John was as corrupt and selfish as the worst of his predecessors; he was certainly not the man to fill the reunited Church with a sense of spiritual purpose and dignity. The patriarch of Constantinople expressed the feelings of the majority when he stood up and shouted out in Latin, 'Who is that man? He deserves to be burned!'

The archbishop of Mainz was driven to fury. He strode out of the cathedral, demanding that all those of his obedience should follow him. He took a boat that same day and went home. The prelates, needing time to confer with their nations and legal advisers, dispersed to their houses.[11]

Tuesday 12th

Bishop Courtenay stood at the black marble table in the great hall of the royal palace in Paris.[12] The huge four-aisled space was filled with the dignitaries and knighthood of the kingdom of France. This sermon was not going to be an easy one. On the one hand he had to ensure that he was seen to do everything within his power to bring about a peace settlement between England and France. On the other, he had to fail.

Actual terms would be laid out formally the following day. Now was the time for a sermon on the prospect of peace. Courtenay took as his theme a line from Isaiah 39: 8: 'Then said Hezekiah to Isaiah, Good is the word of the Lord which you have spoken, for there shall be peace and truth in my days'.[13]

The French prelates would have known the context of that verse. It was Hezekiah's response to a warning that Isaiah had given him. Hezekiah had showed 'all that is in my house' – all his gold, silver, spices, ointments and armour – to some messengers who had come to him from the king of Babylon. Hearing this, Isaiah had said to Hezekiah, 'Hear the word of the Lord of hosts: Behold, the days come, that all that is in your house, and that which your fathers have laid up in store until this day, shall be carried to Babylon, nothing shall be left, says the Lord. And your sons . . . shall be eunuchs in the palace of the king of Babylon.' This warning was what had prompted Hezekiah to say, 'There shall be peace and truth in my days' – a declaration of peace despite the threat of war.

We do not know exactly what Courtenay said in elaborating on this theme, but we can see that it would have cast the prospect of peace into the shadow of war. According to the French chroniclers, Courtenay talked at length about justice. He emphatically declared that no peace was possible without it. As we have seen, justice was indeed something that principally motivated Henry. But Courtenay was referring to a particular form of justice. It amounted to the injustice of the French refusal to accept Edward III's claim to the throne of France, and to flout the terms of the Treaty of Brétigny of 1360.

Courtenay seems to have claimed that no permanent peace was possible unless the terms of a treaty that had been set aside as unworkable and irrelevant for the last fifty-five years were now implemented.

Wednesday 13th

The day after Courtenay's speech, the French royal family staged a show of strength. The ambassadors of John the Fearless – including the duke of Brabant, Margaret of Holland, the bishop of Tournai, the seigneur de Ront and William Bouvier – and the representatives of the county of Flanders, of which John was the overlord, swore on pieces of the True Cross that they and he would preserve the peace of Arras, which they had confirmed the previous month. The duke of Brabant and his sister also 'certified that their brother [John the Fearless] had made no alliance with England' and nor would he make any in future that were to the detriment of France. Following this, the old duke of Berry swore the same oath on the relics, and so did Charles, duke of Orléans, the duke of Alençon and the duke of Bourbon. The count of Eu and the count of Vendôme followed them, as well as the chancellor of France, other officials of the royal household, and a large number of archbishops and bishops.[14]

The oath-taking had a double purpose. The first was to strengthen confidence in the actual reconciliation with Burgundy. The second was to show the English representatives that the French royal family was once more united. If there had been any implicit threat in Courtenay's sermon the previous day, then it was received with a demonstration of unity.

Courtenay himself would have been quietly amused, for he knew of Henry's secret dealings with John the Fearless. Philip Morgan, who had met the dukes of Burgundy and Holland the previous year, was there in Paris with him. But this was certainly not the time and place to use such knowledge; rather this was the time to present Henry's demands plainly, and in such a way that they would be refused.

Courtenay probably did all the talking. He began by reiterating the decisions of the previous embassy. He reminded the French that, on that occasion, he and the other English ambassadors had claimed the throne of France on Henry's behalf. This being acknowledged as unacceptable to the French in principle, the English ambassadors had reserved Henry's right to repeat the claim at a future time, and had proceeded to examine other opportunities for a permanent peace. They had demanded the lordship of the duchy of Normandy in full sovereignty, the lordships of Touraine, Anjou and Maine in full sovereignty, sovereignty over the duchies of Aquitaine, Brittany and Flanders, and lordship of all the lands between the Somme and Gravelines, together with the restitution of all the other lands ceded to Edward III in the Treaty of Brétigny in 1360 and half the county of Provence. On top of this, they had asked for 1.6 million crowns in full repayment of King John II's ransom, and two million crowns (£333,333 6s 8d) for the dowry of Princess Katherine, who would be handed over to be married to Henry.[15]

Having outlined the full scale of the English demands the previous year, Courtenay repeated the official and very generous response of the duke of Berry – how the French were prepared to cede the parts of Aquitaine conquered from the English in lordship, but not in sovereignty. He went into detail about each of the lands that the duke had offered, naming each one specifically in a long list. As for the princess's hand in marriage, he reminded the French how the duke had said they were prepared to stretch to 600,000 crowns (£100,000).

The subtle impression Courtenay gave was that the French had already done much to compromise. So now it was the English turn. He declared that, in the interests of peace, and to avoid the shedding of Christian blood, the king of England was prepared to shift considerably with regard to the marriage. Although the girl was of such high rank that she could hardly be offered to Henry for less than the full two million crowns, Henry would take her off King Charles's hands for just 1.5 million crowns (£250,000). He might even be prepared to accept a million, hinted Courtenay, if the French were to equip her suitably with enough clothes and jewels. As to the other matter – the matter of justice, as Courtenay now overtly described it – the king would be prepared to accept just the implementation of the Treaty of Brétigny in full and the restitution of the Lancastrian inheritances of Nogent and Beaufort. And there was one further requirement: that if Henry and Katherine were to have two sons, the lordship of Ponthieu and Montreuil – the dower lands of Queen Isabella, wife of Edward II – should be inherited by the second-born.[16]

We have already seen how manipulative and subtle Courtenay could be. He had strung Jean Fusoris along, 'buying' astrolabes and texts from him and repeatedly failing to pay for them. He had told the Frenchman all sorts of lies, feeding him disinformation about the poor state of Henry's health, and pretending to be worried that the king would die. He had even gone so far as to seek Fusoris's advice on whether this mission to secure a permanent peace would be successful. In all these matters he was being duplicitous, pretending to be hopeful of peace when he knew Henry was already set on war, and projecting a false sense of vulnerability. Now he was doing the same with the French court. He had reminded them how much they had *already* compromised, and how reasonable the old duke of Berry had been in August 1414. In this way he encouraged the French into a feeling of complacency, building upon the sense of satisfaction with the morning's show of unity and loyalty. And on top of this he projected a sense of English vulnerability by dramatically lessening Henry's demands for a large dowry, and stressing that Henry sincerely wanted a permanent peace. In this way he encouraged the French to believe that they held all the cards, and could press him for further compromises.

The French took the English demands, which were written in Latin, and translated them for the king's benefit. The English would receive an answer the following day.

*

Sir William Bourchier arrived back at Westminster.[17] Sir John Phelip and William Porter had arrived back a few days earlier.[18] Their part in the peace negotiations had been negligible. In fact, probably their whole purpose in travelling to Paris was to investigate the route they had taken – via Harfleur, the fortified port where the French kept their northern fleet. Like the messengers from the king of Babylon to Hezekiah, they had examined the treasures and armour in the enemy's house. Armed with this information, Henry was in a better position to consider carrying away 'all that which [King Charles's] fathers have laid up in store'. For the French royal family had, like Hezekiah, said in their over-confidence: 'there shall be peace and truth in my days'. As with Hezekiah, it amounted to a declaration of peace despite the threat of war.

Thursday 14th

The French replied to Courtenay concerning the terms on which the English offered a permanent peace. With regard to the marriage of Katherine of France – which was, as far as the French were concerned, the substantive issue – they were prepared to offer 800,000 crowns (£133,333 6s 8d). They would also equip her honourably. But in the matter of 'justice' as Courtenay described it, they were prepared only to repeat their earlier offer, namely to restore the lands of Aquitaine in lordship, not in sovereignty. They claimed that these would be more than adequate compensation for the 1.6 million crowns of King John's ransom. Nothing was said about Ponthieu or the rights of a second son born to Henry and Katherine. Or Nogent and Beaufort.[19]

At this point Courtenay must have felt satisfied. He had been seen to lessen demands for the royal marriage by a full million crowns; the French had shifted their position by only 200,000. Although further negotiations could have settled the matter at somewhere in the region of 900,000, this was not the point. His mission was to demonstrate that the French position as a whole was unreasonable. This was also the case in the matter of justice: Henry had reduced his territorial demands by a very large margin, including sovereignty of several northern duchies. The French had responded by not shifting their position at all. Courtenay and his fellow ambassadors could now withdraw from the negotiations on the grounds that they could not agree to a peace in which they obtained nothing more for their king, as they had no authority to settle for so little.

On hearing this, the ever-optimistic duke of Berry suggested that the French would send an embassy to England to seek another path to secure the royal marriage. The English could hardly refuse; one can just imagine their thin-lipped smiles. Thus they had to recommend this as a course of action. The great seal of France was then applied to the French version of the terms offered, and the document was handed to the English ambassadors. Courtenay and his companions left court that same day, and returned hastily to England.

As soon as they had gone, an order was issued in the name of King Charles to levy a tax on the whole kingdom. The English were gathering money, ships and men, and intended to invade, it was declared. They would not find the French unprepared.[20]

*

At Constance a petition was presented to John XXIII on behalf of the nations of France, Germany and England. It contained five requests. It was first asked that, as the pope had publicly promised to abdicate, he should now appoint proctors for that purpose, ready to perform the act when the council required him to do so. Second, that the council not be dissolved until the reform and reunification of the Church had been achieved. Third, no one should leave the council without giving his reason and obtaining permission. Fourth, that under no circumstance should the pope leave the council. Fifth that he should issue letters circulating his promise of abdication.[21]

John replied immediately to three of these points. He endorsed the proposal that the council should continue to sit until its work was finished. He forbade anyone to leave without permission under pain of excommunication and he agreed to issue the bull containing his promise of abdication. As to the other matters – the appointment of proctors and his detention in Constance – he declared he would consider this further and respond at a later date.

*

In line with his promise four days earlier, Henry sent 'certain lords of his council' to request that money be made available by the citizens of London. The lords in question were five of the six highest-ranking men in the country: namely his brothers, John and Humphrey, his cousin Edward, duke of York, his uncle, Henry Beaufort, chancellor of England, and the archbishop of Canterbury. Only his least-favourite brother, Thomas, duke of Clarence, was absent.

With such eminent men gathered in the Guildhall, there arose the question of who should take precedence. Normally in a medieval hall, a lord yielded up his own seat if a more important lord was present. But should the mayor give up his seat to the duke of Bedford, the king's brother, or the archbishop of Canterbury? Given their mission, the two men settled on allowing the mayor to retain his seat.

The archbishop and Bishop Beaufort sat on the mayor's right hand, and the three royal dukes sat on his left. No doubt Thomas Falconer felt hugely honoured to be occupying a position that otherwise only the king had enjoyed.

Having seen to the formalities, the royal lords set about their business. They asked the mayor and aldermen to loan Henry 10,000 marks.[22] They told him that the king hoped that certain merchants and important citizens would offer him loans from their personal fortunes. Being surrounded by so many great men, Falconer was not in a position to refuse.

Sunday 17th

Today was Passion Sunday, when the clergy swapped their white robes for red ones, in expectation of the last two weeks of Lent.[23]

At Constance, Robert Hallum, bishop of Salisbury, preached in the cathedral. It was not an occasion for celebration. A clear decision about John XXIII's abdication had been reached, and yet the pope was refusing to appoint proctors or to rule out leaving the city. He failed to understand that these were not matters for discussion; they were demands. How much more time would it take him to accept them? The Germans were as frustrated as the English. Both nations resolved not to leave Constance until they had forced John to appoint proctors and thereby secured his resignation. They communicated this resolution to the French. The French, wishing not to be pushed into anything by either the Germans or the English, decided to debate the issue on the 19th. The Italians decided they would wait and see what the French decided.[24]

Tuesday 19th

Yesterday the formal commission had been drawn up for Henry's agents to obtain ships in Flanders.[25] Today the earl of Arundel was ordered in his capacity as warden of the Cinque Ports to summon and array seamen for the king's fleet. They were to be ready to sail with fifty-seven ships from the Cinque Ports for forty days. The usual fees would be payable: 6d per day for each master and 3d for every other mariner.[26]

John Gibbe, roper of Bristol, was commissioned to take on more workmen and make cords, cables and canvas until 1 July.[27] An order was despatched to the deputies of the admiral of England, Thomas Beaufort: all ships in English waters were ordered to be arrested 'for urgent causes now moving the king'. No vessel with a carrying capacity of twenty tuns was permitted to leave port for any reason. A similar order went to the earl of Arundel in respect of the Cinque Ports. All these requisitioned ships were to be taken to Southampton by 8 May.[28]

Henry's ambassadors were still on their way back from Paris and he had yet to hear the outcome of the negotiations. Nonetheless he had already set the date for the invasion fleet to assemble.

*

The French prelates were gathering in the Dominican monastery of Constance. With them were five cardinals born in France, including Guillaume Fillastre, the cardinal priest of St Mark, who was keeping a private record of events. Suddenly, without any warning, the representatives from England entered. So did the Germans. Then the emperor arrived, surrounded by all the secular princes of Germany. The French were somewhat alarmed at this intrusion, but did not know what to say. Naturally the emperor demanded the place of honour, and was given it.

When everyone was assembled Sigismund declared that the Germans and English had come to a view on the necessity of the pope appointing proctors. Now they wished to see what the French had to say on the matter.

The French refused to continue their discussions, saying they wished to deliberate by themselves.

Sigismund was furious. He could not believe he had come so far, and had persuaded two popes to agree in principle to resign, only for the French prelates to stop all progress on the grounds of national pride. He compromised, agreeing that the English and German representatives did not have to attend, but insisting that he should have the right himself to remain for the debate. As he pointed out, there were prelates from Provence and Savoy present, and these parts of the French nation were part of the Holy Roman Empire. Despite this, the French prelates insisted that he leave too. Sigismund lost his self-control completely. As he got up, he bellowed to all the prelates there, 'Now we shall see who is for the union of the Church and loyal to the Holy Roman Empire!'[29]

The French were left stunned. In the discussions that followed, they quickly agreed that John XXIII should indeed be forced to appoint proctors, as the English and Germans had demanded. They sent a message immediately to inform the emperor.

Wednesday 20th

It was the second anniversary of his father's death. From tomorrow all official documents would be dated the third year of Henry's reign. Perhaps his mind went back to his conversation that night, two years earlier, with the hermit in Westminster Abbey, William Alnwick. About this time he decided to ask Alnwick to be the first confessor general in his new monastery at Syon. Alnwick accepted. But within a year Alnwick had had enough of listening to women's confessions. He preferred the life of a hermit.[30]

*

Sigismund was growing suspicious. Several times now he had seen Frederick, duke of Austria, holding quiet conversations with John XXIII. At an appropriate moment he took the duke aside and said what was on his mind. He asked the duke outright if he was going to help the pope escape from Constance. Duke Frederick assured Sigismund that he had no intention of aiding the pope in such a manner – in fact, he had never even considered it. Sigismund had no option but to let the matter rest.

That night, in the early hours of the morning, John XXIII dressed himself in a grey cape and covered his head with a grey cowl, disguising his identity. Mounting a small grey horse, he rode out of Constance with a crossbowman, an esquire and a priest. It was three days before full moon. At Ermatingen he rested at a clergyman's house, and had something to drink. Then he went down to catch the boat that was to take him to the city of Schaffhausen.

Despite his assurances to Sigismund, Duke Frederick provided the boat. He also provided the soldiers aboard – who were to guard the pope from here until he reached the sanctuary of the duke's city.[31]

Friday 22nd

In 1400, when Henry IV had been intent on leading a very large army into Scotland, he had ordered all those who had received a grant of land from him or from his royal predecessors to join him in his campaign or lose the lands in question.[32] It had proved an effective way of marshalling extra forces and at the same testing the loyalty of his subjects. Today Henry V, acting on the advice of his council, followed his father's example. He ordered the sheriffs of London to proclaim to all knights, esquires and yeomen holding their estates by grant from Edward III, the Black Prince, Richard II, John of Gaunt, Henry IV or Henry V, 'and any one else of his livery', to hasten towards London 'for urgent causes now nearly moving the king'. They were to assemble there on 24 April at the latest.[33] From there they would march to Southampton, ready to embark on 8 May. Further similar orders to sheriffs of other counties would follow in due course.

Saturday 23rd

At Constance, there was turmoil. If the pope had fled, how could this continue to be called a council? Was it not futile to continue? If they had failed to persuade John XXIII to resign, what hope did they have of persuading the other two popes to do so, now that they knew his promises were worthless?

Into this crisis stepped Dr Jean Gerson. He preached a powerful sermon in which he declared that the Church as a body was bound to Christ, its head, through the Holy Spirit. All Christians, including the popes, were therefore bound to accept the authority of Christ, and this took precedence over all canon law.

It was the right sermon at the right time. It steadied the nerves of those present. But from our point of view it is particularly interesting, for it encompassed the key debate of the Christian world in the year 1415. In questioning whether the Church owed obedience to the pope or directly to Christ, Gerson was asking the same question as Jan Hus. And he was coming to the same answer: the Church's relationship with Christ took precedence over all mortal authorities. Such a line of thinking was very dangerous for it amounted to a licence to rebel against the ecclesiastical authorities in the name of Christ. It was thus a mandate for spiritual independence and even political insurrection. What right did men like Henry V have to claim they were king by God's will if their rebellious subjects could claim to be acting in Christ's name? In Jean Gerson's burning of Jean Petit's *Justification of the duke of Burgundy*, treason had been equated with heresy. In the trials of John Oldcastle's rebellion, heresy had been equated with treason. Who had the right to declare what was heretical? And if the nature of heresy was in doubt, and if all lesser figures than Christ could be disobeyed, even popes, might not Christ condone treason?

All across Europe, the authority of religious and secular leaders was under attack. It was far from clear whether it would withstand the pressure – or collapse into spiritual anarchy and civil wars.

*

Henry was doing his part to maintain both his divine right and his political power. Today he granted an annuity of £40 to Gerard Sprong, one of the men in charge of his guns at the Tower, for good service to both himself and his father.[34] As he understood well, questions of spiritual authority and political power could not be resolved simply as matters of theory, at least not permanently. But one could demonstrate God's will, and resolve the question of treason at the same time, through war.

Sunday 24th: Palm Sunday

Excitement about the end of Lent had been growing for a week now, since the beginning of Passiontide. Today, Palm Sunday, the feeling grew more intense. Holy Week had finally begun. In churches up and down the country, men and women listened to the story of Jesus's entry into Jerusalem, as it appears in St John's gospel. In the chapel royal Henry would have watched his clergy bless branches of willow or sallow – palm leaves being unavailable in England. He would have watched as the consecrated bread and wine was placed in a shrine and carried in procession out of the chapel. He and the lords with him would have joined a second procession, holding the branches behind a priest bearing a cross. Each procession would have halted to hear the St Matthew version of the entry of Christ into Jerusalem. After this, the processions merged at the south door of the chapel and listened to a choir of seven boys singing *Gloria Laus et Honor*. Entering the church again through the west door, the veil over the crucifix was drawn aside while Mass was sung.[35]

Not surprisingly, very little official business was enrolled during Holy Week. One of the few items we can associate with the king is his grant today of 40 marks yearly for life to an esquire, John Steward, who had served him since before his accession.[36]

*

In his prison cell, Jan Hus set pen to paper and composed the following letter that he sent to Lord John of Chlum:

All my guards are leaving already, and I shall have nothing to eat. I do not know what will become of me in prison. Go with the other lords to the emperor, I pray, so he might make some final disposition of me, and so he may not commit sin and shame on my account . . .

Noble Lord John go quickly with Lord Wenceslas [of Dubá] and the others to the emperor, for there is danger in delay. It is necessary that you do so at the earliest possible moment . . .

I fear that the master of the papal court will carry me away with him in the night, for he will remain today in the monastery. The bishop of Constance sent me the message that he wishes to have no dealings with me. The cardinals have done the same.

If you love the poor *Anser* [Lord John's nickname for Hus] arrange that the emperor give me his own guards or free me from prison this evening.

Given in prison (O Lord, do not tarry!) on Sunday, towards the evening.

Monday 25th: Lady Day

Today was the feast of the Annunciation, or Lady Day: the commemoration of the announcement to the Virgin that she would give birth to Christ. It was also the day on which the year of grace changed. Although 1 January was the day for 'New Year' gifts, and 21 March was the day on which the 'official' year changed (*anno regis*, the year of the king's reign), the year 1415 *anno Domini* began on 25 March.

Tuesday 26th

At Constance the council held a full session without a pope – an unprecedented event. Leadership naturally fell to the emperor, who wore his crown and his imperial state robes for the occasion. A number of the cardinals had left Constance to chase after John XXIII – some to persuade him to return (including Fillastre), some simply to follow him out of loyalty – but those who remained had been reassured by Jean Gerson. They attended the popeless session, giving weight to its declarations.

Cardinal Zabarella took the role of spokesman. He declared that the council had been rightfully convened at Constance, and the departure of John XXIII in no way nullified it. The council would not dissolve nor leave Constance, even to transfer to another place, until the schism had been brought to an end and the Church reunited. This last clause was emphasised because a notice from the pope had appeared on the door of the cathedral requiring all members of the papal curia to follow him to Schaffhausen.[37]

That evening after vespers Cardinal Fillastre and two other cardinals returned to Constance. They bore a promise from John XXIII that he would appoint proctors. He proposed to select eight of the four nations' thirty-two deputies, and if three of them agreed that he should abdicate, then it would be so. This seemed to be an attempt to circumvent his earlier public agreement to abdicate.

The emperor was outraged. He declared that he was henceforth at war with the duke of Austria, who had by now also left Constance. The other prelates there urged him to remain calm, for such a war would undoubtedly break up the council, and many would see John XXIII as being justified in fleeing from the city. Sigismund's anger was not to be soothed easily, however, and he sent word to the duke that a state of war now existed between them.

Quite what the English lords at the council thought of all this is not known. But about this time they packed up and set out on the return trip.[38] Their role as ambassadors to the emperor had been performed; and the emperor himself was more concerned with his own affairs than those of a distant English king.

Wednesday 27th

As Henry knelt at Mass today he listened to the account of the rending of the veil in the Temple of Jerusalem. As the words rang out, so a priest dramatically tore the silk veil away from the crucifix above the rood screen, revealing the sculpture of the crucified Christ.[39]

After Mass, Henry made the first of several grants to the priory of the Virgin and St Thomas the Martyr at Newark, Surrey.[40] He also temporarily appointed his servant Roger Assent to the office of forester of Cank Forest in Staffordshire.[41]

That evening the first of the Tenebrae – the services of shadows – took place in the chapel royal. Twenty-four candles were placed on a large triangular candleframe to the south of the altar, representing the apostles and prophets. As the service progressed that evening, one candle was extinguished as each response was sung until only one was left alight in the vast darkness of the church. The king and other attendants then departed in silence, leaving the one candle burning.[42]

Thursday 28th: Maundy Thursday

Maundy Thursday, the commemoration of the Feast of the Last Supper, had always been important for the English royal family. As long ago as the reign of King John, the king had made presents of money and clothes to thirteen paupers on this day (relating to the number of people present at the Last Supper). Edward II had personally undertaken the *pedelavium* – the ritual of washing the feet of the paupers who were to receive the gifts – as a demonstration of his humility. Edward III and Richard II had regularly made quite large donations to the poor on this day. But it was Henry IV who had transformed the occasion, for he had a special connection with Maundy Thursday, probably being born on that day. From the age of fifteen he had given a shilling or clothes and shoes to as many poor men as there were

years in his age on Maundy Thursday. By the end of the decade, his
wife had started to follow his example, and made donations according
to the number of years in *her* age. Henry himself continued these traditions, including the *pedelavium* and the age-related donations.[43]

The practice of the monarch making monetary gifts to poor men
and women continues to this day. However, it is not clear that Henry
related his Maundy Thursday gift to his age in 1415. Two years earlier
he had donated fourpence to each of 3,000 paupers – a total distribution of £50.[44] But we can be sure that Henry would have marked the
day in a fitting manner, mindful of his father's example. And at the end
of the day he would have again attended a service to hear the Tenebrae
sung again in the chapel royal.

Friday 29th: Good Friday

In the early part of the previous century on Good Friday the English
kings had laid hands on people suffering from scrofula, a form of tuber-
culosis called the King's Evil. Imagine a line of several hundred sick men
and women, whose necks had swollen like those of pigs, queuing up to
see the king. The semi-divine position of kings meant they were supposed
to be able to cure this ailment simply by touching. In reality the kings
tended not to touch the sufferers themselves but rather to bless a penny
that was given to each of them. The practice had fallen temporarily into
abeyance in the 1340s, but in its place Edward III had introduced the
blessing of cramp rings – medicinal rings that were worn to cure the
wearer from epilepsy.[45] This was the way in which Henry V displayed
his thaumaturgical powers. Although the 1415 account for Good Friday
does not survive, the 1413 one reads 'In money paid to the dean of the
chapel for the money paid for the making of medicinal rings 25s'.[46] Henry
would also have demonstrated his piety by joining the clergy in 'creeping
to the Cross'. Two priests held up a veiled crucifix behind the high altar
during the singing of the responses; they then uncovered it and laid it
on the third step before the altar. The king and priests then crawled
towards it, shoeless – although it is likely that the king was given a
comfortable carpet, so the crawling did not hurt his knees.[47]

*

At Schaffhausen the weather was cold and stormy. The trees were swept up in the wind; and the rain lashed down, mingled with sleet and snow. Pope John XXIII, who had been anxious to leave, now set out for Laufenburg, despite the weather. He had heard that the emperor had declared war on the duke of Austria. Such was his consternation that he attended no public religious services on either Maundy Thursday or Good Friday. When he set out in the snow and rain, not a single cardinal followed him. They simply watched him go – heading off into the storm with the duke of Austria and his guards.

As Cardinal Fillastre noted, the pope was now all but a prisoner of the duke. He had escaped one danger for another – potentially far worse.

*

Henry sat with his council today, listening to a series of eight petitions. An extant set of minutes records his responses to each one. In one instance, the keeper of the privy seal was ordered to draw up letters to Robert Louvel esquire, acting on information presented in the petition of John Wyse of Pembrokeshire. In another, the case of a Lancastrian servant from Bolingbroke was referred to the chancellor of the duchy of Lancaster. Two women who sent their separate grievances to Henry were both curtly told to pursue their cases in the law courts; Henry did not want to intervene.[48]

Bishop Courtenay, Bishop Langley, Thomas Beaufort and the rest of the English delegation arrived back in London. In all probability, they went straight to the king and duly reported all that had happened during their time in Paris, including the public show of unity in the French royal family and the oaths sworn over pieces of the True Cross. No doubt Henry was very pleased to hear they had succeeded in their mission to force the French to dig in their heels. Similarly he would not have been greatly troubled by the show of unity between the Burgundians and Armagnacs. Although this has led historians for years to believe that his diplomacy had failed, Henry had in place his own secret agreements with John the Fearless, of which the French royal family was not yet aware.

In addition, something may have been said concerning an insult to Henry delivered in Paris. Since this has become the stuff of legend, it needs to be mentioned. In Shakespeare's *Henry V*, Henry ask the

First Ambassador of France, 'Tell us the Dauphin's mind'. To which the First Ambassador replies:

> ... the prince our master
> Says that you savour too much of your youth;
> And bids you be advis'd there's naught in France
> That can be with a nimble galliard won; –
> You cannot revel into dukedoms there.
> He therefore sends you, meeter for your spirit,
> This tun of treasure; and, in lieu of this,
> Desires you let the dukedoms that you claim
> Hear no more of you. This the dauphin speaks.

Henry replies: 'What treasure, uncle?'
'Tennis balls, my liege,' says Thomas Beaufort.

Henry responds carefully:

> We are glad the dauphin is so pleasant with us;
> His present and your pains we thank you for:
> When we have match'd our racquets to these balls,
> We will, in France, by God's grace play a set
> Shall strike his father's crown into the hazard.

Scholars down the years have enjoyed dismissing this story as highly improbable or even impossible. Of course, it goes without saying that it is exceptionally unlikely that the dauphin made remarks about Henry's youth – as Henry was a grown man of twenty-eight and the dauphin himself only just eighteen. Likewise, it is very unlikely that a tun of tennis balls was actually despatched; the French were desirous of peace. But the 'tennis balls' story is evidenced in near-contemporary chronicles. Thomas Elmham, writing before 1418, mentioned it in his *Liber Metricus*; John Strecche, writing in 1422, also mentioned it, and located the event at Kenilworth. As Strecche had been a canon of St Mary's Kenilworth and was, at the time of his writing, living in a cell in Rutland that was dependent on Kenilworth, it seems likely that a story about Henry did circulate. Strecche reports that the ambassadors whom Henry sent to France in his second year had only a short discussion with the French on this matter [the royal marriage] without reaching any conclusion consistent with the honour or convenience of our king, and so they returned home. For these Frenchmen puffed up with pride and lacking in foresight, hurling mocking words at the ambassadors of the king of England, said foolishly to them that as Henry was but a young man, they would send to him little balls to play with and soft cushions to rest on until he should have grown to a man's strength. When the king heard these words, he was much moved and troubled in spirit; yet he addressed these short, wise and honest words to those standing around him: 'If God wills and if my life shall be prolonged with health, in a few months I shall play with such balls in the Frenchmen's court-yards that they will lose the game eventually, and for their game win but grief. And if they shall sleep too long on their cushions in their chambers, I will awake them, before they wish it, from their slumbers at dawn by beating on their doors.'[49]

This can hardly relate to the first embassy Henry despatched in his second year, as that had been warmly welcomed and received such concessions that Henry was forced to send a second. But the second embassy only had a very short meeting with the French royal family, having been kept waiting for several weeks. Henry is very unlikely to have been at Kenilworth on their return – there is no evidence that he was there – but if the story came to Strecche by way of St Mary's, Kenilworth, and as he was writing seven years later and knew that Henry liked to spend time at Kenilworth as often as he could, it is not impossible that he simply misplaced the event when he came to write it down. And significantly Strecche does not state that tennis balls were actually sent, merely that they were part of the mocking of Henry by the French nobility.

Thomas Elmham and John Strecche are not the only writers to record that Henry's ambassadors were insulted. Another anonymous fifteenth-century chronicle in English relates the tennis balls story, saying that the dauphin actually sent the tun of tennis balls, as Shakespeare states; the same story appears in the *Brut* (which was probably Shakespeare's source, either directly or indirectly).[50] Adam Usk wrote in his chronicle how the ambassadors were 'treated with derision'.[51] And the ageing Thomas Walsingham wrote in his *Chronica Maiora* that

On their return from France the second time, our envoys there, the bishops of Durham and Norwich declared that so far the French had been using trickery. The king was annoyed at this and decided to put a stop to their jokes and to punish those who mocked him in the courts of war, showing them by his deeds and actions how mad they had been to arouse a sleeping dog.[52]

As most of these writers were contemporary, it seems that a story about Henry being mocked by the French did circulate at the time. But did the actual mocking take place? No French writer records any insult; and we can be confident that no tun of tennis balls was delivered. Whoever informed Walsingham of the event would have mentioned the delivery if something so extraordinary had taken place. However, something of a mischievous nature probably happened. It may be that no overt insult was intended but some conversation took place that was interpreted as mockery. Perhaps during the royal joust in Paris the conversation turned to Henry's reluctance to joust, and this led to a mocking question from the French about whether Henry preferred to play tennis. We do not know. But it seems that a throwaway remark of a tricking or mocking nature was amplified into an insult of suitably grand diplomatic proportions, and this exaggerated response found its way to John Strecche in Rutland, to Thomas Walsingham at St Albans, and to Thomas Elmham at Lenton (Nottinghamshire), as well as to the author of the *Brut*. Who was responsible? We might blame the ambassadors for the exaggeration – but that would mean they were inciting Henry towards a war that he was clearly determined to start anyway. It seems far more likely that the king himself picked up on something that his ambassadors reported about their brief audience in Paris – something that may have been of minor interest, of no consequence – but which nevertheless deeply injured his pride.

Saturday 30th

Holy Saturday saw a plenary session of the council of Constance in the cathedral. It turned out to be one of the most important days in the history of the Catholic Church.[53] Those present were now prepared to act on the idea that the council as a whole had greater authority than the pope. They had no choice. A number of papal officials had left Constance to follow John XXIII. Those prelates who remained could either enforce their own superiority over the pope, as both Cardinal Fillastre and Dr Gerson had proposed, or pack up and go home.

Cardinal Zabarella was deputed to read the following momentous declaration, the first version of the decree known as *Sacrosancta*. The key passages read as follows:

> First this synod, lawfully assembled in the Holy Spirit, constituting a general council and representing the Catholic Church Militant, has its power directly from Christ, and all persons of whatever rank or dignity, even a pope, are bound to obey it in matters that relate to faith and the ending of the present schism.
>
> Further our holy lord Pope John XXIII shall not remove or transfer the Roman Curia and the public offices or his or their officials from this city of Constance to another place, nor shall he compel directly or indirectly the persons holding the said offices to follow him without the decision and consent of the holy synod . . .[54]

There was a problem, however. Cardinal Zabarella was the most junior cardinal. He could not bring himself to read these words. His nerve gave way. After he had read the less contentious parts of the decree, and the prelates realised he was not going to read the above lines, a huge argument broke out. In the end it was decided to reconvene to discuss the matter at greater length in a week's time.

There are bureaucratic nightmares in all political arenas and ages – but few compare with those of the medieval church.

Sunday 31st: Easter Sunday

After forty-six days of Lenten fasting, the joy of Easter Day can barely be imagined. Late the previous night the Tenebrae – which had been sung each night since Wednesday – were sung for the final time. The candles in the chapel were extinguished one by one and then the final candle was put out. In the darkness the priest struck a new flame with a flint and dry moss, and used it to light the great paschal candle – the immense candle that marked the coming of Easter. Early in the morning on Easter Day the spiritual celebrations started, with the opening of the sepulchre: a miniature tomb in which the figure of Christ was laid. Anthems were sung, and the crucifix and host were carried around the chapel in procession. All the figures of saints in the chapel, which had been veiled throughout Lent, were now unveiled to look on the glory of the risen Christ.[55]

The feast that ensued was a true celebration. Eggs, which had been forbidden throughout Lent, were brought to the chapel and blessed – a custom that may be the origin of our modern Easter egg ceremony. Everyone who could afford it was now able to indulge in meat-eating again. The scale of the royal feast Henry would have presided over late that morning may be gauged from the fact that in 1403 his father spent £160 2s 10d on his household expenses on Easter Day, compared to about £50 on a normal day.[56]

In Cheshire – the home of the finest English longbowmen – the day was marked with archery competitions.[57] It being both a Sunday and a feast day, men would have practised their archery up and down the country. This was in line with Edward III's order of 1363, which had been reinforced by legislation passed by Richard II in 1388 and Henry IV in 1410. Longbows had been crucial in Edward III winning the battles of Halidon Hill (1333), Sluys (1340) and Crécy (1346), and practice was essential if England was to continue the tradition of dominance in archery. Years of experience were required for archers to draw the powerful 6ft longbows back to their ear – a draw weight of 120–170lbs – and control the arrow sufficiently well to hit a man-sized target 220 yards away. But how many Cheshire men shooting at the butts today anticipated that the long-maintained Sunday tradition was shortly to be put to the ultimate test?

April

Monday 1st

The celebrations of Easter, like those of Christmas, remind us that although medieval life was 'nasty, brutish and short' it was many other things as well. The joys of feasting, drinking, dancing, music and story-telling were every bit as significant for medieval people as the constant presence of death. The annual rhythms of light and dark, food and music, love and faith, make that 'nasty, brutish and short' generalisation a somewhat blinkered, morbid view of medieval existence. Easter, just like Christmas, was a period of exuberance and fun as well as religious drama. Following Easter Day there was Hocktide: a two-day period of merrymaking. Its chief characteristic was the practice of 'hocking' or capturing members of the opposite sex and holding them to ransom for a fee. On Mondays women set out in groups on the streets of towns and in the lanes of villages to capture men. On Tuesdays the custom was reversed: men captured women. In some places it was only married women who were allowed to take a role in tying up the trapped men; in others it was just maidens. Perhaps it was because the men had more money than the women – or perhaps the frisson of being tied up by women appealed to something in the medieval male imagination – but much more money was raised for the church coffers by the women.[1]

Henry was not the sort of man to engage in such frivolities. Not only was the court almost totally devoid of women, his serious nature and religious conviction did not incline him to join in such japes. But whether he had any other sort of fun on this day is unrecorded. It seems to have been rather a case of business as usual. Among the grants made today we may notice one of £40 yearly to Nicholas Merbury, the master of the ordnance.[2]

Another gift made this day was the apparently unremarkable sum of 40 marks yearly granted to Sir Ralph Rochford, in return for surrendering Somerton Castle to the king.[3] As later events show, Henry wanted Somerton Castle back so he could give it to his brother, Thomas, duke of Clarence. This in turn causes us to pause. Clarence was notable by his absence on several royal occasions in the first half of this year. At the meeting at the Guildhall on 14 March, when the king's other brothers, together with the duke of York and the archbishop of Canterbury, had all met the Londoners, Clarence was the only duke not present. At several council meetings both his brothers were present but Thomas was not.[4] As we have seen, relations between Henry and Thomas had never been warm, and had verged on hostility; but it looks as though Henry had reassessed their relationship, and realised that he needed to keep his brother and heir apparent close.

Also today Henry finalised the foundation of his new Carthusian priory at Sheen. He paid the prior of the great Charterhouse of Mount Grace £100 for copying books that would be required in the new priory.[5] And he saw the priory's foundation charter sealed, making the priory dependent on Mount Grace.[6] Its endowment was to be drawn from the lands of recently confiscated alien priories, including those of Ware, Lewisham and Hayling, and the substantial grant of £400. Originally the estates of these alien priories had been given to friends and family; so Henry had to compensate those from whom he now clawed them back. These compensatory grants were also made today. Queen Joan, Henry's stepmother, received 1,000 marks annually for her loss of income from the priory of Ware and other religious houses.[7] Sir John Rothenhale was granted £100 annually in compensation for the alien priory of Hayling and its estates.[8]

The foundation charter gives further details about Sheen. On a site of about ninety-three acres, forty monks were to live like hermits in separate cells, these being arranged around a large quadrangle, two hundred paces (about 350ft) on each side. The scale of the church was similarly ambitious: at over 100ft in length, the nave was twice as long as that of any other Charterhouse yet built in England.[9] The monks were to say prayers every day for the king's health during his lifetime and to sing Masses for his soul after his death. They were also to sing Masses for the souls of Henry's parents and ancestors, and 'for the peace and quiet of the people and the realm'. As for the name of the priory, Henry liked his works to have grandiose names – as we have seen with respect to 'the Monastery of St Saviour and St Bridget at Syon'. Sheen Priory was to be known formally as 'The House of Jesus of Bethlehem at Sheen'.[10]

It appears that today Henry also resolved the future of the third of his new monasteries, the Celestine house on the other side of the river. Surprisingly, although the building was already well underway, he scrapped the project entirely. He granted the land to his trustees, Thomas Beaufort, Sir Henry Fitzhugh, Sir John Rothenhale and Robert Morton, together with the Celestines' endowment from various alien priories.[11]

The land intended for the Celestines amounted to a triangular shape of about thirty-one acres on the north side of the Thames, adjacent to the land granted to Syon Abbey. From this we can see that Henry's original plan had been for a trinity of three monasteries and a manor house – two monasteries on the north side of the river and Sheen Manor and Sheen Priory on the south. Sitting on either side of the river like this they formed part of a larger architectural scheme. Anyone being rowed up the Thames would have passed several series of imposing royal and ecclesiastical buildings on the way. First, the visitor would have seen the Tower of London opposite Southwark Abbey (now Southwark Cathedral). Next, three miles upstream, the Palace of Westminster and the royal mausoleum at Westminster Abbey would have come into view, opposite Lambeth Palace. Twelve miles further on, the visitor would have arrived at this splendid arrangement of three monasteries and Sheen Manor. The effect of such a three-stage royal progress along the river would have been stunning. Foreign ambassadors passing by these buildings would have been impressed, especially if they were travelling on to Windsor Castle further up the Thames.

Henry's contribution to this stately progress was not to be quite so grand. The three Celestine monks whom Richard Courtenay had brought back from France refused to swear homage to a king who was determined to make war on their own kingdom. Nor could they accept the means whereby Henry intended to fund them – from the estates confiscated from French abbeys. So the negotiations fell apart.[12] The three monks stayed in England for a few more months but their land was taken away from them.[13] Henry's notorious pride had been pricked by the peace-loving vegetarian French monks, and he tore up his plans for a Celestine foundation to spite them.

*

A clergyman was making his way furtively through the streets of Constance. Jerome was a short, stout man, with a broad thick black beard.[14] He knew the dangers of being caught. He knew that his fellow radical theologian, Jan Hus, was already in prison. Beneath his cloak Jerome carried a placard. It stated that Jan Hus taught and preached the truth, and that all the charges against him had been made out of enmity. At an opportune moment, he placed the placard in a prominent place and hurried away. He left Constance that same day, seeking refuge in a priest's house in the forest outside the city. Unfortunately he left his sword behind at the house in St Paul's Street where he had stayed the previous night. It was handed over to the authorities.

Jerome continued to preach his interpretation of the relationship between Man and Christ. He told those whom he met at the priest's house that the council of Constance was a school of Satan and a synagogue of all iniquity. He insisted that no one there could refute Jan Hus's prodigious learning, nor his own. In this way he announced himself. So the Church authorities pondered, and sent out people to find the man who had come amongst them, stirring up further trouble.[15]

Thursday 4th

Henry's anticipated debts to the mayor and aldermen of London required him to respect their generosity. He could hardly ask for massive loans from them and almost immediately follow up that request by prohibiting them from employing the carts and boats necessary for their own building projects. He issued a licence for the mayor to maintain four boats and four named boatmen, and four carts and four named carters, to carry stone into the city for the rebuilding of the Guildhall. The men, carts and boats would be free from impressment during the forthcoming campaign.[16]

The official commission to Richard Clitherowe and Reginald Curteis to hire ships from Holland and Zeeland was finally issued today. The diplomatic agreement necessary for their mission had been conducted the previous year, the money had been handed over to them at the end of February, but not until 18 March had the first commission been drawn up. And when it was, it named Richard Clitherowe and Simon Flete (not Reginald Curteis) as Henry's shipping agents.[17] Such bureaucratic errors – and there were doubtless many similar minor slips of which we are unaware – did not make the task of preparing for war any easier.

*

Pope John XXIII today wrote this letter to the prelates at Constance:

> John, bishop, servant of the servants of God, to all the faithful of Christ who shall see this present letter greetings and apostolic benediction. Let it be known to you all that we were driven by the fear that can beset even the constant man to leave the city of Constance and go to the town of Schaffhausen believing that there we could accomplish everything that would promote the peace and union of the Holy Church of God . . . But through the agency of the enemy of the human race such difficulties obstructed us there that on Friday of Holy Week, after celebrating Mass, we were compelled to leave in the height of a violent storm because of these fears, in order that we might find a place and a time both plainly suitable and secure for the general council, where and when it might be safe to come.
>
> Although death is considered the crowning terror of all, we dread neither it nor any of the serious dangers that threaten us so much as the chance that Pedro de Luna and Angelo Corario, previously styled Benedict XIII and Gregory XII by their obediences, may seize this occasion to allege the force put upon us and may retract their intention of resigning the right that they claim to the papal office, and that thus the achievement of peace and union in the Church may suffer delay. Our supreme desire is to press towards that true and salutary achievement, and so far as in us lies, we shall omit nothing nor slacken our efforts to bring about that peace and union. Dated at Laufenburg in the diocese of Basel, 4 April, in the fifth year of our pontificate.[18]

The hypocritical meaning was clear. Far from working towards the unity of the Church, John XXIII was actively trying to prolong its divisions. Although he had promised to resign, he was still insisting that the prior resignation of the other two popes was a prerequisite. He counted the mere possibility that Benedict XIII and Gregory XII might not fulfil their resignation promises as enough of a fear to drive him from Constance. In reality he feared nothing but losing his own authority, status and power.

Saturday 6th

Henry today granted custody of the 'temporalities' (secular income) of the see of St David's to the newly appointed bishop, Stephen Patrington.[19] This means that he had received news from Constance that Patrington had been confirmed as the next bishop by John XXIII. If the messenger bearing this news had set out from Constance within a couple of days of the formal appointment there (on 1 Febraury), then we can be sure that Henry would now have been aware of events there up to and including Candlemas.[20] He would have heard that the English were sitting as a nation in their own right, and that the bishop of Salisbury had preached sermons in Latin before the whole council. He would have heard that Jan Hus had been arrested and was to be charged with heresy, and so would the arch-reformer, the late John Wycliffe. He would have heard about Cardinal Fillastre's memorandum – that the council of Constance had a greater authority than any pope – and that the envoys from Sweden had secured the second canonisation of St Bridget. No doubt that last news gave him cause for satisfaction, in view of his recent foundation of 'The Monastery of St Saviour and St Bridget at Syon'. Less welcome would have been the news that the emperor wanted Henry to continue to negotiate with the French, and was even prepared to come in person to England to mediate between the two kingdoms.

*

At Constance itself Emperor Sigismund was enthroned in his imperial robes, a witness to the fifth plenary session of the council. The archbishop of Rheims had said Mass. Now Cardinal Orsini, who was presiding, invited the bishop of Posen to read the final version of *Sacrosancta*. Cardinal Zabarella simply looked on.

In the name of the Holy and Indivisible Trinity, Father, Son and Holy Spirit, Amen. This holy synod of Constance, constituting a general council ... does hereby ordain, ratify, enact, decree and declare the following:

First it declares that ... it has power directly from Christ, and that all persons of whatever rank or dignity, even a pope, are bound to obey it in matters relating to faith and the end of the schism and the general reformation of the Church of God in head and members.

Further it declares that any person of whatever position, rank or dignity, even a pope, who contumaciously refuses to obey the mandates, statutes, ordinances or regulations enacted or to be enacted by this holy synod ... shall, unless he repents, be subject to condign penalty and duly punished, with recourse if necessary to other aids of the law ...[21]

And with that, the council's obedience to the pope was set aside. A page had turned in the divine script. No one quite knew what the consequences would be.

Sunday 7th

Henry grew impatient as the day of his great council approached. Just as he had been short-tempered with the Celestines, to the detriment of his own religious building programme, so now he showed a similar short temper with the French. The duke of Berry had suggested to the English ambassadors at their last meeting that a French embassy should come to England to discuss the peace. The English had had no choice but to agree with this. But where were the French ambassadors now? 'We still have not heard news of the arrival of this embassy, nor do we know the names of those who will be part of it, even though the terms of the truce between us are about to expire,' wrote Henry to the French king.[22] Although only nine days had passed since hearing of the proposed embassy, Henry demanded that the ambassadors come 'without delay'.[23]

Henry's letter repeatedly protested that he was a seeker of peace. 'May there be peace during our reign' he said in his preamble. He went on:

We bring glory upon ourselves through knowing that, ever since the day we took possession of our throne . . . we have been quickened by a living love of peace, out of respect for Him that is the author of all peace, and we have worked hard with all our forces to establish a union between us and our people, and to put an end to these deplorable divisions that have occasioned such disasters and caused the shipwreck of so many souls in the sea of war. This is why we have repeatedly and most recently again sent our ambassadors to your serenity for, and touching, this important concern of peace.[24]

The repetition throughout the letter of the word *peace* amounted to a rhetoric that actually said nothing but assailed the reader with the implications of the very opposite. Henry's very insistence on peace was bellicose.

On the same day as he sent the letter to the French king, Henry sent a writ to all the sheriffs of all the counties in England in which he repeated his instructions to the sheriffs of London of 22 March. All those knights, esquires and yeomen who held their estates by grant from Henry or his predecessors were to hasten towards London 'for urgent causes now moving the king'. They were to assemble there on 24 April – a date chosen to allow them to march to Southampton in time for the planned muster on 8 May.

With only one month to go, Henry's impatience was understandable.

Monday 8th

Any English king planning to lead an expedition overseas had to recognise that the security of the borders was essential. Edward III had taken many precautions to protect the northern counties against the Scots when preparing to cross the seas. As Henry was clearly studying his great-grandfather's preparations in 1346, and almost regarding them as a set of guidelines, so now he followed Edward's example. He sent writs to the sheriffs of Cumberland, the North Riding of Yorkshire, and Westmorland and Northumberland, and to the bishop of Durham. These writs ordered them to proclaim in the king's name that no knight, esquire or yeoman should leave his county, under pain of forfeiting his lands, but should remain in the north ready to resist the king's enemies, the Scots, 'as the king has information that his said enemies are minded shortly to invade the realm with no small power'.[25]

Tuesday 9th

It was the anniversary of Henry's coronation in Westminster Abbey. He can hardly have failed to remember that day. He had been dressed in cloth-of-gold and red samite, and crowned. No expenses had been spared – as that day's household expenditure of £971 testifies.[26] Just as importantly for Henry, it was the occasion on which he had been anointed with holy oil, as God's chosen ruler, and had become a semi-divine person.

Writing a letter to the duke of Brittany he informed the duke that he was in good health and expressed wishes that the duke was well too. And he thanked him for the gift of a gold cup. This may have been brought back by Henry's negotiator, John Chamberlain; but given that two months had passed since Chamberlain had been paid for his services, it is more likely that the cup had been presented more recently, perhaps by agents of the duke of Brittany in England.[27] Having secured the duke's agreement that he would not hinder him in his argument with the king of France, such diplomatic niceties mattered.

Wednesday 10th

In the early fifteenth century there were two forms of medical practitioner. There were physicians, who diagnosed medical conditions and prescribed medicines and treatments to cure the inner workings of the body; and there were surgeons, who dealt with matters relating to the skin and cutting into the body. The skill of the latter was somewhat more practical than the former because surgeons quickly gained considerable experience of ailments that had an obvious cause: a broken limb, for example, or an arrow sticking in the body. Physicians' skills were by contrast largely recitations of rehearsed diagnostic rituals from ancient medical treatises and astrological calculations. Despite this, there were a number of unscrupulous surgeons in the city of London. Today a report reached Thomas Falconer, the mayor of London, and the aldermen that some barbers of the city, who are inexperienced in the art of surgery, do often take under their care many sick and maimed persons, fraudulently obtaining possession of very many of their goods thereby; by reason whereof they are often worse off at their departure than they were at their coming. Because of the inexperience of the same barbers such people are often maimed, to the scandal of such skilful and discreet men as practise the art of surgery, and the manifest destruction of the people of our lord the king.[28]

In order to remedy this situation Thomas Falconer ordered that, as members of the Guild of Barbers supervised their own members, a list of all of them who were skilled in surgery should be drawn up, and two of their number should be elected to enquire into cases of malpractice. It is a timely reminder that there was no regulation of the medical trades in fifteenth-century England. There was no college of physicians, nor of surgeons. Six years after this there was a determined attempt to found a college of physicians, and although it met with Henry's approval, it was doomed to failure due to the inability to train sufficient graduate practitioners to administer physic throughout the realm.[29]

While Thomas Falconer listened to the problems of barbers practising surgery, a privy council meeting took place at which the dukes of Bedford and Gloucester, the archbishop of Canterbury, Chancellor Beaufort and the guardian of the privy seal were present. Their purpose was to discuss the case of a Flemish widow, Katherine Kaylewates, who had had various goods seized by men of Sandwich. This was contrary to the terms of Henry's Statute of Truces, as there was a truce in force between Henry and John the Fearless, duke of Burgundy; and, in line with the statute, local officials had impounded the goods and arrested the malefactors. However, the culprits had been released by the keeper of the gaol at Sandwich without the king's permission. Katherine now petitioned the council to take action, as she claimed she had lost goods to the value of £80. The councillors agreed, and issued instructions for the constable of Dover to recover the goods or, if they could not be recovered, to levy a fine of £80 on the men of Sandwich. They also ordered that the keeper of the gaol be arrested.

Exactly what Katherine's standing was, beyond her status as a

Flemish widow, is not clear but, as a subject of the duke of Burgundy, her case was clearly an infringement of the Statute of Truces. With so much depending on the continued goodwill of John the Fearless, and every diplomatic issue being a potential threat to Henry's plans, the council stamped hard on the people of Sandwich.

In the meantime, further preparations were made for the defence of Calais. Adam Chancellor was commissioned to take ships and mariners, carts and labourers, as well as timber, stones, lime and other building materials for the defence of the town.[30]

Thursday 11th

Nicholas Maudit, a royal esquire and sergeant-at-arms who had served in the royal household for a number of years, received two grants today: one of 20 marks a year and another of £10 – on top of his wages of a shilling a day.[31] Thus encouraged, he was ordered to set out with Robert Spellowe to arrest all the ships with a capacity of twenty tuns and upwards from ports between Bristol and Newcastle, and to bring them to Winchelsea, London or Sandwich by 8 May.[32] In this way Henry hoped to gather all those vessels that had evaded the command of 19 March issued to Thomas Beaufort, admiral of England. Maudit and Spellowe were to act independently; nevertheless the area they were expected to cover was vast. Maudit set out with 100 marks immediately. John Wenslowe, clerk, was given another £300 to pay the owners of ships that Maudit seized and William Tresham, clerk, was given £300 to pay for all the ships requisitioned by Spellowe.[33]

Ships with a carrying capacity of just twenty tuns were relatively small – capable of carrying twenty large barrels on deck. In requisitioning every one of these vessels in the south coast ports, in the port of Bristol, and in all the ports on the east coast as far north as Newcastle, Henry was taking over almost the whole merchant fleet of the kingdom. Given that Thomas Beaufort had not managed to fulfil his obligation to bring all these ships to Southampton, it was very unlikely that Maudit and Spellowe could achieve the task within four weeks.

Friday 12th

It was almost time for the great council, at which Henry would announce his expedition to the lords of the realm. Even now they were assembling in the city of London. The bishops' and earls' houses along the Strand and in the city were filled with the returning lords, ladies, knights, esquires, priests and servants. Amid this bustle, Henry took a barge along to the Tower and called the privy council to meet him there to discuss the last political arrangements before Monday's meeting. Those present were the archbishop of Canterbury, Henry's brothers John and Humphrey, his uncles Henry and Thomas Beaufort, the bishop of Durham and the keeper of the privy seal.

According to the agenda, the first matter dealt with was Henry's correspondence. Two letters needed to be written and sent: one to the duke of Berry and the other to Master Jean Andreu, the king of France's secretary. Safe conducts had to be drawn up and sent to the ambassadors of the king of France. Philip Morgan, the lawyer, had to be given instructions and empowered to prolong the truce. Instructions were also needed for the English delegates remaining at Constance, as Henry required them henceforth to act as his ambassadors to the emperor. It was agreed that it was necessary to speak to the earl of Salisbury 'about Gascony' (although exactly what was to be said is not known), and to give him instructions prior to the meeting of the great council on the following Monday. The last item on the morning's agenda was to speak to the mayor of London about the price of armour. Henry wanted military hardware sold at the lowest rate possible in advance of his coming campaign, and he wanted the mayor to make a proclamation to this effect. Henry told his council what he expected and then despatched them to continue the meeting and draw up the exact documents in accordance with his instructions in the afternoon, at the usual council meeting place of the Dominican friary.[34]

Henry had to face the fact that a sailing date in May was unrealistic. Although as recently as yesterday he had ordered his sergeants-at-arms to bring all the substantial ships in the realm to the three ports by 8 May, in line with his earlier instructions, there was no way he would be ready to sail within a month of that date. No doubt he was loath to alter his plans. He had ordered all those who held their land by a royal grant to assemble in London on 24 April; if he put back the date of sailing their presence near the capital would no doubt cause problems, especially if he did not pay them. However, the sheer logistics of the invasion demanded that he do something. Philip Morgan was empowered to prorogue the truce until 8 June. The new embarkation date was the feast of St John the Baptist, 24 June.

Saturday 13th

With Henry growing impatient, and Chancellor Beaufort breathing down his bureaucrats' necks, it is hardly surprising that the safe conducts for the French ambassadors were drawn up immediately.[35] It was a huge embassy – comparable in size to the English one that had been left waiting in Paris in March. It was led by Guillaume Boisratier, archbishop of Bourges, who was permitted to bring sixty persons in his household. It also included the bishop of Lisieux travelling with fifty persons; the count of Vendôme travelling with a hundred; Guillaume, count of Tancarville, with a hundred; Charles, seigneur d'Ivry, royal chamberlain, with fifty; Guy de Negella, lord of Offemont, with fifty; Braquetus, lord of Bracquemont, with fifty; John de Roucy with fifty; Master Jean Andreu, the king's secretary, with ten; Master Gontier Col, another of the king's secretaries, with ten; Jean de Villebresme with six; and finally Stephen de Malrespect with six. That was a total of 554 people. Henry was dismayed. Large numbers of people always took time to assemble, transport and supply. He clearly hoped that they would come quickly, fail quickly, and go home quickly. To speed their mission, he ordered that the safe conducts should expire on 8 June.[36]

Monday 15th

The day of the great council, which Henry had been planning since at least 4 February, had finally arrived. The spiritual and temporal peers arrived at the Palace of Westminster and gathered in the council chamber: a hall overlooking the Thames called the Star Chamber, on account of it being decorated with stars.[37] Forty-three men were there, besides the king and his officers.[38] All four dukes were present: the king's three brothers and his cousin Edward, duke of York. Both archbishops were present. Eight of the nineteen other bishops were there, namely the bishops of London, Winchester, Lincoln, Ely, Norwich, Worcester, Llandaff, and Durham. Five mitred abbots and the English head of the Order of the Knights Hospitaller were present. Nine of the thirteen earls were there, namely the earls of March, Norfolk, Arundel, Dorset, Salisbury, Oxford, Suffolk, Huntingdon and Westmorland. Fourteen other lords responded to Henry's summons. It was an impressive array.

Of those who were not there – who had presumably not been summoned – the majority were absent for a good reason. Of the eleven absent bishops, three were at Constance (the bishops of Salisbury, Lichfield, and Wells). A fourth, Stephen Patrington, had only just had his election as bishop of St David's confirmed by the pope and had yet to be enthroned. The bishops of Bangor and St Asaph were probably busy maintaining watch over their dioceses, which had been disturbed in recent years by Glendower's revolt. The bishop of Chichester was near death. The bishops of Exeter, Hereford, Rochester and Carlisle were old and frail. Among the secular lords, the earl of Warwick was at Constance, and the earl of Northumberland was in prison in Scotland. The earl of Devon was nearly sixty years of age and blind. The only earl whose absence cannot easily be explained was Richard of Conisborough, earl of Cambridge.

Richard of Conisborough has not so far been mentioned in this book. But that does not mean he was an unimportant figure. He was Henry's first cousin twice-removed: the younger brother of both Edward, duke of York, and Constance of York, Lady Despenser. He was thus in a delicate position. While his brother Edward was one of Henry's closest companions, Richard's sister was the widow of a man who had tried to kill Henry. She herself had plotted to release Edmund Mortimer and his brother from Windsor Castle in 1405. But that does not go even halfway to illustrating how compromised the twenty-nine-year-old Richard was. As the second son of the previous duke of York, he had probably been named by Richard II as third in line for the throne in April 1399.[39] He was Richard II's godson, and possibly his nephew too, being probably the natural son of Richard II's half brother,

John Holland, duke of Exeter, who had had an adulterous affair with Isabella, duchess of York.[40] That meant that his natural father was a man who had been butchered in the course of rebelling against the Lancastrians, during the Epiphany Rising. On top of all this, his first wife had been Anne Mortimer, the sister of the earl of March – the man widely regarded as having a better claim to the throne than Henry. In the event of the earl of March dying without a child, Richard's three-year-old son stood to inherit all the titles and claims of the house of Mortimer – and that included the family's claims to the thrones of England and France. Richard of Conisborough cannot have been unaware that all the enmity of Richard II, John Holland and the dis-inherited and wrongfully imprisoned Mortimers was concentrated in his son. Only his elder brother's closeness to the king could be considered a factor influencing him to remain loyal.

To what extent did Henry understand that Richard of Conisborough felt he had been cheated by the Lancastrians? Perhaps a little. He did make some effort to win Richard's approval. He created him earl of Cambridge in 1414, made him 'almoner of England', and confirmed an annuity on him of 350 marks.[41] But that was all – and even this was less than it seems, for the title earl of Cambridge had originally been held by Richard's father (the duke of York), and the 350 marks had originally been granted him by Richard II in response to a dying request by his mother to give him an income of 500 marks.[42] It was hardly enough, given that Richard had been discussed in terms of being third in line to the throne in 1399. Nor could he look forward to inheriting another title or further lands. Unlike his elder brother, who had inherited the dukedom of York, Richard had seen his star eclipsed. This was especially vexing as he now had two children of his own: Richard and Isabella. His meagre allowance was insufficient for himself let alone two children of the royal blood.

Given this situation, the fact that Richard was the sole absent earl is significant. We have already seen how long Henry had been preparing for this great council, and how important it was. So his absence is evidence of some collapse of trust on one side or the other. Richard must have been disappointed that Henry's annuity (granted the previous year) had not been paid in full. Whereas an earl was expected normally to have an income of £1,000 per annum, to maintain the dignity of the rank, he seems to have received just £285 in the two years since the start of the reign. Henry had promised to find a better means of supporting him but had not actually done so. It was all very well Henry giving him an earldom but that only added to the embarrassment of not being able to keep a large household; he not only wanted a larger income, he needed it. This is why Henry and Richard of Conisborough had a difficult relationship. The king regarded Richard as greedy and ungrateful, and Richard regarded the king as disrespectful to him as a leading member of the royal family.

Another significant absence from this council meeting was that of Henry, Lord Scrope of Masham. As we have seen, Lord Scrope was one of Henry's most trusted advisers, and had been for many years. He had fought in Wales with the king, and had conducted Henry's secret negotiations with the duke of Burgundy in 1414. He was close to the king spiritually too, owning copies of *The Revelations of St Bridget* and making gifts to Bridlington Priory, where one of the king's patron saints, St John of Bridlington, was buried. Scrope was not the only baron not to attend this great council but he was certainly the most surprising absentee.

The king himself opened proceedings, thanking all those present for coming, and then passed over to the chancellor. Beaufort reminded those present that, at the parliament held in November 1414, all the estates of the realm had declared their support for Henry making a voyage to France to reclaim his heritage. However, out of honour and reverence for God, it was deemed necessary first to send ambassadors to the French in order to seek a peaceful solution to the king's demands for justice. The king had 'very graciously' agreed to send another embassy to his 'adversary of France' and that embassy had now returned with nothing new to report – despite the fact that

> in order to come to a good peace and accord, and to put an end to all debates, questions and wars between the two kingdoms of England and France, our said lord the king had offered to his adversary of France to lessen the great part of that which was due to him by right. In view of such a default of justice on the part of his adversary, our said lord the king proposes to undertake his voyage, praying that the said lords temporal named below, many of whom were among those at the said parliament [of November 1414] who offered to serve our lord the king in the same voyage with such retinues as it may please our said lord

the king to number and assign, praying payment for the first quarter
at the beginning of the said quarter, and for the second and third quarters at the end of the second quarter.

Thus was war declared. However, it had become apparent that the
schedule of payments claimed by the lords could not be met, as the
subsidies granted in the said November 1414 parliament would not all
be gathered in time for the second payment. Thus the chancellor
enquired on the king's behalf whether the following arrangement
would be satisfactory. Payment for the first three months would be
made in advance, as agreed, and payments for the second and subsequent quarters would be made in arrears.[43]

The temporal lords there withdrew and discussed this among themselves. Their reply, delivered to the king by Thomas Beaufort, was
general approval. But as the troops were to be raised by indenture, the
lords knew they would be responsible for paying the men and then
reclaiming the expenses from the crown. So they asked for sureties
that the payments would be made. The king thanked them for being
so understanding and asked that they gather again 'in the same place
on the next Wednesday coming' to declare what sureties they would
require.[44]

Having dealt with this matter, the king then turned to the prelates
present. He thanked them for what they had granted him in their
convocations but asked them further to discuss amongst themselves
what aid they could offer him with regard to his forthcoming expedition, by way of loans or gifts. After this, Henry dismissed the lords
and prelates until Wednesday.

Following this first session of the great council, Henry sent another
letter to the king of France. He confirmed that he had now received
the names of the French ambassadors.[45] He added that he did not
wish to comment on their number but thought that the length of
time requested for their safe conducts was too long. If they brought
good news on their arrival, said Henry, then their safe conducts could
be extended. 'And if this peace that we are looking for and pursuing
cannot be made, we will live to regret having lost valuable time without
profit, instead of working to the public good, when we could have
done.'[46] Henry was worried that a new embassy seeking peace would
force him to delay his invasion plans, so that the men he had summoned

to London would simply disperse, and the ships he had ordered to be brought to the ports of London, Sandwich and Southampton would lie idle until their masters reclaimed them.

The rest of Henry's letter is fascinating with regard to his vision of a united England and France, or at least how he wished to express that vision in public:

> Recall how the kingdoms of England and France, when they have been united, have been glorious and triumphant in past centuries, and how, in contrast, the divisions between these two kingdoms have resulted in the loss of Christian blood. If the prophet of prophets, the great Jeremiah, were alive today, he who lamented so bitterly on the misfortunes of one single town, would he not turn the arms of pity to stronger force, seeing the plains inundated with torrents of blood that have run from the deadly divisions of two sovereigns? Look how we knock in opportune times at the door of your conscience, but with no success. You invite peace, so we hope that by force of knocking we will ourselves make an entry. For this deplorable division cannot be contained within these limits; it goes far beyond them – it evidently maintains the schism in the Church and foments disorders that upset the whole world.[47]

Henry was almost claiming that the kingdoms should be reunited as one, under one king, in the same way that the Church should be reunited as one, under one pope. He was suggesting that Charles VI of France was acting like Pope John XXIII – claiming to be seeking unity and peace but privately doing all he could to maintain his own power. Such divisions in Church and state were to God's displeasure, Henry claimed. The world's problems would not be rectified until the kingdoms of England and France were unified. If this were just politicking, or an outrageous claim for the sake of improving a negotiating position, then it would perhaps have been understandable. But it was not. As we have already seen, Henry was already determined on war. He actually meant to invade France – not for the sake of England but for the sake of God's will. Amazingly, he ended the letter by saying, 'we should not look to encroach upon the rights of the one or the other by false points of honour or to wrestle against the truth by subterfuges or specious arguments . . .'

All leaders who go to war in the name of God are either zealots or hypocrites. Reading this letter, one cannot help but feel that Henry was both.

Tuesday 16th

As the payments on the Issue Rolls make clear, Henry had already decided that he was going to attack Harfleur. Today John Bower, turner, was paid for 'helving [making handles for] axes and mattocks for the king's works on his voyage to Harfleur in Normandy'. Thus the destination of the expedition had already been decided, and so had the point of embarkation (Southampton). Given the number of entries relating to the defence of Calais in early 1415, it is probable that the point of re-embarkation had also been decided. The whole plan might have been settled by today. Yet none of these details were announced at the great council. Two days later, when schedules of payment were being discussed, the region to which they would be sailing was left ambiguous: it might be France or it might be Gascony. Later in the month, when the indentures of service were drawn up, the same ambiguity was preserved. As the author of the *Gesta Henrici Quinti* stated, 'having concealed from all save his closest councillors the destination of the ships, he prepared to cross to Normandy.'[48]

It is somewhat surprising that Henry did not let even these forty-three lords know his plans. Why not? If he did not trust someone, all he needed to do was not summon them, as with Richard of Conisborough. To this we may answer that the problem was not one of trust so much as control. Henry could not control the future conversations of these men – they might be overheard by a spy. As he knew from the chronicles of Edward III's expeditions, the way to ensure a safe landing was to leave the enemy completely confused as to where he intended to land. In 1346 Edward III had concealed the destination of his Crécy campaign from almost everyone, not even telling the ships' captains.[49] They were instructed to follow the leading ships in the fleet and had sealed instructions regarding their destination that they were only to open in the event of a storm scattering them. This extreme secrecy regarding his destination seems to be another part of Edward III's scheme for a French invasion that Henry followed.

But why Harfleur? Why not simply invade via Calais, which was already an English port, thereby saving on the costs and delays of a possibly lengthy siege? Or why not land in Gascony, which was already under attack? Or do both: attack in the south as well as via Calais? After all, the indentures drafted later this same month allowed for a campaign in Gascony, and a southern front had formed an essential part of the Crécy campaign, to which Henry seems to have paid such close attention.

Henry wanted to prove himself a second Edward III, victorious in France, and to do that he needed to perform military feats similar to those Edward III had accomplished at the battle of Crécy and the siege of Calais. In order to show that God favoured him in the same way, he needed a battlefield victory or a successful siege of an important town, or preferably both. Battles were difficult to bring about but sieges were easy: all one had to do was attack. Moreover, they could be simplified and shortened using heavy artillery. Thus there was the chance of an easy symbolic victory in attacking the town. While this could be said for towns in Gascony too, Harfleur was much nearer, and thus easier and cheaper to reach. It would have been very difficult to transport heavy cannon to Gascony, and to use them to his advantage; Thomas Beaufort's experience in 1414 had shown that it was difficult to make progress of any sort in that region. Indeed, since the truce in Gascony had ended on 2 February, French forces had advanced through the Saintonge. On this very day the duke of Bourbon's army was in Pons.[50]

There were good strategic reasons to attack Harfleur too. It was a port on the north bank of the Seine estuary: to control it was to control both the seas of Normandy and one side of the river giving access to Paris. It had also been a royal naval boatyard for the last century, and a fortified haven for many of the French ships that preyed on English merchant vessels in the Channel. If Henry could secure it, he would win twice over: firstly by removing the threat to English shipping and secondly by threatening the French navy.[51]

So Harfleur it was. Henry had received enough intelligence about the town and port from his close friends Bishop Courtenay and Lord Grey in 1414, supplemented by more recent information from Sir William Bourchier, Sir John Phelip and William Porter, and probably many others too. He had made up his mind.[52]

Wednesday 17th

The second session of the great council took place in the council chamber at Westminster. The lords assembled and the king entered. At his command Chancellor Beaufort announced how the king had decided to appoint his brother John, duke of Bedford, as keeper of England during his absence on the forthcoming overseas expedition. John's salary was set at 5,000 marks per year (£3,333 6s 8d). Beaufort also announced that the king had appointed a privy council of nine men to advise Bedford. This consisted of the archbishop of Canterbury, the bishops of Winchester and Durham, the earl of Westmorland, the prior of the Knights Hospitallers, Lord Grey of Ruthin, Lord Berkeley, Lord Powys and Lord Morley.

Attention then switched to the defence of the realm in the king's absence. Beaufort announced that the Scottish borders were to be under the command of the earl of Westmorland, Lord Morley and Lord Dacre. The East March of Scotland would receive an extra two hundred men-at-arms and four hundred archers. Wales would have one hundred more men-at-arms and two hundred archers. Calais would have 150 men-at-arms and three hundred archers; and the sea would be guarded by 150 men-at-arms and three hundred archers. The advice of the privy council, which had discussed this in February, was set aside. So too were the naval provisions for Sir Gilbert Talbot. Only the provision for Wales remained unchanged. Fewer men were to guard the seas and more were stationed at Calais and on the East March. Whether these changes were the result of discussions with those present at this great council, or whether they were simply announced, is not clear.[53]

It is probable that this business occupied just the morning session, after which the lords dispersed to discuss what securities they would accept in lieu of payment for the second and third quarters of the forthcoming campaign. Henry's business later that day included giving instructions for Sutton House to be demolished and its timber, stone and lead to be used in his 'great work' at Sheen – the construction of his new manor house and monastery. The doomed Sutton House had been begun by Richard II in 1396 and completed by Henry IV in 1403, but Henry V did not like it. Having held one council meeting there at the start of his reign, he seems not to have visited Sutton again before ordering its destruction.[54]

*

The council of Constance had decided to ask the cardinal of Ostia, Jean Alarmet de Brogny, to preside over sessions in the pope's absence. This was logical, as the cardinal was John XXIII's vice-chancellor and usually acted on official instructions on his behalf. Thus a vestige of normality was reintroduced to the workings of the papacy, and business could continue. With the cardinal and the emperor presiding, several decrees were today promulgated by the increasingly ambitious and determined prelates.

The first eight of these decrees were to ensure that John XXIII was forced to abdicate. Two delegates were named on behalf of each of the four nations to go to John XXIII and ask him whether he wished to abdicate in Constance, Ulm, Ravensburg or Basel. He had two days to make this choice and to name his proctors. After that he was to have ten days to follow through with the business. If he failed, it was agreed that 'proceedings will be started against him as law and reason dictate'.[55]

The ninth decree read as follows:

> In the matter of faith against Jan Hus, by authority of this sacred council, the archbishop of Ragusa on behalf of the Italian nation, the bishop of Schleswig on behalf of the German nation, Master Ursin of Talamand for the French nation and Master William Corfe for the English nation, masters of theology, shall investigate the case of the said Hus and his adherents and proceed in it as far as, but excluding, the imposition of a definitive sentence.[56]

For Jan Hus, now being kept in isolation in the bishop of Constance's castle at Gottlieben, the end was in sight. There was no hope of being found innocent. The very next decree, the tenth, dealt with his inspiration and guide: the late John Wycliffe. 'The said commissioners shall also receive the report of the cardinals of Cambrai, of St Mark and of Florence on the action taken towards the condemnation . . . of the memory of John Wycliffe.' As the council openly sought Wycliffe's 'condemnation' it followed that his supporters must also be condemned.

For this reason Jerome of Prague now also appeared in their reckoning. The eleventh decree accused him of heresy and of disseminating libellous pamphlets. Jerome too was about to feel the power of the fanatical reformers within the Church hierarchy at Constance.

Thursday 18th

The third session of the great council at Westminster was given over to the scales of wages to be paid to various men on the forthcoming campaign. Two scales had to be agreed: one for Gascony and one for the kingdom of France. By the end of the session the chancellor was able to declare that the wages for each duke would be 1 mark (13s 4d) per day of service, for each earl half a mark (6s 8d), for each baron 4s, and each knight 2s. If the expedition was directed into the kingdom of France then each esquire would receive 12d per day, each archer 6d per day, and a company of thirty men-at-arms would receive 100 marks per quarter. If the army were to fight in Gascony, a salary of 40 marks per year would be paid to each man-at-arms and 20 marks to each archer.[57]

Friday 19th

The payments on the Issue Rolls for today are a reminder that the costs of the forthcoming expedition and the defence of the realm were not the only financial burdens on the treasury. There were many annuities too, granted by Richard II and Henry IV, varying from 4½d per day pensions paid to long-serving messengers to 20 marks per annum to Henry IV's barber. Ten years earlier, such payments had hugely encumbered the government, tying it down with a thousand financial strings, but as Henry had found to his cost when acting as prince regent, failing to honour these obligations was not an option. To fail one's faithful supporters and retainers after years of hard work was a sure way to leave those currently serving the king disillusioned and demoralised.

On this section of the roll we find more payments relating to Henry's secret letters, such as one sent 'in all haste to Sir John Grendon for certain causes contained in the said letter, 18s 14d' and a similar letter sent 'in all haste' to the mayor of Winchelsea. The king's youngest brother, Humphrey, duke of Gloucester, was paid 500 marks (£333 6s 8d) that had been granted to him and his heirs as an annual sum. But the most interesting payment is that of £23 12s 'for a *jantaculum* [breakfast] in our palace of Westminster for the duke of Clarence and others of the council advising the king about his voyage to Harfleur and Normandy'. The suggestion made above, in respect of the reclamation of Somerton Castle – that Henry was working closely with his brother Thomas – is hereby confirmed. Thomas's rivalry with Henry was no longer the uppermost feature of their relationship. The fact that Henry had passed over him in choosing his younger brother John to be keeper of the realm does not appear to have been a problem. Thomas, as a thoroughbred war leader, knew where he belonged – fighting, in France, alongside his king.

Saturday 20th

With the great council out of the way, the organisation of the war shifted on to a new level. The first of all the many indentures for service on the forthcoming expedition was sealed, this one being for the earl of Huntingdon, who undertook to serve in the army with twenty men-at-arms and forty archers.[58] Henry also ordered new bowstaves to be made, and commissioned Nicholas Frost, bowyer, to requisition all the bowyers and necessary labourers he needed, with power to 'arrest' men for the purpose.[59] Henry's new foundations were not forgotten either. John Pende, glasier, was commissioned to take glass for the king's use, presumably for the windows in the manor house of Sheen.[60] The confiscated alien priory of Otterton in Devon was allocated to Syon Abbey, in anticipation of the arrival of the nuns from Vadstena.[61]

Sunday 21st

So freely had Jerome preached about the iniquities of the council of Constance that the clergy in the area where he was staying were alarmed. They went to the local lord yesterday evening to urge him to take action. The lord in question sent men to watch for Jerome this morning. When he knew the preacher had been surrounded, he came to him and said, 'Master Jerome, yesterday you said something to me of the council. I must ascertain whether it is true or not, and you shall accompany me to Constance.' Jerome then realised he was trapped. He was taken to Constance and handed over to the bishop's men, who imprisoned him in 'a special dungeon' in Gottlieben Castle, where Hus himself was being held.[62]

When news of Jerome's arrest was announced, 'many were glad, and lauds were rung', wrote Ulrich Richental in Constance. Something of the medieval sense of bloodletting as a remedy for illness seems to have taken hold of the people. The Church as a body was sick; its humours were out of balance. Thus to restore the Church to health, some blood needed to be let. Jerome and Hus would provide that blood.

*

At Westminster, a decision was made by the king and council to act on information from Calais that the ale and food supply for the town was failing. In the past, supplies had been shipped from the town of Gosseford in Suffolk, which had had a royal monopoly on the business. Henry now ordered that the necessary victuals should be obtained from the Kent towns of Sandwich, Faversham, Dover, Deal and Mongeham, suspending Gosseford's monopoly for one year.[63] Unsurprisingly, given the timing, the rights of a small Suffolk town were unimportant by comparison with a sanctuary in France to which Henry was probably already planning to lead his army.

Monday 22nd

The clerks in Westminster recording the payments from the exchequer noted another 10 marks paid for keeping Mordach, earl of Fife, locked up in the Tower of London. They also noted that William Bolton, one of the king's messengers, was sent to Winchelsea, Rye and Hastings with letters to the mayors of those towns ordering ships within the Cinque Ports to go to sea 'to resist the malice of the king's French enemies'.

Henry himself was probably at Windsor Castle by supper time.

English kings since Edward III normally spent a couple of days travelling by barge up the River Thames to the castle, in preparation for St George's Day.[64] If the king was abroad, then the keeper of the realm had to take his place. There was no question of the royal family not celebrating the feast of St George at Windsor.

Tuesday 23rd: St George's Day

The Order of the Garter had been formally established by Edward III on St George's Day 1349.[65] It consisted of the monarch and twenty-five knights, together with support staff and officers. According to its ordinances, each knight had to come to Windsor Castle to celebrate the saint's feast day every year, without fail. If the knight could not attend, he was required to explain his absence and to celebrate the feast wherever he was, in the same way as he would have done if he had been at Windsor, wearing the appropriate robes.

Henry himself had been nominated to a Garter stall soon after his father's accession in 1399, and his three brothers had been nominated the following year. No doubt they travelled up the river together for the feast. With them would have been a number of the lords who had attended Henry's great council a week earlier. The full list of Knights of the Garter on this day in 1415 was as follows:[66]

Henry, king of England
João, king of Portugal
Gilbert, Lord Talbot
Thomas Fitzalan, earl of Arundel
Edward, Lord Charlton of Powys
Henry, Lord Fitzhugh
John, duke of Bedford
Eric, king of Denmark
Sir Thomas Erpingham
Henry, Lord Scrope of Masham
Humphrey, duke of Gloucester
Thomas, Lord Morley
Sir Robert Umphraville

Sir John Daubridgecourt
William, duke of Holland
Ralph Neville, earl of Westmorland
Edward, duke of York
Sir John Cornwaille
Thomas Beaufort, earl of Dorset
Thomas, duke of Clarence
Hugh, Lord Burnell
Richard Beauchamp, earl of Warwick
Richard, Lord Grey of Codnor
Thomas, Lord Camoys
Thomas Montagu, earl of Salisbury
Sir Simon Felbrigg

Obviously not all of these men were in attendance. The kings of Portugal and Denmark and the duke of Holland were heads of state; they hardly ever attended the Garter feasts in person. The earl of Warwick and Lord Fitzhugh were still on their way back from Constance. But most of the others would have travelled to Windsor. The three knights raised to the Order during Henry's reign – the earl of Salisbury, Lord Camoys and Sir John Daubridgecourt – would certainly have attended. They were among at least sixteen Garter knights who were preparing to set out on the expedition to Harfleur.[67] There cannot have been many other occasions since 1415 when so many Knights of the Garter took part in an overseas military expedition together. Even the duke of Holland was playing his part, in providing the ships.

Henry was not the only one celebrating St George's Day. All around the country people were carrying dragons in processions. Town guilds carried figures of St George and the dragon around their parishes and churches.[68] But nowhere did the celebrations compare with the solemnity of the gathering at Windsor, where religious services, swearing of oaths, and a lavish royal feast took place. The main procession would have seen the Knights of the Garter walking slowly together in their long deep-blue mantles, lined with scarlet, and wearing their garters on their left legs. Beneath their mantles they wore miniver-lined surcoats. Long hoods hung down their backs.[69] The king's own mantle had a longer train than the others, and was lined in ermine, not scarlet – one appears in the inventory of Henry's possessions at his death: 'a mantle of blue velvet, embroidered with an escutcheon of St George and a garter and furred with ermine, value £20'.[70] Ahead of the knights in the procession would have been the thirteen canons of the Order, all dressed in long mantles of purple marked with the shield of St George, and thirteen other priests, dressed in red mantles. There would probably have been dragons and St George figures in the Windsor procession too. Looking through Henry's inventory we find references to 'a gold dragon with a cross, the gold being worth 37s 11d', 'a little silver-gilt dragon, worth 8d', 'a little gold chain and a gold cross for a dragon, worth 23s 6d', 'a gold dragon set with a sapphire and 12 pearls, worth 40s' and 'three silver-gilt dragons, worth in all 12s 4d'.[71] On top of these dragons, which Henry may have worn as badges, we find that he owned a silver-gilt image of St George containing a relic of St George himself, the gold in this saint-shaped reliquary being worth £13 3s 4d.[72]

Due to the rigid formality of the Order, we can say a few things about proceedings on this day, even though not a single Garter-related document survives from this particular feast. Those attending would have witnessed the formal installation of the sixty-year-old Lord Camoys, whom Henry had recently nominated to the Order following the death of Lord Ros the previous year. Thirteen ladies were given robes and attended the feast, in line with the precedent set by Edward III in the 1370s and continued since by Richard II and Henry IV.[73] We even know the order in which the knights sat in the chapel and at the feast that followed: in the exact order in which they are named above. In the chapel they sat in designated stalls, each bearing their arms; during the feast they sat at two large round tables that used to be kept at Windsor Castle specially for the purpose. Each table accommodated thirteen knights, and so must have been about 9–10ft in diameter. Each place had the name of every knight who had sat there in the past inscribed on it in French.[74]

As to what the knights said to one another as they sat at these tables, we have no way of knowing. But for Henry, looking across at his brother John and Sir Thomas Erpingham on the opposite side of his table, there were only two subjects on his mind: religion and war. And in celebrating the feast of St George, the warrior-saint, he was celebrating both of them.

*

Cardinal Fillastre, Cardinal Zabarella, and several other prelates had set out from Constance on 19 April to tell John XXIII the news of the decree promulgated against him on the 17th. He had two days to decide where he wished to abdicate; those two days would be reckoned from the moment they informed him of the news. However, when they reached Freiburg, where they believed he was staying, under the protection of the duke of Austria, they found he had abandoned the place and made his way to Breisach, on the Rhine. He was staying at a public hospice.

The cardinals and the rest of the deputation arrived in Breisach and sought an audience with John. His servants declined to admit them.

The cardinals refused to accept this response and sent their messenger back to ask again. And again. The pope's servants claimed they did not know where he was, for they did not go into his chamber. Not until seven o'clock in the evening could the cardinals establish for certain that John was still in the hospice, when a nobleman who had served him in his chamber confirmed his presence there.

When the pope realised he could not conceal his whereabouts any longer, he asked to have a private audience with the two cardinals before meeting the delegation. The cardinals refused, saying they had to acquit themselves of their duty to the council first. Reluctantly the pope invited the entire delegation to come to him at the hospice the following day.[75]

Wednesday 24th

Full moon was about an hour before dawn. Most men would have been aware that the nights were bright enough to travel by, even if they were not up before dawn. John XXIII must have wondered whether he should not just flee, and get as far away from Breisach as possible before he had to confront the delegation. There was a bridge over the Rhine at Breisach, and he knew that he might find shelter on the far side. It must have been tempting. But for the moment he stayed where he was, and waited for the embassy.

When the deputation assembled, Cardinal Fillastre did the talking. He read out the council's decree of the 17th and also the emperor's letters of safe conduct. At the end, the pope declared that it was still his intention to bring peace and unity to the Church, and that he was prepared to abdicate – according to the council's own formula. He denied that he planned to return to Italy but said that he would rather go into France, on the other side of the river. He had already written to the duke of Burgundy, John the Fearless, who was sending two thousand men-at-arms to be his armed guard. He added that he would respond to the council in due course, and would speak to the two cardinals after dinner.

The news about the pope seeking shelter with John the Fearless was astounding. The delegation agreed Cardinal Fillastre and Cardinal Zabarella should return to the pope's hospice that afternoon and try to dissuade him from leaving. They did so – and they pleaded with him to abdicate straightaway. As they told him, by complying with the council's wishes he might yet preserve some dignity and some material provision for himself. If he did not resign he risked losing everything, for legal proceedings would undoubtedly be brought against him. But like Jan Hus in his prison cell at Gottlieben, John XXIII refused to change his mind. The cardinals departed, empty-handed and despondent.[76]

*

Turning to the Issue Roll payments made today – handed out by royal clerks to messengers in the great hall of the Palace of Westminster – we find certain signs of personal intimacy. Historians are normally reliant on chronicles and private papers for descriptions of friendship; these are often suspect, chronicles being subject to bias and private papers from this period almost non-existent. Official records are far too formal to note personal closeness; the king's feelings have to be inferred from grants, appointments and signs of continual proximity. However, with respect to today Henry made a special provision for his friend, the earl of Arundel. Arundel was being paid only 100 marks (£66 13s 4d) for his salary as treasurer. Despite the financial pressure he was under, Henry thought this too low and directed that a further £300 be paid to Arundel out of 'special regard' for him. This was similar to a special allowance he made to his uncle, Henry Beaufort, for attending council meetings. Such indicators of 'special regard' are doubly significant when they appear in account books. Men and women often lie or exaggerate their feelings in their letters to one another – especially heads of state – but they rarely lie in their account books.

The king seems to have had just such a 'special regard' for Sir John Phelip. He was a household knight and one of the men who had travelled via Harfleur on the embassy to Paris in January. Over the year he received several grants and gifts from Henry. Today he received three – one of £20, another of 40 marks and, with his wife Alice, an annual grant of £100. Alice was the daughter of Thomas Chaucer, the king's butler, and the granddaughter of Geoffrey Chaucer. Phelip was thus not only a friend but a man whose past and present were interwoven with the Lancastrian tapestry, and an example of the sort of enforcer Henry relied upon heavily in preparing for his campaign.

Unremittingly, the payments in these accounts are for pensions and war. Another £60 was paid to Roger Salvayn for timber for the defence of Calais. Another £5 was paid to John Bower, turner, in return for 'helving axes, mattocks and picks for the king's voyage to Harfleur'. Thomas Strange received £282 for the wages of his troops keeping the peace in North Wales. Henry bought another ship from three Breton merchants, paying £500 for the *St Nicholas of Guérande*. Nicholas Merbury paid £10 to William Founder for more gunpowder for the expedition to Harfleur, and William Catton received 25 marks for repairs to the king's ships.

Among all these payments for war and pensions to supporters is a payment to John Hull for the maintenance of Mordach, earl of Fife. In itself this is nothing special – payments for Mordach's upkeep appear regularly in these accounts – but for the first time we see the payments given a terminal date: 27 May. By that date the heir of the regent of Scotland was expected to be back on his home soil. Henry's representatives in the north must have agreed an exchange for the earl by this date. It is another small sign of the diplomatic game at which Henry excelled. Over and over again we find signs of diplomatic initiatives that collectively contributed to his grand strategy of isolating France and maintaining the stability of England's borders.

Another terminal date appears in these same rolls today, and it was even more significant. At Calais on this day, Philip Morgan secured a prolongation of the truce with his French counterpart, Jean Andreu. Peace was guaranteed – until 8 June.[77]

Thursday 25th

Pope John XXIII arose early. At sunrise he slipped out of Breisach with only one servant, saying goodbye to no one and telling nobody where he had gone. His plan was to make for the bridge over the Rhine and seek shelter until he could make contact with the duke of Burgundy's men. John the Fearless himself was still at Dijon, and showed no sign of coming to the aid of the pope in person.[78] But John's men – if the pope was right in thinking they were nearby – could easily spirit him away. Then the council of Constance would have to depose the pope in his absence, and both the other popes too. That would put the council's authority to a very severe test.

When John XXIII came to the bridge there was a man there waiting. In what must have been a very awkward confrontation for both parties, he stopped the pope. The pope turned back. But he met another man along the road by the river. This man took the pope to a barn, and told him to wait there while he went to fetch horses and an escort. When he returned the men in the escort were, of course, not those of the duke of Burgundy but the duke of Austria. They took John to Neuenberg, where there was no bridge across the river.

When the emperor learned that the pope was intending to head into France and seeking the protection of John the Fearless, he was furious. Messengers rode through that afternoon and evening, ordering local lords to take action. Rumours spread: that the emperor was preparing an army to ride north and storm Neuenberg, or that the men of Basel were being ordered to march to Neuenberg to apprehend the pope. The emperor sent ambassadors to the duke of Burgundy – they met him on the 28th at Is. He also wrote to the duke of Ludwig of Bavaria-Ingolstadt, palatine count of the Rhine, the duke of Austria's cousin, urging him to bring the duke of Austria to reason. Every possible form of influence was brought to bear on the duke of Austria.

By 8 p.m. Duke Ludwig had contacted the duke of Austria and told him emphatically that John XXIII was a lost cause. The pope himself was by now terrified and powerless. He had been reduced from his state and greatness to something less than a normal man – unfamiliar with his surroundings and uncertain how to behave. When the duke of Austria decided that enough was enough, and that he would take the pope back to the cardinals at Breisach, he simply instructed his men to dress the pope in common clothes and lead him to Cardinal Fillastre. The pope was in no position to object; he donned a white jerkin and a black mantle and mounted a small black horse. In this guise they led him back through the night to Breisach. The pope and his escort were forced to wait for more than an hour outside the gates before they were finally admitted by the night watch.[79]

Friday 26th

In France the optimism of the show of unity on 13 March had completed dissipated, and the mood was one of deep concern. A week earlier a message had been sent to the bailiff of Rouen ordering him to prepare against an English invasion. Today an official letter was sent out from the French court confirming that the king had heard that Henry V was collecting a large fleet and an army.[80] The additional news that the English refused to prolong the truce for more than five weeks would have heightened the tension. It would have hammered home the point Henry had made in his letter of the 15th: that he saw the French refusal to comply with his demands as an act of disobedience to God.

For the princes of France, English bellicosity was only half the problem. The other reason for concern was their own divided government. The king was undergoing a severe bout of sickness and could not possibly grasp the seriousness of the situation. Nor could the septagenarian duke of Berry, for he had now left court. The duke of Orléans could not be given command without infuriating – and further alienating – John the Fearless; and likewise John could not be given command either. The 'fearless' duke was perhaps the one member of the French royal family who had the military experience, the political skills and the sheer energy to organise a successful defence of the realm – but of course the Armagnacs could not risk him exercising military authority. Nor would the dauphin tolerate his presence. Thus, in the absence of any member of the royal family who was sane, competent and politically acceptable, the fat, eighteen-year-old dauphin was himself appointed captain-general of France, with orders to resist the English invasion.

The dauphin's appointment only worsened the situation. He was wont to sleep all morning and have his dinner at four in the afternoon, and his supper at midnight, spending the night hours playing music and dallying with his mistress, la Cassinelle – so called because she was a daughter of one Guillaume Cassinel.[81] He had never resisted anything, let alone an invasion. The responsibility for actually organising the defence of the kingdom fell to the constable of France, Charles d'Albret – and herein lay yet another problem. Charles was an experienced commander, having been constable of France for eleven of the last thirteen years. Nevertheless he had no authority over the great dukes and princes. He could hardly command the duke of Burgundy, or the duke of Brittany, or the duke of Bourbon. All he could do was advise the dauphin. But the dauphin was quite a law unto himself. The chronicler Monstrelet relates a story about how the dauphin and his mother in this month commanded all the dukes of the royal blood to come to them at Melun. When the dukes had arrived, they were detained there and ordered not to return to Paris while the dauphin and his mother went back to the capital. The dauphin, having tricked his mother into placing herself in his power without the other members of the royal family, sought out the three men in Paris who had command of her treasure. He forcibly entered their houses with his supporters and removed his mother's wealth to his own *hôtel*. After this act of theft, he summoned the principal men of the city and the university to the Louvre where he had the history of the realm since his father's coronation read aloud, with particular attention to the waste of money by various men over the years, including the duke of Burgundy. As dauphin, he declared, he would not permit this to continue; but instead would henceforth take on the whole government of the realm himself. Charles d'Albret could do little in the face of such overbearing and threatening inexperience.

In reply to Henry's letter of the 15th, the French government today wrote that the king of France would do all he could to arrive at the peace that was 'so desirable for all mortals', and that to this end he sought the prolongation of the truce and was sending his ambassadors.[82] It was a predictable letter, drafted in line with the dauphin's wishes, and aimed at forcing Henry to talk, not fight. But as Chancellor Beaufort had said to the English parliament in November 1414, there was a time for all things, and the time for talking had passed.

*

At Westminster too the time for talking had passed. Now it was the time for action. Richard Clitherowe and Reginald Curteis, who had been commissioned to raise ships for the king's voyage from the duke of Holland, were advanced a further 3,250 marks (£2,166 13s 4d) by Giovanni Vittore, a Florentine merchant, for the wages of the masters and mariners of those ships.[83] Thomas Chalton, mercer of London, was sent abroad with £400 to buy 'cannon, saltpetre and other necessary things of war' for the forthcoming voyage, and £225 to buy other mercery ware'. Lord Grey of Codnor, keeper of the town of Berwick, was paid £1,092 for the wages of 120 men-at-arms and 240 archers defending the East March. Robert Rodyngton was paid £40 for the safe conduct to Southampton of certain wine-laden ships, captured by Sir Thomas Carew, John Clifford and himself.[84] And the colossal sum of £4,316 10s was paid to Sir Roger Leche, treasurer of the royal household, by the cofferer William Kynwolmersh, 'for the victuals and stuff required for the household for the forthcoming voyage to Harfleur'.

One last payment here ought to be mentioned: another gift to Thomas, duke of Clarence, this one being an annuity of 100 marks to him and his wife Margaret. It was to be followed (tomorrow) with the re-grant of the manor of Hawardyn, the stewardship of Chester, and the castle and town of Mold. These had already been given to Thomas by Henry IV but the documents had proved invalid, so Henry re-granted them to his brother.[85] Clearly Henry was determined that Thomas would have no cause for complaint. As the French royal family began to disintegrate, the English one was more united than ever.

Saturday 27th

Every day was valuable for the raising of men and ships for the expedition. Messengers were heading out from Westminster in all directions. They were riding out with letters under the great seal to the sheriffs of the counties, and the mayors, bailiffs and burghers of towns, to assign men-at-arms and other defensible men and archers to be arrayed 'in thousands, hundreds and twenties to patrol the coast of the sea and other places . . . to the extent necessary to expel the enemies of the king by war and to defend from time to time'. John Wenslowe, Nicholas Maudit and William Tresham received money to pay the masters and mariners of the ships they were requisitioning, in line with their commissions of 11 April. More money was paid to the bowyers working for Henry. John Sewale, messenger, was 'sent with all speed with the king's letters to the customers and controllers of the port of Kingston upon Hull to be at Westminster on the last day of the month of Easter'. Two more messengers took similar urgent messages to the customers and controllers of the ports of Lynn,

Melcombe and Exeter on the same day. And a gift of £100 was made to John Wilcotes, receiver general of the duchy of Cornwall, on account of Henry's 'special regard' for him.[86] Henry had in mind a job for Wilcotes, which he would put to him the following month.

*

Cardinal Fillastre and the other delegates had left Breisach by the time the pope had returned on his small horse, on the night of the 25th. But having heard of the duke of Austria's capitulation, and the return of the pope to Breisach, they turned around and rode back in that direction. They met the pope and the dukes of Austria and Bavaria-Ingoldstadt on the road, heading towards Freiburg. As they rode with them they laboured hard to persuade John to resign his papal title. He only had two options, they told him: either he could abdicate honourably, with provision being made for him, or he could allow himself to be deposed ignominiously. They argued with him for the rest of that day, and even into the night. Nothing was decided.

Sunday 28th

This morning, John XXIII repeated his willingness to abdicate to Cardinal Fillastre and the rest of the delegation from Constance. But once more he attached conditions to his decision. He wanted financial provision for himself, and for the emperor to forgive the duke of Austria. He wanted to be made a cardinal and to be head of the whole college of cardinals, as well as a papal legate and a perpetual vicar of Italy, with papal power over the whole of the Italian nation. He declared that he would abdicate on these grounds – as long as the abdication could take place on neutral territory, such as Burgundy, Savoy or Venice. A statement to this effect was signed by the pope himself and taken off to Constance.[87]

*

Henry was at Lambeth Palace, the London house of the archbishop of Canterbury. A petition of the earl of Salisbury for the payment of his expenses while serving on the embassy of 1414 had been drawn up in early March; for some unknown reason only now did Henry grant it.[88] Perhaps it had not previously been presented? For our purposes it is interesting to note that it shows that the earl of Salisbury had also had a good look at Harfleur on this expedition in 1414.

Later in the day the king took a barge back across the river to Westminster. His business there included granting permission for the prioress of the Dominican nuns at Dartford, who had become a recluse, to appoint proctors for her official roles.[89] Henry also commissioned George Benet, cordwainer of London, to take sufficient hides for 'the king's works' – but whether these were for the buildings at Sheen or the forthcoming expedition is not clear.[90]

Monday 29th

Today was a key date in the move towards war. All the leading lords and knights came to the palace of Westminster to seal indentures detailing the numbers of troops they were expected to provide for the forthcoming campaign. Top of the list was the king's brother, Thomas, duke of Clarence, who was required to raise 240 men-at-arms and 720 archers. The duke of York was expected to raise 100 men-at-arms and 300 archers. The earl of Salisbury was to provide forty men-at-arms and eighty archers; Lord Scrope thirty men-at-arms and ninety archers, and so on.

The indentures that the lords sealed were agreements written out twice on a single piece of vellum in duplicate that, when both texts had been sealed, were divided by cutting the vellum in two with a wavy line. Any disagreement over the terms could then be resolved – if necessary by checking the king's half of the indenture against the lord's half, and making sure the two married up. Each lord agreed to serve Henry for a whole year in person, either in Gascony or in France itself, and the indentures stipulated the wages each lord was to receive as well as his retinue (at the rates stipulated on 18 April). In most cases it was specified that wages for the first quarter would be paid in advance in two halves: half at the time of the agreement and half on the mustering of the requisite number of men. These indentures stipulated that jewels would be given to the lords in order to guarantee that they would receive payment for the second and third quarters. The agreements also stipulated that the cost of shipping the lords, their men, their equipment, harness and horses would be borne by the king. For the duke of Clarence and other great lords there were specified limits: the king would pay for the transport of fifty of the duke of Clarence's own horses, twenty-four horses for each earl, sixteen horses for each banneret, six horses for each knight, four horses for each esquire and one horse for each archer.[91]

It was not just fighting men who sealed these indentures. Henry had to make provision for other necessary officers, such as a number of surgeons and physicians. Master Nicholas Colnet, the royal physician, agreed to serve on the campaign on the same terms as the fighting men – for a full year – in Gascony or France, with his transport paid for, and bringing three of his own archers and horses. His wages were to be a shilling a day in France and 40 marks for the year in Gascony. The same wages and terms were to apply to Henry's surgeon, Thomas Morstede, except that Morstede was also required to bring along a staff of fifteen men: three archers and twelve more surgeons. The assistant surgeons were, like the archers, to be paid a wage of 6d per day.[92] Even minstrels were contracted to serve in this manner, under the command of the sixty-year-old John Greyndour.[93] Presuming that all these indentures were checked, agreed, sealed and cut up in the hall at Westminster, it must have been a busy gathering.

As the agreements make clear, this was to be a longbow-dominated army. Although some indentures required lords to provide two archers for every man-at-arms, the majority required three. This 3:1 ratio had become established as the norm in Wales over the course of the first decade of his father's reign, and Henry himself employed just such a ratio in Wales. His army would thus be three-quarters archers, excluding support staff. It was no wonder that Henry had continuously employed Nicholas Frost, John Bower and Henry Bower to produce bowstaves since the start of his reign. The armies of longbowmen, pikemen and men-at-arms that had won Edward III his great victories at Sluys and Crécy had now been refined to produce a cheap, manoeuvrable, and devastatingly effective destructive force. Because it specialised in projectile warfare, it could expect to suffer fewer casualties and could thus tackle far larger armies than a force composed only of men-at-arms. And there was also a surprise factor. Apart from the thousand archers that the earl of Arundel had taken to help John the Fearless at St-Cloud in 1411, the French had not seen a mass of English longbowmen for several decades.[94] Even those archers could not be considered representative. The benefits of projectile weapons increased exponentially with numbers; one archer would be lucky to be able to bring down one knight or man-at-arms, but, as Edward III had showed, five thousand archers were more than a match for twenty thousand knights and mounted men-at-arms. It was the massed arrow-power that was so effective. And the French had never in their history come face to face with the full force of seven thousand English archers.

Almost everything was now in place. The plan to sail from Southampton to Harfleur was set, the reconnaissance of Harfleur had been undertaken, the security of the realm had been organised, the interim government had been arranged, the agreements to serve had been settled, the safety of Calais had been seen to, the defence of the seas and the coastline was in order, and gunpowder and bowstaves had been manufactured and laid in store. Yet much more still remained to be done. Henry might have been growing impatient by this stage but once again he had to set back the date of the invasion. The new date for sailing was 1 July.[95]

May

Wednesday 1st[1]

Mayday saw the beginning of summer. Across the country, men and women rose early and went out looking for wild flowers and greenery to deck their houses and streets. In the city of London and the surrounding parishes dancing took place around maypoles; a particularly large one was set up in Cornhill. In some places the people staged Robin Hood plays and held feasts called May ales, with tables laden with mutton, chicken, bread and pastries – and of course lots of ale. May queens and May kings were chosen and given garlands; they were crowned and paraded in procession, with May officers supervising the celebrations, and everyone settling at the end of the evening around a great bonfire.[2]

In the Palace of Westminster, the exchequer clerks were busy enrolling notes of payments. Nicholas Merbury was reimbursed for obtaining a thousand lances for the Harfleur expedition, and for more saltpetre and sulphur for making gunpowder. The clerk recorded a payment of 40 marks to Robert Rodyngton for guarding the ships laden with wine that he had arrested and escorted safely to Southampton for the king. Payments were also made showing that Henry had recently taken steps to mobilise the clergy for war. Sums were paid to various messengers to deliver letters issued under the great seal, commissioning the archbishops and bishops to hold a view of the clergy within their dioceses, 'counting the multitude and members of the clergy and notifying them to the chancellor by certificate on the 8th day of July next coming'. And in the wake of the great council, at which Henry had asked for the bishops and archbishops to consider what loans they might make to assist his expedition, Richard

Norton and John Sewale, messengers, were paid 'for taking eight letters under the king's signet to various bishops and abbots for money lent by them to the king as well as certain letters sent under the privy seal to Hankyn de Mitton for money lent by him to the king for his voyage across the sea'.[3]

Under today's date we also find evidence that Henry had made a personal visit to Southampton (his intended port of embarkation) within the last few weeks. John Drax, sergeant-at-arms, was paid for arresting Christopher Rys by the king's order, whom he 'brought to the presence of the said king at Southampton'. How recent this visit was, it is not possible to say; the longest prolonged gap in Henry's itinerary is early March; but it is possible that he had inspected the town more recently, perhaps in Holy Week.

Under this day's date we find other references to Southampton. William Soper was paid £280 'for making the new ship named *Holyghost*' as well as a further £20 'for paintings on the king's new ship the *Holy Ghost* at Southampton'. The exchequer clerks also paid messengers for carrying letters to various sheriffs for them to assemble cattle and lead them to Southampton to feed the army about to muster there. This is the first sign of the great drive of men and provisions towards Southampton that would take place over the subsequent months, and which everyone in Southern England would have seen taking place along the highways and byways around their parishes.

Thursday 2nd

The previous day, at 4 p.m., the messengers carrying the signed notice of the pope's decision to abdicate had arrived in Constance. They were told that the twelve days the pope had been allowed for his decision had expired the previous night. Today a general session would be held at which the pope would be formally accused by public edict for his crimes, damages, and other offences.[4]

The citation against the pope had already been drafted, and the cardinal of Ostia received a copy at about 7 a.m. this morning. Few other cardinals had time to read it as they were being summoned into the cathedral. When all were assembled in the emperor's presence, the deputation from John XXIII was read aloud. Sigismund responded that

HENRY · · · THE FIFTH

Portrait of Henry V, painted on wood *c.* 1520.
Although this is a later image, it is probably a copy of a lost original.
All the other portraits of the king are based on it.

Henry's father, Henry IV. The relationship between these two deeply religious, fiercely proud men was often difficult – due as much to their similarities as their differences.

Henry V's stepmother, Queen Joan. In the year 1415 Henry showed her great respect. Later he accused her of being a witch and confiscated her income.

Thomas, duke of Clarence.
Henry's brother – just one year younger –
was a ruthless and reckless warrior,
and Henry's greatest rival.

John, duke of Bedford. The third of
the four brothers. An intelligent, pious
and capable man, Henry entrusted the
keepership of the realm to him in 1415.

Humphrey, duke of Gloucester.
The fourth and youngest brother, and
arguably the most cultured. He fell to
the ground at Agincourt, whereupon
Henry stepped over him to protect him.

Henry Beaufort, bishop of Winchester and chancellor of England. Henry's uncle and one of his most trusted confidants.

Henry Chichele, archbishop of Canterbury. He shared Henry's zeal for the reform of the Church and, in particular, the extirpation of Lollardy.

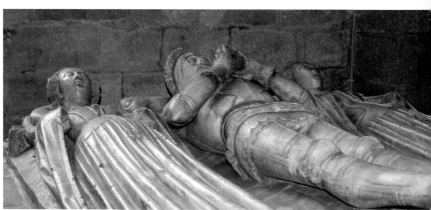

Ralph Neville, earl of Westmorland, and his wives. Henry depended on him for the security of the north. The effigy on the right represents Joan Beaufort, Henry's aunt.

Thomas Fitzalan, earl of Arundel, and his wife Beatrice. One of Henry's closest friends, he became treasurer on Henry's accession. He contracted dysentery at the siege of Harfleur and died shortly after returning to England.

Richard Beauchamp, earl of Warwick. Another of Henry's closest friends, a diplomat and a military commander. He led the English embassy to the council of Constance.

London in 1483. Charles, duke of Orléans, is shown writing poetry in the Tower of London during his long captivity there (1415–1440). London Bridge and Old St Paul's can be seen in the background.

Westminster Hall. A place for great feasts and royal bureaucracy. A marble throne used to be on the daïs at the far end.

Westminster Palace. In the seventeenth century the chapel royal was used by parliament. However, the skyline was largely unchanged from 1415.

Ciuitatis Westmonasteriensis pars.

Parlament House — the Hall — the Abby

The Holy Roman Emperor, Sigismund, king of Hungary. Without his leadership the council of Constance would not have met, let alone been successful.

The Cathedral of Constance in 1819. Here the plenary sessions of the council of Constance were held. Here too Jan Hus was defrocked prior to his execution on 6 July.

it was too late: he refused to accept it. The representatives of the four nations were similarly scornful of the pope's advances. Nothing more was said on the matter. The opening Mass began, and the other prelates who were late arriving took their seats. After the Mass, the citation was read out. John was accused of heresy, promoting the schism, simony, maladministration, wasting the property of the Church, and sinful acts in his personal life. At the end of each charge, the representatives of each nation responded, '*placet*' – it is pleasing.

The cardinals present heard the accusations, and were not pleased. The text had been received by the cardinal of Ostia only just before the session. The bishops from the nations were lesser men than the cardinals; yet the bishops had been privy to proceedings. The college of cardinals had been deliberately overlooked, as if superfluous to the discussions. It amounted to contempt – and now they rose and gave vent to their feelings. How was it that the English nation, with fewer than twenty churchmen and only three bishops, could cast a vote on this matter, and yet they, the cardinals, could not? There were sixteen cardinals present, and they all took precedence over all the English churchmen. They had a good point.

Eventually, after much wrangling, the cardinals were refused permission to form a nation of their own. Instead they were fobbed off with the right to appoint six deputies who could sit with the representatives of the nations. The determination of the emperor to end the schism, supported by the prelates of the German, French and English nations, was greater than the traditional authority of the papal curia. The latter had lost much of their respect, and with it they had lost power.

Friday 3rd

Henry gave orders today for William Kingston, master of the *Katherine of the Tower*, to equip his ship and be ready to enter the king's service. Similar orders were delivered to John Piers, master of the *Little Trinity of the Tower*, and to William Robinson, master of the *Nicholas of the Tower*, and to Stephen Thomas, master of the king's great flagship, the *Trinity Royal*.[5]

In the great tapestry of the whole fifteenth century, the most important thing that happened today was a birth, and its significance was a complete unknown to all those present. It had nothing to do with Henry himself, nor his ships, nor the council of Constance, nor France. A baby girl was born, and the mother was Joan Beaufort, Henry's aunt. The father was the stalwart Ralph Neville, earl of Westmorland, on whom Henry relied for the defence of the north. Henry's newborn cousin was called Cecily, and she would grow up to marry Richard, son of Richard of Conisborough, earl of Cambridge. Her husband would begin the dynastic struggle that we know today as the Wars of the Roses; and she would give birth to twelve children. Two would become kings of England: Edward IV and Richard III.

History, through its linear stories, encourages us not to think in such terms. But just as Henry was giving his orders for his flagship, the *Trinity Royal*, to be made ready for his forthcoming invasion of France, a group of women in a chamber at Raby Castle were wiping his aunt's brow, washing her body, and changing the sheets on her bed – and bathing the crying infant whose sons would one day kill Henry's son and grandson, obliterating the Lancastrian dynasty.

Saturday 4th

Henry's business today was principally taken up with German shipping. He ordered officials at Kingston upon Hull to de-arrest the ship called *Holy Ghost of Lubeck*, which was then in the port, and to allow the master Herman Sasse to return to his homeland.[6] A licence was drawn up at his instigation for two German merchants to ship wheat and malt to Norway.[7] And a commission was issued to two men to take the sail, anchors, cables and armaments of a German ship lately wrecked in the port of Kingston upon Hull, and to deliver them to one of his mariners.[8] It was perhaps no coincidence that three items of German business should be dealt with by him on the same day. One might speculate that he had received a German delegation of sorts, or that he had appointed a specific clerk to deal with German affairs.

*

At Constance, the day of reckoning had come for the soul of the late John Wycliffe – at least in terms of its earthly fate. Forty-five articles against him – forty-five possible instances of heresy in his writings – were re-examined and condemned anew. To these were added a further 266 examples of his heretical teaching. Regardless of any good he had done in his lifetime, a sentence was drawn up condemning not only his books but also his memory.

For Henry, this was justification of his condemnation of the Lollards. For Jan Hus, Jerome, and their supporters, it was a declaration of ominous intent.

Monday 6th

Rogationtide – the days between Rogation Sunday and Ascension Day – saw more religious processions. Most communities carried crosses around their parishes, asking for God's blessing upon the fertility of the soil. Church bells were rung and banners carried, but there was no feasting. Instead, men and women were expected to fast again, eschewing meat for three days as in Lent, until Ascension Day itself.[9]

Henry granted £10 to his servants Thomas Green and John Mede, this sum having been confiscated from the constable of Berkhamsted Castle as a fine for allowing the escape of two felons from the castle.[10] He issued a commission of inquiry into the circulation of false coin in Cambridgeshire – his second inquiry of this year into the treasonable practice of counterfeiting money.[11] And he commissioned Sir James Harrington, the duke of York's lieutenant of the East March, and eight other men to arrest a total of thirty-one named men who had breached the truce agreed between Henry and the Scottish regent, the duke of Albany. They were to be imprisoned in Berwick Castle 'until they have made due reformation of their incursions'.[12]

*

At Constance, at the time of vespers (early evening), the emperor publicly took back the duke of Austria into his favour. In the Franciscan monastery, the duke went down on his knees three times before the emperor and submitted himself, his castles, cities, towns, vassals and subjects unreservedly to Sigismund. He begged to be forgiven for his crimes against the emperor and against the Church, and everyone present. He submitted himself absolutely to the authority of the council and begged only that the pope's life be spared, and promised that, if this was granted, he would bring him back to Constance.

Sigismund was satisfied. He took the town of Freiburg, where John XXIII was staying, into his own hands, and ordered that the pope be guarded day and night, with twelve guards during the day and twenty-four at night. Cardinal Fillastre noted in his record of events that things had turned out as he had foretold: the pope had exchanged one threat for a far worse one. Now he stood to lose everything.[13]

Wednesday 8th

Henry granted two lords, his brother Thomas and his cousin the duke of York, letters of protection for his forthcoming voyage.[14] He ordered that the royal revenues from Carmarthen should be handed over to the mayor and burgesses of the town 'as the Welsh rebels razed the walls and the citizens are robbed nightly as a result'.[15] And Sir John Tiptoft – the long-standing Lancastrian supporter who had risen to prominence as Speaker of the Commons during his father's reign – was formally appointed seneschal of Aquitaine.[16] This seems to have been the first positive move Henry made with regard to Gascony since his uncle's return in the summer of 1414.

The same day the constable of Dover was commissioned to levy £80 from the people of Sandwich in the case of Katherine Kaylewates of Flanders. The patent letter explained how she had been robbed of goods to that value, contrary to the truce between England and Flanders, and how the king wished to provide remedy for her.[17] Henry was allowing nothing to threaten the fragile series of alliances and non-aggression pacts that he had carefully built up since his accession.

Thursday 9th: Ascension Day

The sixth Thursday after Easter was Ascension Day, the commemoration of Christ's ascent into Heaven. The church bells were rung once more, and processions were held in which the clergy of the great churches carried their valuable relics through the streets of their towns. Those who had been fasting for the last three days found relief in the form of the great feast.[18] And, in Henry's case, special oblations were made. In 1413 he had marked Ascension Day with a gift of £2 to a Franciscan friar, on top of his usual gifts.[19]

At about this time, Henry left Westminster and headed west, to Reading. Before he did so, he granted authority to Sir Robert Umphraville and Sir James Harrington to prorogue the truce with Scotland, or to negotiate a new one. This was merely a precautionary measure, pending more specific arrangements that would follow in a week's time.[20]

Friday 10th

At Reading Henry dictated a letter addressed to an unnamed group of men – possibly the mayor and aldermen of London.[21] 'In the name of the Holy Trinity we have taken our road along our next voyage, to be made personally by us . . . and have promised to pay our lords and others of our retinue for a quarter of a year, and have promised each of them to pay another quarter, the one following, at the time we embark, which is not far off,' he declared. He went on to explain what had been explained at the first day of the great council in April: that the grants and subsidies would not be sufficient to cover the second payment in advance. However, he did not mention that various lords had agreed to accept payment for this second quarter in arrears; instead he asked that the recipients of the letter loan him as much money as they could, sending it to Sir John Pelham and William Esturmy, who would deliver such security for the loan as necessary.

Henry's presence at Reading at this time has convinced some writers that he was on a pilgrimage. This might have been the case; the *Brut* also refers to Henry riding about the land on pilgrimages before his voyage to France. But if that was the purpose of his journey he did not go much further than Reading, and certainly did not visit St Winifrid's well, or Holywell, in North Wales, as some writers have supposed.[22] Holywell was about eight days' journey from Westminster, each way; and Henry, having left Westminster on the 9th, was soon back there.[23]

Most probably he had set out for Winchester or Southampton and today received news that sent him hurrying back to London.

While Henry was dictating his begging letter at Reading, Bishop Courtenay was compiling a dossier of the promises made by the Armagnac lords in the time of the late king, Henry IV. When John the Fearless had been in power, the Armagnacs had taken it upon themselves to promise Henry IV that they would help him recover his inheritance of Gascony, and recognise his sovereignty over the duchy of Aquitaine. The Treaty of Bourges had been proof of their acknowledgement of Henry's right to the whole of the region. It had not escaped Courtenay's notice – nor Henry's – that the Armagnac lords had reneged on their earlier promises. For the purposes of demonstrating the justice of Henry's cause, the Treaty of Bourges was now dug out from its coffer in the Tower of London and sent to Lambeth, where Courtenay started reading it. It would have no bearing on the negotiations with France but it would have great importance in persuading those at the council of Constance of Henry's right to feel aggrieved – among them the Holy Roman Emperor.[24]

Also today, four men were commissioned to enquire into a long-running dispute at Lynn (now King's Lynn) in Norfolk. Lynn was at this time a large and very prosperous town with a population in the region of five thousand, with valuable trading connections with the Baltic. However, it was within the lordship of the bishop of Norwich. Prior to 1406, the bishop of Norwich had been Henry Despenser, 'the fighting bishop'. At the time of Henry IV's return to England in 1399, the men of Lynn had sought to overthrow Despenser by attempting to place themselves directly under the patronage of the new king. Costly legal battles had followed, in which the mayor and burgesses and the rest of the community had become heavily indebted to the gild merchant of the town, owing more than £450. After Despenser's death, the gild merchant sought to recover this money from the mayors who had led the legal battle to oust Bishop Despenser. The result had been a bitter row that no man seemed able to sort out. Henry's instructions, enrolled today, mark yet another royal attempt to solve the dispute, which would carry on for another couple of years.[25]

*

In France, in the seneschalcy of Nîmes, the *arrière-ban* was proclaimed.[26] This type of call-out was the most severe: any man who did not obey it was to forfeit all his lands. The reason for this proclamation was that Henry's subjects in Gascony 'had taken many towns in France'. The truce had run out, the duke of Bourbon had recommenced hostilities at the head of 6,000 men and the English were responding. Whether they had really taken many towns is open to question, but the fact that the war was opening up not just in the Saintonge – where the duke of Bourbon was now threatening Blaye, on the north side of the Gironde – but also near Nîmes in the south of France reminds us that Henry's Gascon policy was proving dangerous. He might have been preparing to go to war with France in order to secure the sovereignty of the region, but he showed little concern for his lands there, or for his Gascon subjects.

Saturday 11th

One possible explanation for the shortness of Henry's visit to Reading is that he had – as he claimed in his letter – set out on the road to war, going to Southampton via Reading, but that some news brought him back the following day to the capital. If this is the correct explanation, then the most likely reason is that he had heard that his ambassadors to Constance had now returned. The earl of Warwick, Sir Ralph Rochford and Lord Fitzhugh entered London today; Sir Walter Hungerford had arrived back yesterday.[27] So there was a very good reason why Henry turned back to the capital straightaway. No doubt he wanted to hear all the news of proceedings against the pope, and how things stood at the time they departed.

*

At around this time two envoys from Prussia were admitted to the king's presence. They were Peter Benefeld and Hans Covolt of Danzig. The Grand Master of the Teutonic Knights, a military order based in Prussia that continued to fight crusades every year in the north of Lithuania, had commissioned them in January to come to England to seek payment of sums totalling over 10,000 marks that Henry IV had promised to pay the Order. They had set out from Marienburg on 27 March, and probably arrived in London about a month later. They had then spent ten days seeking an audience with Henry, and they may have seen him just before he set out for Reading.

Their first audience amounted to very little. They received no promises – only the news that the king was very busy. He was also not inclined to smile on knights from distant lands asking for large amounts of money, even if he did owe them. They were told it would be three weeks before he could see them again.[28]

Sunday 12th

Of all the families that had rebelled against Henry IV, none had done so with greater force and greater losses than the Percy family. The three principal members of the family – Henry Percy, earl of Northumberland, his brother Thomas Percy, earl of Worcester, and Henry 'Hotspur' Percy, son and heir to the earl of Northumberland – had originally sided with Henry IV, and supported him, becoming his most trusted advisers. But they had sought to control him, and Henry IV was not the sort of man who looked kindly on attempts to influence his royal prerogative. Nor had the Percy family realised that, in becoming responsible for the safeguarding of the north, they would end up more indebted than they had been under Richard II. So they had rebelled. At the battle of Shrewsbury Hotspur and the earl of Worcester had paid with their lives. At the battle of Bramham Moor in 1408, the old earl of Northumberland followed them into the grave.

Although this was in many respects a victory for the Lancastrians, it was not a satisfactory permanent state of affairs. The heir to the earldom of Northumberland was the young Henry Percy, Hotspur's son, who had been abandoned in Scotland by the old earl and imprisoned by the Scots. Thus there was no hereditary lord locally to guard the East March. That responsibility had been given officially to the duke of York who performed it through a deputy, Sir James Harrington. This was not the same as having an earl on hand to raise his feudal tenants and wider retinue to resist the Scots. As Henry Percy was now of age, his release, restoration and return to Northumberland would be strategically useful to Henry.[29]

Henry's plan was to exchange Mordach, earl of Fife, for Henry Percy. He had already set a provisional date of 27 May for taking Mordach from the Tower and sending him back to his father, the duke of Albany. Today at Westminster he gave instructions for drawing up the safe conducts for the Scottish magnates who had been designated to negotiate and agree the transfer of the two men. These included Mordach's own son and heir (Robert Stewart), George Dunbar (son and heir of the Scottish earl of March), three other lords, the duke of Albany's secretary, and twenty servants.[30]

Monday 13th

The emperor, the cardinals and the prelates gathered this morning in the cathedral at Constance. The bishop of Salisbury said Mass, and afterwards it was declared that the citation against the pope had been promulgated throughout the city, being posted on doors as well as read aloud. At this point Cardinal Zabarella rose and declared that the cardinal of Cambrai, Pierre d'Ailly, had received a papal bull from John XXIII yesterday evening in which he had declared that his proctors would be cardinals d'Ailly, Zabarella and Fillastre. Cardinal Zabarella added that he had only just seen this instruction, and was unsure what to do. Cardinal Fillastre stood and declared that he had only heard of his appointment that morning at 7 o'clock, and he did not intend to accept it.

All this sounds remarkably petty, but proceedings were about to take a turn for the ridiculous. The bishop of Posen went into the pulpit and declared that three cardinals should accompany the representatives of the nations and go to the door of the cathedral and formally summon the pope (who was still at Freiburg, as everyone there knew). Only the nations' representatives went; not a cardinal stirred. The cardinals started arguing about which ones should go to the door. The cardinal of Pisa declared that it should be two junior cardinal deacons who should perform the duty. The cardinal of Bari replied that in his thirty years of being a cardinal, it had always been the representatives of the three ranks of cardinal who performed such functions. This led to an argument about whether there had been a similar case in the past. The reason why the nations and the emperor had so strongly resisted the cardinals becoming a nation in their own right is very vividly revealed by this event. They were like a bunch of old hens clucking away about whose role it was to summon a non-existent cockerel into the hen house. In the meantime, the prelates representing the four nations had gone to the door, summoned the pope, come back and announced he was not there, as everyone knew.

Cardinal Fillastre and Cardinal Orsini and eight bishops, two from each nation, were then deputed to hear witnesses give evidence against the pope in the Franciscan friary. This took place in the afternoon. Ten witnesses came forward, including several bishops – enough 'to prove the pope's waste and maladministration . . . through simony and corruption, etc, especially his reckless alienation of church property for his own profit . . . all leading to the conclusion that he should be suspended'.[31]

The proceedings against the pope clearly fascinated all those who took part in them. Cardinal Fillastre described them in detail, and they were also mentioned by the papal notary, Jacob Cerretano, and Ulrich Richental. None of them even mention that a petition on behalf of Jan Hus was presented today, in the same Franciscan friary, or that a number of important lords came in person to see it presented to the cardinals and bishops. Among them were Lord Henry Lacembok, Lord John of Chlum, Lord Wenceslas of Dubá, nine other named lords, and several others unnamed. It was an impressive delegation on behalf of a man whom many already regarded as a condemned heretic.

The petition was read out by Hus's friend, Peter of Mladoňovice. He told the cardinals how Lord John of Chlum and Lord Wenceslas of Dubá had been requested by Sigismund to induce Jan Hus to attend the council under an Imperial safe conduct. He explained that Hus had agreed, in order to remove the stain of ill-repute from Bohemia, and had come of his own free will to Constance. But although he had been neither tried nor convicted, he had been imprisoned, even though everyone else was allowed to come and go freely, including representatives of the popes Gregory XII and Benedict XIII. Hus was now 'so cruelly chained and reduced to so slender a diet that it is to be feared that, his strength being exhausted, he might be in danger of losing his reason'. Peter insisted that the reverend fathers observe the emperor's safe conduct and bring the case of Jan Hus to a speedy end, stating that 'the lords put particular confidence in the eminent rectitude of your paternities'.[32]

Wednesday 15th

Henry met his council in the Star Chamber at Westminster. One might have thought that the matters to be discussed would have touched on the affairs at Constance. Somewhat surprisingly, the only subject mentioned for which we have any evidence was wine. Or more particularly, what to do with wine-laden vessels captured at sea. Henry decided that warrants should be drawn up under the privy seal and directed to the mayor and bailiffs of Winchelsea, to value the wines that had been taken there, and to deliver them to Thomas Chaucer, the king's butler. It was also decreed that letters should be sent to William Soper and John Eastgarston, customs officials at Southampton, declaring what should be done with Scottish, French and Breton wine-laden ships taken at sea, and what was to be done with wine in Flemish ships. Along these lines, another warrant was sent to Sir Thomas Carew, John Clifford and Robert Rodyngton, who were instructed to deliver their captured ships to the customs officials of Southampton, unless they were Flemish.[33]

Following the return of the ambassadors from Constance, including Sir Ralph Rochford, Henry formally handed over the castle of Somerton to his brother Thomas, duke of Clarence.[34] The temporalities of the see of Coventry and Lichfield, which should have been handed over to the new bishop, John Catterick, soon after his appointment on 1 February, were now finally made over to him in his absence – just ten weeks late.[35] One cannot help thinking that the government had taken advantage of Catterick's absence at Constance to keep as much of the episcopal revenue as they could. Also today, letters of protection were drawn up for Edmund Mortimer, earl of March, who was going to France on Henry's expedition.[36] Mortimer might have been a weak soldier but it was vital that he should be with the army. Left in England, with such a strong claim to the throne, who knows what treason might have been effected in his name? His presence on the expedition was an example of Henry keeping his friends close and his enemies closer.

Llywelyn ap Madoc Ddu, one of the last followers of Owen Glendower, had finally given up his adherence to the Welsh cause. Today Henry pardoned him 'for all treasons, rapes, murders, rebellions, insurrections, felonies, conspiracies, trespasses, offences, negligences,

extortions, misprisions, ignorances, contempts, concealments and deceptions committed by him', and returned to him all his lands within the
lordship of Builth, which Henry IV had confiscated on account of his
rebellion.[37] Glendower was still in hiding but he had been deserted by
almost every lord who had served him. Gradually, one by one, Henry
was accepting them back into the English fold. He might not necessarily trust them, but at least he could give them an opportunity to give
up fighting.

Thursday 16th

Although Henry had already delegated authority to Sir Robert
Umphraville and Sir James Harrington to negotiate a new truce with
Scotland, he now decided to appoint new negotiators: Lord Grey of
Codnor, Robert Ogle and Master Richard Holme. They were to meet
with the duke of Albany's commissioners on 6 August.[38] In so doing
he replaced the duke of York as warden of the East March with Lord
Grey of Codnor, who was not going on the campaign but remaining
behind as one of the council. Both the duke of York and Sir James
Harrington would now be following Henry to France.

Further arrangements were made for the shipping of the king's
household. The king had a writ drawn up for Robert Hunt, sergeant
for the carriage of the royal household, to find sufficient carts and
four-wheeled wagons to transport the royal household abroad. Also
he was to find 'timber, iron, carpenters and smiths for the same carts
and wagons, newly constructing them where necessary, and sufficient
horses for the same, and all manner of other necessities wherever they
may be found, both within liberties and without (excepting the estates
of the Church), paying a reasonable sum for the same; and arresting,
paying and providing sufficient men to govern the said carts.[39] At the
same time, he gave orders for ships and harbourage for his newly
appointed seneschal of Aquitaine, Sir John Tiptoft.[40]

Henry was mindful of the fact that the first men for the expedition would have started gathering in London, in line with his orders
for them to assemble there on 24 April, ready to march to Southampton
by 8 May. Ships were already gathering at Southampton, Winchelsea,
London and Sandwich, in line with his orders of the previous month

to assemble by 8 May. These deadlines had already passed – and it was still another six weeks before his planned sailing date. Today he ordered Richard Woodville, castellan of Dover Castle, to look over the men mustering at Dover. He expected five knights and eight esquires with retinues totalling 203 men-at-arms and 621 archers to be there.[41] One of these knights, Sir John Grey, was supposed to be gathering forty men-at-arms and 120 archers to serve on the campaign.[42] None of the other knights and esquires is recorded as serving on the expedition, so presumably they and their retinues were intended for the defence of Calais (as men sailed there from Dover) or for the defence of the seas.

Friday 17th

A large number of letters of protection and safe conduct was issued today to those going abroad in the king's service. The recipients included Sir John Tiptoft, going to Gascony, and many lesser knights and esquires heading to France: men such as William Shore from Hertfordshire, William Wingate from Bedfordshire, James Grigg from London, John Baskerville from Herefordshire, and James Ethevenes, gentleman of Cornwall. It is a reminder of how the preparation for war was fast becoming a countrywide movement, drawing in men from all across the kingdom, and that men were travelling long distances, staying in inns, buying food and drink, armour and horses, arranging safe conducts and responding to writs. The whole country must have been buzzing with expectation.

Saturday 18th

Five days had passed since the Bohemian and Polish lords had delivered their petition on behalf of Jan Hus to the council of Constance. Two days ago they had received a formal reply from Géraud du Puy, bishop of Carcassonne. The lords had been astonished to hear a number of reasons given justifying the imprisonment of Hus. Although the basic demand of the petition had been agreed – that Hus be given a fair trial – it seemed from the council's responses that he had already been judged. Now the lords returned, fired up, and Peter of Mladoňovice responded in a powerful and uncompromising manner, in defence of his friend and teacher:

> First, whereas to the lords' statement that Master Jan Hus came here to Constance of his own will and freely under the safe conduct and protection of the emperor and the empire, you responded that the lords had been ill informed concerning the safe conduct . . . for you said that Master Jan Hus had procured the safe conduct only fifteen days after his arrest . . . On the very day of the arrest of Master Jan Hus, Lord John of Chlum, when he was asked by the pope in the presence of amost all the cardinals as to whether he [Hus] had the emperor's safe conduct, replied 'Most holy father, be assured that he has'. None of them requested at the time that the safe conduct be shown. Immediately on the next and the third day and thereafter Lord John loudly complained in respect of the pope that Master Hus, under the safe conduct of the emperor, was detained as a prisoner, and showed the safe conduct to many. Moreover to verify what he is saying, he calls on the counts, bishops, knights, esquires, and the notable citizens of this city of Constance for their confirmation and testimony, for they all saw the safe conduct at the time and heard it read aloud.[43]

This set the tenor for the rest of the speech: sheer anger that the council could dare to fob these lords off with such blatant untruths.

The second response the prelates had given to the lords was treated with similar anger. The lords claimed that Hus had been condemned as a heretic and a heresiarch – an inventor and preacher of new heresies – and excommunicated for failing to appear at the papal curia five years earlier. However, they pointed out that the excommunication had been issued by one of Hus's enemies, Archbishop Zajic of Prague, who had been acting in a personal capacity. When Hus had been summoned to appear before the papal curia, he had sent proctors, as was proper; but they had been refused an audience and had been imprisoned for several months and cruelly treated, and Hus himself had been condemned in his absence. Cardinal Zabarella had reviewed the case, and had declared the actions against Hus invalid on account of his proctors not being heard; but Michael de Causis, one of Hus's enemies, persuaded the pope to take the case away from Cardinal

Zabarella and give it to another who was certain to uphold the sentence of excommunication. As for the council's third response – that Hus had preached heresy since coming to Constance – the lords objected that this was impossible. He had been arrested soon after his arrival, and in the intervening period he had been in the company of Lord John of Chlum who was prepared to swear that Hus had not preached at all.

Such was the strength of Peter of Mladoňovice's case that he chose to prefix it by saying that the lords 'do not hereby accuse your paternities of dissimulation in this matter but wish that . . . you may discern and judge it more clearly and effectively'. It was a polite sop to the cardinals and prelates. One can understand why: Hus stood to suffer if the lords should be dismissed. But the implication that the prelates of the council were lying is equally understandable. It was true.

★

Huge amounts of money were now being laid out for the forthcoming expedition. Sir Roger Leche, treasurer of the royal household, and his assistant, John Spenser, received a large number of payments for the costs of 'the king's voyage to Harfleur', totalling more than £3,000. John Rothenhale, controller of the king's household, had received £400 for the expenses of 'boys and other persons of the king's household to attend the voyage to France'. Stephen Flexmer and Henry Bower and others had been paid £6 and 100 marks for making more bows, But these amounted to just a fraction of the total handed out by the exchequer clerks today. Among the many other payments we find:[44]

- Richard Clitherowe and Reginald Curteis, for the provision of ships from Holland and Zeeland for the king's voyage abroad £449 6s 9d
- Richard Woodville esquire, castellan of the king's castle of Dover, for the wages of ships' masters and mariners to guard various ships sent from Zeeland and Holland by Richard Clitherowe and Reginald Curteis £140
- William Catton, clerk of the king's ships, for repairing and mending ships £100
- For the earl of Dorset, admiral of England, and other officers attending to the preparation of ships within the waters of the Thames 60s 6d

- Roger Hunt, going to the port of Plymouth with £1,883 6s 8d to pay the wages of Sir John Tiptoft, seneschal of Aquitaine, and his retinue in Aquitaine £10
- Sir John Neville, custodian of the town of Carlisle and the West March, for the wages of his men-at-arms and archers: two payments, of £148 and £312 10s
- Various messengers sent to all the ports of England with letters under the great seal to prohibit the passage of anyone foreign going abroad 63s 4d
- Sir Richard Arundel for his expenses in keeping the castle of Bamburgh £120
- The earl of Arundel, treasurer of England, for his expenses in going to parts of Wales for certain difficult matters moving the king £18 12s
- John Wele and Thomas Strange, for the wages of men-at-arms and archers remaining with them for the safe custody of North Wales £263 5s 6d
- John Everdon, clerk of the king's wars, for conducting certain sums of money for various men-at-arms and archers in South Wales to join the king's voyage to foreign parts 66s 8d

On top of all these payments there were a large number of annual pensions to be paid – £20 to a confectionary cook in the royal spicery, £10 to a royal attorney, £100 to Sir John Robesart, £40 to Nicholas Merbury, £40 to Gerard Sprong . . . Among them we find a payment to Richard of Conisborough, earl of Cambridge, 'to whom Richard king of England granted a 100 marks twice yearly for life'. However, today Richard received only £40 of the 100 marks owing to him. If he was feeling aggrieved that Henry was not making sufficient provision for him, this partial payment is hardly likely to have helped. He was an earl – yet the king expected him to get by on an income of £80 per year.

No doubt the reason why Henry did not pay Richard in full was his pressing need to send his money elsewhere. No money was sent to Sir John Talbot in Ireland, even though he had an army in the field. Even the treasurer, the earl of Arundel, had to accept that he could not take the full sum he was due in respect of his wages. Henry realised he would have to rely on loans from now on. As the lords and prelates at the great council had demonstrated, they were prepared to accept deferred payments on the basis of the king handing over the crown jewels as security. There was a precedent for this in Edward III putting his treasure up as security – even pawning the great crown – in order to pay for his campaigns in 1338–40. Today we find the first evidence that Henry had given instructions to do likewise. John Coppleston junior was paid for coming up from Devon with £573 6s 8d in loans from the dean and chapter of Exeter Cathedral, the mayors and corporations of Exeter and Plymouth, the abbots of Tavistock and Buckfast, the priors of Plympton and Launceston and four gentlemen: Robert Cary, Alexander Champernowne, John Beville and John Copleston. In return he took back jewels worth £800, namely 'a large tabernacle of gilt silver, garnished with gold, which had belonged to the duke of Burgundy, having twenty balas rubies, twenty-two sapphires and 137 pearls'.[45]

Today we also find evidence that Henry expected the French ambassadors to come sooner rather than later, for he laid aside £200 'for the expenses of the French ambassadors coming from Dover to the presence of the king at Winchester'. Already he was anticipating where he would be when they arrived.[46] Like so many other things, he had a tendency to stick to his plans once he had made up his mind. In this case it was not to be to his advantage.

Sunday 19th: Whitsunday

Whitsunday – or Pentecost – commemorated the inspiration of the Holy Ghost, and so was of particular significance to a man like Henry who believed so zealously in the Holy Trinity. Two years earlier he had spent £151 16s on the feast held this day, and gave alms of a noble (6s 8d) in the abbey of Westminster.[47] No doubt he did something similar in this year – and the religious character of the day is probably the reason why we find no royal business conducted.

Monday 20th

Whit Monday saw processions of all sorts in parish churches, towns and cities. In some places images of the Virgin were carried in procession. At Exeter a huge May garland was carried through the streets along with the colossal figure of an elephant.[48] Quite what the relevance of the elephant was is unclear; few Exonians had ever seen one; even the thirteenth-century carving of an elephant on a misericord in the cathedral would have been known only to a very few people. But the sense of celebration was in the air – and, in some places, for good reason. For example, today, at Vadstena in Sweden, there was a great procession overseen by Henry's sister, Philippa, as the first nuns stepped out from the monastery for the boats that would take them to their new Bridgettine monastery at Syon.[49]

A payment of 6s 8d is noted today to John Brown, who was sent 'with all speed' to Sir John Wilcotes, whom the king had assigned 'to provide for the ambassadors of France until they come to the king's presence'.[50] Henry had perhaps had this duty in mind when he had made the grant to Wilcotes in April. Coupled with the £200 he had provided for the ambassadors' expenses, it reveals that Henry genuinely expected the French to send their representatives to him quickly. As they well knew, they had nothing to gain from sending their men on a futile mission – but they had everything to gain by delaying tactics, forcing Henry to put off his embarkation, and causing him thereby to waste money and resources.

Tuesday 21st

Henry met with his council today at Westminster to discuss the instructions to be issued to John Hull and William Chancellor: two esquires whom Henry had chosen to conduct Mordach, earl of Fife, back to Scotland. It was agreed that Mordach should be taken to Newcastle upon Tyne and handed over to the mayor and sheriff of the town with letters from the king instructing them to convey him safely to Warkworth Castle. The two esquires were also to carry similar letters to the sheriff of Northumberland and the constable of Warkworth Castle, letting them know of the arrangements. At Warkworth, Mordach was to be safely guarded until it was clear that Henry Percy was out of Scotland and in Berwick Castle. The esquires were ordered to take royal letters to the constable of Berwick Castle instructing him to receive Mordach and keep him safely. When the hand-over had been effected, the esquires were to inform Sir Robert Umphraville or Sir John Widdrington or 'other notable persons who know Henry Percy well' and once these men were sure that it was indeed Henry Percy who had been delivered, they were to release Mordach to the Scots and to bring Henry Percy swiftly to the king. The hand-over was to take place by 1 July at the latest, and Mordach was not to be permitted to speak to anyone prior to his release.[51]

A commission was issued to John Hawley, John Clifford and Robert Rodyngton to find out who now had in their possession 'certain vessels of the king's enemies laden with wine lately captured by Thomas Carew and other subjects of the king at sea [who] took them to other ports in Devon and Cornwall without Thomas's permission'. These ships were not those that Robert Rodyngton had taken to Southampton by 26 April but others that Carew had captured. This is made clear by a second commission issued to the same men: to find out who owned the vessels and to conduct them safely 'to the king's presence at Southampton'.[52] It might have been the wine the king was after – he had recently paid the victualler of Calais £128 for Gascon wine for the royal household – but, given the destination to which these ships were to be taken, it was more probably the vessels themselves.[53]

Friday 24th

A council minute dated 'Friday 25 May' [sic] notes that four members of the privy council – Henry Beaufort, Thomas Beaufort, the earl of Arundel and the keeper of the privy seal – met at Blackfriars to discuss extorting money from the Italians. Henry's need for money for his invasion was about to take an ugly turn.

Merchants from Italy might have thought they had nothing to do with the war between Henry and the king of France. It did not concern them. But they had been increasingly drawn into it. Henry's recent prohibition on foreigners leaving the country was a significant threat to their international trade; so was his requisition of all ships with a carrying capacity of over twenty tuns. A number of Venetian galleys in English ports were commandeered for the purposes of his invasion. But far more threatening was Henry's demand for cash.

The four privy councillors interviewed six Florentine merchants, four Venetians and two merchants from Lucca. Bishop Beaufort addressed them, and informed them that it was customary for men trading in foreign countries to make grants to the kings so that they could undertake expeditions. He hoped that they would loan the king what they could. If they did not, they would be imprisoned.

This was nothing short of tyranny. But that did not help the Italian merchants whom Beaufort had seized in Henry's name. When told that they profited greatly from their trade in England, and that they should give up their gold and silver and other jewels to the tune of £1,200 in the case of the Florentine merchants, £1,000 in the case of the Venetians, and £200 in respect of the men of Lucca, they refused. 'And because they refused to lend such sums to our lord the king, they were committed to the custody of the Fleet Prison'.[54]

Was there any justification for their seizure and arrest? Taking a view sympathetic to Henry, we may speculate that his thinking was as follows. Since the leading English merchants in London were being leaned on very heavily to loan money for the expedition, for the safe-guarding of England's trading links among other things, there was no reason why other merchants profiting from trade in England should not equally be required to do so. Indeed, the Italians may have been considered to have had an unfair competitive advantage in retaining their capital while the English merchants had to pledge theirs. In addi-tion, we may remark that there was a precedent: Edward III had given orders for all the Italian merchants in England to be arrested in 1337, saving only those of the Bardi and Peruzzi companies, on whom the king was reliant for future borrowing. As Henry V regarded so many aspects of his great-grandfather's reign as instructive for his own expe-dition, he may have known about this from the same chronicles that he was using for his military preparations. Although in 1337 the Genoese had been supporting the French in their antagonism of England – providing them with ships and mercenaries – Henry seems not to have been bothered by such details. Thus the king may have wholly believed that what his council was doing in his name was justifiable. But from a more objective standpoint it smacks of the sort of tyranny that Richard II perpetrated in the late 1390s, which Henry's father had returned to England to stamp out in 1399.

The above business concerning the merchants – like all direct requests for money – was not conducted by the king in person but on his behalf by powerful men. Henry himself was concerned with the building of a bridge. He appointed Robert Welton, one of the clerks of the exchequer, to be the surveyor for 'the construction of a bridge to be made by the king's advice, to take carpenters, smiths and other workmen, artificers and labourers, and timber, iron, hides and other necessaries'.[55] Where his new bridge was to be is not clear, but presumably it was a replacement of a dilapidated structure on the king's highway.

The formal order for the delivery of Mordach, earl of Fife, to John Hull and William Chancellor was drawn up today at the king's personal command.[56]

Saturday 25th

Robert Thresk – one of the clerks of the exchequer whom Henry had rewarded in February – had recently submitted a petition to the chamberlain. He wished to have permission to found a chantry of three chaplains to celebrate divine service daily at the altar of St Anne in his church at Thresk in Yorkshire (Thirsk, as it is called now).[57] The beneficiaries of these prayers would be Robert Thresk himself and the king – for their good estate in their lifetimes and for their souls and the souls of Robert's friends and relatives after death. Henry granted the petition.

One other order is extant for today. Stephen Ferrour, the royal farrier, was ordered to take iron and 'horsenails', and to enlist black-smiths for shoeing the king's horses on his expedition to France.[58]

Sunday 26th: Trinity Sunday[59]

Trinity Sunday was, for Henry, one of the most important religious feasts of the year. His devotion to the cult of the Holy Trinity featured in almost every aspect of his life, and the lives of those around him. From the character of his prayers to the decoration in the stained glass windows of royal palaces and chapels, and the salutations in his letters, he was a sincere follower of the three-in-one: God the Father,

God the Son and God the Holy Ghost. Of the twenty or so ships in the royal fleet, three were called *Trinity* and one was the *Holy Ghost*. In 1413, he had travelled to Canterbury Cathedral to see his father entombed in the Trinity Chapel on Trinity Sunday. He may have had a difficult relationship with his father but, in their complete devotion to the Trinity, they were as close as father and son could be.[60]

For this reason it is all the more surprising to find Henry conducting business as normal on this day. Other important religious feasts noted above saw little or no recorded royal business. In contrast, several matters were attended to today. Only one of them was of a religious character. Henry ordered a charter to be sent to the House of Jesus of Bethlehem at Sheen showing that the priory had been granted the possessions of Ware and other alien priories.[61]

A letter was sent to the sheriff of Chester on the king's command, stating that, on the advice of the chancellor, Henry had decided that no general or special assizes were to be held during his absence abroad.[62] This was not out of any clemency for those accused of heinous crimes; they were left to languish in their gaols until their moment of justice should come after the campaign was over. Henry's motive was to free up his men preparing to travel with him by releasing them from any obligation to serve on juries or to have to worry about turning up in court to give evidence.

Henry made preparations for feeding his army. The sheriffs of Kent, Oxfordshire, Wiltshire and Hampshire were ordered each to send two hundred oxen to Southwick, Tichfield, Beaulieu and Southampton respectively by 25 June.[63] All four of these writs were authorised by Henry in person – as indeed were the great majority of preparatory writs. Also he heard his chamberlain recite a petition from the royal surgeon, Thomas Morstede, asking for a sum of money sufficient to obtain all the surgical consumables he had been ordered to provide for the duration of the voyage, and for the king to arrange carriage for everything to France. In addition, Morstede asked the king to appoint men to serve at the given wages: one suspects that he anticipated some difficulty persuading surgeons to give up their lucrative, safe London practices in return for 6d per day in a war zone. As one would expect, Henry granted Morstede's petition in all respects.[64]

It is worth pausing at this point, on Trinity Sunday, to reflect on how much business was falling personally to the king. When books about Henry's reign state that Henry spent most of the first half of 1415 preparing for the forthcoming campaign, they fail to draw attention to the extraordinary level of work that this entailed, and how much of it was dealt with by the king. As we have seen, Henry even involved himself in such matters as the provision of meat for the army when it assembled – even though this was a religious feast day when he might have chosen not to work. We have seen him over and over again personally attending to such matters as the provision of horseshoes and horsenails, or the manufacture of bowstaves. One would have thought that much of this would be delegated. But in 1415 there was no War Office. Matters such as carriage could be delegated, but otherwise each individual aspect of the forthcoming campaign had to be attended to by the king and council. And, with the council largely composed of clergymen or earls absent on royal business, for the most part that meant by Henry himself.

Monday 27th

This morning at the Tower the earl of Fife was released into the custody of John Hull and William Chancellor, in accordance with Henry's directions of the 21st.[65] His long journey back to Scotland had begun.

Elsewhere in the Tower, Henry was presiding over the council meeting held today to delegate various duties. First on the agenda was the duke of Burgundy. Instructions needed to be drawn up for men going to see John the Fearless. What the exact nature of their business was we cannot tell; the instructions themselves are no longer extant. But we know that Henry himself chose the archbishop of Canterbury, Hugh Mortimer, Master Philip Morgan and Master John Hovingham to deal with the matter, adding Lord Scrope 'when he will arrive'.[66] Apart from the archbishop, all of these men had been on the embassy to John the Fearless in June 1414, and Lord Scrope had secretly been back since. The wording of the note referring to Scrope suggests that the men were to sit down to draw up the instructions straightaway. Clearly the secret negotiations with John the Fearless were ongoing.

The next items on the agenda were the crown jewels and the treaty that Sir John Tiptoft was required to negotiate in Gascony. With regard to the crown jewels, the lords had decided at the April great council that, in return for accepting late payment of wages, they would take jewels as security. Some had already been dispersed, such as the 'large tabernacle of gilt silver' recently sent back to Henry's creditors in Devon. To control the dispersal of such treasures, Henry appointed a committee consisting of his brother John, Henry Beaufort and Richard Courtenay, bishop of Norwich. Another committee – namely his brother Humphrey, Thomas Beaufort, and the keeper of the privy seal – was appointed to draw up precise instructions for Sir John Tiptoft with regard to Gascony.

The various committees indicate that Henry was beginning to delegate more tasks. The chancellor, Henry Beaufort, was given the duty of arraying men for the defence of the realm in each county. Beaufort was also instructed to inform all the archbishops and bishops to enter into their registers 'the malice of the Lollards'. He was to organise the building of beacons – warning fires, in case of invasion – in each part of the country. To the treasurer of England (Thomas, earl of Arundel) and the controller of the royal household (John Rothenhale) fell the responsibility for obtaining and transporting victuals to Southampton. The treasurer (Arundel) and the admiral of England (Thomas Beaufort) were given the task of paying all the mariners. And these two men were also entrusted with sorting out the terms of an agreement for provisioning Calais and its English-held hinterland.[67]

Despite this increased level of delegation, Henry did not lessen the burden on himself. He commissioned several men to enquire into those rights in his manor of Sheen formerly enjoyed by his tenants there, which they had lost as a result of his new initiatives.[68] And he personally dictated a letter to the sheriff of Hampshire firmly ordering him to proclaim throughout the county that people should bake bread and brew ale to provide for the king's army due to assemble at Southampton.[69] Although this was the same day as he appointed a committee to oversee provisions for the army, it still fell to the king to issue this letter. And one small detail it contains explains just why it had become so important for the king to start delegating to the newly constituted committees. The people of Hampshire were ordered to bake and brew until the feast of St Peter ad Vincula (1 August).

That was a full month after Henry hoped to sail. Clearly he anticipated yet further delays.

Tuesday 28th

Chancellor Beaufort was quick to act on his commission to array the
clergy. The king dictated – or Beaufort drafted in the king's name –
a letter to be sent to all the archbishops and bishops. By the end of
the day, the chancery clerks had written out the necessary copies to
be sent to the twenty-one prelates of England and Wales, requiring
them

> to assemble with all speed the able and fencible clergy of the diocese . . .
> compelling them to be arrayed and equipped according to their estate
> and means, sparing none, and keeping them in array so as to be ready
> to resist the malice of the enemies of the realm and Church of England
> and of the Catholic faith when need be . . . and to certify in chancery
> under his seal by 16 July their array and equipment and the number
> arrayed.[70]

Nor were they to restrict their array to the parish clergy. The order
expressly stated that the regular clergy were to be included, thereby
requiring even those canons and friars who lived in near-monastic institutions to be arrayed. Even those who had exemptions from serving
were required to be arrayed. During the king's forthcoming expedition
the clergy were to assist in 'the defence of the realm and the church
and of the faith, for which all Christians are bound to fight if need be
to the death'. Quite what the motley crew of canons, precentors, rectors,
vicars, priests, friars and hermits looked like when they were arrayed,
together with their households, is anybody's guess, but they assembled
in large numbers. And between them they provided a large number of
archers. A total of 6,759 eventually gathered in just six dioceses, so probably twice as many archers were arrayed by the clergy as sailed to France
with Henry. Those Sunday archery training sessions, compulsory since
the reign of Edward III, were now paying off.

The stream of orders preparing for the campaign continued. John
Rothenhale, controller of the household, who had been delegated to

find provisions for the expedition, issued a bill straightaway for Sir John Phelip and six other men 'to take coals, wood, bowls, pots, vessels, and all other things necessary for the scullery of the royal household, as well as carpenters, labourers, carts and horses as needed'.[71] He issued a similar order to Alexander Smetheley, yeoman usher of the king's hall, to procure sufficient 'timber, carts, horses, litters, saddles, carpenters and labourers' for his office on the expedition.[72] Other orders of Rothenhale included a commission to David Andever to take sea fish in the south and west of England for the royal household, and a commission to Richard Scalle to gather enough bacon for the king's voyage.[73]

Amidst all this organisation and determination, one small, rare chink of personal affection is visible. Today Henry gave an order for Blanche Chalons to receive £20 yearly from the duties levelled on cloth in East Anglia.[74] Blanche was the daughter of Hugh Waterton, one of the most trusted of all Lancastrian retainers. Hugh had first served John of Gaunt and then had become treasurer to Henry's father in 1377. He had remained in the future king's service for the rest of his life, becoming his chamberlain in 1396 and travelling with him on his crusade to Prussia and his pilgrimage to Jerusalem. In 1393 his daughter Blanche had married Robert Chalons esquire, who had also travelled on the crusade to Prussia. Thus she was by inheritance and by marriage intimately connected with Henry's family. But most of all, she had looked after Henry and his brothers and sisters in the 1390s, when they had been in Hugh Waterton's guardianship.[75]

As Henry is increasingly revealed as a man who desired spiritual blessings and military victory above all else – to reassure him of the justice of his kingship – it is something of a reassurance to find that he had not forgotten those who had looked after him in his youth.

Wednesday 29th

Many of those observing the proceedings of the council of Constance must have wavered in their confidence that the prelates would be able to depose the three popes. Things had changed a lot since the last time three popes had been removed (at the council of Sutri, in 1046). There was a more formal election process, so to set aside the pope necessitated the setting aside of the opinions of a majority of the cardinals. Whole kingdoms and 'national' interests were now represented by each pope, and so each man had his secular following as well as his cardinals and prelates. And yet the council had done enough to continue to inspire confidence. It had shown enough conviction in its dealings with John XXIII; and Gregory XII had maintained his willingness to resign his title, despite John XXIII's machinations and subversions. So the council had managed to weather its difficulties – largely due to the leadership of the emperor, the courage of the radical intellectuals who were prepared to elevate the council above the power of any pope, and the compliance of Gregory XII.

Today was the day that all those who had kept their faith in the council were rewarded. Today was set for the deposition of Pope John XXIII. The sentence had been written, the agreement had been achieved. Now all it required was the performance of the act.

The man selected to read the sentence was the deep-voiced Martin Porée, bishop of Arras, the chief spokesman of John the Fearless. The pope himself was not present, being in custody at Radolfzell.[76] When the emperor was seated, following Mass, the bishop of Ostia signalled for Porée to begin. First he declared that, in the case of a vacancy, the council prohibited anyone taking any steps to fill that vacancy without the assent of the council – a wise precaution. The second decree stipulated that none of the three current popes should ever be re-elected to the papacy. And then came the words of the deposition itself:

In the name of the Holy and Indivisible Trinity, Father, Son and Holy Spirit, amen. The sacrosanct general synod of Constance, lawfully assembled in the Holy Spirit, invoking the name of Christ and keeping God only before its eyes, has noted the articles formulated and presented in the case against the lord pope, John XXIII . . . The clandestine departure of the said pope from this city of Constance and the sacred general council at a suspicious hour of the night, in an unsuitable disguise, was and is unwarrantable – a notorious scandal to the church of God and the council, a disturbing obstacle to the peace and union of the Church, an act to prolong the schism and a violation of the vow sworn by the same pope John to God and the Church and this sacred council. Pope John was and is a notorious simoniac, a notorious waster of the property and rights of the Roman and other churches, and of other pious institutions, and an evil administrator . . . By his detestable and dishonourable life and character he has notoriously scandalised the church of God and Christian people . . . Therefore, for these and other crimes . . . he deserves to be unseated, removed and deposed from the papacy and all administration, spiritual and temporal, as unworthy, unprofitable and dangerous. And the said holy synod hereby unseats, removes and deposes him, declaring all and every Christian of whatever rank, dignity or condition released from obedience, fealty and obligation to him . . .[77]

That was emphatic. It could have been more so – earlier drafts of the sentence had included charges of adultery, incest, and murdering his predecessor.[78] But in the formulation of the final decree it had been decided that the more scandalous charges would bring shame upon the whole Church, and so only those above were read out. They were enough. John XXIII was no longer pope, and no one would ever again address him as one.

About the time of the pope's deposition, John Catterick packed his bags and began the journey back to England. Ostensibly he carried a commission from the council to collect papal revenues, but in reality his main purpose was to relay all that had happened back to the king. He may have carried a copy of the deposition with him; the chronicler Thomas Walsingham included an amended version of it in his *Chronica Maiora*. Walsingham also mentioned that when the news was proclaimed in London, the chest containing the papal revenues in St Paul's Cathedral was unlocked and emptied.[79] The English were only too keen to be rid of John XXIII. Another chronicler, Adam Usk, found out that the pope had originally been charged with crimes far worse than simony and wasting church property. 'Extraordinary to relate,' he began, 'because he [Pope John] was recalcitrant, and because of his former perjuries, homicides, adultery, simony, heresy and other crimes, and because he had twice ignominiously fled in secret in disguise, he was sentenced to perpetual imprisonment'.[80]

Pope John XXIII, the man who had summoned the council, was destined to be locked up in Gottlieben, the castle of the bishop of Constance, where Hus and Jerome were lying in chains.[81]

*

Henry Fitzhugh, acting in his capacity as chamberlain of England, drew up a list of the king's minstrels whose wages were due to be paid on the forthcoming expedition. There were fifteen in total, which sounds like a large number until one remembers that music in the royal household at this time was not simply a matter of sweet harmonies while relaxing with a goblet of wine. Medieval secular music was either 'high music' or 'low music'. 'Low music' was indeed tuneful and created in order to delight the listener. 'High music' on the other hand was loud – horns, sackbuts, clarions and trumpets – not intended to delight so much as to warn, impress or command. With this in mind, it is worth noting that two of the names of these minstrels were 'Tromper' and a third man was Thomas Norreys, *tromper*. Three other men were surnamed Pyper, relating to their profession of playing the English bagpipes.[82] Six of the fifteen at least were retained for making 'high music'. These were the men who were to serve under John Greyndour in France – not to sweeten the sounds of the camp or soothe the king's furrowed brow but to impress ambassadors and organise and inspire the troops in the face of the enemy.

Having already ordered the clergy to be arrayed in the various dioceses, it was now the turn of the county gentry to array the common men. As yet there was no formal militia in England – that would not develop until the sixteenth century. Nevertheless there was a long tradition of ordering the knights and esquires in each county to array men for the defence of the realm. Commissions were sent out today to the gentry in twenty counties.[83] Henry, having experienced the turbulent years of his father's reign, knew that he was opening himself up hugely to attack by taking an army abroad. Whether the threat was the Scots, the Lollards, pro-Richard II supporters, Glendower, or just French or Scottish piracy, he could not afford to leave the safety of the realm to chance. He needed the gentry to have men at their disposal.

The above commissions of array hint at the vulnerability of the kingdom while the king was away. But uppermost in the minds of many men who were planning to travel to France was their own vulnerability. In the medieval period, when fortunes were liable to alter greatly over the course of a year, men generally left the making of wills until they were seriously ill or otherwise anticipated their demise. War overseas forced them to contemplate their own destruction and the fate of their immortal souls, and to make a will and arrangements for their estate before setting out.

The first such arrangements were those of Thomas, earl of Arundel, the treasurer. With estates spreading from Sussex to the Welsh border, it was necessary for him to grant his estates to trustees, with power for them to grant them back to him in the case of his survival, or, in the case of his death, to his wife, Beatrice, and their children. As a tenant in chief of the king, he needed Henry's permission to be able to grant the estates in this way. But as one of the king's closest friends there was no problem gaining such permission; the necessary letters were drawn up today.[84]

Thursday 30th: Corpus Christi

The feast of Corpus Christi, or the Body and Blood of Christ, was an unusual religious celebration in that it did not relate to a saint or an event in Christ's life. In fact it was not even of ancient origin. A thirteenth-century nun, Juliana, had petitioned several bishops for the celebration of the Eucharist; after her death, one of the bishops became pope. When he heard a story of the Eucharist being seen to bleed, he sanctioned her proposal, and issued a papal bull in 1264 proclaiming that the feast of the Body and Blood of Christ should be celebrated throughout Christendom.

In England the most noticeable ceremonies connected with this feast were the plays and processions performed around the country. For the last forty years an increasing number of the principal towns and cities had seen religious plays performed on this date. In some places (York and Coventry, for instance) a whole series of religious plays was staged – ranging from enactments of the building of the Ark to the flight into the Holy Land. Juliana's vision of a holy celebration was sufficiently abstract to allow medieval people to celebrate their faith in whatever way they wanted. In other places (Lynn and Exeter), the Holy Eucharist was paraded around the town in a tabernacle, followed by all the townsfolk.[85]

These celebrations were modestly observed in the royal household. No great feast was held to mark the day; household expenses were only a little more than usual.[86] The main event of the day was rather

Henry's formal instruction to Richard Courtenay, keeper of the king's jewels, to deliver valuables to each of the lords, knights and esquires serving on the forthcoming expedition. The process was for the treasurer to supply a personally signed (not sealed) bill authorising the amount due for the second quarter's service, and for Bishop Courtenay to assign gold and jewels to that value.[87] Those receiving items of treasure had to seal an indenture acknowledging receipt – this somewhat recklessly promised they could keep the gold and jewels if they had not been redeemed by a certain time.

Friday 31st

Henry had as yet experienced no signal failure in his reign – but that did not mean that all was well throughout his realm. Gascony in particular had seen him exercise almost no authority since the truce of February 1414 and the end of Thomas Beaufort's campaign. For many Gascons this was exactly as they wanted things; the less interference from the king of England the better. But for others, especially those who were directly threatened by the advancing French, it was quite the opposite. If they sided with the French, they were prey to attack from the English lords in Gascony. If they stood loyally by Henry, they were liable to be attacked by the French. Each attack cost them dearly in destroyed lives, ruined fabric, robbed churches, violated women, burnt buildings and heavy financial penalties. A light-touch approach was all very well for Henry but it was calamitous for many of his Gascon subjects.

As a result of this situation, some Gascon lords and even some ladies had decided to take matters into their own hands. One such was Jehanne d'Armagnac, the widow of Guillaume Amanieu de Madaillan, lord of Lesparre and Rauzan. Hitherto her husband's family had been loyal to the king of England, being relatively safely situated on the west coast, south of the Gironde; but now Jehanne decided to shift her allegiance. She decided to marry the count of Foix, who had already deserted the English cause, and to arrange the marriage of her daughter with his son. Such an alliance threatened to open up the way for the French to exercise influence in Médoc, close to Bordeaux, the seat of the English administration in Gascony. With French forces pushing in from the north towards the Gironde, and Lesparre to the south threatening to turn French, Henry stood to lose control of the river – and with it access to the region. Seated in his chamber at Westminster, Henry must have felt frustrated. Sir John Tiptoft had been appointed seneschal of Aquitaine, and he had received his instructions for negotiating a new treaty; but he had yet to set sail – and it was a three-week voyage to Gascony. All Henry could do was to order that the lordship of Lesparre be confiscated (which he did today) and hope that no more lords – or indomitable widows – chose to swear loyalty to the French king.[88]

*

Jan Hus's friends, including all the lords who had presented their petition on 13 May, reassembled. There had been a second meeting in the interim, on the 18th, when certain implications of the lies being spread about the state of the Church in Bohemia had been discussed. Now Bohemian and Polish lords replied to accusations made at that hearing and protested against the continued detention of their preacher.

Once more Peter of Mladoňovice spoke up for Hus. In the first of two documents that he read aloud, he argued against certain heretical acts that Hus's enemies had dreamed up to attack him. Again he argued that Hus should not be tarred with the same brush as Wycliffe himself, for, although Hus was a follower of Wycliffe, he himself was not responsible for anything that Wycliffe had written. Peter asserted that Hus had never promoted errors or erroneous beliefs, and he stressed that Hus had worked hard to eradicate errors and misunderstandings. In the second document he referred to the recent hardships of Hus, and the support he enjoyed in Bohemia. As to Hus's own writings, Peter argued that it was obvious that Hus sought only the truth, and never to preach anything heretical or erroneous. Many of the heretical quotations supposedly found in his books were not written by him at all. Peter stressed how much of the ill-fame Hus had suffered was due to personal enemies spreading lies about him and declaring he had uttered heresies that had nothing to do with him. But the situation could yet be redeemed. All that was necessary now was for Hus to 'be fairly heard by learned men and masters of sacred scripture . . . in regard to each and every article laid to his charge, in order that he may explain his intention and meaning'.[89]

> May it therefore please your most reverend paternities to free the said Master Jan Hus, neither convicted nor condemned, from the chains and shackles in which he is now cruelly detained, and to place him in the hands of some reverend lord bishops . . . in order that he, Master Jan Hus, may regain his strength and thus may be more carefully and readily examined . . . The lords and nobles of Bohemia offer to give a guarantee . . . until his process and trial has been settled.[90]

It was a powerful, passionate performance. Both documents were carefully copied and submitted to the deputies of the nations and also sent to Sigismund. Two other documents were submitted at the same time. The first was a record of the public testimony of the bishop of Nezero, the head of the inquisition into heresy in the city of Prague, stating that, after many conversations with Hus, he had discerned no heresy in him. The second was a letter of support from the lords of Moravia.

The patriarch of Antioch, a French theologian called Dr Jean Maroux, replied: 'Whether his [Hus's] protest proves to be valid will become evident in the course of the trial'. As for the false abstractions from Hus's works and accusations made by his enemies, Dr Maroux declared that their veracity would be reflected in the final sentence on Hus. Concerning the main tenor of the petition, Dr Maroux said that the deputies of the nations 'were willing to grant him a favourable public hearing' and that 'they were willing to deal kindly with him'. The trial would take place on 5 June.

There was just one fly in the ointment. Dr Maroux stated that Hus could not possibly be released from prison, regardless of the number of lords standing guarantee for him, 'for under no circumstances is he to be trusted'. However 'kindly' and 'favourably' the deputies might treat him at his forthcoming trial, there was no avoiding the fact that, in their minds, he was guilty.

June

Saturday 1st

Ever since the meeting of the lords during the great council of 15–18 April, Henry had known that royal jewels, treasures and precious artefacts would have to be pawned out. But for Richard Courtenay, the prospect of handing out the mass of precious items in the Jewel Tower of the Palace of Westminster must have been daunting. Here were golden collars, brooches, plain coronets, crowns dripping with rubies and diamonds, and swords with gilt handles. Here was the sword garnished with ostrich feathers, which Henry had used in Wales. Here too were helmets with golden circlets, jewel-encrusted belts, rings with precious stones, gold and silver spurs, gold and silver collars for hawks and hounds, gilt-silver candlesticks, golden dishes for spices and salt, gold plates, gold bowls for hawks, gold aquamaniles (water jugs), ewers and basins, and enamelled gilt-silver cups and goblets. Even if Courtenay was familiar with the sight of it all, never before could he have faced the prospect of giving it all away. It would be a difficult task to make sure everything was redeemed within two years.

Here and there among the chests of gold and silver were some real treasures – priceless items that would be a heavy responsibility to pass over to a creditor. The Iklington Collar was a heavy gold collar worn by Henry when he had been prince of Wales, 'garnished with four rubies, four great sapphires, thirty-two great pearls and fifty-three lesser pearls'. Courtenay reckoned it was worth about £300. Even more valuable, at £458 13s 4d, was a pair of large gold basins, each weighing 14lbs 4oz, chased in a rose pattern and enamelled with the arms of St George in the centre, and around the rims with the arms of St Edward, St Edmund, the emperor, England and France, the principality of Wales and the duchy of Guienne. The Tigre was another great treasure: an alms dish of gold, shaped like a ship carried by a bear, garnished with nineteen balas rubies, twenty-six pearls, weighing more than 22lbs. Courtenay placed a value of £332 on that. There was another great ship: a warship made of gilt-silver, with castles at the prow and the stern and the figures of twelve men-at-arms fighting on the deck. Its value was £156 12s. And then there was the Pallet of Spain: a helmet with a crown attached, garnished with thirty-five balas rubies, four sapphires, fifteen large emeralds, three hundred small emeralds, and three hundred small pearls, the crown alone weighing 8lbs 6oz.[1]

All these named and exquisite treasures paled into insignificance when compared with the Pusan d'Or. It lay in a leather case. Open that case and you would have seen, in the dimness of the Jewel Tower, a great gold collar worked with antelopes and set with dozens of precious stones. It was worth ten times as much as any of the above items. And Courtenay was going to give it away.

The bishop must have looked at the thousands of precious items and mentally allocated the most valuable and important ones. The Iklington Collar would be suitable security for a large loan expected from the prior of St Mary's Coventry and the mayor and corporation of the town. The Pallet of Spain would be suitable return for a large loan from John Hende, one of the richest London merchants; or perhaps an earl.[2] The basins similarly would be good collateral against a large loan. The Tigre would suffice as security for the wages due to be paid to his men by the duke of York. And the gilt-silver ship would suffice for the wages of the earl of Salisbury's soldiers. As for the Pusan d'Or, it could really only go to the mayor and aldermen of London – in return for the loan of 10,000 marks that the royal embassy had requested at the Guildhall on 14 March.

Then there were the crowns, and most of all the great crown: the Crown Henry. This was the crown of the Lancastrian kings, worn by Henry IV and probably made for him. It was made predominantly of gold. Rising from its circlet it had a series of gold fleurs-de-lys interspersed with pinnacles of jewels. The fleurs-de-lys were each garnished with a ruby, a balas ruby, three great sapphires and ten great pearls. Each pinnacle was garnished with two sapphires, one square balas ruby, and six pearls. But whatever the intrinsic value of its gold and jewels, it was worth far more than the total of the gold and jewels. It was the great crown of England, and the *Lancastrian* crown at that; it had huge symbolic value. It could not be given to just anyone, however rich, not even for a loan of £10,000. When Edward III had first pawned the great crowns of England he had placed them with Italian bankers; but this was not something that Henry needed or wanted to do. It would have been politically unwise. There was only one person to whom it could realistically be entrusted: the man who was in line to inherit it – Thomas, duke of Clarence. Having contracted to serve Henry with 240 men-at-arms and 720 archers, thereby taking on the burden of a monthly wage bill of £1,000, it would be necessary to find something magnificent for such a lord. It would suffice to pay the wages of his troops.

The treasures mentioned above were all of a secular nature. What is most surprising about Henry's allocation of treasure is that he ordered many religious artefacts – his reliquaries, crosses, tabernacles and altar tablets – also to be pawned. These too were given out as collateral for the payment of soldiers' wages. The royal chapels at Windsor Castle were inventoried, and any valuables that could be spared were removed. Censers, chalices, coffers, lecterns, holy water stoups, ampulae, crucifixes and reliquaries – the whole range of chapel fittings and accoutrements was taken away, valued and allocated. Even the relics themselves were mortgaged: a piece of the Holy Tunic and a piece of the True Cross were marked down to be pawned. So were relics of St Christopher, St Chad and St Thomas Becket, and the head of one of the 11,000 Virgins (women supposedly martyred in Roman times). Painted icons of the Virgin, the Trinity, St Thomas, St Edward the Confessor, St Michael, St Catherine, St John and St George were similarly identified. Everything was listed by Edmund Lacy, dean of the royal chapel at Windsor and handed over today to Bishop Courtenay, to serve as a down payment for the soldiers sent to France.[3]

This mixing of secular and religious treasures, and the use of saints' relics as military collateral, requires some explanation. If Henry was so fanatically religious, how did he justify the distribution of holy relics to pay for a war of aggression? On the face of it, Henry was employing religious artefacts for purely secular ends. But as we have seen, there is an explanation: he really did see the forthcoming expedition in religious terms. The letter he had sent to the king of France on 15 April made clear how he saw the unification of England and France as a religious duty. His quotation, 'he will turn where He wills', from the *Codex Justinianus* also points to his belief that his will was God's will, so that it was his religious duty to invade France. Whether it was God's will that he should be victorious remained to be seen; but because Henry believed his determination to fight was divinely inspired, this was a religious conflict. Henry was simply acting as God's instrument, as if he had no free will of his own. Hence it was wholly justifiable for him to call for the clergy to be arrayed to defend the realm, regardless of whether they were regular or secular, or had been granted an exemption from military service. Similarly it was wholly justifiable for him to requisition the Church's property and pawn it to pay his soldiers' wages. In his eyes, he and they were simply doing God's work.

Courtenay did not disperse everything straight away. The Crown Henry remained where it was for the time being. So did the Iklington Collar, the gold basins, the Pusan d'Or and everything else except the £800 tabernacle of the duke of Burgundy, which had already been sent to Devon. But on this day, the same day as he took possession of the relics and other valuable religious artefacts, Courtenay began to allocate everything, in line with his royal commission.[4] No doubt some lords were very keen to know what exactly they were going to be given – whether a jewel-encrusted belt or the skull of one of the 11,000 Virgins.

Sunday 2nd

Henry commissioned one Hankyn Pytman to employ mariners and prepare his ship called the *Rude Cog of the Tower* ready for action.[5] That the 'red cog' in question was normally harboured at the Tower suggests it was English – despite the German name of the captain. Few foreign merchants would have brought their ships to England at this stage for fear of them being requisitioned by the king. Considering that ships in English ports were unable to leave, in line with Henry's instructions of 19 March and 11 April, international trade must have now gone into a serious decline.

Monday 3rd

When Henry V had become king, he had dismissed almost all of the senior officers in the royal household. On 21 March 1413, the first day of his reign, he had sacked the old chancellor and treasurer and appointed Henry Beaufort and the earl of Arundel in their places. Two days later he had replaced his father's steward and keeper of the wardrobe with, respectively, Sir Thomas Erpingham and Sir Thomas More. Within two weeks he had removed the chamberlain and the chancellor of the duchy of Lancaster, appointing Lord Fitzhugh and John Woodhouse in their respective places. Only one senior officer had remained in post throughout: the keeper of the privy seal. This was John Prophet, who had been appointed by Henry IV in 1406. Now Prophet's time was up. In his place Henry appointed John Wakeryng, a man who had a long track record in government administration, having been appointed chancellor of the duchy of Lancaster in 1402 and later keeper of the rolls in chancery. Apart from replacing Thomas More with Sir Roger Leche as treasurer of the royal household in late 1413, this was the first significant change to the senior ranks of the household since the start of the reign.

Other royal business today included Henry's order for his secretary, John Stone, to be inducted as the dean of St Michael's le Grand, and a royal pardon to the bishop of Hereford for all his crimes 'except murders committed after 19 November, provided he be not a counterfeiter of money'.[6] Already twice this year Henry had ordered commissions into the counterfeiting of coin; clearly it was a major concern.[7]

Henry assigned three Dorset manors, Christchurch, Canford and Poole, as places where the earl of Salisbury's men were to assemble and wait, ready for the expedition to set sail. This was not just for their convenience. A story appears in one of Thomas Walsingham's chronicles about Sir John Arundel in 1379. He and his men were planning to sail from Southampton to Gascony, and took shelter in a nunnery because the wind and the tide were against them. In their boredom, the men became drunk and violent; they raped the nuns and stole from the nunnery and a local church.[8] Henry, by locating his troops in specific places, was not only providing for his soldiers but was also minimising the threat to communities of a large number of nervous, armed men being located on their doorstep.[9]

*

In Paris, the dauphin called a meeting of the royal council, to assemble in his father's presence. The royal dukes were all away from the capital. Those who attended included Charles d'Albret; Louis, count of Vendôme; Jean de Werchin, seneschal of Hainault; Raoul de Gaucourt; and Nicholas d'Estouteville, seigneur de Torcy. The business to be discussed was the threat of invasion. A letter was drafted from the council to the constables of the cities and towns in Normandy, ordering them to instruct the nobility and gentry to make ready to resist the English and to ensure they had sufficient armour and equipment, and to keep watch day and night, and to ensure that the walls of towns were repaired.[10]

This was not the only council meeting that the dauphin had held. Monstrelet records that the dauphin

> held many councils and recalled the duke of Berry and other lords to Paris, with whom he had several meetings to know how he should act in this matter, for the king was confined by his illness at this time. It was determined that men-at-arms and archers should be assembled in various parts of France ready to march against the English the moment it was known that they had landed; that garrisons should be placed in every town and castle on the coast; and that as much money as possible should be raised with all speed.[11]

As yet the duke of Berry had not yet returned. While the dauphin waited for him, he said goodbye to another of his councillors. The count of Vendôme was setting out immediately for England with the other ambassadors to whom Henry had granted safe conducts. Archbishop Boisratier and the others had gone on ahead.[12] They were travelling slowly, via Amiens, Montreuil, Boulogne and Calais, taking a full two weeks on their journey to Dover.[13] The longer they delayed, the more money and men the dauphin could raise – and the more King Henry's time would be wasted.

Tuesday 4th

Henry commissioned Nicholas Mynot, fletcher, to find twelve more craftsmen to make arrows and bolts, taking whatever timber, feathers, silk and wax they needed for the work.[14] Although we have come across many references in 1415 to Henry ordering and paying for bows to be made, this is the first explicit reference to him ordering arrows. This is somewhat surprising, given that modern commentators on longbows frequently talk about archers being able to shoot ten or more arrows per minute. Were all the arrows used by Henry on his expedition made by these twelve men?

The fletchers in question would have had to obtain the ash rods, make sure they were not rotten, then cut them, shape them, and smooth them, making sure the shafts were not bent. They would then have needed to trim each shaft to fit inside the socket of its arrowhead, and fix the arrowhead in place with bone glue. They would have needed to trim the shaft to length to suit a standard bow, and give it a nock, and strengthen this nock with a piece of bone. It would then have had to be flighted with goose feathers, and these had to be glued into place and bound tightly with silk. The finished arrow then needed to be laid aside long enough for the glue to set. Apart from this last element, the whole process cannot have taken less than half an hour for each arrow. If you consider that it would also take an experienced blacksmith twenty minutes to make each arrowhead, then every sheaf of twenty-four arrows represented twenty man-hours' work (not including making the quiver). If Henry was intending to take seven or eight thousand archers with him on his expedition, he would have understood he needed in the region of 130,000 such sheaves – the equivalent of 2,600,000 man-hours' work.[15] Fletching this number of arrows would have taken Nicholas Mynot and his twelve companions more than forty years.[16] Henry's arrows were not all made by twelve men in the two months before the expedition set sail.

So where did they come from? Henry already had a large store. He kept thousands of bows at the Tower, and no doubt he kept thousands of arrows there too. And the Tower arsenal represented just a fraction of the number of arrows available in England. Edward III's archery ordinances of 1363, which required men to practice archery every feast day, and to abstain from other sports and games, had two consequences – that archery skills were kept up, and that arrows and bows continued to be produced in large quantities in peacetime as well as war.[17] Further legislation in the 1360s made it illegal to export these bows and arrows. On top of this, Glendower's rebellion had required many more new arrows to be produced, and to a higher standard than before. An Act of 1406 stated that henceforth 'all the heads for arrows and quarrels shall be well-boiled or brased, and hardened at the points with steel'.[18]

From this it can be seen that the majority of Henry's arrows were not newly made. Old arrow-heads could be re-used many times over, the damaged shafts thrown away and new ones added when necessary. Hence this was probably the prime purpose of commissioning the fletchers mentioned above: the renovation of old arrows. The bulk of Henry's arrows were made on a continuous basis throughout the realm; and probably most of them by 1415 were of the new steel-point type, capable of penetrating armour.

This was not the case in France, where archers were somewhat looked down upon. One of the most common questions asked about the English victories of the Hundred Years War is this: if the longbow was such a significant weapon, why did the French not develop it too? The answer is implicit in the entry above. No other country had such a strong archery tradition – and this applies to the making of bows, the making of arrows, the renewal of old arrows, the legal requirement to practice archery, and a pro-archery popular culture (as reflected in the earliest Robin Hood ballads). And since the real devastation was caused by the *massed* use of longbows, no other country quite managed to create the killing assemblies that Edward III pioneered. Even though most of the bows were made of Spanish yew, the Castillians never developed a great archery tradition. It was an English idiosyncrasy, arising from the breakdown of law and order in England in the last years of the reign of Edward I and the reign of Edward II. Charles V of France had tried in vain to build up the French longbow and crossbow forces in the 1360s and 1370s; French people saw no reason at that time why they should become archers, nor why they should make so many bows and arrows. And kings of France could not command the men of the autonomous duchies of Burgundy and Brittany to practise archery. The kings of England *could* command their subjects, and they did. And when they required three million arrows for a campaign, they did not have to wait for them to be made: they simply ordered them to be gathered.[19]

Wednesday 5th

The prelates of the council of Constance gathered in the refectory of the Franciscan friary, preparing for the trial of Jan Hus. Hus himself was not present, still locked in his cell. The prelates ordered the public reading in his absence of the articles of his work that had been found to be heretical. As the heresies were declaimed, the Bohemian and Polish lords in attendance realised that the prelates were still accusing Hus of statements that were not actually made by him, or, if they were, they were being quoted out of context to give them an inflammatory and heretical meaning. They hurriedly sent a message to the emperor to tell him that Hus was being condemned without a fair trial – even though the prelates of the council had promised to deal with him 'favourably' and 'kindly'.[20]

As two of the lords ran to Sigismund, the condemnation was read out, quoting from Psalm 50.

> To the sinner then God said: why do you expound my justice? Why do you take my covenant into your mouth? You indeed hate discipline and have cast my words behind you. If you saw a thief, you ran with him; and with adulterers you took your portion. Your mouth abounded in malice and your tongue concocted deceit . . .

The emperor listened to Hus's supporters. He gave curt instructions to two important German lords to go directly to the Franciscan house and inform the prelates gathered there that they should not pass a verdict on Hus without hearing him in person. If Hus stood by his books, and if they were found to contain heretical articles, and if he refused to abjure them, *then* they could condemn him. But not before.

The two lords entered the refectory and passed on the emperor's message. The prelates were not in a position to argue. Had Sigismund wished to enforce the safe conduct he had granted Hus, he could have removed the prisoner from their power. So, reluctantly, they complied.

They directed Hus's friends to choose the books on which Hus was to be judged. Lord John of Chlum and the others chose four to be submitted for inspection, including his principal work, *About the Church*. And Hus himself was sent for.

When Hus entered the refectory, his friends tried to follow him but they were barred. Hus stood alone before the prelates. He was asked whether the books they were examining were his. He looked at them, and held them up, and declared them loudly to be his works, and if anyone found error in them he was prepared to amend them accordingly.

This was his moment of truth, the hearing for which he had risked everything.

One of the prelates started reading the articles on which Hus had been condemned, concentrating on specific heresies such as whether transubstantiation actually took place or whether the bread of the Holy Sacrament remained mere bread. Hus tried to speak but he was told to remain silent. When he again tried to speak to clarify that a clause had been misquoted, a great many prelates told him to be quiet, and started denouncing him. Hus cannot have failed to realise that there was real anger in the refectory. These men were doing all they could to unite the Church after its disgraceful leadership failure under three failed popes. The Church needed a strong single authority, which would speak to all Christian men on behalf of God. They believed that God would direct them to find that single new unifying voice – and here was this lone Bohemian priest trying to preach a gospel of spiritual anarchy and chaos. Of course they were angry.

Hus did his best to defend himself, but his attackers were not looking to debate with him. Nor did they wish him to amend his ways. They wanted to condemn him, and force him to admit he was wrong. Enemies like Michael de Causis were calling with the rest of the prelates for Hus's books to be burned. When Hus tried to explain some of the finer doctrinal points underpinning his books, he was shouted down. When he tried to respond to a difficult question with a difficult answer he was told, 'Leave off your sophistry. Answer yes or no!' He began to realise that no one was listening to his arguments. He had been a fool to believe that the council would. So he decided to be silent. Some of his more ardent opponents jeered at him further: 'Look – he cannot answer! He admits these errors!'

The meeting came to an end. Clearly, given the sensitivity of his case with regard to his lords and the apparent support of the emperor, the prelates could not condemn him straight away. Instead they adjourned his case until the following Friday. The bishop of Riga was instructed to return Hus to his cell.

As Hus left the refectory, and passed the lords gathered outside the door, he reached out to them, saying, 'Do not worry for me.'

'We do not fear,' they replied, grasping his hand as he was led away. 'I know, I know well,' he told them.

The bishop and his guards led him up some steps. At the top he turned and saluted his friends before being walked back to his cell.

That night he wrote to the lords who had helped him that day. In this respect he was better off than he had been in Gottlieben Castle, where he had been from 30 March to 2 June, and from which he had been unable to send any messages at all.[21] He did his best to be optimistic:

> Almighty God today gave me a courageous and stout heart. Two articles are already deleted. I hope however that by the grace of God more will be struck out. Almost all of them shouted at me like the Jews did to Jesus. So far they have not come to the principal point – namely that I should confess that all the articles are contained in my works . . . The presidents said that I should have another public hearing. They do not wish to hear arguments about the Church.[22]

*

Henry's most important business today was issuing the warrant for Master Philip Morgan to go to Calais and liaise with Sir William Lisle, acting lieutenant of the town, to prorogue the truce with France.

Much to Henry's annoyance, his attempt to hurry the French diplomats by extending the truce only to 8 June had failed. They had disobeyed him, taking their time when he had urged them to hurry. Henry did not like to be disobeyed in this manner, but he had no choice. He could not be seen to be refusing peace initiatives. Morgan and Lisle were thus empowered to extend the truce for as long as they deemed necessary. It took five days for the warrant to reach Calais – presumably carried by Philip Morgan – and they extended the peace to 15 July, probably as a result of verbal instructions given to Morgan today.[23]

All the time Henry was putting back the departure date for the expedition. First it had been 8 May, then 24 June, then 1 July, and now it was possibly as late as 15 July. Surely he could now expect the ambassadors to hurry up and arrive?

The rest of Henry's business was a series of grants and petitions. The people of Winchelsea were given authority to reduce the size of their town. Edward I had refounded it on a new site in 1288 – just as the old site slipped beneath the waves of the Sussex coast – and had made sure it was laid out on a grid pattern. More recently the French and Castillians had attacked the town and damaged it; so in 1414 a programme of strengthening the defences had begun. Now, however, the area being enclosed within the defences seemed too large: could the townspeople please enclose a smaller area? Henry, 'liking such places to be strengthened,' and considering the important position this port occupied on the south coast, granted their request.[24]

Henry granted to Master Richard Dereham, archdeacon of Norfolk, the wardenship of King's Hall, Cambridge, with his fees and gowns to be paid for by the sheriff of the county.[25] Also today he ordered that the people of Northampton be granted a tally acknowledging that they had lent the king £66. He appointed John Hayne to be chief ranger in the forest of Wolmere and Aliceholt, Hants, and granted his servant John Green, keeper of the king's beds, one third of the tolls for crossing the Tweed.[26]

Last but by no means least there was a grant of £20 to his old nurse, Joanna Waring or Waryn, the woman who had suckled him in infancy.[27] Along with the gift to Blanche Chalons (on 28 May), it is one of the very few signs of intimacy in 1415 between Henry and female companions. It is interesting that both women's relationship with Henry was that of looking after him in his youth.

Thursday 6th

Henry's preparations for the forthcoming campaign had to meet a wide variety of challenges. For example, he was taking cannon to attack

Harfleur, with the intention of effecting an entry by smashing the walls down. Although it was to be expected that the townsmen would quickly surrender when they realised they were facing large cannon, it was probable that there would be some damage. Therefore, presuming he was successful in taking the town, he would need to rebuild the walls again very quickly, to make them defensible and capable of with-standing a reprisal siege. Likewise he was bound to come across bridges that had been destroyed. He would need craftsmen by the dozen. For this reason he ordered Simon Lewis and John Benet to 'arrest' (the usual word for requisitioning workmen) one hundred masons for the forthcoming expedition. He also commissioned Thomas Mathews and William Gill, to 'arrest' 120 more carpenters; and William Marsh and Nicholas Shockington were commissioned to take on forty more black-smiths. All these men were to come from the city of London and the home counties (Sussex, Surrey, Kent, Essex, Hertfordshire, Buckinghamshire and Middlesex), and they were all to assemble in London on 17 June. There was not much time. John Southmead was ordered to find an extra sixty carts and bring them to the city by that date, to transport everything necessary down to Southampton.[28]

Friday 7th

This morning at 7.12 a.m. there was a near-total eclipse of the sun. The fact is known from contemporary chronicles as well as modern astronomical calculations. At Constance, Peter of Mladoňovice noted the second day of the trial of Hus as taking place 'about an hour after the almost total eclipse of the sun'.[29]

The atmosphere was even graver than before. The Franciscan friary was surrounded by armed guards – men of the city armed with swords, crossbows, axes and spears. The emperor himself came, bringing with him Lord Wenceslas of Dubá and Lord John of Chlum. All the prelates were in attendance.

The prosecution took a new direction, concentrating on Hus's affinity with Wycliffe. Many of Wycliffe's teachings had clearly inspired Hus – such as there being a single universal Church whose head was Christ, the limited authority of the pope, and the necessity for the Church to return to its poor and humble roots. But these had all been declared heretical. It therefore followed that if Hus could be shown to have preached the same things, he too was guilty of heresy. Hus's Bohemian enemies now swore that he had preached Wycliffe's heresies openly in Prague in 1410, and they specifically accused him of teaching that the bread and the wine of the host remained bread and wine even after its consecration.

Hus denied the accusations vehemently, but first Cardinal d'Ailly interrogated him on the subject and then a whole succession of English theologians did so. The third of the Englishmen to rise and speak was Master William Corfe, who had been appointed by the English nation to deal with Hus's case. 'Look!' declared Corfe, 'He is speaking evasively, just as Wycliffe did, for he too conceded all the things that this man concedes and yet held that the material bread remains on the altar after consecration.' Then one of Henry V's own representatives at the council, John Stokes, took up the accusations. 'I saw in Prague a certain treatise ascribed to this Hus in which it was expressly stated that the material bread remains in the sacrament after consecration.' It was as if the English felt they had a monopoly on assigning Wycliffe's guilt where they wanted, using their nationality as a qualification for the right to lay accusations of heresy.

Hus's dilemma was that Wycliffe *was* the foundation of his questioning of the Church. He could not simply shift the blame onto his teacher's shoulders; Wycliffe had not forced him to follow his teachings. Although he might answer the English theologians, and even prove them wrong, he had been condemned as soon as Wycliffe had been condemned. The argument grew more and more bitter. He was challenged as to why he had not condemned the heretical articles in Wycliffe's writing himself – he answered that he had refused to do so on the grounds of conscience. The bishop of Salisbury attacked him over the question of whether the payment of tithes could be refused. Other Englishmen poured scorn on him for his claim that a miracle had prevented Wycliffe from being tried in St Paul's Cathedral. The longer the inquisition went on, the more farcical the trial became. Eventually, under tremendous pressure, Hus declared, 'I do not know where Wycliffe's soul has gone; I hope that he is saved but fear lest he be damned. Nevertheless I desire and hope that my soul were where the soul of John Wycliffe is!' At this apparent confession to suffer the same fate as a condemned heretic, there was general laughter.

Hus had no hope of escape. Eventually Sigismund intervened and gave a speech that went to the heart of the matter.

Listen, Jan Hus! Some have said that I gave you the safe conduct fifteen days after your arrest. I say, however, that that is not true ... I gave you the safe conduct even before you had left Prague. I commanded Lords Wenceslas of Dubá and John of Chlum that they bring you and guard you in order that, having freely come to Constance, you would not be constrained but be given a public hearing so that you could answer, concerning your faith. The council has given you a public, peaceable and honest hearing here. And I thank them, although some may say that I could not grant a safe conduct to a heretic or one suspected of heresy ... I counsel you to hold nothing obstinately but, in those things that were here proved against you and that you confessed, to offer yourself wholly to the mercy of the council; and they ... will grant you some mercy, and you will do penance for your guilt. But if you wish to hold all that obstinately, then they know well what they must do with you. I told them that I am not willing to defend any heretic; indeed, if a man should remain obstinate in his heresy, I would kindle the fire and burn him myself. But I would advise you to throw yourself wholly on the mercy of the council, and the sooner the better, in case you involve yourself in greater errors.

The formal charges were then read out against Hus, and he was led away by the bishop of Riga, back to his cell.

*

At Westminster the king's clerks began drawing up the rest of the warrants to pay the companies of men-at-arms and archers. It took them another nine days to complete the task. Henry commissioned two men to find appropriate manors near Plymouth for the safe harbourage of Sir John Tiptoft and his men making their way to Gascony.[30] He also made a grant to the bailiffs of Sudbury who had lent 40 marks towards his voyage.[31] It was a modest acknowledgement. A far greater one came from John Hende, the richest London merchant of the day, who handed to the treasurer 2,000 marks (£1,333 6s 8d).[32]

Saturday 8th

This morning, at about eight o'clock, the bishops of Carcassonne and Evreux were about to set out through the forest on the border between Lorraine and Bar in France. They were on their way from Constance to Paris, their mission being to arrange for the emperor to travel through France later in the summer. Sigismund hoped to meet with King Ferdinand of Aragon to arrange the deposition or resignation of Pope Benedict XIII. He also hoped to meet with the French and English kings to persuade them to come to terms peaceably.

Eighteen men of their company had already gone ahead, to arrange accommodation for the large households of the bishops for the next night. Among them was Master Benedict Gentien: a theologian from the University of Paris. Suddenly 'ten men with drawn swords rushed out at us from the forest behind us, and beating and wounding us, forcibly dragged us to the castle of Souci, where they promptly stripped us of money, horses and clothing'. One of the priests in the company suffered a head wound but otherwise everyone was unharmed. That was not the end of the matter, however, for these were not merely thieving brigands. They wanted the bishops who were following. Later that day, about three o'clock in the afternoon, they found the main group and attacked them too, killing a priest. The two bishops were forced to ride to Souci, arriving there about three hours after midnight.

The culprit was one Henri de la Tour. When the bishops demanded to know why he had taken them prisoner, he told them who had ordered it: Charles de Deuil, lord of Removille. And why? As representatives of the king of France attending the council of Constance, they had often spoken against the honour of John the Fearless, duke of Burgundy. Now they were to pay the penalty.

*

Henry's navy was beginning to take shape. Two dozen royal ships were on their way to Southampton. Most of the English merchant fleet was heading similarly to one of the three designated ports. Benedict Espina, an agent of the Jurade of Bordeaux, wrote from London to the mayor of Bordeaux today, stating that Henry was planning to write himself asking for two siege engines called *brides* to be sent to him (the letter in question was indeed sent a few days later). Espina added that in England cannon and brides were being loaded every day, and twenty-two thousand mariners had already been employed to assist with the crossing.[33] Seven hundred ships were expected to arrive shortly from Holland. 'It is also said that the son of the king of Portugal is coming with a large company of galleys and men.' How many ships were really being prepared in Holland is open to question, for a report from Bruges stated that 125 cogs had been collected for Henry's navy, plus 181 other vessels.[34] But these three hundred may have been just the start of a larger flotilla. In addition, Henry could rely on the Cinque Ports to send out their core fleet of fifty-seven vessels; more ships would come from other ports.

From the point of view of the French, the situation looked even worse, for it was rumoured there too that Henry's ally, King João of Portugal and his three sons (Henry's first cousins) had gathered 225 ships in Lisbon and Oporto, and were intending to help the English. The Portuguese were as keen to conceal their intended destination as the English were to conceal theirs; it was to their advantage if the Moors believed that they were sailing to join the king of England. But the French could only have blanched at the thought.

Henry himself gave instructions to Richard Beauchamp, earl of Warwick and captain of Calais, to proclaim that all the hired soldiers then in the town of Calais should remain there for the time being at the king's expense, not leaving except with special permission.[35] Calais was to prove of critical importance to his plan – it was his one safe harbour in Northern France.

To help the royal finances, Henry's uncle Henry Beaufort made the largest personal loan of the year, depositing 2,945 marks (£1,963 6s 8d) with the treasurer. It is not recorded what security he asked for in return, if any.[36]

*

Jan Hus was forced to stand before the prelates of Constance in the refectory of the Franciscan friary for the third and final time. Now there were no personal attacks on his views about transubstantiation. Nor was there discussion of whether he had said heretical things – a list of thirty-nine errors had been abstracted from his works. The only question now was whether he would repent and recant.

Of the thirty-nine articles read today, twenty-six were from his book *About the Church*. It is not difficult to see why members of the council were so perturbed. The first offending article echoed Wycliffe's concept of one universal Church to which only those predestined for salvation had membership. This did not necessarily include the pope or the cardinals. The fifth read 'no position of dignity, or human election, or any outward sign makes one a member of the Holy Catholic Church'. As all the cardinals, archbishops, bishops and abbots there had all been in some way raised by 'human election' this was insulting. That Hus had said this in the context of Judas not being a member of the Church did not make any difference; he had dared to cast aspersions on their religious status. The ninth article insisted that St Peter was not and never had been the head of the Church – with the implication that the pope, as St Peter's successor, was not head of the Church either. Hus, of course, insisted that Christ was always the head of the Church. The tenth article stated that if the pope followed the Devil, then he was not the vicar of Christ but the vicar of the Devil. The twelfth stated that the pope took his pre-eminence from the power of the Roman emperors, and the thirteenth and fourteenth questioned whether popes had any right to be called head of the Church. As appointing a new head of the Church was one of the council's main tasks, Hus could expect no flexibility or tolerance on these issues. The seventeenth article extended these questions about the holiness of office holders to the cardinals themselves, stating they were not the successors of Christ's disciples unless they lived after the manner of the apostles. The nineteenth article exhorted secular lords to compel priests to live saintly lives. The twentieth – arguably the most threatening – seemed to equate all ecclesiastical authority with the power of men, stripping it of spiritual justification altogether. The twenty-third stated that priests living in accordance with Christ's laws, with a knowledge of scripture and a desire to edify the people, should continue to preach even if they be excommunicated. The twenty-sixth argued that no interdict could be brought upon a kingdom or nation by any authority, as Christ had never done such a thing.[37]

No one wanted to argue the merits of any of these statements; they were far more safely treated with contempt. So was their author.

The prelates did not ask Hus any questions but took the opportunity to express their anger. The subject shifted rapidly from things he had written to the thing he was, a heretic, and whether he would change. Would he abjure the articles laid against him? How could he abjure them, he said, when many of them had been quoted out of context? To abjure was to renounce a formerly held error. But he did not acknowledge that any error had been proved against him.

Once again it was the emperor who brought the meeting to its decisive point.

> Listen Jan Hus! As I told you yesterday, I still say to you and cannot keep repeating to you; you are old enough; you could well understand if you wished. You have now heard that the lords here have proposed two ways forward: either you surrender yourself in all things to the grace of the council, and the sooner the better, and revoke all the errors in your books . . . Or, if you wish to defend them stubbornly, the council will surely proceed against you according to its laws.

Once again Hus insisted he had come freely to the council to be instructed in any error. And once again he was accused of being stubborn, and speaking captiously, and refusing to accept the authority of the council. It could not go on. The shadow of heresy increasingly darkened the refectory; there was no more mocking, no more laughter. The prelates increasingly fell silent as they realised what the outcome of the trial would be.

Hus was once more led away by the bishop of Riga. As he walked past the armed guards, Lord John of Chlum stepped forward to grasp Hus's hand, consoling him. As Peter of Mladoňovice noted, 'Hus was very glad that Lord John was not ashamed and did not hesitate to greet him – already rejected, despised and regarded as a heretic by almost all'.[38]

The last word fell to the emperor. Sigismund delivered a devastating speech that, although it was spoken in Constance, would be heard across Christendom.

> Most reverend fathers! You have heard that just one of the many things that are in Hus's books, and which he has confessed to writing and which have been proved against him, would be sufficient to condemn

him. Therefore if he will not recant his errors and abjure, and teach the contrary, let him be burned, or deal with him according to your laws . . . And send these articles here condemned to my brother in Bohemia and alas! to Poland and to other lands where he already has his secret disciples and his many supporters, and say that any people who hold these beliefs will be punished by the bishops and prelates in those lands, and so uproot the branches as well as the root. And let the council write to kings and princes that they show favour to their prelates who in this sacred council have diligently laboured to extirpate these heretics . . . Also make an end of others of his secret disciples and supporters . . . and especially with him, him – Jerome![39]

Sunday 9th

In Souci castle, Henri de la Tour was confronted with the safe conducts his prisoners had been carrying. They had been granted by the king of France. De la Tour also heard today that the duke of Bar was furious at the treatment of the bishops, and was determined to hang the perpetrators and level the castle where they were being held. De la Tour accordingly separated out the wealthiest of his captives and took them with him, leaving the majority of poorer men there with his wife, who was ill with puerperal fever. Benedict Gentien and twenty of his companions were 'thrust into a dungeon, horribly deep and small, with little light and bad air, filthy and foul'. As he commented, 'Two men could scarcely stay alive there for two days – what then of twenty? I was lashed with a rope whip like a thief.'[40]

*

Another hostage situation was developing, in the north of England. For the last two weeks Mordach Stewart, earl of Fife, had been travelling in the company of his custodians, John Hull and William Chancellor. Their detailed instructions had been to deliver their prisoner to the sheriff of Newcastle, and then to ride on to Berwick to arrange the actual handover with Henry Percy. But today as they passed Kippax, near Leeds in West Yorkshire, they were set upon by

Henry Talbot of Easington-in-Craven.[41] Henry Talbot was a kinsman of Sir Thomas Talbot, an outlawed Lollard knight – and a determined opponent of Henry V.

What was the purpose of this? It is difficult to be absolutely certain because the only direct evidence we have is later and comes from men on trial for their lives. Certainly Mordach was not kidnapped at Kippax for his own benefit – this was not a Scottish rescue. Given Talbot's connections, it is possible that disaffected supporters of Wycliffe were willing to play their part in disrupting Henry's plans to invade France. But there were other disaffected men in England who wanted to see the king's plans disrupted. They had been biding their time for such an opportunity as this. As events later in the month revealed, there is a good chance that the person who was behind Henry Talbot's actions was actually a member of the royal family.

Tuesday 11th

The duke of Bar had been serious when he had declared that he wanted to hang the men who had seized the bishops of Carcassonne and Evreux. Yesterday his men had started to besiege Souci. By the evening the captain was so fearful he had fled. Today the remaining defenders surrendered the castle and submitted to the duke's mercy. The duke himself liberated Master Gentien and all the other prisoners. Soldiers were sent out in all directions to scour the forest in search of the missing bishops and their captor.

As good as his word, he then stripped the castle of its valuables and gave orders for the whole place to be destroyed. One only hopes he spared a thought for the lady of the castle, suffering from her post-childbirth illness.

*

Loans were beginning to come in steadily. The bailiffs of Canterbury were given a letter allowing them 100 marks from the customs duties of the city in return for a loan; and the executors of Simon Tonge, having also lent the king 100 marks, were given assurances that they would be repaid after Midsummer's Day (24 June).[42] Note the very short repayment period – just two weeks. Sometimes the treasurer took money in and repaid it within a matter of days. Perhaps it was considered more efficient to consolidate sums owing. Whatever the explanation, the treasury was working hard to maintain the cash flow. As fast as money came in, it was going out again. Thomas Chaucer, the king's butler, was assigned £310 today for wine and reimbursement of his trips abroad.[43]

The king had previously issued a proclamation pardoning all those who had long-standing debts to the crown at the start of his reign. He made a number of exceptions to this pardon: anyone still living was a key one; only debts inherited from dead forebears were to be pardoned. If the debtor had died since the coronation, then this too would be an exception, and other exceptions included those who had accounted for their debt at the exchequer or who had jointly entered into bonds with others . . . The whole system was so complicated that no one could easily tell if they had been pardoned or not. The intent of the pardon – to encourage a feeling of goodwill for the king – was totally lost in the ensuing confusion. So Henry sent a writ to all the sheriffs in England to proclaim that all royal debts owing as of 21 March 1413 (the first day of his reign) would be pardoned, and that people who wished to have charters to that effect should apply to the exchequer before Michaelmas (29 September).[44]

Wednesday 12th

For a certain sum of money paid in advance, men and sometimes women could obtain a corrody: a place within a monastic precinct where they would be fed and sheltered for the rest of their lives. In some cases the corrodian was given this position as a gift of the monastery and, in a few cases, the king might direct that a place be made available for one of his ageing servants. Today Henry sent a letter to the abbot of Selby ordering him to note that one of his corrodians, John Gregory, wished to sell his place to a Lancastrian supporter, John Totty, and the king was content that this should happen.[45] No doubt the abbot of Selby was less happy; the place had been for John Gregory's life; if it carried on going to new people, the monastery would be keeping a supposedly aged retainer not for one or two years but for decades.

Two other personal pieces of Henry's business were dated today.

He confirmed on his friend Sir John Phelip the manor of Grovebury, alias Leighton Buzzard.[46] And he assigned the revenues of the towns of Great Stanmore, Little Stanmore, Edgware and Kingsbury to pay the salary of his new keeper of the privy seal, John Wakeryng.[47]

Thursday 13th

Although Henry had lifted the monopoly on supplying food and ale to Calais, one Peter Pret, master of a ship with wine and victuals for the English castle of Merk in the Calais hinterland, had come to the attention of the mayor of Faversham. As Faversham had been one of the towns that Henry had expressly allowed on 21 April to supply Calais, the mayor decided he was within his rights to impound the ship, as its goods and wine had been purchased in London, which was to the detriment of his town's trade. Henry must have been exasperated. Here he was, trying to arrange a war – and a provincial merchant was trying to hinder him, mistakenly believing that the monopoly had been extended to Faversham for the benefit of the town. Needless to say, Henry gave an order to de-arrest the ship immediately.[48]

Self-interested mayors were a relatively small problem; the finances of the kingdom were far more significant. Even if he pawned all his disposable relics, chalices and church plate, as well as his jewels and treasure, he would not have enough money to meet his liabilities over the next year. It was not just the costs of the expedition that were going to bankrupt him, it was the cost of paying for the defence of the realm in his absence. A projection of the income and expenditure for the year from 24 June was drawn up by the exchequer, and made for uncomfortable reading:

Income (estimated):

Customs and taxes on wool in English ports:	£36,000
Small customs in English ports	2,000 marks
Tax on imported wine	£10,000
Revenue from royal estates in South Wales	2,000 marks
Revenue from royal estates in North Wales	1,000 marks
Revenue of the hanaper in chancery	£1,000

Revenue from the duchy of Cornwall	4,000 marks
Revenue from the sheriffs at the exchequer	1,000 [marks]
Revenue from sale of wardships and marriages	1,000 marks
Revenue from the king's mint within the Tower of London	£500
Revenue from mints elsewhere	200 marks
[Total as given on the account]	£56,966 13s 4d
[actual total	£54,966 13s 4d]

Expenditure on defence (including sums owing)

Wages of the captain of Calais town and his retinue from 6 Aug. 1414 to 1 Nov. 1415	£9,031 2s 4d
Wages of the treasurer of Calais town and his retinue from 6 Aug. 1414 to 1 Nov. 1415	£2,933 7s 2¼d
Wages of the captain of Calais Castle and his retinue from 6 Aug. 1414 to 1 Nov. 1415	£569 11s 5¼d
Money still owed to creditors in Calais for the period before 6 August 1414	£1,540 17s 3½d
Wages for those at Hamme Castle, near Calais, from 6 Aug. 1414 to 1 Nov. 1415	£705 13s 6½d
Wages for those at Sangatte Castle, near Calais, from before 6 Aug. 1414 to 1 Nov. 1415	£651 3s 2d
Wages for those at Guisnes Castle, near Calais, from before 6 Aug. 1414 to 1 Nov. 1415	£3,176 19s 1¾d
Wages for those at Merk Castle, near Calais, from before 6 Aug. 1414 to 1 Nov. 1415	£1,504 6s 0d
Wages for those at Oye Castle, near Calais, from 6 Aug. 1413 to 1 Nov. 1415	£1,247 9s 8¼d
Wages for those at Rysbank Tower, Calais, from 6 Aug. 1414 to 1 Nov. 1415	£379 10s 10½d
Wages for those at Balyngham Castle from before 6 Aug. 1414 to 1 Nov. 1415	£782 6s 10d
Wages of Richard, Lord Grey, and the East March from 10 June 1415 to 31 Dec. 1415	£1,884 13s 9d.*

* This sum of £1,884 13s 9d is the amount that was originally assigned. It appears that part payment only, of £583 6s 8d, was authorised.

Wages of Sir John Neville and the West March of Scotland from 24 June 1415 to 31 Dec. 1415	£2,444 16s 0d
Wages of Sir Robert Umphraville and his men at Roxborough from 24 June 1415 to 31 Dec. 1415	£628 9s 10d
Wages of Sir John Talbot and his men in Ireland from 30 January 1415 to 31 Dec. 1415	£2,445 12s 4¼d
Wages of Thomas Strange and his men in North Wales from 25 March 1415 to 24 June 1415	£546
Wages of Thomas Strange, John Merbury and their men-at-arms in North Wales from 24 June 1415 to 31 Dec. 1415	£1,900
Wages of the admiral and those defending the coasts from 24 June 1415 to 1 November 1415	£1,231 15s 0d
Wages of the duke of Bedford in the king's absence (per annum)	£5,333 6s 8d
Total	£38,937 1s 1¼d

Although the planned assignments covered amounts owing from past years, they only covered ongoing defence expenditure up to 1 November 1415 (in France) and 31 December 1415 (in the British Isles). At these rates a whole year would see total expenditure on defence exceed £60,000. Clearly there was a deficit – and it was not just a few thousand pounds. In addition to defence expenditure, Henry needed to pay the running costs of the royal household, which in recent years had amounted to between £20,000 and £25,000.[49] And then there were all those annuitants receiving sums at the exchequer and drawing cash directly from the receivers of the ports. There were also his four great building projects at Sheen to be paid for. Although the revenues cited above do not include the extra subsidies Henry had been granted by parliament and the convocations, his expedition was obviously going to leave the government owing tens of thousands of pounds. Even if he added the income from the duchy of Lancaster – which under his grandfather had sometimes reached £10,000 per annum – there was going to be a serious short-fall. The wages on his forthcoming expedition for all the archers, men-at-arms, grooms, masons, carpenters and other support staff could be expected to total about £500 every day. The three months in the field, which he was planning to pay in advance, was going to cost in the region of £45,000 – and the second quarter the same. Within a year his liabilities might exceed £200,000. But he had gone too far to stop now. He was prepared to throw everything he had at the forthcoming expedition. Hence today he issued the order for many of the daily utensils of the royal household to be pawned, namely all the non-essential 'basins, cooking pots, ewers, cups, hanaps, goblets, jars, mazers (silver-rimmed drinking vessels), saucers, skillets, scummers, spoons, standing cups, bowls, plates, dishes, chargers, chafers, spiceplates, funnels, salt cellars, flasks, ladles, gridirons and candlesticks'.[50]

No doubt that is where his new set of 'twelve dishes of pure gold' went, never to grace the royal table again.

*

At about this time two envoys came to England from Count Louis of the palatine county of the Rhine. When Henry's sister Blanche had married Louis in 1402 she had been promised a dowry of 20,000 marks, half of which was due immediately.[51] Although Blanche had died in 1409, at the age of seventeen (probably in childbirth), the count still wanted the remainder: 4,000 marks. This was the wrong moment to ask for such a sum. Henry gave the envoys an audience, verbally acknowledged the debt, and then directed them to the duplicitous Bishop Courtenay.

Also around this time the two envoys from the Grand Master of the Teutonic Knights managed to see the king for a third time. Peter Benefeld and Hans Covolt were still in search of the 10,000 marks promised by Henry's father. After their first meeting with Henry in early May, they had had to wait three weeks to see him again, at about the start of June. Again they had been shrugged off with diplomatic politeness. But unlike the envoys from Count Louis of the Rhine, Benefeld and Covolt were insistent. They had come even further and were seeking an even larger amount of money. And their tenacity knew no bounds.

The Teutonic envoys noted that they met Henry after he had been on a pilgrimage. Where that might have been, or when, we do not know.[52] But when they were admitted to his presence they found him with his brothers and a great assembly of knights. When they asked for the money he replied, 'You see we are busy just now'.[53] That was not good enough for the envoys who pressed for an answer on whether they would get their money or not. Henry could not simply refuse to pay what he owed; it would be to the detriment of his honour, just as being seen to refuse to negotiate with France would have damaged his honour. So he delegated the matter. 'You will receive an answer from the council,' he replied, and dismissed them.

Friday 14th

If Henry thought he could avoid the Teutonic envoys, or that the council could convince them to return to Prussia, he was much mistaken. Benefeld and Covolt went to the council the very next day, and addressed the chancellor. With him they could be more demanding – a mere chancellor did not require the same level of respect that a king did. Chancellor Beaufort expressed surprise that these men were so demanding when it was surely obvious that the king had much to do, organising his expedition to France. The envoys pointed out that when they had received their commissions, the Grand Master of the Order had not known that Henry was planning to start a war; but even so, this was not the first time the matter had been raised. The kings of England had been petitioned many times for this money over the years, so Henry had started his war knowing what his level of indebtedness was. They used their words well, suggesting that the king was trying to back out of the debt with dishonour. Beaufort insisted that that was not the case: the king honestly meant to pay; but now was not a good time to ask for money. The chancellor said that he would make sure that they received a letter promising payment at a future date that would surely satisfy the Grand Master. And with that he refused to take part in any further discussion of the matter, and left the council chamber.[54]

Henry acknowledged two further loans, including one of £1,000 from John Victore and 50 marks from the town of Bury St Edmunds. These sums went straight out in payment of £1,214 1s 5d for wine to Thomas Chaucer, the butler, and £250 on more wine to John Burgh, vintner of London. Wine remained a high priority in the royal household, even when the household goods were being pawned. Henry seems to have had no personal interest in ale. And kings did not drink milk or water.[55]

*

The condemnation and humiliation of Hus was a catalyst not just for the reformation and unification of the Church but for the elimination of heresy within its ranks. This necessitated action in a number of directions. First there were the Hussites themselves and similar sects of men, whose crimes amounted to following subversive religious practices. For example in some places laymen as well as clerics were accustomed to receive the wine as well as the bread when they took communion (the blood of Christ was normally reserved for the clergy). The extirpation of such errors and heresies was today delegated to a committee set up under four cardinals and fourteen prelates and theologians, headed by Dr Jean Gerson. At the same time a number of decrees were promulgated against the more obvious errors in Hus's teaching.[56]

Despite their growing numbers, the private heretics were only part of the problem. More pressing was the fact that heresy was a political issue. All across Europe it was becoming fused with treason in one politico-religious crime. John the Fearless, as the most prominent and vocal 'traitor' of the day, was the spokesman for all those who believed that treason was a purely political crime and in no way heretical. There could be no putting off discussion of Jean Petit's *Justification of the duke of Burgundy*. Dr Gerson himself had already proclaimed this work to be heretical as well as treasonable, and had overseen it being publicly burnt in Paris. A petition was now submitted to the council to confirm that verdict.

The emperor was personally in the firing line in this matter. Sigismund had heard from the duke of Bavaria-Ingolstadt, brother of the queen of France, that when the emperor went to Nice to meet Benedict XIII he was unlikely to arrive safely, for John the Fearless was plotting to kill him on the way. Did this amount to a heretical act? Was the suggestion more than propaganda? The very idea was alarming to John's ambassadors at Constance, who reported the matter to their lord. John the Fearless wrote directly to the emperor claiming that this story was false and that he had never imagined or contemplated such a crime, but rather would pay the emperor the highest honour. The emperor read out John the Fearless's letter, so that all might know of his self-professed innocence, and also that the accusation had been made.

The story was circulated by the duke of Bavaria-Ingolstadt on behalf of the French. The main issue was John's supposed heresy in murdering the duke of Orléans. He was being tried by proxy, in the form of the *Justification of the duke of Burgundy* by the late Jean Petit. Those representatives of the French king who had spoken against Petit, and declared this work heretical, were implying that John himself was a heretic. Accusations that he was trying to kill Sigismund, if taken seriously, would undoubtedly weaken his case.

This was the context in which news of the capture of the bishops of Carcassonne and Evreux was about to reach Constance.[57] John could see exactly what damage it would cause. They had spoken against him and Jean Petit. So if he were to be blamed for the kidnapping of these French bishops so soon after being accused of attempting to murder the emperor, he would be condemned out of hand. Hastily he dictated another letter to the emperor:

Most serene prince and invincible king, ever august, my dearest lord and kinsman. It has come to my knowledge that certain foreigners, far beyond the bounds of my domain, recently took captive some ambassadors of my lord the king of France, alleging (I am told) that they had learned these ambassadors had impugned my honour on many occasions at the council of Constance and elsewhere, and had expected by this act to gain or increase my favour. They have discovered their mistake. In truth I did endure my injuries patiently for a time, setting my hopes on the Most High who awards to each his deserts, rather than disturb by revenge the council of the universal Church, your majesty and my said lord [the king of France], whom I am bound to reverence in person and in his envoys, and to whom I would offer no offence. But as soon as I heard with indignation the aforesaid news, I sent messengers immediately to command the captors instantly to release their prisoners with all their possessions unharmed, adding threats of possible vengeance if they did not obey. Thus by great exertion and difficulty I have prevailed on them to release their captives with all their goods.

I make haste to report this to your serenity, whose grace can deliver men from prison, in the hope that your highness will grant amnesty to all who took part in this affair, confirmed by Imperial letters. Humbly I beseech your majesty not to trust malicious men who may attempt to distort or find sinister meaning in what I truthfully relate here, nor those who delight in telling sinister and disturbing stories to your highness. I pray you to accept without hesitation my own assurance that I am guiltless as regards the capture of these men, and have done all I can to set them free; and that in all ways I hope to please the sacred council, your majesty and my lord [the king of France]. May the Almighty preserve you and fulfil your desires. Written at Dijon, 14 June. Your majesty's most humble kinsman, John, duke of Burgundy, count of Flanders, Artois and Burgundy.[58]

Whether the emperor believed this or not is not known. But he would have been wrong to take it at face value. According to Benedict Gentien, the bishops were not located until the duke of Lorraine discovered them in the forest on 16 June, and handed them over to the duke of Bar. Therefore John the Fearless was lying when he wrote in this letter that they had been freed on his orders. It is approximately 110 miles from St Michiel (where the duke of Bar took the bishops after rescuing them) to Dijon, where John was at the time[59] The timing is more than just suspicious. The only way John could have heard of their capture on the 8th, then sent orders for them to be released *and* heard back by the 14th that they had indeed been freed, is if the news was sent to him as soon as the attack had happened and then he *immediately* sent orders to the perpetrators to release the bishops. That implies he knew who they were, and had power over them. Even more incriminating is the fact that the bishops were not found until two days after John's letter stating they had been released on his orders; so his letter to the emperor was written in the sure knowledge that they would soon be located. As if these two points of information were not enough to incriminate John, at the end of July he openly forgave the duke of Bar for his part in rescuing the bishops. So this letter was an utter lie from start to finish. It is worth reading again in that light – if John could be this duplicitous, what was an agreement with him worth? Was the first letter he sent to the emperor also a lie – did he really plan to kill Sigismund? The line,

'I did endure my injuries patiently for a time' might well have been as threatening as it sounded.

Saturday 15th

Henry and his council dealt with two cases of wrongful dismissal this morning. The first was a petition from Robert Darcy. The previous keeper of the writs and rolls of the common bench had resigned in favour of Darcy, and Darcy had taken over the keepership; but he had been ousted by John Hotoft, who had then pocketed the revenue.[60] Henry granted the petition, and gave Darcy an income of £60 per year by way of compensation. Then he and the council heard the case of John Wykes. Richard II had appointed Wykes to be marshal of the household, and he had been dismissed 'without reasonable cause'. The council agreed he should be restored to the marshalcy, and Henry gave instructions accordingly.[61]

Henry's officers had recently bought goods worth £667 11s from the famous ex-mayor of London, Richard Whittington. He directed his customs officers at Chichester to pay the sum. Whittington was a long-standing and substantial financial supporter of the Lancastrians, ever since the days of John of Gaunt. Nevertheless even his patience could grow thin. The Chichester customs officers were trying to levy tolls on some goods of Whittington's that had already been taxed once but which had been recovered after the ship they were on sank. Whittington, having seen his goods sunk once, had no wish to pay a second round of tolls. Henry gave orders for his goods to be released without further payment. He also directed that customs officers in the port of London should undertake to repay 1,000 marks that Nicholas Molyn and some Venetian merchants had lent the king.[62] Perhaps the imprisonment of the Italian merchants on 24 May had convinced others that it was as well to loan the king the money he required.

After seeing to his business of the morning, Henry said a formal farewell to his stepmother, Queen Joan, and set out in a solemn procession to St Paul's Cathedral with the duke of York and the earls of March, Dorset, Arundel, Oxford and Huntingdon, Lord Ros and Sir John Cornwaille. At the cathedral, he listened to a solemn Mass near the tomb of his grandparents, John of Gaunt, duke of Lancaster, and his duchess, Blanche. Afterwards they processed through the city with the same lords and the mayor of London, Thomas Falconer, and 340 of the leading citizens. The procession followed him across London Bridge to Southwark Abbey, where he attended another service, before setting out on the road towards Winchester. The Londoners followed him as far as Kingston upon Thames, where the earl of Arundel turned back. The king said farewell to him. Then, turning to the Londoners, he asked them to return to the city and look after it. 'Christ save London!' he exclaimed as he departed from them.[63]

*

Back at Westminster Bishop Beaufort was preparing for his journey down to Winchester. He must have groaned inwardly when he saw Peter Benefeld and Hans Covolt approaching. They noted he was preparing to leave; could they have their money now? If not, could they have the letter he had promised them? Beaufort told them to go and ask the king's secretary, John Stone, to write it out for them. And without another word he mounted his horse and rode off.

Benefeld and Covolt went to see John Stone. He was too busy, he said. So they went away. And then they came back. Seeing that these envoys were so insistent, he directed them to go and see the keeper of the privy seal, who was responsible for issuing writs for official letters in the king's absence.[64]

Sunday 16th

Before Henry had left London, he had given instructions for a number of appointments and grants to be drawn up.[65] Four royal justices were appointed and a grant of 110 marks yearly made to each of them.[66] More loans were acknowledged by the king – £400 from the old bishop of Lincoln, Philip Repingdon; £100 from the bishop of Hereford, and £20 from the royal esquire, Richard Woodville and his wife – and provision was made for their repayment.[67] Henry confirmed that the temporalities of the see of St David's that he had granted to Stephen

Patrington on 6 April, were now his (Patrington's) to keep. Lastly he appointed Richard Beauchamp, earl of Warwick, Richard Beauchamp of Abergavenny, Lord Berkeley, Sir John Greyndour, Hugh Mortimer and Walter Lucy to govern the Welsh Marches and the counties of Hereford and Gloucestershire, guarding them against rebellion and invasion. In view of the events shortly to unfold, that last named man – Walter Lucy of Richard's Castle, Herefordshire – is a very interesting addition. Clearly Henry trusted him. Whether he was wise to or not is another matter.[68]

Thomas Falconer, mayor of London, and Bishop Courtenay, keeper of the king's jewels, met today for the formal handing over of the Pusan d'Or, the golden chain that would be the security for the loan of the Londoners. It was described in the agreement as

> one great collar of gold, worked with crowns and beasts called antelopes, enamelled with white esses [the letters SS] and the beasts surcharged with green garnets, the charge being two pearls, and each beast having one pearl about the neck. And each of the crowns is set with one large balas ruby and nine large pearls; and in the principal crown that is in front there are set in addition to the balas ruby and the pearls, two large diamonds in the summit; and besides the crowns there are eight other balas rubies. The collar weighs in all 56 ounces. It is enclosed in a case of leather and sealed under the arms of the bishop [Courtenay].[69]

The agreement went on to state that it was put in pledge against the loan of 10,000 marks from the citizens of London, and the king was bound to redeem it before 1 January 1416. That was optimistic, in the extreme.

*

Benefeld and Covolt must have been becoming fairly familiar with the way the English court worked by now – and how men shifted their responsibility for difficult business. Beaufort had gone, and John Stone had sent them on to John Wakeryng, the newly appointed keeper of the privy seal. Could they now have their letter promising payment of the money? No, Wakeryng said; he could do nothing for them because he lacked any instructions from the king. As the king had gone to Winchester, they would have to see the clerk of the council. And where was he? Unavailable. He would see them in two days.[70]

It was not easy being a foreign envoy to Henry's court.

*

This evening, Henry and his companions reached Winchester.[71] There he gave permission for his youngest brother, Humphrey, to make a settlement of his estates. Humphrey's trustees were his two uncles Henry and Thomas Beaufort, the bishop of Durham, Sir John Tiptoft, Sir William Beauchamp and three other men.[72]

Having left London, and set out on the first stage of the road to war, Henry's companions had begun to ponder the possibility that they would not return.

Monday 17th

The loans that Henry had been offered for his expedition so far give the impression that people were giving readily in response to his request. Further evidence suggests the process was not that simple. At Salisbury, the mayor and burgesses had received a letter asking them for money; Bishop Beaufort and the duke of York had even visited in person to ask that they give £100. It was a small sum compared to the 10,000 marks requested from London. But although Salisbury was one of the ten largest towns in the country, the citizens were reluctant.[73] They resented being asked for yet more money on top of their subsidies and customs. Eventually they agreed they would send the king 100 marks, and that eighty-five citizens would find the money between them. Even so, at least one man, Thomas Pistour, refused to pay on principle. The mayor was forced to board up Pistour's house, and an almighty row broke out, in which Pistour roundly cursed the mayor and was almost sent to gaol. But the real blow fell today. Walter Shirley informed the mayor and burgesses that no security had yet been forthcoming for their loan. He had returned from Westminster with the citizen's money still in his purse and the angry voice of Bishop Beaufort ringing in his ears.[74]

*

At Dover the French ambassadors disembarked, not knowing that Henry had left London. It is likely that they were following the dauphin's orders in going as slowly as possible, for they did not leave Paris until four days before their safe conducts were due to expire. But in so doing they missed the king. Henry was not keen to conduct yet more negotiations. His departure from London may have been timed to avoid them. Given the delays he had experienced already, one can understand his reluctance to wait any longer.

From Archbishop Boisratier's point of view, the prospect of nego-tiating must have been just as disagreeable. The king whom he had to persuade was clearly already preparing for war – Boisratier could see that from all the men on the move in Southern England. Henry would not have spent so much on men and equipment without expecting a substantial return. When Boisratier reached London and found the king had already set out, he must have been deeply concerned. The fact that Henry had deputed Sir John Wilcotes to lead them to Winchester was probably a very small reassurance.[75]

Not all the ambassadors named in the letters of 13 April had arrived. The count of Tancarville, the lord of Offemont, John de Roucy, Jean de Villebresme and Stephen de Malrespect had not come. The arch-bishop of Bourges, the count of Vendôme, and all the others attended, together with their households. The total of 360 was more manage-able than the 554 originally envisaged.[76] And with them was Jean Fusoris, who had insisted on attending the delegation. He was still after the money that Courtenay owed him from his visit to Paris the previous year.[77] Given the number of foreigners already in England seeking money from the king, his chances of success were slim indeed.

*

Sir Thomas Gray was riding back from London to his estates in Northumberland. As he was in the vicinity of Conisborough Castle in Yorkshire, the seat of his kinsman Richard of Conisborough, earl of Cambridge, he turned that way. The earl of Cambridge was at home – and had something important to say.

Sir Thomas was solid northern gentry: thirty years old and very well connected. His wife was Alice Neville, the daughter of the earl of Westmorland, one of the staunchest of all Lancastrians. But on his mother's side he was related to a large number of rebels and potential rebels. She was Joan Mowbray, daughter of John, Lord Mowbray, and sister of Thomas Mowbray, duke of Norfolk – the man whose argument with Henry's father had caused the Lancastrians to be banished and disinherited, prompting the Lancastrian revolution of 1399. That made Sir Thomas Gray first cousin to the duke's son and heir, Thomas Mowbray, who had been summarily executed by Henry IV for joining Archbishop Scrope's rebellion in 1405. Another of his first cousins was Walter Lucy of Richard's Castle, a retainer of the earl of March, the Mortimer claimant to the throne; and the earl of March himself was his third cousin once-removed. The countess of Oxford, who had rebelled against Henry IV in 1404, was his mother's first cousin once-removed, and the late earl of Northumberland and his son, Hotspur, who had both died fighting Henry IV, were his second cousins, once-removed.

For years Gray had been a loyal man. Like so many of Henry V's friends, he had fought in Wales, and had been rewarded with an annuity of £40 by Henry's father. But Henry himself had not greatly liked Sir Thomas – he preferred his brother, Sir John Gray – and Thomas's annuity had been stopped. Sir Thomas had fallen into debt and consequently had been outlawed twice. Over the years he had found common cause with that other man whom Henry had little or no time for, the equally impecunious earl of Cambridge. So close had the two men become that they had sealed their connection with a marriage: Sir Thomas's eldest son had married Isabella, Cambridge's daughter by his first wife, the late Anne Mortimer, sister of the earl of March.

This alliance was a potent one. Although the children were still young, they were related to almost everyone of high rank who had lifted a finger against the Lancastrians. Moreover, the earl of Cambridge was resentful at having seen his prospects collapse – from being third in line to the throne in April 1399 to being the lowest and most impoverished member of the royal family. He understood that the forthcoming campaign was principally a trial of Henry's dynastic right in the eyes of God; but why should he fight to prove the king had a greater right to the throne than the earl of March, his kinsman? Given the way he had been treated, it was hardly surprising that he wished to stop the war, and prevent Henry putting his dynastic right to the test. He stood to lose too much if Henry won.

When they were alone, Cambridge let Sir Thomas into a secret:

Henry Talbot had kidnapped Mordach, earl of Fife, on his way back to Scotland. Cambridge may have ordered the kidnapping, for he told Gray he planned to exchange Mordach for two prisoners in Scotland. One of these was Henry Percy, which was straightforward enough, as Henry himself had already agreed this transfer. The other was Thomas Warde of Trumpington – the impostor who claimed to be Richard II. If the duke of Albany had to admit that the pseudo-Richard was now dead (as in fact he was, as Cambridge probably knew), then those who supported Warde as a living symbol of the injustice of the Lancastrian dynasty would naturally switch their allegiance to Edmund Mortimer, earl of March. Henry Percy would raise the men of Northumberland on behalf of March (his cousin), and Cambridge himself would take March into Wales, and rouse the Marcher lords, the Welsh partisans and the Lollards. There they would make a stand against Henry V and the Lancastrians.

Over the years many people have regarded the earl of Cambridge as hare-brained for hatching this plot. And with good reason – he vastly overestimated the revolutionary spirit of those whom he tried to enlist. He simply presumed that anyone with a grudge against the Lancastrians would risk their necks and join him. He also seems to have given very little thought to the fact that he would have to kill all three of Henry's brothers (as well as Henry himself) before he could have eliminated their claim to the throne, which had been ratified by parliament. A quadruple royal murder was never going to be easy. However, given Cambridge's many anti-Lancastrian connections, he might not have been a complete fool. A Percy–Mortimer alliance, supported by Welsh partisans, was not a new idea.[78] A similar plan had originally been hatched by Henry Percy, Owen Glendower and Sir Edmund Mortimer (uncle of the earl of March) in 1405. Together they had decided to divide all of England and Wales between their respective families. They had been inspired by an ancient prophecy that a dragon out of the north (Percy), a wolf out of the west (Glendower) and a lion out of Ireland (the earl of March, who was also the earl of Ulster and Connaught) would drive Henry IV from his kingdom and divide the kingdom between them.[79] So what the earl of Cambridge envisaged was not simply his own hare-brained scheme; it had deep roots, going back to the betrothal of Henry 'Hotspur' Percy and Elizabeth Mortimer way back in 1379.

The framework of prophecy and past rebellion had become a little rickety with the passing of the years. Glendower was a dying man, and although he still commanded considerable support in North Wales – so much so that no attempt was made to recruit any archers there – the willingness of the Welsh to venture into England for the benefit of the earl of March was unknown. Henry Percy still needed to be recovered from the Scots, and his loyalty was also untested. But against these weaknesses and doubts, Cambridge could set some new strengths. In Wales a royal esquire called David Howel had promised that if there was a stirring in the north, he would put Llanstephan Castle at Cambridge's disposal. The Lollards were another factor: Sir John Oldcastle would rise, along with Sir Thomas Talbot and other heretic knights in various parts of England. Cambridge would secure Henry Percy and invite him to avenge his father's and grandfather's deaths by joining them and becoming the prophesied 'dragon out of the north'. Perhaps the relations of other men who had been killed by the Lancastrians would join them – those of Archbishop Scrope and the Despensers, for example, or the Holland family, Richard II's half-brothers. And then there were Cambridge's and March's own kinship networks. The eldest son of the old earl of Devon was a brother-in-law to the earl of March. Lord Clifford was brother-in-law to both Cambridge and Henry Percy, and a first cousin of the earl of March. According to Cambridge, Clifford had already sworn to join them. In fact he was expected to come to Conisborough in another three days. If Sir Thomas Gray would wait, they could discuss the plans together.

Sir Thomas decided not to wait, but agreed to come and meet both Cambridge and Lord Clifford on a future occasion. Cambridge asked him to speak to Sir Robert Umphraville and Sir John Widdrington – the men who had been deputed to remove Henry Percy from Berwick. They had both sworn to take the side of Henry Percy in a war against Henry V. This was probably a lie; and Sir Thomas was sceptical, for he never spoke to either man. But the whole scheme appealed to him. It promised not just revenge on the Lancastrians who had killed his uncle and cousin but wealth and power in a closer association with a new king and a new dynasty.

This is perhaps the most important aspect about the earl of Cambridge's plot. It was more to do with getting rid of the Lancastrians than making the earl of March king, or championing the cause of

Richard II, or helping the Lollards, or dividing up the realm three ways. Sir Thomas did not even like the earl of March – he called him a hog.[80] It was not realistic to hark back to the three-way division of England envisaged in 1405. But all these things were options, they all had their precursors, and they were all more attractive than the status quo. Cambridge was right in this respect: many people preferred the idea of Henry V dead rather than leading an army through France – including a number of provincial merchants as well as the Lollards, Welsh partisans and English political players. They may have had their different reasons but they were mutually sympathetic with regard to their distrust of the Lancastrians.

As a result of the chief character of the plot being one of opposition, it is hard to describe exactly how the protagonists intended to meet their objectives. In this sense it may be compared with some of the attempts on Henry IV's life, such as the Epiphany Rising or the Percy Rebellion and (most of all) the Northern Rebellion in 1405. Thus it has confused many historians, who prefer to see neat plans and processes laid out in evidence of a coherent and achievable strategy. Opposition plots like Cambridge's tend to be vague because their ambitions are destructive, not creative, and they have to appeal to a wide range of disillusioned parties. They also have to be adaptable as the circumstances of their intended target or victim change. In this regard the earl of Cambridge's plot was typical. If it turned out that Thomas Warde was dead, then they would publicise the fact. If he was alive, they would expose him. If Henry Percy was not keen to rise with the rebels, or if they could not exchange Mordach for Thomas Warde or Percy, then they would abandon both Percy and Warde and concentrate on proclaiming the earl of March king of England.

On that last issue it was especially important to be adaptable. While Gray and Cambridge were chatting about their rebellion at Conisburgh, an esquire called Ralph Pudsay found where Mordach was being held, and took him back into the king's custody.[81]

Tuesday 18th

Normally the signet – the king's personal seal – travelled with the king wherever he went. It was kept by his secretary, and it was used to send letters conveying the king's personal instructions. For this reason it is normally the best guide to where the king was. However, as we have seen, Henry left his secretary in London when he departed for Winchester – and it would appear that John Stone still had the king's signet with him. He used it today to authenticate a letter from Henry, dated at Westminster, to the Jurade of Bordeaux, asking them to assist Sir John Tiptoft, the new seneschal. Probably at the same time he wrote a second signet letter to the same recipients, asking them to send the king 'two of the best siege engines called "brides" and a master and carpenter to look after them'. Henry, having promised in 1414 to send siege equipment to Gascony, was now asking them to send some to him.[82]

At Westminster the Teutonic envoys finally managed to see the clerk to the council. Did he provide them with the promissory letter they required? Not at all. He said he could find no record of any decision in this matter and they would have to return the following day to see the council.[83]

Wednesday 19th

Predictably enough, Benefeld and Covolt returned to see the privy council as directed. There were only four councillors present: the archbishop of Canterbury, Bishop Langley of Durham, the earl of Arundel (treasurer of England), and John Wakeryng (keeper of the privy seal). And they met purely to record their decision that they agreed that the treasurer should have power to make assignments of the royal customs and subsidies on wool, leather and hides.[84] They did not grant a hearing to the Teutonic envoys. As soon as their morning's business was dealt with, the archbishop of Canterbury departed for Maidstone, to join Bishop Courtenay of Norwich and the bishop of London in consecrating Stephen Patrington as the new bishop of St David's.[85]

Benefeld and Covolt accosted Bishop Langley. Langley told them he could do nothing in this matter without the approval of Henry Beaufort, the chancellor. He advised them to go to Winchester and take the matter up with him again. Benefeld prepared to ride to Winchester in person. What else could he do?

Thursday 20th

Men up and down the country were busy enlisting archers. This was especially the case in the north of England and in Wales, where the archery tradition was strongest. In Cheshire, 247 archers were recruited for the campaign. In Lancashire, five hundred archers had been assembled by the local gentry. North Wales was still a sensitive area, but recruitment in the south, in the lordship of Brecon and the counties of Carmarthen and Cardigan, had yielded five hundred archers, including twenty-six mounted men. All of them were packed off to Southampton to join the general muster there.[86]

*

Probably in London, and probably about this time, Lord Scrope had a conversation with Sir Walter Lucy, lord of Richard's Castle and a close friend and retainer of the earl of March. Lucy was also a first cousin of Sir Thomas Gray, and although he probably did not know yet of the meeting between Gray and Cambridge on the 17th, he knew the two men very well, and understood their antipathy towards Henry V. His purpose in meeting Lord Scrope was to tell him, in the strictest secrecy, that he was worried lest the earl of Cambridge and Sir Thomas Gray would incite the earl of March to claim the throne.[87]

The evidence for this conversation comes from Scrope's own testimony. The original document is badly damaged but these two men seem to have met and discussed the earl of Cambridge and Sir Thomas Gray between the council's instructions to release Mordach and hearing the news of his recapture.[88] It may be that Lucy already knew that Cambridge was planning to ask Sir Thomas Gray to join him. The key three facts that seem incontrovertible are that (1) Lucy raised the matter with Scrope; (2) that he did so in the wake of another Lollard mass gathering; and (3) that Scrope asked for more information about the plot.[89] At this point Lucy, who realised he had already spoken too freely, said nothing more and was 'hard' with Scrope.

Why did Lucy tell a close friend of the king about the plot, endangering himself and the earls of March and Cambridge and Sir Thomas

Gray? The explanation lies in the fact that the king had discovered that the earl of March had not only obtained the appropriate papal dispensation to marry Anne Stafford but had already completed the act. Henry was furious when he found out – so much so that he told the earl of March that he was going to fine him 10,000 marks for his effrontery. This is the same sum for which March had bound himself to the king in his indenture, sealed at the beginning of the reign lest he rebel against the king; it was utterly shocking that the full sum should be laid upon him just for marrying without permission, at the age of twenty-four. Normally fines for this were between £100 and £1,000. But Henry was merciless: he insisted that the earl pay the full amount – and if he did not have the money, then he was to borrow it. Walter Lucy himself had lent the earl 500 marks, and the earl of Arundel and Lord Scrope had provided the rest. This is why Lucy and Scrope had fallen into conversation: they were both creditors to a man who was on the verge of rebellion. Lucy warned his fellow creditor that the earl might easily fall prey to the conniving of his rebellious kinsman, the earl of Cambridge and Sir Thomas Gray. Then they would not only lose their money; the kingdom might slip into a civil war.

Scrope was profoundly shocked. All he knew at this stage – as far as we can tell – was that March was on the edge of rebellion, and that Lucy knew something was afoot between Cambridge, Gray and March. But Lucy would not tell him more.

Scrope was determined to find out. He was aware of how Edward, duke of York, had foiled the Epiphany Rising in 1400 – by joining the plotters and then revealing all to the king – and had saved the entire royal family.[90] Scrope decided to do likewise, to ingratiate himself with the plotters to determine what they were planning.

Friday 21st

By today news had reached Winchester that the bishop of Chichester had died. Henry instructed that a letter be sent to the dean and chapter giving them permission to elect another bishop. It seemed as if he was going to allow the canons to elect one of their own number. But Henry nominated his own preferred candidate – his confessor, Stephen Patrington – almost immediately. This was in spite of the fact that Patrington had only recently been consecrated as bishop of St Davids. It seems a little high-handed, and it seems almost certain there was a financial motive. Patrington – an aged Carmelite friar – had little need for a large personal income; he was probably more than satisfied with the temporalities of the bishopric of St David's, which Henry had granted him in April and delivered just two weeks ago. Henry may have nominated Patrington on the understanding that the new bishop would not demand the Chichester income straightaway. In the end Henry took the temporal income from the bishopric of Chichester for well over a year. [91]

Henry's cash flow was helped today by the largest single loan he received. The treasurer of Calais, Roger Salvayn, deposited £10,936 3s 8d with the treasurer in London.[92]

The long-suffering envoy from the Teutonic Knights, Peter Benefeld, arrived in Winchester today. Beaufort greeted him with the words, 'Aren't you settled yet? I'm exceedingly sorry but I'll see about your letter tomorrow'.[93] And Benefeld had to make do with that.

Saturday 22nd

At Westminster a second recognition of a debt to an Italian merchant was made – this one for a loan of 200 marks and a debt of £478 18s 8d to a merchant of Lucca, Paolo de Melan.[94] Clearly the council's bullying tactics were working, in the short term at least.

From Westminster more letters went out under the authentication, 'by the king'. These were addressed to the bishops of Lincoln and Ely, ordering them to muster the clergy of the dioceses to defend the realm and the Catholic Church. The instructions were as those of 1 June but they carried the added proviso that they were not to meddle with the students and clerks of the universities of Oxford and Cambridge.[95] Students obviously could not be expected to defend the realm.

Two other royal letters are extant, both dated at Winchester, and so closer to where Henry himself was at this time. One gave orders that a joiner called John Widmore should be paid £25 for delivering a thousand lances to the king.[96] The other directed the sheriff of Oxfordshire to send a further two hundred oxen, bullocks and cows to Fareham as speedily as possible, for the troops to eat.[97] That was the equivalent of twenty-five plough teams. The folk of Oxfordshire and Berkshire were going to have a harder task ploughing their fields next year.

*

Peter Benefeld was still not having any luck with Chancellor Beaufort. He went to see him, as instructed, but was told that Beaufort was busy on account of the impending arrival of the French envoys. He would be unable to see him for at least eight days.

Sunday 23rd

It was the eve of the feast of St John the Baptist. People up and down the country lit ceremonial bonfires this evening to mark the night before Midsummer's Day. In some towns, people rolled burning hoops through the streets. In other places they built wakefires around which they drank and danced, or 'St John's fires', piled with wood and bones. The inclusion of bones in these St John's fires was to ward off evil spirits – the only problem was having to dance through clouds of smoke that smelled truly revolting.[98]

From Winchester Henry sent out another letter concerning the University of Cambridge. This was to the sheriff to keep the peace in the town 'as the king is informed that certain scholars of the university have made riots and unlawful assemblies there, and are striving day and night to continue to make them, to the disturbance of the people and in breach of the peace'.[99] In contrast to his letter of the previous day, ordering the bishop of Lincoln not to force the Cambridge students to array for the defence of the realm, it sounds as though these scholars would have been ideal conscripts.

*

Henry, Lord Scrope of Masham, dictated his will to his clerk, John Bliton, and set his seal to it.[100] Given his closeness to Henry, and given his political associations, it is not a document that can be passed over lightly.

The first thing one notices about the document is its size. The printed version extends to 8½ folio pages – more than 5,000 words of Latin. The most important lords mentioned were the king, Henry Beaufort, Thomas Beaufort, Bishop Langley of Durham, and Lord Fitzhugh. Although there are references to Masses to be sung for the souls of Richard II, Henry IV and Thomas, duke of Gloucester (the murdered uncle of Richard II and Henry IV), the rest of the royal family does not appear. In other words, there is no evidence here of strong political connections outside the king's immediate circle. Scrope made bequests to more than a dozen of his own family members and more than fifty other men of his household – everybody who served him was given a considerable sum, even the boys and the pages who served in his household were to be given a noble (6s 8d) – but the earls of March and Cambridge, Lord Clifford, Sir Thomas Gray and Sir Walter Lucy do not appear at all.

Normally we would be surprised to find pages and boys given significant bequests in a lordly will. But Lord Scrope was one of the most generous men of his time – loaning money to lords during life as well as giving it away in death. However, money was not half the story, for he was among the most religious men of the age too. We have already come across his ownership of a copy of *The Revelations of St Bridget*, and his will amplifies this religiosity to a quite remarkable extent. Most of his bequests were of religious things, not money. For example to the king he gave a gold figure of the Virgin Mary garnished with balas rubies and pearls. To Henry Beaufort he gave a small breviary covered in blue velvet. To Thomas Beaufort he gave a book of meditations; to Bishop Langley, an illuminated Apocalypse in Latin and French, a book of Mattins; and to Lord Fitzhugh he gave two books containing the *Incendium Amoris* and *Judice me Deus*, both by Richard Rolle, a Yorkshire hermit and mystic. These set the pattern for all his other personal bequests too – almost everyone of high rank received a valuable book of spiritual devotion. He had dozens in his possession.

Reading Scrope's will, the overwhelming surprise is the sheer number of religious bequests. He left sums of money, holy books and costly vestments to about forty named churches and monasteries. Some of these were substantial: to the shrine of St John of Bridlington he bequeathed his 'gold collar with white swans and small flowers', to the prior of Bridlington he gave a religious book and a gilt-silver crucifix;

to the king's new priory at Sheen he gave £10; and he gave 5 marks to every other Charterhouse in the kingdom. But then one sees that he made a bequest of at least a noble (6s 8d) to every single recluse or anchorite in the whole country. Having given 1 mark, £1, £2, or a book, to specific anchorites and recluses at Westminster, Beverley, Pontefract, Stafford, Newcastle, Peasholme, York, Wigton, Chester, Gainsborough, Leake, Stamford, Dartford, and seven other places, he stipulated that 6s 8d should be given to every anchorite and recluse in London and its suburbs, and in York and its suburbs, and to every other anchorite or recluse who could be found within three months of his death.

Given all the above, it is no surprise to find that Scrope made extremely detailed arrangements for his burial. He spoke of his lowly state in terms reminiscent of self-abasing Lollard wills. He left his soul 'to Almighty God, the Virgin Mary, St John the Baptist, St Katherine and all the saints' and expressed a wish to be buried in the north side of the chancel of York Minster, between two columns. If that was not possible he wanted to lie near his father in the chapel of St Stephen in the same minster. He hoped his wife would choose to be buried beside him, when her time came, and bequeathed her goods to the value of £2,000. He asked to be buried in a table tomb of marble, with an effigy of alabaster representing him in armour, with St John at his head and St Katherine at his foot. He made many gifts of gilt-silver figures to the minster, and gave specific instructions about the size of the candles he wanted to be used at his funeral – two, each of 24lbs – and how many Masses were to be sung for his soul, and for how many years after his death.

All in all, the impression we have of Lord Scrope is that he was the most deeply religious temporal lord at Henry's court – with the exceptions of the king himself and possibly Lord Fitzhugh, a co-founder of Syon Abbey. He was in every way an asset to the king: as a diplomat, a religious man, and as a trusted confidant. His recently acquired knowledge of the wavering of the earl of March was worrying not because he was inclined to support him or the earl of Cambridge but rather because of the danger they spelled to the royal family, with whom he was intimately connected. The only thing possibly dividing him from the king was his outlook on war. He had not attended the great council in April and was late turning up to the council meeting at the end of May to discuss Henry's secret diplomacy with Burgundy. As a deeply religious man, who had visited the shrine of the peace-loving St Bridget in person, it is possible that he did not approve of unnecessary military aggression.[101] But even so, his will shows that the king and the king's most trusted confidants remained the men closest to his heart. The earls of March and Cambridge did not even merit a mention.

Monday 24th: the Feast of St John the Baptist

Midsummer's Day itself saw the Midsummer Eve celebrations continued, with more bonfires, dancing and drinking. In some towns pageants were held. In others Midsummer marches or processions were arranged, with the men of the town parading with weapons, torches and music. Mummers might join in these marches, dressed as giants or dragons. Sometimes naked boys took part, painted black to represent Moors. Houses were decorated with greenery brought in from the country, and shop fronts and streets were festooned with leafy boughs, garlands and birch branches.[102]

At Winchester, Henry issued another order for meat for the army, in addition to that of the 22nd. This one went out to the sheriffs of Wiltshire and Hampshire; Henry wanted them each to find a hundred cattle and take them to Lymington, Romsey, Alderford, Fareham and Titchfield, paying whatever price may be agreed.[103] Such orders as these allow us to imagine the sheriffs' officers attending every market in the vicinity, buying cattle, and the roads filled with animals as well as men on the move, the cows being herded together for their march towards the towns around Southampton.

Tuesday 25th

Letters were being issued from three places in the king's name. Yesterday's two orders had been issued from Winchester and Southampton. Today another patent letter went out as 'by the king' from Westminster. This confirmed the settlement of some confiscated alien priories' property on a royal esquire, John Woodhouse, whom Henry had recently appointed chamberlain of the exchequer.

The recipient was to acknowledge his service by 'rendering to the king a red rose at Midsummer' every year thereafter.[104]

The king was actually based at Wolvesey Castle, the bishop's palace near Winchester Cathedral. A letter was sent out from there in his name to Richard Courtenay, bishop of Norwich, licensing him to grant a portion of a manor to the collegiate church of Ottery St Mary, Devon, in aid of the maintenance of the Courtenay family altar, dedicated to St Catherine.[105] Another letter was sent out from Winchester awarding an annuity of £20 to Ralph Pudsay esquire, who had recaptured Mordach, earl of Fife.[106]

*

In York, about this time, Gray would also have heard the news about Mordach's recapture. A man called Skranby brought him a letter at his lodgings, written by the earl of Cambridge in person. It explained that Lord Clifford had not come on the 20th, as he had promised, and so Cambridge had not sent for Gray to join them. Whatever else it said we have no way of knowing, for Gray tore it up and threw it into a cesspit.[107]

*

In his cell in the Franciscan friary in Constance, Jan Hus wrote to his friends.

> Our Saviour restored Lazarus to life four days after his decomposition. He preserved Jonah for three days in the whale and then sent him to preach. He drew up Daniel from the lions' den to write prophecies . . . Why could He not now liberate me, a miserable wretch, from prison and death, in the same manner . . . ?
>
> A certain doctor told me that whatever I did in submitting to the council would be good and lawful for me; and he added that 'if the council said that you only had one eye, even if you had two, you should confess to the council that it was so'.[108]

And that last passage just about summed up his position. He would not recant because, for him, matters of faith were matters of truth.

For the council, his refusal to recant was a refusal to accept their authority. The failure in this lay not with Hus but with the Church. The onus was on the council to show Hus and the rest of Christendom that he was wrong to deny that he had only one eye when he believed he had two. Hus was about to demonstrate that the truth was more important than mere authority. It was more important, even, than his life.

Wednesday 26th

Although Peter Benefeld had been told a few days earlier that Chancellor Beaufort could not possibly see him for another eight days, he was surprised one morning to see him out walking. They greeted one another and Beaufort walked with him for about a mile, talking about Poland and events in Prussia. At the end of this diversion, Beaufort asked for three days' more grace, so he could talk things over with the king's secretary and the keeper of the privy seal. By this stage, Benefeld knew better than to take any leading member of Henry's court at his word, and decided personally to go and see the king's secretary, John Stone, at Westminster.

Henry himself was concerned with St Werbergh's church in Chester. This had been founded by King Athelstan, and so Henry regarded it as having been founded by one of his ancestors. Maintaining it was something that touched upon the royal dignity and, as it was 'in a dilapidated and impoverished state', the king declared he would take it into his own hands. Accordingly, he appointed his uncle, Henry Beaufort, to remedy the condition of the abbey.

Today Henry also issued an order to the constable of the Tower of London to deliver Brother John Matthew, a canon of Carmarthen, to the abbot of Waltham Holy Cross. The abbot was to keep this renegade Welsh canon a prisoner until further notice.[109]

Thursday 27th

Peter Benefeld probably arrived back at Westminster this evening, having ridden the 63 miles from Winchester in a day and a half. He met with John Stone and asked him when he was expecting to go to Winchester. Tomorrow, Stone replied, explaining that he planned to be in Southampton on the 30th. He added that the best person to see in this matter would be the archbishop of Canterbury. So Benefeld went to see the archbishop. But Chichele declared that, although the king had acknowledged the debt, he had not given any instructions for anything to be done about it, just as the keeper of the privy seal had said. Given this impasse in London, Benefeld reckoned his best option was to take Chancellor Beaufort at his word and see him when he and John Stone met. Therefore he prepared to ride back to Winchester the following day with the king's secretary.

Friday 28th

Henry and his circle had already proved their fondness for the strict order of Carthusian canons. Henry's priory at Sheen was a Charterhouse, and Henry Scrope made provision for all the Charterhouses in England in his will. A week ago, on the 21st, Henry had made a grant of the manor of Hinckley to Mount Grace priory in Yorkshire, at the request of Thomas Beaufort, on condition the monks pray for the king and his uncle in life and for their souls after death. Now he followed that up with a confirmation of several manors granted by the Mowbray family to the Carthusian house of Eppeworth, in Lincolnshire. Henry also added a gift of his own, granting the Carthusians two pipes of wine yearly from the royal wines landed in Kingston upon Hull. These of course were not for the monks' general enjoyment; they were, as Henry stipulated, 'for the celebration of Masses in the said house'.[110]

Saturday 29th

The French ambassadors were nearing Winchester, so they sent ahead for safe conducts so that they might come to the king's presence. Henry dictated these today, naming the archbishop of Bourges and his companions. Hearing that he could expect them tomorrow, Henry sent out a welcoming party. The bishop of Durham had now joined

Henry at Winchester, so he and Bishop Courtenay rode with Thomas Beaufort and the earl of Salisbury to greet their diplomatic opposite numbers. They met them on the road, about a mile from the city, and escorted them in honour to their lodgings at the Franciscan Friary.[111]

Sunday 30th

Henry's relationship with his stepmother, Queen Joan, had never been a close one. In later years he banished her Breton companions, accused her of witchcraft, and confiscated her income. But in 1415 they were probably as close as they were ever likely to get. Queen Joan had shared her husband's ardent faith in the Trinity, and this gave her something in common with her stepson. Henry had shown respect to her when he bade her a formal farewell at Westminster on the 15th. Today he specified which royal estates she might stay at during his absence. While he was abroad she might live at Windsor Castle, Wallingford Castle, Berkhamsted or Hertford Castle.[112] In addition, he gave her the royal manor of Langley outright. This latter gift was not a mark of affection or generosity, however; it was compensation for Hertford Castle, which her late husband had granted her but which Henry now wanted for himself.[113]

*

The ambassadors from France finally arrived at Winchester. They found the king in the great chamber of Wolvesey Castle, seated at a table, with his head uncovered – without a crown. He was wearing a long robe of cloth of gold. Near his bed was a magnificent chair adorned with golden tapestries. To his right sat his three brothers and the duke of York, the earl of Huntingdon, and several other lords. To his left sat Chancellor Beaufort and the bishops of Durham and Norwich.

The French humbly genuflected before the king on entering, in the correct manner. Archbishop Boisratier passed the formal sealed letters he carried from the king of France to another man to pass to Henry, together with similar letters from the duke of Berry. As these were opened for the king, Archbishop Boisratier said:

Most excellent and most powerful prince, our sovereign lord the king
of France greets you affectionately, and the duke of Berry humbly
recommends himself to your serenity. The king's letter you have there,
dated 1 May, begins as follows: Our very dear cousin, we send you our
special ambassadors, praying that you receive them on our recommen-
dation, and wishing that you hear them favourably. For we are hoping
that by their mediation, you will have satisfaction on the subject of the
agreement that you wish to conclude between us.

Henry kissed the letter and handed it to his chancellor and asked after
the king of France's health.[114] When told all the details he spoke to
the ambassadors. 'You are welcome', he said, inviting them to take
spiced wine with him and his lords. As the drinks were being served
he invited the ambassadors to return and dine with him on the
following day. Then they would have a public audience in the hearing
of all the bishops and lords then present.[115]

*

While all this formal posturing was taking place, Peter Benefeld and
the king's secretary arrived from Westminster. Benefeld immediately
went to the bishop's palace and asked to see the king. He was told
that a royal audience was quite out of the question. The French envoys
had arrived; it would be at least nine days before the king or the chancellor could attend to his letter.

By this stage Benefeld must have been wishing he had never left
Prussia.

July

Monday 1st

This morning, Henry prepared to receive the French envoys at Wolvesey Castle. They were expected for dinner: about 11 or 11.30 a.m. by our reckoning.[1]. While he waited he dealt with various items of business, including commissioning four men to look after the temporalities of the see of Chichester, which were in the king's hands following the death of the bishop.[2]

The French envoys came early. They joined Henry for a special Mass sung by twenty-eight chaplains, and afterwards were led to the great chamber where they had seen the king the previous day. He sat on the golden-tapestry-covered chair near the royal bed, with the same people to his left and right as on the previous day: secular lords on one side and prelates on the other. Archbishop Boisratier opened his address with a sermon on the theme of Kings I, chapter 19. 'Peace be to you and your household'. He developed this to praise peace in general terms without mentioning the subject of their mission. He quoted various texts of the Old and New Testaments, and stated that 'he had come in the interests of peace', demonstrating how it would be better to be certain of this peace, which all men desired, than run the risk of the horrors of war.[3]

When the archbishop had finished, the chancellor responded, saying the king had heard the archbishop's speech with great pleasure and considered it most eloquent. He was particularly pleased to hear that the king of France was prepared to do all he could in the interests of peace. In the past he had been tardy in sending negotiators, and this slackness was very dangerous; he hoped that in future the French king would be speedier about matters of peace.

At the dinner that followed, Archbishop Boisratier and the bishop of Lisieux were seated on one side of the king and his youngest brother Humphrey on the other. The count of Vendôme and the seigneur d'Ivry sat next to Humphrey. After the dinner, the king returned to the bishop's great chamber where he was staying and addressed the ambassadors graciously, saying to them that he was happy that they had arrived because 'they wished to work efficaciously for peace'. And then he dismissed them, delegating the actual discussions to his ambassadors.[4]

★

Michael de la Pole, earl of Suffolk, today set his seal to his will. He was fifty-four years of age, and a grandfather. Knighted by Richard II in 1377, he had seen his family fall completely from grace when his father was impeached in the parliament of 1386. It had taken him a long time to recover his family dignities, but eventually he had done so. He had been appointed to the privy council in 1402, and in 1408 he had been one of the representatives at the council of Pisa. Now he would be heading to France, to war. It was time to contemplate the end of life, as many men were doing in the few quiet moments they were permitted, lying in their beds or kneeling in chapel.

De la Pole wished to be buried in the Charterhouse at Kingston upon Hull, with no tomb but just a flat stone on him, between the tomb of his parents and the altar. But interestingly he declared this was to happen only if he died in the north of England. If he died anywhere else, he desired to be buried in the collegiate church at Wingfield, Suffolk, on the north side of the chapel of the Virgin. To his son he left a small Latin primer. To his wife Katherine he left a small book and the coronet that once had belonged to her father, the earl of Stafford. She was left in charge for the rest of his estate, in conjunction with his aged uncle, Edmund de la Pole.[5]

★

In the Franciscan Friary at Constance, Jan Hus was also contemplating death. Today he had to make his final declaration to the council – whether he would recant or not. Would he accept that men could act in God's name against him? He wrote the following momentous letter:

> I, Jan Hus, a priest in hope of Jesus Christ, fearing to offend God and fall into perjury, am unwilling to recant any or all of the articles produced against me in the testimonies of false witnesses. For God is my witness that I neither preached, asserted nor defended them, as they said . . .
>
> If it were possible for my voice to be heard across the whole world – as it will be at the Day of Judgment, when every lie and all my sins will be revealed – I would most gladly recant before all the world, taking back every falsehood or error I have ever said or thought of saying.
>
> This I say and write of my own free will. With my own hand.[6]

And with those few small words, in the silence of his cell, Jan Hus decided that he would obey his conscience, and die a martyr's death.

Tuesday 2nd

The French ambassadors assembled this morning 'in the chapter house of the small church' with the bishops and lords whom they had met the previous day. In the king's absence, Chancellor Beaufort presided. He outlined his authority to all those present, and urged the French to cut straight to the main point because the delays so far encountered were prejudicial to the king and contrary to his recommendations. The king had decided they had until the following Saturday to discuss the subject of peace, and after that there would be no more discussion.

Archbishop Boisratier could see that his authority was not great enough to secure peace. No power in the world could have stopped Henry on his march to war. In his letter to the French king, Henry had said that he would extend the time of the ambassadors' safe conducts if the peace negotiations looked promising. Now he had already set a final date for their discussions: in just four days' time. And there was to be no let up to the military preparations. Nevertheless the archbishop had to do what he could.

The king, our master, takes as witness the whole of Christendom, which has always wished for peace, and states that he has always searched to come to it by the road to justice, in offering to dismember the realm and to cede to the king of England more important towns in Aquitaine, more counties and lands of an almost unappreciable value, and the hand of his illustrious daughter Katherine with a dowry of 800,000 gold crowns. History does not show a daughter leaving her father's palace with such a large sum of money. Would you tell us whether you are agreeable with these propositions?

According to the official French chronicler who recorded these words, the English chancellor replied that Henry did not intend to withdraw from his initial demands – specifically his *first*, most excessive terms. Beaufort maintained that in the course of the year 1414 the king of France had written to Henry stating that he was sending an embassy to treat with him in the way of justice and of the peace treaty, and to conclude the marriage, and to bring together certain key points and particulars in order to hasten the success of negotiations. Henry had been given to understand that the French ambassadors had sufficient authority to offer much more than they had to date. The archbishop of Bourges objected that the letters of authority that he had been given in France should not be supposed to convey more powers than they actually did. However, he had been authorised to offer to augment Princess Katherine's dowry by 50,000 francs (not crowns), and he promised that the young princess would be sent to England with rich clothes and valuable jewels.[7]

At this the meeting broke up to confer further.

Wednesday 3rd

Archbishop Boisratier sent a formal request to continue the negotiations in the chapter house. After they assembled, Chancellor Beaufort, as spokesman, let it be known that Henry had reduced his demands from 1,000,000 crowns of gold to 900,000. The archbishop responded that he was not authorised to agree to such a sum, unless it be done subtly, by a change of text. There had been discussion in both currencies: francs and crowns. Ten gold crowns was the equivalent of about

10.5 francs.[8] The French could stretch to 900,000 francs. But how much income might be assigned to Princess Katherine, when she was queen?

The whole process of negotiations was tiresome to the English; it was a charade. They were going to war – there were no two ways about it – and so the usual negotiating postures were meaningless. Having said that, if the French raised new objections, these could be used as further means to hasten the breakdown of the negotiations with no loss of honour. So the English replied that Katherine when queen would have the use of 10,000 marks (£6,666 13s 4d). The archbishop was appalled and argued that this was not enough, pointing to the illustrious birth of the princess, and stressing the advantages that the union would bring to both kingdoms. He also insisted that the sum allowed her should be relative to the immense wealth that she was bringing Henry in her dowry. Chancellor Beaufort would have none of it.

Discussions on the subject of the marriage stopped there, and the ambassadors departed.[9]

*

Henry was not present at these discussions in the chapter house. Only one instruction of his is known for today. He ordered that the keepers of passage in fifteen ports were not to allow anyone at all to leave.[10] This was a wise precaution; it was usual to close the ports immediately after the death of a king, for reasons of security, and Edward III had extended this to times of war, to conceal news of his expeditions' destinations leaking out. But one wonders what the people of the French ports thought, when no more vessels docked from England. They would have known their ambassadors were still overseas. The empty seas must have been ominous.

Thursday 4th

'A happy and famous day,' wrote Cardinal Fillastre in his journal at Constance. In the presence of Sigismund, wearing his imperial insignia, the representatives of Gregory XII – by far the most amenable of the three popes at the start of 1415 – came to abdicate on his behalf. Carlo Malatesta, Friar Giovanni Dominici, cardinal of Ragusa, and the patriarch of Constantinople, sat before the emperor and listened as Gregory's last two papal bulls were read out, conferring on his delegates the authority to represent him at the council, and on Carlo Malatesta the authority to resign his papal title.

Giovanni Dominici preached a sermon on the theme of 'Who is he and we will praise him? For in his lifetime he has done marvellous things', relating this to Pope Gregory XII. After this he reiterated his master's support for the council and all its acts to date, and all acts to be performed thereafter. Following this Friar Dominici was received into the college of cardinals at Constance – no longer a schismatic – and the patriarch of Constantinople was likewise honoured with a cardinal's red hat.

Then it was the moment for Carlo Malatesta to read his written permission to abdicate in Gregory XII's name, when it was considered expedient. The archbishop of Milan declared on the council's behalf that it was expedient now. The nations all agreed, and following a few words praising his master, he read out the carefully prepared text:

> The authentic bull of our most holy lord aforesaid, just read, shows him to be free from pressure and coercion by violence and seduced by no error, so that all may clearly perceive by his deeds with what sincerity and heartfelt love he has laboured and will labour for the sacred union and restoration of Christendom in the unity of the Holy Mother Church. He accepts even the way of his own abdication, honestly, freely and sincerely. Therefore as proctor on behalf of our most holy lord Pope Gregory XII, in the name of the Father, the Son and the Holy Spirit, I abdicate and resign as set forth in these letters, in reality and effect all right, title and possession that he holds as pope, and in the name of our said lord I hereby renounce the papal office and every right, title, and possession of the papacy that he now holds, in the presence of our lord Jesus Christ, the head and bridegroom of His Holy Church, and before this sacrosanct synod and universal council, representing the Holy, Roman and Universal Church.[11]

And with that Gregory XII was once more Angelo Corrario. Where there had been three popes there now was only one.

*

The French ambassadors came before Henry, in response to his command; they bowed and knelt before him. There too were the archbishop of Canterbury, Chancellor Beaufort and many other lords.[12] The king addressed them directly and coldly on the subject of justice: how his kingdom of France had been withheld from him.

As soon as he had finished, Archbishop Boisratier, the count of Vendôme and the seigneur d'Ivry stepped forward and showed Henry the letters of credence that they had been given by the king of France. Henry kindly and courteously asked them to expand on the theme. So the archbishop of Bourges spoke as follows:

> To the honour of Jesus Christ, king of kings, I declare here that our serene king – having by your letters the assurance and certainty that you desire peace and an alliance by way of a marriage between you and his illustrious daughter, my lady Katherine, and knowing the fine qualities that distinguish your person – has himself a vital desire to conclude this peace and to establish, by way of kinship and justice, a lasting alliance between you in the interests of both kingdoms. We have been charged, if we find you well disposed to this accommodation, to offer you a further five towns, seven counties and many lordships, which you have been proposed before: the town, the castle and all the lordship of Limoges, including two populous towns, Limoges and Tulle, and by further addition another 50,000 crowns of gold on top of the 800,000 crowns that have been promised for the dowry of Madame Katherine.[13]

It seemed to the French ambassadors that the king was pleased with this offer. He answered them that he would reflect on it at greater length, and would reply to them on Saturday. With that they were ushered out; the interview was over.

As the ambassadors left the chamber they met Jean Fusoris, who had been waiting there. He did not have permission to enter the rooms where the ambassadors of the two kingdoms met, but he had waited outside the door each day, hoping to meet Richard Courtenay. The bishop had been doing his best to avoid him, but now he came up to him and greeted him in a kindly way. 'You are most welcome, Master Jean,' he said. They talked further, and Fusoris asked for the money that Courtenay still owed him. Courtenay told him to come back in the morning.[14]

Friday 5th

Fusoris went to Wolvesey Castle next morning, accompanied by two esquires. He looked for Bishop Courtenay. The man was nowhere to be found. Fusoris then enquired of Courtenay's whereabouts from a doctor of theology he encountered – who was probably Edmund Lacy, the dean of the royal chapel at Windsor. Lacy informed him that he was a little late; the privy council was already sitting and Richard Courtenay would be with the king. But they would not be long; would Master Fusoris care to have some wine while he waited? The esquires declined but Fusoris said yes, and spent some time chatting to Lacy. They talked about exchanging students – two from France studying in England and two from England in France – and they agreed that such a scheme depended very much on whether peace could be achieved. Dr Lacy asked about astrology and wondered whether there were many astrologers in Paris. Fusoris responded that there were many amateurs but few professionals, as it was not a science that paid great rewards. At this Lacy took out a sextant he had with him, which was marked with the revolutions of the heavens since the king's birth. Fusoris refused to touch it, on account of the likelihood of war between their countries; not only were the negotiations going badly, he had seen a herald in Winchester wearing the livery of the duke of Burgundy.[15] No doubt he suspected that Henry might agree a treaty with John the Fearless, and the two of them jointly attack France. Lacy did not press the matter but said instead how much he would have liked to spend some time in Paris, maybe a year or two. It might have been possible 'if only your ambassadors had come sooner,' he added, with the obvious implication that the advanced state of military preparations meant that peace was no longer a possibility. Then he paused and reflected that perhaps he was being too negative; maybe an English embassy might achieve some significant breakthrough after Henry had actually taken his army across the Channel?

The wine was finished and Fusoris joined his friends waiting in the hall of the castle. A little while later he saw Bishop Courtenay leaving the great chamber and walking down to the chapel to sing Mass. Fusoris followed him into the chapel, and while the bishop prepared the altar for the service Fusoris asked him again for his money. Bishop Courtenay explained that he would have sent it sooner but he could not find a reliable enough messenger to take it to Paris. But he assured the tenacious old Frenchman that he would give him what he owed him, but that he had not a penny with him at that time. He asked whether Fusoris had brought any gifts for the king? Fusoris said he had brought an astrolabe and some copies of tracts that he had discussed with Courtenay in Paris. Hearing this, Courtenay asked him to bring them to him the following morning at Mass, when he would present them to the king. In fact, he and Henry had often talked about Fusoris, he said, and suggested that Fusoris might like to meet the king.[16]

Some idea of what the king and the council had been discussing can be gained from the patent letters issued as 'by the king' from Winchester today. Legal cases were being prepared by royal officers in the court of the exchequer against the duke of York for monies owed by him in respect of his custody of the Channel Islands and the alien priories there: Henry ordered these to be dropped, and pardoned his cousin everything he owed the exchequer. He ordered that two men whom he had pardoned for murder in the first year of his reign, and who had subsequently been detained by royal officers, should be released. And a shipbuilder called William Godey was commissioned to take boards, timber, iron, pitch, tar, carpenters and smiths for making a new ship for the king. Given the advanced stage of proceedings, this must have been a ship for use in a future campaign.[17] But why Henry was looking so far ahead at this precise juncture, when he was running short of money and there was no guarantee he would survive this forthcoming expedition, is a mystery. Perhaps it was simply that Godey's services were now available.

Finally, a commission was sent 'from the king' to Sir Gilbert Talbot empowering him to draw up a treaty with Owen Glendower. Just in case the Welshman saw an opportunity to rise for one last time while Henry was out of the country, a process of negotiation should be started, to persuade Glendower that he had more to gain by being loyal to Henry than by fighting a guerrilla war against him.[18]

*

In Constance, the emperor sent Lord Wenceslas of Dubá, Lord John of Chlum and four bishops to the prison cell in the Franciscan Friary. It fell to Lord John, Hus's closest friend at Constance, to do the talking.

> Look, Master Jan, we are laymen and do not know how to counsel you. Therefore see if you feel that you are guilty in anyway of what you have been charged with. Do not fear to be instructed therein, and to recant. But if you do not feel guilty of those things with which you have been charged, then follow your conscience. Under no circumstances do anything against your conscience, or lie in the sight of God, but rather be steadfast until death in what you know to be the truth.

At this Jan Hus began to weep. But he replied,

> Lord John, be sure that if I knew that I had written or preached anything erroneous against the law and against the Holy Catholic Church, I would humbly desire to recant – as God is my witness. I have always desired to be shown better and more relevant scripture than my own teachings and writings.

One of the bishops there could not restrain himself. 'Do you claim that you are wiser than the whole council?'

Turning to him, Hus responded: 'I do not claim to be wiser than the whole council; but, I pray, give me one member of the council who would instruct me by better and more relevant scripture, and I am ready instantly to recant!'

'See how obstinate he is in his heresy!' declared the bishop triumphantly. And with that exclamation they led Hus back into his cell and locked the door.[19]

When they had gone, Hus began to write his last letters.[20] He addressed one to his friends in Constance, and another to his friends back home in Bohemia. He gave his last remaining possessions away to those who had stood by him. And then he wrote his very last letter, addressed 'to the entire Christian world'. In this he tried to give a synopsis of his trial. He repeated the words he had used before: 'I had supposed that in this council would be greater reverence, piety and discipline'. The letter was never finished. But it did not matter. He would address the entire Christian world the following day.

Saturday 6th

It was John Wycliffe who was dealt with first by the council of Constance. The first forty-five heretical articles to be identified were execrated once more, and then another 260 were likewise dealt with. Any memory or memorial of him was condemned. And then it was time for Hus.

The archbishop of Riga led him into the cathedral. The emperor was there, wearing his crown, and so were a crowd of prelates. In the middle of them all was a table and a pedestal where the vestments and chasuble were arranged for the purpose of unfrocking him. Hus fell to his knees when he saw the table and pedestal, and stayed there a long time, praying silently. As he knelt there the bishop of Lodi went up into the pulpit and preached a sermon about heresy, stressing how heresy does so much harm to the Church, tearing it to pieces, and how it is the duty of kings to eradicate any and all such heresies.

After the sermon, the charges against Hus were read out. He heard, stopped praying and stood up. He tried to reply but he was forced to be silent. 'I beseech you, for God's sake!' implored Hus. But he was forbidden to speak. He fell to his knees and began praying again.

They began the unfrocking ceremony. Seven bishops forced him to his feet and adorned him in the vestments of the priesthood as if he was about to celebrate Mass. They took no notice as he called out 'My Lord Jesus Christ was mocked in a white garment when he was led from Herod to Pilate!' They led him up onto the table, and put a chalice in his hand. Standing there, in tears, facing the multitude of priests, he declared, 'These bishops exhort me to recant and abjure. But I fear to do so, lest I be a liar in the sight of the Lord, and also lest I offend my own conscience and the truth of God.'

Taken down from the table, the bishops began to unfrock him. They took the chalice from him, declaring, 'O cursed Judas, because you have abandoned the counsel of peace and have counselled with the Jews we take away from you this cup of redemption!'

'I trust in the Lord God Almighty,' Hus replied, 'for whom I patiently bear this vilification. He will not take from me the cup of redemption, but I firmly hope that I will drink from it today, in his kingdom!'

They cursed him with every holy garment they took from him. And when he stood in just his gown and black coat they took a pair of scissors and obliterated his tonsure, removing most of his hair. They placed a paper mitre on his head, which bore the images of two devils and the word, *heresiarch*, shouting 'we commit your soul to the Devil!'

'And I commit it to the most merciful Lord Jesus Christ, who bore a much heavier and harsher crown of thorns!' replied Hus.

They led him out of the cathedral and delivered him into the hands of the executioners. His books were being burned nearby, the smoke drifting across the city. Crowds had gathered to watch him go, and more now arrived, accompanying him through the streets. The emperor and authorities had foreseen this, and there were more than a thousand guards ready. Hus sang psalms as he was led along, and called out 'Have mercy on me, oh God!'

So many people were crowding around Hus that, to avoid the masses, the guards had to force them back from the bridge out of the city. Once across, Hus's executioners led him off the road that led to Gottleiben Castle and around the edge of a meadow beside the road, to the place where the stake was. Two wagon loads of straw and brushwood stood ready. People in the crowd following started shouting that he should have a confessor before he died but a mounted priest, wearing a green suit with a red silk lining, shouted back that he had been excommunicated, and deserved no confessor.

More people were flocking to the place of execution. Soldiers started running towards Hus, lest matters get out of hand. Ulrich Richental, who was an eyewitness, estimated that there were three thousand armed men there. He was standing near as Hus approached the stake; Richental saw him fall to his knees and scream to Christ for mercy. At the place of execution he was offered a confession on the condition that he recant. 'I am no mortal sinner!' he yelled, terrified. So they proceeded.

Hus was tied to the stake with ropes, his hands being tied behind his back. He was made to stand on a stool, and a sooty chain fastened around his neck. The executioners took brushwood and straw from the wagons and piled it around him. They scattered a little pitch over it, and lit the fire.

Hus began to sing. 'Christ thou son of the living God, have mercy on us.' As he sang the wind caught the flames and the smoke and flames began to rise into his face, and for those who saw him it seemed his lips were moving but they could hear nothing. Soon they heard not singing but the cries and screams of excruciating pain, as the fire burned his gown and his skin. The executioners piled on more straw and brushwood. And so he died.

The paper mitre on Hus's head did not burn straightaway, according to Richental, so the executioners knocked it off into the flames with a stick. They had orders to ensure that no trace of him remained. No artefact of his had been removed in the cathedral: everything he wore on the day of his death was to be obliterated with him. His purse, his coat, his clothes, his belt – even his knives. And the full extent of this order became clear as the flames died down. The executioners knocked his charred flesh into the fire, and broke the bones with clubs so that they would be burned more thoroughly. As the fire died down they found his skull, dragged it out, and smashed it open with their clubs. The pieces they threw back into the flames.[21]

The ashes were guarded. When cold enough, they were gathered up and cast into the Rhine. The very determination to remove Hus entirely from physical existence – like the will to eliminate any memory of Wycliffe – shows how seriously the council regarded him. The first great battle of the year 1415 was over; and although Jan Hus had lost his life, the cause for which he fought had a new martyr and was immeasurably stronger. Christendom was never the same again.

*

Fusoris went to Wolvesey Castle next morning with his servant, Jean du Berle, taking the astrolabe and astrological tracts that he had mentioned to Courtenay. The French ambassadors were still with the king when he arrived, and he waited in the hall. Eventually the meeting broke up and the king and all the negotiators, including Courtenay, came down the stairs from the great chamber and went into the chapel. Fusoris followed them, and heard Courtenay celebrate Mass. When it was over, Courtenay signalled to him to approach, and led him to the king's pew.

'My lord,' said Courtenay, 'this is Master Jean Fusoris, that I spoke of, who, thinking there would be a treaty of peace, has brought with him a composition for your solid sphere, another for an instrument wherein may be seen the motions of the planets, their conjunctions, oppositions and aspects, together with a figure of the heavens at all hours, a small astrolabe and a practical guide on how to use it, and a sextant that he offers to your majesty.'

'Thank you,' said the king in Latin, as Fusoris – on one knee – produced the articles and passed them to the bishop one by one. '*Grans merci*,' he added afterwards.

'I hope they are pleasing to you, serene prince,' replied Fusoris, in French.

The king said nothing more but Courtenay told Fusoris he was invited to dine with them.[22]

This tendency to say very little was Henry's usual manner. However, today he was particularly disinclined to make small talk with a visiting French astrologer. The negotiations had to be brought to a close. He had recalled the French ambassadors to the palace for the final day of negotiations and had delivered his verdict on their offer made on Thursday. He wanted the ambassadors to tell him exactly when he could expect Princess Katherine to be delivered to him with her jewels and 850,000 crowns, and when the towns and lands would be delivered to him. He declared he was happy with these terms on one condition – that the ambassadors agree a truce to last fifty years. Of course he knew well that the ambassadors had no authority to agree this term – so he would send his own ambassadors to Paris to put the proposal to the king of France while the French ambassadors remained here in England. Much lively debate had followed this. Henry Beaufort had insisted the girl be handed over with the money and jewels on St Andrew's Day (30 November). The French objected, on the grounds that it would be impossible to gather all the money by then. And they maintained they could not agree to the fifty-year truce because they had insufficient authority, and they could not assure the king of the terms on which he was to hold these new lands. He wanted full sovereignty and the French ambassadors would not say exactly on what basis the offer was made.[23] At this point they broke to attend Mass and then eat dinner.

After dinner Courtenay came up to Fusoris and shook his hand. The final stage of the embassy now had to take place. Courtenay informed Fusoris that there would be no deal, no peace treaty and no marriage. He expressed his regret, for he believed that had the French envoys come sooner then the whole matter could have been settled. In this way he once more turned reality around to suggest it was all the fault of the French. Fusoris objected that, regarding the marriage, that was the fault of the English, for the usual amount of money had been offered – and more besides. It was Henry's obstinacy and his excessive demands for the peace that were to blame. Courtenay replied that, no, Henry was a good, wise man. He was chaste and pure – the bishop was sure that he had not slept with a woman since becoming king. But what did Fusoris think of him, now he had met him?

Fusoris's answer is very revealing. Henry had a great stateliness, and the fine manner of a high lord, but he seemed better suited for the Church than for war. The real soldier in the family was not Henry but his brother Thomas, duke of Clarence – or so it appeared to Fusoris.[24]

That afternoon the king and the ambassadors reconvened in the great chamber. Fusoris was with them this time. There was no further debate. Henry Beaufort reiterated the whole process of the peace negotiations, from the original demands in 1414 down to the debate that morning.

> But you do not have the power or the will, as each of you knows, to agree with our lord the king about the manner and the form in which he will hold these lands: if, for example, it will be as King Edward III of happy memory held them, and without prejudice to his rights, or otherwise. You are no better when it comes to the prolongation of the truce and avoiding the effusion of human blood, nor on the exact date and time of the handing over of the Princess Katherine with the money and jewels.[25]

Beaufort went on to juxtapose these supposed failings on the part of the French negotiators with the fact that Henry had showed himself prepared to forego 'great, important and notable things' such as his claim to the throne of France, the duchies of Normandy and Touraine, the counties of Anjou and Maine, overlordship of Brittany and Flanders, and other lands claimed 'in the time of Edward of venerable memory' and delivered to him by treaty. As a result of this, claimed Beaufort, it seemed that the French king had no sincere intention of working towards a permanent peace.

According to the chronicler Enguerrand Monstrelet, it was the archbishop of Canterbury, not Beaufort, who delivered the speech. He states that he ended with the declaration that unless the French delivered Henry everything that had been owed to Edward III by the Treaty of Brétigny, he would invade France and despoil the whole of the kingdom, and that he would remove Charles VI from the throne with his sword. To this Boisratier is supposed to have replied,

> O king, how can you consistently with honour and justice, wish to dethrone and iniquitously destroy the most Christian king of the French, our very dear and most redoubted lord, the noblest and most excellent of all the kings in Christendom? O king, with all due reverence and respect, do you think he has offered, by me, such an extent of territory and so large a sum of money with his daughter in marriage, through any fear of you, your subjects or allies? By no means! But moved by pity and his love of peace he has made these offers to avoid the shedding of innocent blood . . . for whenever you will make your promised attempt, he will call upon God, the blessed Virgin, and on all the saints, making his appeal to them for the justice of his cause . . . We have now only to entreat you that you will have us safely conducted out of the realm and that you will write to our said king under your hand a seal, the answer you have given us.[26]

Henry ordered that a letter summarising the final response be drawn up and sealed with the privy seal. It would be ready by the end of the day. The peace negotiations were over.

A later source states that Archbishop Boisratier lost his temper at this point and declared that Henry had no right to claim the throne of France as he had no claim to the throne of England; and he and his fellow ambassadors should have been negotiating with the heirs of Richard II, not Henry.[27] We cannot be certain whether this preserves a real event – a loss of control that could not have been allowed to stand in the official record – or whether it was just an imaginative embellishment. If Archbishop Boisratier did lose his temper, who could blame him?

*

Back at Constance, the king of France's ambassadors succeeded in having the propositions of Jean Petit refuted. Although Petit was not actually named in the edict condemning tyrannicide, it was clear in which direction it was intended. Drafted by Dr Jean Gerson, it stated:

> The holy synod, being particularly desirous of finding measures to extinguish the errors and heresies now springing up in various parts of the world, as it is bound and was convened to do, has learned recently that certain propositions have been published, erroneous and scandalous on many counts, both to faith and good morals, and aimed at the overthrow of the whole fabric and order of the state. Among these propositions the following is reported. 'Any tyrant may and should be rightfully and meritoriously killed by any of his vassals or subjects, even by methods of secret conspiracy, blandishment and flattery, notwithstanding any vow or league the vassal may have made with him and without waiting for a sentence or mandate from any judge whatsoever.' In order to oppose this error, the holy synod . . . decrees and affirms that this doctrine is erroneous in faith and morals, and disapproves and condemns it as heretical, scandalous and seditious, opening the way to craft, deceit, falsehood, treachery and perjury. In addition, it declares and decrees and affirms that those who obstinately maintain this most perilous doctrine are heretics and as such should be punished by the rules of the canons and the law.[28]

By this reckoning, John the Fearless was a heretic and deserved the same punishment as Jan Hus had just received. His lawyers Martin Porée and Pierre Cauchon were going to have a hard time refuting this decision and exonerating their lord.

*

After the French ambassadors had left, Henry attended to a few more items of business at Wolvesey with his council. He dictated a letter to the Jurade of Bordeaux on behalf of the earl of Dorset, to whom they owed money. He declared he had already asked them once to pay; he now requested they do so immediately, so he did not have to write to them again on the matter. The earl of Westmorland and eight other men were commissioned to enquire into the abduction of Mordach of Fife in Yorkshire, and to arrest and imprison the offenders.[29] And finally he consented to see Peter Benefeld, the tenacious envoy of the Teutonic Knights.

Hearing Benefeld's case, Henry beckoned the chancellor and his secretary to him and asked what was being done about the matter. Beaufort declared that a friendly letter was going to be drafted to the Grand Master of the Order explaining that no money was currently available but that the debt would be honoured in due course. Beaufort would be riding back to the capital on the following day; perhaps Peter would care to travel in his company. Then the letter could be written when they were back at Westminster.

Henry was satisfied. He dismissed Benefeld, and called for supper. Then he set out for Titchfield Abbey, near Southampton.[30]

Sunday 7th

Fusoris knew the French embassy would be leaving Southampton this morning, so today was his last chance to get his money. He rose early and went to the town house in Winchester where Courtenay was staying. The bishop was apparently still in bed, but a servant went to a chest and took out 100 nobles for the tenacious Frenchman. Fusoris pointed out that when he had tried to change the last 100 nobles in Paris he had lost out to the tune of 33 crowns. The servant assured him these were all good – in other words, they were all of the correct weight.[31]

Fusoris had finally got what he came for. His servant came to the house with his horses and belongings, and he set out on the journey back to Paris, catching up with the ambassadors shortly afterwards.

Wednesday 10th

Henry stayed at Titchfield Abbey with the remaining members of his privy council. They discussed the dossier of diplomatic agreements

with the French, which Bishop Courtenay had compiled on 10 May.
Key to them all was the Treaty of Bourges of 1412: the document in
which the Armagnac lords ceded sovereignty of Aquitaine to the king
of England. In order to win the approval of the council of Constance
for his war, and especially the emperor, he needed to show that his
cause was a just one. It was somewhat ironic that the Treaty of Bourges
– a document that Henry had been forced to swear to uphold by his
late father – was now the best justification for his forthcoming
campaign. The French could indeed argue that he had no right to the
English claim on the throne of France, but they could not deny that
the lords now in authority had once confirmed that Henry was the
rightful sovereign lord of Gascony, and had offered to help him regain
sovereignty of the duchy.

Henry directed the archbishop of Canterbury to draw up copies of
the agreements and to have them witnessed and sealed by a notary
public – a common means used on the Continent for authenticating
documents – as well as by the archbishop himself. When this was
done, the whole file was sent to Sigismund as an explanation for the
forthcoming war. According to a contemporary writer, Henry hoped
that 'all Christendom might know what great acts of injustice the
French in their duplicity had inflicted on him, and that reluctantly, and
against his will, he felt compelled to raise his standards against the
rebels'.[32]

*

Fusoris and the French ambassadors had now been travelling for three
days. An English esquire came among them, asking where the count
of Vendôme was staying. He had presents, he said, for the ambassadors. He was pointed in the direction of the right inn, and all the
Frenchmen in the party crowded around to see what the squire had
brought. Jean Fusoris failed to get near, but met the squire later and
was given 40 nobles (£13 6s 8d) in return for the astrolabe and the
books he had given the king, together with a message of thanks.

Fusoris was grateful and walked along with the esquire. When he
was asked why the ambassadors had taken such a long time to arrive,
thereby forcing the kingdom to go on to a war footing (in the esquire's
opinion), Fusoris replied that, as far as he knew, it was because there

had already been one embassy; it was not thought that a war was likely. And the king of England was a fool to press for war – he had much more to gain from a marriage than a war. After all, Fusoris had seen that a number of people in England thought the earl of March should be king. Some preferred the idea that Thomas, duke of Clarence, should have inherited the throne instead of his elder brother, and hoped that Henry would die soon without an heir so Thomas would inherit. There had been a rising against Richard II when he had left the country, and Richard had lost his throne; perhaps Henry would find that the same thing happened to him? War was dangerous, in more ways than one. And what did he hope to gain? If he meant just to make a short raid, he would not be met with much of a welcome when he returned – having taxed the country so heavily and forced so many towns and lords to make loans to him. And if he meant to undertake a longer campaign, he would find armies more numerous and better-trained than his army now gathering at Southampton. Henry could not rely on the king of France and the duke of Burgundy fighting each other.

In response to all this the esquire could only say that, with God's help, there would yet be peace. The two men then parted, Fusoris to ride on to Dover and sail for France with the ambassadors and the Celestine monks from Sheen. If Henry was not going to build them a monastery, and insisted on going to war with their country, they were not going to stay. As Fusoris said, for a Frenchman in 1415 England was a good country to have visited but a bad one in which to linger.

Thursday 11th

When Henry Beaufort had left Winchester he had carried a number of Henry's instructions back to London with him. These were all issued in formal letters over the next few days. Henry instructed the collectors of customs in London and various other ports to repay a loan to the Venetians of 1,000 marks, to pay £285 0s 6d for sails, ropes and tackle for the king's flagship, *Trinity Royal*; and to repay £9,000 to the treasurer of Calais.[33] Sir Ralph Rochford was reimbursed £102 6s 8d for his expenses in going to the council of Constance; and Dr Jean Bordiu, archdeacon of Médoc, was reimbursed £171 16s 8d for his mission to negotiate with the king of Castile at Fuenterrabia, from which he had returned in February. A number of sergeants-at-arms were appointed; and Henry ordered that the wages of the keeper of the privy seal be paid.[34] A royal judge, William Loddyngton, was given permission to celebrate Mass in an ancient chapel. Formal assignments were drawn up concerning the major jewels pledged. In particular, an indenture conveying the Crown Henry to Thomas, duke of Clarence, was sealed, stating that he could dispose of it as he saw fit if the king had not redeemed it by 2 February 1417. This document also stipulated that he should not break it up – a direction that Thomas ignored, dividing it among his followers as security for future payment of their wages.[35]

Friday 12th

Henry arrived at Southampton. He wrote a letter under the signet to the council – probably those members with Chancellor Beaufort in London – enclosing a schedule of four carracks that the earl of Huntingdon had been promised. He urged that a warrant be issued to the masters of these ships for each of them to take a hundred mariners to serve in them.[36]

With the king was one of the royal 'esquires of the body', John Cheney. He was about to set out with three men-at-arms on the mission to Harfleur. Today he penned one of the few private letters to survive from this year, addressing Sir John Pelham, who was also due to sail:

Right worshipful and worthy Sir, I recommend myself to you with all my heart thanking you for the great kindness and gentleness that you have shown me up to now without fail, praying you might always be of good continuance; and you will wish to know that the king and all the lords here are well blessed by God. And as regards my lord the earl of Huntingdon now at sea at last, the bearer of this letter shall declare it more plainly by mouth than I can write it at this time. Furthermore, right worshipful and worthy Sir, you will want to know that I am here, and have been at great costs and expense, wherefore I need to borrow a notable sum before I go and fare from my house, and from other friends of mine, save only you, worthy Sir, having full hope and trust in your gracious and gentle person to help and succour me at this time in my greatest necessity, to lend me some notable sum of gold such as the bearer of this, Thomas Garnetier, my servant, shall truly declare ... praying the Holy Trinity send you honour prosperity and joy. Written in haste at Southampton, the 12th day of July.[37]

So the first ships were at sea already, with the earl of Huntingdon. And Henry was not the only one feeling the financial strain of the expedition.

Saturday 13th

About this time the Teutonic envoys had a final meeting with the chancellor in London. At last he was honest with them: they could expect nothing in the immediate future. If the money was to be paid, it would only be in small instalments, at long intervals; and there really was no point in them pressing for more than that.[38] And with that even Peter Benefeld realised he had come to the end of the road. All there remained to do was to write up the whole episode for the benefit of the Grand Master, and to sail back to Marienburg.

Tuesday 16th

It is not clear exactly why the earl of Huntingdon was already at sea. One might speculate that he was guarding against a pre-emptive French attack. However, as the French ambassadors were still on their return journey, this seems unlikely. Rather it seems we should connect the earl of Huntingdon's expedition with an assault on the Norman town of Fécamp, which took place today.[39] People in the area and all along the coast now knew they could not rely on the French government to protect them. Many packed up their belongings and left. The war had begun.

Wednesday 17th

From Bishop's Waltham, Henry sent out an order to the sheriff of Norfolk. He had been informed that certain men of Norfolk had refused to keep watch for the safety of the coast. He ordered that the sheriff make a proclamation that the king declared that this remained their duty, and they should not fail to do perform it adequately.[40]

*

At Constance, Sigismund and the council had achieved the feat of deposing one pope and persuading another to resign. Now they turned their attention to Pope Benedict XIII. The conference to discuss his abdication had been planned to take place at Nice in June, but it had been delayed, partly by an outbreak of the plague in that town and partly because of concerns for Sigismund's safety, following the threats made against him by John the Fearless. But now the time had come to act. Sigismund appointed the duke of Bavaria-Heidelberg to preside over the council in his absence and urged the deputies to discuss the reform of the Church but not to make any final decisions until his return.[41]

Sigismund did not want to run the risk of coming across John the Fearless. He set out to travel through Savoy, to the south of the duke's lands, keeping his route secret.

Friday 19th

In Portugal, at the royal estate of Odivelas, Henry's aunt, Queen Philippa of Portugal breathed her last. She was fifty-five years of age, and a much-loved woman in her adopted country. Among the children she left were such figures as the future king, Duarte I of Portugal and Enrico (Henry the Navigator). But to Henry her death would have meant little beyond the gradual breaking of a diplomatic bond. She had married João I of Portugal in Oporto in February 1387 – when Henry was only a few weeks old. In all probability, Henry had never actually met her.

*

Sir Thomas Gray of Heton had come down from the north and had spent about a week in London. Yesterday he had saddled up and started his journey westward to Southampton. He had spent last night at Kingston upon Thames, and was riding to Southampton along the road through Guildford.

Treason was on his mind. After throwing the earl of Cambridge's letter into a cesspit at York, he had been visited by a man called Cresswell, who was a retainer of the imprisoned Lord Percy. Cresswell had shown him some copied documents: an indenture between Sir Robert Umphraville and someone – possibly the duke of Albany – and a copy of a letter from Percy to the earl of Cambridge and Lord Clifford. Gray had commented to Cresswell that the king would like neither the indenture nor the letter. But Cresswell had told him that it was God's will that Henry Percy should come from Scotland with a strong hand in the name of King Richard II, as the earl of Cambridge and Lord Clifford were urging him to do in their letters. Gray seems to have promised nothing; he had yet to make up his mind about the earl of Cambridge, whose plan to exchange Mordach for Lord Percy had been thwarted and whose new plans were even more dangerous. Cambridge was now considering kidnapping one of eighteen important English lords on a list provided by the duke of Albany, any one of whom he would exchange for Lord Percy.

As he was travelling, an esquire rode up alongside him. It was his cousin, Walter Lucy. They greeted each other and before long their conversation turned to Henry Percy and King Richard II. Lucy asked Gray what had happened about Henry Percy. Gray replied that he did not know, although he added that he had seen 'an indenture which was not likely to be fulfilled'. Then Lucy told him about the heavy debts that the earl of March had undertaken, and how the earl had borrowed heavily from the earl of Arundel and Lord Scrope, as well as himself, in order to pay back the punitive fine that Henry had levied on him for marrying Anne Stafford. Lucy added that Arundel and Scrope had always been good to the earl of March. Gray was sanguine. It meant nothing, he said, for the earl of March 'was but a hog'.

At this point the conversation shifted on to more dangerous ground. Lucy said to Gray that the earl of March 'should be found a man and challenge his right', meaning that the earl of March should make a claim for the throne. He added that he understood from the earl of March that Lord Scrope had been to see him of his own free will, and 'the highest and the haughtiest' had spoken to the earl also, encouraging him to pursue his claim. Scrope had told him that he had the support of the earl of Arundel too, for they had both been intent on helping the earl of March for the last three years. Scrope had finally presented the earl with three alternative strategies. One was to go to France and return at the head of a mercenary army (as the earl's ancestor, the first earl of March, had done in 1326). Another was to attack the king at sea. The third was to go into Wales and start a rising against the Lancastrians there.

The testimonies on which the above account relies are suspect, being delivered by Gray at a later date, in prison. But even so one can see that Lucy was not being wholly honest with him. The earl of Arundel was one of the king's closest friends; he was not a man to favour the earl of March's claim to the throne. Nor was Scrope. But both men had lent the earl money. When Lucy told Gray that Arundel and Scrope would support the earl of March's claim to the throne, he was lying. When Scrope and Arundel had resolved in 1412 that they would help the earl of March's cause, they had only meant as far as marrying Anne Stafford. Neither man wanted the earl to be king. And Scrope's recent visit to the earl was rather more sensitive than either the earl himself or his steward, Lucy, realised. Scrope wanted to know more about the plot – not in order to join it but to learn what was afoot. His observation that the earl of March had three strategies open to him was not delivered as conspiratorial advice but an observation: a warning. He later repeated these same strategies – to show the flaws in each of them.

Nonetheless, Lucy convinced Gray that Lord Scrope and the earl of Arundel would support the cause of the earl of March. He had fooled himself into thinking this, and now he fooled Gray into thinking it too. At this point Gray began to think that the earl of Cambridge's plot might not be so far-fetched after all. If they could bring about a revolution between them, Gray surmised, then he stood to gain mightily. His son would be married to the king's niece.[42]

Saturday 20th

At Southampton Henry ordered Richard Redeman and John Strange, king's clerks, to supervise the mustering of the men about to set sail under the command of the duke of Clarence.[43] The reason for having royal clerks look over the lordly retinues was in order to count exactly how many had gathered, and to make sure that they were all fit to fight. Henry did not want to pay the wages of useless men, or archers who could not draw a longbow, or men who had simply failed to show up.

At Westminster the king's clerks acted on an instruction that Henry must have issued some days before. They searched the patent rolls in accordance with their instructions – presumably conveyed by Chancellor Beaufort on his return to London – and drew up a commission to two clerks to assist the prior provincial of the Dominican Order in England to investigate the nuns of Dartford. The Dominican nuns' house had been founded by Edward III; being a royal foundation, the prior provincial had to petition the king for permission to intervene.[44] The king had granted the petition and given the clerks power 'to enquire into and punish with the said prior provincial any defects, excesses and trespasses in these things and to reduce all the sisters to obedience according to the form of apostolic bulls and letters patent dated 10 November in the 30th year of the reign of Edward III.'[45]

*

Sir Thomas Gray received a message at Hambledon, in Hampshire.[46] If he should hasten on to Southampton he would hear a 'new thing' from the earl of Cambridge. So he did.

When he arrived, Gray told Cambridge about meeting Walter Lucy the previous day, and hearing from him that Lord Scrope and the earl of Arundel had been supporters of the earl of March's cause for the last three years. That seems to have been the catalyst for Cambridge to discuss his new plans with Gray in detail. Cambridge had decided to shift his attention directly to the earl of March. The idea was to take the earl into Wales, and there proclaim him king of England, declaring that Henry V was a usurper. The earl of Cambridge – whose maternal grandfather had been King Pedro of Castile – had in his custody the Pallet of Spain, a piece of head armour which incorporated a real crown. The earl of March could be crowned with that. He also owned a banner decorated with the arms of England. With a genuinely royal opposition leader to fight for, many of those who did not want to go to France, many Lollards and many Welshmen would be attracted to their cause. Or so he thought.

*

William, Lord Botreaux, of Cadbury in Somerset, was preparing to set out with sixty men in his retinue. He was twenty-six years old, and normally would not have considered making his will for another twenty years. But like many young men on the verge of setting out for France, he decided that the time had come to consider his final resting place and the final disposal of his worldly goods.

First he declared that he wanted to be buried in the parish church at Cadbury. With regard to his possessions, he bequeathed to his wife Elizabeth 'all the utensils, ornaments and furniture of my hall, chambers, kitchen, pantry and buttery except the drinking cups, basins and ewers and other vessels of gold and silver'. He also left her 'a basin and ewer of silver, five newly-made goblets, a drinking cup of gold made in the form of a rose, and suit of vestments for her altar, adorned with peacocks' feathers and velvet'. He left £1,000 to be shared between his two daughters, for their marriage portions, but if they inherited his estate due to the lack of a son then the £1,000 was to be 'distributed by my executors to the poor and needy, and to buy books and vestments for such parish churches of my patronage as may want them, and to help the poor tenants in my lordships'. He directed that three priests should celebrate divine services at Cadbury for his soul and the souls of his ancestors, until a college could be founded there according to his directions. He left bequests of £2 to each of the four orders of friars at Bristol and to various friaries and monasteries from Bodmin in Cornwall to Salisbury in Wiltshire. And on every Wednesday and Friday for ten years after his death, his executors were to distribute a penny to each of twenty-four paupers.[47]

Sunday 21st

Three envoys arrived from King Ferdinand of Aragon with a present of two fine coursers and a jennet for Henry. Their instructions were to negotiate a new alliance between Aragon and England, and to propose a marriage between Henry and Maria, King Ferdinand's eldest daughter. They found the king pleasant and open to negotiation on their initial interview but were informed that he was about to cross to France. So they went on a pilgrimage to Canterbury by way of Winchester and London at Henry's expense. Henry deputed John Waterton and Master John Kempe to meet them on their return to Southampton and to sail to Spain with them to meet Ferdinand.[48]

The instructions he gave Waterton and Kempe were guarded. They were to admit that Henry was unmarried but they were to stress that it would be 'a very difficult matter' to arrange a marriage, even if Maria was a suitable bride. Rather he instructed them to offer the hand of one of his two unmarried brothers (John and Humphrey), with a request for a dowry of 200,000 crowns, although the envoys might allow themselves to be beaten down to 160,000. Henry still intended to take a French princess for himself.[49]

*

When Sir Thomas Gray awoke in the guesthouse of the Greyfriars in Southampton, he found Lord Scrope standing at the foot of his bed. Scrope asked how he liked the prospect of the voyage to France. Gray admitted that he was averse to it, and told Scrope about his meeting with Walter Lucy two days earlier. Gray had believed Lucy's story about Scrope supporting the earl of March's cause. He further believed that Lord Scrope was prepared to consider rebellion against the Lancastrians on account of the fate of his uncle Archbishop Scrope of York, who had been executed on Henry IV's personal authority in 1405. So he asked Scrope directly: did he favour the earl of March's claim to the throne?

Scrope knew that if he simply denied that the earl of March had a claim, then Gray would realise that he had been misled. Gray would inform Cambridge, and he would be unable to find out anything more about the plot. So he answered evasively. He told Gray that he had visited the earl of March and heard him speak about his claim to the throne, following his outrage and frustration at being fined so heavily by the king for marrying Anne Stafford. It was enough to convince Gray that the conversation was worth continuing. As each man had a separate commitment for dinner that morning, Gray suggested they meet up again later.

That afternoon, Sir Thomas Gray went looking for Scrope and met him in the street. Together they went to see the earl of March. Walter Lucy was with him. In their presence Scrope asked Gray what he reckoned the earl of March should do? He had three options, Gray said, repeating the three strategies which Lucy had told him Scrope had outlined. He could take the field, he could go to Wales, or he could attack Henry at sea. The earl of March confirmed that 'his heart and his will was full thereto', if he had sufficient forces at his disposal.[50]

Scrope asked the earl of March if he had discussed any of this with anyone before now.

'Why?' asked the earl of March.

'Because I have heard the earl of Cambridge and Sir Thomas here have spoken in this manner to you.'

'Who told you?'

'Walter Lucy.'

Scrope then went on to expound on the dangers the earl faced. As Scrope put it,

if [the earl of March] drew near to Lollards they would subvert this land and the Church; if he drew to Wales it should undo both him and this land; if they made him take a field [the king] would come on him with all [his] host and destroy him; and if he went into Wales he should be enfamined and lost; and if he went by sea with vessels of advantage, he should be taken and undone . . .[51]

Hearing these things, the earl promised Scrope that he would do nothing hasty – he 'would not be stirred until [Scrope] came again'. Walter Lucy promised likewise that he would not do anything treasonable for the time being. After this, the earl and Lucy took to their horses and left.

Following their departure, Gray told Scrope 'that the earl of Cambridge and he and others . . . would meet with the earl of March at his house at Cranbury' on the following day. Scrope was not tempted to join them. Instead he left Gray and took the ferry across the River Itchen to his lodgings. And he sent a verbal message by one of his servants to Walter Lucy – the man who had originally informed him of the emerging plot – stating that he was amazed that such things were being discussed at this present time, for plainly the king 'had men on every side to espy such governance'.

The reply came back that 'they did but hunt' and they were not yet ready to take action. Scrope had to be content with that.

Monday 22nd

Business was conducted in Henry's name today from both Southampton and Bishop's Waltham.[52] It was at Bishop's Waltham that he had a letter drawn up directing the council to pay £500 per year to his brother Thomas during the minority of Henry Beaufort, son of the late John Beaufort, earl of Somerset. The king specified that the arrears since 1410 should be paid, and that 2,000 marks a year should be paid since 14 July 1413.[53] The total was £5,166 13s 4d – hardly an easy sum for the treasurer to find at short notice. At Bishop's Waltham too a letter was drawn up in Henry's name ordering that a great tabernacle of gold, which had once belonged to his grandfather, John of Gaunt, should be delivered to the archbishop of York, the bishop of Durham and several other northern prelates, as security for the repayment of £993 that they had lent him.[54]

Also today, but at Southampton, Henry granted the duchy of Lancaster to sixteen trustees with the power to regrant it to his heirs. Like all the other men who were making their wills, he was beginning to consider putting his affairs in order in case he died. Those named as his trustees were the archbishop of Canterbury, Henry and Thomas Beaufort, Thomas Langley, Richard Courtenay, the duke of York, the earls of Arundel and Westmorland, Lord Fitzhugh, Lord Scrope, Sir Roger Leche, Sir Walter Hungerford, Sir John Phelip, Hugh Mortimer, John Woodhouse and John Leventhorpe. The name that sticks out in that list is that of Henry Scrope. Despite any differences they may have had about the king's war policy, Scrope was clearly still very much in the king's favour.[55]

*

The duke of Albany knew there were plots afoot in England. The list of eighteen names handed to the earl of Cambridge indicates that the Scots were aware of discontented factions. They probably also knew that some men were waiting for news of a northern rising before they would take action in the name of the earl of March. They were also aware that Mordach was back in Henry's custody and was not now going to be handed over as agreed. Consequently about this time they sent two armed expeditions into the north of England. One, led by the earl of Douglas, went into Westmorland and burnt the town of Penrith; the other went into Northumberland. The latter managed to penetrate just six miles before coming across Sir Robert Umphraville at Yeavering, near Kirknewton. Umphraville had only four hundred men with him but managed to rout the Scots, killing sixty men, capturing four hundred and sending the remainder running for twelve miles back into Scotland.[56]

If the copied indenture that Cresswell had showed Gray the Friday just past was Umphraville's promise to allow the Scots to pass, then either it was a forgery or part of a plan of entrapment. Umphraville never meant to observe its terms. Cambridge had been quite foolish to believe it.

*

Gray and Cambridge gathered this evening for supper at the earl of March's house at Cranbury, five miles north of Southampton. The plot was no doubt discussed, and so too the warnings of Lord Scrope. There was clearly a feeling that if they actually *did* nothing, they were innocent. The promise they had given Scrope not to act in the immediate future did not extend to not planning or plotting – or 'hunting', as Lucy put it.

*

In Paris, the five hundred Cabochien supporters of John the Fearless who had been exempted from the Peace of Arras were finally banished from the city.[57] No doubt most went straight to John himself, who was then at Rouvres. Their part in the drama of the year 1415 was not yet over.

Wednesday 24th

The Portuguese fleet finally set sail from Lisbon. To the great relief of
the French spies who were watching, it did not move north but south,
towards the Straits of Gibraltar. It was not going to join with Henry's
fleet in an attack on France; it was heading to Ceuta, in Morocco.

*

The duke of Clarence's retinue was mustered on St Catherine's Hill. The
duke of Gloucester's was at Romsey; the earl of Oxford's was at
Wallopforth; and the earl of Huntingdon's on Swanwick Heath with
the companies of Lord Botreaux, Lord Grey of Ruthin, Roland
Leinthal, and much of the royal household. The men of Sir Thomas
Erpingham and Sir Lewis Robesart gathered on Southampton
Common; other contingents were at Hampton Hill.[58] More than twelve
thousand men were now in the area, and even more horses.

It was inevitable that there would be discontent. Henry directed a
proclamation to be made telling all those who felt they had been
harshly treated to complain to the steward of the treasury or the
comptroller of the royal household. He also had it proclaimed that
all knights, esquires and yeomen in the army were to find sufficient
provisions for themselves in France for three months. This was an
extraordinary amount of food for each man to provide: feeding the
army was a serious concern.[59]

Part of the problem was that Henry was very late in setting out.
Even if his original orders to take ships to Southampton by 8 May
had been drawn up in the expectation that they would not actually
set out until 1 June, that date had already slipped by almost two months.
Even the second revised departure date of 8 July was over two weeks
ago. Henry must have been getting frantic. Much more of a delay and
there would be little time left for a campaign in France. And his finances
were going more awry all the time. Today he had to reiterate his
pledge that jewels would be made available to cover the second
quarter's wages.[60] And he issued more licences for lords who had
received jewels or plate as security to dispose of the said items if they
were not redeemed within a certain time. Two days ago, when he

had ordered John of Gaunt's tabernacle to be handed over to the prelates, he had licensed the recipients to sell it if he had not redeemed it within a certain time. Now he issued a licence for Sir Robert Chalons to dispose of a cup of gold, two bowls of silver gilt and a little basin of silver gilt delivered to him for security of £45. Without these licences, the pledges were of only notional value.[61]

A sense of financial desperation in the royal household may be inferred from such changes of strategy. When Henry had originally planned to sail, he had envisaged paying for the campaign through subsidies and loans. The need for money had grown more intense over the first half of the year; and by the end of April he was resigned to offering items from the royal treasure as security. By early June he was pawning religious artefacts too; and by mid-June he was selling off or breaking up the non-essential utensils of the royal household. Now he had been forced to allow treasures that had been handed over as security to be broken up and sold. The whole six-month progress of financial retreat must have taken a heavy toll on the nerves of the men around Henry who had to deliver this news to the king. He cannot have been pleased to hear that valuable treasures owned by his ancestors had to be broken up to pay for his war. It was not his idea of great kingliness – to *dispose* of his inheritance. The pressure told on one officer in particular. Today the aged Sir Thomas Erpingham was replaced as steward of the household by Sir Walter Hungerford. One suspects he may have asked to stand down, on account of his age and his inability to cope with the administrative pressure.

*

Art MacMurrough, the native Irish lord of Norragh, was granted a two-year safe conduct for two of his men to come to see the king.[62] What it was the erstwhile rebel had to tell Henry we do not know; but what is striking about this reference is that it is practically the only Irish business which we can associate with Henry all year. After appointing Sir John Talbot to govern the country in 1414, he had simply left him to it. So little had been his involvement with the country he had not even paid Talbot – even though he had budgeted for Talbot's salary in June. And if Art MacMurrough's representatives had anything to report to the English council it was about the utter ruthlessness and severity with which Talbot was treating the people. In February he had ordered the arrest of all traitors, outlaws and felons, and the arrest of all the children of rebels, be they Irish or English, so that they could be brought up with the loyal English. He had then proceeded with a savage attack on anyone who dared to oppose English rule, plundering where he went and hanging rebel warriors and their sons. The Irish annals were most indignant on his plundering from the poets of Ireland.[63]

The irony is that Henry did not deal with even this piece of Irish business. By the time the representatives of Art MacMurrough arrived to let him know what was being done in his name, Henry was in France.

★

Henry's will was finalised today. Unlike his father's will, this was not written in English but in Latin, the language of the Church. It began with the dedication to the Holy and Indivisible Trinity and was immediately followed by acknowledgement of the saints by whom Henry was particularly moved, namely:

The Virgin Mary,
St Michael, Gabriel and all the angels and archangels,
St John the Baptist and all the patriarchs,
St Peter, St John and all the apostles,
St George, St Thomas and all the holy martyrs,
St Edward, St John of Bridlington and all confessors
St Anne, St Mary Magdalene and St Bridget
Catherine, Barbara, Ursula and the Eleven Thousand Virgins, and all the holy virgins, and all the celestial court

Henry specified that he wished to be buried in Westminster Abbey, to the east of the shrine of St Edward, in the place where the relics were then kept. He wanted a fine stone tomb and requiem masses sung in vast numbers, three each day by every monk of the abbey. He wanted a special altar to be set up in front of his tomb, dedicated to the Virgin; and he wanted further Masses to be said daily at the altar. So strong was his instinct to control his reputation in death that he even went so far as to stipulate the types of Masses that were to be sung each day and which times of day each of these Masses was to be sung. He left £100 per annum to pay for all these services.

This was just the beginning of the religious requests. As one would expect, he was generous to his new foundations, Syon Abbey and the Charterhouse at Sheen, to each of which he left 1,000 marks. He left vestments, patens, chalices, candelabra, crucifixes and other religious artefacts to Westminster Abbey. In addition, he wanted thirty paupers to be kept in food and clothing for a whole year after his death: they had to be men who were genuinely in need and they all had to pray to Almighty God every day for Henry's soul. The king willed that another three thousand Masses should be sung in honour of the Holy Trinity for the benefit of his soul. And fifteen Masses should be sung every day of the year in honour of Christ's wounds. Five thousand Masses were to be sung in honour of the five joys of the Virgin Mary. Nine more were to be performed in honour of the nine orders of angels, three hundred in honour of the three Patriarchs, twelve in honour of the twelve apostles, and 4,125 in honour of all the saints. And all of these Masses had to be celebrated as soon as possible after his death.

With regard to the individual beneficiaries, the first-named was the Holy Roman Emperor Sigismund, to whom Henry left precious stones to the value of 500 marks. The list of names that follow Sigismund's is the clearest and fullest indication we have of Henry's friends among the aristocracy and his servants in the year 1415:

1. The Holy Roman Emperor
2. John, duke of Bedford
3. Humphrey, duke of Gloucester
4. Henry Chichele, archbishop of Canterbury
5. Henry Beaufort, bishop of Winchester, chancellor
6. Thomas Langley, bishop of Durham
7. Stephen Patrington, bishop of St David's, Henry's confessor
8. Joan Bohun, dowager countess of Hereford, Henry's grandmother
9. Edmund Mortimer, earl of March
10. Richard Beauchamp, earl of Warwick
11. Thomas Beaufort, earl of Dorset

12. Thomas Fitzalan, earl of Arundel
13. Ralph Neville, earl of Westmorland
14. Joan of Navarre, queen of England, Henry's stepmother
15. Edward Holland
16. Gilbert, Lord Talbot
17. Henry, Lord Fitzhugh, royal chamberlain
18. Sir Walter Hungerford, royal steward
19. Sir John Rothenhale
20. John Woodhouse
21. Sir Gilbert Umphraville
22. Sir John Gray
23. Roland Leinthal
24. William Porter
25. John Cheney
26. Roger Salvayn
27. John Steward
28. Lewis Robesart
29. John Waterton
30. William Bourchier
31. John Brown
32. Nicholas Merbury
33. John Botteler
34. John Stone, royal secretary
35. Stephen Payne, royal almoner
36. Nicholas Colnet, royal physician
37. John Wickham, royal chaplain
38. Henry Romworth, royal chaplain
39. Thomas Rodburne, royal chaplain
40. Richard Cassy, royal chaplain

Only after listing all these men by name, and many other servants by their offices, did Henry make a bequest 'to our successor,' meaning of course Thomas, duke of Clarence. This included his best two crowns, two pairs of astrological spheres, the sceptre of the kingdom, an ensign of Spain, a queen's crown, and all his armour.[64]

In many ways Henry's will confirms all the things that we have known or suspected of him to date: extreme religiosity – excessive, even for the period – huge self-importance, a great favouritism for his uncles, no personal love for his brother Thomas, and no acknowledgement of any women except his grandmother and his stepmother. There was a single note of conscience in the will – he ordered that the 25,000 marks that he still owed to his fathers' executors should be paid in full – but otherwise the document was a statement of Henry's vision of his own importance and piety.

His choice of men to be executors was largely predictable: Bishop Beaufort, Bishop Langley, Bishop Courtenay, the earl of Westmorland, Lord Fitzhugh, Sir Walter Hungerford, Sir John Rothenhale, John Woodhouse and John Leventhorpe. Nevertheless, there are some surprising inclusions and omissions. It is interesting that Lord Scrope's name does not appear – as he had been appointed a trustee of Henry's Lancastrian inheritance as recently as 22 July and was to be re-appointed later this same month. Probably the most surprising beneficiary was the earl of March, who was also a witness to the sealing of the will.

Henry signed his will as follows: 'This is my last Will subscribed with my own Hand. R[ex]. H[enricus]. Jesu Mercy and Gremercy Ladie Marie help.'

It is the last word that resonates.

Thursday 25th

Sir Thomas Gray and the earl of Cambridge made their way to Hamble in the Hook, where the earl of March was lodging. They wanted to know whether March was still with them or whether Lord Scrope's warnings had dissuaded him. No, said the earl. He was still in favour of the rising. After further discussions about March's role, Gray and Cambridge left him and went to the Itchen ferry, where they met Lord Scrope.

There are two accounts of what happened next, one by Gray and the other by Scrope. According to Gray, he and Cambridge met Scrope at the ferry and they discussed the expedition to France. Cambridge asked Scrope what he thought, and the latter declared that it was 'best to break the voyage' if at all possible. Cambridge agreed, and the two men asked Gray how this might be achieved. Gray responded that he did not know how they could drive so many men away from Southampton. Scrope suggested it could be managed by burning the ships; and Cambridge agreed. If Gray's testimony on this point is correct,

Scrope was contributing ideas that might lead to the disruption of the campaign.[65] However, Gray's testimony also named men such as Robert Umphraville and the earl of Arundel as fellow plotters; it seems that he was out to implicate as many people as he could, Scrope included.

According to Scrope's own testimony, he spoke to Edward Courtenay, who was brother-in-law to the earl of March, and to Lord Clifford, the earl of Cambridge's brother-in-law. He tried to show them what folly the rising would be, and to put them in fear of taking action against the king, or helping those that did. On the way home from seeing Lord Clifford he met Cambridge and Gray at the Itchen ferry. They told him they had just been to see the earl of March, and asked him when the ships would set sail. Scrope said he was not sure but said 'I believe our tarrying should lose us all'. He left it at that, supposing that once the men had set sail, and Gray and Cambridge found themselves with the army on enemy soil, they would see the danger of taking up arms against the king.

Before Cambridge and Gray left him, they urged Scrope to call on the earl of March. He agreed to do so, if the earl was not yet in bed. As it happened, the earl was still up, so Scrope talked to him about the plot. Once again he tried to persuade the earl not to go through with any of Gray's and Cambridge's plans, whatever they might be.[66]

In all this, Lord Scrope's behaviour and testimony concerning his own actions is consistent with the way that Edward, duke of York, had gathered information about the Epiphany Rising in 1400. York had attended the secret meetings of the conspirators without telling the king for more than two weeks; and when they had been about to act, York had sent an urgent message to the king, warning him.[67] Scrope's evasive and ambiguous answers were clearly designed to lead Cambridge and Gray into revealing more information about their plans. Apart from Gray's assertion that Scrope thought it best to 'break the voyage' and had suggested burning the ships, Scrope was consistently a receiver of information fed to him by others – and someone who warned others about the implications of what they were doing. Even if he had suggested burning the ships, this may have been no more than an attempt to win the trust of the plotters. Still there were things that Scrope did not know, as the earl of Cambridge later pointed out; and so he still had good reason to stay in with the conspirators. But he was not one of them. Why otherwise did he try to dissuade the earl of March and Walter Lucy from rebelling? And why did Cambridge hold back some crucial details about the plot?[68]

Friday 26th

Archbishop Boisratier and the other envoys who had left Southampton on 7 July arrived back in Paris. They went straight to the *hôtel de St Pol* and delivered their report to the dauphin and the rest of the council. It cannot have been well received. They had found Henry intractable and, despite his honeyed words of peace, they had themselves seen thousands of troops pouring into the Southampton area, as well as cattle for victuals on the campaign, and carts and wagons full of bows, arrows, armour and supplies. There was now not the slightest doubt that Henry meant to follow up his attack on Fécamp with a full-scale onslaught on France.[69]

Some Englishmen were not waiting for the invasion to start. About this time the garrisons of the castles around Calais prepared to raid the Boulogne region as soon as the truce came to an end.[70]

*

John the Fearless could see the mood at Constance shifting against him. The French had been successful in their attempts to have Jean Petit condemned as a heretic. The *Justification of the duke of Burgundy* looked as if it was going to go the way of John Wycliffe and Jan Hus's writings. But Duke John still had some cards to play. He had to lift this condemnation, otherwise he too could be classed a heretic, and all hope of regaining influence in France would be lost. So he authorised his ambassadors in Constance to start bribing the cardinals – with good Burgundy wine.[71]

Saturday 27th

At Southampton the king was growing desperate. Already late setting out, he was paying the wages of the crews manning the ships that had arrived from Flanders and Holland, and yet he was still short of vessels. So Henry ordered John Acclane and John Scadlock to seize all the ships they could find in the port of London, regardless of whether they were English or foreign, and to bring them straightaway to Southampton. He did not have enough arrows either, and a second commission was issued to John Acclane to acquire bows, arrows, bowstrings and artillery.[72]

*

In Bordeaux, the mayor and jurats of the city wrote back to Benedict Espina, their agent in London, telling them that one of the two siege engines called 'brides' that Henry had asked for was now ready, and that they would send it whenever he required it. As for the other, it would be ready when Benedict Espina arrived in person, in several weeks' time.[73]

Sunday 28th

Sir Jean le Maingre – better known as Boucicaut – had once been the most feared jousting champion in Christendom. He had fought at the famous St Inglevert tournament of 1390, when he and two other knights had faced more than a hundred knights one by one, all of them jousting with sharpened steel lances – including Henry's father. He had attended his first battle at the age of twelve, had been knighted at sixteen, and had fought on crusades and campaigns from Prussia to Nicopolis. Now all his experience was to be put to the test. He was commissioned to serve as the King's Lieutenant and captain general of the French, with responsibility for the defence of Normandy, among other places.

Unfortunately the duke of Alençon had previously been appointed captain general for Normandy. The division of responsibilities was now unclear. It was also a mistake to fail to consider the duke's pride: he did not take kindly to being overlooked in this way.[74]

*

Henry ordered a final letter to be drawn up to send to the king of France. As it is one of the most remarkable documents of the year

– indeed, in all English medieval history – it justly deserves to appear
here in full:

Most serene prince, our cousin and adversary, the two great and noble
kingdoms of England and France, formerly joined as one but now
divided, have been accustomed to stand proud through all the world
by their glorious triumphs. The sole purpose of their unification was
to embellish the house of God, that holiness might reign and peace be
established throughout the Church, and to join their arms by a happy
accord against her adversaries, to subdue the public enemies. But, alas!
The discord that plagues families has troubled this harmony. Lot, blinded
by an inhuman feeling, pursued Abraham: the honour of his brotherly
union is buried in the tomb, and hatred – the sickness inherent in
human nature and the mother of fury – comes to life once more.
Nevertheless, the judge of all, who is susceptible neither to prayers nor
to corruption, is the witness of our sincere desire for peace; we have
done in conscience everything within our power to achieve it, even to
the extent of an imprudent sacrifice of legitimate rights that we have
inherited from our ancestors, to the prejudice of our posterity. We are
not so blinded by fear that we are not ready to fight to the death for
the justice of our cause. But the law of Deuteronomy commands that
whoever prepares to attack a town begins by offering it peace; thus,
since violence, the enemy of justice, has ravished for several centuries
the prerogatives of our crown and our hereditary rights, we have done
out of charity everything within our power to re-enter possession of
our rights and prerogatives, so that now we are able by reason of the
denial of justice to have recourse to the force of arms. Nevertheless
as we wish to be confident of a clear conscience, we now address you
with a final request, at the moment of setting out to demand from
you the reason for this denial of justice, and we repeat to you in the
name of the entrails of Jesus Christ, following the example shown us
by the perfection of evangelical doctrine: friend, give us what we are
owed and by the will of the Almighty avoid a deluge of human blood,
which has been created according to God; restore to us our inheritance
and our rights that have been unjustly stolen, or at least those things
that we have demanded earnestly and repeatedly by our various ambassadors and deputies, and with which we would be contented in respect
of God and in the interests of peace. And you will find us disposed on

our part to forego 50,000 crowns of gold of the sum that we have been offered as dowry, because we prefer peace to avarice, and because we would prefer to enjoy our paternal rights and this great patrimony which we have been left by our venerable predecessors and ancestors with your illustrious daughter Katherine, our very dear cousin, than to acquire guilty treasures in sacrificing to the idol of iniquity, and to the disinheritance of the posterity of the crown of our realm, which would not please God, to the eternal prejudice of our conscience.

Given under our privy seal in our town of Southampton, upon the coast, 28 July.[75]

'Upon the coast:' Henry was on the brink. But the most interesting thing about this extraordinary letter is the line concerning the law of Deuteronomy: 'whoever prepares to attack a town begins by offering it peace'. This explains Henry's approach to the peace initiatives since the start of his reign: he was always offering peace while moving to war, as if he was a king before the walls of a town who felt bound to offer the citizens peace first before destroying them and their town – not for their benefit but to justify his actions in the eyes of God. Herein lies the philosophy he was following: he was only offering peace, and sending and receiving ambassadors, because that was what he believed a warrior of God should do prior to attacking.

Before Henry could set sail there were still some administrative issues to deal with. He made a grant for life to John Sutton of Catton, yeoman of the chamber of the duke of Bedford.[76] John Waterton, who had now left Southampton with the Aragonese envoys, had to be given formal instructions as to what he might or might not offer, especially with regard to Henry's brothers' marriages; these were now issued. At the same time Dr John Hovingham and Simon Flete were empowered to treat for a continuation of the alliance with the duke of Brittany.[77] It was important not to let the diplomatic isolation of France weaken.

*

The earl of Cambridge and Sir Thomas Gray met at Otterbourne, a village a few miles north of Southampton. The earl showed Gray a letter from the earl of March, written in his own hand. It stated how March had been to the king and how badly he had been treated by Henry in connection with the business of his marriage, being fined 10,000 marks. According to Gray, the letter stated that March saw no solution to his jeopardy but to 'undo' the king; and therefore he wished the earl of Cambridge to come to him on the following day, or else to suggest how he should act, for he was now ready to do so.

Monday 29th

Henry decided the time had come to set the date for embarkation. From Portchester Castle he sent a writ to the sheriff of Hampshire to ensure, on pain of 'the king's grievous wrath,' that all those encamped in the area should be ready to board on Thursday 1 August at the latest. The term 'grievous wrath' is repeated in several letters at this time – a note of desperation, one feels, after all the various delays.[78]

A number of letters and orders were issued from Portchester at the same time. Henry settled his personal inheritance from the late earl of Hereford, his grandfather, on his executors. He named as his trustees the same sixteen men he had with regard to his settlement of the duchy of Lancaster on 22 July – including Lord Scrope.[79] The confiscated estates of the French priories that had been intended to endow the abandoned Celestine monastery at Sheen were also granted to trustees.[80] And lastly the mayor and bailiffs of Southampton were ordered to put three men in prison until further notice. Presumably they were among the thousands mustering around the town, waiting to sail and fight, who were causing disturbances in their hungry boredom.[81]

*

Sir Thomas Gray and the earl of Cambridge rode to Hamble in the Hook to see the earl of March. It was there that the final plans were made. Lord Scrope was not present. It was decided that Sir Walter Lucy would join the earl of Cambridge on the morrow, and then the earl of March would meet them at Cranbury on 31 July – the night before the voyage set out. After supper they would ride to Beaulieu.

And there they would proclaim the earl of March and call those who would stand with them to that place. If enough men from the army joined them, they would fight Henry; if not, they would take the earl of March into Wales until Henry Percy had been released, and start a rising in the north. To this end the earl of Cambridge had sent a man to Sir Robert Umphraville to enquire how he might take custody of Percy and the pseudo-Richard II (if he was still alive) without offering the recently recaptured Mordach in return.[82]

Tuesday 30th

In Paris it had long been a bone of contention that John the Fearless had not sworn to observe the terms of the Peace of Arras. His representatives had done so on 13 March, and had promised that he would do so too. But he had delayed, claiming that if his five hundred supporters were not also pardoned, then he would not swear. Further procrastinations had followed, forcing the government to take further action. First they had sent three ambassadors to the duke; but these men arrived shortly after John had heard that the dauphin had sent away his wife in order to spend more time with his mistress. As the dauphin's wife was John's own daughter, John had rebuked the dauphin, stating he would not help the French royal family against the English if he did not mend his ways.[83] Recently the dauphin had sent two more diplomats to John asking him to swear to abide by the peace.

The new diplomats were more successful: John the Fearless swore the oath today at Rouvres. Of course, it was not a plain capitulation: discussions had been in progress at Dijon throughout June and July, and there were a number of contingent clauses and subtexts. John agreed to forgive the dauphin on certain conditions. He promised to make peace with the duke of Bar, following the duke's rescue of the envoys of France whom John had kidnapped on their way back from Constance. He instructed his envoys to protest against those who asserted that he had an agreement to help the king of England – technically his agreement was not to hinder Henry – and to state that he was ready to march against the English as soon as he was commanded to do so.

The reason for this change of tone was partly because of the shift of opinion made against him at Constance – and there was only so much John could achieve by bribing cardinals. He wanted the French government to put pressure on the University of Paris, forcing them to discuss Jean Petit's *Justification* anew and to clear it of heresy, thereby undermining Dr Gerson's case. He also wanted all his Cabochien supporters pardoned, including the five hundred previously excluded. The dauphin had no option but to agree that the duke's demands would be met in full. Just in case the dauphin reneged on his promise, the wily John made his oath conditional on the implementation of all his terms.[84]

Wednesday 31st

The earl of March was due to ride to Cranbury today to meet the earl of Cambridge, Sir Thomas Gray and Sir Walter Lucy. But when he set out from Hamble in the Hook, he turned a different way: he went to see Henry at Portchester Castle. There he betrayed the conspirators who would have fought to make him king, telling Henry everything he knew.

It must have been a tremendous shock. Henry believed he was performing God's work. And yet these men – unimportant in God's eyes, as far as Henry could see – could take it into their heads to rise against his great mission and his divine status.

The implications were even more horrifying. He did not know how many other men were involved. It would have been reasonable to think that all those who stood to benefit from March's accession would have supported him. That would have included Edward Courtenay, the heir to the earldom of Devon, and Lord Camoys, who was married to the earl's aunt. It would have included various members of the Holland family – some of whom not only wanted revenge for the Epiphany Rising but also were related to the earl of March through his mother, Eleanor Holland. Then there were the relations of the other plotters: Lord Clifford, Lord Percy, Sir John Gray, Lady Despenser and maybe even the duke of York. What did the duke know about his brother's plot?

As for Lord Scrope – how could he have known about this plot and not said anything? Scrope had been in Wales with Henry; he had served him and his father loyally for well over a decade. He was a member of the privy council, and one of the trustees of Henry's estates. The chronicler Monstrelet asserted that Scrope 'slept every night with the king'.[85] It was like Oldcastle's rebellion all over again – a trusted friend had betrayed him and sought his death. Thomas Walsingham's *Chronica Maiora* made it clear how this betrayal was perceived by contemporaries. Being so close to the king, and so important, Scrope was presumed to have been the leader of the conspiracy; and being so often in France, it was presumed that he must have been bribed by the French. Walsingham describes him as 'the first and chief' plotter, and a man

in whose faith and constancy the king had trusted his whole heart . . . He was so much esteemed by the king that when the latter held public or private deliberations, the discussion was decided by his advice. He pretended, moreover, such gravity of demeanour, such modesty in his bearing, so much religious zeal, that whatever he said the king decided it must be done, as if he were an oracle descended from Heaven. If a solemn embassy had to be sent to France, the king thought that it should be carried out by the ability and person of Henry Scrope. But he entered into negotiations with the enemy, as a hidden foe to his lord the king, whom he soothed with false assurances.[86]

From this distance in time, and with the original records available to us, we can see that Scrope had not had any dealings with the French other than his official diplomatic ones, and was not part of the conspiracy at all. As we have seen in his will, written only a month earlier, he did not just pretend to be religious, he was deeply devout. His absence at several key meetings – most notably that at Hamble in the Hook on the 29th – shows that he was not a leader of the plot. From the evidence we have it is clear that he was inveigling himself with the conspirators in order to learn when and where they were planning to strike, just as the duke of York had done in 1400. As Scrope himself put it, if he had 'heard a grounded purpose', he himself would have come to tell the king.[87]

Henry ordered the conspirators to come to him at Portchester Castle; the guards who carried this message to Cranbury no doubt were instructed to accompany them. Scrope was also located and asked to speak to the king. He came that evening, possibly of his own volition, although other members of his household were later arrested.[88] He told the king everything he knew, naming all those whom he believed would have joined the conspiracy, including several Lollards. Henry sent an urgent message to the mayor of London warning him of the danger and urging him to keep the city safe, perhaps alarmed by the Lollard link.[89] He also issued a commission to make enquiries into the plot, to find out who was implicated and what they hoped to achieve. The commissioners were four earls, four barons and two royal justices. They were collectively to report on 2 August, having enquired into

> all kinds of treasons, felonies, conspiracies and confederacies committed or perpetrated in the aforesaid county by whomsoever and in any way, and to hear and determine the same treasons, felonies, conspiracies and confederacies according to the law and custom of our realm of England.[90]

It is difficult to appreciate what emotions the king must have experienced over the course of this one day. Any apprehension or sense of divine commitment arising from his confidence that he would be sailing on the following day must have been dashed against the shock of the conspiracy; and of course the consequent feelings must have been mixed with further frustration that he was going to have to postpone the expedition yet again. And now, with an enquiry underway and several treason trials to be held, he could not say when he would be able to set out.

August

Thursday 1st: the Feast of St Peter ad Vincula

The feast of St Peter ad Vincula – St Peter in Chains – was also known as Lammas Day, or the day on which the 'loaf mass' was celebrated. It was the formal beginning of autumn, and with it the start of the season of harvesting and agricultural celebrations. Whole families – old and young alike – took themselves into the fields to reap the corn. Peasants working for manorial lords could look forward to three months of better food: white bread rather than rye, roast meat and fresh ale. Girls working in the fields were singled out for their prettiness and crowned as harvest queens by their fellow workers. Across the country, merchants and traders began packing up their wagons and carts to attend the many fairs that took place over the subsequent three months. People had a chance to buy rarer and more exotic things, such as dyes, silks, spices and perfumes. The fairs also gave market traders the opportunity to sell goods such as wool and hides in bulk to exporting wholesalers.[1]

At Southampton, the celebrations of the season were of little importance to Henry. Whereas the invasion had previously dominated his waking hours, now he had to cope with the reality of betrayal. According to the earl of March and Lord Scrope, the conspirators had discussed proclaiming the earl of March king today – the very day on which Henry hoped to set sail. It was the anniversary of the death of the late duke of York, the supposed father of the earl of Cambridge, and the man whom Richard II had designated as the heir to the throne.[2] Was that the reason for the conspirators' timing? Was this a Yorkist plot? Did Lord Scrope really want to stop the invasion? So many doubts and questions must have pained Henry as he went about his business. And all he could do was wait for the findings of the inquiry.

Lord Scrope was probably the first person to be interrogated by the commissioners. A lengthy letter of confession was drawn up and presented on his behalf. After a humble preamble in which he acknowledged that his life lay in Henry's hands, he implored the king to show mercy, on the grounds that he had never offended him in any way before, nor ever would again, and because, he said, Henry had shown mercy 'so abundantly' to every man in the realm. Following this he reiterated in great detail the whole process by which he had come to hear of the plot, putting into writing what he had verbally communicated to Henry at Portchester Castle the previous night. He mentioned his first conversation with Walter Lucy about the earl of March, and gave a day-by-day account of his communications with the plotters from the time of his meeting Sir Thomas Gray on the morning of 21 July. He was quite candid about how he had advised them – of how they should be lost whatever course of action they took against the king. Repeatedly he had told the earl of March and Walter Lucy what folly it would be to follow the earl of Cambridge. According to his account, after the 25th the plotters had had nothing more to do with him; he did not even know about the meeting at Cranbury. He ended his testimony stating that if he had heard 'a grounded purpose' or plan connected with the plot, he would have come straight to Henry and declared all he knew to him; but the earl of March had beaten him to it. He ended by repeating that not telling Henry sooner was 'the first trespass that ever I fell [into]' and he prayed 'to all my lords' that they should be merciful on him, clearly indicating that he expected to be judged by his peers.[3]

The earl of Cambridge was probably also interviewed by the commissioners today. In the first and most badly damaged of his three surviving letters, he confessed to his plan of taking the earl of March into Wales. He also confessed to his plan to exchange the earl of Fife for the fake Richard II and Henry Percy – and mentioned Sir Robert Umphraville, Sir John Widdrington and Sir Thomas Gray as being complicit – although he was keen to point out that Lord Scrope knew nothing of this part of the plot. He added that Davy Howell had offered to hand over castles in Wales to the plotters if there was a rising in the north. Unfortunately much of this letter is lost, and so it is difficult to tell the full extent of information that it originally contained; but a revised version was drawn up, perhaps by the earl himself, which included further incriminating details.⁴ For example, he claimed that Scrope had approved of the plan to take the earl of March into Wales, and that he (the earl of Cambridge) had had the form of proclamation drawn up in which Henry V was referred to as 'Harry of Lancaster, usurper of England'. Interestingly, Cambridge actively tried to remove any blame being attached to certain other people. He did not try to implicate the earl of March, nor Walter Lucy. Twice he asserted that Scrope was ignorant of certain aspects of the plot. He did name other people who might have helped them, such as Sir John Heron, but he stated that he only heard this from Sir Thomas Gray.⁵

In view of the circumstances it is unlikely that Henry had much to do with the routine business of government conducted by the officers at Southampton today. A charter confirming Queen Joan's estates was drawn up for her security during the king's absence. Thomas More, a long-standing Lancastrian officer, was granted a licence to alienate land so he could endow a perpetual chantry for Masses to be sung for his soul. And John Grawe, a royal bailiff of Kirkton in Lindsey, was pardoned for non-production of 78s of the king's rent, which had been taken from him by highwaymen.⁶

Friday 2nd

Sir Thomas Gray was led before the commissioners to be interviewed. His was by far the fullest and most damning of all the confessions drawn up. The surviving portion is badly fragmented but even what survives shows that he was ready to reveal all – even down to the wavering between the various strategies. He stated that he had heard from the earl of Cambridge that Sir Robert Umphraville, Sir John Widdrington and Lord Clifford were involved, and he confessed that he had personally spoken with Walter Lucy about the possibility of putting the earl of March on the throne. He repeatedly stressed that the earl of March was assenting to the plot, right up to the end; and stated this as a matter of personal knowledge, not just hearsay. He even suggested that the earl of Arundel was assenting to the idea, as well as Lord Scrope; but otherwise his only line of accusation against

Scrope was to suggest that he (Scrope) had said that it was 'best to break the voyage'. As for the meetings that took place, these all correlate with Scrope's own testimony.

Following the extraction of these confessions, the trials could take place. Twelve Hampshire men, selected from an empanelled total of thirty-six, were appointed to the jury. In the castle of Southampton, in the king's presence, they listened to the cases against each man. The constable of the castle, Sir John Popham, led the accused from the dungeon and into the hall where the jury was sitting. The charge was read out – that all three accused men had

> falsely and treacherously conspired . . . having gathered to themselves many others, both of the retinue of the lord king and of his liege subjects, to take Edmund earl of March to the parts of Wales . . . to elevate him to the sovereignty of the realm of England in the event that the lord Richard II after the Conquest, lately king of England, was found to be dead, and to make a certain proclamation in the said parts of Wales in the name of the aforesaid earl of March, as heir to the crown of England against the said present lord king, by the name of Henry of Lancaster, usurper of England to the end that many of the lieges of the same present lord should join themselves to the said earl of March and quickly adhere to him.[7]

There followed three more specific charges, levelled against just Cambridge and Gray. These were that they were planning to redeem Thomas Warde of Trumpington and Henry Percy from Scotland and to bring them and the men of Northumberland to do battle with the king; and that they would hold castles in Wales against the king. The last was a shock: they were charged with plotting to kill the king and his brothers.

As we now know, this charge was false, trumped up by the government in order to bring the trial to a speedy conclusion.[8] It was an inference based on the character of the plot to make the earl of March king. If Edmund were to be crowned, then Henry and all three of his brothers would have to be removed from the order of succession. Therefore the plotters were assumed to have compassed this crime, and therefore they were charged with plotting to kill all four of Henry IV's sons. Moreover, it was not just Cambridge and Gray who were charged with conspiring to murder the king: Scrope was too. The charge specifically laid against him was that he

> was consenting to destroy and kill the present lord king and his brothers, and lords, magnates and liegemen aforesaid, and to commit and perpetrate other aforesaid evils, as already stated; and so these things should be done he communicated with the same earl of Cambridge and Thomas Gray, and with divers other lieges of the said present lord king, and falsely and treasonably concealed these things from the same present lord king.[9]

The accused men must have been profoundly shocked. When asked how they wished to plead, Cambridge and Gray both stated that they were guilty of each and every one of the charges in the form stated, even though the murder charge was simply an inference drawn by the judges. Frantic with fear, they submitted themselves to the grace of the king, imploring his forgiveness. Scrope was the only one who kept his head. He admitted discussing these matters but had never done anything to aid them. As for killing the king – he had never even considered that. He claimed that he had communicated with the others

> with the intention of ascertaining the malice of the aforesaid Richard earl of Cambridge and Thomas Gray in the premises. And so, having obtained knowledge aforesaid in that matter, his intention was to impede that malicious purpose of theirs. And as to the concealment of the aforesaid treasons from the lord king . . . he put himself in the grace and mercy of the lord king. And concerning the imagining of the death of the lord king and his brothers, or of any other persons whatsoever, as was previously put to him, he said that he was in no way guilty of it. And moreover he said that he was a lord and one of the peers of the realm of England, and asked that he should be tried and judged by his peers . . .[10]

There could be no refusal to this request without a severe infringement of lordly rights, and so Scrope and Cambridge were both returned to the custody of Sir John Popham to await trial. Gray was not a peer, however. Having pleaded guilty, he stood to be judged and punished forthwith. The justices presiding decided that, as he was by his own admission a traitor to the king and the realm, he should be drawn, hanged and beheaded. At this the king spoke that he remitted the two first penalties, namely the drawing and the hanging. He needed only to be beheaded, and his head sent to Newcastle upon Tyne to be fixed above the gate for all to see.

Later that day Gray was led on foot through the middle of Southampton as far as the North Gate. There he was beheaded in public. His goods and chattels, lands and tenements were all declared forfeit to the crown. As for the other two accused men, Cambridge and Scrope, the duke of Clarence was commissioned to empanel twenty lords to hear their cases. The trial would take place on the 5th.

Henry himself then turned his attention to the north, and the implications of a Scottish invasion in the wake of Cambridge's plot. He ordered a writ to be sent to all the sheriffs that all the 'fencible lieges' or militia should be arrayed ready to defend the kingdom against the Scots and the king's enemies 'as the king has particular information that those enemies and their adherents are purposing shortly with no small power to invade the realm by divers coasts'.[11]

*

In Calais, anticipating that Henry would have set sail already, the extra men-at-arms stationed there began to make raiding parties into the area around Boulogne. Perhaps Henry had ordered this, to create a diversion. But his ships were still at Southampton, going nowhere. The dauphin sent David, seigneur de Rambures, and Jacques de Longroy with five hundred men-at-arms to defend the country.[12]

Sunday 4th

In all the preliminary arrangements over the years, nothing had prepared Henry for this becalmed frustration. Many men were now urging him to cancel the campaign. The contemporary author of the *Gesta*, who was there with the army at Southampton, put it well in describing affairs in the camp at this time:

Many of those most devoted to the king wanted him to abandon his resolve to make such a crossing, both in case there should be any similar acts of treason still undiscovered and also, and especially, on account of the madness of Sir John Oldcastle and those of his persuasion – rumours spreading of an insurrection by him after the king had sailed.[13]

The Lollards were indeed again on the move. Not so much in London, where Henry had perhaps expected them to make a stand when he sent his letter on the 31st. The reply from the mayor, Thomas Falconer, promising he would keep the city safe, arrived back in Southampton today; in it he gave no indication that there was a Lollard threat.[14] Rather the Lollards were stirring in the Welsh Marches, where Oldcastle had taken shelter. According to Thomas Walsingham, 'as if by agreement, and as if they knew about the plot [of the earl of Cambridge], there was a rising of the Lollards'.[15] Cambridge had repeatedly discussed arranging a Lollard rising to support his own plot. Interestingly, Walsingham described them 'vomiting blasphemies against the king', drawing attention to how deeply ran the idea that rebellion and blasphemy, like treason and heresy, were intertwined. He added that the Lollards wrote tracts that they fixed to the doors of churches, aiming for 'the overthrow of the king, the subversion of the orthodox faith, and the destruction of the Holy Church'.

The Cambridge plot had one serendipitous result for Henry. Because the fleet had not set sail as intended on 1 August, he was still in England when Oldcastle came out of hiding. The Lollard lord had been sheltering near Malvern. He assumed that Henry must already have set sail and so chose this moment to send threatening letters to Sir Richard Beauchamp, lord of Abergavenny. Sir Richard responded by sending out messengers in the king's name to Worcester, Pershore and Tewkesbury that same night, summoning his loyal men to come to him armed at daybreak at Hanley Castle. The prelates of these towns also supported action against Oldcastle and urged their flocks to obey. Enough men gathered to drive Oldcastle back into hiding. Several Lollards were captured by Sir Richard and forced to reveal where their leader had hidden his weapons and money. Breaking down a false wall in the identified house, Sir Richard discovered not just weapons and money but other symbols of the heretical revolt, such as:

a standard on which had been painted a chalice and the host in the shape of a loaf of bread, just as if that was the element in the sacrament that was to be worshipped . . . And there was also seen there a sort of crucifix with scourges, and a spear with nails, which he had had painted on his banners to deceive the simple-minded, if ever he had had a chance to raise the banners in support of a public show of madness.[16]

Had Oldcastle waited until the king had actually set sail, perhaps many more Lollards would have taken up the cause. As things were, the king was still in England at the head of an army. It was just too risky.

Nevertheless, these stirrings were ominous. After all the months of preparations, all the diplomacy, financial arrangements, musters, gathering of weapons and supplies – there were religious factions who wanted to stop him. There were still secular lords who wanted to see him dethroned. And although their little rebellions were easily quashed, and the tracts of Lollards were easily denounced, there was no knowing when one of these objectors might get lucky. Historians, intoxicated with the great-man view of Henry V, have often remarked how these rebellions were of little consequence – that he easily overcame them. But they were important at the time on account of what they represented. Each one was another sign of dissent and delayed him more. But his resolution held firm. Those telling him he should cancel the expedition were ignored. In this respect he was very like his father. No matter what obstacles were placed in his way, he was determined to overcome them all.

Monday 5th

For the trial of Cambridge and Scrope, the duke of Clarence enlisted all the most senior lords then present at Southampton: himself, his youngest brother, Humphrey; his cousin the duke of York; the Earl Marshal; the earls of March, Huntingdon, Arundel, Salisbury, Oxford and Suffolk; and lords Clifford, Talbot, Zouche, Harrington, Willoughby, Clinton, Maltravers, Bourchier and Botreaux. The duke of York asked to absent himself from the trial; so the earl of Dorset took his place. The reason publicly given for York's withdrawal was that Cambridge was his brother. Perhaps we should also bear in mind the fact that the model for Lord Scrope's actions was precisely what

York himself had done in 1399–1400. On that occasion York had with-held information about the attempt on the king's life for a full two weeks; there could easily have been a dramatic scene if Lord Scrope objected that among his peers was a man who had committed the same crime as him.

Sir John Popham led the two accused men into the hall of Southampton Castle. Their confessions were read out to the nineteen seated lords. Both had drawn up a final letter imploring mercy; these were also read out. Scrope's letter is now very damaged, and beyond a few words clarifying his intention that key parts of his will be carried out, especially his desire to be buried in York Minster, it is difficult to determine what he wrote. Cambridge's last letter is complete:

> Mine most dreadful and sovereign liege lord, I, Richard of York, your
> humble subject and very liege man, beseech you of grace and of all
> manner of offences that I have done or assented to in any kind, by stir-
> ring of other folk egging me thereto, wherein I know well I have highly
> offended to your highness; beseeching you at the reverence of God
> that you like to take me into the hands of your merciful and piteous
> grace, thinking you will, of your great goodness. My liege lord, my
> full trust is that you will have consideration, though that my person
> be of no value, your high goodness where God has set you in so high
> estate to every liege man that to you [it] belongs plenteously to give
> grace, that you [will] accept this my simple request, for the love of Our
> Lady and of the blissful Holy Ghost, to whom I pray that they may
> induce your heart to all pity and grace for their high goodness.[17]

There was never any doubt that both men would be found guilty. The duke of Clarence had been commissioned not only to hear the case but to proceed to execution immediately thereafter.[18] The king had clearly washed his hands of Scrope and wanted him executed. The proceedings of the previous trial on the 2nd were read out once more and the actions of these men were 'unanimously adjudged and judici-ally affirmed as high treason damnably and wickedly imagined, conspired and confederated against the lord king and realm of England', in line with the false accusation of attempting to kill the king. They were condemned to be drawn, hanged and beheaded, and their families were to forfeit all their goods and chattels.

The earl of Cambridge's confidence that the king would forgive him was misplaced. As a member of the royal family, Henry did spare him the drawing and hanging but insisted that he be beheaded. Lord Scrope was spared the hanging but not the drawing. He was downgraded from his membership of the Order of the Garter, dragged through the town from the Watergate to the North Gate, and there beheaded. Henry ordered that Scrope's head be taken and stuck up on one of the gates of the city of York.[19]

So ended the plot of the earl of Cambridge. It was an incompetent series of protests from two angry and frustrated men. And the manner of its ending was equally angry and frustrated. Cambridge and Gray had actually *done* nothing; they had no 'grounded purpose', to quote Scrope's words. The charge that they had planned the death of the king was completely false: it was concocted by either the commission of enquiry or (more probably) by the king himself, through his lawyers, to hasten the process of dealing with the plot.[20] It was later circulated in order to justify the killing. Scrope was not a leading protagonist, and he was less culpable than the earl of March or Walter Lucy. Neither March nor Lucy was charged with any crime – even though the whole plot was largely down to Lucy's loose tongue, encouraging Scrope to believe the earl of Cambridge was more dangerous than he really was, and leading Gray to believe that the plot had the backing of Scrope and Arundel. March was certainly guilty of treasonable intentions, even if he did eventually betray the plotters. Scrope by comparison had no more to hide than Lord Clifford, Sir Robert Umphraville and Sir John Widdrington, whom Gray and Cambridge also implicated. But although Henry sent for Umphraville this same day, and suspended him as constable of Roxburgh Castle, he took no further action against any other men.[21] Those he initially arrested were condemned, all the others were forgiven.

None of Lord Scrope's religious bequests was honoured by Henry. All his money and possessions were taken by the king. In this we can see a money-hungry side to Henry V, also reflected in his extortion of 10,000 marks from the earl of March and his later confiscation of his stepmother's income on a charge of witchcraft. But it was not just about money: Scrope was not allowed his cherished place in York Minster. Whatever doubts Henry may have had about his loyalty, Scrope was the victim of a vindictive and cruel act, for Henry showed himself disinclined to give him the slightest benefit of the doubt. In this case – as in that of the claim on the throne of France – Henry was more interested in exercising authority than justice.

Scrope's sentence was a significant lapse of Henry's judgment. Were there any mitigating circumstances? Of course: Henry was under huge pressure, he had been delayed and he must have seen the chances of a successful campaign vanishing with the approach of autumn. Money was flowing rapidly out of the treasury, the debts were piling up, and he had nothing to show for them. If he was hasty in proceeding to try the lords as if they were commoners, then he had good reason. But many aspects of this process seem fundamentally unjust. The concoction of the charge of regicide in particular was unjust. The inclusion of both March and Clifford on the panel to condemn Cambridge and Scrope can hardly be seen as fair; they were certainly not disinterested. And we cannot simply dismiss the trial as a miscarriage of justice. It led to a terrible precedent, for the trials of traitors in the court of the steward of England, at the king's personal command, dates from this event. Many men in later centuries were executed in consequence of Star Chamber trials under the authority of the steward of England, as a result of this angry exercise of power.[22]

Edward duke of York absented himself from all these proceedings. His brother had specifically stated that he had urged the others not to let him know anything. Cambridge had wanted to protect his brother, and this may be considered a sign of genuine fraternal affection, as well as a failure to think through his plan. Edward was no doubt deeply shocked and saddened by the events. His day was spent otherwise engaged: he was granted a licence allowing him to settle some of his estates on trustees for the completion of the collegiate church at Fotheringay that he had started to build and where he intended to be buried.[23] It is fitting that this took place on the day of Cambridge's execution – Cambridge's son would one day come to lie in the same church.

Henry's other deeds after the grim business of the morning included dictating the letter conferring on Richard, Lord Grey, Sir Robert Ogle and the lawyer Richard Holme the necessary authority to treat with the representatives of the duke of Albany for a new truce between England and Scotland.[24] He also pardoned one John Prest of Warwickshire for sheltering Sir John Oldcastle. The latter at least shows he retained at least some measure of mercy.

Tuesday 6th

Lord Scrope had hardly been dead twenty-four hours before Henry started distributing his lands as gifts to his supporters. Henry, Lord Fitzhugh, was among the first to benefit, acquiring all of Lord Scrope's manors, rights, income and possessions within the franchise of Richmond.[25] Two of Scrope's Suffolk manors were parcelled out as grants to the king's friend Sir John Phelip and his wife Alice.[26] He also instructed Robert Clitherowe and David Cawardyn to go to London and seize all the goods in Scrope's London house and hand them over to the mayor of London for safe keeping.[27]

It was obviously a day for grant-making and gift-giving. Sir Thomas Chaucer, the king's butler, who was also heading to France, was pardoned all his debts to the crown; and Robert Orell was granted the forestership of the forest of Snowdon.[28]

*

Richard de Vere, earl of Oxford, who was waiting to set sail with his twenty-nine men-at-arms and seventy-nine archers, drew up his will. He wished to be buried with his ancestors in the priory church of Colne, in Essex. He left all his goods and chattels to his wife, Alice, and gave her power to dispose of all the rest of his possessions. It was a very modest will by comparison with some. But he was not alone in not wanting a great fuss or a huge ceremony. Sir Thomas West, who was also about to set out, had written a will a few days earlier in which he requested only that no more than £40 was to be laid out in meat, drink and candles on the day of his funeral, and that £24 be paid to two priests to celebrate divine service each day on behalf of his soul and his ancestors' souls for two years after his death.[29]

Wednesday 7th

The day had at last come. But before Henry went down to his flag-ship and embarked, there were some last minute necessities. One was a pardon for the earl of March 'for all treasons, murders, rapes of women, rebellions, insurrections, felonies, conspiracies, trespasses, offences, negligences, extortions, misprisions, ignorances, concealments and deceptions committed by him'.[30] No one can have had much doubt that 'the hog' (as Gray had called March) or the 'daw or simpleton' (as Sir John Mortimer later referred to him) was anything but complicit in the plot to make him king.[31] But he had been the one who had informed Henry and that necessitated a reward of some kind. Not to lose his life and lands was an appropriate one.

Another essential item of business was a royal order to all the sheriffs 'on pain of grievous forfeiture, for particular causes moving the king and council' to proclaim that men shall keep watch, night by night, until Allhallows (1 November) to protect the towns as well as the shores, and that 'no man who holds a public inn shall receive or suffer a stranger to stay more than a night and a day without knowledge of the cause of his abode there'. This was in case of rebels as well as French and Scottish spies. Henry added that any man who did not confess his reason was to be arrested; clearly he had been shaken by the earl of Cambridge's plot and knew that he was taking a huge risk by leaving the country at this juncture with two of his three brothers.[32] The duke of Bedford was the sole potential Lancastrian heir left in England. Henry's third and final precaution before leaving Portchester Castle was a repeat of his earlier order to array the clergy of the diocese of Lincoln against the Lollards during the king's absence abroad.[33]

Finally Henry went down to the barge that was to take him out to his flagship, the 540-tun capacity *Trinity Royal*, which was moored between Southampton and Portsmouth. With a crew of three hundred sailors, it was one of the two largest ships in his navy. It had a huge purple sail and the great banner of the Trinity on the main mast, together with streamers a dozen yards long and other smaller flags bearing the arms of St Edward and St George. The top-castle of the mast was decorated with a large gilt-copper crown, a golden leopard was on the prow and on the capstan was a sceptre with fleur-de-lys. As soon as he stepped on board Henry ordered the yard supporting the great sail to be half-raised to indicate his readiness to set out straightaway, and to signal to all the other ships scattered along the coast to start to make their way to the king.

Henry did not set out immediately. He still had to wait for the ships to gather – and this would take some time. It was reported by eyewitnesses that he had 1,500 vessels in his fleet. In addition, more than 12,000 horses needed to be transported, and in each case the poor animal had to be put into a sling and hoisted on to deck with a crane: this was not a quick or easy task.[34] For the next few days the *Trinity Royal* did not move. In that time she became known as the King's Chamber. Another vessel – perhaps the *Holy Ghost* – was functionally named the King's Hall.[35] On these two ships the 101 men of the royal household attended on the king and the members of his council, coming and going from other smaller ships moored nearby – the King's Larder, the King's Kitchen and the King's Wardrobe.

Thursday 8th

The first day waiting for the ships to assemble was spent seeing to some final pieces of administration. Diplomatic loose ends needed sorting out. An order was sent to Henry Kays, the keeper of the hanaper in chancery, to pay some money in advance to Dr John Hovingham and John Flete, the ambassadors to Brittany (who had been given their instructions on 28 July).[36] A similar order was sent for Philip Morgan to be given 100 marks enabling him to return to the Burgundian court of John the Fearless to conduct 'secret discussions'. Morgan had been part of the committee on 27 May to discuss this mission; his departure had been delayed by his journey to Calais to prorogue the truce. His instructions, which were formally drawn up by the chancellor two days later, empowered him to treat anew with John the Fearless, seeking to establish exactly what help the duke might offer Henry.[37]

As the earl of Arundel, the treasurer of England, was about to sail with Henry, a new treasurer was needed. Henry appointed his friend Sir John Rothenhale, controller of the royal household, to the post.[38] New orders were issued allowing the export of tin. And the paperwork allowing the heads of Lord Scrope and Sir Thomas Gray to be transported to their various places of exhibition needed to be drawn up. We might consider medieval society unsophisticated for beheading men and exposing their rotting heads in public but it was sufficiently sophisticated to require eight separate letters to be written to the sheriffs of eight counties ordering them to permit the passage of the said heads to York and Newcastle, where they were to be impaled on spears.[39]

Before he set sail Henry made some final grants. To his friend Sir

John Gray, younger brother of the executed Sir Thomas Gray of Heton, Henry granted custody of all the family lands during the youth of Sir Thomas's heir.[40] To William Porter, king's esquire, Henry gave one of Scrope's Leicestershire manors. To Lord Fitzhugh he gave Scrope's inn at Paulswharf, London, in addition to his earlier grant of Scrope's Richmond franchise. Scrope's estate had by now become something like a displayed carcass, complete with pecking vultures. But it was a hasty and reckless dismembering of an estate – and another thing that Henry would later come to regret. It emerged in later years that Scrope's family estates were all legally entailed on his father's male heirs, so they could not be confiscated by the king at will. Henry had no right to re-distribute them among his friends.[41]

Sunday 11th

Nearly all the ships that Henry was expecting had assembled in a vast flotilla around him. He ordered the formal custody of England to be given to his brother John, duke of Bedford, the keeper of the realm. With this formal transfer went the right to summon parliaments and councils, to grant licences for the election of bishops and abbots, to restore and take temporalities and to accept fealty.[42] John was instructed to summon a parliament immediately, to meet on 21 October to agree further financial support for the campaign. Then, about 3 p.m., with the handing over of the final documents, the last messengers left the *Trinity Royal* and the great purple sail was raised to its full height.

Henry's voyage was underway. As the ships started to move, a large number of swans settled in the sea and started swimming among the boats. This was seen as a good sign. Less propitious was the smoke that started rising in the sun. Three ships had caught fire. They burnt to the waterline before the fleet left English waters.[43]

Monday 12th

The figure of 1,500 ships has long been accepted by historians. It was estimated by an eyewitness, and it tallies – more or less – with the 1,600 ships mentioned in some French sources. In addition it is a reasonable figure if one considers how many men, horses and supplies were on these ships. Recent historical research in this area – particularly that undertaken by Anne Curry – is most significant. For example, the chronicler who stated that there were 1,500 ships also implied that there were more than 12,000 fighting men in the fleet. Professor Curry has demonstrated this was true by checking the financial records for the wages of the army and correlating these with the numbers of men required by indenture. Her findings are as follows:

- twenty-six peers undertook to provide a total of 5,222 men (including themselves);
- fifty-seven knights undertook to provide 2,573 men;
- lesser captains undertook to provide 1,306 men;
- a further thousand archers were drawn from Lancashire and South Wales;
- 650 archers and 50 men-at-arms were summoned from Cheshire (but only 247 of them were paid, suggesting that only this smaller number turned up);
- the royal household provided in the region of 900 men.

Taking the lower figure of 247 Cheshire archers (a safe minimum), this adds up to at least 11,248 men, of whom 2,266 were men-at-arms. In addition there was a number of other support staff, such as cooks, clerks, chaplains and servants for the lords and clerks for the men-at-arms. The account of the earl of Oxford suggests that it was usual for the men-at-arms each to bring their own page with them at their own expense.[44] So, although these pages do not figure in the royal accounts (being paid by the men-at-arms), it is safer to presume there were as many pages as men-at-arms – in excess of two thousand. Furthermore, there were all the miners, smiths and carpenters whom Henry had ordered to come on campaign: a total of 560 of them. If each lord and knight had a chaplain and two non-combative servants, we can be certain that the *minimum* number of men with Henry today as he crossed the Channel was more than 14,000 men, not including the mariners. Additional financial records detailing several hundred more fighting men are known to have existed once, being quoted in older historical works. If these are included, then the total number of non-mariners was in the region of 15,000. And, as Professor Curry points out, the travel allowances of horses were regularly taken up, with some lords taking several dozen beasts. There were more horses in the army than there were fighting men.[45]

Those 1,500 ships must each have been carrying a minimum of ten men and ten horses, not including mariners. Given that the ships used to patrol the coasts carried between ten men-at-arms for a balinger and forty or fifty for a ship or barge, an army of this scale would have required 1,500 vessels, especially as each man was required to carry food sufficient for three months. Each ship also had to carry heavy artillery and weaponry – millions of arrows and thousands of bows, gunpowder and stone cannonballs – as well as more basic provisions for a siege: such as timber and animals for food in the first days. It was the largest army to leave England since the siege of Calais in 1347 (when Edward III had employed about 32,000 men over the course of a year).[46] And at the time it was probably the largest fleet ever to have set out from England. In this context, one can understand Henry's frustrations and occasional hastiness over the past months. He was taking a massive risk.

Tuesday 13th

It was the fishermen off the coast of Boulogne who first noticed the fleet approaching the French coast.[47] The region around their town had been ransacked over recent days by the English of Calais, so they were alert to the danger. But one imagines that they looked at the huge fleet in the Channel with considerable alarm. Especially if they believed that it was heading to their own town.

The men of Boulogne were lucky: Henry was heading elsewhere. At about five o'clock in the afternoon *Trinity Royal* sailed into the mouth of the Seine and dropped anchor near a small hamlet called Chef de Caux, about three miles from the walls of Harfleur on the north bank of the Seine estuary. The banner of the council was unfurled on the *Trinity Royal*, calling all the councillors to a meeting. It was decided that a royal proclamation would be issued to all the ships forbidding anyone, on pain of death, from landing on French soil before the king himself, unless they had the king's express permission. Everyone was to prepare to land early on the following morning; if the men dispersed in search of plunder, or women, the captains of the army were liable to lose control. There was also the heavy risk of men in small groups being picked off by the French defenders. Henry had no need to take such risks at this stage of the campaign.

A group of men was selected to go ashore that night and to reconnoitre the immediate vicinity. Henry chose the hugely experienced Sir John Cornwaille, and Cornwaille's brother-in-arms, William Porter, king's esquire; and Cornwaille's stepson, the young and talented earl of Huntingdon. With them went Sir Gilbert Umphraville and John Steward, and a number of mounted men-at-arms.[48] Prior information from the men who had travelled through Harfleur over the preceding year led Henry to believe there was a hill nearby, Mont Leconte, on which it would be suitable to make a first camp. The expedition was to explore the area and establish first whether there were Frenchmen guarding this hill. Second, they were to find a suitable place for quartering the royal household. They went ashore in the early hours.

Wednesday 14th

Henry's attitude to the landing suggests a high state of anxiety. This is entirely understandable: he had 15,000 men and probably twice as many mariners in an extremely vulnerable position. Years of planning, preparation and reconnaissance were being put to the test. Cautious all the way through, he waited until Cornwaille, Porter and Huntingdon had returned before he began to plan his own landing.

Those in the ships around him looked at the beach where they were expected to land. They felt uneasy. As the author of the *Gesta Henrici Quinti* noted,

> the shore was very stony, with large boulders against which the ships were liable to be dashed, and with other smaller stones, pebbles handy for throwing, with which the enemy (had they wished to oppose our landing) could have attacked us and defended themselves. And at the back of the shore, between us and the land, deep ditches had been dug that were full of water; and behind these . . . earth walls of great thickness, furnished with ramparts and angles in the manner of a tower or castle; and between every two ditches the ground was left intact for the breadth of a cubit, permitting only one man at a time to enter or leave.[49]

The site had been chosen because it was thought to be left unguarded. But there was a good reason why: it was very difficult to land a large force here. A few ships could unload here quickly, maybe – but 1,500? The whole process would take such a long time. About a mile away, to the south of Harfleur, there were fewer stones – but that was no easier a landing place as there was a marsh there that led far inland, with ditches and gullies. The narrow tracks through that marsh would have allowed a few men to hold up several thousand.

Henry and his men took to the barges 'between the sixth and seventh hour' – which in this case probably means 6–7 a.m. (reckoning from midnight).[50] When Henry landed he fell to his knees and prayed that he might do justice on his enemies. This gesture may have been a spontaneous act – or it may have been a deliberate emulation of his predecessors. It is worth remembering that Edward III had fallen on landing in Normandy on the Crécy campaign, and declared it a welcome embrace from the kingdom of France. This in turn was probably a deliberate emulation of William the Conqueror, who had fallen on landing in England in 1066 and got up with his hands full of sand, declaring he held the kingdom of England in his hands. Also in emulation of past practice, Henry knighted a number of men there on the beach – among them William Porter, Thomas Geney, John Calthorp and John Radcliffe – just as Edward III had knighted his son and other men on landing in 1346.[51] Following these ceremonies, he was quickly led to the Mont Leconte, where his priests were able to celebrate Mass, and where the army would camp.

*

For the French in the vicinity, there was no question of resisting such a large army. Although the English feared attack, and knew they were hugely vulnerable as they stepped ashore, to stop them would have required a large force of men to be ready to intercept them. The nearest such force (as the crow flies) was one of 1,500 men commanded by Charles d'Albret at Honfleur, on the south side of the Seine. Boucicaut was on the north side of the river – but at Caudebec, about 25 miles to the east.[52] He also had about 1,500 men: too few to tackle the English after they had begun to come ashore in large numbers. As for Harfleur itself, there were at most only two small forces present: one hundred men-at-arms under Jean, seigneur d'Estouteville; and thirty-four men-at-arms in the town, under the command of Lyonnet de Braquemont, Olivier de Braquemont and Jean Bufreuil, together with a small number of crossbowmen under Roland de Gérault.[53] These forces could hardly take on an army of more than 11,000 fighting men. Three hundred more men-at-arms were mustering on this very day, commanded by the redoubtable knight, Raoul de Gaucourt; but they were still more than three days' march away from Harfleur. What defensive precautions had already been undertaken were due to the townsmen themselves. Apart from the possibility that de Gaucourt might yet reach the town before the blockade started, the people of Harfleur and the small garrison were on their own.

Thursday 15th: the Feast of the Assumption

The problems posed by the landing site meant that it would take several days for all the men, horses, equipment and provisions to be taken off the ships. As thousands of men moved in and around the beach, and up the hill to the tents, Henry probably relocated himself to the priory of Graville. Perhaps it was in the church here that he celebrated the feast of the Assumption.

Outside the burning and looting had already started. Pigs, geese and hens were taken, granaries and houses robbed and burnt. The Englishmen – all with the red cross of St George painted on their surcoats – scattered quickly, searching for plunder.[54] After a week of being restricted within small ships, they revelled in being on dry land and able to take what they wanted from the country that they had come to destroy.

Friday 16th

Henry had been gathering information on Harfleur for months. Members of his first embassy in 1414 had travelled to France via Harfleur, including Bishop Courtenay, the earl of Salisbury and Lord Grey.[55] As we have seen, certain members of the recent embassy had also travelled that way, namely Sir William Bourchier, Sir John Phelip and William Porter. And these were just the ambassadors who had passed through Harfleur; there must have been many other men besides. So Henry knew more or less what to expect when he looked down over the town and port from the hill to the west.

Harfleur was a medium-sized town, with a population of about five thousand people. A high 2½-mile stone wall, punctuated by two dozen watchtowers and surrounded by ditches, encircled the church of St Martin, the public buildings and houses of the citizens. The wall also enclosed *le clos de galées*: an inner fortified naval port whose walls were higher even than those of the town. The River Lézarde ran down from the north and divided into two: one part ran around the western wall of the town, like a deep moat; the other ran through sluices in the town walls, through the centre of the town itself and into *le clos de galées*. This guaranteed a water supply in a siege, and gave power to two mills just inside the walls. There were three gates: the *Porte Leure* on the west, the *Porte Montivilliers* on the north, and the *Porte Rouen* on the south east. Two large towers guarded the water gate leading to *le clos de galées*; these could raise a great chain between them, preventing the entry of any ships. To the south, on either side of the Lézarde, the town was protected by the marshes that ran down to the sea; these were the same marshes that the English attackers had noticed while waiting to disembark on the rocky shore further to the west.[56]

Not everything was familiar to Henry; some changes had recently taken place. Around each of the three gates substantial barbicans or bulwarks had been built. These were circular enclosures of tree-trunks lashed together and part-buried in the ground, strengthened with earth mounds and surrounded by water-filled moats. They had spaces in them for small cannon and crossbows to fire at approaching attackers. The road to Montivilliers had been in part taken up, and the stones taken into the town to use in the town's catapults.[57] The river approach to the town had been blocked with sharpened stakes below the water line. Most worrying of all, the sluice gates had been closed on the north, flooding the entire valley. To go around in order to attack the town on the east side now required a journey of nine or ten miles.[58]

But Henry had set himself upon a path. Since April he had described the expedition's first aim as seizing Harfleur. It was a matter of pride that he would do what he had set out to do. He ordered the houses in the suburbs to be burnt and the whole area to be cleared, ready for his siege engines and cannon. The attack would begin the following day.

Saturday 17th

The final provisions, horses and equipment were unloaded from the ships, and the siege began. Henry divided his army into three 'battles' or battalions in order to facilitate organisation. His own battle was centrally positioned, facing the *Porte Leure*; the other two were established on his flanks, probably commanded by the dukes of Clarence and York.

The actual order of events thereafter is not easy to determine. In all likelihood Henry set a high priority on bringing up the cannon and the siege engines from the coast. At least one great gun, 'Goodgrace', and one siege engine were positioned directly opposite the *Porte Leure* and its barbican.[59] He held a council to determine the best way of attacking the town and of supplying the soldiers who were now encamped in the fields to the west. Groups of men were sent out to find food in the villages and farms nearby; they quickly covered a huge area. A twenty-eight-year-old priest from Harfleur, Raoul le Gay, was captured by an English foraging party on the road seven miles east of Harfleur. He was taken back to Santivic, three miles from the main army, and told by a French-speaking English knight that he would be ransomed for 100 crowns. Unfortunately for him, he could not pay. The English decided to take him to the main camp, at Graville.[60]

It appears likely that it was today that Henry issued his military ordinances – the set of codes of conduct for the campaign. These had been issued to armies since at least Edward III's campaign in 1346, when an edict had stated that

> no town or manor was to be burnt, no church or holy place sacked, and no old people, children or women in his kingdom of France were to be harmed or molested; nor were [the soldiers] to threaten people, or do any kind of wrong, on pain of life and limb.[61]

For Henry to attack in France and yet be seen as the leader of a moral war he needed to do his best to control the more violent and less humane tendencies of his soldiers. The military ordinances were proclaimed by the captains of the army, and copies were to be given to the captains to ensure that they were obeyed.

Various versions of the ordinances issued by Henry V over the years 1415–21 are extant. The set most likely to have been issued in August 1415 is known by historians as Upton's ordinances.[62] There were fourteen sections, the first being to protect churches and religious buildings and not steal from them, and to respect the Eucharist and the pyx; and the second not to capture or harm any clergymen or women, or to take prisoner any clergymen unless they were armed and hostile, and not to rape any women, on pain of death. The third section stipulated that everyone in the army – including merchants and other non-combatants riding with the army – should obey without question any order from the king, the constable and the marshal of the army. The fourth section specified how the night-time watch was to be maintained, with the constable and marshal again in charge. The fifth ordered captains to be ready to muster their men-at-arms and archers whenever the king or his officers required, on pain of arrest and forfeiture of arms and horse; and the sixth was designed to prevent insurrection and loss of control within the army. For instance, no one was to 'cry havoc' – 'havoc' being the order by which men on the battlefield could break ranks and steal whatever they wanted – and no one was to 'cry montez' (to horse) or other cries that might bring danger to the whole host. No one was to let old feuds and duels govern their conduct in the camp; and no matter what news came to the army, no one was to break ranks.

The remainder of the ordinances were similarly intended to strengthen the army through discipline. No one was to ride out from the host without permission, or to go forging ahead on their own. No one was to raise a banner or pennon of St George to lead a group of men away from the main army, nor to go ahead of the host under a banner unless he was a messenger. No one was to burn any buildings without special command of the king. If anyone found victuals or wine he should take only enough for himself and not destroy the remainder but leave it for the army. Men were not to rob each other of any vict-uals they found or otherwise received. No one except the king, constable or marshal was to give safe conduct to anyone from outside the army.

Particular ordinances treated the problem of prisoners. For most soldiers the main lure of war was the attraction of wealth – to be gained not by looting but by taking and ransoming important men. Hence disputes often arose over who had taken whom prisoner. It was now made clear that there were to be no disputes over captives – nor over weapons, coats of arms, or lodgings. Grooms and pages who got involved in such arguments were to have their left ear cut off. When a man took a prisoner, he was to take his helmet and gauntlets as a sign that his victim was already claimed. Two men who collectively defeated a knight could share the rights and subsequent ransom. It was clearly anticipated that, in the heat of battle, rivalries between men could lead to one trying to kill the other's prisoner. This was forbidden. The killing of a man who was trying to submit was similarly not allowed. No man was to sell his prisoner or to ransom him without the king's permission, and everyone who took prisoners was liable to pay his lord one third of the eventual ransom.

There was one last moral ordinance in this set, and it is very revealing of Henry's attitude to women of easy virtue and his view of sex. Although earlier English kings had tolerated prostitutes in the royal household, Henry had a much stricter moral view. He prohibited any women from staying in the camp at all, or even being located nearer than three miles. His ordinance laid down that the first time a woman was found in the camp, she was to be warned. The second time she was to have her left arm broken.[63]

*

In his pavilion, the duke of York sealed his last will and testament. Like Henry IV and Henry V himself, he adopted the self-demeaning language of extreme abasement. The document, which was in French, began:

> In the name of God the Almighty, and the Son, and the Holy Ghost, and the Holy Trinity, and the glorious Virgin, Our Lady St Mary, and St Thomas our glorious Martyr, and of St Edward the Holy Confessor, and all the Holy Saints in Paradise, I, Edward of York, of all sinners the most wicked and blameworthy . . .

He desired to be buried in the chapel at Fotheringay, 'in the middle of
the choir, near the steps, under a flat marble slab'. He stipulated that
his debts should be paid and the expenses of his funeral should not
exceed £100. His first bequest was to the king: 'the best sword and the
best dagger I have'. Next was

> to my dear wife Philippa my bed of feathers and leopards, with the
> furniture that goes with it; also my white and red tapestry of garters,
> fetterlocks and falcons; my green bed, embroidered with a compass,
> my two large vessels of silver, the covered basins in her keeping, with
> the falcons and fetterlocks in the middle, with a blue background.

Those servants of his who had been in his service for a whole year
before sailing to Harfleur were to be paid their wages in full for the
six-month term after his death: £2 10s to each esquire, £1 to each
'*garçon*' and half a mark (6s 8d) to each page. All his houpelands (full-
length, long-sleeved and high-collared gowns) were to be divided
among the servants of his chamber and wardrobe; his saddles and
harnesses were likewise to be divided among his servants. In all the
Masses that might be said for him, he willed that Richard II, Henry
IV, his father Edmund of York, and his mother Isabella should also
be mentioned. He continued:

> I will that all my vestments, crucifixes, images, tabernacles, basins,
> ewers, censers, sconces and other jewels in my chapel, excepting the
> goods and jewels that I pledged to enable me to go in that voyage to
> France in the company of my lord the king, be after my decease given
> to the master and his brethren of my said college [of Fotheringay], to
> be perpetually kept by them and their successors . . .

Other personal bequests included £20 to Thomas Pleistede 'in memory
of the kindness that he showed me when I was a prisoner at Pevensey';
a sword, a coat of mail and £10 in cash to Philip Beauchamp; a suit
of jointed armour covered in red velvet and £10 in money to Thomas
Beauchamp; and a new suit of jointed armour covered in velvet, his
helmet and his best horse to Sir John Popham.[64]

*

In London, the talk was of Lollardy. In the wake of the letter from Henry at Southampton, the mayor, Thomas Falconer, had renewed his searches for dissidents. And on the information of his new servant, the fifteen-year-old Alexander Philip, he had been alerted to John Claydon. The mayor had ordered a search of Claydon's house in St Martin's Lane, where the copy of *The Lantern of Light* had been found.

Today Claydon was brought before Henry Chichele, archbishop of Canterbury, and a large gathering of theologians and lawyers, in St Paul's Cathedral. Claydon admitted that he had been accused of Lollardy repeatedly, for more than twenty years. He further admitted that he had been locked in the prison at Conway for two years on account of his supposed heresy, and for three years in the Fleet Prison in London. He added that, having been released by order of the chancellor at the time, John Scarle, he had publicly abjured the heresies of Lollardy, and had promised to abstain from the company of other Lollards.

Archbishop Chichele began to interrogate Claydon. Had he any books in English? Yes, many, replied Claydon. Chichele beckoned the mayor forward to give evidence. A book in English, bound in red leather was produced. Handing it to Chichele, Thomas Falconer declared it had been found in Claydon's house and was 'the worst and the most perverse book that he had ever read'. The archbishop asked Claydon whether he recognised the book; Claydon admitted that he had had it written at his own cost. Chichele demanded that Claydon name the author. 'John Grime,' Claydon replied.

Now Chichele began to press his victim. *What* was John Grime, he demanded, presumably expecting the answer 'a Lollard'. Claydon did not answer. Chichele was insistent. Had Claydon read this book? Claydon admitted he could not read but had heard parts of it read by John Fuller. And were any parts of this book Catholic, profitable, good and true? Claydon replied that he was very fond of the book, and found many things there that were profitable for his soul, especially the text of the sermon that had been preached at Horsleydown. And did the accused have any communication with Richard Gurmyn, a baker suspected of Lollardy, since his abjuration? Yes, admitted Claydon, Gurmyn often came to his house.[65]

Following this confession, Chichele passed the book over to a doctor of divinity and a doctor of law to be examined. He prorogued the case until the following Monday, when the judgment would be delivered.[66]

Sunday 18th

Harfleur was now all but cut off. The captain, Jean d'Estouteville, must have looked at the gathering horde of Englishmen to the west with foreboding. There were so many of them, drawing up their cannon and siege engines – and he himself had probably fewer than two hundred soldiers and the services of about a thousand able-bodied townsmen. No help could reasonably be expected now. But if he despaired of reinforcements the feeling was premature, for riding to join the people of Harfleur in their hopeless struggle was Raoul de Gaucourt.

Raoul de Gaucourt was a Picard knight – and one the of the most determined, courageous and resourceful military leaders in France. He had fought against the Turks on the Nicopolis crusade in 1396 and was one of the thirteen knights of the duke of Bourbon's new Order of the Prisoner's Shackle. Boucicaut, the most famous knight in Christendom, was one of his personal friends and comrades in arms. De Gaucourt also understood the dangers of the English archers, having faced them at the battle of St Cloud in 1411.[67] That Henry had already surrounded the town, and was pillaging the countryside far to the east of Harfleur did not dissuade this man from bravely riding with his three hundred men-at-arms straight for the gates on the eastern side of the town.

Henry was taken by surprise. With his groups of knights going far to the east beyond Harfleur, he did not imagine for a moment that reinforcements would arrive this late in the day, and risk a battle. But he had failed to take into consideration the water defences of Harfleur. Henry could not send troops arrayed for battle around the south of the town to intercept de Gaucourt, due to the salt marshes and the river Lézarde. Nor could he send a force of men around the north side due to the flooding of the valley. He could do nothing but watch as Raoul de Gaucourt led the last contingent of fighting men into the town, to the great joy of those within.

The boldness of de Gaucourt's entry into Harfleur infuriated Henry. It was an obvious sign of his failure to seal off the town properly at the outset. But it is a noticeable feature of Henry's character that, when his pride was hurt, he did not let the matter lie or accept the injury but took decisive action. Now he decided to employ one of his most efficient weapons of war: his brother, Thomas of Clarence. That very night he ordered Clarence to take his battle and find his way around the flooded valley, sealing off the town on the east side. Clarence was to take a cannon with him, and start bombarding the town. At the same time Henry ordered his ships to shift to the mouth of the Lézarde and prevent any reinforcements or supplies reaching the town by the water gate. He would not be made to look foolish again.

Monday 19th

At dawn, when the people of Harfleur roused themselves to face the day ahead, they looked up at Mont Cabert, the hill overlooking the town on the east, and saw the forces of Thomas, duke of Clarence, arrayed around a chapel on the slopes. They saw the cannon of the king of England to the west, facing the gate, and the banners of the lords of England all around their beautiful town. The huge weight of Henry's determination to demonstrate that God was on his side had come to bear on them, and the pressure must have been terrifying. They knew that, unless the king of France sent a relieving army, they had no hope. Many would die, and those who survived could expect to lose all they had worked for all their lives.

Henry's herald began the proceedings. The king sent him to the *Porte Leure* to offer,

in accordance with the twentieth chapter of Deuteronomic law, peace to the besieged if, freely and without coercion, they would open their gates to him and, as was their duty, restore that town, which was a noble and hereditary portion of his crown of England and of his duchy of Normandy.[68]

This repetition of Deuteronomic law – mentioned in Henry's extraordinary letter of 28 July – must have been chilling to those who heard

it, especially in respect of claiming Harfleur as a hereditary possession. For the law as laid out in Deuteronomy 20, verses 10–16, was
very explicit as to what should happen to those who resisted a hereditary lord:

10. When you come to a city, in order to attack it, first proclaim
    peace to it;
11. And it shall be: if it gives an answer of peace, and opens its gates
    to you, then all the people that are found therein shall be your
    subjects and shall serve you;
12. And if it does not give an answer of peace, but makes war against
    you, then you should besiege it;
13. And when the Lord your God has delivered it into your hands you
    shall smite every male therein with the edge of the sword;
14. But the women, the children and cattle and everything that is in the
    city, including all the spoil, you shall take for your own; and you shall
    enjoy the spoil of your enemies that the Lord God has given you;
15. Thus shall you do to all the cities that are distant from your home-
    land, which are not of the cities of these nations;
16. But of the cities of those people that the Lord God gives you as
    an inheritance, you shall save alive nothing that breathes.

Despite this horrific threat, according to the author of the *Gesta*, the
inhabitants of the town made light of the offer of peace and the threats
of destruction. Henry responded by 'informing them of the penal
edicts contained in the aforesaid law [of Deuteronomy] which it would
be necessary to execute upon them as a rebellious people should they
persist thus in their obstinacy to the end'.[69] As Henry regarded the
town as part of his inheritance from God this meant that the women
and children, and even the cattle of the town, could also expect to be
slaughtered along with the men.

But still the people of Harfleur did not give in.

*

There were various methods employed in the middle ages for the
destruction of a town. Water supplies could be cut off or poisoned;
buildings set alight in the hope that the fire would spread throughout

the town; the town could be blockaded to prevent food from entering; the walls could be over-run by large numbers of troops using scaling ladders and battering rams on the gates; and cannon and other siege engines could be used to smash down the walls. Harfleur was a difficult prospect whichever method Henry chose. The volume of water flowing through the town (despite the closure of sluices to flood the valley to the north) made it difficult to cut off the water supply. The barbicans prevented any direct attack on the gates, and an attempt to scale the walls would inevitably lead to a massive loss of life. Henry's own ordinances prohibited burning – and even though he could have rescinded those instructions, the town would not have been worth possessing if he had burnt it to the ground. His model for a successful siege was Edward III's seizure of Calais, which had been effected by a combined landward and seaward blockade, both of which Henry had already put in place. However, it had taken Edward III eleven months to starve Calais into submission, and Henry did not have eleven months to spare. He could not afford such a long campaign, nor could he risk a battle before the walls with an oncoming French army without a port from which he could retreat.

Henry chose to deploy his heavy guns from the outset. Having cleared the last buildings from the suburbs, the great iron-bound cannon blasted stones of 400–500lbs at the defences. Although there was a large number of cannon in the English arsenal in England, Henry had brought no more than a dozen with him, and perhaps fewer.[70] These monsters weighed up to two tons and could only fire at a very slow rate; but when they did fire, and struck the target, the effect was devastating. One stone hitting a castle tower could easily bring the whole edifice crashing down. Henry's father had been at the cutting edge of gunnery technology, designing cannon himself, and deploying them with great effectiveness in his sieges. At Warkworth in 1405 he had forced the defenders to surrender after one of his great guns had fired seven times; shortly afterwards at Berwick he had demolished the external walls of the castle with small cannon and then, with a single shot from one of his great guns, had blown apart one of the towers, after which the defenders surrendered.[71] This was the technology that Henry himself now proposed to use to reduce the town of Harfleur, and show that a siege that took Edward III eleven months could be accomplished by his men in a few days.

Henry did not just bring up his guns. He built deep ditches and earth ramparts around them, to defend the gunners and other men shooting at the walls. In front of each cannon he positioned a screen made of heavy planks of wood; these were hinged at their midpoint on each side, so that when the top was tilted back, the lower part allowed the cannon to blast a stone towards the selected target. Similar defences were placed directly opposite the strongest barbican, to allow a round-the-clock watch to be stationed there, in case the enemy should attack from it. Those digging the protective ditch around this defence continued excavating day after day, thereby making a trench that almost reached the water in front of the *Porte Leure*.[72] And then the gunners – twenty-five of them, including four master gunners, with fifty assistants – were instructed to destroy the town walls, to destroy the barbicans, and to fire indiscriminately into the centre of the town, to kill the inhabitants and to demoralise the enemy.[73]

Meanwhile Henry sent a messenger to the duke of Brittany to make sure that their truce still held good.[74] As he knew, it was all very well having alliances with subjects of the king of France before the fighting started; whether they would actually support him with men and arms now they could see their services would be required was a totally different issue. Henry had obviously given similar instructions to his brother and the chancellor before leaving England, as the duke of Bedford was set to publish (on the 20th, tomorrow) the truce with the duke of Brittany at Dartmouth, Plymouth and Exeter. When that was done, the embassy led by John Hovingham and Simon Flete would leave London, with powers to renegotiate a new alliance with the duke of Brittany. They would remain there, reminding the duke of his diplomatic obligations, until Henry had left France.[75]

*

Raoul le Gay had been kept at Santivic for the last two days. This morning he was brought to the king's camp at Graville where his guards told him to sit on the ground. There they left him, without food or drink, until midday. While Henry was with his council deciding on how to blast a hole in the side of Harfleur, a young Englishman came up to Raoul and spoke to him in Latin. Raoul told him he was hungry and thirsty, and the Englishman relayed the message to the guards. The guards helped him up and took him into the precincts of the priory. Here he met several English lords who, noticing his tonsure, asked him in French if he was a priest. When he said yes, he was, they asked him where were the English soldiers who had captured him, for in arresting him they had clearly contravened one of Henry's most important ordinances. But Raoul did not know.

The young Englishman who had first spoken to him in Latin was then given instructions from the king to send Raoul to Thomas Beaufort, the constable of the army, who was lodged nearby. On arrival at Beaufort's camp, the earl himself questioned Raoul in French. When he was done, he told him to sit down on a millstone and not to stir. There he was left until nightfall, still without food or drink. Only then, when the stars were appearing, did one of Beaufort's men give him a piece of bread and some ale, and find him somewhere to sleep. Things could still be tough for a priest in English custody, despite Henry's ordinances forbidding the arrest of unarmed priests.

*

In Paris, the dauphin and the government started sending out letters to the regions announcing that the English had landed, and summoning forces and appealing for money. The earliest extant such letter was despatched to Verdun.[76]

*

In London, in St Paul's Cathedral, the trial of John Claydon resumed. Archbishop Chichele presided, supported by Bishop Clifford of London, Bishop Catterick of Lichfield and the king's confessor, Stephen Patrington, bishop of St David's. The general examiner of the province of Canterbury opened proceedings, and called on the doctors of law and divinity to give their evidence. They named the book by John Grime as the notorious *The Lantern of Light* and proceeded to read sections from it and to condemn them as heresy. Fifteen particular passages were singled out, and read aloud, and condemned. And then the book was solemnly burned in a fire prepared for the purpose.

After John Claydon's confession had once more been read out, he was told formally that the archbishop judged that he had lapsed into his former heresy, and, with the assent of the three bishops and all the doctors of law and divinity present, he decreed that Claydon be handed over to the secular authorities for capital punishment.

It fell to the mayor, Thomas Falconer, to write to the king informing him that he proposed to carry out the sentence of burning Claydon to death.

Tuesday 20th

It was full moon. Henry had ordered that the bombardment of the town should continue day and night. For the people of Harfleur the sound of a stone whistling through the air and striking a building with tremendous force, sending it crumbling into the street, was becoming a normality. The screams of those men, women and children injured in the constant bombardment were no doubt just as demoralising as the missiles themselves.

Henry was taking advantage of the extra moonlight to keep the bombardment going. He himself stayed up at night – 'he did not allow his eyelids to close in sleep', as one chronicler put it – going through the camp and seeing that his men were prepared and organised, visiting the sentries, checking the positions of his guns and siege engines.

It is not known for certain who was now in control within Harfleur. It is possible that Raoul de Gaucourt had taken over as captain of the town. Alternatively he may have simply taken charge of the defences, so d'Estouteville was still the man giving the orders.[77] Either way, probably both men also stayed up, inspecting the defences by moonlight and ordering the masons to repair the walls – while outside the walls Henry encouraged his men to fire their cannon again.

Thursday 22nd

The mayor of London, Thomas Falconer, wrote to the king about John Claydon:

Forasmuch as the Almighty King and the Lord of Heaven, who lately taught your hands to fight, and has guided your feet to the battle, has now during your absence, placed in our hands certain persons who not only were enemies of Him and of your dignity but also, in so far as they might be, were subverters of the whole of your realm: men commonly known as Lollards, who have laboured for a long time for the subversion of the whole Catholic faith and of Holy Church, the lessening of public worship and the destruction of your realm, as also the perpetration of very many other enormities horrible to hear; the same persons, in accordance with the requirements of the law, we have caused to be delivered by indenture unto the Reverend Commissaries of the Reverend Father in Christ, Lord Richard, by Divine permission, the Lord Bishop of London. Whereupon one John Claydon by name, the arch-parent of this heretical depravity, was by the most Reverend Father in Christ and Lord Henry, by Divine permission, the Lord Archbishop of Canterbury, Primate of all your realm, and other bishops, his brethren, as well as very many professors of Holy Scripture and doctors of law, in accordance with the canonical sanctions, by sentence in this behalf lawfully pronounced, as being a person relapsed into heresy, which before had been by him abjured, left in the hands of the secular court; for the execution of whose body and the entire destruction of all such enemies, with all diligence, to the utmost of our power we shall be assisting . . .[78]

The sentence was pushed before Henry with no expectation that he would intervene to try to stop the killing, as he had done with John Badby in 1410. Those days of clemency had long since given way to a rigid application of the ultimate penalty. In order to create a horror of religious deviation Falconer's letter linked the Lollard cause to treason. Claydon was portrayed as 'an enemy of Him and of your dignity' and 'a subverter of the whole of your realm' seeking 'the destruction of your realm'. This was all blatantly untrue. Claydon was just a conscientious man who felt bound to follow his conscience in religious matters over and above the institution of the Church. Once again we can see how heresy and treason were being linked, amplifying the heretical nature of treason and the treasonable nature of heresy.

This is why Mayor Falconer did not expect a messenger to come galloping back from the coast with orders to stop the burning.

Friday 23rd

By this stage Harfleur was completely cut off. Yet the commanders within had managed to get a message out to Charles d'Albret, then at Rouen, saying their land routes were in enemy hands and that the only hope of reaching the town was by boat; they asked for more supplies. D'Albret commissioned a galley and sent it out today.[79] If the oarsmen managed to find their way between the English ships in the Seine and into Harfleur, then it would have been the last contact the people of Harfleur had with the outside world.

Saturday 24th

The formal reply to the letter that Henry had written 'on the coast' at Southampton was drawn up and sealed in Paris.

The blessing of peace, beloved of God and nature, to which after the example of our Lord Jesus Christ, which He left to his disciples and gave to us as a legacy, we have always sought and desired by every means in our power, and which for the honour of God, we desire most earnestly to procure, for the advantages that attend it, and to avoid the effusion of human blood, and the innumerable evils produced by war. As this we believe is manifest and clear to you, your council and others, you have occasioned us great surprise, and not without cause, after such great overtures and other points discussed between your people and ours, with a firm intention of establishing peace, to the great sin of your party. And as we never did refuse justice, nor shall we, if it please God, to all who may demand it of us; as it is lawful for every prince in his just quarrel to defend himself, and to oppose force by force; and as none of your predecessors ever had any right, and you still less, to make the demands contained in certain of your letters, presented to us by Chester your herald, nor to give us any trouble, it is our intention with the assistance of the Lord, in whom we have singular trust, and especially from the justice of our cause, and also with the aid of our good relations, friends, allies and subjects, to resist you in a way that shall be to the honour and glory of us and of our kingdom, and to the confusion, loss and dishonour of you and your party.

With respect to the marriage of which you write at the end of your letter, it does not appear that the means that you have adopted to make a request or demand, and especially of affinity or marriage, is proper, honourable, or usual in such a case; and therefore we will not write to you upon any other matter at present but send you this letter in answer to that which you wrote us by the said Chester.[80]

It was entirely understandable – and the 'great surprise' of the attack was probably genuine in the sense that, when negotiations for peace had been in progress in 1414, an invasion on this scale could not have been anticipated. The French government, like the French people, could not see what they had done to warrant such an attack.

★

Troops were now gathering to defend the north of France, and to guard against the anticipated march on Paris. Jean de Werchin, seneschal of Hainault, marched into Amiens today with 120 men-at-arms and sixty archers. The count of Vendôme either had or was raising a company of three hundred men-at-arms and 150 archers. The duke of Berry was raising a thousand men-at-arms and five hundred archers. As can be seen from these figures, whereas most English companies had thirty longbowmen to every ten men-at-arms, the pattern for the French was to have five archers (mostly crossbowmen) for every ten men-at-arms. Thus the resisting force was very different in its composition from the attacking one. Each French man-at-arms would have had a page, like his English equivalent, and there would have been a number of grooms and servants too, and these men also needed to be fed and watered.

Although these forces by themselves could do nothing to stop the English from attacking Harfleur, they could impede the progress of the foraging parties by restricting their movements. According to Monstrelet, Boucicaut, Clignant de Brabant and the seneschal of Hainault were all in the field, harassing the English along with Charles d'Albret. They prevented them from taking any other towns in the region, despite the widespread incursions of the English foragers.[81]

Sunday 25th

The siege had now been underway for a week, and the siege engines and cannon had continued bombarding the town, day and night. The author of the *Gesta* remarked that

> within a few days, when by the violence and fury of the stones the barbican was in the process of being largely demolished, the walls and towers from which the enemy had discharged their offensives were rendered defenceless with their ramparts destroyed; and truly fine buildings, almost as far as the middle of the town, were either totally demolished or threatened with inevitable collapse or, at least, their framework falling apart.[82]

For Henry, this was now becoming a problem. He wanted to take Harfleur and hold it; but if the inhabitants and soldiers under Raoul de Gaucourt held out until the town was destroyed, he would not be able to defend it against the French counter-attack, whenever that might come. Then he would find himself defending nothing but a pile of rubble, and trapped against the coast. The truth was that his strategy of taking the town quickly was likely to leave the town in ruins long before the inhabitants' food supplies ran out. The effect on his nerve and the nerves of his fellow councillors cannot be known; but it would be foolish to suppose that the situation was anything but deeply worrying.

The destruction of the town was not Henry's only concern. Raoul de Gaucourt was rallying the defenders to fight with crossbows, guns, catapults, and siege engines of their own. From the barbican outside the *Porte Leure* they shot and fired at the attackers, and also from behind screens erected in the openings of shattered walls and broken towers. In addition, by night, when it was difficult for the archers to pick off the defenders, they started to rebuild the damaged walls and the barbican, re-laying the stones and placing large tubs filled with earth, dung, sand and stones. Walls teetering or collapsing they shored up in a similar way, using bundles of faggots set solid with clay, earth and dung. They also lay clay, dung and earth over the streets and lanes to soak up the impact of crashing stones and masonry, so that projectiles would not bounce off the hard ground into buildings but would get swallowed up in the mud.

For Henry the obvious next step was a full-scale assault on the walls with scaling ladders, or through the breaches he had made. Overcoming the defenders in this way would preserve what remained of the defences. But his first attempts to overwhelm the walls proved futile. The defenders had filled jars with a compound made from sulphur and quicklime to throw in the eyes of the men who attacked. They had also gathered barrels of inflammable powders, oils and fat; if any siege equipment came close – such as a wooden tower to launch an onslaught on the walls – then they set light to the barrels and poured them over the wooden apparatus. The author of the *Gesta* remarked that 'people under siege could not have resisted our attacks more sagaciously, or with greater security to themselves, than they did'.[83]

*

Raoul le Gay had languished in Thomas Beaufort's camp for a whole week now. In that time he had been practically famished; no one wanted to waste good food on a Frenchman. His predicament was that he had been taken illegally and yet no one wanted to let him go, given how much he had seen of the English quarters. He continually asked to be released but this request was denied. In the end he was taken before the king. Henry demanded to know whether he had been taken in arms – in which case his imprisonment did not contravene Henry's military ordinances. Raoul protested that he had not. Henry seems to have paid little attention otherwise to the man but ordered that he be taken to Bishop Courtenay's tent, which was close to the king's pavilion, and quartered there.[84]

Wednesday 28th

The French council sent out letters summoning forces to assemble at Rouen. The actual form of the summons was a *semonce des nobles*, to be proclaimed in Normandy and the surrounding areas. This stated that, although the king of France had sent envoys to England in the hope of avoiding the bloodshed and inconvenience of war, the English had invaded and laid siege to Harfleur. So the king had directed the dauphin as lieutenant to gather an army at Rouen. All the nobles and men-at-arms of the region, and all the archers and crossbowmen, were to gather there as soon as possible. As they journeyed, men were to wear a white cross – in contrast to the English red one – and were under strict instructions not to pillage any places through which they passed, nor to stay anywhere longer than one night. All those attending would receive protection for six months from any legal cases in the courts against them, and they would be paid. King Charles himself would join the army soon, in order to raise the siege and lead his subjects in the fight against the English, in the eyes of God.[85]

One lord was exempted from this *semonce des nobles*: John the Fearless, duke of Burgundy. Perhaps his agreement with Henry V was suspected. Perhaps it was just too dangerous to the Armagnacs to allow the duke to ride at the head of an army across Normandy. Either way, it was a diplomatic gamble, for it gave a clear message that the duke was out of favour.

*

Bishop Courtenay attended Mass in his tent at about nine o'clock this morning. Afterwards he took Raoul le Gay and went to hear a religious service in the king's chapel. Raoul was astonished to hear such beautiful music. One of the more incongruous images of the siege is Henry V listening to his choristers singing pious anthems while his cannon boomed out in the valley below, blasting at the walls of Harfleur day and night.

After the service, Courtenay spoke to Raoul about Jean Fusoris. He explained that Fusoris was a canon of Notre Dame in Paris, and a famous astronomer. If Raoul would carry a message to Fusoris, the bishop would set him free. Raoul had never been to Paris himself, and so he refused. But when Courtenay threatened to ship him back to England to be imprisoned, he accepted the mission. Courtenay would give him the letter to Fusoris tomorrow.

*

Down in the valley, the men of Harfleur were taking the fight to the English. As Henry tried new tactics to break their defences, so they devised new methods of defeating him. When Henry planned to fill in the ditches on both sides of the town with bundles of faggots ten feet long, the defenders simply got ready to pour burning oil into the same ditches and set light to the faggots and the men laying them. So Henry abandoned that plan. Instead he decided to try to fight his way into the town by having two mines built, to tunnel beneath the walls' foundations and then bring them crashing down by setting light to the pit props. A 'sow' or protective shelter was built for each mine and digging started. Raoul de Gaucourt knew exactly how to tackle that threat. He ordered counter-mines to be dug, in which the besieged men dug towards the miners and fought for control of the mine, and then filled it in. Such measures were hard work and terrifying; it was a race in great heat, darkness and barely any air – conducted with the sole intention of breaking through and meeting a desperate, murderous enemy. On both occasions the defenders proved the better miners and managed to thwart the attackers, breaking through and bringing down their shaft before the walls could be pulled down. The sole English achievement as a result of the mines was that the watchmen guarding one of the mines saw an opportunity to attack the outer ditch on the king's side, and managed to capture it. From there they could bring the siege engines a little closer to the walls, and use the ditch as protection while they attacked the defences.[86]

On the east side of the town, Thomas, duke of Clarence, was having his men-at-arms and archers dig ditches. Thomas had impressed everyone with the ferocity of his onslaughts on the walls; but he was in a very dangerous position. He was on the exposed side of the town – open to attack from companies of Frenchmen. His messengers had to run the gauntlet of crossing the flooded area north of the town in small boats in order to get to the king, and then get back. And having fewer men than Henry at his command, he was also prone to attacks from the town itself, from guns as well as crossbows and sallies of men-at-arms. Nevertheless he kept up the pressure, following Henry's initiatives and keeping up the bombardment. Now his men were constructing a long defensive ditch in front of his own lines, copying the Harfleur townsmen's own method of driving tree trunks into the ground, and heaping up earth from the ditch against them, to protect his men while they continued the assault.

Thursday 29th

In his tent near the king's pavilion, Courtenay wrote his letter to Jean Fusoris. He wrote with his own hand, in Latin, and said how he recalled their previous conversations, and how a clerk who knew Fusoris had recently passed on news of him. He asked that Fusoris write back with news within the next eight or ten days but not to mention either of their names in the correspondence, as no one knew of it except the king, 'who is very close, as you know'. He then sealed the letter and handed it to Raoul le Gay, together with a purse containing twenty half-nobles, which Raoul hid beneath his shirt. Another man in Courtenay's service handed Raoul a letter to take to Paris, to a friend of his. Courtenay himself gave Raoul a small parchment list of fruit, pumpkins and other things he wanted from the prior of the Celestines in Paris, and promised to pay for them on delivery. He also told Raoul to tell Fusoris that Henry had landed with fifty thousand men, four thousand barrels of wheat, four thousand casks of wine, sufficient supplies for a six-month siege of Harfleur, and twelve large cannon. Probably all of this was exaggerated; he had fewer than a third as many men, and had only ordered food for three months. Besides, according to Monstrelet, many of his supplies had been damaged at sea.[87] But the instruction fits with what we know about Courtenay's relationship with Fusoris on previous occasions – he fed him misinformation in the hope that it would be passed on to the French court, while seeking intelligence of his own.[88]

There was one particular question that Courtenay did not put in writing but asked Raoul to put to Fusoris: whether the duke of Burgundy was responding to the call to arms. This seems to have been a genuine area of concern for the bishop. Despite the agreement between Henry and John the Fearless, the latter had proved duplicitous throughout his career, and still was not wholly trusted. Henry and Courtenay suspected he might break the terms of his agreement and fight on the French side simply because the enormity of fighting against his fellow French subjects on behalf of an English claimant to the throne was too great. As it

happened John the Fearless was still at Argilly, where he had been since
he himself had entertained the ambassadors of the duke of Brittany,
who had arrived there on the 15th.[89] John the Fearless's ambassadors
were no doubt discussing the implications of the English invasion with
their Breton counterparts, and reviewing possible strategies. Courtenay
would not have known this, of course, but the English council was very
eager to know which way the two dukes with English treaties would
choose to act.

Saturday 31st

Raoul le Gay had left Bishop Courtenay's camp on the 29th with letters
of safe conduct, so he could pass through the English lines. He had set
out as intended in the direction of Paris. But later that night he turned
back and made his way in the moonlight to Montivilliers. At sunrise,
when the gates to the town opened, he passed into the town. The
French guards demanded to know who he was and where he had come
from. He said he had come from the English army, and showed them
his English safe conduct. The guards tore it up, but they allowed him
into the town. He wandered around until he found some friends of
his, and went to a tavern and had a drink with them; but later, as he
walked in front of the town hall, he was pointed out to the town
officials as having come from the English camp with English letters of
safe conduct. He was arrested and locked up in a chamber in the
abbey.

Today Raoul was brought out of his prison and taken to the town
hall. A French Benedictine monk, who had also been arrested by the
English, detained and then released, recognised Raoul and said he was
carrying a secret letter. Raoul admitted it, and, realising the gravity
of his situation, declared that he had no intention of delivering it. But
of course he had to produce the said letter. When the recipient was
identified as Jean Fusoris, it seemed to the authorities that they had
discovered one of Henry's spies: a trusted astrologer, right in the heart
of the city with access to the court. A message was despatched to
Paris straightaway.[90]

★

In Paris the French king's councillors were facing a crisis. The taxation they had levied on 14 March was not going to be sufficient to pay for an army strong enough to counter the English. They therefore decided they needed 24,000 *livres tournois* (about £4,000) as soon as possible. Of course this was unpopular; one writer in Paris described it as 'the heaviest tax that had ever been seen in the whole age of man'. Many Parisians began to recall the duke of Orléans and his high taxes and lax morals, and saw the return of them both in the new taxation and the dauphin's immoral lifestyle.[91] As Pope Benedict had not yet been forced to resign, the French government set about obtaining permission from him to levy a tax for the war on all the clergy throughout France. And all this was to pay the expenses of an army of just six thousand men-at-arms and three thousand archers. The French government was having difficulty even raising a mediocre force to resist the English. There was a failure to recognise the gravity of the situation.[92]

One development in France's favour did take place today. The five hundred Cabochien supporters of John the Fearless were granted an amnesty, in accordance with the conditions of John swearing to uphold the Peace of Arras. With this measure in place, the oath should have held firm. There should have been no doubt in French minds that John the Fearless would oppose the English, and the dauphin indeed issued a letter today declaring him a good and loyal subject.[93] As for what John actually intended to do, no one knew. On the one hand, he was promising to support the dauphin. But on the other, the dauphin's failure to include him among those who received the summons of the 28th, and another on 1 September, was an insult that he could use diplomatically to his advantage – to the point of refusing to fight.

*

At Harfleur the bombardment continued. The siege was now two weeks old, and still there were few signs that the inhabitants were prepared to give up. Some chronicles suggest that Raoul de Gaucourt had held negotiations with the English, offering to surrender the town; but these are equally likely to have been malicious rumours circulated in the wake of the defeat, when the various noble families in France all sought to blame each other for the failure to resist the English invasion. Just as likely to be true are the references to sorties from Harfleur, as the inhabitants sought to carry the fight to the English. What is certain is that a third mine was commenced about this time, in the hope of bringing the siege to a speedy end with no further destruction to the fabric of the town. It too was bound to fail, like the others. The approach to the centre of the town from the *Porte Leure* was now a broken mass of stone and timber; and yet still the inhabitants were determined to hold on. No matter what Henry threw at them, Raoul de Gaucourt and his fellow defenders held out. And they were in turn inflicting serious injuries on Henry's men. Thomas Hostell, a man-at-arms in Sir John Lumley's company, later recalled how at Harfleur he had been hit by a crossbow bolt, which had entered his head, destroying one eye and his cheek.[94] Incredibly, he went on to fight at Agincourt.

One cannot fault Henry's personal resolution in all this, nor that of his brother Thomas in commanding the second army on the eastern side of the town. The king continued to make nightly inspections of his lines, encouraging his men and making sure that watches were in place and the shift pattern for firing the guns was maintained.[95] But several strategic miscalculations were now obvious. One has already been mentioned – that in order to bring about a swift end to the siege using guns, Henry was having to destroy the defences he hoped to gain. So he had miscalculated the determination of the townsmen. But another, worse problem was becoming apparent. His army was too big for its purpose. An army suitable for fighting a battle was far larger than the size of force one needed for a successful siege. He could not risk a full-scale attack as he would lose too many men whom he would need later to fight a French army. But all the men with him needed food. They needed wine and ale. They needed money, and they needed clean accommodation. And although that last aspect might seem a minor one, it was actually very important. For now another obstacle in Henry's path emerged – not from the defenders but recognisable from the foetid hot air of the drying flooded valley north of the town, and the ever-present effluent of fifteen thousand men camped in a small area with no sanitary provision.

Dysentery.

September

Sunday 1st

Explanations of how and why people fell ill were confused in 1415. Sometimes astrological predictions were put forward for contagious diseases – planetary alignments leading to a miasma, or a polluted environment, which in turn led to pollutants entering the body through the pores of the skin and upsetting the balance of the four humours. Sometimes a miasma was associated with a particularly noxious smell. Alternatively diseases were attributed to God's will: either as punishment for a sinful act – as in the diseases heaped upon Henry IV for ordering the judicial murder of the archbishop of York – or as a means of attaining redemption from such sins. In the latter case, God was supposed to have visited sufferings on people so that they might atone for their behaviour and, through dying an agonising death, repent by bearing it well and thereby enter Paradise.

In the case of dysentery, people realised that large camps of soldiers attracted diseases, and that men chose to assemble large armies, so therefore the astrological explanation did not apply. Obviously God's will did apply, and it could be understood that, through disease, God sought to demonstrate to men that He did not approve of some sieges. In that sense, however much Henry claimed to be fighting a just war, and acting as an agent of God's will, the appearance of dysentery in the camp could be seen as a sign that God did not, after all, approve of Henry's war or his cause. Those who were loyal to Henry therefore looked for other explanations, and hit on other polluting factors. One contemporary chronicler, John Strecche, presumably writing on the basis of information sent back by combatants, pointed to the eating of unripe grapes and bad shellfish as the cause. Another writer, Thomas

Walsingham, gave a vivid explanation for the causes of the stomach diseases and dysentery. He claimed

> These deaths were caused by eating fruit, the cold nights, and the foetid smell from the bodies of different animals that they had killed throughout the English lines but which they had not covered with turf or soil, or had thrown into the waters of the river so they were forced to endure their decaying stench.[1]

Certainly the presence of rotting animals cannot have helped, especially considering it was an uncommonly hot summer.[2] The sixteen-year-old Lord Fitzwalter, serving in the company of the duke of Clarence, became one of the first casualties of the siege, dying today.[3]

Another factor contributing to the hardship of the besiegers was that they were beginning to run short of food. Although Henry had ordered that each man bring sufficient food for three months, in reality supplies had only lasted three weeks. In London today one Richard Bokeland was ordered to provide two ships to convey victuals, including fish, to the army at Harfleur. And over the next two days 700 marks was assigned to Richard Whittington to repay him for his expenses in maintaining the siege of Harfleur, and two men from Henley were ordered to provide one hundred quarters of wheat for the king's household at the siege.[4]

*

For those in the town, things were even harder. They had even less food, could not sleep for the fear and the noise of the incessant destruction, and water-borne diseases were beginning to spread within the town too. Knowing this, Henry sent a herald about this time to invite Raoul de Gaucourt and the other leaders in Harfleur to discuss terms. They came, under safe conduct, and met the king. Henry attempted with 'sweet words' to persuade them to surrender the town. He had his title to the throne of France repeated to them too, and his claim to the duchy of Normandy. But Henry had underestimated the townsmen's resolve. De Gaucourt insisted that the king of France would not leave the town to fend for itself for long but would soon arrive with an army. So he refused Henry's invitation. Instead of surrendering, he sent a messenger to the dauphin urging that he send an army as soon as possible to relieve the town.[5]

*

The dauphin left Paris this morning and journeyed to St Denis, the royal abbey just north of the city. Here he prayed for victory. He also sent out letters to the dukes of Orléans and Burgundy, and the count of Nevers (brother of John the Fearless, duke of Burgundy) requiring each of them to send five hundred men-at-arms and three hundred archers. John the Fearless was requested not to come in person but to send his son, Philip, count of Charolais, in his place. This was no doubt intended to avoid the risk of the duke leading an army that might suddenly turn and fight against the dauphin, on the side of the English. Nevertheless, John was bound to take offence.

Tuesday 3rd

Henry wrote a letter to the mayor and jurats of Bordeaux telling them that he and his company were in the best of health, for which 'in all humility, we give thanks to our lord God the Almighty, hoping that by His grace, He will give us in pursuit of our right, the fulfilment of our desire and undertaking, to His pleasure, and for the honour and comfort of us and you . . .' With God's help, he said, the enemy would be less capable of doing harm to his Gascon subjects in future, alluding to the danger of Norman ships attacking the Gascon wine trade. He asked them to assist Sir John Tiptoft in guarding against any French assault in Gascony. As for himself, he stated he was in need of wine and other victuals, which he asked them to send straight-away, promising payment in full on delivery.[6]

At the same time, Dr Jean Bordiu, archdeacon of Médoc, who was with the king at Harfleur, wrote a more detailed letter to the Jurade. He noted that the king himself had just written, and gave much more detail regarding the real state of affairs at Harfleur. He stated that, although the fields were still providing the army with sufficient corn, they could not be expected to meet the future requirements of the army, especially as more men were coming from England 'every day'.

This alerts us to the fact that reinforcements were arriving – a fact that is supported by careful analysis of the accounts relating to some of the companies with Henry.[7] Bordiu mentioned that Henry had asked for more wine to be sent; in this respect he specified that the king required between five hundred and seven hundred tuns. And he urged the townsmen to look to this with diligence, stating that Henry wished to come in person to Bordeaux before he returned to England.

Bordiu went on to say that, 'with the help of the Holy Spirit', he expected the town to fall within eight days. This was because the defences on the landward side and on two flanks had now been 'well and truly breached'. The town within the walls was 'totally destroyed'. The English had now managed to cut off the water supply below Montivilliers, thereby diverting the River Lézarde, draining the flooded area and cutting off the town's water supply. When the town finally fell, the king was not going to enter it but 'stay in the field' meaning he meant to continue his planned march through France. On this Bordiu was quite specific: 'he intends to go to Montivilliers, and from there to Dieppe, afterwards to Rouen and then to Paris'.[8]

Much of this was wishful thinking. Regardless of how long the town held out, it was now surrounded by thick, stinking mud, suffused with inedible fish and animal entrails, bones and excrement . . . It could only grow more dangerous – especially as the English troops had to trudge through it to get closer to the breach in the walls. The dysentery was not going to go away, and the town would require a substantial workforce to rebuild it as well as to maintain it. And the food was running out. About this time Henry issued an order, via his brother the regent in England, to the constable of Dover Castle and the warden of the Cinque Ports, to send each and every fisherman with his boat and tackle to Harfleur, there to provide fish for the king's army.[9] The chances of Henry marching on Paris in the near future were non-existent.

*

The messenger who had left Harfleur two days earlier had travelled through the night to Paris, and then on to St Denis, to convey de Gaucourt's plea for help to the dauphin. At first the dauphin was reluctant to receive him, having other business to attend to; but after the urgency of the situation had been established, the messenger was granted an audience.[10] He can have left the dauphin in no doubt as to the conditions in the town, and pleaded for a relieving army. If none was forthcoming then the town would soon have to surrender, to the detriment of the throne of France.[11] The dauphin was able to say that a large army was already gathering: the summons of 28 August and the letters to the royal dukes of 1 September would result in a large force assembling at Rouen. If the town could hold out for a little while longer, the French would drive the English into the sea.

There was just one problem. Henry had declared that, after he had taken Harfleur, he would march on to Rouen. We do not know if this news was publicly being circulated – it only appears in the letters sent to Bordeaux. But if the French did know, then it would have soon become apparent that both sides were going to converge on the same town.

Saturday 7th

The letter from Richard Courtenay to Jean Fusoris, carried by Raoul le Gay and confiscated in Montivilliers, arrived in Paris yesterday. On receipt, Fusoris was arrested and thrown into the prison known as the Little Châtelet. He was taken out today and led before the president of the *parlement*, Jean de Vailly, and charged with high treason.[12] Poor Fusoris had been duped by Courtenay. His presence in England that summer, coupled with the incriminating evidence supplied by Raoul le Gay, did not help his case. The old astrologer-clockmaker must have been in fear of his life from the moment the men-at-arms knocked on his door.

*

In London, Richard Gurmyn, the baker accused of Lollardy in the trial of John Claydon, was led before the authorities in St Paul's. His trial probably took much the same form as Claydon's, involving the decla-ration that he was a manifest heretic. The sentence of burning was inevitable. Some protested that he had taken advantage of the king's offer of a pardon, made on 9 December 1414. Thomas Falconer, however was having none of it. When the church authorities turned over Gurmyn to him for punishment he did not allow any time for the guilty man to locate his letters of pardon – if indeed he had them. Nor did he bother writing another letter to Henry. He simply had the pyre built at Smithfield, had Gurmyn dragged there, and burned him to death.[13]

Tuesday 10th

In Paris, the old king attended a solemn procession and Mass in the cathedral of Notre Dame, praying for victory 'with the help of God and the intercession of the saints'. When this had finished he travelled to the abbey of St Denis and there heard another Mass. The relics of the patron saint were exhibited, and the king was handed the sacred war banner of France, the *Oriflamme*, which he then passed to the similarly aged Guillaume Martel, seigneur de Bacqueville. With that symbolic gesture, France was now at war. If the banner was unfurled on a battlefield, it was an instruction to the French to take no prisoners.[14]

*

In London, it was John Claydon's turn to face the wrath of the pyre. No pardon was forthcoming from France. Indeed, Falconer's letter had probably only recently been received. His friend Gurmyn had gone before him, and that perhaps gave him strength. Claydon was taken out of prison and put into the barrel, which was surrounded by faggots, and made to endure the agony of the killing flames. He had probably never even heard of Jan Hus. Yet he shared the same fate – for daring to seek spiritual consolation in a book.[15]

*

As Claydon screamed his last, one of the king's best friends, Richard Courtenay, fell ill. It was the men around the king who were suffering most now from the dysentery. His tent was positioned close to the king's, and sometimes during the siege Courtenay had shared the king's own quarters. It must have been personally worrying for Henry to see one of his closest friends taken ill with the fever. It must also have been deeply psychologically disturbing to realise that, if God felt inclined to smite Bishop Courtenay with what men called 'the bloody flux', the king and all his army might die before the rubble and foetid muddy ditches of the town that had been Harfleur.[16]

Bordiu had predicted the town would fall within eight days. This was the eighth day.

Wednesday 11th

In Constance, Jerome's nerve failed. Rather than face the terrible fate of being burnt, he chose to recant and publicly assent to his faith in the Catholic Church. To this end he had written a confession in his own hand, which he read out at a special session of the council to judge his case. However, the form of his confession was not considered explicit or full enough, so he was required to rewrite it more explicitly. The date of 23 September was assigned for him to read this revised confession, which included his abjuration of the doctrines of John Wycliffe and his friend Jan Hus. On that day he would go so far as to approve of the burning of Jan Hus.[17]

This is the last time Jerome will appear in this narrative; but it is worth noting that, on 26 May 1416, he withdrew his recantation and his renunciation of his faith in the teachings of Wycliffe and Hus. He stood up for himself, revoked his earlier confession and boldly declared himself to be a follower of Hus. He was burnt four days later and died in great agony, for he endured the flames much longer than Hus had done, screaming terribly throughout the ordeal. His bones and ashes were broken up and dumped in the Rhine, like those of his friend.[18]

Friday 13th

Another messenger from de Gaucourt reached the dauphin. This man was called Joven Lescot, and he had originally been smuggled out of the town in order to solicit aid from the constable, Charles d'Albret, who was then at Rouen. D'Albret had sent him with the Montjoye herald to the dauphin, who was at Vernon-sur-Seine. The message he delivered was similar to that of the earlier messenger, only more desperate. Again the dauphin promised that his father the king would soon be riding at the head of an army – but that is all he seems to have done directly to respond to the appeal for help.[19]

Sunday 15th

A month and a day after the army landed in France, Bishop Courtenay died of dysentery – dehydrated and feverish, excreting bloody diarrhoea. Henry was with him in his tent when he passed away, and closed his friend's eyes with his own hands. So, this was God's judgment on him, his ambitions and his expedition. Henry knew that many people in the outside world would see it that way. And he had lost a great friend, which must have affected his thinking. His judgment was so askew that, wiping the feet of the dead man, he ordered that the bishop be taken to Westminster Abbey to be buried among the kings of England. It was not an appropriate resting place for a bishop of Norwich, but Henry could not see that. Grief, worry and pressure were clouding his mind. The monks of Westminster did as they were asked, of course; they could hardly refuse their king and patron; so the body of Bishop Richard Courtenay was taken to the royal sanctuary at Westminster Abbey and laid to rest. There it remains to this day, in the same grave – and in the same coffin – as Henry V himself.

Just when the king was at this low ebb, the men of Harfleur rallied to drag him down further. The watchmen and guards on the main barbican outside the *Porte Leure* made a sally against the English guard, and set fire to the English defences. From his position at Graville, Henry would have left Courtenay's tent to see the smoke of the burning faggots drifting down the valley and the enemy troops attacking his own soldiers. Later, inspecting the lines, he would perhaps have heard how the Frenchmen were shouting insults at the English for being so half-awake and lazy.[20]

At about the same time, there were barges and galleys in the Seine, attempting to break through the English maritime blockade of the town. There seems to have been an attempt to break out from the town, timed to coincide with an attack from the river. De Gaucourt's messengers to the dauphin and d'Albret were not only getting information out of the town but somehow they were getting information back in. Although Henry had sent the ships from Flanders home long ago, and had also sent back many English ships, those that remained with him held their defences, and when the sortie from Harfleur retreated, so too did the barges and galleys.[21]

At Southampton, in the wake of the earl of Cambridge's plot, when Henry had been urged to cancel his expedition, he had shown the necessary resolve of a great leader. Others might have seen the death of a close friend – and a bishop at that – as a sign that God was against him; Henry seems to have seen it rather as a personal test. Through such sacrifices he was being tempted to seek terms, or shelter, or retreat. But, of course, this was Henry V – and this is one part of the popular legend that is true: he would never give in. Tenacious in the extreme, this setback simply caused him to order an all-out attack on the barbican of the *Porte Leure* the following day.

In preparation for the assault, Henry ordered that faggots be prepared to fill in the defensive ditches in front of the barbican. This was done through the night. From references to his watchfulness at night, one gets the impression that, as the men moved silently through the darkness, carrying the bundles of sticks, the king was watching, surveying, calculating and praying.

Monday 16th

It was Henry's twenty-ninth birthday. No celebrations were likely. All he wanted was revenge for the previous day's torments.

The onslaught on the barbican in front of the *Porte Leure* was led by the young and 'high-spirited' John Holland, earl of Huntingdon, supported by his father-in-law Sir John Cornwaille and the newly-knighted Sir William Porter, as well as Sir Gilbert Umfraville, John Steward and Sir William Bourchier.[22] These were the same men who had commanded the first reconnaissance of the shore at Harfleur on landing, and so may have formed a recognised crack squadron within the English army. In the afternoon a contingent of Frenchmen sallied out, trying to build on their success of the previous day. But Holland

and his men met them head-on. Then, by shooting burning arrows, flinging torches and laying incendiary powders, they managed to set enough of the barbican on fire to force the defenders back to the main gate. Amid the burning parts of the barbican, shattered by cannon, the first English troops entered, and torched the rest of the defensive enclosure. Some Frenchmen were still there in the smoke, trying to beat down the flames; they were set upon by the English. Most realised their dire situation and fled inside the walls, blocking the entrance behind them with timber, stones, earth and dung.[23]

The English, having taken the barbican, now worked to put the fires out. It was a struggle: it took two days to extinguish the blaze. The smoke rose in thick pungent wafts from the dung for another two weeks.

Tuesday 17th

Chroniclers differ in their explanations as to how negotiations began for the surrender of Harfleur. The eyewitness who wrote the *Gesta* claims that the English approached Raoul de Gaucourt, acting captain of the town, threatening the full application of the law of Deuteronomy – death for all the inhabitants, including women and children – but he spurned the offer, prompting Henry to order an all-out assault for the following day.[24] This plan to storm the town is also mentioned in a letter that Henry himself later wrote to the citizens of London, but the townsmen decided to negotiate again this same night. Thomas Walsingham wrote that on the night of the 17th a man-at-arms was sent over the walls to the camp of Thomas, duke of Clarence. He entreated the duke to send word to his brother, the king, begging that a truce be called.[25]

Both sources may be right. The townsmen may have first approached Thomas, rather than the king himself. By this reckoning, Henry sent messengers to demand the surrender of the town in the morning and, on being refused, organised a massive onslaught. His trumpeters proclaimed that all the seamen should join with the soldiers in a combined land-and-sea attack on the town. Henry had decided he could not wait any longer: the whole army would mount the walls that lay in patched ruins around the town. To facilitate this, towards dusk he ordered all the guns to start firing, blasting the remaining houses and walls with stones, and to continue all night. In this situation, knowing the fate that awaited them the next day, it would have been quite understandable if the men of Harfleur had decided that enough was enough and sent the man-at-arms to parley with Thomas, duke of Clarence. Thomas then told his brother. After this, Henry sent out Thomas Beaufort, and the elderly warriors, Lord Fitzhugh and Sir Thomas Erpingham, to negotiate with the townsmen in the middle of the night.

The above vacillation on the part of the defenders suggests that they were now utterly desperate. But why did they first refuse to negotiate, and subsequently plead for peace, on the same day? There are several possible explanations. The first is that they learned over the course of the day that Henry was planning an all-out attack, and decided that it was better to surrender and hope for mercy than to fight to the death. (This is the explanation Henry himself gave in his letter of 22 September.) Another possibility is that Henry had so far refused to consider anything but an unconditional surrender whereas the duke of Clarence, who may well have himself been sick with dysentery by now, was known to be more amenable. The fact that de Gaucourt was now severely sick with dysentery himself probably sapped some of his fighting spirit.[26] The position of the dauphin may have also been a factor. Two weeks earlier the men of Harfleur had entertained hopes of a French army coming to relieve them. But as yet the troops had not assembled in sufficient numbers, and neither the king nor the dauphin was at Rouen. The king was still at Poissy, where he ate dinner, before moving on to Meulan that afternoon.[27] The dauphin was at Vernon. If the defenders had received confirmation of the lack of any approaching army during the course of the day, then they may well have despaired of their cause. If the French king did not move to help them, why should they risk their wives' and children's lives for his sake?

Wednesday 18th

It was full moon. In the early hours, Thomas Beaufort, Lord Fitzhugh and Sir Thomas Erpingham returned to Henry and passed on the terms offered by the townsmen. They begged the king of England, out of charity, to suspend the attacks on their town until the Sunday of Michaelmas (29 September).[28] If the king or the dauphin had not come with a relieving army by then, they would surrender the town.

Picture the king hearing these words, with the glow of a warming fire on his cheeks. It was at last the offer of a capitulation that he had wanted for so many weeks. But even Michaelmas was too long a delay, and if the French army caught him here, at the walls of Harfleur he would be trapped. Henry's strategy was to take the town and then move his army away from the place as quickly as possible, drawing the French royal forces *away* from Harfleur, and thereby allowing his men to rebuild it. So he told his uncle and the other two envoys to return to the town and tell de Gaucourt that, if the town was not surrendered when daylight came, there would be no further discussion of the matter.

The men of Harfleur, who had held out heroically, were at the end of their strength. De Gaucourt himself later admitted that they were on their knees due to sickness and starvation.[29] Their town was in ruins, and many of the townspeople had been killed. So they urged the English envoys to go back again to the king and to beg him for a truce to last until Sunday, 22 September, the feast of St Maurice. To guarantee their offer, they promised to send an embassy of lords, knights, esquires and burgesses of the town, today, at one o'clock in the afternoon. Twenty-four men would be hostages of the English. If a French army had not arrived by early afternoon on Sunday 22nd, the town would be surrendered unconditionally. The people of the town as well as the hostages – their bodies as well as their possessions – would be at Henry's command, to do with as he wished. The sole proviso was that they should be allowed to send messengers to the king and the dauphin to inform them of this deadline.

When the three envoys reported to Henry in the early hours, he knew he had won. The French army was still assembling, the French king and the dauphin were not yet at Rouen; there was no chance of them sending a relieving army so soon. And by accepting the surrender now, having threatened them all with death, he could show mercy in the hour of his triumph, exactly as Edward III had done at the siege of Calais, sparing the lives of the six burghers who came, with ropes around their necks and carrying the keys of the town. So he agreed. The cannon fell silent.

*

Lying on his bed in his pavilion, Michael de la Pole, earl of Suffolk, was breathing his last. The man who had seen his father impeached by the enemies of Richard II, who had worked for so many years to recover his family dignities, and had done so, and had written his will in June, died from the dysentery that was now rife in the English camp. Two of his sons were with him: his twenty-year-old heir, Michael, and his younger son, William, who was also sick. In accordance with the earl's wishes, his body would be taken home to be buried in the church at Wingfield, Suffolk. Or at least his bones would.

Medieval armies often carried with them a large cauldron. When an important man, like the earl of Suffolk, died on campaign, and if it was impossible to embalm his body and send it home intact, his heart was cut out and preserved, and his body was dismembered and boiled for a long time, so that the flesh was stripped from the bones, like so much meat. The bones were then gathered and sent back with the heart for burial. Boiling and removing the flesh and cooked organs from a man's ribcage and skull must have been one of the most unpleasant duties of a soldier on campaign – short of actually killing people.

*

At one o'clock this afternoon, two processions approached each other beneath the walls of Harfleur. That from the English side, which had come down from Graville, was led by the bishop of Bangor, with the thirty-two chaplains of the king's chapel singing behind him. With them came the English envoys, and clerks with the indentures drawn up for the surrender of the town, accompanied by many other lords, knights and esquires. From the town came Raoul d'Anquetonville and twelve other seigneurs, and twenty-four other knights and esquires, accompanied by a large number of Harfleur's leading citizens.

When they met, just outside the *Porte Leure*, the commanders of the town swore on the consecrated host that they would abide by the terms of the agreement. Proctors on behalf of the king (who was not present) did likewise. The terms were read and sealed, and the French half of the agreement handed over. When this formality was complete, the twenty-four knights and esquires submitted themselves as hostages; following this they were invited into a royal tent nearby where they were given food and drink. After the meal, they were each assigned to a different lord, so they might be honourably treated while the French envoys went to seek a relieving army. Guillaume de Léon, seigneur de Hacqueville, was chosen to ride to the dauphin, and set off immediately with twelve men-at-arms.[30]

De Léon's mission was bound to be in vain. It was likely to take him at least fifteen hours in the saddle to reach the dauphin at Vernon, which was more than 75 miles away by road. He did not have time to ride on to see King Charles at Meulan if he wanted to be back in time for the deadline of three o'clock on 22 September.

*

In Paris, the deadline for gathering the new tax was fast approaching; but little money had come in. The sheriffs and collectors of taxes were ordered to hasten their collections. This did nothing to endear the administration to the people of Paris, who now began to speak about inviting John the Fearless back to the city to take charge of the government. In country areas, it was said, men and women and their children were retreating into the woods with their possessions and living there like savages rather than await the royal tax collectors, whom they feared more than the English. We may doubt that this was actually the case, just as we may doubt the story that some Frenchmen turned to brigandage as a result of the taxation; but as these stories come from a contemporary local source, they are indicative of how bitterly this new tax was viewed by the Parisians.[31]

Friday 20th

De Léon probably arrived at Vernon either late the previous evening or early this morning. He delivered his message. In reply he was told curtly that the army had not yet gathered, and could not reach Harfleur in time. His journey had been in vain. The French were abandoning the people of Harfleur to their fate.

De Léon mounted his horse and rode back to Harfleur, to tell the townsmen the sad news.

*

King Charles was now at Mantes.[32] The previous day he had been at Meulan, from where a letter was sent out today, in his name and that of the council, to various places in Northern France. The text addressed to the bailiff of Amiens reads as follows:

Whereas by our letters we have commanded you to make proclamation throughout your bailiwick, for all nobles and armed men experienced in war immediately to join our very dear and well-beloved son [the dauphin], whom we have nominated our captain-general of the kingdom. It is now some time since we have marched against our adversary of England who has, with a large army, invaded our province of Normandy and taken our town of Harfleur, owing to the neglect and delay of you and others in not punctually obeying our orders; for, from want of succour, our noble and loyal subjects within Harfleur, having made a most vigorous defence, were forced to surrender it to the enemy. And as the preservation and defence of our kingdom is the concern of all, we call on our good and faithful subjects for aid, and are determined to regain those parts of which the enemy may be in possession, and to drive them out of our kingdom in disgrace and confusion, by the blessing of God, the holy Virgin Mary, and with the assistance of our kindred and loyal subjects.

You will therefore by these letters strictly command everyone within your jurisdiction, on the duty they owe us, to lose no time in arming themselves and in hastening to join [the dauphin] . . . In addition to the above, you will likewise ensure that all cannon, engines of war, and other offensive or defensive weapons that can be spared from the principal towns be sent to our aid without delay, which we promise to restore at the end of the war. You will use every possible diligence in seeing to the execution of these our commands; and should there be any neglect on your part, which God forbid, we will punish you in such wise that you shall serve as an example to all others who offend in a similar manner . . .[33]

The French government was in a state of panic. They had already started to blame minor officials for allowing the English to seize Harfleur, even though there were still two days left before the siege would be over. They had also received information that John the Fearless had written to his Picard vassals urging them not to obey 'the command of any other lord, whoever he might be', which was the reason why these men had failed to muster.[34] So now they saw fit to blame John the Fearless personally. This pattern of creating scapegoats and blaming political adversaries for the failures would continue for years. Burgundians blamed Armagnacs, and Armagnacs blamed Burgundians. And still the king and the dauphin had no real knowledge as to whether the dukes of Orléans and Burgundy were going to send sufficient men to help fight the English. According to the chronicler Monstrelet, messengers were sent out again today to the two dukes with further letters repeating the order for them each to send five hundred men-at-arms immediately. The government was without money, short of armed men, short of leadership, and short of a strategy. It did not bode well for those who were setting out to muster at Rouen, let alone the starving men, women and children sheltering in the ruins of Harfleur.

Saturday 21st: the Feast of St Matthew

In Wales, about this time, and in some unknown location, Owen Glendower died. The great Welsh patriot who had evaded Henry and all his soldiers in life now evaded him in death. Few men knew where he was, and those who did know were not going to say. They were not even going to announce his death; his burial place would forever remain a closely guarded secret. He would live on in the hearts of his countrymen – defeated by the English but unbowed and unrepentant in striving to make an independent princedom of Wales.

Glendower's achievement ultimately had not been the independence of Wales. It had not even been to the benefit of most Welshmen. Hundreds of families on both sides of the border had been impoverished by the war: the English through the many harassments of Glendower's men; the Welsh through the reprisal attacks of Henry and his men as well as the annual expeditions of Henry's father. Extreme anti-Welsh legislation had been passed in parliament as a result of constant pressure from the English representatives, so that no Welshman could marry an English wife, or own property in England, or even sue an Englishman in an English court. Even now there were swathes of the country where ruined farms and barns lay burnt out, and no income was generated, and no tithes were paid. Glendower's real achievement was symbolic: a sense that resistance against the English landlords and parliament was not only possible but might lead to a better and prouder, more confident Wales. Since the beginning of his rebellion in 1400, he had never been caught; he had suffered through the loss of sons, brothers and friends in battle; but he had reigned as Prince Owain IV, and he had presided over a Welsh parliament, and he had inspired people. That inspiration would outlive him by centuries. In that respect he had much in common with Henry himself.

Eventually news did filter through to the English. No further mention is made of Glendower in English sources; royal commissioners were henceforth directed to negotiate with his son. Contemporary Welsh chroniclers began to refer to 1415 as the year in which the Welsh rebellion finally came to an end.[35]

Sunday 22nd: the Feast of St Maurice

The date set for the surrender of Harfleur was not an arbitrary one, plucked out of thin air. St Maurice might not have been a saint familiar to everyone at Harfleur, and his was not one of the major feasts; but what he symbolised was relevant. He had been a Roman soldier who had refused to kill Christians, and had been martyred as a result. That mercifulness towards Christians was exactly what Henry V wanted to stress now. It was a religious propaganda exercise: Henry had promised to destroy the inhabitants in line with Deuteronomic law; but by showing mercy and sparing their lives he was associating himself with the values of a saint and a follower of Christ's teaching.

At eight o'clock Guillaume de Léon, the seigneur de Hacqueville, returned to tell the townsmen the bad news. There would be no relieving army. At one o'clock the ailing Raoul de Gaucourt, together with Jean d'Estouteville and the other commanders, Lyonnet de Braquemont, Olivier de Braquemont, Jean Bufreuil and Roland de Gérault, and all those who had previously sworn to observe the terms of the truce, walked out of the ruins of the *Porte Leure* and through the still-smoking remains of its barbican. They followed the English heralds along the road and up the nearby hill to where the great pavilion of Henry V had been placed. There was a throne in front of it, and all the lords of England who were sufficiently healthy were seated in a circle, wearing rich robes. Sir Gilbert Umphraville stood to the right of the seated king, bearing Henry's crowned helm on a staff. As the twenty-four hostages were near at hand, they too were invited to join their countrymen in the formal surrender, making the total of Frenchmen present about sixty-six.[36] According to Adam Usk, those who had come from the town wore ropes around their necks in emulation of the burghers of Calais.

At this stage, the Earl Marshal was still well enough to conduct his official duties, so it fell to him formally to receive the men of the town. He announced on the king's behalf that the men of Harfleur and their fellow Frenchmen had resisted Henry, king of England and France, and therefore had tried to withhold a part of his inheritance, so they were liable to be put to death *en masse*. However, as they had surrendered of their own free will, albeit tardily, he assured them that, 'they should not depart entirely without mercy, although he [the king] might wish to modify this after further consideration'.[37]

All the while the Earl Marshal was speaking, Henry was staring fixedly ahead – making a point of not even looking at those who had dared to defy his will.[38] Once again the king's fierce pride was in evidence. Given this personal feeling on the king's part, we should not assume that he had always intended to let the men, women and children of Harfleur survive. His great uncle, Edward the Black Prince, had spared no one when he had attacked Limoges in 1370 – killing women and children as well as men, in line with the full Deuteronomic sentence. Indeed, it is worth bearing in mind what happened at Limoges in order to understand Henry's clemency on this occasion and his cold-hearted lack of it on others. As Froissart described the sack of Limoges,

On the next day, in line with the prince's order, a large section of the wall was blown up, filling in the ditch at the place where it fell. The English were pleased to see this happen, for they were all prepared, armed and drawn up in their ranks, ready to enter the town when the moment should come. The foot soldiers were able to enter this way with ease: on entering they ran to the gate, cut the supporting bars, and knocked it down, together with the barriers. And all this was done so suddenly that the townspeople were not expecting it. Then [the Black Prince], the duke of Lancaster [John of Gaunt], the earl of Cambridge, the earl of Pembroke, Sir Guiscard d'Angle and all the others, together with their men rushed in . . . all prepared to do harm and ransack the town, and to kill men, women and children; for this is what they had been ordered to do. This was a most terrible thing: men, women and children threw themselves on their knees before the prince crying 'Mercy, gentle sires, have mercy!' But he was so enraged by hatred that he heard none of them; thus none – neither man nor woman – was heeded. All were put to the sword . . . wherever they were found . . . men and women who were in no way guilty . . . More than three thousand persons, men, women and children, were put to death there that day.[39]

Nor can this be dismissed as an extreme form of retribution in war, from which Henry wished to distance himself. Just as his father had done, Henry lauded the Black Prince as a great warrior and a firm believer in the Holy Trinity. And Henry himself was more than capable of ordering just such a massacre. He did so two years later, in 1417, at Caen, after his men forced their way into the town. On that occasion he ordered that no priests or women were to be killed; but all their menfolk were to be slaughtered. Eighteen hundred men were put to death.

When de Gaucourt, d'Estouteville and the others had handed the keys of the town to the Earl Marshal, Henry told them that their lives would be spared. He ordered two standards – the royal standard and another standard bearing the cross of St George – to be hoisted over the gates, and appointed Thomas Beaufort lieutenant of the town. He invited the prisoners to dine with him. Later, he had his secretary write a letter in French about the success of the siege to the mayor of London.

Very dear, trusted and well-beloved. We greet you, letting you know for your consolation that we are personally in very good health, thanks be to God who grants this to us. After our arrival on this side, we came before our town of Harfleur on Saturday the 17th day of August last past, and laid siege thereto, in the manner described before now in our other letters sent to you. And by the good diligence of our faithful lieges at this time in our company, and the strength and position of our cannon and our other ordnance, the people within the town urgently tried to negotiate divers agreements with us; yet notwithstanding this, we decided to make an assault upon the town on Wednesday 18 September; but those within the town had realised this, and made great efforts to confer with us, over and above their earlier attempts. And to avoid the effusion of blood on both sides, we inclined to their offer. Thereupon we answered them, and sent to them the final terms of our intent; to which they agreed, and for this we do render thanks to God, for we thought that they would not have so readily assented to the said final terms.

On the same Wednesday there came out of the said town the seigneurs de Gaucourt, d'Estouteville, de Hacqueville, and other lords and knights who had governance of the town, and delivered hostages; and all the lords and knights as well as the hostages (of whom some are lords and knights and some notable burgesses), swore upon the body of Our Saviour that they would deliver our town to us and submit the persons and goods therein to our grace unconditionally, if they should not have been rescued, by one o'clock on the following Sunday, by battle given to us by our adversary of France or his eldest son, the dauphin. Thereupon we gave our letters of safe conduct to the said seigneur de Hacqueville and twelve other men to go to our said adversary and his son to inform them of the treaty so made. The seigneur de Hacqueville and others of his company returned today at eight o'clock in the aforenoon into our said town without any rescue being offered by our said adversary, his son, or any other party. And the keys of the town were then fully delivered and put in our hands; and all those within were submitted to our grace without any condition, as above stated, praised be our Creator for the same. And we have put in our said town our very dear uncle the earl of Dorset [Thomas Beaufort] and have made him captain thereof with a sufficient staff of people of both ranks. And we will that you render humble thanks to our Lord Almighty for this news, and do hope by the divine power and the good labour and diligence of the people on this side to do our duty still further in gaining our right in these parts; and we do desire also that, by way of those passing between us, you will certify us from time to time as to news regarding yourselves. And may our Lord have you in His holy keeping. Given under our signet in our said town of Harfleur, 22 September.[40]

Monday 23rd

Henry had apparently not wanted initially to enter the town of Harfleur. Presumably he felt it was beneath his dignity to confront the wreckage of the homes of merchants, families and clergymen. However, he needed to enter the city, if only to gauge the scale of the destruction for himself. Only by seeing the place with his own eyes could he assess how many men he would have to leave in order to guard and rebuild it. And only by seeing the town for himself would he understand its future strategic potential.

The gates, surmounted with the royal banner and the flag of St George, were thrown open to receive their new lord. The envoys and commissioners riding with Henry entered the town; but Henry dismounted right in front of the *Porte Leure*. He took off his shoes and socks and walked barefoot through the streets to the parish church of St Martin. Buildings on either side of the main street were smashed: timbers at odd angles, stone walls crumbled into the road. When he saw the church of St Martin, he could see for himself that his ordinances against damage to church property had not stopped his cannon wrecking it. The steeple and tower had collapsed, and the bells within had crashed to the ground.

Henry walked around the town with his closest friends. After surveying the damage, he ordered all the women and children to be rounded up, and all the poor too. As for the men: those who were prepared to swear fealty to Henry as their liege lord could stay in Harfleur. Those who were not would be imprisoned and ransomed for as large a sum as they could pay. The clergy were also gathered together. They would learn their fate on the following day.

According to Monstrelet, the two towers on either side of the water gate refused to surrender, holding out for a further ten days. This is unlikely – the English sources do not mention it – but it does suggest that there were disagreements within the town about whether or not to surrender.[41] These too could have contributed to the vacillation of the night of the 17th, which saw the first serious discussions. Either way, the defenders had acquitted themselves with great honour. They certainly did not deserve to be blamed for the fall of the town, when the rest of France had failed to come to their aid.

Tuesday 24th

Where the women, children, priests and paupers who had been gathered spent the night is not known; presumably they had been lodged in secure barns, halls or other large buildings. Today they were greeted by armed guards and led through the gates of the town. Given 5 sous each to buy food, the women were told they were free to go wherever they wished, taking their clothes and as much as they could carry in their arms. There were said to be about two thousand of them, including their children. Many – fifteen hundred according to one source – were accompanied in a convoy by the English guards to Lillebonne, where they were handed over to Marshal Boucicaut and placed under his protection. Their menfolk, including their teenage sons, had to remain behind. One French chronicle notes that the women from Harfleur – whether those handed over to Boucicaut or those who went their own way – were systematically rounded up, robbed and raped by French soldiers. Other French chroniclers attest to how badly the French troops treated their own countrymen and women; however, it is possible that this story of pillage and rape was just another result of the culture of blame and incrimination that developed in France over the subsequent months.[42]

Of course, all the English sources point to the expulsion of the women from Harfleur as an act of mercy by the king, as they considered he had every right to 'enjoy' or slaughter them all. Such an attitude overlooks the actual degree of misery that these people must have endured, and how little the people of Harfleur had done to deserve such treatment. For a full month they had suffered from a lack of sleep and food; they had lived in fear that the English siege engines would destroy their homes and families. Then, at the end, after a month of hellish torment, they were driven away from their homes and husbands and sons, losing all they owned. And it needs to be remembered that in medieval times, it was a far worse fate to be driven out of your hometown than it would be today. It did not just mean you lost your friends and family – you also lost those who would defend you physically and those who would defend your good name. For many of the women forced to walk to Lillebonne, life can hardly have seemed to have improved since the end of the siege. What lay before them was hardship, penury, alienation from their husbands, and the unknown. 'It was pitiful to see and hear the sorrow of these poor people, thus driven away from their dwellings and property,' wrote Monstrelet. The eyewitness who wrote the *Gesta* agreed, noting that the women left 'amid much lamentation and grief, and tears for the loss of their customary habitation'.[43]

Henry's plan was to turn Harfleur into a military base. All the town records were burnt in the square, thereby removing any knowledge of who owned what.[44] The houses needed to be repaired and then granted out to those who had followed Henry. Other Englishmen would follow in due course, invited to settle in the town. Burghers who did not swear loyalty were told they would be shipped across to England, where they might be ransomed, if they were lucky enough to have wealthy friends.[45] Those who did swear fealty were allowed to remain in the town but they were not allowed to own property. Young men were conscripted into the defence of the town – though presumably this was just to serve as boys and pages.

The first and main object was to make Harfleur defensible once more. As the boys would be of little use and even the men who swore fealty were bound to be of dubious loyalty, Henry needed to give the town a significant garrison. In this he had an important decision to make: did he make the town his headquarters for the winter, and keep his whole army there? Or should he leave a garrison there while he himself led the army through France, as he had planned and as Bordiu had stated in his letter of 3 September? The French king's letter, requiring that siege engines be brought up to Rouen, clearly anticipated that Henry would remain there through the winter. Bordiu's letter stating that Henry intended not to enter Harfleur but to remain in the field, suggests the plan was still to march through France, presumably to Calais. It was a tricky problem. If he remained in Harfleur he would be trapped, and he could expect no mercy from the French king. If he left the town then he would be compromising the security of both the town and the army, for Harfleur itself would require a large contingent of men to defend it, and so many men were ill with dysentery – perhaps as many as two thousand men were incapable of fighting – that he did not have enough men or supplies to stuff the town with defenders. If he wished to march on

Rouen as he had announced, he would be taking an enormous risk, marching against the forces of a larger and richer kingdom, with no escape route.

★

John the Fearless had been at Argilly for over a month now. Four days ago, on the 20th, the ambassadors of the French government, led by the duke of Lorraine, had arrived. Their mission was to try to persuade John to send men to help the dauphin in his struggle against the English and, at the same time, to keep John away from Paris. With Paris in a heightened state of anxiety, and experiencing a particular cynicism with regard to the government, the appearance of John the Fearless in the city threatened to cause mayhem, if not an insurrection.

Today the ambassadors were given three letters, one of which had been written by John the Fearless himself. Of course, the duke revelled in the chance to cause more upset in Paris, and saw the slight to himself in the earlier letters as being the perfect excuse to push the dauphin into a corner. John professed his deepest loyalty to the kingdom of France but complained bitterly about the request that he remain at home, and not come to the rescue of France in her hour of need. Was he not the dauphin's father-in-law? Why had all the other lords of Northern France been summoned and he had not? It was nothing more than an attempt to belittle him, and to undermine his honour, which 'he valued higher than everything else in the world'. Instead of the paltry five hundred men-at-arms he had been asked to send, he would attend in person with a far larger number, as it was his duty to save the kingdom in its current peril.[46]

Another of the letters that went back with the duke of Lorraine was written by vassals of John the Fearless on behalf of their lord. They complained that John had not been given command of his own men. This was most unfitting; the men of Burgundy saw their prime loyalty being to the duke of Burgundy, not the king of France. The lords also supported the tenor of the duke's own letter. How come the dauphin required so few troops? Why had there been such a delay in requesting them from the duke of Burgundy? Why had the duke himself been asked not to fight for the kingdom? Had not the seriousness of the English threat been registered by the government?

For the envoys who had to carry these letters back to the dauphin, the menace of John the Fearless must have seemed as dangerous as that of Henry V. And although the duke's own letter seemed to suggest he was wholeheartedly on the side of the French, they could not be sure he would not switch at the last moment and side with the English. They could not be certain that he would not simply take his soldiers and ride into Paris, betraying both the king of France and the king of England. The only thing they could be certain of was that no one could trust him.

As it happened, John the Fearless had already started to gather his forces together. He might have spent four days arguing against the king's order of 1 September to send more troops, but in fact he had issued orders to his marshals on 15 September to start gathering the men required.

Wednesday 25th

The losses to the English army did not end with the fall of Harfleur. In fact it seems likely that the majority of the casualties from the siege died after its capitulation. The end of September saw several prominent men expire. Today, Sir John Chidiock, Lord Fitzpayn, succumbed.[47] His is just one of the many names that do not appear noted in the chronicles as casualties of Henry's campaign; those writing such works had no wish to commemorate anything but the glory of Henry's victories and the paucity of the English casualties. As a result, many men who gave their lives for Henry were simply ignored. References to their deaths made for uncomfortable reading.

Thursday 26th

As noted several times already, Henry repeatedly followed the pattern of Edward III's Crécy campaign of 1346. Now he chose to enact another of Edward's wartime measures: a challenge to a duel. Edward III had first offered to fight a duel with his rival King Philip of France – with the prize being the kingdom of France – in 1340.[48] The idea was that the king could parade his courage and his Christian

virtues – offering to fight alone to avoid shedding Christian blood
– while at the same time being very sure that his rival would not
actually meet him in battle. Today he issued a challenge to the
dauphin, to be carried to him at Vernon by the English herald
William Bruges and Raoul de Gaucourt.[49]

Henry by the grace of God, king of England and of France, and
lord of Ireland, to the high and puissant prince, the dauphin, our
cousin, eldest son of the most puissant prince, our cousin and
adversary of France. From the reverence of God and to avoid the
effusion of human blood we have, in many times and in many ways,
sought peace; and although we have not been able to obtain it, our
desire to possess it increases more and more. And well considering
that the effects of our wars are the deaths of men, destruction of
countries, lamentations of women and children, and so many general
evils that every good Christian must lament it and have pity, and us
especially, whom this matter particularly concerns, we are minded
to seek diligently all possible means to avoid the above-mentioned
evils, and to acquire the approbation of God and the praise of the
world.

Whereas we have considered and reflected that, as it has pleased
God to visit our said cousin your father with infirmity, in us and you
lies the remedy. And so everyone may know that we do not prevent
it, we offer to place our quarrel at the will of God between our person
and yours. And if it should appear to you that you cannot accept this
offer on account of the interest that you think our said cousin your
father has in it, we declare that if you are willing to accept it and to
do what we propose, it pleases us to permit that our said cousin shall
enjoy that which he has at present for the term of his life, out of reverence for God and considering he [King Charles] is a sacred person,
whatever it may please God to see happen between us and you, as it
shall be agreed between his council, ours and yours. Thus, if God shall
give us the victory, the crown of France with its appurtenances shall
be immediately rendered to us as our right, without difficulty, after his
decease; and that all the lords and estates of the kingdom of France
shall be bound to accept this, as shall be agreed between us. For it is
better for us, cousin, to decide this war forever between our two persons
than to suffer the unbelievers by means of our quarrels to destroy

Christianity, our mother the Holy Church to remain in division, and
the people of God to destroy one another . . .[50]

Here we see all the familiar arguments: that really all Henry wanted
was peace, that he was simply doing God's will, and that the unification of England and France was desirable in the eyes of God as it
would help heal the schism in the Church. Perhaps the most interesting line it contains is the overt statement that Henry sought 'the
approbation of God and the praise of the world', which seems a neat
summing up of what truly motivated him.

Bruges and de Gaucourt were told to inform the dauphin that
Henry would wait for eight days at Harfleur for the reply. The implication was that he would not wait much longer than that before
leaving. But then where would he go?

*

Sir William Butler of Warrington died today.[51] He had been made a
Knight of the Bath at Henry IV's coronation, alongside Henry V's
three brothers. Thus, although he does not figure prominently in this
book, he was a man whom the king had known for many years and
whose loss would have mattered to him personally. Henry ordered that
Sir William's body should be dismembered and boiled, and sent home
in the same ship that was carrying the bones of the earl of Suffolk.
There was also the matter of who was going to take charge of his
retinue. Butler had led a party of fifty Lancashire archers to Harfleur,
in addition to his own retinue of four men-at-arms and twelve archers.[52]
His death was a strategic blow to Henry, as well as a personal loss.

Friday 27th

Another knight, Sir John Southworth, died today. Coming straight
after the deaths of Sir John Chidiock and Sir William Butler, it causes
us to ask how many Englishmen were sick at this point? And how
many men had actually died or were dying?

When Henry had landed on 14 August, he had had a minimum of
11,248 fighting men, of whom 2,266 were men-at-arms. In addition

there were the servants, pages and support staff, resulting in at least 15,000 men with the king, excluding mariners. As shown in Appendix Three, the long-accepted method of assessing the proportion of sick men is based on the assumption that the whole army was equally infected, and all at the highest rate. This has normally been followed by historians in their keenness to justify the long-established figure of just 5,900 Englishmen at Agincourt, with the implication that the magnitude of the victory was as great as English legend and Henry V's propaganda claims. A less nationalistic and more considered approach – using the lists of those invalided back to England – allows us to establish an accurate minimum of 1,693 for those sent home. Unfortunately these lists are incomplete, and we do not know how many names might be missing. However, as we know the army was divided into three battles – under the command of the king, Clarence and York – we can estimate casualty rates in all three areas where the English army was camped. This gives us a level of infection of about 17% across the whole army. The total number of men sent home was very probably between 1,693 and 2,550, of whom between 1,330 and 1,900 were fighting men, with the greatest concentration among the men situated in close proximity to the king.

As for the number of deaths, there were actually very few deaths at Harfleur. One chronicler, Monstrelet, states that two thousand Englishmen died at Harfleur but it seems that, writing thirty years later, he confused two thousand 'lost' (i.e. invalided home) with two thousand dead. A close examination of the surviving accounts shows there is only evidence for thirty-seven English deaths, including those who died from attack as well as disease. Probably fewer than fifty Englishmen perished at Harfleur.

*

Raoul de Gaucourt was given leave to depart today, possibly in the company of William Bruges. But what was Henry to do with the other knights and men of honour who had surrendered at Harfleur?

He decided to release them temporarily, after they had sworn an oath to present themselves at Calais at Martinmas (11 November). There they were to surrender themselves to the king himself or his lieutenant, or a specially appointed deputy. Sixty knights (including de

Gaucourt) and more than two hundred other gentlemen were thus released in the expectation that they would voluntarily give themselves up into custody in just over six weeks' time.[53] If a battle had already taken place, he told them, they were simply to pay their ransoms. If no battle had taken place, they were to submit themselves to imprisonment.

*

The people of Paris were in confusion. Some did not believe that Harfleur had yet fallen. Others thought that there must have been some betrayal – that it had been sold to the English. Others said that Henry had already admitted this publicly. And still more were in despair that the royal family was dealing with the war so badly. They bitterly resented the new taxation, and openly sang songs in praise of the duke of Burgundy.[54]

Around this time a Frenchman called Colin de la Vallée, one of the Burgundian faction who had been exiled from Paris, wrote a letter to his wife telling her to meet him at a certain town on 20 October, and to bring with her twenty crowns, for John the Fearless was planning to be there by that time with a large army. Not having the money, she went to a friend to borrow it. Unfortunately she left the letter with the said friend, who was an Armagnac supporter. In no time at all the streets of Paris were seething with this news about an intended Burgundian rising. The gates were barricaded, and everyone in Paris was preparing for the city to be attacked – not by Henry V but by John the Fearless.

Saturday 28th: the Feast of St Wenceslas

St Wenceslas was the patron saint of Bohemia. At Sternberg today, fifty-four noblemen of 'the famous marquesdom of Moravia' in the kingdom of Bohemia put their seals to a savage attack on the council of Constance for the illegal burning of Jan Hus. They refused to accept that Hus had been anything other than a good man, or that the charges against him had been anything but false and malicious. 'And being thus unmercifully condemned, you have slain him with a most shameful and cruel death, to the perpetual shame and infamy of our kingdom of Bohemia . . . in reproach and contempt of us.'[55]

It was a particularly nationalistic letter, but, in reading it, we can see how Hus's misguided and stubborn but conscientious refusal to conform had unleashed forces that were set to wrench apart the whole of Christendom.

> We declare unto your fatherhoods and to all faithful Christians . . .
> that any man of whatever estate, pre-eminence, degree, condition or
> religion who says that in the kingdom of Bohemia heresies have
> sprung up that have infected us and other faithful Christians . . . lies
> falsely upon his head as a wicked traitor and betrayer of the said
> kingdom . . .

Henry V and his advisors, and the French king and his, might all have been trying to bring about a Catholic kingship, in which heresy was treason and treason a religious crime as well as a secular one. John the Fearless might have been doing his best to separate the two at Constance, making a clear distinction between treason and heresy. But the Hussites in Bohemia had taken things a stage further, creating a form of nationalist kingship in which one could argue that, if a religious act was popular, and was not treasonable, it was not heresy. Jan Hus's death was going to have a profound effect on the development of Europe. Today's letter gives a hint as to why he was already widely regarded as a martyr.

*

Henry's decision to send the sick back to England was forced upon him. To leave them at Harfleur would have been counter-productive, in respect to both the likelihood of infecting others and their consumption of food and other resources. To take them with him on a march across France would have been impossible. As the sick were returning without their horses and stores, they required relatively few ships – perhaps twenty large vessels sufficed. The ships from Holland had returned to their own country shortly after the landing, and a number of English ships had returned to their ports on 12 September, but enough remained for the task.

The sailing started today. The earl of Arundel was put aboard a vessel with a guard of five healthy men-at-arms and many of his sick followers. One of his men-at-arms died in the process. Other important lords who were carried on board the ships included Thomas, duke of Clarence; Edmund Mortimer, earl of March; and John Mowbray, the Earl Marshal. A significant proportion of the high-ranking lords who had undertaken to come to France had been lost. A total of twelve dukes and earls had mustered at Southampton in July: two earls were now dead (Suffolk and Cambridge) so, with a further three earls and a duke lost to ill-health, Henry had lost half of the original contingent of magnates. Furthermore, Henry had decided to leave his uncle Thomas Beaufort, earl of Dorset, in charge at Harfleur, and to send the earl of Warwick directly to Calais by ship, to defend the town and receive the prisoners.[56] At a time when rank meant so much in terms of the structures of command, Henry was running out of leaders. Apart from Beaufort, there were only four members of the pre-campaign royal council with him: his youngest brother, Humphrey, duke of Gloucester; the duke of York; Lord Fitzhugh; and Sir Thomas Erpingham.

Sunday 29th: Michaelmas

In England, the regent John, duke of Bedford, sent out a writ to all the sheriffs, prelates and lords proroguing parliament from 21 October to 4 November.[57] He had received a message from Henry, who seems to have expressed a desire to be present at the said parliament. Henry had allowed himself five weeks to make the journey back to Westminster.

What was his strategy at this juncture? He had appointed his uncle Thomas Beaufort lieutenant of Harfleur, so clearly he did not intend to stay there to command personally. This accords with the information about his intended march through Montivilliers, Dieppe, Rouen and Paris, mentioned in Bordiu's letter of 3 September. It also tallies with his letter to the dauphin challenging him to a duel, which stated that he was going to stay at Harfleur for eight days – implying that he was going to leave shortly afterwards. Clearly he never intended wintering in the town but was planning to march through France.

But where was he heading? Rouen and Paris, as Bordiu stated – or Calais?

As we have seen, and as Henry knew, the French army was gathering in Rouen. To attack it would be risking disaster. English longbow armies were most successful when they managed to force an enemy to attack them when they themselves were in a static position; then they cut down the troops charging towards them, using the first fallen ranks as a means to slow up the ranks behind while they shot at them. Henry might have gone looking for a fight, and tried to attract the French to attack him near Rouen but, had he done so, he would have had no escape plan, being too deep within Normandy. If the French failed to be drawn into the attack, they could slowly strangle his army by withholding supplies – besieging the English in the field, as it were. And they could call up more and more men; Henry could not call up reinforcements. Thus there was a good strategic reason why he was not intending to head to Rouen. This part of Bordiu's letter was probably deliberate misinformation, in case it fell into French hands. By the time it arrived in Bordeaux, it would not have mattered what it said about Henry's strategy.

Calais, on the other hand, did offer an escape route, for it was a port. Henry had been fortifying and provisioning the town all year for this very reason. For his troops to embark anywhere else, he would have needed to arrange for a fleet to go to that place, and wait there in fear of being attacked. He would then have to lead his men to the waiting ships, and make sure that they all embarked without being attacked by a following French army. Disembarking had taken three whole days before; it was a risky operation. Thus Calais was his only realistic option – it was his only safe port of embarkation. All the English-held alternatives were in Gascony, hundreds of miles to the south. In addition de Gaucourt, d'Estouteville and the other French prisoners from Harfleur had been instructed to make their way to Calais, and to surrender there to Henry in person or, if he was not there – if he had already departed for England, for example – then a specially appointed deputy. This deputy would have had to be someone of high status, probably the earl of Warwick (the lieutenant of Calais), who was sent directly there by ship.[58] There is no doubt that Henry was sticking steadfastly to the plan to march to Calais that he had developed many months earlier.

Although it seems clear that marching to Calais was, and always had been, his intended strategy, we have to ask whether this destination was chosen in order to attract the attention of the French army gathering at Rouen. In short, did he intend to do battle? Answering this question is a developmental process. As Henry proceeded towards Calais, he could have expected his circumstances to change. So it is worth attempting to answer this difficult question at various stages, including the outset, to see whether the answer changed as the march altered course and ran into difficulties.

The answer at this initial juncture is *yes*. He did intend to fight the French. There are several reasons for this conclusion. First, Henry wanted a battle because his religious outlook demanded it. He had come to France to put God's will to the test, and that could only properly be done by a conflict in which he might lose his life. Second, he had come with an army that was too large for just a siege; it was an army designed to fight a pitched battle. Although he had lost many men, he still had the majority, and so could stick to his original plan. Third, he was determined to follow a path previously trodden by Edward III's army to Blanchetaque, a point at which the River Somme could be forded. Edward III's march, which culminated in the battle of Crécy, had been chosen specifically to encourage the French to attack the English in Ponthieu. Henry, having sent Raoul de Gaucourt with William Bruges to deliver the challenge to the dauphin, knew that the dauphin would have learnt from de Gaucourt that the English were marching to Calais. He had even told him roughly the time he was going to depart – after eight days. Telling all 260 gentlemen prisoners to meet him in Calais was similarly a guarantee that the French would know where he was going. He was thus encouraging the French to come after him and attack him. In his instructions to the 260 prisoners he even referred overtly to the likelihood of a battle. Thus he was not just following Edward III's route, he was adopting similar tactics.[59]

A fourth reason can be seen in the personal nature of Henry's decision to march to Calais. It is clear from several sources that the majority of the leaders still with the army at this point were strongly opposed to the idea of the march precisely because a battle would be too dangerous. One source claims that even the warlike duke of Clarence was in favour of bringing the campaign to an end – a division with

Henry that perhaps led to his departure from the English army as much as his suffering from dysentery.[60] Leaving this aside, another well-informed chronicler, writing some time after 1446, stated that 'the majority of the councillors were of the opinion that a decision should be made not to march on', due to the shortage of fighting men following the ravages of dysentery.[61] The author of the *Gesta* wrote very much the same thing:

> although a large majority of the royal council advised against such a proposal as it would be highly dangerous for him in this way to send his small force, daily growing smaller, against the multitude of the French which, constantly growing larger, would surely enclose them on every side like sheep in folds, our king – relying on divine grace and the justice of his cause, piously reflecting that victory consists not in a multitude but with Him . . . who bestows victory upon whom He wills, whether they be many or few – with God affording him His leadership, as it is believed, did nevertheless decide to make that march.[62]

The later source gives a similar justification for the decision, stating that Henry said 'he would rather throw himself and his men on the mercy of God in determining the outcome of events, not shirking the dangers, than offer himself to the enemy as grounds for elevating their pride, diminishing the reputation of his honour by flight'.[63] From these accounts it is clear that Henry went against the consensus and took what his councillors considered to be a great gamble – deliberately risking a battle. This contrasts with his considerable aversion to taking any risks in the course of landing in August. What made him switch from being so risk-averse then to being so risk-taking now? It can only have been a defiance of the very risk that so worried his council – a chance to do battle. Thus his decision to march to Calais was not just a testing of God's will, and it was not just a strategic calculation based on Edward III's success in 1346, it was also a matter of pride.

The above motivations – religious fanaticism, a confident strategy based on a historical precedent, and pride – are not particularly edifying. Looking at Henry at the end of September, one would hardly call him a great man. He had obtained one small town – a key target – but had destroyed it in the process. He had lost a good proportion of his fighting force and left the remainder perilously situated in a hostile kingdom with a large army gathering in the field. As far as any reckoning of God's judgment went at the moment, his cause had been cast into doubt by the death of Bishop Courtenay and the sicknesses of his brother and heir, Thomas, and his great friend, the earl of Arundel. The dissent revealed by the earl of Cambridge's plot had not added to his glory, nor had the continued activities of the Lollards. Yet it was at this moment that he stepped out from the clouds of fallibility and made the decision that made him, and changed him, and altered the balance of European politics in England's favour. Through it he set himself on the path 'to acquire the approbation of God and the praise of the world'. If Henry had shown any sign of greatness up until this point, it was as an organiser and a man convinced of his own infallibility, arranging for the circumstances of this march to be as promising as possible. But in going against the council's decision now he showed that he was far more than just an organiser and a facilitator. It must have taken complete determination – after all the delays, and after losing so many men to dysentery – to give the order to march on. And in so doing he took on all the responsibility, and all the danger. He knew that he was himself a far greater prize than the ruins of Harfleur – he knew the French would think they could retake the town any time and so they were bound to come after him. Then Henry and his army would lead the enemy away from the near-defenceless Harfleur, like a lioness leading a predator away from her cubs.

At this moment in time, we can see Henry V throwing everything behind his faith. This is the moment when, having mapped out a path to greatness, he actually set foot on it. Like Jan Hus, he was prepared to die in pursuit of what he believed he had to do. Historians have sometimes called this 'the madness of unreasoning pietism'; but they forget that, if a man truly believes God is on his side, no reasoning is necessary – or even possible. For him, God really *is* on his side, and it would be madness to pretend otherwise.

That is what is so frightening about Henry V at the end of September 1415.

October

Wednesday 2nd

Sir John Phelip died today, aged thirty-one. He was one of the household knights, the head of a company of thirty men-at-arms and ninety archers, and a trusted advisor – one of the men who had spied on Harfleur at the start of the year. When he travelled through the port then, little can he have imagined what a heap of rubble it would become, or that he would die there. His death is another reminder of the personal losses Henry was suffering. Phelip had been a witness of the king's last will in July. His wife was Alice Chaucer, granddaughter of Geoffrey Chaucer, whom Henry would have remembered from the poet's twilight years at the court of Richard II. In tribute to his friend, Henry ordered Sir John's body to be boiled, and his bones sent back to England.[1]

Thursday 3rd

In Paris, orders were issued to repair the walls and defences of the city. Not against the English but against John the Fearless, as the enthusiasm for his return was inflaming the people to riot.[2] The very idea that John might return to the capital and seize control prevented the king and the dauphin from moving down the Seine, and taking control of the army, for their worries were focussed as much on the city as on the English. Parisian officers who showed Burgundian sympathies were replaced with Armagnac men. No city troops were to leave – not even to fight the English. They were required to defend Paris against the Burgundians. In effect, the French were fighting a two-front war within their own borders: a civil war and an invasion.

The civil war was not confined to France. In Constance John the Fearless's principal representative, Martin Porée, bishop of Arras, was defending his lord's reputation with every weapon at his disposal. Silver, wine and jewels had already been issued by the various ambassadors as bribes. Threats and violence had aided the duke's cause. Bishop Porée had already forced the original condemnation of Jean Petit's *Justification* to be reconsidered, and the duke himself had sought the reinvestigation of its supposed heresy by the University of Paris. Now it was Porée's intellect that forced the council to cower at the duke's name. For Porée was not just defending Jean Petit; he was attacking possible heresies in the works of the great man Gerson himself. The most influential theological thinker of the council was coming under attack.[3] From this point forward Porée would prove himself to be a great advocate for his master, defending Jean Petit so ruthlessly that the nine charges originally laid against him by Gerson at the University of Paris, and repeated at Constance in June, were all called into question. Eventually, on 15 January 1416, the condemnation of Jean Petit by the bishop of Paris was annulled.[4] In defiance of the king of France, the council only condemned tyrannicide in general terms: they refused to condemn the murder of the duke of Orléans and they passed no resolution directly condemning Jean Petit for writing his *Justification of the duke of Burgundy*.

Friday 4th

The eight days Henry had told the dauphin he would wait at Harfleur were now up. It was time to act.

Of the 11,248 or more fighting men with whom Henry had landed on 14 August, he had approximately 9,600 left.[5] Thus he did not have a great deal of flexibility as to how many men he should assign to the defence of Harfleur. He knew from his experiences in Wales that small garrisons proved costly in the long term, and so he had to leave enough men to make the town defensible; on the other hand he could not leave so many as to render the rest of his army weak.

He decided to leave 1,200 men, in his usual proportion of three archers to every man-at-arms. Thus nine hundred archers and three hundred men-at-arms (including about thirty knights) prepared to remain at

Harfleur to defend it, along with the majority of the carpenters and masons. In charge of these, under the overall command of Thomas Beaufort, were a number of captains, including Lord Botreaux, Lord Clinton, Sir John Fastolf and Sir Edward Hastings.[6] Everyone else would march to Calais. This would involve between ten and eleven thousand men: 1,500–1,600 men-at-arms, a similar number of pages, 6,600–7,000 archers, and a few dozen chaplains, clerks, surgeons and royal servants, plus any of the reinforcements who had arrived since 15 August.[7] They would start to set out from the following Monday or Tuesday.

Saturday 5th

A storm was brewing in the Harfleur area. Although most of the English ships had by now departed, and the hired vessels had long since returned to Holland, there were still a number in the waters at the mouth of the Seine. Some were being loaded with cannon to return to England; others were shipping the last of the dysentery victims back home.[8] Others were arriving, bringing grain and reinforcements. Perhaps some vessels owned by the fishermen of Dover and the Cinque Ports remained. All were now in danger, unable to take shelter in the ruined harbour at Harfleur. A number of them were dashed to pieces before the end of the day. As the chronicle of Ruisseauville has it, 'the navy of England was partly or completely lost at sea by the exceptionally heavy rain that had fallen as a result of a storm'. Nor did all of the ships that survived the tempest make it back to their home ports: some were captured over the subsequent days by Breton pirates, laying in wait for the stragglers.[9]

*

At Westminster the duke of Bedford was doing his best to make good the shortfall in the numbers of troops in his brother's army. He wrote to the sheriffs of London ordering them to proclaim to all the knights, men-at-arms and archers who wished to go to Normandy that they should present themselves to Chancellor Beaufort to claim their wages in advance.[10] How many did so is not known. But none of those who did set out could have joined Henry's army. Even if they had sailed immediately, they would not have arrived at Harfleur in time. The ten thousand men preparing to set out with Henry on the march could expect no further help.

Sunday 6th

The duke of Bedford's efforts to help his brother did not just stop at trying to provide more men. Today he commissioned one John Fisher of Henley to provide corn for the sustenance of the king's army in Normandy, and charged him with transporting it to Harfleur for the next six months.[11] It might have helped sustain the garrison but not the army itself.

*

At Boulogne a messenger arrived from Abbeville, with news that Henry had placed a garrison at Harfleur and was now marching to Calais.[12] Although it is certainly possible that the first troops began to leave Harfleur today – some exchequer accounts specifically state that they did – there is no way this information could have reached Boulogne the same day.[13] It seems that it was circulated by the French, following William Bruges and Raoul de Gaucourt's delivery of the challenge to the dauphin. Henry's decision to announce his destination was likely to lead to more dangers than simply having a French army following on his tail.

Monday 7th

Henry had despatched the experienced earl of Warwick to Calais by ship, to defend the town and to receive the prisoners whom he expected to arrive at Martinmas. Warwick had not yet arrived, however. In the meantime the town was under the command of Sir William Bardolph, who had been appointed as successor to Sir William Lisle. Thus it was Bardolph who wrote today in response to a request for news from the duke of Bedford.

> To the most high and mighty prince and my most honourable and gracious
> lord . . . thanking you most humbly and often, as far as I am able, on my
> own behalf as well as that of all my companions in these Marches, that

your noble lordship is pleased to have so dearly and so tenderly taken to heart the wellbeing, ease and prosperity of all of us and of the said Marches, as written not long ago in your honourable and most gracious letters.

Having sent to these parts the sheriff of Kent, the lieutenant of Dover Castle and the victualler of that town, your commissioners . . . to find out how things were and in what state, I have signified and reported to them the truth of this matter orally and to your lordship . . . in writing and otherwise.

Hearing from these esquires, it is well understood that it is your will that we make the hardest war that we can against the French, enemies of our most feared noble lord, in order to prevent those on the frontier crossing or advancing near to where he is now in person . . .

As for news of this area, may it please your lordship to know that several good friends who have come to this town and the Marches both from the areas of France and of Flanders, have told and reported to me clearly, without doubt, that our lord the king will do battle with his adversaries within fifteen days next coming at the very latest. And that also, along with the others, the duke of Lorraine will assemble very soon, according to what they say, with fifty thousand men; and that once they are all assembled they will be no less than one hundred thousand, or indeed, even more. Also they say for certain that a noble knight accompanied by five hundred lances has been ordered to wait on the frontier under the governance of the seigneur de la Biefville in defence of the Marches on the part of the enemy . . .[14]

Obviously the lieutenant of Calais had no idea how long it would actually be before Henry could do battle with the French. Calais is 144 miles from Harfleur, and the very fastest messengers would have taken at least three days to cover the distance. So if Bardolph's knowledge about the battle plan had come from Henry it must have been sent before the 4th. This is not impossible for, although this letter states that the news about the planned battle came 'from the areas of France and of Flanders', Henry may have sent a message to Calais for three hundred men-at-arms to ride south to secure the ford over the Somme at Blanchetaque.[15] Alternatively, Bardolph's information could have been obtained from spies coming from Boulogne the previous day, or from Abbeville. It was probably from Flanders that he had heard about the duke of Lorraine's mobilisation. News about this had most likely been

fed back to Calais by Henry's ambassador to John the Fearless, Philip
Morgan, for the duke of Lorraine was a close ally of John the Fearless.
Information from Morgan had certainly been carried back in recent
days through Calais to England.[16] His news that the duke of Lorraine
was preparing to join the French king cannot have cheered the English.

*

At Vernon, the aged King Charles finally met up with his son, the
dauphin. They had with them the Oriflamme. Troops were gathering
downstream at Rouen. They would stay at Vernon for two more days
and then set out, arriving in Rouen in five days' time.[17]

Tuesday 8th: the Feast of St Denis,
Patron Saint of France

Upon landing, the English army had been divided into three battles.
One had been led by the duke of Clarence, one by the duke of York,
and one by Henry himself. These battles now served as the arrangement in which the army would march to Calais. One battle, the
vanguard, would take the lead. The main battle would be in the centre;
and the third battle would take up the rearguard.

The commanders of two of these battles are known. Henry himself
led one, the main battle; and another was led by the duke of York. Henry
had probably meant Clarence to lead the third, but his departure from
Harfleur prevented it. It is not clear who took his place. Precedence
would have pointed to the only remaining duke without a command:
Humphrey, duke of Gloucester; but he was only twenty-one and inexperienced in war, so precedence was set aside. Humphrey was placed in
the main battle, with the king. There were still four earls with the army
– Huntingdon, Oxford, Salisbury and Suffolk – but the new earl of Suffolk
was even younger and less experienced than Gloucester, and the earl of
Huntingdon was with the king. Salisbury's role is unknown.

The inconsistent and partial chroniclers' accounts place the duke of
York in charge of both the vanguard and the rearguard. One possible
explanation is that York was in charge of the notional 'rearguard' while
the army was at Harfleur; and that after Clarence's departure he assumed

control of the vanguard on the march itself. He was certainly in charge of the vanguard during the latter part of the march, supported by Sir John Cornwaille and Sir Gilbert Umphraville – two leaders from the 'crack squadron' that had led the initial reconnaissance after landing and led the assault on the *Porte Leure* on 16 September. York was also appointed constable and marshal of the army, because the previous constable, Thomas Beaufort, was going to stay at Harfleur.[18] Command of the rear-guard on the march was probably entrusted either to Sir Thomas, Lord Camoys (who commanded it at the battle), or to the earl of Oxford (who was later made a Knight of the Garter for his deeds on the campaign).[19]

The vanguard may have set off the previous day, or even as early as the 6th. Be this as it may, the main battle marched this morning, according to the author of the *Gesta*, who was with the king.[20] Before setting out, Henry declared that the army could expect to march for eight days and they should take sufficient supplies (mainly dried beef and walnuts).[21] As it was 144 miles to Calais, and most able-bodied men could easily ride or walk twenty miles a day, this was quite reasonable. In fact, it left the best part of a whole day in reserve. What he seems not to have told them was that the spare day was set aside to fight a pitched battle.

By dusk the English had suffered their first casualties. Although Henry ordered his men to skirt around the fortified towns and castles they came to, and kept his lines half a mile away from Montivilliers, there was a skirmish as they passed the town. Six men were taken prisoner by the town garrison and one was killed.[22] It was a taste of the difficulties to come.

Wednesday 9th

In line with Henry's orders, the English army camped in the open. Not only did this enable him to keep control, it also allowed the captains to patrol the moral behaviour of the men, keeping them away from the temptations of theft and women. The military ordinances (first proclaimed on or about 17 August) were read for a second time before the army set out. The *Gesta* specifically mentions the repetition of instructions not to burn or lay waste, or to take anything except food and necessities for the march, or to capture any Frenchmen (other than those offering armed resistance). In addition it is evident that Henry sought to minimise the effect on the local population by enforcing the ordinance stipulating that no one should ride ahead of the army except messengers and herbergers (men seeking food and places to stay). There was a practical reason for this. Henry proposed to use his power to destroy French property as a bargaining position when he came to the towns and castles that lay between him and Calais. If his men were disciplined, he could offer not to burn the towns and villages in return for safe passage.

The bulk of the army travelled via Fauville. But those companies on the flanks of the army were travelling at a distance of several miles – presumably foraging for supplies. One of these attacked the partially deserted town of Fécamp, which had been the subject of a naval attack in July.[23] The seigneur de Rambures had gathered many men in the abbey, having burnt the suburbs in anticipation of a fight. According to French sources, it was de Rambures's men who took advantage of the townswomen there, who had crowded to the abbey for protection. One English man-at-arms, William Bramshulf, and two valets, Edward Legh and John Rede, were captured before the troops were steered away towards Dieppe.[24]

Thursday 10th

At Arundel Castle, Henry's great friend Thomas Fitzalan, earl of Arundel, the treasurer of England, felt that he was drawing near the end of his life. He had been carried aboard ship at Harfleur on 28 September and had arrived back in Sussex a few days afterwards. Since landing he had been tenderly nursed by Elizabeth Ryman, the wife of one of his retainers.[25] But although she was a good nurse, and although the earl had not been one of those who had felt the need to make a will before setting out, the time had now come for him to put his affairs in order.

Thomas asked to be buried in the choir of the collegiate church of the Holy Trinity in Arundel Castle, where he wanted a new tomb chest and effigy made for him. He also willed that a suitable monument be erected over the grave of his late father, Richard Fitzalan, earl of Arundel, who had been judicially murdered by Richard II. He allowed 200 marks for his funeral expenses, and made the following specific bequest:

in regard to a vow made by me to St John of Bridlington, when I was there with my lord the king (when he was prince of Wales), namely that I would once every year in person offer to that saint, or send the sum of 5 marks during my life, I will that my executors forthwith pay all the arrears thereof, beside the cost of the messenger sent for that purpose.[26]

His other last requests included that a chapel be built in the Mary Gate at Arundel, dedicated to the Virgin; and that 'all those soldiers who were with me at Harfleur in France be paid all the arrears of their wages'.

*

At Oudenaarde, the nineteen-year-old Philip, count of Charolais, the son and heir of John the Fearless, wrote to officials at Lille:

Dearest and well-beloved, my father has recently informed me of his departure with all his power to advance against the English in the service of the king . . . and he wishes to have with him everyone in his lands who is accustomed to bear arms, including us ourselves, in person, and the knights and esquires of Flanders and Artois.[27]

At the same time the French royal council were reading letters from John the Fearless stating that, regardless of the dauphin's request that he stay away from the royal army, he was planning to serve in person. The council decided by a majority vote to approve of his action. This cannot have been easy, for there was no saying what he would do when he had an army behind him. Letters of peace between John the Fearless and Henry V, negotiated by Philip Morgan and sealed with the duke's own seal, arrived at Westminster this very day.[28] The duke was playing off one side against the other – promising the French he would ride to help them against the English, and promising the English he would not impede their progress.

Friday 11th

The English army converged on Arques, a small town and a castle four miles from Dieppe. Before the town was a river, the Béthune, crossed by narrow bridges. Henry ordered his men to draw up in their three battles, as if preparing to attack. The townsmen opened fire with their cannon, holding the English at bay.

Henry halted the advance. He ordered his heralds to remove their cote-armour, to address the townsmen in a friendly manner, and to present themselves at the main gate.[29] He knew he was in a strong position, with ten thousand men behind him, so he proposed a deal. If the men of Arques would let the English pass through the town, and if the townsmen would provide them with a fixed quantity of bread and wine, then he would not harm the town or any of its suburbs, nor allow his men to burn the vicinity. The townspeople agreed. According to the *Gesta*, they gave up hostages to guarantee the safety of the English as they passed through the town.[30]

The tension must have been great when the English walked into Arques. As they did so, they saw the trunks of large trees that had been felled and dragged to the town in a rudimentary attempt to defend the gates. One imagines the frightened people of the town peeping out of their windows with their shutters ajar as the enemy troops passed, almost holding their breath as they watched them, hoping that the fragile agreement would hold.

It did hold. And when the English soldiers had passed through, they did not turn towards Dieppe, as Jean Bordiu had stated they would in his letter of 3 September. Nor did they turn towards Rouen, where he had said they would head next. In line with Henry's original plan, and his clearly expressed desire to get to Calais within eight days, they kept on going – riding and marching north.

The king and dauphin could now join the troops gathering at Rouen and start to chase Henry out of the kingdom. They knew exactly which road he was taking – they too had history books to inform them. Messengers rode hard for Boulogne to inform them that Henry was following the path of his great-grandfather Edward III. The English were heading for the ford across the Somme, at Blanchetaque.[31]

And so were the French.

Saturday 12th

Arques had been a small town, only too ready to let the English pass by peacefully. Eu was a different matter. It was well defended by high walls and steep slopes, standing above the River Bresle, with a population of about a thousand.

Henry must have arrived in the evening.[32] There were bodies on the ground before the walls. He heard that, as his outriders and scouts had approached, bearing the standards of the English, the garrison of Eu had made a sortie on horseback and 'attacked them with much noise and aggression. There was loud battle on both sides but the French did not restrain the Englishmen for long, and being forced back to the gates, they defended themselves with arrows and missiles'.[33] Both sides suffered fatalities. One of the French dead was Lancelot Pierre, 'a valiant and much renowned man of war' and a companion of the count of Eu. An Englishman had driven his lance through the plates of armour protecting Pierre's stomach – but Pierre's own lance had similarly gone right through his assailant's body, killing him too.[34] But individual acts of valour like these – although they impressed the chroniclers – could not hold up the approach of the English vanguard. Before long the French had withdrawn to defend the town.

Although the temptation to storm the town must have been great after the hostile reception, Henry decided to follow the same course of action as at Arques. He sent heralds to the gates to offer the inhabitants peace in return for food and drink. If they would supply bread and wine, and send hostages for the safe conduct of the garrison, Henry would not burn the town and the villages nearby. If on the other hand they refused, he would destroy everything.

While the men of Eu were considering this offer, the English made camp at a little distance. It was not an easy night. By this stage they had heard that a great army had gathered ahead, at Blanchetaque, the very crossing point to which Henry was heading. Frenchmen who had been taken captive were saying that there would be a battle the following day, or on Monday. The author of the *Gesta* was unsure what to think. Some of those with him thought that the French would be unlikely to come up from the interior of the country so quickly. After all, the French could not be sure that the duke of Burgundy would not attack Paris, or even join Henry. On the other hand, there were those who pointed out that the noble kingdom of France could not be expected to withstand the indignity and dishonour of an English army marching through Normandy and into Ponthieu. They were bound to attack.

What Henry himself thought is not known. He was probably placing his hopes in getting to Blanchetaque before the French. He knew the dauphin and the royal dukes were still a long way behind him. If he had to face an army, it would be composed of men gathering with Boucicaut and Charles d'Albret, the marshal and constable of France, on the north side of the river, and not the full array of the royal dukes.

As the sun went down over Eu, everything still seemed to be on course for a relatively safe passage for the English through to Calais. The chances of this were further enhanced when the men of Eu agreed to offer hostages and sustenance to the army.

It was eighteen miles to Blanchetaque. The English would get there the following day.

*

John the Fearless had spent the early part of October at Chalon. On the 10th, he had made his way to Germolles.[35] From there he despatched an embassy to the French king, supporting what his son the count of Charolais had declared two days earlier – that he intended to mobilise his forces and join the king very soon.[36]

Despite this, he did not set out. He remained at Germolles for the next seven days. His vassals in Picardy, however, were responding to his summons. They were not joining the army at Rouen but the separate French army now gathering north of the Somme, under Boucicaut and d'Albret. The French king might have been mad and the dauphin inexperienced but Boucicaut and d'Albret knew what they were doing. The English would soon find themselves sand-wiched between two armies – and forced to fight.

*

Other French magnates were riding to the aid of the French king. Today the old duke of Berry, the dauphin's great uncle, arrived at Rouen, where he had mustered one thousand men-at-arms and five hundred archers.[37] The king himself also arrived at Rouen today, accompanied by the dauphin. Other French lords were already there; so now the army had a direct chain of command. This was important, for it was being rumoured today that the duke of Clarence had landed at Calais with another large army.[38] Which way were the French in Normandy to turn their attention? To Henry? To the defence of the towns? To the river crossings, to the Marches of Calais, or to the defence of Boulogne?

About this time, the newly gathered French royal family and the other members of the council drew up a battle plan, probably with the intention of stopping Henry at Blanchetaque. The vanguard was to be commanded by Boucicaut and Charles d'Albret. They would be followed by a second battle, under the duke of Alençon, the count of Eu, and other lords. On each wing of the army there would be a battle of foot soldiers, the one on the right commanded by the count of Richemont, and the one on the left by the count of Vendôme and Guichard Dauphin. David, seigneur de Rambures, would command a contingent of heavily armoured cavalry, with the mission to charge into and break up the ranks of English archers; and a separate squadron of several hundred mounted men-at-arms under Louis de Bosredon was given charge of attacking the English baggage.[39] The anticipated army would be composed of the troops gathering at Rouen as well as those waiting beyond the Somme, gathering at Abbeville and Péronne.[40] Wherever the English positioned themselves – whether their backs were against the Somme or elsewhere – the French were prepared to attack.

Sunday 13th: the Feast of St Edward the Confessor

The feast of St Edward the Confessor had special significance for the Lancastrian dynasty. Not only was it the feast of the principal English royal saint; Henry's father had been sent into exile on this day in 1398 by his cousin Richard II. Exactly one year later he had been crowned king of England, in Richard's place. As a result Henry IV had built a chapel in Canterbury Cathedral dedicated to St Edward the Confessor. Henry V had shown himself to be no less fond of the English king-saint than his father: one of the banners he was carrying now bore the arms of St Edward.

The English army must have set out for Blanchetaque shortly after packing up their tents, at first light. Already there had been worrying reports from prisoners taken along the way that there was a huge French army waiting to intercept the English at the ford.[41] These reports received confirmation late this morning, when the army was still six miles away from the crossing point. According to Monstrelet, a Gascon gentleman serving in the company of Charles d'Albret was arrested. Waurin's chronicle describes him as being mounted and armed; Monstrelet's refers to him as a devil. As a Gascon it may be that he crossed the Somme and came to the English purposefully – out of a greater loyalty to Henry, as the duke of Aquitaine, than to his feudal lord (the d'Albret family having been once subjects of the English kings).

The man was taken before the duke of York, the leader of the vanguard, and questioned. He said that he had left Charles d'Albret at Abbeville. When asked about the ford at Blanchetaque, he told them it was very heavily guarded. Guichard Dauphin and Boucicaut were both there, with six thousand fighting men.[42] If all this was true, it meant that the English were trapped between two armies: one under d'Albret and Boucicaut between Abbeville and Blanchetaque, and the ducal retinues gathering at Rouen.

The duke of York realised the significance of this information, and sent the Gascon to the king. There he was questioned again. Henry heard everything he had to say. Then he dismissed him, halted the advance, and called an immediate meeting of his council.

The meeting lasted two hours. We cannot know for certain what was said but it proved to be a turning point for Henry – a breaking point, even. Everything he had done all year had been carried out with the greatest resolution. There had been those who had said he should have cancelled the campaign when the earl of Cambridge's plot had been revealed; he had ignored them and pressed on. The siege of Harfleur had hugely sapped the strength of his army, and there had been those who had said he should not have started on this march. Nevertheless he had ignored them and set out, determined to make his way to Calais. He was equally determined to meet the French in battle – even to the point of telling them exactly where he would be. And now he was being forced to acknowledge that he had been out-manoeuvred. His resolution to march on regardless, and to test his cause against God's will, had only succeeded in endangering the tired and hungry survivors of the long siege. If at this point he tried to persuade his councillors otherwise, he failed to win them over. Their advice was that the army should find another crossing.

No doubt Henry had already sent scouts ahead to examine the conditions at the ford and they had probably come back with information that many French troops were stationed there. The number of six thousand men was probably not a huge exaggeration. If Boucicaut, d'Albret and the seigneur de Rambures had been joined by the duke of Alençon, as was likely, then there would have been at least four thousand fighting men north of the Somme.[43] By now Henry may have learned that the three hundred men-at-arms who had left Calais to take control of the crossing had been annihilated by a Picard army.[44] Henry's strategy was falling apart. His council were sensible to put their faith in avoiding battle rather than deliberately seeking it.

It must have been a depressing meeting. It was not possible to advance by way of Blanchetaque. Retreat was out of the question. And if they marched inland, along the Somme, there was a good chance that the enemy troops north of the Somme and those gathering at Péronne would starve them in the field. It seemed that the French had indeed 'enclosed them on every side like sheep in folds', as several councillors had warned they would before they had set out. And the eight days' rations were almost all used up – this was the seventh day of what was supposed to have been an eight-day march to Calais. The bread and wine the men had received at Arques and Eu had not gone far, and most men had been drinking unhealthy river water for the last week. Some of them were carrying festering wounds; others were still suffering from dysentery.

Henry probably considered advancing his men to the ford and trying to fight his way across. He knew that Edward III had done so in 1346 – and, on that occasion, as if by a miracle, the tide had come in after the last of the English were across and stopped the French from crossing. Surely God would work some similar miracle for him? But if he suggested this, the councillors would have countered that Edward's army had fought a way across the Somme against no more than three thousand men. According to the Gascon informer, the ford was further defended now with sharpened stakes driven into the bed of the river, allowing the French crossbowmen to rip the English apart in midstream. Fighting against six thousand in these conditions, including crossbowmen, would be very difficult.

Thus it was, at this point, six miles short of the ford, that Henry abandoned his original plan. He ordered the army to head inland, following the banks of the Somme.

As they made their way along the river, looking for a crossing nearer Abbeville, the scouts reported that all the bridges had been be broken by the constable and marshal of France.[45] So they proceeded until that night, cold, hungry and weary, they came to the villages of Mareuil and Bailleul-en-Vimeu, where they camped.[46]

★

In London, the mayor Thomas Falconer had come to the end of his eventful year in office. At the Guildhall, accompanied by many aldermen in their robes as well as the recorder and the two sheriffs of the city and 'an immense number of the commonalty', he presided over the election of his successor. This was Nicholas Wotton, a member of the Drapers Company. He would be sworn in on 28 October.[47]

★

At Arundel Castle, the earl of Arundel died.[48] It was a sad end, considering his extraordinary career. After his father's execution in 1397 he had been treated as a servant and regularly humiliated by his guardian, John Holland, duke of Exeter. Locked up in Reigate Castle, he escaped – although still only seventeen – and managed to get to the continent where he joined his uncle, the archbishop of Canterbury, in exile. Together they went to meet Henry's father in Paris, and joined with him in his attempt to wrest the throne from Richard II. Thomas was thus the very first Lancastrian supporter, and had remained loyal to the dynasty thereafter – taking part in putting down the Epiphany Rising in 1400, fighting alongside Prince Henry in Wales after Glendower's revolt, and taking action against Archbishop Scrope in 1405. By 1407 he was the prince's principal retainer, and served on the prince's council during the regency of 1409–11. He was sent by the prince to fight for John the Fearless at St-Cloud in 1411, and proved himself efficient in battle. As his will shows, he shared the prince's devotion to the Holy Trinity and to the cult of St John of Bridlington; and very soon after Henry's accession he was loaded with titles and honours: warden of the Cinque Ports, constable of Dover Castle and, most important of all, treasurer of England. Apart from Henry's uncles and brothers, only Richard Beauchamp, the late Richard Courtenay, and the duke of York were as close to the king. Thomas now became the second of that number to die as a result of Henry's will to fight a war in France.

Monday 14th

The bridge at Pont Rémy was Henry's next target, about four miles east-north-east of his camp. Seeing a large number of men drawn up on the opposite bank, he believed battle to be imminent, and dubbed a number of knights. Among these were Lord Ferrers of Groby, Ralph Greystoke, Peter Tempest, Christopher Moresby, Thomas Pickering, William Hodelston, John Hosbalton, John Mortimer, James Ormonde and Philip and William Halle.[49] Knighting men was a good way to inspire them to feats of valour in the forthcoming battle, as they would seek to win glory and prove themselves worthy. As he approached the bridge, however, he saw that it was broken. So too were the causeways leading to it. The river here had a broad marsh on either side – hence the causeways – so no bridge-building was possible, even though Henry had specifically brought carpenters who were experienced in the craft.

It was at this point that the hearts of the English fell. They had run out of food. They had no way forward, no way back, and there were thousands of French troops on all sides tracking their movements, and hoping to kill them. The head of the Somme lay sixty miles away. They had no option but to march inland, deep into hostile territory. To desert at this stage would be certain death for any Englishman; otherwise many men would have simply run away. The words that the author of the *Gesta* used to describe the plight of the English at this moment were clearly heartfelt:

At that time we thought of nothing else but that, after the eight days assigned for the march had expired and our provisions had run out, the enemy, who had craftily hastened on ahead and were laying waste the countryside in advance, would force us – who were already hungry – to suffer a really dire need of food. And at the head of the river, if God did not provide otherwise, they would with their great and countless host and the engines of war and devices available to them, overwhelm us, for we were few in number, fainting with a great weariness, and weak from a lack of food.

I, the author of this, and many others in the army, looked up in bitterness to Heaven, seeking the clemency of Providence, and called upon the Glorious Virgin and St George, under whose protection the most invincible crown of England has flourished from of old, to intercede between God and his people, that the Supreme Judge, who foresees all things, might take pity on the grief all England would feel at the price we would pay with our blood, and in His infinite mercy, deliver from the swords of the French our king and us his people, who have sought not war but peace, and bring us to the honour and glory of His name, in triumph to Calais. Without any other hope but this, we hastened on from there in the direction of the head of the river . . .[50]

What the author of the *Gesta* does not say at this point is that Henry's high-minded intentions not to lay waste 'his' kingdom of France were starting to wear thin. It was all very well for him to declare that no burning, raping or killing should take place; but the men were now hungry, and the scouts were taking matters into their own hands. Henry may or may not have condoned their actions, but the English burned and looted as they marched to Airaines.[51]

Tuesday 15th

The Issue Rolls for this day record an interesting payment. It reads: 'to Master Robert Benham sent to Calais with divers medicines ordered for the health of the king's person and others in his army who went with him'.[52] This obviously postdates the actual delivery of the medicines by some weeks; but it suggests that Henry had not escaped the siege of Harfleur totally unscathed. What he had been suffering from, and whether he was still afflicted, we can only guess. But the knowledge that he was ill, and had not yet reached Calais to benefit from the medicines in question, makes his leadership in the face of many adversities all the more striking.

*

The dejected English army approached the city of Amiens. Two days earlier, in the same town, the orders for the defence of the Somme had been read out. Charles d'Albret had chosen to concentrate the bulk of his forces at Abbeville, in an attempt to trap Henry against the river. The people of Amiens had been ordered to send reinforcements – large numbers of crossbowmen and all their artillery. This they had done, albeit very reluctantly, for it left them vulnerable. Now at Abbeville there were several thousand fighting men and twelve heavy cannon, more than two thousand cannon balls, and large stocks of saltpetre, sulphur, gunpowder, and various other machines of war.[53] At Amiens there were no stockpiled munitions.

The people of Amiens were lucky. The English marched straight past, at a distance of about three miles. It is likely that the soldiers from Abbeville, who had been tracking them along the far bank, had bolstered the defences of the town. Also troops stationed upstream at Corbie and Péronne may have shifted to Amiens in response to the English advance. D'Albret's plan was flexible enough to defend the inland towns. The dejected English had no option but to press on into the dangerous interior of France.

Wednesday 16th

At first Henry's progress had been fast – sixteen or seventeen miles per day – as fast as one could reasonably go with ten thousand men and several hundred carts and wagons. But since the council meeting six miles short of Blanchetaque, that speed had fallen off. From that moment to the end of today the army had covered between ten and eleven miles per day.

There were several reasons for their slowness. The main one was that they were desperate to find a way across the river. Although the army was travelling along a line of hills nearby, frequent forays had to be made down to the water to investigate every bridge and every possible ford, and every potential site for a new temporary bridge. Of course, the bridges were all broken, and the fords guarded. No doubt the consequent frustration led to the burning and looting along the way – another delaying factor. They had to find food as well; their supplies of dried beef and walnuts had all long since gone, so they had to forage for everything they ate and drank. The weather did not help. It rained hard and was windy, and the nights were very cold.[54] Riding or marching for hours in such miserable conditions must have been difficult, especially when the men were starving, weak, and frightened.

Boves was a town in the overlordship of the duke of Burgundy, being held for him by the count of Vaudémont, brother of the duke of

Lorraine. Although the count was with Boucicaut at the time, the question remained, would the townsmen fire on the English? Or would they hold to John the Fearless's promise not to impede Henry in his quarrel with the king of France? It is perhaps significant that Thomas Elmham, writing three years later, notes that Henry 'chose' to stay at this town, perhaps seeing his reception by the garrison of the castle there as a test of John the Fearless's loyalty. The garrison, situated on a well-defended rocky outcrop, fired no cannon, nor did they make a sortie and attack. Instead they negotiated with Henry for the safe passage of the army. They surrendered hostages, and under cover of night they sent out eight massive baskets of bread, each one carried by two men, to help sustain the army. Henry also asked the captain of the castle to look after two very sick knights in the army, directing the men in question to give up their horses as an advance payment of their ransoms.[55]

A number of low-status men, presumably archers, today broke into the vineyards and presses in the region around Boves, looking for wine. Not surprisingly they found it – in large quantities. When this was reported to Henry he was very angry. Some men asked why he had forbidden them to drink wine, asking to fill up their bottles with it, now they were here. Henry replied that

> he was not troubled by the idea of bottles but that the problem was that many would have their stomachs as their bottles, and that was what bothered him, for he was worried they would get too drunk.[56]

No wine and no women. One does not imagine there was very much song either – apart from the pipes and drums of war. What with the lack of food and lack of comfort, campaigning with Henry V was a grim experience.

One man did get his reward today. Henry promised his esquire, William Hargrove, that when they returned to England he would make him the usher of the Order of the Garter, together with the house in Windsor Castle that went with the office, receiving the usual wages as his predecessor. This position carried the right to bear the black rod before the king and his heirs on feast days, and is today known after the symbol of the office: Black Rod.[57]

Thursday 17th

Henry left Boves this morning, making his way over the River Avre and setting out on the road towards Nesle. There was no saying where the next meal would come from. Nor when the rain would stop, and the wind let up. For his men, it was vital to keep going regardless of the soaked and stinking state of their clothes and bodies. The French were gathering all along the other bank of the Somme, moving from town to town, concentrating on potential crossing points. Today, as the English passed through the villages on the way to Nesle, the French made a sortie from Corbie and sent out a group of cavalry to attack the English archers passing the adjacent fields.

The sudden presence of cavalry at this point shows that a bridge or ford at Corbie – a walled town on the north side of the river – had not been destroyed. This in turn suggests that the English reluctance (or failure) to cross here was due to the numbers of French troops able to defend the place. The English archers responded swiftly to the sortie and put the men-at-arms to flight, taking two of them prisoner.[58] But there was no attempt to cross.

This sudden cavalry attack seems to have warned Henry of the danger that a charge could break up his ranks of archers. With this in mind he gave instructions that every archer should cut himself a thick stake, six feet in length, sharpened at both ends. The idea was similar to that employed by the French at Blanchetaque, where stakes had been driven into the river bed to stop the English men-at-arms riding across. When the French horses tried to break the lines of archers, their horses would either be impaled or would take fright.[59]

A short while afterwards, as the army moved through the villages towards Nesle, looking for food, the cry went up that a gilt-copper pyx containing the Holy Eucharist had been stolen from a church. This was directly in contravention of the ordinances that Henry had proclaimed at the start of the march. It was also a very obvious affront to God – and, since Henry's greatest source of inspiration was his confidence that God would favour him because 'victory consists not in a multitude but with Him . . . who bestows victory upon whom He wills, whether they be many or few', he had no option but to find the culprit and make an example of him. He stopped the army and ordered the captains to search all their men. An archer was found with the pyx concealed in his sleeve. Henry ordered that it be returned to the church. He then had the man hanged from a tree in the sight of the rest of the army, before ordering them to continue on their way.[60]

*

The duke of Bourbon joined the king, the dauphin, the duke of Berry and the other lords today at Rouen, adding his contingent to the army gathering there. Bourbon and Berry (Bourbon's father-in-law) had both withdrawn from court earlier in the year due to their disgust at the dauphin's behaviour. Now France was in danger, these old quarrels were being set aside. The duke of Orléans was still at Cléry, not far from Orléans, but he was about to ride north in haste. Even the duke of Brittany, who had recently renewed his agreement with Henry's negotiators, was on his way from Falaise to Rouen, albeit slowly.[61]

There was one obvious exception to this collective unity against the English. John the Fearless was still two hundred miles away, making a leisurely trip between dinner at Chaigny and supper at Beaune.[62] It seems he had decided to honour his agreements and letters of peace with Henry in a manner of speaking – he would not *personally* involve himself in the quarrel with the king of France. At the same time this allowed him to obey the order from the king of France not to join the host advancing against the English in person. His promises to attend the army in person were just bluster. By an extraordinary coincidence, the duplicitous duke's mind had been made up for him by the fact that both the kings he was playing off against each other wanted him to stay away. So he decided he would.

Friday 18th

The English army continued towards Nesle. Being further away from the river, they did not look for crossings and thus made faster progress. From leaving Boves yesterday morning and arriving this evening at Nesle, they covered between twenty-five and thirty-five miles, depending on whether they travelled via Corbie and Harbonnières or via Caix.[63] It was a full moon today, so it is likely that the king ordered the army to march later into the evening, pressing on to his destination.

At Nesle they met an unwelcome sight. The townsfolk knew that a large French army under d'Albret and Boucicaut was gathering at Péronne, just sixteen miles away; so they hung red banners over the wall, signifying their refusal to surrender. Henry angrily gave orders that the villages around Nesle be 'burned and utterly destroyed' on the following day. As he had stationed his men in these same villages, the burning was presumably to be carried out as the army departed their quarters.[64] It is a sign of the desperation into which Henry himself had now sunk – that he was prepared to issue orders for indiscriminate burning, contrary to his own ordinances.

But at this very moment, when he had already led his men 170 miles from Harfleur, he had a stroke of luck. Someone told him that there was an unguarded ford in the vicinity. It may have been someone from Nesle who informed him, hoping thereby to save the threatened villages. Or it might have been someone who had remained in one of the villages when the English had arrived. One chronicle states that the location of the crossing was revealed by some prisoners who were being dragged along with the army.[65] Perhaps an English scout noticed for himself that a broken causeway led to a broken bridge that was still passable – another chronicle tells a story along these lines.[66] Whatever the source, Henry's scouts delivered the news either in the night or in the early morning. The ford lay near Bethencourt, about three miles away. The author of the *Gesta* reckoned it would save the English army eight days' marching if they could cross there.

Saturday 19th

Henry sent an advance party of mounted men to investigate the ford at first light. He instructed them to test the conditions of the ford and the depth and speed of the water. They returned with good news. A mile short of the Somme was another very marshy little river, which the army would have to cross, and they would be in great danger if they were to be attacked at that point. But beyond it there were two long, narrow causeways leading up to two fords through the Somme itself. These had been broken in several places, so that one could barely pass in single file. Nevertheless, the river could be crossed. The depth in the middle was only a little higher than the belly of a horse.

Henry immediately gave the order to advance. Any delay would increase the risk of the French discovering the plan. Before leaving he ordered the villages where the army had sheltered overnight to be pulled apart so that doors, shutters, window-frames, stairs, structural timbers, straw and every other suitable commodity should be used to make good the causeways. After this, the remnants of the buildings in the villages were set alight, in accordance with his earlier order.[67]

Sir Gilbert Umphraville and Sir John Cornwaille led the crossing party, taking a number of men-at-arms and archers from the vanguard over the ruined causeways on foot, and then through the river, to set up a defensive position protecting the ford on the far side. When sufficient men were across, the doors and timbers from the villages were brought up and laid down, so the horses and carts could be drawn to the river and across. Henry ordered that one ford be used for the fighting men – whom he needed quickly on the other side – and the other for the horses and baggage. He himself stood by the entrance to the soldiers' causeway, making sure that the men did not pack themselves in too tightly in their urgency to cross. In this way, quickly, Henry achieved a bridgehead on the far side of the water.

How come Henry had been able to cross at this point, despite the shadowing French scouts? The answer is that, in marching to Nesle, the English soldiers had moved several miles away from the river and so the French had lost track of them. It was fortunate, to say the least; Henry had only taken the route to cut off a bend in the river, near Péronne. But as a result of his unplanned and unpredictable troop movements, only now did the French scouts relocate the English army. They must have been aghast to see the English on the *north* bank, in the process of crossing. They hurriedly called up reinforcements and made as if to attack, but realised that they did not have enough men there to force the English back. For a while they remained at a distance, gauging whether to fight or not; but all the while the English force on the north bank grew stronger, and eventually the French scouts abandoned the place altogether.

According to the author of the *Gesta*, the army started to wade through the Somme about 1 p.m. and continued until an hour short of nightfall.[68] According to the later Burgundian chroniclers, the attempt to make the crossing had started at 8 a.m. and continued until nightfall. If the advance guard went across earlier than the main battle, as soon as Henry ordered, then both accounts are probably correct. When all the men were across, they marched by moonlight to the villages to which the herbergers directed them.[69] Henry himself was found a suitable house at Athies. Others were lodged at Monchy-Lagache.

The English troops were in higher spirits than they had been for days. 'It was a cheerful night that we spent in those hamlets,' wrote the author of the *Gesta*.[70]

*

Just ten miles from Bethencourt lay Péronne, where the leaders of the French army north of the Somme were meeting in council. The duke of Bourbon was apparently one of those present; he must have spent many hours in the saddle over the last two or three days, covering the 120 miles from Rouen. Also present were Charles d'Albret and Boucicaut, the duke of Alençon, the count of Richemont, the count of Eu, the count of Vendôme, Guichard Dauphin and Jean de Werchin, seneschal of Hainault.[71] The duke of Bourbon declared that King Charles had resolved to do battle with Henry 'in the coming week' and that both the king and the dauphin were intending to be there at the battle in person. Probably as a result of Bourbon's news, the other lords at Péronne joined him in writing a letter to the duke of Brabant at Louvain, requiring him also to participate in the forthcoming battle with his men-at-arms.[72]

Despite the explicit reference in this letter, the strategy of bringing the English to battle so soon did not originate in Rouen. King Charles himself did not yet know of it. Discussions regarding general strategy were still underway among the courtiers, and an important council meeting to settle the matter was scheduled for the following day. The decision for the army north of the Somme to do battle 'in the coming week' seems to have been a decision made by the duke of Bourbon, either by himself or in conjunction with those at Péronne. Bourbon may have hastened to Péronne specifically to encourage these moves to war. It was noted by one chronicler that Bourbon was particularly keen to attack the English.[73] And the duke certainly had already shown an eagerness to fight. Only in January he had founded the Order of the Prisoner's Shackle for the purpose of fighting Englishmen. It looked as though Bourbon was going to have his chance sooner rather than later.

*

Although Henry's ploy of leading the French away from Harfleur by using himself as bait had worked brilliantly, allowing the garrison of 1,200 men to rebuild the defences without interruption or danger, the problems they faced within the town were far from over. The dysentery had infected the townsmen too during the siege, and had contributed to its surrender. Now those busy rebuilding the place were having to work in the same unsanitary conditions. They were also going down with the disease.

Lord Botreaux was one of those who fell seriously ill after the army departed. No doubt he had visions of the church at Cadbury where he had declared he wished to be buried, just three months earlier. Perhaps he recalled the bequests he had made to his wife Elizabeth and young daughters. He was sent back to Dover by ship today. But as things turned out, he was one of the lucky ones. His last will would remain in a chest at Cadbury for another forty-seven years before he finally passed away.[74]

Sunday 20th

The English soldiers rested in the villages where they had spent the night, finding food left by the villagers and the French scouts. No doubt Henry held another council meeting. His army was now on the same side of the Somme as the French, and they had an army waiting to intercept them.

Three French heralds came and presented themselves to the duke of York, leader of the vanguard, who sent them to the king. As if to pour scorn on their morality, an English chronicler noted that one of the heralds, Jacques de Heilly, had absconded from prison in England and had fled secretly to France 'carrying a beautiful woman'.[75] According to the French herald Gilles le Bouvier, the dukes of Bourbon and Bar and Charles d'Albret had met the count of Nevers (youngest brother of John the Fearless) at Corbie, and collectively they had sent the ambassadors to Henry, challenging him to battle. Le Bouvier added that they told Henry they would fight him at Aubigny in Artois on the following Thursday. Henry accepted the challenge, and gave de Heilly and his companions gifts.[76]

The author of the *Gesta* also stated that Henry accepted the challenge but added that he prepared to do battle the following day.[77] The two accounts appear incompatible – until one remembers that the armies were in very close proximity to one another. Unless Henry had been ready to do battle immediately, he could easily have been surprised by the French. Hence he prepared to fight straight away.

*

At Rouen, the French king presided over a great council of thirty-five noblemen. The duke of Anjou had now joined the lords gathered there, and so had the duke of Brittany. The main item on the agenda was whether to attack the English army or not. There is no sign that they had any idea of the duke of Bourbon's resolution to attack by the 26th.

Thirty of the thirty-five men present were for fighting. Of the five against, the most important was the duke of Brittany. He declared that 'he would not make one step [towards the English] unless his cousin the duke of Burgundy were there'.[78] His reference to Burgundy suggests that he and Burgundy knew of each other's agreements with the king of England and that, through Brittany's ambassadors in mid-August, the two dukes had decided they would act together. However, Brittany and the other four objectors at Rouen were heavily outnumbered. The other councillors claimed that the troops in the French army north of the Somme were already sufficient for the French to attack safely. If Brittany wanted to hold back or withdraw, his decision would have to be a personal one.

The council resolved to send word immediately to the constable, Charles d'Albret, telling him of the decision to fight. They also resolved to send orders throughout the kingdom requiring all the lords accustomed to bear arms to hasten to him, day and night, from wherever they were. But contrary to the duke of Bourbon's assumption, neither the king nor the dauphin would join the army. The duke of Berry (whose father King John II had been captured by the English at Poitiers) put forward reasons of security in support of this, arguing that there was no point in risking losing the king or his son, and his argument was convincing. The dauphin was apparently much put out that he would not take part in the fight but he was forced to accept the council's decision.[79] It was also decided that two other dukes would not fight: the duke of Berry, who was too old; and the duke of Anjou, who was suffering from a bladder disease. Anjou's six hundred men would be led to join the main army by the seigneur de Longny.[80]

The duke of Orléans was chosen to represent the royal family at the forthcoming battle. With this in mind – contrary to the earlier policy that both he and Burgundy should stay away – a new plan was formed by the council. Orléans was to have overall command and take charge of the main battle, along with Charles d'Albret and the dukes of Alençon and Brittany (despite the latter's objections). The vanguard ahead of them was to be led by Boucicaut, the duke of Bourbon, and Guichard Dauphin. The rearguard was to be led by the duke of Bar and the counts of Nevers, Charolais, and Vaudémont. On the wings Tanneguy du Chastel and the count of Richemont were each to be in charge; and the seneschal of Hainault was to lead the specialist heavy cavalry needed to break the ranks of the archers.[81]

Monday 21st

The English marched north from Athies and Monchy-Lagache this morning. Henry rode in armour, and ordered all his men-at-arms to do likewise.[82] He may even have gone looking for a fight, for he led his troops straight to Péronne. But the army passed the town 'a short distance away to our left'. A number of French men-at-arms approached at a gallop but a group of English men-at-arms responded immediately by riding forward to intercept them. Before they clashed, the French turned their horses and rode back into the town.

By the time the English passed Péronne, most of the French had already left. Nevertheless, looking at the mud churned up by many thousands of horses, deep fear caught the hearts of those in the English army. As the author of the *Gesta* put it, about a mile beyond Péronne,

> we found the roads remarkably churned up by the French army, as if it had preceded ahead of us by the thousand. And the rest of the troops – to say nothing of the commanders – fearing that battle was imminent, raised our eyes and hearts to heaven, crying out, with voices

expressing our inmost thoughts, that God would have pity on us and in His ineffable goodness, turn away from us the violence of the French.[83]

As the troops marched on towards the River Ancre, they were looking for a place to camp. They hoped the day's march would be over quickly. 'Their hearts were quaking with fear,' Thomas Elmham wrote. Some skirmishing with the French took place, and at least one man-at-arms was captured.[84] The fights were probably much more serious than this single statistic suggests, for any Frenchmen would have needed a considerable number of compatriots to warrant their attacking a group of armed English scouts. And these conflicts on the periphery of the army, which were now happening every day, cannot have done anything but make the English more despondent.

*

In line with the French council's decision to attack, the duke of Brittany set out from Rouen with a large body of men – six thousand, according to Monstrelet. He must have been leading many soldiers besides his own contingent. But the English ambassadors, Dr John Hovingham and Simon Flete, had not yet departed from Brittany. As they had no doubt reminded him quite recently, the dangers to the duke of breaking his agreement with Henry, and fighting for the French against the English, would be calamitous – if Henry should win.

*

In his castle at Louvain this evening, at about eight o'clock, Duke Anthony of Brabant received the letter that the dukes of Bourbon and Alençon and the other lords had written to him on the 19th. The messenger must have ridden hard – the distance he had covered was about one hundred miles. If the duke of Brabant was going to respond in time to join a battle scheduled to take place before the 26th, he had no time to lose.

His response is very interesting. John the Fearless might have promised Henry that he would not hinder him in his war, but such an anti-French strategy did not affect his brothers' loyalty. The youngest of the three brothers, the count of Nevers, had already taken the field. Now Anthony followed his lead. He ordered his secretaries to write letters to all his vassals requiring them to be in arms at Cambrai as soon as possible. And he sent an esquire to the city of Antwerp this same evening with similar orders.[85]

Tuesday 22nd

Duke Anthony went to the council chamber in the town of Louvain this morning. He asked the town council to give him men-at-arms, archers and crossbowmen to fight against the English. There was not much time; only a few men could be mustered before he departed for Cambrai, where he would gather his vassals.

★

Henry's passage across the River Ancre may have been at Ancre itself, from which he would have marched in a direct line northwest through Forceville to Acheux, where the army camped tonight. Alternatively he may have crossed at Miraumont, and then turned westwards to Forceville. The latter route would explain why Gilles le Bouvier's chronicle states that Henry turned away from the road towards Aubigny, where the French had told him they would fight him on Thursday. Other chronicles seem to support this view.[86] But why might Henry have changed course at this point, if he was so determined to fight the French?

One possible answer is food. Henry was not negotiating with any towns north of the Somme for safe passage; his men were simply grabbing what they could from the villages through which they passed. But the only reason to suppose that the villages on the way to Aubigny were very poorly provisioned is that the French had already looted them (French chroniclers repeatedly note that the French did more damage in looting than the English). Another explanation is fear. Not necessarily Henry's own – but that of his men, certainly. Even many years afterwards, the chroniclers' accounts reflect the terror of the English at this stage. They were marching straight to where they knew a larger French army was waiting for them, on ground that the French had chosen. One day's rest had not been enough to refresh them. It would have been irresponsible of Henry to force his men along a road through villages where they could find no food on their way to what they believed would be a fatal battle. Accordingly he turned away, so he could reassure his commanders and his men that, if there was to be a battle, he would choose the site.

Once this point is realised, it becomes apparent that, even if we are wrong in supposing that Henry crossed at Miraumont and changed direction, and that really he crossed at Ancre, the same argument applies. If he rode constantly northwest after passing Péronne, then he had simply decided not to follow the French to Aubigny at an earlier point – when he saw the mud churned up by their horses' hooves and cart wheels. In order to keep his men's spirits up, he had to be seen to be taking the initiative himself, and not simply leading them despondently to their deaths at Aubigny.

Did Henry still hope to fight a battle? It is clear that the decision to march to Calais from Harfleur was originally his, and that he fully expected to fight a pitched battle on the way. But it is equally clear that he did not imagine being one hundred miles from Calais after two weeks. The failure to cross the Somme had cost him dearly, for now he was leading a starving, weak and dispirited army. His refusal to follow in the path of the French army to a designated battlefield does seem to suggest that the collective decision-making of the king and council had turned away from actively seeking an engagement. We have seen how the English refused to tackle the French in battle at Blanchetaque; now this deviation seems to indicate that the English were deliberately trying to avoid the French by moving as fast as they could along an alternative route to Calais, not stopping to parley with any towns for food. The question is thus a difficult one to answer; and the truth is that there were differing opinions within the English camp. Even if Henry personally still hoped to engage the enemy, very few of his council and his army shared that hope. And not even Henry was prepared to fight the French on ground that the French themselves had chosen.

Wednesday 23rd

Over the last two days Henry had kept the army moving at fifteen miles per day – almost as fast as he had been travelling when first setting out from Harfleur towards Blanchetaque. Now he pressed on harder than ever, making them go at least twenty miles. The troops rode or marched in their weary state in a straight line from Acheux to Thièvres. Here they crossed the River Authie, and then passed the next small river, the Grouche, between the walled town of Doullens and the castle of Lucheux. The main army encamped at Bonnières and the villages to the south of Frévent, while the duke of York pushed on to Frévent itself.[87] There he led his men against the French men-at-arms in the town; and having put them to flight, set about repairing the broken bridge there, ready for the following morning.

*

The French army had probably marched from Péronne towards Aubigny after hearing back from the heralds on the 20th. It would have appeared to them best to arrive first, to choose their positions and rest, before doing battle. At some point their scouts must have reported that the English had turned away from Aubigny and were heading fast on the northwest road. On hearing this, the French commanders, knowing Henry's men were tired and malnourished, probably imagined that Henry had decided to try to outmanoeuvre them and get to Calais without a fight. In order to bring the English to battle by the 26th, they had to position themselves between the English and the road to Calais. And they had to do so quickly.

Turning away from the road to Aubigny, the French made their way to St Pol on the River Ternoise. From there it was an easy march along the north bank of the river to cut off the English at Blangy. A letter was sent to the town of Mons (by which route the duke of Brabant was riding) declaring to the townsmen that the battle would take place on the 25th.

Thursday 24th

The English crossed the River Canche this morning and proceeded directly northwards, towards Blangy, where they could cross the River Ternoise. The duke of York and the whole of the vanguard was ahead, clearing a way for the English army. The French were in the same area. Advance English troops regularly came under attack from squadrons of French men-at-arms. Seven Lancashire archers were captured in one engagement.[88] It was becoming clear that both sides were racing to the Ternoise, and if the French stopped them crossing, there would be a battle – with no safe retreat for the English. There was no time to go looking for food. Although most of the troops had not eaten properly for several days, and were growing weaker all the time, their hopes of survival rested on speed, and avoiding a pitched battle with the better-fed, better-equipped and more numerous French men-at-arms.

Henry himself was nervous, distracted. Along the route to Blangy he was told that his herbergers had identified a place in a particular village where he could eat and briefly rest. But he continued, ignorant of where the town was. When informed that he had ridden a mile and half past it, he refused to go back, explaining he was in his cote-armour and it would not do for him to turn up at a village when dressed for war. He could have added that he did not have time. So he rode on, taking the main battle of the army with him, and ordered the duke of York to lead the vanguard further ahead.[89]

When the duke of York came to the hill overlooking Blangy, he saw French troops desperately trying to destroy the bridge. Immediately he attacked, and fought the men-at-arms there, killing some and taking others prisoner. Having secured the bridge, he sent scouts up the hill on the far side. One returned 'with a worried face and anxious gasping breath, and announced to the duke that a great countless multitude was approaching'.[90] Another account states that the scout who first spotted the French

> being astonished at the size of the French army, returned to the duke with a trembling heart, as fast as his horse would carry him. Almost out of breath he said 'be prepared quickly for battle, for you are about to fight against such a huge host that it cannot be numbered'.[91]

Soon other scouts returned, and confirmed this sighting. The duke reported the locations to the king.

It was twelve miles to Blangy-sur-Ternoise, so the valley must have come in Henry's sight about noon or a little later. The author of the *Gesta* notes that the main battle caught their first sight of the enemy here: they were emerging further up the valley, to the right. The

English crossed the Ternoise and climbed rapidly up the hill on the far side. And when they reached the brow of the hill, they were suddenly confronted by the French army.

In describing the moment, the author of the *Gesta* uses the words 'grim-looking' to describe the French. It was not their expressions to which he was referring; he could not see their faces. 'Their numbers were so great as not even to be comparable with ours . . . filling a very broad field like a swarm of countless locusts,' he later wrote.[92] It was a sentiment echoed by every writer on the English side, and very probably every man in Henry's army.

This brings us to a most important question. As the army ascended the hill from Blangy to Maisoncelle, and looked for the first time across the field of Agincourt, what did they really see? How many men were there this afternoon? Were the English truly outnumbered thirty-to-one as the author of the *Gesta* relates? Or six-to-one, as Jean de Waurin claimed? Or three-to-one, as reported by the French chronicler Le Fèvre, who was actually in the English army at the time. Or 'three or four-to-one', as the French monk of St Denis stated? Or did the French outnumber the English just three-to-two, as the chronicle written by a Parisian cleric said?

As shown in Appendix Four, the actual ratio of Frenchmen to Englishmen at the battle cannot have been more than two to one. Indeed, it was probably slightly less than that: the English army of between eight and nine thousand fighting men found themselves facing between twelve and fifteen thousand Frenchmen. There simply is no evidence to support a larger French army. Those who have opted to maintain the vast disparity mentioned in chronicles like the *Gesta* have done so largely because of national pride and tradition, not because of a body of supporting evidence. On the other hand, those who have sought to correct such views have themselves failed to answer a crucial question arising from their revisionism: why were the English astonished as they climbed the hill above Blangy and saw the French army? Or, to put it another way, why do so many chronicles on both sides agree that the French hugely outnumbered the English?

The most likely answer – which has not been put forward before – lies in the different make-up of the two armies and the numbers of their respective non-combatants. English companies had thirty archers to every ten men-at-arms, and thus only ten pages: an extra 25% non-combatants. In the French army, for every thirty archers there were sixty men-at-arms, and thus sixty pages: an extra 66% non-combatants. Whereas the English had about 1,500 pages, the French had between eight and ten thousand. In addition, all the men-at-arms on both sides would have had spare horses, and the easiest and safest way to move these was to allow the pages to ride them. From a distance of three or four miles, it would have been very difficult to distinguish between the men-at-arms and the pages. So when the French looked at the English army they saw no more than eleven thousand men in total (eight to nine thousand fighting men, plus the pages and support staff). But when the English looked at the French army, they saw at least eighteen thousand mounted men – not including the four or five thousand archers and crossbowmen, and the extra infantry raised from the locality. If there were ten thousand men-at-arms, as the Burgundian chroniclers and Gilles le Bouvier suggest, then the English probably really did see an army about three times the size of their own fighting force.

From the point of view of the French, another factor has to be considered – the prejudice against low-status archers. French archers had won no major battles, and had contributed very little to French military prestige over the centuries. Crossbowmen employed in French wars were often mercenaries; and the French saw their archers as relatively insignificant. Also, crossbows were slow and weak in battle; it is unlikely that many Frenchmen knew how destructive a coordinated mass of English longbows could be – the most that any of them had faced in living memory was the thousand or so archers at St-Cloud in 1411. For the English, on the other hand, the archers were crucial. So, while eight thousand English soldiers came to terms with the prospect of fighting what appeared to be an army of 24,000 or more Frenchmen (three-to-one), the French saw that their own men-at-arms outnumbered the English men-at-arms six-to-one. The contemporary chronicler Edmond de Dyntner adopted this form of reckoning: 'there were ten French nobles against one English,' he stated, slightly exaggerating.[93] The social prejudices of the French military elite, in addition to variations in the two kingdoms' military traditions, meant that both sides thought the French army outnumbered the English heavily, whether three-to-one, or six-to-one.

The feeling the English had of being outnumbered three-to-one was exacerbated by the fact that they could not see the whole of the French force. They knew the size of their own army, of course, having marched in three battles and camped together for the last three weeks. But for them, the whole of the surrounding area might have been populated with French troops. The villages could not be presumed to be unoccupied; a large number of scouts had attacked French troops at villages and river crossings. The very character of the medieval landscape meant that coppices, barns and houses obscured the forces of the defending army.

On top of this, both sides would have been aware that not all the French troops had yet arrived. It seems the count of Nevers was not actually with the French army at this stage.[94] It is possible that his men-at-arms had delayed at Corbie, and had been the cavalry whom the English had seen at Péronne on the 19th. Certainly his brother, the duke of Brabant, was still hurrying to the army, staying at Lens this evening, thirty miles away. The duke of Brittany was still at Amiens, although he had sent ahead his brother the count of Richemont with some of his men. The duke of Anjou's six hundred men-at-arms also had not yet arrived, being led by the seigneur de Longny. The commander of the Parisian garrison, Tanneguy du Chastel, who was also in the battle plan, was also absent. Even the newly appointed overall commander of the French forces, the duke of Orléans, was not yet with the army. For the already-outnumbered English the prospect of becoming more heavily outnumbered on the following day can only have demoralised them further.

*

Henry's reaction to the news that a huge army lay ahead of him was to set spurs to his horse and ride ahead to join the duke of York. Having seen the French army for himself, he returned to the main battle and 'very calmly and quite heedless of danger, he gave encouragement to his army and drew them up in battles and wings, as if they were to fight immediately'.[95]

The troops began to make their confessions. They knelt and prayed. According to some reports, it was at this juncture that Sir Walter

Hungerford said to Henry that he wished they had another ten thousand of the finest archers in England. According to the *Gesta* Henry replied,

> that is a foolish way to talk because, by the God in Heaven upon whose grace I have relied and in whom is my firm hope of victory, even if I could I would not have one man more than I do. For these men with me are God's people, whom He deigns to let me have at this time. Do you not believe that the Almighty, with these his humble few, is able to overcome the opposing arrogance of the French who boast of their great number, and their own strength?[96]

Another source has Henry replying less lyrically to a request by Hungerford for just one thousand more archers:

> Thus, foolish one, do you tempt God with evil? My hope does not wish for one man more. Victory is not seen to be given on the basis of numbers. God is all-powerful. My cause is put into His hands. Here he pressed us down with disease. Being merciful, He will not let us be killed by these enemies. Let pious prayers be offered to Him.[97]

Did such a conversation take place? Other chroniclers do mention it – but in very similar words. All the accounts might have been based on a story circulating in the wake of the *Gesta*. The authors were writing with the benefit of hindsight, and keen to expand on the religious virtues of the king. But even if the story is true, and verbatim, it was not wholly original. It has several precedents in biblical speeches attributed to Judas Maccabeus, the Old Testament king to whom Edward III had been compared, and with whom Henry's father had associated himself.[98] For example, in 1 Maccabees 3: 16–19, one reads:

> When he reached the city of Beth-Horon, Judas went out to meet him with a few men; but when they saw the army coming against them, they said to Judas: how can we, few as we are, fight against such a mighty host as this? Besides we are weak today from fasting; but Judas said: it is easy for many to be overcome by a few; in the sight of Heaven there is no difference between deliverance by many or a few; for victory

in war does not depend upon the size of the army but on the strength that comes from Heaven.

Other speeches are to be found in the various chronicles for the evening – but these too are of uncertain veracity, and written with the benefit of hindsight. Henry supposedly made a speech in which he declared that he would rather die than be taken by the enemy. He might have done, he might not. Similarly, some French chronicles state that Henry sent heralds to the French asking that the battle be put off until the following day. As not all the French had arrived, such a plan suited them well.[99] If Henry did seek a short truce, he did not trust the answer. He kept his troops drawn up in battle formation until sunset, and for much of that time he made them kneel and pray.[100] Only when it was clear that there would be no pitched battle did he tell them to take shelter for the night in the houses, gardens and orchards of Maisoncelle.

It was then that it began to rain.

*

The night of 24–25 October 1415 cannot have been easy for anyone anywhere near Agincourt, whether they were French or English. For the Englishmen camped in the tents in the orchards and gardens of Maisoncelle, and for their lords and masters in the houses and barns, there was the sheer nervous anticipation of the following day. Few could have slept well. Some were still suffering from dysentery.[101] As they lay or sat there, listening to the pounding of the rain – if they were not actually feeling it soak through their clothes – most would have believed that on the following day they would die. Men who survived the battle but who were captured and could not afford to pay a ransom would be killed, normally with a knife through the windpipe or an axe blow through the skull. It was being said that the French were casting lots for which English lords they were going to take prisoner, such was their confidence. The rain was the least of their worries. Their lack of food, their tiredness and fear – tomorrow everything would be over, the whole hellish episode.

For the Frenchmen things cannot have been much easier. The rain was a bother. They had to go into the villages and take what straw and hay they could find to try to soak up the mud where they were camping. Many men had been billeted in villages until now, and so lacked any tents or other shelter, and so grew depressed as they sat waiting in the heavy rain. They were also tired, having tracked the English army for two weeks, and having had several hard days' riding in order to cut off the English advance. They too were hungry and miserable. They had been forced to live off the land, and had had to requisition or steal food from their own people. Groups of them had regularly confronted the English and been wounded. Large portions of their army were absent. The duke of Orléans seems to have caught up with the rest of the army during the night, or first thing in the morning, so presumably he was riding through the dire weather.[102] But that meant their overall commander was tired and unfamiliar with the territory as well as the troops. And where were the other ducal companies? Where was the duke of Brittany? Where were the duke of Anjou's men? Where was the duke of Brabant? Where was the duke of Lorraine? Where were John the Fearless and his son, the count of Charolais?

Henry was lodged in a small house in Maisoncelle. His night was no doubt spent in prayer – in part at least. Everything he had worked for was to be put to the test on the morrow. Every decision he had made was likewise to be tested. But most of all, his faith was on trial. If God was not on his side after all, then tomorrow he would be a prisoner of the king of France, and in his absence his enjoyment of the throne of England would depend entirely on the loyalty of his brothers. How loyal would they be, after he had forsaken the advice of his brother and heir, Thomas, in undertaking this march across France? The very reason he was here in France was to prove his right to the throne of England by demonstrating it was God's will that he should be king of France. If he lost this battle and many hundreds of men, he stood to lose not just his claim on the French throne but the security of his English title too. He had staked everything on victory. It was all or nothing.

In this light one has to give Henry credit for holding his nerve and providing such controlled leadership, especially in the wake of his own ill health. Few other men could have done it, in such appalling circumstances. But he did not let up for a moment. In line with his strict discipline on the march, he ordered that the whole camp was to remain silent throughout the night. Men-at-arms making a noise were to have their horses and armour confiscated. Archers and servants who were not silent were to have an ear cut off. This rule of silence served two purposes: it encouraged prayerfulness, and it permitted careful attention to the sounds of the night. Had the English been making a clamour, and with the rain falling so heavily, it would have been very easy for a French sortie to make a sudden night attack and cause confusion and panic throughout the English army. The two camps were no more than 1,200 yards apart; one source says their front lines were as close as 250 paces.[103] Because of the danger, Henry also ordered his men to build bonfires by which to keep watch through the night.

The moon was now in its last quarter. With the rain clouds above, there was virtually no moonlight. Nevertheless it appears that the count of Richemont advanced to the English lines with two thousand men, and came close enough to be noticed and attacked by archers before he withdrew.[104] Henry also sent out men to reconnoitre the land. Despite the darkness and the rain, it was worth getting to know as much as possible about the site of the forthcoming battle.

Friday 25th: the Feast of
St Crispin and St Crispinian

It is unlikely that Henry slept. At the best of times he needed very little rest. In the hours before dawn he probably stayed in his house in Maisoncelle, discussing the battle ahead with members of his council, hearing reports of the attack of the count of Richemont, and waiting for the return of the scouts he had sent to spy out the land during the night.

Before dawn, wearing his armour, he attended his first Mass of the day, sung by the priests of the royal chapel. He heard two more Masses, then rose from his knees, and lifted his helmet and spurs. He ordered an esquire to take ten men-at-arms and twenty archers and to guard the horses and the baggage wagons, which would remain in Maisoncelle. They would also guard the high-status pages with the army and the sick who could not fight.[105]

Outside it was growing light. It was time for the army to move out.

Henry called for his horse – a small white one – and rode with his councillors through the mud of the village towards the battlefield. The sodden remains of the overnight bonfires were around them. Captains were raising and ordering the men who had sheltered in tents and in barns, in the gardens and orchards. Henry instructed his trumpeters to remain quiet; he did not want the French to hear the English, nor to break the solemn air about the camp. Just as the English had passed the night in disciplined silence, so now they grouped together to face the French without a sound.[106]

Further up the field, about three-quarters of a mile away, the French were also deploying their men. Like the English, few of them had slept. Some of the English soldiers had heard them talking and shouting through the night, as they re-organised themselves in the rain. Many were soaked and tired. Some remarked that their horses had not neighed all night, as if sensing some calamity would befall them. But the lords, who were dry, were far more positive. They had succeeded in trapping the king of England. Tomorrow they would lead him and the dukes of York and Gloucester to Paris and Rouen as prisoners of the king of France.

In arranging their forces, the French seem largely to have ignored the royal plan drawn up at Rouen a few days earlier. That had stated that the duke of Bourbon, the marshal of France (Boucicaut) and Guichard Dauphin were to lead the vanguard, and the main battle was to be led by the duke of Orléans, with the dukes of Brittany and Alençon, and the constable (d'Albret). The third battle, the rearguard, was to be led by the duke of Bar and the counts of Nevers, Charolais, and Vaudémont. Thus the original plan was for three battles, plus the two wings (led by Tanneguy du Chastel and the count of Richemont) and the special cavalry (to be led by the seneschal of Hainault). The plan had to be adapted to a certain extent, as the duke of Brittany, the count of Charolais and Tanneguy du Chastel had not yet arrived; but also there were lords there who were ardent for glory, and they did not want to be in the rearguard. Those at the front, in the vanguard, would see all the best action – and capture all the most valuable prisoners. Whoever managed to seize the king of England would not only become famous but very wealthy. Consequently, many of those in the rearguard and main battle asked to be in the vanguard. Most of them got their way.

The result was that the French started arranging themselves in just two proper battles: one huge vanguard of about 4,800–5,000 men-at-arms, and the main battle (as it was termed), consisting of about three thousand men-at-arms. Six hundred men-at-arms gathered on each wing, with their backs against the woods on each side. There may also have been men-at-arms in the rearguard; but if so, there were no more than six hundred of them.[107] Some sources claim there were crossbowmen in the vanguard; but other chronicles indicate that the French lords' eagerness to take prisoners meant that they placed their archers in the rearguard, just ahead of the infantry and pages, who were with the wagons and baggage. One source expressly notes that the four thousand crossbowmen who were originally intended to be at the front, to begin the battle, were 'given permission to depart' by the lords, as they would not be needed. Presumably they took up their position at the rear. The author of the Gesta notes that they shot from the back and wings of the French army, and their bolts did little damage.[108]

Not long after dawn, the French were ready. So many men were in the vanguard that the lines stretched right across the field and into the woods on both the Agincourt and Tramecourt sides. As a result, the six hundred men-at-arms on each wing had to stand forward of the vanguard, so they had enough room to charge without riding into the back of their fellow men. In order to make their lances more rigid, and easier to wield in a relatively confined space, they were told to cut the narrow end off the wooden lance and fix the steel head back on the sturdier shortened shaft. The lack of room may also have led to the decision to send the crossbowmen to the back of the army; they could not help but be charged down by the French knights if they were at the front. Besides, the French decided they would not need their crossbowmen to break up the English formation; they would do that with the heavy cavalry, as the Rouen plan had instructed.[109]

To what extent these decisions were those of the duke of Orléans, who was still a month short of his twenty-first birthday, is unclear. One has to presume that he listened to the advice of the experienced military men like Boucicaut and d'Albret, and weighed it up against the advice of the other royal dukes, Bourbon, Alençon and Bar. But this generalship by advisory committee was bound to lead to difficulties. It was probably the reason why so many men went into the vanguard. The young duke of Orléans no doubt thought that he should take a lead position in the vanguard, and so positioned himself at the front, rather than in the main battle; this was after all an opportunity for him to demonstrate to the absent duke of Burgundy that he and the Amargnacs would uphold the honour of France. Having thus broken the plan set at Rouen, it was difficult to prevent the other important lords from taking their places in the vanguard too, if they so wished. This was a great mistake, for it resulted in the crossbowmen being crowded out and sent to the back of the army, where they proved ineffective. Such errors indicate that there was no real generalship in the French army – there was only politics.

This advisory-committee form of generalship led to other problems. For example: when exactly should the fight begin? Although the count of Richemont had arrived with his Breton troops, his brother the duke of Brittany had not. Everyone expected that Brittany would arrive shortly, not knowing that he had no intention of turning up. In the meantime his absence raised the question of whether the French should attack straightaway or wait. The same question had been discussed the previous day, when the two sides had first faced each other. The duke of Bourbon and other courtiers were then all for attacking immediately. The experienced military men – most notably the constable and the marshal – were more wary and inclined to wait for the rest of the army.[110] This was wise counsel, for the seigneur de Longny was still eighteen miles away, with the six hundred men-at-arms of the duke of Anjou. As for the duke of Brabant, he was still at Lens, thirty miles away. To be exact, at prime (about seven o'clock) he was attending Mass. At the moment he took Holy Communion, one Robert Daule hurried into the chapel to tell him that the battle with the English would take place before midday. Immediately, the duke told his companions to mark their clothes with the white cross, and set out to fight.[111]

Another failing which arose from the lack of generalship was the choice of battleground. The French might have succeeded in cutting off the English advance to Calais but in doing so they had placed themselves in a narrow confined space between two woods, and with ground sloping away on either side. Moreover, they were encamped in a ploughed field that had turned into a quagmire as a result of the recent heavy rain – and conditions were going to get worse, with thousands of horses churning up the mud. The ground between the two armies was no firmer, and dangerous for galloping horses. Orléans did not have the experience to order a change of location, and no one else had the authority to suggest they move. No doubt some lords said that it would be dishonourable to back away in order to find better ground, especially when they had six times as many men-at-arms as the English. Those aware of the danger might have found it difficult to suggest a better place to do battle. But the experienced military men could suggest nothing but waiting. The English were dispirited and hungry, and they relied on *being* attacked – responding to a French advance. The French could continue to starve them in the field. They had time on their side.

As Henry rode out of Maisoncelle on his small white horse and looked across the fields towards the French lines, he saw the undulations of the terrain, and realised how the ground fell away in the trees on either side. There was scope there for arranging an ambush to distract the charging French cavalry. His scouts would have informed him how soft the ground was, and how slippery; but now he would have seen the churned-up mud for himself. He also would have seen the lines of the French vanguard forming up ahead of him, 'their spears like a forest', and the wings of mounted cavalry extending towards him.[112] The task facing him must have seemed daunting.

The English army began to form up in the same three battles as they had marched from Harfleur. The vanguard under the duke of York took the right-hand side of the field, the Tramecourt side. Henry himself would lead the main battle, which formed up in the centre. On the left-hand side of the field, the Agincourt side, the rearguard formed up, under the command of the old but experienced Sir Thomas, Lord Camoys. The archers hammered their sharpened wooden stakes into the ground before them, and presumably resharpened the points, hoping thereby to prevent a direct onslaught of the French cavalry.[113] On their flanks were thorn bushes and hedges, and directly in front of them was a small depression in the ground, meaning that anyone riding against them would have a short but decidedly uphill struggle at the end, before hitting the sharpened stakes. This position was defensible, and the best to withstand a French charge.

As the hour approached prime the last arrangements were made to bring the army into a state of readiness. The archers were ordered to replace their bowstrings. On the right flank Henry sent an esquire with two hundred archers to skirt around the bushes and hedges and to hide in the woods on the Tramecourt side. On the left flank he sent a group of men-at-arms to conceal themselves in the woods on the Agincourt side.[114] Those archers in the centre battle were placed to the sides of it, in two 'wedge' or triangular formations, close to the archers on the wings. This served to create a tapering corridor through which any French troops would have to charge directly to reach Henry; they would not be able to sweep across the field towards him, or come at the main battle from an angle, due to the stakes as well as the archers themselves. This was important, as Henry knew that the prime objective of the French was to capture or kill him. He had experienced a similar situation when fighting at Shrewsbury in 1403; on that occasion Henry's father had employed the tactic of having two men-at-arms clothed in royal armour, so that the enemy could not tell which man was actually the king. Guillaume Gruel's chronicle of the life of the count of Richemont asserts that Henry V employed this same tactic at Agincourt; this was probably an unfounded assertion, based on a later, malicious attempt to detract from Henry's military reputation.[115] Nevertheless, the idea it embodies – that the person of the king was all-important to the outcome of the battle – was undoubtedly true. Hence at the centre of the main battle was a concentrated mass of men-at-arms around the king. Here also were placed Henry's five banners – representing the Trinity, the Virgin, St George, St Edward the Confessor and of course the royal arms of England – and the banners of the lords whose retinues were present.

There are many speeches recorded for Henry at this point. One chronicle, the *Brut*, has him asking what time it was; on being told that it was prime, he stated that it was a good time to be about to fight a battle on behalf of England, for many people in England would be at prayer at that hour. Several other chronicles echo this. One has Sir Walter Hungerford's line about wishing for more men, together with Henry's Maccabean response, attributing the outcome to God alone. Thomas Elmham's chronicle has the king recalling the victories of Edward III and his eldest son, the Black Prince, which had been won with fewer men. Thomas Walsingham gave Henry patriotic lines culled from the Roman poet, Lucan. All the English writers, writing long after the event, felt obliged to give Henry suitably patriotic, stirring words – proving him an inspiring leader – even though any precise recollection so long after such a tumultuous event would have been impossible, even for those who had been present. Having said this, it is worth noting that le Fèvre, who was present in the English army, noted that Henry went along the battle line making many speeches, not just one. According to him, Henry told the archers how they could fight secure in the knowledge that the war was a just one, and that the throne of France was his rightful inheritance, and that they had all been born in England where their mothers, fathers, wives and children now were at that very moment, and that 'the French had boasted that if any English archers were captured, they would cut off the three fingers of their right hand so that neither man nor horse would ever again be killed by their arrows'.[116]

While le Fèvre's account of Henry's speech has a ring of truth, and has a claim to authenticity, it is difficult to know what to make of the speeches attributed to him by the other French writers. For example, Juvénal des Ursins' version of Henry's speech has him outlining his claim to the throne of France and that it had fallen to him to make good that claim by conquest.

> He had not come as a mortal enemy, for he had not consented to burning, ravaging, violating nor raping girls and women, as they [the French] had done at Soissons; but he wished to conquer gently all that belonged to him, not to cause any destruction at all.[117]

Quite how one could 'conquer gently' is an interesting question; but more importantly the reference to the attack on Soissons in 1414 – when a victorious French army had killed large numbers of Burgundians and raped many women, including nuns – shows that des Ursins' main reason for making this point was a moral one, and not simply a historical reflection. It was part of the tide of French accusations and blame that immediately followed the battle. He went on to stress how Henry ordered his men to lay aside their personal animosities and embrace each other (implying that the French themselves should have done this), and promised his men the full value of any prisoners they took. He even went so far as to claim that Henry promised that all those fighting there that day would henceforth enjoy the same privileges as noblemen.

The fact is that most of the Englishmen present would not have heard the king's speeches – only those near enough, as he rode up and down the lines. But the importance of Henry's speech-making was not so much that he was heard by his men as that he was *seen* by them. Just to know he was there was an inspiration to many. His appearance was noted by most of the chroniclers; one described him as

> clad in safe and very bright armour: he wore on his head a splendid helmet, with a large crest, and encompassed with a crown of gold and jewels; and on his body a surcoat with the arms of England and France; from which a celestial splendour gleamed on the one side from three golden flowers planted in an azure field; on the other from three golden leopards sporting in a ruby field. Sitting on a noble horse as white as snow, having also horses in waiting royally decorated with the richest trappings, his army were much inspired to martial deeds.[118]

The king's appearance was thus of importance to both sides. For the English it was important to know he was sharing their danger, and in control of the army. For the French, the dazzling spectacle of him in his surcoat, armour and crowned helmet was the bait that would draw them charging down the corridor of stakes and archers.

★

Henry was impatient, waiting for the French to attack. They had made no move for an hour at least. A small number of men-at-arms had ridden out from the French lines and had approached the English army at a gallop, but these had been warned off with a volley of arrows, at Henry's order.[119] Now more riders were approaching – heralds.

The English army were jittery. The time for negotiation had passed. Still, if negotiators were seen to be pursuing a dialogue, Henry had to be seen to listen to them.

The chroniclers, writing about these negotiations at a later date, concealed the terms under layers of post-battle propaganda. Some French writers claimed that Henry had previously sent his heralds to the French army asking for safe passage to Calais, offering to cede Harfleur and the castles below Calais, to restore the prisoners he had taken, and to pay 100,000 crowns in recompense. Obviously none of the English writers mention such a shameful request.[120]

Negotiations of some description did take place, however. It appears most likely that the French sent negotiators to Henry.[121] They may have offered him safe passage to Calais in return for significant concessions – including his renunciation of the throne of France.[122] But the French were not serious; they were playing for time. Among the negotiators were Guichard Dauphin and Jacques de Heilly.[123] When their terms had been formally presented to the English council, and dismissed, the heralds were told to depart. It would appear that de Heilly then offered to fight a personal duel with anyone in the English army who claimed he had escaped his custody in England against the laws of chivalry. Duels before a battle were not uncommon: it was a chance for a man-at-arms to win great prestige, fighting in front of a large crowd of soldiers. But on this occasion it was just another delaying tactic. The troops were anxious; by now it was probably past nine o'clock, and they had been standing still in their battle formations for the best part of three hours. So Henry tersely denied Jacques de Heilly his duel, and told him he could expect to be a prisoner of the English again later that same day.[124]

While these discussions were taking place the French were also growing restless. Some men received the honour of knighthood: it was said that five hundred French knights were dubbed before the battle. One of them was Philip, count of Nevers, who was knighted by Boucicaut.[125] Eighteen men in the company of the seigneur de Croy swore an oath that, when the two sides came together, they would either knock the crown off Henry's head or they would die trying.[126]

For Henry, the time wasting was a cause of concern. His men were eager to get the fight over and done with; they were starving. The author of the *Gesta*, sitting on a horse at the back of the army, thought the French were trying to defeat the English through hunger. Others in the ranks could not understand the reluctance of the French to do battle, considering they had so many men-at-arms. What were they doing? Perhaps this was where the rumour that the French were playing dice for the honour of imprisoning the great lords of England came from. Whatever the cause, the tension was threatening to break the discipline of the army. Henry therefore put the question to his council. What if the English were to do the unthinkable – and attack?

This strategy sounds entirely logical now but it was counter-intuitive to the English military mind of 1415. The textbook longbow victory was achieved by having archers on the flanks, in a defensive position – just as Henry had arranged them – and shooting at the charging enemy as they approached. That had been the secret of the first massed-longbow victory at Dupplin Moor in 1332, and Edward III had perfected the strategy at Halidon Hill in 1333 and Crécy in 1346. Henry was simply following a technique that had been tested over the last eighty years. But to *attack* with massed longbows was unusual. Henry would have known it could be done on a relatively small scale – he himself had probably used the tactic in Wales, and the late earl of Arundel had helped win the bridge at St-Cloud through an English longbow attack in 1411 – but it was a risky manoeuvre. For a start the English would have to abandon their defensive position and move forward, on foot, for a distance of seven or eight hundred yards – two-thirds of the distance between the two armies. They would have to remove the stakes and reposition them, while exposed to the risk of the French heavy cavalry. Shooting accurately and fast, and advancing quickly in formation, were incompatible.

The situation was best summed up by one English chronicler, in the following passage:

The king, considering that a great part of the short day was already past, and firmly believing that the French were not inclined to move from their position, consulted the most experienced officers of his army whether he should advance with his troops, in the order in which they stood, towards the enemy that was refusing to come towards him. Having fully considered the circumstances of such an important matter, they wisely decided that the king should march with his army towards the enemy, and attack them in the name of God. For they considered that the English army, very much wearied with hunger, illness and marching, was not likely to obtain any refreshment in the enemy's country, and that the longer they remained there, the more they would suffer from weakness and exhaustion, whereas the enemy, being among friends, could easily obtain whatever they needed, and as a result of the delay, accumulated new and greater strength by the arrival of fresh troops. Therefore the king's advisers finally concluded that further delay was damaging to the English but advantageous to the French.

The king considered it would be difficult and dangerous to leave his position; yet to avoid greater dangers, with the greatest courage, he set his army an example of how they should march towards the enemy, preserving their current formation. He commanded that his own chaplains and all the priests of the army should start to pray, and that heralds should attend only to their own duties, and not take up arms.[127]

This account is convincing. Henry was frightened to leave his position but he did so anyway. We have noted that Henry was extremely cautious in his strategic moves to this point. He demonstrated a high degree of caution in his choice of landing place at Harfleur, he was very cautious in his attacks on the walls of that town, preferring to blast at them rather than risk sustained assaults. After leaving Harfleur he did not attack any other town and avoided confrontation wherever he could, at Blanchetaque and after leaving Péronne. So for him now to be reluctant to give up his defensive position was entirely in character and understandable. That he did so, and gave the order to advance banners, was a mark of outstanding courage. It proved to be the single most important decision of his life.

★

One struggles to imagine what went through the minds of the English archers when the word went around to advance. They – the few, hungry and fatigued – were going to advance against this seeming mass of French men-at-arms, their social and military superiors. In order for their bows to work effectively, they would certainly need to be within two hundred yards of the enemy, and preferably less than half that to shoot accurately. A charging mounted man-at-arms could cover a distance of one hundred yards in ten seconds; so the archers could be charged down before they came within effective killing range. The one advantage they had was that they could shoot rapidly. Crossbowmen in such a situation would have been helpless, because they could not shoot quickly enough; but archers could loose a dozen or more arrows a minute. Against a thousand charging knights on horseback, each weighing half a ton and travelling at six hundred yards per minute (twenty miles per hour), this was crucial, for only by bringing down enough horses, could they slow the charge.

The question was: could the English archers get close enough to bring down enough horses?

When the order was given to prepare for the banners to advance, the English were terrified but ready. All the men-at-arms had dismounted, and were ready to run in their armour. Some of the archers were preparing to take their stakes with them; others just knew that they had to advance quickly, and decided to leave their stakes behind. Others were probably too scared to know what they should do.[128] Many men were praying; many were bending down and putting a small piece of earth into their mouths, preparing for the moment of their death and the Last Judgment. Then, out in front of the massed army rode old Sir Thomas Erpingham with his complement of men-at-arms. At the back, seated on a horse was the author of the *Gesta*, with the other priests, all of them praying desperately, with their faces turned towards Heaven. 'Remember us, O Lord, our enemies are gathered together and boast of their excellence. Destroy their strength and scatter them so that they may understand that there is none other that fights for us but You, our God . . . Have compassion upon us and upon the crown of England . . .'[129]

All eyes were fixed on Sir Thomas Erpingham. Those hidden in the woods on the flanks were watching him; the archers in each wing were watching him, and so too was the king. So were the men-at-arms in the main battle. And then, in full view of them all, he yelled out 'Now Strike!' and threw a white baton spinning high in the air, for all to see.

A huge shout went up across the English lines and men began moving forward. Everyone was running through the wet mud – archers, men-at-arms, knights and lords – even the king. Sir Thomas Erpingham and his men hurriedly dismounted and joined in the king's battle, Sir Thomas running forward despite his advanced years. The archers were lightly armed, and were able to run much faster than the men-at-arms in the thick mud. But even they had a struggle; they had to get within range of the French front lines and start shooting arrows before the French cavalry charged into them, and broke their ranks. As they ran, they must have looked ahead and seen that the French had realised what was happening. Some Frenchmen were mounting their horses and beginning to move. Others were shouting to one another to take arms.

Henry's decision to attack was a stroke of genius. The French were taken by surprise. Gilles le Bouvier noted that at the moment the French heard the English shout, 'some had gone off to get warm, others to walk and feed their horses, not believing that the English would be so bold as to attack them'.[130] Clignet de Brabant, who had been instructed to lead the Tramecourt-side wing in a charge to break up the archers, could only find 120 of the six hundred men he had for the purpose. He could not wait for them all, there was no time. He shouted to those who were ready and charged. The English trumpets sounded, and the archers stopped and loosed a first barrage of arrows at Clignet de Brabant and his cavalry, sending them one by one into the mud or making them crash into one another, leaving riderless horses to charge into the French vanguard, disrupting their advance. At the same time on the Agincourt side of the battlefield, only three hundred men could be found of the six hundred men to form the charge on that wing. They were met with a terrifying hail of arrows from the English and they too turned back, with the exception of Guillaume de Saveuses and two of his men, who charged on fearlessly to their deaths – when they came close enough for the arrows to penetrate their armour.[131]

A few minutes earlier the French commanders had been wholly confident of victory. Suddenly they had cause for grave concern as their sole means of breaking up the ranks of English archers had shattered on the hailstorm of arrows. The problem was the mud. It was so thick that the men-at-arms on the wings could not gallop. The lightly-armoured English archers were thus able to get close and send showers of steel-headed arrows at them while the French ponderously trudged through the churned-up sludge, slipping this way and that. The horses were terrified at the shouts and trumpets as well as their lack of footing in the quagmire of trodden ground. And it was even worse than they had imagined, for the untrodden land on to which they had charged was a newly ploughed field, with soft earth that had soaked up the rain and now gave way between the horses' heavy hooves. The English archers were able to run forward again, and shoot for the weak points in the horses' head and chest armour, and for their legs. If they got within thirty yards, close enough to puncture the steel armour, they could target the men-at-arms themselves, sending the riderless horses careering back terrified into the French vanguard.[132]

The French commanders could only look on with dismay and

mounting consternation as the riders on the wings rode chaotically back into the vanguard. Even those who had not lost their horses, and who had clung on, had great difficulty controlling their steeds as they careered in panic away from the arrows. No horses could have been trained to face such an onslaught, and nor could their riders have expected their sudden inability to ride together in formation. There was only one option left open: to sound the trumpets commanding a full onslaught of all the troops, and to overwhelm the English through sheer force of numbers. To this end they followed what must have been a pre-arranged plan, dividing into three columns – one for each of the English battles. They charged together – men and steel spears aiming for the hearts of the English commanders, where the standards of the duke of York, the king and Lord Camoys were being held aloft.[133]

Few Englishmen can ever have seen a charge of eight thousand men-at-arms. None of the Englishmen at Agincourt that day had done. No one can have been confident that they would withstand such a colossal attack. But they all knew what they had to do. They were engaged in a fight for their lives. They had been facing death since leaving Harfleur, and it showed in their readiness to throw themselves into the fray. The French on the other hand had thought up until now that they were simply engaged in a quest for glory – it had not occurred to them that they might actually lose this battle. Their confidence had been rocked. And it was shaken even more as they charged, alarmed, and in confusion, for the two hundred English archers hidden in the woods on the Tramecourt side of the battlefield opened their shoulders and let fly a barrage of arrows. Turning to face them, the French on the duke of York's side were distracted; and the next thing they knew, the duke of York's archers ahead were advancing towards them. Between them, the English archers were shooting about a thousand arrows every second, penetrating their armour, killing the horses beneath them, and making them rise up and fall over. Barrages of arrows were loosed, the coordinated flights of steel points a testimony to Henry's determination to bring his own self-doubt and all the questioning of his legitimacy to a final, deadly resolution.

At the back of the English army, the priests had thrown themselves on the ground at the first sign of the French advance, begging that God in His Mercy might 'spare them from this iron furnace and terrible death'. If they had looked up at that moment, they would have seen the strange fruit that grew from the seed of the massed archers' arrows: huge piles of dead and dying men and horses, higher than the height of a man – more than two spears' height. It had been remarked on at the first great longbow victory, at Dupplin Moor: the charging men could not retreat, so they had to scramble over the dying men and horses in front of them. But at a rate of a thousand arrows a second, no one could escape for long – and those climbing were also shot, making the barrier higher. Those at the bottom were held immobile and crushed. Some suffocated. The French could not find a way around the dead and dying, as the woods on either side held them to the same small patch of ground. Those in the third rank of one column of the French vanguard were so tightly packed they could not use their swords. And they could see their heroes being struck down and turning in flight. For those near them, it was deeply disturbing to see men like Guichard Dauphin and the count of Vendôme yelling at their men to retreat.[134]

Such were the numbers of French men-at-arms clambering over the dying front ranks that it seemed to the English that God was holding their enemies helpless for them, presenting them to be slaughtered. But not all the English were finding it easy to pick off the men-at-arms. The column of Frenchmen that pressed hardest was that facing the duke of York. It was here that the fighting was fiercest. The archers may have run out of arrows, allowing the French the advantage as they came on. And wearing quilted leather, not steel armour, they were no match for the fully-armed men-at-arms. Their best hope in the hand-to-hand fighting was a previously unknown weapon: a weighted, sharp-pointed mallet designed for penetrating steel armour and helmets: a poleaxe.[135] With these, and normal axes, the archers fought against the French knights and esquires, hacking and bludgeoning them with short, rapid sweeps. But the French men-at-arms were trained to deal with hand-to-hand warfare. Gradually they advanced on the duke of York's standard. The battle was so furious, so bitter, that all thoughts of taking prisoners had long since vanished. Englishmen tried to use their poleaxes to crush the helmets of the attacking Frenchmen; the French wielded their swords to cut and kill the English archers. In the duke of York's own retinue ninety men were killed as they fought to protect their lord.[136] Despite their great struggle, the French managed to break through and strike the duke himself. Down went the king's much-loved cousin into the mud, fighting to his death for his king. All his regrets about his brother's treason died there in the mud with him.[137]

York was not the only English casualty. The young earl of Suffolk, eager to prove himself after his recent inheritance, was killed. So too was the recently dubbed knight, Sir John Mortimer of Worcestershire, and Sir Richard Kyghley of Lancashire, Sir John Skidmore of Herefordshire, Dafydd Gam of Breconshire, and many archers.[138] At this stage of the battle the English began to sustain terrible wounds from the swords of the French. But even on the hard-pressed duke of York's side, the lords who were second-in-command (probably Sir Gilbert Umphraville and Sir John Cornwaille) rallied the men so that the line did not break. And gradually the English became aware that they were actually holding the French and forcing them back. The French had no room for all their heavily armoured men. They could not retreat, due to the press of men behind them, nor advance, due to the strength of the English ahead. So the French onslaught turned into a supply chain of victims as each man fell and left room for another cumbersome man to wield his sword against the English poleaxes. The English, still in a state of terror, killed every Frenchman they could see in a few crazed minutes of frantic, panic-stricken killing. For these few minutes, as the men in the central French battle pressed forward, those in the column attacking the king were simply pushed towards the English men-at-arms, who slaughtered them bloodily in a kill-or-be-killed frenzy. Indeed, the word 'kill' is the operative one in most accounts of this stage of the battle. 'No one was captured; many were killed,' commented one chronicler, continuing 'the English were increasingly eager to kill for it seemed there was no hope of safety except in victory. They killed those near them and then those who followed . . .'[139] Thus the French were pushed to their ignominious, bloody deaths in the mud.

When the French did stop pushing forward, it was not because of a general's command: the men at the rear were beginning to withdraw. This allowed the English men-at-arms with Henry to break through the central column of the vanguard. When that happened, all was suddenly confusion in the French army – there were no columns, no vanguard, no main battle, just a mass of desperate men fighting for their lives, or trying to surrender and being killed as they tried to give themselves up. Few Englishmen had time to take prisoners. It was at this point, when the English were making real advances into the French ranks that the intensity of the fighting around the king increased to an uncontrollable level. Some French knights – some French chronicles give the credit to the duke of Alençon – burst through and hacked their way towards the king. The king's bodyguard came under attack, and fell back. The king's brother, Humphrey, fell backwards under the force of the French onslaught, wounded in the groin, and was lying in a precarious position until Henry himself stepped forward and stood astride him, swinging his battle axe, fighting directly against the front rank of the enemy. In those long, exposed moments, while Henry fought in person, the French realised that the king of England was within their reach and redoubled their efforts to kill him. Someone – perhaps the duke of Alençon, or perhaps one of the eighteen men of the seigneur de Croy who had sworn to knock the crown from Henry's helmet – managed to break through and bring an axe down on his head. But they only succeeded in hacking off a portion of the gold crown; and as soon as the blow had landed the protagonist was beaten back by the knights who came to Henry's assistance, rescuing both the king and his brother in the same forward movement.[140]

This was the scene that confronted the duke of Brabant as he arrived now, about midday, having ridden hard from Lens, thirty miles away. He must have been exhausted. His horses must have been similarly exhausted. He stopped near a thicket and, seeing the dire situation in which the French army now found itself, realised that he had little time to prepare for battle. His armour, surcoats and accoutrements of war were all in his baggage many miles behind – so he had one of his chamberlains, Gobelet Vosken, take off his armour. He ordered one of his trumpeters to tear off the Brabant coat of arms hanging from his trumpet and, having made a hole in the material, put it over his head as a makeshift surcoat. Another trumpeter handed over the Brabant arms to serve as a flag for the duke's lance. Then, together with the few companions who had been able to keep up with him on the road from Lens, he yelled his war cry, 'Brabant! Brabant!', and set his spurs to charge into the fray.[141]

One chronicler stated that the duke of Brabant arrived with very few men – just those of his household – 'right at the point of defeat'.[142]

In one respect this was true; the balance had shifted. Many French were lying in the mud, bleeding to death, or trapped by their horses, or suffocating under a mass of bodies. Some were in flight. One of the duke's own men, John de Grymberg, who had the hereditary right to carry the Brabant banner, took one look at the battlefield and galloped as fast as he could in the opposite direction.[143] But according to the Burgundian writers, the rearguard – or some body of men-at-arms that amounted to a rearguard – was still mounted at this point. The French who had taken flight were regrouping in companies.[144]

In the confusion, few people could establish what was happening. This regrouping by the French seems to have coincided with an attack on the English baggage wagons. The way almost all the chroniclers describe this attack is as an opportunistic looting spree; but there are good reasons to believe it was a planned attack on the English, directed by a French commander. This would mean that the point at which the duke of Brabant arrived was not the end of the battle. It only appeared to be so with the benefit of hindsight.

When Henry had given the order to advance banners, he had also taken the precaution of ordering the baggage wagons to close up on the rear of the English army. Only ten men-at-arms and twenty archers had been guarding the baggage, so it fell to them and the carters to bring forward the wagons and the horses, and to help the sick and the injured, and to protect the pages stationed at the rear. They had only partially accomplished this task – if, indeed, they had started it. So the baggage and horses remained largely in and around the village of Maisoncelle. It was attacked here by Isambard d'Agincourt, Riflart de Clamance, Robinet de Bourneville and other men-at-arms, together with six hundred local men, mainly drawn from Hesdin.[145] The fact that men-at-arms were involved suggests that this was not meant to be a self-seeking raiding party, even if it turned into one. Nor was it without organisation – an attack on the English baggage had been envisaged in the first battle plan, drawn up at Rouen on or about the 12th. The French were attempting to do what the Black Prince had done at Poitiers when the battle was turning against him. On that occasion the prince sent a small body of men to unfurl his banner at the rear of the French army, and to attack the king of France's battle from behind; it only took a small number of troops on that occasion to cause confusion throughout the whole army. Such distractions could be decisive. But bringing them about was not easy. Hence local men, who knew the land, had been sent to find their way around to attack the English from behind. The problem was that they had taken too long. When they came across such rich plunder as the English horses and the king's jewels, they delayed further, to help themselves. They found a sword set in a jewel-encrusted gold scabbard that was supposed to have belonged to King Arthur, and two crowns of gold, the orb, many precious stones and a gold cross containing a piece of the True Cross. This failure to bring the baggage forward was a huge piece of luck, for the raid did not distract the English at all, and they continued to hold the French onslaught.[146]

By the time the men of Hesdin attacking the baggage wagons had been driven off, it was too late. The French line of defence was breaking up. The army was in flight. Those still mounted probably got away quite easily, as their opponents could not chase them and the archers had run out of arrows. But many – probably the majority – had lost their horses. Hundreds were lying under the huge piles of dead men, their limbs broken, or bleeding heavily from arrow wounds, or simply unable to extricate themselves from the piles or from under their dead horses. Those in armour knew their part was done. They could await discovery, and would in due course agree a ransom. For them there was no danger. Any wounded infantry on the battlefield knew their fate would be quite different; those who could still walk were no doubt trying to flee, or hide themselves as well as they could.

*

In London, shocking news reached the capital today, 'replete with sadness and cause of endless sorrow': there had been a great battle in which the English army had been defeated.[147] The particulars were shrouded in mystery; it was not even known whether the king had been killed or taken prisoner. No doubt Henry's brother, the duke of Bedford, and his uncle, Chancellor Beaufort, enquired of the mayor-elect what he had heard from merchants coming from France. But no further information was available.

*

It was about one o'clock in the afternoon. Henry was still anxious, lest the many men-at-arms who had fled managed to regroup and launch another attack; but most of the French had dispersed. Attention now turned to the piles of dead and wounded. The English pulled corpses off the piles, looking for lords trapped alive underneath. They checked the men lying in the mud. Lords and men-at-arms were dragged to their feet and forced to relinquish their weapons, their gauntlets and helmets; then placed under guard, to be led away by their captors. In this way, the marshal of France, the great Boucicaut, was captured by a humble esquire called William Wolf, and the belli-cose duke of Bourbon was taken prisoner by Ralph Fowne esquire. Sir John Gray took the count of Eu; Sir John Cornwaille captured the count of Vendôme. Ghillebert de Lannoy, chamberlain of the count of Charolais, was found amid a pile of dead men with a wound in his knee and another to his head. The duke of Orléans was pulled out from under a pile of dead men by Sir Richard Waller. The young count of Richemont had been covered in so much blood from the dying men on top of him that no one recognised the arms on his surcoat.[148]

These were the lucky ones. Those of no great value would have had their throats sliced open with a sword, or had a final vision of an axe suddenly coming down into their face. There were some exceptions. Two of the prisoners claimed by Lord Fitzhugh were a man-at-arms called Jean Garyn and his servant. The servant would normally have been despatched with a knife through his windpipe – but in this case his master was prepared to pay a ransom for him.[149] Some men managed to escape from the battlefield despite their wounds. Even then they had to hide themselves: they were liable to be killed by the local men, who hated the Armagnac army on account of the pillaging and rapes they and their communities had endured. If they found a defenceless man-at-arms they killed him and stripped him of his clothes and possessions.[150]

Suddenly, while the English were occupied taking prisoners, there was a shout of alarm: the French were about to launch a new attack. The chronicle of Ruisseauville claimed that this was due to Clignet de Brabant having rallied the remaining French men-at-arms. Basset's chronicle states the men had been rallied by Guillaume de Tybouville. Des Ursins' account states the new threat was not a case of men being rallied but the appearance of a wholly new force, led by the duke of Brittany. While we know this last suggestion is wrong – for the duke was still at Amiens – it was quite credible at the time; indeed we know that the seigneur de Longny was just three miles from the battlefield with the duke of Anjou's six hundred men-at-arms. Other writers assumed it was the arrival of the duke of Brabant that caused the alarm; and although the duke himself was probably already a prisoner, the rest of his men might have been spotted approaching the battlefield. What is certain is that the new threat was sufficient to cause Henry to panic. He ordered all the prisoners who were not of the royal blood to be killed immediately.[151]

Of all the events connected with Agincourt, this massacre is by far the most controversial. It causes anger and division among English and French historians even today.[152] Some have suggested Henry's order amounted to a war crime – and although the modern concept of war crimes did not exist in 1415, Henry's order was against contemporary morality, against the law of chivalry (which demanded that one spare one's prisoners), against Henry's own ordinances of war, and against Christian teaching. These prisoners were, after all, unarmed, fellow Christians, and had given themselves up. On the other hand, many historians have wanted to stress that Henry had no choice; he had to ensure that he won the battle and protected his men. This self-defence argument has two dimensions: first, that Henry could not spare the men to guard the prisoners because he needed every hand to fight the enemy; second, if he had not killed the prisoners they could have started to fight for their fellow Frenchmen. For the majority of English historians, still wedded to the post-Shakespearian 'great-man' view of Henry, this is the only way of presenting him: he made a hard decision in the nick of time, and saved his army.

In determining which line to tread between these two extremes – or, indeed, whether to accept one of the extremes – a number of points need to be carefully considered. The first is that we may dismiss the often-repeated notion that it was the attack on the baggage wagons that caused Henry to order the massacre. Although this is to be found in some fifteenth-century chronicles, this reflects an attempt in later years to shift the blame for the massacre on to the French looters. The vast majority of early accounts point to a second or regrouped army as the cause of alarm.[153] In addition, there is a logical point

ruling it out. Ghillebert de Lannoy wrote a memoir in which he
described being taken to a house with ten or twelve other prisoners,
after being pulled out of one of the piles of dying men.[154] There was
thus a considerable delay between the taking of prisoners and the
massacre: long enough to take the prisoners back to Maisoncelle to
lock them up in houses. As the baggage wagons were also still in
Maisoncelle, an attack by several hundred local men here cannot have
occurred so late in the day without considerable fighting: there would
have been enough armed Englishmen around to fight them off.
Certainly Isambard d'Agincourt and his men would not have had
unfettered access to the men-at-arms' horses and the king's jewels.
The attack on the English baggage belongs to the earlier phase of
the battle, while the main fight was still in progress, long before
Henry ordered the massacre.

How significant was the new threat? Three years after the battle,
Thomas Elmham wrote, 'there was indeed a great throng of people.
The English killed the French they had taken prisoner for the sake of
protecting their rear. Praise was given to God.'[155] Tito Livio Frulovisi,
writing many years later, also referred to large numbers of new men,
claiming that

> Henry immediately prepared to fight another army of the enemy, no
> less than the first. Considering that the English were exhausted by so
> long and hard a fight, and because they saw that they held so many
> prisoners – so many that they came to the same number as themselves
> – they feared they might have to fight another battle against both the
> prisoners and the enemy. So they put many to death . . .'[156]

These English statements about the arrival of a substantial new army
do not tally with the English and Burgundian eyewitness accounts.
They also clash with the French accounts, which associate the massacre
with the arrival of new forces. De Lannoy and Thomas Basin both
mention the arrival of the duke of Brabant in person as the cause –
though how much de Lannoy could have known, being locked in a
house in Maisoncelle at the time, is doubtful. And as we have seen
the duke of Brabant did not bring a numerous army; he had travelled
too fast for more than a few dozen men to accompany him on his
thirty-mile dash from Lens. It cannot have been the remainder of

The rue Vieille du Temple, Paris, where John the Fearless murdered the duke of Orléans on 23 November 1407. The rue des Blancs-Manteaux, along which the murderers fled, is by the no-entry sign on the far left; the rue des Rosiers is by the no-entry sign on the near right.

John the Fearless, duke of Burgundy. His achievements were few and his acts enormously divisive; but almost everything he did was surprising.

La tour Jean sans Peur, Paris. John the Fearless built himself a bed chamber and bathroom high above the ground, supported on massive stone columns, so he would be safe from assassination at night.

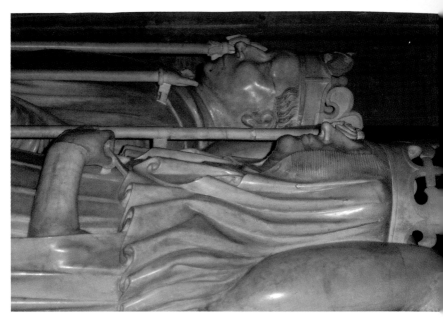

Charles VI, king of France. He reigned for more than forty years but suffered from a mental illness, allowing ambitious members of the royal family to vie with each other for power.

The keep of the Château de Vincennes, near Paris. A royal residence, largely rebuilt by Charles V. On 31 August 1422 Henry V died in a house at the foot of the great tower.

The duke of Berry, Charles VI's uncle. One of the wisest of the French royal dukes, he presided over the peace negotiations in Paris in 1415, even though he was seventy-four – unusually old for the middle ages.

View from the top of the keep of Portchester Castle, Hampshire, showing the harbour where the king's fleet gathered. Henry was at the castle from 29 July until he embarked for France on 7 August.

Harfleur. The River Lézarde used to run both through and around the town, where there was a fortified naval base. St Martin's Church was badly damaged in the siege that began on 17 August.

On the march from Harfleur to Calais, Henry had to pass several defensible towns and castles, such as this one, at Arques (now Arques-la-Bataille).

Thomas, Lord Camoys, who commanded the English left wing at Agincourt, and his wife, Elizabeth Mortimer. She was the aunt of the earl of March and the widow of Henry 'Hotspur' Percy.

Sir Thomas Erpingham. A veteran commander at Agincourt, Erpingham gave the dramatic signal for the English army to advance.

Michael de la Pole, earl of Suffolk, who died at the siege of Harfleur. Like other important casualties, his body was boiled and his clean bones sent back to England for burial.

The view from the left-hand side of the English position in front of Maisoncelle, looking north towards the position of the French army. The cross marking the site of the supposed French mass grave is in the small clump of trees in the centre.

The battlefield of Agincourt. This is the view towards Maisoncelle from the road a little way south of the supposed site of the French mass grave. The English would have drawn up across the horizon, near the trees in the distance.

Calais, from a drawing of 1535–50. Henry's numerous preparations for provisioning the town in early 1415 suggest that the embarkation of the army here was planned from the outset.

This letter from Henry, concerning the duke of Orléans and the security of the north of England, is widely believed to be in the king's own hand.

his men who were arriving, as they can hardly have travelled the thirty miles so quickly. However, even if it was the rest of the duke's men, then we must remember that he had undertaken to bring a total of 1,400 men-at-arms and six hundred crossbowmen in total – and some of them had travelled with the duke and some were already at Agincourt. So the largest new force that can have been seen approaching must have been considerably less than two thousand men, accompanied by fewer than a thousand pages. As the English had lost no more than six hundred men, the 'new army' cannot have amounted to more than a third of the English army. The same argument applies to the men of the duke of Anjou. If Henry ordered the massacre because of intelligence that the seigneur de Longny had a force of six hundred men-at-arms three miles away, then his decision was clearly an over-reaction. To constitute an imminent threat, the French 'new army' would have had to be both substantial and visible; but if any large, new force actually appeared *on the battlefield*, the majority of chroniclers would have noted its appearance. Not one does. Thus we may be confident that any 'new army' was distant from, as well as much smaller than, the English force, and did not push Henry into ordering the massacre.

The majority of accounts, including those of eyewitnesses, state that it was the regrouping of French men-at-arms that caused Henry to kill the prisoners. This is a far more credible explanation. A large body of men gathering on the actual battlefield would have constituted an immediate and serious threat. That it was a snap decision – albeit one taken in conjunction with leading members of the council – is made clear by the fact that it eventually proved an unnecessary precaution. In the end there was no second French attack. Nor can the massacre itself be said to have prevented that second attack, as it took place out of sight of the regrouping Frenchmen, in and around Maisoncelle.[157] It was thus a decision made suddenly, and unfortunately, in the face of a perceived imminent risk.

According to the author of the *Gesta*, the order to kill the prisoners was made as a result of the French 'rearguard' re-establishing their position and line of battle in order to attack. The official French chronicle, written by a monk of St Denis, vaguely parallels this, stating that a group of warriors on the edge of the vanguard made a movement to the rear to withdraw from the blind fury of the fighting, and that

their withdrawal triggered the massacre. Clearly this does not fit with
the time needed to take prisoners like de Lannoy from under the piles
of dead and remove them to a house to lock them up; but it tallies
in referring to a regrouping of men-at-arms at the rear of the French
army. If the Ruisseauville chronicler was correct in stating that it was
Clignet de Brabant who organised the regrouping, then this also tallies
with the official chronicle, as Clignet had led one of the first attacks
on the archers and must have withdrawn to re-organise his men. Finally,
and most crucially, the two Burgundian eyewitnesses, le Fèvre and
Waurin, state that the rearguard and 'centre division', which had previously been put to flight by Henry's main battle, regrouped and showed
signs of wanting to fight: 'marching forward in battle order'.[158]

In this last statement we have a version of events that is both
supported by the eyewitness accounts and consistent with the
chronology of events and the scale of imminent threat necessary to
provoke a sudden and (as it turned out) unnecessary massacre. But if
the above analysis leads us to an understanding of the circumstances
in which Henry made his decision – reacting to a large number of
men marching towards him across the battlefield, not a small second
army three miles away – it still does not allow us to say it was wholly
justified. How many men had regrouped? How many prisoners were
there? How real was this threat?

The key word in the account of Waurin and le Fèvre is 'marching'.
The French could no longer use their horses due to the large piles of
dead and dying men and horses that littered the battlefield. The narrow
shape of the field prevented the regrouped men from riding around the
piles of the dead in formation. One might add that, if the regrouped
men *had* been able to charge, there would have been no time for the
killing of the prisoners to be carried out. Thus we may be sure that the
regrouped force was on foot. It must have been numerous too, to consider
attacking the English again – at least as many men-at-arms as the 1,500
on the English side. But many French men-at-arms were dead, many
had been taken prisoner, and many had fled (the seigneur de Longny
encountered some of the latter, and they persuaded him also to flee).
The best-informed French chronicles mostly agree with the number of
fatalities around the four thousand mark – a figure that includes the prisoners now killed by the English. Even if three thousand men-at-arms
had actually fled, this still left two or three thousand men-at-arms possibly

rallying, and perhaps they still had some vestiges of the infantry and crossbowmen with them. Although the English had lost relatively few men – the chronicles of Ruisseauville and Monstrelet suggest six hundred English fatalities, and only le Fèvre and Waurin give a higher number (1,600) – they had run out of arrows. Hence, the advance of two or three thousand men-at-arms was a very serious matter.

The problems with this line of argument are the manner and scale of the killing. According to le Fèvre and Waurin, the Englishmen at first did not want to kill their prisoners, as that would render them worthless. This would be in line with English military tradition. At St-Cloud, when John the Fearless ordered all the prisoners to be executed for treason, the English had refused, saying that 'they had not come as butchers, to kill the folk in market or in fair' but to ransom them.[159] However, the very reluctance of the Englishmen to kill their prisoners at Agincourt suggests that a number were not convinced of the danger. As some of the prisoners were locked up in houses, like de Lannoy, this is not surprising. But when Henry realised his men had lost focus, and were more mindful of profit than their strategic position, he assigned the task to an esquire and two hundred archers, who set about cutting the prisoners' throats. Two hundred: if the action had to be done hastily, then two hundred men could not have quickly cut the throats of a much larger number of men in armour without risking being overpowered. That the matter was indeed a matter of urgency is clear from the account of de Lannoy – the house in which he and his companions were being held was simply set alight, so his fellow prisoners were burnt alive.[160] If, say, a thousand prisoners had been divided to be killed separately or in small groups, this itself would have taken time; in which case the two hundred archers might as well have guarded the prisoners as killed them. Unless le Fèvre and Waurin were completely wrong in their estimate of two hundred archers being assigned to the job, then it is simply not credible that there were more than three or four hundred prisoners at this stage of the battle – at the very most. The suggestion that there were thousands massacred is not only without direct evidence, it conflicts with the eyewitness evidence that we do have. In all probability, the majority of the four thousand dead Frenchmen were lying in the mud on the battlefield, and were not slaughtered in cold blood by the English; and lying there among them were the majority of the prisoners who were later found alive and eventually ransomed.

On this basis we can start to evaluate the second of the key strategic decisions that Henry made during this battle (the first being the order to advance). A mass withdrawal by the French men-at-arms took place, allowing the English tentatively to think they had won the day, and to start to take prisoners. They had gathered a few hundred French men-at-arms, who were disarmed and taken back to Maisoncelles – a process that must have taken at least half-an-hour, if not longer. The English were thus taken by surprise when the French, who had been regrouping on the far side of the field, perhaps in the vicinity of their camp, began to advance on foot in formation towards them. Realising the sudden danger, and probably aware that other French armies were in the vicinity, Henry had the task of bringing his arrowless archers to order, and found they were more mindful of profit than strategy. When they failed to respond to his immediate order to put the prisoners to the sword, Henry delegated the task to an esquire and two hundred men, while having the trumpets sound for the remainder to form up once more. The esquire and his men did their duty as quickly as possible, going to Maisoncelle and burning some men alive and cutting other men's throats. While the killing was in progress, it seems that Henry sent heralds to the advancing army asking them whether they meant to fight or whether they would leave the field.[161] It is likely that Henry told the advancing French that he had killed the prisoners, thereby removing one profound reason for them to renew the fighting, for many of the men-at-arms would have felt obliged to try to rescue their fellow men. As it was, they were too few in number to overwhelm the regrouping English, and lost the element of surprise in their long march over the fields. When told of the deaths of the prisoners, their resolution to continue the fight must have dissolved, and they dispersed.

The above allows us to understand the closing phase of the battle, and why Henry gave the order to kill the prisoners. It was not that there were so many he feared they might constitute a second front; it was because the regrouping French took him by surprise and he suddenly needed his men to concentrate once more on the battle, not on the value of their prisoners. There was also a strategic advantage in killing them. But although we may thus understand his decision, and why he made it, there can be no getting away from the fact that it was made in haste and was to his everlasting shame. If telling the advancing French that he had killed the prisoners was of strategic advantage, then he could have told them this without actually killing them. Better still he could have threatened to kill them. By all the standards of the time, the killing was an ungodly act, and no way to win the love or respect of the people whom he sought to rule as king.

★

The battle was over. According to Monstrelet, Henry summoned the French heralds to him, to ask them to whom the day belonged. The French and English heralds agreed that it was an English victory. Henry then delivered a speech, thanking God, and asking the name of the castle nearby. On being told it was Agincourt, he named the battle after the site – a scene famously repeated in Shakespeare's play. However, this dialogue was probably a literary device. The herald le Fèvre, in his account of the naming of the battle, fails to mention the presence of any heralds, French or English. He states Henry asked his fellow lords for the name of the castle, and named the battle after it. And even this detail is open to question. Henry would have known the name of the castle – he had been controlling the movements of thousands of men in the immediate area for the last twenty-four hours. Had he not known the name of the only visible castle, the most significant landmark near the battlefield, that would not have filled his commanders with confidence.

How long had the battle taken? Sources on the whole are keen to stress how little time it took. One chronicle – Ruisseauville – states that it was all over in half an hour; another, that of the count of Richemont, suggests less than an hour.[162] The author of the *Gesta*, who had been watching the whole battle from the back of the English lines, stated that it took two or three hours for the English to put the vanguard to flight.[163] The arrival of the duke of Brabant ahead of his men is perhaps the best indicator. Having heard about the battle at prime, and ridden thirty miles at the fastest speed possible, with men in armour along muddy roads, he cannot have arrived much before noon, even if he and his men had a change of horses. If the English advance took place at ten o'clock, and the vanguard had not quite been put to flight at noon, then probably another few minutes passed before the French were in flight, and it was not until one o'clock at the earliest that the regrouped French advanced and Henry gave the order for the prisoners to be killed.

It then began to rain again.[164]

Still Henry held his men in formation. Probably not until four o'clock did he return to Maisoncelle to dine.[165] His reason for holding his men there, in the rain, was not just defensive. He wanted them to be silent, and to reflect on the day, and to listen to him. He gave a speech – or again, more probably several speeches – in which he thanked them for their courage, and encouraged them to remember that day as a sure sign of the justice of his cause, and of the efforts he was making to recover the lands of his ancestors. He also told them not to be blinded by pride, or to attribute the victory to their own strengths but to acknowledge that all the credit for the victory belonged to God, who had given their small number victory over a larger army and laid low the French lords in their pride. Finally he urged them to be grateful that they had lost so few men.[166] He ordered that the bodies of the duke of York and the earl of Suffolk be boiled that evening, and their bones sent home to England to be buried in the places specified in their wills – York at Fotheringay and Suffolk at Wingfield. As for the rest of the English dead, which probably numbered six hundred, he ordered their bodies to be gathered and placed in houses and barns in Maisoncelle, and there burnt.[167] The army would march towards Calais in the morning. He did not have time to give the few hundred Englishmen who had died in his cause a Christian burial.

After Henry returned to Maisoncelle, and the army was told to stand down, archers crossed the battlefield stripping corpses of their armour. Where living men of rank were found, they were hauled back to the village as prisoners. In this way, although the soldiers had lost their first few hundred ransoms, they replaced those with almost everyone they could find alive. Contemporary English estimates of the total number of prisoners taken were between seven and eight hundred. The names of nearly three hundred prisoners are known.[168]

As they searched for prisoners, they found the bodies of the French lords, their ostentatious armour covered in mud, rivulets of rain running over the metal and their cold limbs. The most impressive suits of armour were the first to be looted. Very soon the corpses of the great lords of France were lying almost naked, in nothing but their linen underwear, soiled with mud and the contents of their bowels. Here lay the duke of Bar and his brother John; there the duke of Alençon. Here lay the counts of Vaudémont and Roucy; there lay the count of Marle and the seigneur of Grandpré. The archbishop of Sens had taken arms and fought with the secular lords: he too lay lifeless in the mud. The constable of France, Charles d'Albret, lay dead, and the seigneur de Bacqueville. So too did the seneschal of Hainault. The duke of Brabant lay some distance away from the battlefield, stripped of the armour borrowed from Gobelet Vosken. No one had recognised him; wearing a torn trumpet banner as a surcoat had made him appear most unlike a duke. Vosken too was dead. The duke's younger brother, Philip, count of Nevers, was also dead. All eighteen of the men of the seigneur de Croy who had sworn to knock the crown from Henry's head had died in the attempt. David de Rambures was dead, lying near the corpses of his three sons. Oudart, the seigneur de Renty, lay dead with two of his brothers. Four sons of Enguerrand de Gribauval were dead. Four thousand men were being stripped of their armour, their clothes and their dignity, and left naked in the mud. About 1,400–1,500 of them were lords, knights and esquires, including one hundred knights banneret. Probably half the French men-at-arms who fought in the battle did not leave it alive or were led away as prisoners of the English.[169]

At supper that evening, Henry directed that he should be waited on by the captured French princes. According to the chronicle of Ruisseauville, he asked them how the situation appeared to them. They had no option but to admit it constituted an English victory. On which note Henry began to preach about it not being an English victory but the work of God and the Virgin Mary, and of St George, because of the sins of the French, who had gone to war proudly, and raped both married women and young girls in the process, and stolen from the countryfolk and robbed churches. 'Look at my men,' declared Henry, 'they never mounted on women, nor robbed men or the Church'.[170] Another account has him saying that it was a great wonder that the French had not fared worse because it was evil and sin to which they had abandoned themselves. They had not kept faith or loyalty with any living soul in their marriages or in other matters. They had committed sacrilege in robbing and violating churches. They had taken by force all kinds of people, nuns and others. They had robbed the whole population and had destroyed them without cause . . .[171]

In the course of the evening some emissaries came to him from the French who had not been captured. They asked for permission to go among the dead and look for their lords and friends. Henry said that, because of the late hour, they could not; but they might the following day. According to the Ruisseauville chronicle, when this answer had been given, Henry ordered five hundred men to go among the dead with axes, to kill anyone who remained alive and to remove what armour they could.[172] This latter point may well be propaganda; for le Fèvre states that Henry, when told that his archers were taking the armour from the battlefield, ordered that no one should take more than he needed. The rest was to be placed in a barn with the collected bodies of the English dead, and burnt.[173]

Quite what the dukes of Orléans and Bourbon thought of this, as they waited on Henry at his table, stretches the imagination. That morning they had been preparing for a straightforward clearing up of the weakened English forces. The duke of Bourbon had been looking forward to this fight all year. The duke of Orléans had been appointed commander of the army. Then they had seen their army crushed, they had seen their friends, family and companions killed and the laws of chivalry flouted in a massacre of unarmed men. They had heard Henry lecture them on the morality of the French troops – as if he was doing God's work in invading the kingdom of France, destroying Harfleur, sending diseases throughout his own army, killing Frenchmen and leading his own people into battle in pursuit of a claim that they did not believe was justified. And on top of all this they must have wondered, why them? Where was the duke of Brittany? Where was the duke of Burgundy and his son the count of Charolais? Where were the king and the dauphin? Where was Tanneguy du Chastel? All of these men had purposely avoided the battle. The count of Charolais had been taken to Aire on his father's orders, and prevented from fighting. For the young duke of Orléans in particular it must have been a very bitter pill. The defeat would be portrayed by John the

Fearless as an Armagnac failure. He would be blamed. The rift in the kingdom of France, which had opened with John the Fearless's murder of Orléans' father eight years earlier, had culminated in a disaster of such magnitude that reconciliation was now impossible.

For Henry, the message of the day was a confirmation that God approved of him. If the French had died because of the mud, then it was so because God had made it rain, so he could show favour to Henry and punish the lustful, greedy, proud French. And although the army had not been exactly a royal one – the king of France had not been present, nor the dauphin – God had delivered him the victory over many members of the French royal family, Burgundians as well as Armagnacs. It served to justify his claim to the throne of France. Thus the day marked a turning point in his life for he was able to portray his victory as a miracle. It was later said that St George was seen at the height of the battle, fighting on the English side.[74] Men who were too weak to draw their bows before the battle miraculously found themselves able to draw and shoot with ease.[175] Chroniclers were encouraged to exaggerate the size of the French army and the numbers of dead, and to minimise the size of the English army. No English chronicler wrote about the hundreds of English dead – most state that fewer than forty Englishmen died. Their numbers were downplayed to enhance the miraculous dimension of the victory, and the names of many of those killed – even some of the knights – were erased in order to enhance the miraculous nature of the victory. So sure was Henry that the victory represented the benevolence of God that he ordered that the names of St Crispin and St Crispinian should be repeated to him in a Mass every day for the rest of his life.[176]

But when at the end of this long day, he finally slept, something essential had changed. Henry had demonstrated to his contemporaries that he had God's blessing in ruling by the sword. His divinely sanctioned victory meant that to carry on fighting was not only justifiable, it was God's work. He had to do it. He was God's instrument.

Saturday 26th

This morning Henry was up very early. He walked across the battle-field, looking at all the corpses. Where his men found Frenchmen alive, they either took them prisoner or killed them. Many Englishmen were amazed that so many of the corpses had already been stripped of all their armour and clothing. Between the pilfering of the local people and the looting of the English, the nobility of France had been left 'naked just like those newly born' in the mud.[177]

After the battlefield had been scoured for any more French lords who had survived the night, and who could be taken prisoner and ransomed, the battlefield was abandoned, and the naked bodies left where they were. Henry ordered the army to move out. It was forty-five miles to Calais. The loss of a large number of horses during the raid by Isambard d'Agincourt and the men of Hesdin meant that many men had to walk. Many of the lesser prisoners also had to walk. For those on foot, it was a three-day journey to Calais.

Sunday 27th

After the battle the servants and friends of the Frenchmen who had been killed returned to the scene. The duke of Brabant's body was found some way from the battlefield. It was naked and showed he had been wounded in the face and neck. He was one of the prisoners killed when the French had regrouped. Those who found the body were amazed that such an important man could be butchered in such a fashion. It seemed like an unchivalric, godless act. Sorrowfully they lifted his body and took it to Saint-Pol, where it was embalmed, ready for transportation to Brussels, to be buried.[178]

News of the defeat reached the king and dauphin at Rouen. The old king, despite his illness, must have recognised instantly that this was the most terrible news of his thirty-five years on the throne. He asked who had died. Seven royal cousins, he was told. The duke of Bar and his brother, the duke of Brabant and his brother, the duke of Alençon, the count of Marle and Charles d'Albret. One can imagine the silent moment of disbelief that followed, as each man came to the king's mind and then was acknowledged as dead. The messengers then told him the full extent of the tragedies – the deaths of the seigneur de Bacqueville, bearer of the Oriflamme, and Guichard Dauphin. The messengers went on to describe the particularly heavy casualties among the men of Hainault. The total of the

French dead, they told him, was four thousand men-at-arms, including 1,400 knights and esquires.[179]

Then they told him about the captured dukes of Orléans and Bourbon, and the counts of Vendôme and Richemont, and all the royal and noble prisoners.

Monday 28th

In London, news about Agincourt had yet to arrive. It was still believed that the English had been defeated, and the fate of the king was as yet unknown. Thus it was in a solemn mood that the people of London prepared to swear in their new mayor, Nicholas Wotton.

The campaign looked to have been a disaster. It had been costly and had succeeded only in taking one town, which could be expected soon to be retaken by the French. Many men had fallen ill. The earl of Arundel was not the only one to have died since being sent home sick. Sir John Daubridgecourt, a Knight of the Garter and a close friend of Henry's, who had attended the siege of Harfleur in the company of the incapacitated duke of Clarence, had also died.[180] If this news about an English defeat was true, and the king was dead, what was it all for? Henry had gambled with the legitimacy of his entire dynasty – everything his father and the Lancastrian family's retainers and supporters had risked their lives for – and lost. The thought must have occurred to many people at Westminster that, if the king had been killed in battle, it was to be expected that the Southampton plot would be praised and the earl of Cambridge seen as a martyr. In time someone else would try to rid England of its dubious dynasty.

*

Henry arrived at Guines, the English-held castle to the south of Calais, and there took up his quarters with his close companions and the most noble French prisoners. Here he held a council meeting to determine whether he should press on and try to extend the war. It occurred to him that, as he had a fully mobilised army with him, he might use it to attack the town of Ardres, which was not far away. There were other French-held forts in the Marches of Calais too; these perhaps were now vulnerable? But his councillors strongly advised him to desist from any further warfare. They told him that such victories as he had received, miraculous as they were, should suffice for his honour for the time being.[181]

Tuesday 29th

Early this morning a messenger arrived in the city of London, tired after riding all night from Dover. He had come from the English army. Far from being defeated, Henry had won a great victory over the French. Countless French men-at-arms lay dead, and the king was marching triumphantly, gloriously, through Northern France to Calais.

This amazing news – an incredible turn-around after the dismal news of four days earlier – was a cause for exultation. It was proclaimed publicly on the steps of St Paul's Cathedral that same morning. Chancellor Beaufort himself preached in the cathedral on the theme of the king's safe delivery. Throughout the city the bells were rung. Joyously the new mayor and aldermen, together with an immense number of the freemen of the city of London, went in procession on foot to Westminster, as if in a great pilgrimage, to give thanks at the tomb of St Edward the Confessor for the safe delivery of the king and the great victory he had won.[182]

Queen Joan, who attended the Westminster service, must have been torn. Her stepson the king had won a glorious victory; but her own sons, the duke of Brittany and the count of Richemont, had been on the opposing side. So too had her cousins, the duke of Brabant and the count of Nevers, and the dukes of Orléans and Anjou. What of them? She cannot have known whether her eldest son, the duke of Brittany, had observed the terms of his agreement with Henry and stayed away from the battle. Nor whether her younger son, the count of Richemont, had fought. So many of her French and Burgundian cousins had died, she was now told, as the bells rang out joyfully over Westminster.

*

The people of Calais had come a long way out of the town to greet Henry, so great was their joy at his victory. The priests and clerks of the town processed behind him as he approached the gates, singing *We praise you, O Lord*. The streets were filled with women and children as well as the men of the town, all shouting 'Welcome, our sovereign lord!' as he passed them with his councillors, leading the captured great lords of France.

Few of his men received such a cheerful reception. The archers were barred entry. The fear was that they would not pay for their food in Calais, and start looting. So they were forced to camp outside the walls. They were desperate for food. Those who had taken prisoners, hoping to ransom them for large sums, were forced to sell them to the men of the town or their social superiors in return for nourishment. Otherwise they could not find enough sustenance to keep themselves alive, let alone their prisoners. It was a bitter stage of the journey for 'the few' who had helped Henry to his victory.[183]

Wednesday 30th

In Bordeaux, the news of the victory was still far off: it would be another three weeks before they heard. The mayor and jurats of the city were still considering Henry's request for siege engines and cannon, contained in a letter he had sent them in June, which they had received on 20 August.[184] It is probable that they had only recently heard of the fall of Harfleur, and so were rethinking their decision to send the guns. After due deliberation, they decided that it was now too late in the season for them to respond helpfully, since the winter would soon be upon them and Henry's campaign would be halted for the winter months.[185]

Thursday 31st

The archers starving outside the walls of Calais were not the only unfortunate English victims of Henry's success. Recently a payment had been made for arresting and bringing John Foxholes (former chaplain of Lord Scrope), Thomas Blase (formerly Scrope's steward) and other men who had served in the household of the late Lord Scrope to Westminster.[186] Today they were led before the king's council to be questioned regarding the goods of the executed traitor. Henry's miraculous victory only heightened the sinful context of Scrope's actions in June. If some of the goods described in Scrope's will had been disposed of in accordance with Scrope's instructions, and not delivered to the king, then the lord's crime of treason had been compounded by his servants' disobedience.

The bishop of Durham and Chancellor Beaufort demanded to know from Foxholes and Blase into whose hands the goods and chattels of their late master had come. They said on oath that they knew nothing of the goods. They said that John Bliton wrote the late lord's will, and that he was now a clerk in the kitchen of the duchess of York. But they did not know what the will said or even where it was. The two bishops continued to interrogate them, knowing that men in Lord Scrope's service had concealed portions of his wealth from the royal coroner. They asked Thomas Blase how many vessels of silver Scrope had possessed. Six dozen and no more, he replied. Another man, Robert Newton, a canon of the king's chapel at Westminster who had previously served in Lord Scrope's chapel, was brought in and questioned as to how many copes Scrope had possessed. One hundred and twenty, he replied.[187]

The upshot of these interrogations is not known. Some of Scrope's possessions were later located at Pontefract Castle, and an order for them to be confiscated issued three weeks later.[188] Others had been found in London by yeomen of the king's chamber at the time of his arrest and handed over to the mayor.[189] But the difficulty in tracking the rest of Scrope's possessions suggests that some of his household servants kept their master's belongings, or disposed of them in their own way, rather than render them to the king. Later an enquiry would be made in Yorkshire as to the whereabouts of goods concealed from the king's officers.[190]

*

In Paris it was said that John the Fearless was pleased by the English victory at Agincourt, for this was a defeat for the Armagnacs.[191] The reality was nowhere near so straightforward. He had tried to play the kings of England and France off against each other and in one sense had succeeded: the Armagnacs had been defeated and humiliated in the most public way possible. But in another sense he had lost terribly, for he had lost both of his brothers: the duke of Brabant and the count of Nevers. Only five days earlier he had attended the christening of the count of Nevers' son. Many more Burgundians, including his vassals from Picardy and Flanders, lay dead in the mud at Agincourt.

Those who saw Agincourt as the work of God must have suspected that the deaths of both of John's brothers was divine retribution for John's murder of the old duke of Orléans in 1407. Medieval chroniclers and moralists liked to trace such full turns of the wheel of fortune. It was an obvious conclusion. It had been that killing that had started the whole civil war and had left France without clear leadership and vulnerable to Henry's ambitions. We have no way of knowing what Jacquette Griffart – the woman who had witnessed the murder – thought of the news of the battle and the deaths, but, if she was still alive these eight years later, the whole period probably struck her as a protracted and sickening bloody mess.

November

Friday 1st: Feast of All Saints

The formal beginning of winter: the season of the dead. Now the light was fading earlier in the afternoon, and the working day was shorter. At this feast of All Saints, men's and women's thoughts turned to the departed. People wore their mourning clothes. Traditionally men around the king wore black funeral robes, and the king himself put on a purple velvet gown. Churches burnt candles late into the night, and in some places torches were carried in procession. Many churches began ringing their bells after the evening service – and carried on ringing them until midnight – in an attempt to comfort the souls of the dead in Purgatory. Had you been walking through the streets of London on this moonless night, you would have heard the bells of many parish churches ringing out in the darkness, across the cold ground. Had you been living in a rural village, from the quiet of your bedchamber you may well have heard the distant ringing coming across the fields. Those in the churches, their faces solemn in the golden glow of candlelight, would have remembered and prayed for their lost family members – fathers, mothers, children, many of whom would have died before their time due to war, childbirth and disease.[1]

In Northern France the candles, prayers and commemorative ringing would have had an extra poignancy. Many of the Frenchmen slain at Agincourt came from the vicinity of the battle, from Artois, Picardy and Flanders. Whole families had been wiped out. In many cases three or four members of one family had proudly ridden out to join the army defending France one week earlier. Now their wives and mothers were bereft, lighting the candles and hearing the bells, not knowing whether their husbands died unshriven of their sins, and without hope of entering Heaven. Many others did not know whether their husbands and sons were alive or dead, hoping against hope that they had been taken as prisoners by the English to Calais. Many women would have understood their fate in terms of a sudden legal danger, realising that their lands would now fall to another member of their husband's family – a brother or cousin, perhaps – with the result that they stood to lose wealth, status and protection. Some women would just have looked at the late-night candles, simply trying to come to terms with the knowledge that the men to whom they had been closest in life were now among the dead, and that the sound of the bells ringing out from the church was their last communication to them.[2]

Saturday 2nd

At Perpignan, in Aragon, the Holy Roman Emperor was furious. He was seeing his entire mission to reunite the Church threatened by another self-interested pope.

Sigismund had left Constance on 17 July and headed towards Nice and then Narbonne. There, at the end of August, he had declared that his purpose in travelling was to secure the resignation of Benedict XIII, and he would wait there for the pope.[3] Benedict had travelled as far as Perpignan, where he had learnt that his protector, King Ferdinand of Aragon, was very sick. Although Ferdinand was still not yet thirty-five, he was dying – and his physicians advised him not to travel to Narbonne. Nevertheless Ferdinand disregarded their dire warnings and had himself carried on board a ship, by which he travelled to Perpignan, there to confront the recalcitrant pope. He invited Sigismund to join them; Sigismund obliged, arriving on 19 September. There had followed six weeks of bitter wrangling.

The problem was that Benedict had no intention of simply abdicating, as Gregory XII had done. Rather, like John XXIII, he wanted to use the negotiations to secure certain advantages. At one point he went so far as to suggest that he himself should personally choose the next pope for the whole Church. He also was keen that the council should be removed to a place more in keeping with his tastes – somewhere by the sea, perhaps. Eventually Sigismund demanded a simple abdication. It was refused.

King Ferdinand watched all this with the impatience of a dying man. He knew that Benedict would be lost without his support – only the Spanish nation was standing by him. But after the weeks of wrangling, Ferdinand could see that if he died of his present sickness, which was likely, it might be said of him that he had abetted Benedict in his determination to cling on to power. The time had come for a drastic measure. Yesterday Ferdinand had sent his son and heir, Alfonso, to Benedict with a summons and a demand that he resign the papal title immediately. Benedict had responded by publicly creating several cardinals and declaring he was going to move his papal court to Peñiscola, a castle on the south coast, south of Valencia. Clearly the purpose was to avoid further negotiations with Sigismund, Ferdinand or any part of the Church outside Spain. Today Ferdinand sent his son back to Benedict, to demand once more that he abdicate. The pope evasively answered that he would send his answer from Peñiscola.

This was the point at which Sigismund lost his temper. Hearing that Benedict had taken ship, he declared he was returning to Narbonne. He did not even bother sending a farewell salutation to Ferdinand but set out immediately for Serrano. Ferdinand hurriedly sent a solemn embassy after him, imploring him to return to Perpignan and promising that he would act in such a way as to satisfy him. But Sigismund had had enough. If Ferdinand wanted to communicate with him further, he would find him at Narbonne.

There could be no more hesitation for Ferdinand. Benedict was no longer worth supporting; he stood alone. All the other nations were insistent on the reunification of the Church. On top of this, if Ferdinand continued to hesitate, then he would jeopardise his agreement with Henry V, who had no regard for the French pope. Accordingly Ferdinand did as Sigismund requested. He sent further ambassadors to Narbonne to negotiate Benedict's abdication. At the same time he sent another summons to Peñiscola. The days of Benedict's pontificate were numbered.[4]

Sunday 3rd

The interim government in England was dealing with the routine business arising from the year's events. Following the death of Bishop Courtenay, the duke of Bedford and the council gave permission for the monks of Norwich Cathedral to elect a new bishop. And Edmund Mortimer, earl of March, was peremptorily reminded that he still owed a fine for his marriage. The first instalment of the 10,000 marks was set at £2,000 by the council; payment was required immediately.[5]

William Zouche, Lord Zouche of Haringworth, died today. He had been at Southampton at the time of Henry's departure, and had sat as one of the judges at the trial of the earl of Cambridge and his co-conspirators. Although it is not certain that he was on the campaign itself, the king had recently nominated him as a Knight of the Garter, to succeed the recently deceased John Daubridgecourt, who had contracted dysentery at Harfleur. He may therefore have been nominated in respect of his good service on the campaign. Either way, he was never installed in his seat of honour at one of the two round tables at Windsor. His place was eventually offered by Henry to the Holy Roman Emperor, Sigismund, who came to England to be installed the following year.[6]

Monday 4th

Relatively few noblemen gathered at Westminster for the parliament that opened today. Most secular lords were still with the king in France. Only nineteen were present in the Painted Chamber alongside the forty-nine prelates and approximately two hundred representatives of the shires and the boroughs to hear Chancellor Beaufort make the opening speech.

How different the mood would have been had the original news received at Westminster – about an English defeat – been true! As it was, Beaufort knew he had a willing and a thankful audience. With the duke of Bedford presiding, Beaufort declared emphatically that those present should 'honour the king, because he himself honours God Almighty above all others' and because the king had protected the rights of the Holy Church. Many of those hearing those words 'honour the king' would have understood the biblical connotation – from the first letter of Peter:

17. Honour all men. Love the brotherhood. Fear God. Honour the king.
18. Servants, be subject to your masters with all fear; not only to the good and gentle but also to the froward.

When Duke John acknowledged the rightness of these sentiments, and officially declared that parliament was in session, Beaufort continued in the same manner of lauding the king. This parliament, he declared, had been summoned for two reasons. He explained that both might be best understood through the biblical line from Judges 15: 11: 'as they did unto me, so I have done unto them'. Except in Beaufort's phrasing it became 'As he did unto us, so let us do unto him'.

The first reason why parliament should 'do unto Henry as he had done unto them' was that he had striven for good government. Ever since his coronation, the king had worked 'for the preservation and reform of the law, and for the peace of the land, and for the benefit, safety and tranquillity of all his subjects'. So they were obliged to offer Henry something in acknowledgement of his labours.

The second reason concerned France. Beaufort explained that although Henry had done all he could to secure a lasting peace and avoid the shedding of Christian blood, he had been unable to secure a restitution of his rights through diplomacy. Thus, 'forsaking all kinds of personal pleasure, comfort and safety, he undertook the same expedition and venture for that reason, believing wholeheartedly in his lawful quarrel and in Almighty God, in accordance with the words of the wise man who says, "strive thou for justice, and the Lord shall fight with you"' (Ecclesiasticus, 4: 33). And with that Beaufort went on to tell the story of the whole expedition – from the siege of Harfleur, 'the strongest town in this part of the world', which had been 'surrendered without the loss of life', to the march across Northern France.

Already the propaganda elements were in place – not the least of which was the obfuscation of the fact that forty or so men had lost their lives in pursuit of the king's ambitions at Harfleur. Beaufort went on to stress that Henry took only 'a small number of men in comparison with the might of his enemies' and that he

encountered and fought with a large number of dukes, earls, barons and lords of France and other lands and countries overseas, and with all the chivalry and might of France and the same lands and countries; and how finally, with the Almighty's help and grace, all the French were defeated, taken or killed, without great loss to the English; and how he, after such a glorious and marvellous victory, has now arrived safely at his said town of Calais with his men and prisoners, praise be to God, with the greatest honour and gain that the realm of England has ever had in so short a time.[7]

Having reminded all those present of the drama of the expedition, and the courage of the king, and above all else the judgment of the Almighty, Beaufort then delivered the rhetorical flourish, repeating 'as he did unto us, so let us do unto him'. He declared that this glorious victory was just the beginning, and that without their continued help, the honourable and profitable expedition would be unable to continue. It was the duty of each and every man present at that parliament to consider how he might make provision for the continuation of the king's military success.

It was a recipe for an ongoing war of aggression. But in the euphoria of the moment, that was exactly what the English parliament wanted. Nothing illustrates better how Henry was a man of his time than the ecstatic reception of the news that the English were going to sustain the war effort in France, on a permanent basis. The English parliament seems to have forgotten that the war aims did not extend beyond the king's dynastic security and personal pride.

Wednesday 6th

Beaufort had concluded his opening address on the 4th with an exhortation to the commons to elect their Speaker immediately, and to present him the following day. There was a delay. But today the commons presented Sir Richard Redman, the duke of Bedford's own councillor. It was a tacit acquiescence of Henry's triumph over parliament as well as over the French nobility. Whatever the king's uncle and brother asked for would be granted.

In the meanwhile the government continued to support the king at Calais. An order was issued from Westminster that no corn should be exported to any port on the continent except Calais or Harfleur.[8]

Friday 8th

The crimes of the earl of Cambridge, Sir Thomas Gray and Lord Scrope assumed a different complexion in the light of Henry's victory. Any public belief in Scrope's innocence was eradicated by the judgment of God in Henry's favour. In that sense Agincourt acted as a sort of baptism in which all Henry's past sins and errors were wiped clean away, and all his decisions justified – however doubtful they may have seemed at the time. Henry's malicious propaganda, concerning the attempt on his life and Scrope accepting bribes from the French, was accordingly accepted throughout the kingdom. Members of Parliament were left in no doubt that Scrope's execution was entirely justified.

The confirmation of the judgments was the business of today's parliament. The confessions of each executed man were read out, and the lords declared that the judgments were all good, just and lawful. The prelates also supported the judgments, in case any trace of guilt remained attached to Henry's name for acting in such a ruthless manner. Every effort was made to present Henry as a scrupulously pious and God-fearing man.

Aside from the business of parliament, the royal council ordered that the prior of the House of Jesus of Bethlehem – Henry's new Charterhouse at Sheen – be paid £20 for the new works he had undertaken there. Presumably finances for this project were limited by the war effort; work was still underway two years later.[9]

Monday 11th: Feast of St Martin (Martinmas)

The feast of St Martin was an especially carefully observed feast. It fell at a date coinciding with several key moments in the agricultural calendar. The first snows could be expected to fall from this date. Those animals that were not going to be fed and kept through the dark months were singled out and slaughtered. Pigs were held down and bled to death slowly, then butchered and salted down for the dark months ahead. Bullocks were likewise felled; and sheep, goats and geese too. It was thus a day of plenty in many larger households: there was more than enough meat to go around and gallons of wine, for St Martin of Tours was the patron saint of vintners, and the day marked the occasion for tasting the new vintage. In addition, Martinmas was still considered the last great feast before the long period of abstinence which was Advent. There was a folklore element to the day too: the weather conditions were a sign of the weather for the rest of the winter – snow on Martinmas was thought to indicate a mild Christmas. Finally, St Martin was famous for cutting his cloak in half to share it with a beggar; hence it was a day when even the poorest people could expect their wealthier neighbours to be generous.

*

At Calais it was the day for the prisoners from Harfleur to present themselves. De Gaucourt, d'Estouteville and the other knights and gentlemen whom Henry had temporarily released thus gathered in the town.

When they had sworn their oaths at the end of September, Henry's representatives had told them that if a battle had been fought before Martinmas, then they were simply to pay their ransoms. They were only required to submit to imprisonment again if no battle had been fought. On account of this assurance, many turned up expecting to pay a sum of money and then leave as free men, after swearing never to fight against the king of England again. However, Henry declared that if they had previously heard that they would be able to leave freely, they had been misinformed. They were now his prisoners once more.

For Raoul de Gaucourt, who was still very ill, this was a bitter blow. They had done the honourable thing and fulfilled their vow to submit; but Henry saw no reason to observe his side of the bargain. He was particularly harsh with de Gaucourt himself. Henry declared that 140 or 160 Englishmen had been captured by the French in the course of the campaign, and if de Gaucourt wanted to be a free man again, he should set about ransoming all the Englishmen who were left languishing in French gaols. The men who had pillaged the English baggage train at Maisoncelle during the battle of Agincourt had looted a number of precious items, all of which Henry wanted back: de Gaucourt was to arrange for their return. Henry also told de Gaucourt that he must provide two hundred casks of Beaune wine, to be sent to him in London. And all this despite de Gaucourt technically being the prisoner of Sir John Cornwaille.

De Gaucourt went to the French noblemen imprisoned at Calais and asked for advice. They told him to do what Henry asked, otherwise he risked spending many years in an English prison. De Gaucourt accordingly asked the king for permission to leave Calais and arrange all the things Henry had requested. He paid the ransoms of all the English prisoners he could find – 120 or 140 of them. He redeemed all the jewels he could trace, and sent them to Henry in London. He also sent the Beaune wine. But although the total cost of all this was in excess of 13,000 crowns (about £2,167), Henry did not remit de Gaucourt's ransom, or allow him his freedom. When de Gaucourt came to England he found that he still owed Sir John Cornwaille his full ransom of 10,000 crowns, and would remain his prisoner until it was paid in full. Despite fulfilling his vows, and despite Henry's own claim to be the protecting sovereign of France and its subjects, de Gaucourt – one of the founders of the Order of the Prisoner's Shackle – remained a prisoner for many years to come.[10]

Most great medieval kings respected the courage and resilience of their adversaries. If they vanquished them, treating them well simply enhanced their chivalric standing. But as far as we can judge, Henry did not see the French knights in a chivalric way. He saw them in a religious context – as the losers in a religious war, to be dealt with according to the law of Deuteronomy in the most extreme situations. With regard to de Gaucourt personally, Henry probably thought he was being merciful by letting the man live. From a more objective point of view, he cheated him. After defending Harfleur so long and so bravely, de Gaucourt deserved better.

*

The death of Sir John Chidiock at the siege of Harfleur had meant the family estates stood to be inherited by his fourteen-year-old heir, John. Custody of these manors was granted to Edmund, earl of March, presumably as compensation for his expenditure on the campaign. Clearly his involvement in the earl of Cambridge's plot had not lost him all favour, even if he did still have to pay the 10,000 marks fine for arranging a marriage without Henry's approval.[11]

Tuesday 12th

In line with the chancellor's announcement to parliament that the government would seek a large quantity of money to pay for the ongoing war, the duke of Bedford ordered the archbishop of York to hold a convocation of the clergy of his province before the next 20 January. The convocation of Canterbury was due to meet on the 18th of this month. The clergy of the two provinces were expected to grant an extra subsidy to pay for the next phase of military operations. No doubt many of the spiritual and secular lords hoped that this taxation meant that the loans they had made to the crown would be repaid sooner rather than later. In reality it would be years before any of them were fully recompensed, and many were never repaid.[12]

Only one statute seems to have been enrolled in this parliament – unsurprisingly, given the king's absence. It too concerned money. Foreign coins that had previously been forbidden or ruled illegal tender were not to be imported into the realm. Presumably the thinking was that the silver content of English coins had to be maintained at a high level, in order to preserve the value of the currency. There was a danger that the value of the foreign coins would outweigh that of the English ones, which had been reduced in weight in 1412 in order to raise money for the treasury.

Another opportunity to gain a large sum of money easily was recognised in reversing a piece of legislation that threatened Welsh landowners. After the revolt of Owen Glendower in 1400 the English parliament had forced Henry IV to pass more and more extreme anti-Welsh legislation. Now, with Glendower's revolution a spent force and the man himself dead, there was less danger. The government therefore issued a proclamation that, in return for a payment of £1,000, the lands of Welsh tenants of the king would not escheat to the crown but would pass directly to the heirs, according to Welsh law.[13]

Wednesday 13th

This, the tenth day of the parliament, was the last. It thus became the shortest parliament in medieval English history. It had served its two major functions: to ratify the king's action at Southampton against the conspirators and to secure an advancement of more money to pay for the expenses of fighting in France. By the end of the day the members had agreed to bring forward the collection of the second instalment of the large tax granted in November 1414 by two months. They had also granted a further tax of a tenth and a fifteenth and declared that the king might receive the wool subsidy and various other customs dues for the rest of his life without having to ask parliament. In reality, the grant of the wool subsidy was a matter of routine, so this is less generous than it at first appears; however, it was very unusual to see members of parliament voluntarily giving up some of their hard-earned rights. This, combined with the grants concerning the increased taxation, is a reflection of the euphoria that the news of Agincourt generated among the English landowning classes.

The duke of Bedford made one exception to this general subsidy of a tenth and a fifteenth. The inhabitants of the most northerly counties of Cumberland, Westmorland and Northumberland were to be exempt from liability as they had suffered 'yearly' attacks, their lands being repeatedly 'burned, despoiled and destroyed by the sudden invasions of the king's enemies of Scotland'. They could hardly be expected to pay for the king's war in France when he was failing to defend their lands in England.[14]

Friday 15th

In Paris the council had spent the last two days in feverish discussion concerning the destruction of the people and dignity of France by marauding men-at-arms, and the chaotic finances of the realm. The intention had been to come to some sort of resolution yesterday concerning future action; but that had proved impossible. So the debate continued today. Five or six masters of the council were deputed to draw up instructions that would govern an embassy to go to the king at Rouen. The purpose of the mission was to draw the king's attention to the problems his people were facing. They also were to outline a solution: a series of *ordonnances*, or regulations for the government of the kingdom, together with certain proposals for the reorganisation of the kingdom's finances.[15]

There was good reason for the councillors to be concerned. John the Fearless was planning to advance on Paris. Distraught and angry at the loss of his two brothers and many of his vassals, and quick to blame the Armagnac leadership, he had set out on the 5th from Dijon and arrived at Châtillon-sur-Seine on the 8th. There he had waited a week, conferring with his council and agents in Paris, who no doubt helped foment the stories that he was about to march on the city and liberate the people from the oppression and incompetence of the Armagnacs. The Burgundians in Paris were furious that the Armagnac government had allowed the royal troops to pillage their fellow Frenchmen in Normandy, and commit many rapes in the process, while the English were said to have been relatively abstemious on both accounts.

Henry's propaganda was working as effectively in France as in England. Despite the shared disaster of Agincourt, the rift between the two warring French sides was as deep as ever.

Saturday 16th

Henry sailed from Calais. In the course of crossing the Channel there were terrible gales. A snowstorm blew up, and the fleet was scattered. Two ships foundered with the loss of all hands; Henry himself did not reach Dover until nightfall. It would have been ironic in the extreme if Henry's own ship had foundered, and people saw God's judgment damning him immediately after he himself had seen his victory at Agincourt as a sign of God's approval. But as things turned out, Henry and his ship survived, and so God was deemed to have acted to preserve the king of England against the elements, thus further underlining Henry's divinely approved position.[16]

Partly due to the storm and partly due to the sheer number of troops awaiting passage across the Channel, many men had some days to wait before they saw the white cliffs. It took more than a week for all the men, horses and prisoners to be ferried back to Dover. Although Henry made provision for each man's voyage – allocating a sum of 2s per man and 2s per horse – the campaign was deemed to have ended when he set foot back on English soil. Even those who had to make their way back to the north or far west of England saw their pay come to an end today. Later they would petition the king for their eight days' wages: their request met with the terse 'the king does not wish it' in reply.[17]

Henry granted the keeping of Louis, count of Vendôme, to Sir John Cornwaille, the man who had originally captured him.[18] Cornwaille was amassing the largest collection of prisoners of all the English lords, dealing with French knights as if they were so many business assets. On the day of the battle itself he had purchased Ghillebert de Lannoy from his captor; at Calais he had bought many more prisoners, including Raoul de Gaucourt and Jean d'Estouteville. Cornwaille had no intention of allowing such men to remain in France to find their ransoms; he had them shipped back to England with him. De Lannoy, for example, could be expected to provide 1,200 crowns (about £200); he was too valuable to risk losing. Cornwaille held de Gaucourt and d'Estouteville for ransoms of 10,000 crowns (£1,666 13s 4d) each, regardless of the 13,000 crowns de Gaucourt had laid out meeting Henry's fraudulent requirements for his freedom.[19]

Sunday 17th

Henry made his way from Dover to Canterbury Cathedral, where he arrived this evening. He planned to stay two days in Canterbury, no doubt spending the following day attending Mass in the cathedral and paying his respects at the shrine of St Thomas of Canterbury and the tombs of his father and great-uncle, Edward of Woodstock (the Black Prince).[20] With Harfleur and Agincourt under his belt he could feel he was fit to be in their company. He had equalled their achievements. One suspects that with regard to his father, with whom he had never had an easy relationship, there was a personal score that had been settled by his proving himself on the Agincourt campaign.

Tuesday 19th

Archbishop Chichele had been at Canterbury to welcome Henry on his arrival yesterday.[21] Presumably he left Henry today to hurry back to London to attend the convocation at St Paul's. The more Henry's victory could be portrayed as a miracle, the easier it was to justify using the Church's money to fund his ongoing war. And the more Henry was dependent on the financial support of the Church, the less likely he was to listen to the reformers in parliament who, since the early years of his father's reign, had called for the Church to return to a state of poverty, with its property being confiscated and distributed by the government.

There was no problem persuading the clergy to give the king money. In addition to the tenth of their income that they had already agreed to give Henry at the next feast of the Purification (2 February 1416), they also granted two further tenths, to be paid at the next two feasts of St Martin (11 November 1416 and 1417). These grants were even to include benefices that normally were exempt from taxation. However, at the request of Adam Usk, Welsh benefices were excluded, as the war with Glendower had left them much the poorer.[22]

Wednesday 20th

Leaving Canterbury yesterday, Henry travelled on to Rochester. Along the way he made various gifts and grants. These were not great rewards for fighting on the campaign; rather they were tokens of the king's appreciation of the services performed by relatively unimportant figures. Henry gave Thomas Rugge two tuns of wine per year, together with two bucks and two does from the forest of Kingswood by Bristol.[23] And he granted to Sir Edward Courtenay the keepership of the New Forest, which the late duke of York had enjoyed.[24]

Back at Westminster, the victory of Agincourt had encouraged William, Lord Ferrers of Groby, to lend the king 500 marks. Provision was made for his repayment at a future date. The business of shuffling money around in order to pay for the next campaign was already underway.[25]

Thursday 21st

Henry personally authorised the granting of letters of protection for John Rippon, abbot of Fountains, returning to the council at Constance.[26] Although the main focus of the council's activities was now on the emperor at Narbonne, and the abdication of Benedict XIII, there were still many prelates at Constance discussing the reform of the Church. These discussions were taking place behind closed doors. As far as Ulrich Richental could see nothing new happened in all the time the emperor was away. All he noticed was that there was a procession and Mass at the cathedral every Sunday and the secular lords present held many jousts and tourneys 'and danced afterwards with the ladies'.[27] But on this very day a session of the council was being held to discuss a disagreement between the bishop of Trent and Frederick, duke of Austria. The latter had confiscated the church and city of Trent and its hinterland and, as there was no pope to whom to make recourse, the bishop appealed to the council.[28] To all intents and purposes the council had become the pope. For this reason it was necessary for Henry to keep up the attendance of the few English prelates there who constituted the English nation.

*

A writ was sent today to Robert Waterton, constable of Pontefract Castle, to confiscate all the goods of Henry Scrope that could be found in that castle.[29] More evidence concerning Lord Scrope's income had recently been found in York, in the form of documents concerning the value of his manors; these were now brought to London by John Grenewode, valet to Scrope's receiver.[30] Gradually the servants of the late Lord Scrope were being forced to give up the secrets of their lord's wealth.

Friday 22nd

There was more bureaucratic tidying for the council to see to before the king's return. At Westminster a commission was issued to Sir Humphrey Stafford, Sir John Moigne, the constable of Corfe Castle, the sheriff of Dorset and two other men to make enquiries as to which townships and tithings in the Isle of Purbeck were bound to keep nightly and daily watches of the coast, and to certify to the king the names of those who had refused, as a result of which various subjects of the king had been kidnapped.[31] Who had done the kidnapping is not clear, but it seems there may have been French reprisal attacks, in the manner of the old 'piracy war' of the previous decade. A failure to guard the coasts after Henry's emphatic orders on this matter, issued on 2 August, could not go uninvestigated.

Saturday 23rd

The traditional place for greeting the most important visitors to London was on Blackheath. The done thing was to go out to meet them – the further you travelled out from the city, the greater the honour to the visitor. It was on Blackheath, four miles from the city, that Henry IV had met the emperor of Byzantium in 1400. Similarly, the mayor and aldermen of London had gone out to Blackheath to welcome back Henry IV and his new wife in 1403, on their return to the capital after their marriage at Winchester. Now it was time again for the Londoners to go out to meet their king – 'whom God had marvellously and miraculously in his clemency led back in triumph from a rebellious and uncontrollable people'.[32]

Citizens were up as soon as it was light, all eager to see the king. The mayor and twenty-four aldermen dressed in scarlet; lesser individuals wore red gowns with parti-coloured hoods of red and white (according to the *Gesta*) or black and white (according to Adam Usk). Thousands of men and women gathered – twenty thousand according to one author, ten thousand according to another – and many of them were on horseback. Men of various trades wore distinct badges, and waited at the traditional place on the common for the king, who was coming from Eltham Palace. At about ten o'clock in the morning they saw him approaching, dressed in purple robes. They readied themselves, lining his way. Behind him rode the most important of the French prisoners – drawn behind him in a sort of Roman triumph. The mayor greeted the king, and thanked him for his labours on behalf of the public, and congratulated him on his success, giving thanks and honour to God for the victory. After this the citizens hastened back joyfully to the city to join in the various processions and celebrations for the king's arrival.

The Londoners saw the return of the king as a chance to make an impact of their own, and to reaffirm the bond between their city and the crown. They had put up a considerable sum of money towards the expedition and they wanted to be able to celebrate its success as much as the king. So when Henry came to the tower guarding the approach to London Bridge he found it guarded by the figures of a giant man and a giant woman, each taller than the walls of the city. The male giant held the keys of the city in his left hand and a great axe in his right; the female giant wore a scarlet mantle and jewellery; and the pair of them appeared to be looking out for the king's return. All around them, in and on the tower itself, were minstrels playing trumpets, horns and clarions. The royal arms were hung out from poles projecting from the walls. One wall had the words *Civitatis Regis Iusticie* (City of the King of Justice) painted on it.

As the royal cavalcade neared the centre of London Bridge, where there was a drawbridge, Henry saw a pair of tall pillars. Each one was built of wood, covered with linen, and painted to resemble building blocks of white marble and green jasper. At the top of the one on the right was a large antelope, standing erect, with a shield bearing the royal arms suspended from its neck, and with its right hoof extended, holding a royal sceptre. On the left-hand pillar was a rampant lion, holding a staff and the royal standard. Proceeding onwards, at the exit from the bridge, was another wooden and painted linen tower; this one had a statue of St George in armour set into a niche above its arch, with the arms of St George displayed on all sides. The statue held a sword in one hand; and from his left hand a scroll hung down with the motto: *Soli deo honor et gloria* (To God alone, honour and glory). Above the niche containing the statue of St George was inscribed the motto *Fluminis impetus letificat civitatem dei* (The force of the river makes glad the city of God), and above that, on top of the linen-covered tower, stood a line of spears and flags displaying the royal arms. In the house directly adjacent was a choir of boys dressed as angels, in pure white gowns and with wings, their hair entwined with laurel, all singing together an anthem – 'Blessed is he who comes in the name of the Lord'.

On went the procession, along the old Roman road through the city that is now Gracechurch Street, past cheering and waving crowds. Fathers and mothers held up their children to see the king. So many people leaned out of the windows of houses you might have thought that the citizens were staying indoors; yet many more people were in the streets, making it difficult for the riders in the procession to pass. Aqueducts had been set up to run with wine, and men and women drank freely. Yet in all this Henry progressed with a cold humourless face, as if none of it moved or delighted him.

When the king turned left into Cornhill, he saw that the tower of the water conduit there had been covered in crimson cloth, like a tent. From the centre it stretched out to the tops of staffs arranged around it; these staffs were also wrapped in crimson cloth. Here, encircling the tower, hung the coats of arms of St George, St Edward the Confessor, St Edmund and the arms of England. And above it all, between escutcheons of the royal arms, was written this quotation from Psalm 20, verse 8: 'Seeing that the king hopes in the Lord and in the mercy of the Almighty, he shall not be moved' – a fitting epithet, considering Henry's determination to lead his army to battle, trusting that God would deliver him victory. Above these, staffs bore flags and coats of arms. Under an awning, at the foot of the tower, stood a number of old men with white hair, dressed as Old Testament prophets, their heads wrapped in gold and crimson turbans. They released a flock of small birds from their cages as the king approached; they flew around the king, and some landed on him, sitting on his shoulders even, before flying away. As they did so, the prophets sang Psalm 98: 'Sing to the Lord a new song, Alleluia, for His deeds are marvellous, Alleluia'.[33]

From Cornhill the procession progressed through the crowds: first into Poultry and then straight on, into Cheapside. Coming to the great conduit in the middle of the street, Henry found the tower turned into another pavilion, like that in Cornhill. This one was of green cloth, decorated with shields bearing the city's arms. As with the Cornhill conduit tower, the ramparts were decorated with staffs bearing flags and coats of arms; and under the awning at the base were twelve old men dressed as the apostles, and twelve dressed as past kings of England, with the names of the apostles and kings written before them. As the king approached they burst into song, singing the words of Psalm 43, verse 8: 'For you have saved us from those who afflict us, and have saved us from those who hate us'. They presented him with baskets of wafers intermingled with leaves of silver, and gave him wine that ran from the pipes of the conduit, in emulation of Melchizedeck, king of Salem, in the Old Testament.[34]

The king, his companions and his prisoners rode further along Cheapside. Normally they would have seen the great Eleanor cross in the middle of the wide street, erected by his ancestor Edward I in memory of his first wife Queen Eleanor. Today there was no cross to be seen. Instead a wide, three-storey wooden castle crossed the crowded street, reaching from St Peter's Church to the other side. It had timber towers, vaulted arches and ramparts, and the linen-covered walls were painted to resemble porphyry, marble and ivory (according to Usk) or white marble and green and crimson jasper (according to the *Gesta*). Some of the vaulted arches were at ground level, so that men could ride through; others were at gallery level. Angels, singers and organs stood in the arches, and music filled the air. Above them were written the words *Gloriosa dicta sunt de te, civitas dei* (Glorious things are said of you, city of God), and above that, at the very top, where the ramparts were, hung the arms of St George, the royal arms, and the arms of the Holy Roman Emperor. In front of the whole edifice was a great gatehouse, joined by a bridge to the main castle: over this bridge a choir of beautiful maidens processed 'very chastely adorned in pure white cloth and virgin attire', singing in English, 'Welcome Henry the Fifth, king of England and France'. Boys dressed as angels above them joined in the chorus, and, as they passed, six important citizens stepped towards the king carrying two basins of gold containing a thousand pounds in gold coins, which they offered to him.

Passing under this great castle Henry was welcomed by more crowds on the far side. Even here men and women were leaning out of windows, and standing in the streets. Some were hurrying along ahead of the king, wanting to see each part of the spectacle. As the author of the *Gesta* noted,

> so great was the throng of people on Cheapside, from one end to the other, that the horsemen were only just able to ride through. And the upper rooms and windows on both sides were packed with some of the noblest ladies and womenfolk of the kingdom and men of honour and renown.[35]

Ahead of them, where Cheapside met the churchyard of St Paul's, there was another conduit; this too had been turned into a fantastic building with arches and niches. Here more girls dressed in virginal white, and wearing symbols of chastity, blew gold dust from gold chalices over the king as he passed. Above them, at the top of the tower, was a sky-blue canopy on to which clouds had been painted; it was supported by four gold angels; above it stood the figure of a gold archangel – and the whole canopy covered a magnificent figure representing the sun in majesty. Drums beat around the base, the virgins sang, musical instruments accompanied them, and boys dressed as angels danced around. The motto on this tower read simply: *Deo Gracias* (Thanks be to God).

As the two most detailed descriptions of all these scenes and displays make clear, the euphoria of the Londoners was beyond anything that anyone could remember. 'No one could recall there ever having been a more noble array or greater assembly in London,' commented the author of the *Gesta*. And yet Henry proceeded to ride through all this exultation not with a smile on his face but 'with an impassive countenance and at a dignified pace'. His progress was slow and solemn, his mood that of silently pondering something. He clearly did not see it as an opportunity to show off, despite wearing imperial purple. He rode from Cheapside and was greeted by twelve bishops, all wearing their mitres; he dismounted, and entered St Paul's Cathedral. At this point we may begin to see why he was so solemn. The last time he had been here, on 15 June, he had been accompanied by his brothers and uncles and his closest friends. His brothers were still alive, so too were his uncles; but of his four closest friends, only the earl of Warwick was still alive. Edward, duke of York, was dead. So too were Thomas Fitzalan, earl of Arundel, and Richard Courtenay, bishop of Norwich. York and Arundel had both been with him the last time he had entered this cathedral.

The bishops led Henry through the nave of St Paul's up to the high altar. There he made an offering in memory of the departed. He made another at the shrine of St Erkenwald behind the high altar, and another at the Holy Cross. No doubt he paid his respects at the tomb of his grandparents, John of Gaunt and Blanche of Lancaster, which was nearby. He seems to have asked that a solemn funeral Mass be held in the cathedral for the dead on both sides who had been killed at the battle of Agincourt. Then he went out into the churchyard, where he had tethered his warhorse. He mounted it, and rode with his knights back to his palace of Westminster.[36]

Much to his astonishment, when he reached Westminster he was greeted by a huge crowd of people there too. The abbot and monks met him and led him in procession into the abbey, to pay his respects

at the shrine of St Edward the Confessor and the tombs of his ancestors, including that of his inspiration, Edward III. After that, he went
back to the palace, to escape the celebrations and hubbub.

*

At Dover, the boats carrying the last archers and men-at-arms who
had fought at Agincourt finally came into port. The horses were craned
off the boats in the cold, and the men set foot again on English soil.
Their pay had stopped a week ago, so now they needed to get back
to their homes as quickly as they could. For many of the archers,
perhaps the majority, travelling back to Cheshire, Lancashire and the
other northern counties, much of their pay would be spent just getting
home. They would have to ask for accommodation and food at monasteries. Hopefully the kingdom's exultation at the news of the victory
meant they were welcome, and could buy a bowl of pottage and some
bread in return for their stories of the campaign.[37]

*

At Bordeaux, the seneschal and Jurade finally heard about the victory,
four weeks after it took place.[38] They probably had mixed feelings.
The people were ordered to make processions to celebrate the great
victory of their king; but the mayor and jurats cannot have been
neglectful of the fact that they had failed to send the king the siege
engines and support he had requested. The outcome of the king's
campaign was also bound to cause problems for those lords whose
lands bordered on French dominions. The easiest way for the French
to seek revenge for the injury to their pride was to set about attacking
English possessions in France; and since Calais and Harfleur were well
defended, the obvious easy targets were going to be in Gascony.

*

At Troyes, in Champagne, John the Fearless was giving an audience
to the ambassadors of the French king and dauphin: the bishop of
St-Brieuc, Reynaud d'Angennes, Jean de Vailly and Jean de Roucy.
What was being discussed is unclear – but it is likely that John was

proposing to take charge of the government again, now that the duke of Orléans had so disgraced the kingdom of France. Armagnacs had led France into its current mess and fought the battle in which both his brothers had been killed. They had let their armies rampage across France, and had taxed the people to the point of despair. It was time to let him take charge. But whatever John actually said, his entreaties failed. The French king's ambassadors left quickly, offering him nothing.

John stayed the next three days at Troyes assembling his men-at-arms. He would march towards Paris at the end of the month.[39]

★

In Paris, the gates were blocked up, as a precaution against the approach of the Burgundians. Troyes was ninety miles from Paris – but that was just one week's march. The Armagnac captains of the city were preparing defences in the streets. All the alleys around the defensible places were taken over, and the inhabitants evicted. Everyone was uneasy; terror prevented people from even talking about the situation. A rumour began to go around among the Burgundian citizens that the Armagnac captains were going to murder them in the night.[40]

It was not just the Parisians who were scared. The French royal family were already on the move back to Paris, worried that they might lose control of the capital again. The king would arrive tomorrow. The queen, who was lying dangerously ill at Melun, was warned by the Parisians that she risked falling into the hands of the duke of Burgundy. She had herself carried in a litter back to the capital, where she took refuge in the *hôtel d'Orléans*, along with her daughter-in-law, the dauphin's wife, John the Fearless's daughter.[41]

It was eight years to the day since John the Fearless had slaughtered the duke of Orléans in the rue Vieille du Temple. The repercussions of that night were still being felt in the streets of Paris – as well as across the rest of France.

Sunday 24th

According to Adam Usk, a funeral Mass was held at St Paul's Cathedral for the dead of both sides, at Henry's command.[42]

Henry's high-ranking prisoners were not going to be kept in dungeons but treated well, according to their status. For this reason they sought and were granted permission to bring a number of their servants over from France. Henry allowed several men to come to the duke of Bourbon. One of them was a valet, Alardin de la Noir, whose safe conduct enabled him to bring two or three coursers and a sumpter horse, as well as the duke's robes and other clothes. Three falconers were licensed to bring the duke's goshawks and hunting dogs. Henry had no reservations about the duke enjoying himself hunting while his ransom was settled. As for the ransom itself, this was to be negotiated by a knight, Gilbert, seigneur de la Fairte, and a clerk, Pierre de Toulon, who were also permitted to come to England.[43] The count of Vendôme, whose keeping had been granted to Sir John Cornwaille, received similar letters of protection for some of his servants coming to England, including men bringing a horse, robes and other things to ease the count's captivity.[44]

Henry was informed that his late father's confessor, the Dominican friar John Tille, who was due forty marks a year for life, had not been paid for the last year. So he issued a new order to the receivers of the cloth subsidy for the city of Winchester to pay the money due.[45] He also sent letters to Norwich confirming the election of John Wakeryng, keeper of the privy seal, as the next bishop of Norwich, in place of the late Richard Courtenay. No doubt Henry was grateful for their election of a man whom he had probably nominated himself. Letters were also despatched to the prelates at the council of Constance confirming the election. As these letters would take several weeks to arrive, a copy was sent addressed to 'the pope', on the basis that by the time the letters arrived, a new pope might have been chosen.[46]

Monday 25th: the Feast of St Katherine

A council meeting took place in the king's absence. Present were Chancellor Beaufort, the bishop of Durham, 'the treasurer' (presumably the acting treasurer, Sir John Rothenhale), John Wakeryng (keeper of the privy seal) and Roger Leche (treasurer of the royal household).

Their business struck quite the opposite of the celebratory tone of the Londoners, just two days earlier. It was decided to send a thousand quarters of oats to Harfleur for the sustenance of the horses there, to be deducted from the £3,640 earmarked for the garrison's wages. As the king's treasury was empty, this sum had to be drawn against the subsidy due on the next St Lucy's day (13 December). At the same time they decided that an influential and discreet person should be sent to Harfleur to examine the state of the town and to make sure that there was sufficient artillery to defend it against a French attack. The same person was to pay the captain and garrison and to report back to the king. A further enigmatic clause states that they should enquire more closely of the king what his plans were for the captain of the town, Thomas Beaufort. Nothing was written in the minutes about this, but one suspects that Henry Beaufort knew that his brother wanted to be relieved of his post. It was suggested that the man sent to Harfleur to examine the place should be able to govern it if the earl of Dorset were to leave. Names to be put to the king as possible candidates for this role included William Loveney and Gere Flour – men of much lower rank than the earl of Dorset.[47]

The men of Harfleur were suffering. Henry had made provision for the manpower to rebuild and defend the town, but his arrangements for feeding them had been less than satisfactory. Occasional orders not to export grain to anywhere but Calais and Harfleur, such as that of 6 November, were not enough to guarantee an adequate supply of food. The captains of the town were regularly having to lead expeditions out to forage from the neighbouring area. One such expedition in the last week of November, led by Sir John Fastolf, ended up within six miles of Rouen. Fastolf captured five hundred Frenchmen in the process but had to let them go, for he suffered a reprise attack on his return journey.[48] The outlook was bleak; the defence of Harfleur over the next twelve months was to become 'an epic of endurance'.[49] Henry Beaufort's subtle attempt to replace his brother with an administrator – if we are right in reading this council minute as such – was thwarted; Thomas Beaufort was only temporarily able to return to England. And rightly so: none of the four men at this council meeting had been on the expedition or knew what conditions were like in Harfleur.

Tuesday 26th

As Henry's solemnity during the procession on the 23rd indicates, his personal reaction to the successful campaign was not one of euphoria. Nor did it result in a wave of thankful rewards. But gradually Henry did make grants to his knights in return for their service. One to Sir Edward Courtenay has already been mentioned. Yesterday Henry granted Sir Walter Beauchamp the manor of Somerford Keynes. Today he confirmed the keeping of a Northamptonshire manor, Whyscheton, on Sir William Bourchier.[50]

The people of Newcastle had failed to make the case for their town to be exempted from the taxes granted in the last parliament, but they managed to appeal to the king. Henry today granted them their freedom from liability, 'because they are much impoverished by the capture of their ships and merchandise by the king's enemies of Scotland and others, the walling and fortification of the town, many watches kept there, and great mortality'.[51]

Wednesday 27th

The position of Lord Warden of the Cinque Ports, left vacant by the death of the earl of Arundel, was awarded by Henry to his brother Humphrey. In view of the important responsibility of ordering the ports to supply a large number of ships for the king's use, this was not a position that could be left unfilled for long. The king also person-ally authorised safe conducts for servants of the duke of Orléans, namely Master Robert Tuilliers, a member of the duke's council; Master Hugh Perriez, the duke's secretary; and two other servants, coming to their lord in England with goods, riding equipment and horses.[52]

Thursday 28th

Henry had decided that the expenses of members of the royal house-hold were to be met by the income from estates in the king's hands due to the heirs being under age, and the sale of the marriages of heirs and

heiresses. He proclaimed that those who had accounts and needed satisfaction should apply to the chancellor or John Rothenhale for repayment from the exchequer.[53] He also fulfilled his promise to William
Hargrove, made in France on 16 October, to make him Black Rod.[54]

Henry issued a proclamation to the sheriffs of London and the
mayors of Great Yarmouth, Lynn, Kingston upon Hull, Newcastle
upon Tyne and the bailiffs of eleven other ports that for the next
twelve months they were not to carry on any more fishing in the
waters of Denmark and Norway, nor in the seas around Iceland.[55]
The reason for this is to be discovered in a petition against the
proclamation delivered at the parliament in 1416: the usual areas
where fishermen had found cod suitable for salting had been over-
fished, and now were barren. So English fishermen had sailed to
the coast of Iceland, where they had found cod in abundance.
Unfortunately King Eric of Denmark, Sweden and Norway had been
petitioned by his subjects there to prevent this; being Henry's
brother-in-law, he had sent to him asking him to prohibit the English
fleets fishing in Icelandic waters.[56] Hence Henry's proclamation
today – and hence the discontent of the English fishermen in the
following parliament.

Incidentally, had these English fishermen sailed even further than
Iceland, and started fishing off the shores of Greenland, they would
have found a community there struggling but surviving in the extreme
Arctic conditions. And its bishop was an Englishman, Robert
Hingman.[57]

*

At Marigny-le-Châtel, John the Fearless arrived and feasted, 'accompanied by many knights and esquires in arms'. This was still eighty
miles from Paris but some of his men had marched on ahead and
were now approaching the capital. Nor was he stopping at Marigny;
the following day he was planning to press on to Nogent-sur-Seine.[58]

By now, both factions within Paris were living in fear. It was said
that the provost of the merchants had prepared four thousand black
padded jackets and four thousand axes with blackened blades – so
they would not be seen in the darkness – to kill all the Burgundians
in the city, if John the Fearless should try to enter. Troops were billeted

about the city for this purpose, and the blackened jackets and arms had been secreted at various locations.[59]

Friday 29th

Henry seems to have practically hidden himself in the Palace of Westminster after his triumphal procession through London. Few acts are recorded, and he seems to have done little bureaucratic work. Today he confirmed a charter that had been granted to the town of Berwick on Tweed by Edward III. Towns regularly sought confirmation of their charters by successive monarchs, in case the new king failed to observe the freedoms and privileges granted by his predecessors.[60]

It is difficult to imagine what life was like for all those thrown together within the palace. For Henry's companions there was the satisfaction of victory and confidence in their king. For Henry himself, things seem to have taken a darker turn. Having proved himself in the eyes of God on the field of battle, he now had set himself a high standard of kingship, which he would have to live up to. At any time God's favour might be withdrawn, and he might suffer a mishap, a defeat, or an illness. He had lost friends and companions, and would probably lose more in the future. The demonstration of God's favour had asked the unexpected question of Henry: what next? Victory resolved the question of whether he should claim to be king of England and France, but it also meant that he had to continue God's work. What might be the extent of that work? Would he have to go on fighting and praying for ever?

For the prisoners this situation must have been very confusing. Although the most important lords were allowed their creature comforts, their hawks, hounds and servants, they had never before been prepared for this change in their fortunes. Nothing in their education had prepared them for being so powerless and so shamed. Moreover the extent of their shame would continue to be discussed for years, as their ransoms were negotiated and paid. Charles, duke of Orléans, was not ransomed – by Henry V's express order. As the obvious leader of the Armagnac claim to the throne, and as the leader of the opposition to Henry's ally, John the Fearless, Henry ordered him never to be released. After Henry's death, his successors continued to maintain this policy of perpetual imprisonment. When he was allowed to return to France in 1440, after twenty-five years of captivity, his wife was dead and people said he spoke better English than French.

One of the saddest stories arising from the imprisonment of noblemen after Agincourt is that of Arthur, count of Richemont, the twenty-two-year-old younger brother of John, duke of Brittany. Arthur had been pulled out from under the piles of dead and dying, soaked in blood. He was taken to London and followed Henry through the streets on the 23rd – a prisoner in the triumphal procession. A few days later, his mother – who was Queen Joan, the dowager queen of England – asked Henry for official permission to see her son. Henry granted this, and so Arthur was told he might visit his mother in the Queen's Palace within the Palace of Westminster. Joan had not seen him since he was ten, when she had first come to England. She was apprehensive. Before her son arrived, she ordered one of her most well-educated court ladies to take her place and greet the young man as if she were the queen. Joan herself hid behind two of her ladies-in-waiting. When Arthur entered, he greeted the pretend queen, and paid his respects to her. To everyone's shock, he clearly believed that she really was his mother. At that moment Joan saw just what she had lost when she had left France. Her son did not know his own mother.

An awkward moment ensued, but the pretend queen gently suggested to Arthur that he should go among the ladies-in-waiting and greet them all. He did so. When he came to his mother she looked at him with tears in her eyes. 'My poor son, you do not recognise me,' she said. It was the young count's turn to be shocked. He embraced his mother, and both of them wept openly. Joan then gave him a large sum of money and provided him with clean shirts and clothes. But he was so ashamed by not recognising her that, even though he remained a prisoner in England for the next five years, he could not bring himself to visit her again.[61]

December

Sunday 1st: Advent Sunday

The period of fasting and prayer in anticipation of Christmas had come. From now until Christmas the diet would be entirely meatless – consisting of fish, spices, vegetables, bread and fruit – until the great feast on Christmas Day. Henry usually heard a Mass every day but, in this particularly holy period of the religious calendar, and in the solemn context of being the recipient of a religious victory, he would probably have attended more religious services. The afternoons grew dark early; the candles were carried in procession around the chapel royal, accompanied by the singing of the chaplains.

At St Paul's today, in line with Henry's orders, a funeral Mass was sung in memory of the duke of York, the earl of Suffolk, and all those who had died at Agincourt – Frenchmen as well as English. Henry and his brothers attended the vigil in the cathedral the previous night along with other members of the royal family. According to Thomas Walsingham, Thomas Beaufort returned from Harfleur at this time and was present at this service. The bones of the two magnates were then taken off for burial at their desired resting places – the duke of York at Fotheringay, in Northamptonshire, and the earl of Suffolk at Wingfield, in Suffolk.[1]

In contrast to the dearth of bureaucratic activity since Henry's return, the early days of December saw him undertake a number of items of business. He personally pardoned Sir John Arundel for failing to deliver £60 to the exchequer, on account of the great losses and expenses he had sustained in serving as the sheriff of Devon. He granted his brother, John, duke of Bedford, that he would never again have to pay any fines or fees to the crown for the rest of his life. He gave to his esquire Lewis Robesart custody of the lands, rents and services owing to the under-age brother and heir of the late Richard Tyndale – a means of rewarding him for his loyal service. He granted a renewal of their charter to the Dominican friars of Hereford, without charge, stating that it was 'for God, because they are poor'; and he officially handed over to Robert Clitherowe and David Cawardyn, yeomen of the king's chamber, a number of furred robes and coats, used linen sheets and linen napery in return for going from Southampton to London in August, when he had ordered them to seize the goods of Lord Scrope.[2]

*

In France, John the Fearless and his troops came to the fortified town of Provins, less than fifty miles from Paris.

Every day the tension in the capital was growing. People were wary of carrying knives now, afraid they would be accused of treason if found to have a weapon in the street, and thrown into one of the city's prisons.[3]

The dauphin entered the city. Yesterday he had passed the church of St Denis but had failed to pay his respects at the tombs of his ancestors or to pray at the shrine of the saint. He took up his lodging in the *hôtel de Bourbon*, near the Louvre. He had brought with him a large force of men-at-arms – six thousand, according to Monstrelet. Billeting them in and around Paris did nothing to calm matters. Whether they were in the suburbs of the city or at Corbeil, St Denis or Melun, they caused all sorts of damage to their hosts and neighbours. They forced their way into people's houses, stealing what they deemed most valuable, thereby increasing the frustration and anger within and around the capital. No one could control them. Nor was the disquiet confined to Paris. At Laon, in Picardy, the people rioted while the bishop pleaded for a garrison to be sent.[4]

France had experienced enough disasters. But soon after returning to Paris the dauphin fell seriously ill, and took to his bed. According to the official French chronicler, he had contracted dysentery.

Monday 2nd

Henry dictated a letter to an official at Newcastle upon Tyne concerning two Flemish ships that had been captured by Robert Hornsee and John del Strotherland. These two men had fitted out two balingers to defend the shores of England against the Scots, in line with Henry's orders, and had captured the two Flemish vessels laden with merchandise. They had taken them to Shields – but there the ships had been impounded and removed to Newcastle. Feeling aggrieved, Hornsee and del Strotherland had appealed to the king.

Henry's letter is peculiar. It shows great concern for the costs that Hornsee and del Strotherland had incurred, and the likely damage to their estates, but pays no regard at all to the fact that their action was against the law. It was an incursion of the Statute of Truces, for there was an agreement in force between Flanders and England. Henry commanded the official to restore the ships to Hornsee and del Strotherland, if it had not already been done, or to appear before the council to explain himself.

Clearly Henry was in the wrong. He might have originally drawn up the Statute of Truces simply to guarantee the security of his alliances against France, but his victory at Agincourt did not mean he could now turn a blind eye to those who broke the law. One can only suppose that the duplicity of the duke of Burgundy, whose brothers had both fought at Agincourt, now caused Henry to lay aside that agreement with Flanders. Such a course of action would have set an extremely dangerous precedent. The council understood this, and corrected the mistake: by the end of January 1416, the vessels had been restored to their Flemish owners, specifically in accordance with the terms of the truce.[5]

*

In Paris the council were facing a whole host of grave problems. John the Fearless was still at Provins but he was about to advance further towards Paris with his army. The collapse of law and order in the city was a further issue. It was decided that Robert Mauger, president of the council, should speak to the dauphin, and present him with the series of *ordonnances* for the better government of the realm, in line with the decision of 15 November.

About this time the council sent for help from Clignet de Brabant and the lords of Barbazan and Bocquiaux. They also sent a message to Bernard, count of Armagnac, who had recently been appointed constable of France (following the death of Charles d'Albret at Agincourt), urging him to hurry to Paris with as many men as he could muster. Until his appointment, the count had been at Perpignan, following the fortunes of Benedict XIII and the emperor's attempts to bring about Benedict's resignation. On being appointed constable he had left Perpignan and hurried towards Paris. Thus he was already on the way, but such was the vastness of France that it would be the end of the month before he arrived.[6]

Tuesday 3rd

At the port of Lynn, in Norfolk, the disputes that had divided the town between the mayoral party (who had sought the removal of the influence of the bishop of Norwich) and the rest of the gild merchant continued unabated. On the death of the mayor, John Lakynghith, the alderman of the gild, Robert Brunham, had taken up the reins as acting mayor. In August 1415 a new man, John Bilney, had been elected mayor by the gild merchant. Extraordinarily, the duke of Bedford wrote to the gild to insist that the election results should be ignored, and that Robert Brunham should continue to act as mayor. Any failure in this respect would result in Bilney paying a fine of £1,000.

The men of Lynn saw this as an outrageous and unjustifiable attack on their privileges, and they resented Bedford's intervention bitterly. A riot ensued, and Bilney declared that he never wanted to be mayor of Lynn in the first place. Bedford replied on 18 October that Thomas Hunt should now be mayor, attempting to mollify the townsmen with the assurance that this imposition of an official by the government would not be a precedent, or lessen their traditional rights and liberties in future. Of course, that was simply a red rag to a herd of bulls. Bedford's attempt at mediation resulted in another riot.[7]

Into this fray stepped the king. In support of his brother, he upheld all of Bedford's actions. Today he commissioned the sheriff of Norfolk and seven other local knights and esquires to enquire as to all the 'evil-doers' who had supported thirty-eight named objectors in hindering Thomas Hunt from exercising office. At the same time he repeated the threat of a £1,000 fine on those who stopped Bedford's appointee from being mayor.

So much for the king observing the liberties of the people. This might have been an attempt at arbitration but it amounted to the imposition of local officers by the crown.[8]

Wednesday 4th

Henry confirmed the provision made on 12 November by his brother the duke of Bedford concerning Welsh lands with respect to the county of Cardigan. He specified that the sum of £1,000 was to be paid in four instalments: on the next two feasts of St Philip and St James (1 May), and on the next two feasts of All Saints (1 November). He also pardoned the sheriff of Kent the sum of £60 owed at the exchequer, due to the dilapidations in old farms in the county, and arranged for one of his aged servants, Stephen French, to be sent to Beaulieu Abbey for his maintenance.[9]

*

This evening, the fear in Paris reached its height. It was tonight that the Burgundian supporters expected to be slaughtered. The monks of St Martin des Champs and other places of refuge kept fires burning all night in their houses, and Burgundians gathered together for security, watching and waiting for the attack.[10]

Thursday 5th

In the summer Henry had deputed John Waterton and John Kempe to accompany the envoys of King Ferdinand of Aragon back to Spain. Waterton and Kempe had taken the Aragonese diplomats to London, and had returned with them to Southampton by way of Winchester, sailing on 8 September with twenty horses in the ship *John the Baptist of Bayonne*. They spent fifteen days at sea. Finding that Ferdinand was at Perpignan, seeing to the business with Pope Benedict XIII, they set off across land with their Aragonese counterparts, finally gaining admittance to the king today.

Henry had been circumspect in his instructions regarding his own marriage to Maria, the king's eldest daughter. Although he had not ruled it out completely, he preferred the idea of one of his brothers marrying her. However, when the ambassadors arrived in Perpignan, it transpired that Ferdinand had betrothed Maria to Henry's young cousin, King Juan of Castile, who was in his guardianship. Ferdinand tried to persuade the envoys that Henry should marry his second daughter, Leonora, who was then thirteen; but the envoys knew that Henry would not even consider marriage with the *second* daughter of the king of Aragon. The possibility that she might marry one of Henry's siblings remained open for discussion – for the time being, at least.[11]

It was going to be a long period of negotiation for Waterton and Kempe. They did not return to England until June 1416 – and with nothing to show for their efforts. Leonora was eventually betrothed to Henry's cousin, Duarte, the future king of Portugal.

*

At Westminster, Henry's focus remained on his bureaucratic duties. He instructed the constable of the Tower of London to accept custody of two men from Lynn, John Wyrom and John Sherman, who had been arrested for resisting the duke of Bedford's mayor, and to keep them in prison until further notice. The receivers of the town of Boston were directed to pay the yeoman of the robes, Henry Somercotes, £10 yearly. Henry granted leave for the abbot of Canterbury not to have to attend court sessions on account of his ill health, and to appoint attorneys in his stead. He also agreed that the prior and monks of the London Charterhouse could alienate the advowson of a church in London, as part of an exchange of property with the bishop of London. Finally, three men from Newcastle upon Tyne were commissioned to requisition coal – or 'sea coal' as it was then known – for the king's use in London. Henry would not have used coal to heat his palaces but it was employed in such industries as smithying, making steel (including armour, swords and arrowheads) and casting bronze (including cannon).[12]

*

In Paris an emergency meeting took place, to discuss the widespread fear of the preceding night and the threat of the approach of the duke of Burgundy. Four hours after dinner, in line with the advice of the great council and the leading men of the University of Paris, Robert Mauger prepared to read out the series of *ordonnances* to the dauphin and the dukes of Anjou and Berry. Unfortunately, the dauphin was indisposed. It was said that he had spent too long eating and drinking, and was not fit to hear anyone speak. Such was his reputation; but it is more likely that the dysentery – which could not be publicly admitted, for fear it would be seen as a sign of weakness, or worse, God's judgment – was keeping him in his bed. The meeting was put off until the following day.[13]

*

Although John the Fearless had had no success with his first diplomatic contacts with the dauphin, at Troyes, he was not inclined to leave it at that. From Provins he renewed his diplomatic offensive, sending ambassadors to the king and dauphin, namely Jean de Luxembourg and the seigneur de St Georges. Through them he begged to be allowed to come to Paris, to explain the reasons for his approach. It was not a ploy likely to succeed. With such a large army behind him, the reasons seemed obvious.[14]

Friday 6th

Various French prisoners sought permission to come to Henry, presumably to ask to return to France to seek their ransoms. Among them were Charles Savoisy, who today received a safe conduct for himself, two esquires and four servants to enter Henry's presence. Among the other French prisoners we read the name of Ghillebert de Lannoy, the man who had escaped from the massacre during the battle of Agincourt by fleeing from a burning house, only to be recaptured. In contrast to his luck that day, he did manage to persuade Henry to grant him a safe conduct to return to France – although he did not actually receive it until the following February.[15]

Henry granted permission for Ralph Neville, earl of Westmorland, to make a settlement of his estates up to the value of £400. Westmorland was fifty-one, so his precaution might have been due to either a feeling of old age or a life-threatening sickness. Had he actually died at this time, it would have been a blow for Henry, as Westmorland was a solid defender of the north of England and utterly loyal to the Lancastrian cause, being the husband of Henry's aunt, Joan Beaufort. But he lived another ten years; in fact, he outlived Henry.[16]

Several of the men who had died on the recent campaign left underage heirs. Some of the wardships that fell to the crown in this way were sold to pay the expenses of members of the household, in line with Henry's order of 28 November; others were handed out to other men as rewards for loyal service. The lands of Sir John Mortimer, who had been killed in the battle of Agincourt, were handed to Sir Roland Leinthal 'in consideration of his great expenses on the king's last voyage', and so was the right to arrange the marriage of the dead man's son and heir. Sir Roland seems to have been knighted on the campaign, as he was not described as a knight in Henry's will in July; no doubt he deserved his reward. Nevertheless, it seems a poor return for the family of a man who had given his life fighting for the king: to see all but a third of his estate (which was reserved to the widow) handed to someone else. Doubly so, in fact, for Sir John's widow had to acknowledge that Sir Roland now had the right to arrange her young son's marriage, and make that all-important family alliance, not her.[17]

Henry handed over Lord Scrope's goods 'to the value of £25' to his servants John Turgess and Richard Hunt in consideration of their service on the recent campaign. This was just the latest in the string of grants he had made at the expense of the late disgraced lord. Within twenty-four hours of Scrope's death two grants of his estates had been parcelled out to William Porter and Sir John Phelip. By 9 October a number of his silver and gold vessels, which had been placed in the hands of the mayor of London, had been sold for £458 on the king's behalf. Another £100 was found in the possession of a London fishmonger; this too was confiscated.[18] Later Henry gave some of Scrope's estates to his grandmother, the dowager countess of Hereford.[19] And many of the late lord's mazers, cups and silverware were retained by the king. Some were still in the king's possession in 1422. Other items were handed out as presents to visiting diplomats and dignitaries. The Danish messengers who had come to ask Henry to stop English fishermen taking cod from Icelandic waters had been given cups that had belonged to Lord Scrope.[20]

*

At the *hôtel de Bourbon*, the dauphin was fit enough to hear Robert Mauger speak. With the dauphin was his brother Charles, count of Ponthieu; his great-uncle, the duke of Berry; and the duke of Anjou, as well as many other members of the great council.

Mauger took as his theme the line 'Lord, save us, for we may perish' and expounded on the dangers to the realm. The cause, he said, was the bitter blood feud that existed between the princes of the blood, which had torn France apart ever since the murder of the duke of Orléans 'to the great destruction of the realm and her poor people'. Evil men were causing disorder and crime everywhere. The problem lay with the enmity between the king and three men in particular: the duke of Burgundy, the duke of Brittany, and the king's own son, John, the seventeen-year-old duke of Touraine. John lived away from the French court, at le Quesnoy, under the influence of the duke of Holland, and so was thought to be under the influence of the duke of Burgundy.[21] Having made this view clear, Mauger read out the *ordonnances* concerning finance, law and order that the *parlement* had decided were necessary to restore the kingdom.

The dauphin heard the sermon and responded with a promise – as the son of the king – that he would do all he could to bring the evil-doers to justice, whatever their rank. He swore to restore the peace of the realm to the people and to the clergy, and to administer justice impartially, wherever necessary.

The representatives of the *parlement* and the university were pleased with the dauphin's response. But saying these things was one thing; doing them was quite another – especially when the principal 'evil-doer' had an army in the field, and was at that very moment marching towards Paris with the duke of Lorraine and an army said to number ten thousand men. Their next destination was Colomiers, thirty-five miles from the capital.[22]

Saturday 7th

John Calverton of Northumberland had suffered heavily due to the attacks of the Scots in the first year of Henry's reign. Because of this, and also because he had served both Henry IV and the present king well, Henry granted him the office of porter in the castle of Newcastle upon Tyne, receiving 2s daily from the sheriff, his duty being to feed the prisoners in the castle 'who suffer great hunger for the lack of victuals'.[23]

*

The English ambassadors to the duke of Brittany – one of the French king's 'three enemies' – returned home today. John Hovingham and Simon Flete had been given their instructions on 28 July; they had left London on 23 August and had sailed from the port of Topsham, near Exeter, with eight men and twelve horses. They had remained in Brittany throughout the period of the English march – and were still in Brittany in October when the duke had been with the king of France at Rouen. Given that the duke was still negotiating with Henry, and already had a treaty with him, it is hardly surprising that he failed to proceed with his army to Agincourt, even if he did send his brother Arthur, count of Richemont, to represent him.[24] He was indeed no friend of the king of France.

Sunday 8th

William Porter had had a successful year. At the start of January he had been a mere esquire in the royal household. Then at the end of the month he had been deputed to go to Harfleur and spy out the place with Sir John Phelip. Returning in March, he had obviously found royal favour as he was named in the king's will in July. On the fall of Lord Scrope he was given some of Scrope's Leicestershire lands. He took part in the advance party that undertook the reconnaissance of the shore prior to the disembarkation of the army in August, and was knighted the next day. He also took part in the attack on the *Porte Leure* on 16 September, and then fought at Agincourt. Now the king wanted to reward him further. Henry granted him the reversion of lands that had previously been granted to Sir John Phelip and his wife Maud, both of whom had died without an heir.[25]

In contrast to William Porter, the de la Pole family, earls of Suffolk, had suffered a double catastrophe on the campaign. First the earl himself had died at Harfleur, then his heir had died at Agincourt.

Granting out the estates would not endear Henry to this potentially important family. Furthermore, it might impoverish the family, alienating the younger son of the late earl. Thus Henry granted the keeping of all the castles, manors and other income to the dowager countess and four other trustees, including Sir Thomas Erpingham and Sir William Phelips. The whole estate was valued at £232 yearly – not a large sum for an earldom, even though that sum did not include the dowers of the countess and the late heir's widow. A further portion of the estate worth £40 was set aside for the late earl's three daughters; this too was granted by the king to the trustees.[26]

Tuesday 10th

The late duke of York left no children. His estate thus fell to the crown, and Henry handed out the manors to various recipients, including the countess of Hereford, Henry's grandmother. She was then aged about seventy and busy rebuilding Walden Abbey in Essex, where she intended to be buried. The dowager duchess of York, Philippa, thus lost not only her husband but was left with only a third of her husband's income. She also lost her estate in the New Forest, which Henry IV had given to her. By way of compensation, Henry granted her the Isle of Wight and Carisbrooke Castle for life.[27]

*

When in June Ralph Pudsay esquire had discovered Mordach Stewart, the kidnapped son of the duke of Albany, he had only stabilised the situation. Mordach had been returned to prison in England where he had spent the intervening months. No change-over of prisoners had taken place before the king had gone to France, and so Henry Percy too had languished in his Scottish prison all this time. Now Henry decided the time had come to rescue his young third cousin, and to restore Mordach while his aged father the duke of Albany was still alive and still regent.

The men he appointed to ride north to arrange the transfer were Sir Ralph Eure, Sir William Claxton, Dr John Huntman and Richard Holme. He directed them to arrange a day before 15 March 1416 when the duke of Albany was to send Henry Percy to Carlisle. They were also to arrange for Mordach Stewart to be brought to Carlisle from his current prison; there they would be exchanged under the command of John Neville, son of the earl of Westmorland and guardian of the West March. In case the Scottish ambassadors did not agree on the transfer taking place without some further security, then the commissioners were to say that the king would authorise the Scottish earl of March to co-supervise the exchange. And if the Scottish ambassadors found fault with this, then the commissioners were to arrange for the earl of Westmorland to send Mordach to Newcastle upon Tyne, and there deliver him to Lord Grey, guardian of the East March, who would then take him to Berwick on Tweed for the hand-over. Official letters for Lord Grey and John Neville empowering them to carry out the transfer would be drawn up the following day.[28]

*

At Colomiers, John the Fearless considered the dauphin's reply to his diplomatic entreaties of 5 December. The dauphin would not tolerate his presence near the capital unless he first disbanded his army. If he wished to come with a few household officers to Meaux to negotiate with the dauphin's representatives, then that would be fine; otherwise that city, like Paris, would be barred against him.

After his late-morning dinner, John set out for Paris. By the end of the day he had come to Lagny-sur-Marne, sixteen miles from the capital. Here he planned to wait and gather more men. Considerable reinforcements were expected to arrive over the next few days from Picardy.[29]

*

This evening, at his house near one of the gates of Paris, a *pâtissier* called Robert Copil was arrested as a supporter of John the Fearless. He was accused of having agreed to open one of the gates of the city when the Burgundian army was within four miles. This would either be the *Porte Montmartre* or the *Porte St Honoré*. He had sent letters to the duke by a lad of ten or twelve years of age, promising to do this, but the boy had been caught and searched.[30]

Wednesday 11th

In the chamber of the chancellor of France, the dauphin, the queen, and the provost and captain of Paris, together with many members of the great council and representatives of the *parlement*, met to discuss the crisis. The duke of Burgundy was approaching Paris, they acknowledged, with a great company of men-at-arms drawn from Savoy, Lorraine and Germany, as well as other places. Already his men had collectively done a great deal of damage in France in the regions of the Seine and the Marne. He claimed he wanted to see the dauphin – but he had refused to go to Meaux to negotiate with the king's ambassadors. Now he had arrived at Lagny-sur-Marne, just one day's march from the capital.

Those assembled were told about Robert Copil. It was decided to take precautions to secure the gates and to prevent sedition causing a commotion within the walls. At Les Halles, Robert Copil was beheaded. His corpse was placed in a gibbet this evening, for all to see. Many other Burgundian sympathisers were arrested and locked up.[31]

Thursday 12th

Henry would have had little knowledge of the crisis in Paris; it is unlikely that he knew that John the Fearless had left Troyes. His concern was rather that of rewarding his brother Humphrey for his service on the Agincourt campaign. He granted him and his male heirs the manor and barton of Bristol, which had previously been a possession of the duke of York.[32]

*

From Lagny-sur-Marne, John the Fearless sent another embassy to the dauphin, this one led by his secretary Master Eustache de Laître (who had been chancellor of France in 1413). De Laître begged the dauphin humbly to allow John to enter his presence. The dauphin consulted the council and decided to send a high-powered embassy, consisting of Bishop Boisgilon of Chartres, Jean de Vailly, president of the *parlement*, and Simon de Nanterre. They were to explain once again that it was not possible for John to come to Paris while he had so many men-at-arms with him. If he were to disband his army and come with just the officers of his household, then he would be welcome in the capital; otherwise he was not to come any closer.[33]

Friday 13th

Icelandic fishing was not the only issue that divided Henry and his brother-in-law, Eric, king of Denmark, Norway and Sweden. An argument had broken out between the men of Lynn and the merchants of the Hanse. Henry IV had issued orders preventing the Hanseatic merchants from trading in the Norfolk town. The Hanseatic merchants now complained that this was a monopoly unfairly obtained by the petition of three Lynn merchants, namely John Copenot, Nicholas Alderman and Thomas Grym.

The clerks of the keeper of the privy seal, having consulted a number of documents from the previous reign, drew up a letter refuting this. In it they stated that the prohibition had been for violent disturbances – including the accusation of murder – which had developed between the men of Lynn and the Hanseatic merchants. This was in fact the case: the original prohibition of 9 September 1411 referred to injuries done to English merchants, so Henry IV had had good reason to impose the ban. The final letter was drawn up yesterday, addressed to King Eric's officials at North Berne in Norway, and sealed today, after the king had inspected it.[34]

Henry's other item of business concerned the estates of the late Lord Zouche, who had died on 3 November. These were due to be inherited by a young heir, who was just thirteen years old. Thus they formed another potentially lucrative wardship – eight years of lordly income. Henry decided to give this income to his uncle Ralph Neville, earl of Westmorland, in recognition of his faithful service guarding the northern border.[35]

*

The most important event took place in Narbonne. This was the agreement of the framework for the deposition of Benedict XIII. After months of persuasion, negotiation, travel and argument, the last recourse of diplomacy had proved fruitless. Now all the secular lords and almost all the prelates had agreed to repudiate him as a spiritual leader. The Holy

Roman Emperor and the ambassadors from the council were described by Cardinal Fillastre as being 'joyful and exultant'.

The agreement took the form of twelve articles. The first outlined the basis for the deposition; the second the right of the council of Constance to summon all the members of the Catholic Church; the third the unity of the members of Benedict's supporters with the rest of the convocation; the fourth the right of the council to quash any and all the papal acts of the three ex-popes; and so on. Most of the actual clauses were technicalities, and in fact another twenty months of wrangling would pass before the final deposition of Benedict XIII. But the text was agreed today and finally ratified by all parties on the following day, at noon.[36] The kings of Aragon, Castile and Navarre, the count of Foix, and representatives of the count of Armagnac – all of them agreed that they would no longer support Benedict. The only kingdom in Benedict's obedience that did not have a delegate at Narbonne was Scotland; but as Benedict was Aragonese and preferred the Mediterranean warmth of southern Spain, it was unlikely that he would seek a final refuge among the Scots.[37]

The end of the schism, which had divided the Church since 1378, could now be foreseen. When the news reached the city of Constance, on 29 December, there was rejoicing in the streets, and lauds were rung five times on all the bells. The emperor's representative, the duke of Bavaria-Heidelberg, ordered everyone to celebrate the next morning as if it were a holy festival.[38]

Saturday 14th

King James of Scotland was the one monarch who did not join in the repudiation of Benedict XIII. He was still languishing in gaol in Pevensey Castle under the guardianship of Sir John Pelham, where he had been since 22 February. Henry had allocated £700 annually for the king's upkeep and safe custody – £421 2s 11½d was paid today.[39]

*

When the dauphin's ambassadors met John the Fearless, they explained the position of the council. John was furious to be told he was not welcome in the capital. He protested that he did not intend to sit back and watch any further downturn in the finances of the realm. Moreover he was a prince of the blood royal, and the dauphin's father-in-law; they had no right to refuse him. But there was no getting around the situation: the dauphin had declared his intention of marching against John at the head of an army, if he approached.[40]

It looked as though a battle was going to take place outside the walls of the capital. That would have pleased Henry V: to see his Burgundian and Breton allies fighting against the French royal family and the Armagnacs. But that was not how things turned out – not in the short term at least.

Monday 16th

At Westminster Henry ordered John Colchester, mason, to 'arrest' men to repair the walls of Harfleur. In particular he was to find stone-cutters, tile-makers and tilers and other labourers for the repair of the town.[41] The recent tension in and around Paris had saved Harfleur from a major direct onslaught, even though some of the French king's counsellors had advised that they should seize the opportunity to take the town and throw the English out before the walls were rebuilt. According to the official French chronicler at St Denis, the troops now billeted around Paris had been raised for precisely this purpose; it was only the danger of John the Fearless's march on the capital that had led to the change of strategy.[42]

For the English at Harfleur, the best form of defence was to attack. Three days later the garrison made an assault on the neighbouring countryside. They rounded up eight hundred peasants, and herded them into the town. Presumably they were ransomed for whatever they could provide. No one in the vicinity of Harfleur can have had much of a Christmas, whether they were within the walls or outside.[43]

Wednesday 18th

The dauphin died today.

His death was an almighty blow for France. Chroniclers knew the man was not faultless: he was fat, self-indulgent, thieving, lazy and immoral, and he had nothing about him of grace. The official royal chronicler at St Denis was just one of several writers who took this opportunity to list his personal failings in great detail. But he had at least shown some aptitude for leadership. Just as importantly, he was loyal to his father. His death left the kingdom of France in the throes of a civil war, led by a king who was mentally unstable and who was estranged from his eldest surviving son, the duke of Touraine. The other leading members of the royal family could hardly step into the gap – the duke of Berry was too old, and the duke of Anjou was also not long for this world. The duke of Bar had been killed at Agincourt, the dukes of Bourbon and Orléans and the count of Eu were prisoners in England, and the duke of Lorraine had taken arms with John the Fearless. With the death of the dauphin, the French royal family had been stripped of a potential leader. The count of Armagnac might be the obvious person to lead the French government in its new crisis, but he was a provincial of insufficiently high birth to restore the dignity of the French monarchy.

As for John the Fearless, he was left in a quandary. He risked a hostile reception if he decided to advance on the city during this period of mourning; yet if ever there was a time to move into Paris, it was now. Not only was the city disorganised and panic-stricken, he could present the death of the dauphin as a sign from God that the government did not have divine approval. But he did not advance. Perhaps he realised his support in the capital was not as strong as it had been. He was still at Lagny-sur-Marne at the end of the month, when the count of Armagnac arrived to take up his role as constable of France. In all he stayed at Lagny-sur-Marne for six weeks, until 28 January, and Parisians began to mock him as 'Jean de Lagny'. Then he marched away.

One would have expected greater resolution from a man known to history as 'the Fearless'. But John was nothing if not suprising.

Thursday 19th

Philip Morgan, to whom Henry had entrusted his 'secret business' with John the Fearless, arrived back in England today. He had left London with eleven men and eleven horses on 19 August and, as far as we know, had been at John the Fearless's court for the entire intervening period. It seems that whatever negotiations he had been deputed to conduct, they did not come to an end with the sealing of the agreement between Henry and the duke, which had been received at Westminster on 10 October. His protracted stay at the court of Henry's Burgundian ally closely parallels that of Henry's envoys to the duke of Brittany. One can only conclude that it was policy, not accident, that kept these diplomatic negotiators in France until Henry himself had returned to England.[44]

Friday 20th

Henry had decided to lodge his most important French prisoners – the dukes and counts – at Windsor Castle for the time being. A royal esquire, the old William Loveney, was appointed to arrange for their upkeep; today he received £26 13s 4d towards their expenses.[45]

Monday 23rd

The lesser lords, those who were not members of the French royal family, were lodged at the Tower of London. Sir William Bourchier, constable of the Tower, was in charge of seventeen of them. In return for keeping George de Clere, his three companions and thirteen other knights 'lately taken at Harfleur' he received £1 6s 8d per day. Given the expenditure of keeping these men – £40 per month – their ransoms were only going to increase with time.[46]

*

In Paris, the day had come for the funeral of the dauphin. His body had been embalmed and laid in a lead coffin at the *hôtel de Bourbon*. Many prelates and lords had come to pay their last respects. This morning the hearse arrived to transport the body to the cathedral of Notre Dame.

The service, which began about 10 a.m., was attended by the aged duke of Berry and the dauphin's younger brother, Charles, count of Ponthieu, and many hundreds of dignitaries and representatives. The king did not attend his son's funeral, being too ill. Afterwards the body

was interred in the same church, as a temporary measure, to be transferred to the abbey of St Denis, the traditional burial place of the French
royal family for the previous eight centuries, when a suitable tomb had
been constructed.[47]

With the dauphin was buried France's hope for the immediate
future. Not until the new dauphin, the duke of Touraine, had been
poisoned, and Charles VI had died would there emerge a king around
whom France could unite to throw out the English. And that would
not happen in Henry V's lifetime.

Wednesday 25th: Christmas Day

A year had passed since Henry had held his Christmas feast in the hall
at Westminster with his brothers, uncles, friends and the rest of the
court. Now the holly and ivy had been cut to decorate the hall once
more, and the fasting of Advent had culminated in the roasting of beef,
pork and goose. The hall at Lambeth Palace where Henry ate his
Christmas feast this year, seated beside Archbishop Chichele, would
have been similarly filled with the light of many candles lifted on great
chandeliers into the beams. As Henry saw the various dishes offered
to him by the archbishop's servants, he had good reason to reflect on
the events of the last twelve months.[48]

A year ago there had been men who said that he was not the rightful
king of England. There had been doubts about the legitimacy of his
entire dynasty. He had silenced them – first by taking direct action
against the plotters at Southampton in early August, and secondly by
proving himself at Agincourt. In so doing he had provided England
with that one thing that writers on kingship for the last hundred years
had said should be the king's highest priority: to establish peace between
the great lords of the kingdom. As recent events in France had shown,
rifts between magnates and their factions threatened the kingdom's
stability and prosperity far more than any external threat; and this was
especially so for England, which had only one international border
(with Scotland). Significantly there had been no backlash against his
actions against Cambridge, Scrope and Gray during his absence in
France. The earl of March was a chastened individual, unlikely ever
to risk incurring Henry's wrath again. As things appeared to the king

this Christmas Day, he had succeeded in doing what only Edward III had achieved in the last hundred years: unifying the English nobility under his kingship. In that respect, everything about his role had changed: the legacy of his father's dubious accession no longer cast a shadow over the kingdom.

There were other things to celebrate too. A year ago Glendower had still been at large, and the Welsh rebellion, although it had lost strength, still prevented the king exercising control over parts of North Wales. The parliament of May 1414 had described Wales as 'a country at war'. That was no longer true. When Glendower was laid to rest, so too was his cause, and even the most ardent Welsh patriots realised the Welsh rebellion was over. Henry could take some of the credit for this, for, although the political will to maintain an English force in Wales had been his father's, and the determination to mount an annual expedition into Wales had also been down to his father, Henry had played his part on the ground, eventually taking command of the campaign against Glendower. As it would have appeared to Henry, he had defeated Glendower himself. Now, with the man dead and no obvious candidate to take his place, he had proved victorious in Wales as well as France.

As Henry talked with Chichele, both men might have considered that Henry's policies in Ireland and Scotland had been equally effective. As it appeared to them, Sir John Talbot had proved a good choice as King's Lieutenant of Ireland. Talbot was a consummate soldier, and had rapidly overwhelmed the Irish rebels and the English lords who had tried to find their own path between the English government and the native Irishmen. Like Henry himself, Talbot had seen outright war as the way to take control, and by the end of 1415 there were few men left who dared to stand against him. In Scotland, the duke of Albany was still negotiating for the return of his son, Mordach; and this policy had clearly succeeded in breaking the 'Auld Alliance' with France, for the time being at least. The only concerted attack by the Scots on the northern border counties during the year had been the simultaneous double raid into Westmorland and Northumberland in July. The latter had been soundly defeated by Sir Robert Umphraville; and although the earl of Douglas had succeeded in burning Penrith, there had been no significant follow-up attacks while the king was in France. Henry's appointment of two reliable commanders to take charge of the East and West Marches had proved sound, and his policy of giving a free rein to the earl of Westmorland to act as an unofficial supervisor of the north was both subtle and successful.

Henry and Chichele might have been more concerned about the situation in Gascony. It was on Henry's mind that he had done so little for his southernmost domain. And over the year the duchy had come under pressure both from external assailants, such as the attacks led by the duke of Bourbon, and from internal disloyalty, such as that of the lady of Lesparre. But in truth Henry did not care very much. For him, Gascony was a low priority. He did not understand the politics of the region, and he knew that it was of little direct use to him in building his war machine. Its prime function, in his eyes, was to supply his household with wine. And there was little danger the merchants of Bordeaux would stop selling wine to England. Until such time as there was a disaster of some sort, affairs in Gascony could be left to manage themselves – which is exactly the policy that many Gascon lords wanted Henry to adopt.

Henry and Chichele would have been far more positive about the implementation of religious policies, especially with regard to the Church. Over the year they had heard about the Holy Roman Emperor forcing the council of Constance to take a strong line against the three popes, so that, one by one, they had all lost authority. Henry may have failed to gain a diplomatic alliance with Sigismund but in religious affairs the two men shared a vision of the reunited, reformed Church. If the news from Narbonne had now reached England, it would have seemed that the third and last pope had now been deposed in all but name. Soon there would be a new pope, and a reform of the whole Church, taking into consideration the programme of forty-six points that Henry himself had commissioned from the University of Oxford. On top of this, the English delegates had succeeded in maintaining the independence of England as a nation, so Henry was now the king of the only state to be represented as a nation in its own right. He had a voice at Constance like no other monarch – even the Holy Roman Emperor had to face opposition within the German nation from other German princes and dukes.

The domestic religious policy was less of a cause for celebration. Sir John Oldcastle was still on the run. He had failed to comply with Henry's threat to revoke the pardon for all the Lollards if he had not submitted before the council in April. As a result there had been more heretics burnt. Nevertheless, as far as Henry could see, his domestic religious policy was by no means unsuccessful. It had received further backing from the council of Constance in the declaration that to celebrate the memory of John Wycliffe was itself a heretical act, and in the decision that burning Wycliffe's followers was justifiable, as demonstrated by the sentence against Jan Hus. Hence the trial and burning of John Claydon (which Chichele had personally supervised) was justifiable, as were similar trials and sentences against other Lollards – even those who never lifted a finger against the king. Such extreme judgments had no doubt helped to suppress any Lollard rising during his absence in France; and Sir Richard Beauchamp, lord of Abergavenny, had been able to defeat Oldcastle very quickly. On a personal level, Henry had further established his credentials in constructing two religious houses at Sheen – the only disappointment was the failure of the Celestine house. Apart from this minor setback, Henry was not only a spiritual king, he was *seen* to be a pious man and the protector of the Church. The only worrying aspect was that Lollardy was not going away, despite the dire punishment. As it must have seemed to Henry, the war of the orthodox faith against Wycliffe and his followers would be a long one, like that against Glendower, and he would need to be prepared to face the threat for many years to come.

Apart from Lollardy, Henry probably felt he had only one significant problem at the end of 1415. Money. His war effort had plunged the kingdom into debt. Parliament and both convocations had been generous, and yet the royal treasury was denuded of valuables. Henry had had to authorise the pawning of many items. The crown of England was in pawn. Huge amounts of royal treasure were in the hands of abbots, bishops and town authorities as security for the repayment of considerable loans. A second year had passed in which he had failed to settle his father's debts. Customs from ports and other sources of royal revenue were increasingly having to be assigned at source, in order to ensure the creditor could be paid. Scrope's manors and possessions had been distributed, even though this was unlawful; and still Henry had massive ongoing debts. On top of all those commitments identified in the budget of June 1415, it would in future be necessary to find several thousand pounds more every year to pay for the defence of Harfleur, including the wages of the captain and soldiers and provisions. How frank the acting treasurer was with the king is not known;

it is perhaps worth noting that Rothenhale was removed from the post and Henry's erstwhile chamberlain, Hugh Mortimer, appointed in his stead on 10 January 1416. But if either Rothenhale or Mortimer had told Henry the real state of his finances, it would have been obvious that Henry was in serious financial difficulties. Humphrey, duke of Gloucester, and the earl of Salisbury were still pressing for the payment of wages to those who had fought at Agincourt in the parliament of 1418, three years later. Most of the artefacts that Bishop Courtenay had handed over as security were not redeemed at the time of Henry's death in 1422; and many were never returned.

All the above – successes as well as a failures – would have been overshadowed by his victories in France. He had planned the French campaign meticulously and carried it off to his enormous advantage. He had succeeded in keeping the French divided among themselves: even after Agincourt, the factions were bitterly opposed to one another. He had demonstrated in the siege of Harfleur that he could seize a fortified town at will, just as Edward III had done at Calais. And he had shown he was right to lead the army to Calais and risk battle, for he had won a great victory. Indeed, that victory justified everything: every controversial decision, every doubt about the legitimacy of his claim to be king of France, and thereby every doubt about his right to the throne of England. It justified his decision to arrest and try Scrope for treason and his very policy of waging war in the first place.

That victory had left him a changed man.

As Henry partook of the Christmas feast, he could reflect that he had proved himself. He had demonstrated he had the vision to confront a major problem and could deal with it successfully. He could plan, he could persuade and he could win. Moreover, he had proved himself not only as an earthly commander but as one who was favoured by God. After this there could be no more championing the 'hog' Edmund Mortimer, earl of March, as the rightful king of England or of France – whatever the legalities of his claim to the throne. All such thinking was expunged at Agincourt: from now on there could only be one king of England – Henry – because that was patently God's will.

Henry had also proved himself in the eyes of all the other leaders across Europe. He was no longer the son of chivalric-but-sick Henry IV; he was a triumphant king in his own right. They had to take notice of him. If God was on his side, then Henry's authority carried that much greater weight with regard to international politics as well as religious affairs. In due course the French complained about the significance given to the English nation at Constance, but the reason for their outbursts was that Henry's prestige had disproportionately increased the authority of the small kingdom of England. In 1416, when the Holy Roman Emperor came to England, Henry did not ride out to Blackheath to welcome him (as his father had done to welcome the emperor of Byzantium). He sent men ahead to greet Sigismund at every stage, and sent the citizens of London ahead to meet the emperor on Blackheath; he himself only rode out a mile from London, proudly forcing the emperor to come to him rather than vice versa.

That was how Henry had changed in other people's eyes. What had changed within him was an awareness of all this. He now had confirmation of what he had long believed: the rightness of his spiritual authoritarianism. Loyalty was still important to him; he was still as vulnerable as he ever was; and describing him, one would still use the words 'circumspect', 'solemn', 'conscientious', 'firm', 'proud', 'virtuous' and 'intense' but now one would add 'divinely favoured'. He had not only proved to everyone else that he had God's blessing, he had proved it to himself too. Henry was conscious he had been handed something exceedingly precious, and, being aware that precious things are fragile, he did not treat it lightly but carefully treasured it. Like a glass vessel of great value, his divinely favoured status had to be looked after with scrupulous care, lest it slip and shatter. There was nothing back-slappingly good-humoured about his victory; there was nothing self-congratulatory. The victory was not his or even that of the English archers. As he himself said, Agincourt was God's victory. Whatever his fellow Englishmen might have thought, he did not do it for them or for England. He did it for God.

This explains his solemnity after Agincourt, why he showed no humour or joy in his triumph, leading his prisoners through London with a fixed expression. It was not just that he had lost several of his closest friends. His sobriety in the post-accession phase of his life, when he had worked so wholeheartedly towards the war, had now given way to religious solemnity – he really did believe himself to be a warrior of God. Fusoris had not been imperceptive in remarking that the duke of Clarence was more warrior-like and that Henry V was more like a priest. Henry had that sanctity, and believed he had a sacred role, and his victory had confirmed it. What Fusoris had not understood – what he could not have foreseen – was that Henry's priestliness would drive him to eclipse even his brother's martial reputation.

Now, and perhaps only now in the wake of Agincourt, Henry began to realise that the task he had been given did not stop at proving his claim to England by proving he was divinely favoured. He had set himself on a path that required him to carry out God's work – through war, and the subjugation of the evils which had beset France. There could be no turning his back on the fact that divine approval carried responsibilities as well as privileges: it had been granted for a reason, and might be withdrawn at any minute. He had to continue to demonstrate his pursuit of God's favour through the pursuit of God's work, and that meant the rest of his life would be devoted to God's justice, war and prayer. There would be no rejoicing, no self-indulgence, no flirtation with women, no complacency, no great building projects, no toleration of Lollardy or any other heresy. Any sign of weakness might incur God's displeasure and the reversal of his fortunes.

On Christmas day 1415, as Henry lifted the wassail cup, and turned to the archbishop of Canterbury, he had become what today we call a religious fundamentalist – or, to be precise, a militant Catholic fundamentalist. As he later described himself, he was 'the scourge of God sent to punish the people of God for their sins'.[49] Everything on Earth was subject to God's will, and he himself, as God's willing instrument, was prepared to wield all the destructive power he could to exercise that will. Of course, he was liable to be accused of tyranny by those who did not believe in his right to interpret God's intentions; but they were among the minority. For most people in England and, indeed, across Europe, Henry was doing God's work, and doing it well.

Some people, it is said, make a pact with the devil in order to achieve their desires. Henry had made a pact with God.

Epilogue

The council of Constance continued to sit until 1418. In 1417, Benedict XIII was finally deposed and Martin V elected pope for the whole of Christendom. Pope John XXIII was then released from prison. He died in 1419, just a few months after the new pope had appointed him Cardinal Bishop of Tusculum. Gregory XII remained a cardinal and became bishop of Porto. He lived out his days at Ancona, dying in 1417. Benedict XIII went to his grave maintaining that he was the one true pope, dying at Peñiscola in 1423.

Charles VI remained king of France until his death in 1422. His estranged son, the dauphin John, duke of Touraine, died in 1417, having been poisoned. Charles was succeeded by his next son, Charles VII. It was this Charles who reunited the French and was crowned king of France by Joan of Arc in 1429.

John the Fearless was murdered during a meeting with the dauphin Charles on the bridge at Montereau in 1419. His death did not end the civil war, however. His son Philip the Good, duke of Burgundy, openly sided with Henry V in his war against Charles VI, having an alliance with the English that lasted until 1435.

Henry himself led a second great expedition into France in July 1417. Thereafter he spent only four months of the remaining five years of his reign in England. In 1419 he took the city of Rouen and thereby secured control of most of Normandy. By the Treaty of Troyes (1420) he was given the hand in marriage of the French princess, Katherine, and was acknowledged as heir to the kingdom of France after Charles VI's death. But he died of dysentery one month before the French king, leaving all his titles to his nine-month-old son, Henry VI. By the time of his death he had exhausted the crown financially, fallen out with his uncle Henry Beaufort (whom he prevented from becoming a cardinal), and seen his brother Thomas, duke of Clarence, killed in the disastrous battle of Baugé (1421).

The custody of the realm during Henry VI's minority fell to John, duke of Bedford (d. 1435), and Humphrey, duke of Gloucester (d. 1447). They vied for power with their uncle Henry Beaufort (d. 1447), who finally became a cardinal in 1426. All three fought over Henry's legacy – which almost immediately became legendary. With an increasingly idealised legend to live up to, and with his powerful guardians exercising a controlling influence over both him and his realms, Henry VI was doomed. His reign was a succession of political disasters. Harfleur was recaptured in 1435. Rouen fell to the French in 1449 and the duchy of Gascony was lost in 1453, leaving the town of Calais the only English possession in France.

The Lancastrian dynasty founded by Henry IV died out in 1471, when Henry VI was murdered on the orders of Edward IV – the grandson and heir of Richard of Conisborough, earl of Cambridge, and the great-nephew and heir of Edmund Mortimer, earl of March.

Conclusion

'Take him all round and he was, I think, the greatest man that ever ruled England': scholars have been mindful of McFarlane's words ever since they were published in 1972.[1] Christopher Allmand, referring to them in the early 1990s, suggested that the debate had some way yet to run, key points being the wisdom of making war against France, Henry's persecution of the Lollards, and his morality in killing the prisoners at Agincourt – all of which left him open to criticism.[2] However, he concluded his study of Henry V with the words, 'a careful consideration of his whole achievement reveals much regarding Henry's stature both as man and king. From it he emerges as a ruler whose already high reputation is not only maintained but enhanced'.[3] Anne Curry writing in the year 2000 was of the opinion that, although academics might have tried to discredit this image of Henry as 'the greatest man who ever ruled England', none to date had managed it. 'For every bad thing one can say about Henry V, there are dozens of good things to say in his defence,' she claimed. As she put it, Henry remains 'the golden boy of fifteenth-century history'.[4]

I do not subscribe to this 'golden boy' view of Henry V. 'Cold steel' would be a better metaphor. While his organisational skills were extraordinary, and his determination to prove himself in war is awesome, his principal achievements were due as much to good luck as good judgment; and his perspective in pursuing his ambitions was prone to two fundamental weaknesses. The first of these weaknesses was the ill-defined objectives and time limits of his vision: he plunged England into a potentially endless and unnecessary war for the sake of demonstrating the legitimacy of his dynasty. The second weakness was his religiously inflated ego. He strikes me as a deeply flawed individual, undermined by his own pride and overwhelmed by his own authority. I find him less politically flexible and less tolerant than his father, Henry IV. I find him less cultured than Richard II; and I find him inferior to Edward III as an exponent of kingship in a number of respects – as a lawmaker, as a strategist and as a cultural leader. Only in matters of faith did he significantly outstrip his predecessors; but even this had its downside, especially for those whom he allowed to be burnt at the stake. I admire his determination, courage, organisational skills, tenacity, leadership ability and his sense of duty; but I find little else to admire and much to dislike.

This is a personal view, however, and while it might excite further discussion, it raises an important question that requires prior consideration. If my view of Henry V is so very different from those of McFarlane, Allmand and Curry, and many other equally well-informed scholars and writers, should I not simply admit that I am wrong and bow to their decades of experience? How can I vary so much from them in judging this icon of English patriotism?

The lazy answer to this question would be that I am not alone in my views. T. B. Pugh, writing in 1988, declared that Henry was 'a man of limited vision and outlook and it is difficult to endorse McFarlane's dictum'.[5] A contemporary view, written by Jean de Waurin after the king's death, was that

> he was a wise man, skilful in everything he undertook, and of very imperious will. In the seven or eight years that his reign lasted he made great conquests in the kingdom of France, indeed, more than any of his predecessors had done before, and he was so feared and dreaded by his princes, knights, captains and all kinds of people that there was no one, especially among the English, ever so near or favoured by him that dared disobey his orders; and likewise the people of the kingdom of France under his domination, whatever their rank, were likewise reduced to the same state; and the principal reason was that he punished with death without any mercy those who disobeyed or infringed his commands.[6]

But one could go on like this, piling up affidavits of greatness, wisdom and cruelty, and agreeing or not as the case may be, and not say anything original. The fact is that my stance has nothing to do with other people's verdicts. Rather, it is because I have employed a different form of history from that previously used to describe Henry V and Agincourt. To be specific, I have chosen to use a different narrative framework – the calendar for 1415 – and considered how the evidence relates to it.

This 'new framework' has been one of my main reasons for writing this book: a concern with the form as well as the substance of history. Historians hardly ever discuss literary form. Indeed, it could be said that most historians do not realise that history *has* a literary form. But the entire genre of historical non-fiction is straight-jacketed by rules, prescribed by educational and heritage-related rituals, institutional procedures and traditions. Academic journals, for example, expect a completely flat, 'objective', neutral stance, with no drama, no pathos, and a minimal display of literary technique. There is no scope to experiment with strict day-by-day narratives in an academic journal; it simply is not done. It is as if academic historians are only interested in *what* they have to say – not the variety of ways in which it can be said. If a leading scholar were to present his knowledge in the form of a pseudo-autobiography of a historical person, he would be criticised heavily for blurring the distinction between fact and fiction, and for stepping outside the prescribed limits of academic history. Yet the exercise would undoubtedly raise new questions, and might actually reveal many of the challenges the historical subject faced. As that example suggests, and as I hope this book has shown, the various ways in which we say something can also be revealing of historical meanings.

Here is not the place to explore why this exclusion of form has come to be the norm. Suffice to say that it has something to do with the educational orientation of historical scholarship in the modern world. But this is an appropriate place to consider how the narrative form adopted in this book is different from the traditional 'life of Henry V', or books about Agincourt. Thus this conclusion first tackles the question of form, in an attempt to understand why it is possible to have a reaction so contrary to the approbation of the scholars mentioned above.

THE FORM

Different structures of historical thought are likely to yield very different insights and interpretations. This book does not cover the full lifespan of the king, nor even his full reign, so its verdict cannot be as full as that of Professor Allmand on Henry's whole life or Professor Curry's on Agincourt. But it is far more detailed on the year 1415 than most biographies of the king. Also, because it is not specifically about Agincourt, it incorporates many religious and social details that would be disregarded as peripheral by the student of that battle. Thus it is more concerned with the interplay of all the aspects of Henry's life at any one time than any other study. This interplay is a hugely important element in coming to understand a historical individual. To present Henry the warrior in isolation from Henry the pious Christian would be misleading, and vice versa. Likewise to consider Henry's lawmaking and law enforcement activities with no reference to his plans for fighting in France would be misrepresentative. The Statute of Truces, which has been held up as an example of his desire for fairness and good government, was not enacted principally for the sake of fairness or good government – and still less for the benefit of foreign princes with whom Henry had truces. It was passed to make sure that, when he had diplomatically isolated the French, he would not see that diplomatic isolation jeopardised by a reckless act of English piracy. It thus appears not so much a quest for justice as a means of social control. In this way the integration of the king's various concerns in this year reveal him in a different light – as a ruthless planner and a brilliant organiser but less concerned with justice than previously thought.

This integration of the various aspects of Henry's life is most valuable when it brings together events which were close in time. For example, the gift of money to Glendower's representatives on the same day as the Burgundians ratified the Peace of Arras and the English diplomats were waiting in Paris, comes across as a deliberate diplomatic snub. John the Fearless's letter to Sigismund about the capture of the French envoys to the council of Constance, when compared with events in their geographical context, reveals inconsistencies in the dissemination of information that point conclusively to his guilt. Similarly the promise that John the Fearless had no treaty with Henry, made on 13 March by John's representatives (including his sister Margaret of Holland) reveals John's diplomacy to be nothing short of outright duplicity when juxtaposed with Henry's payment of £2,000 to his agents to obtain a fleet from Holland. The realisation that Henry maintained diplomats at the courts of both the duke of Burgundy and the duke of Brittany throughout his campaign in France, and that these lords had themselves sent ambassadors to one another in this period, sets a different context to the agreements of non-hindrance that Henry had with both of these dukes. We realise the same with Henry's intention to go to war: every official statement that he did all he could to avert war rings hollow. Direct juxtapositions like these need no conclusion; they place the facts in the hands of the reader so that the reader can make up his or her own mind as to Henry's intentions, or those of John the Fearless. If any reader seriously believes that Henry had not resolved to go to war long before the negotiations had ceased then they have not read this book properly. Presented within a rigid chronological framework, it is as plain a fact as the black and white of the print.

Another consequence of the strict chronological form employed in this book is the inevitable inclusion of more evidence than is normally considered necessary in books about Henry or Agincourt. Any historian constructing a narrative or argument selects his or her evidence and discards certain details as superfluous to requirements. In a book like this, in which we are trying to explore as many days as possible, it would be wrong to discard some days and not others. The consequences are significant. Consider Henry's pawning of religious artefacts and relics from the royal chapels from 1 June. Pawning relics to pay soldiers' wages does not accord with the traditional image of Henry as a pious man. Nor does his dissolution of more then fifty priories. Historians – especially English writers – have tended to present Henry in the best possible light, and have accordingly downplayed or ignored these details. But their place in the calendar structure forces us to confront the apparent inconsistency head-on. It cannot be downplayed or eliminated without distorting our understanding of the man.

This tendency towards comprehensiveness has a literary side-effect. Henry's chief characteristics are repeated with ongoing force. No one can read this book and not be struck by the number of references to his piety. Similarly, no one can fail to notice the extraordinary degree of organisation and planning required to make the whole Harfleur expedition happen. In a normal history text we would remark on these aspects once or perhaps twice; they would not be repeated so many times. The journal form, highlighting the potential importance of the timing of every reference, forces their repetition. Thus Henry's main personality traits are amplified in the narrative. The whole picture is thus proportional to the reality of the man's daily life (as far as it can be determined from the sources). The references to the difficulties on the march from Harfleur clearly underline the depth of the king's determination. Similarly the continued paucity of references to women, coupled with the repetition of Henry's ordinances concerning prostitutes and rape, hammer home the fact that Henry wanted his men to be like him and to love chastity more than the attractions of the fair sex. The result is a behaviour study that represents historical reality in a very different way from a thematic overview.

The form of the chronological year has two further methodological implications. Sometimes it simply is not possible to account for his actions over a period of days. When this happens in a normal history book, it tends not to be obvious; indeed, the historian may not even realise there is a gap – especially if he or she is writing an interpretative account, with a non-narrative structure. In this book, any chronological lacuna is immediately apparent, and it behoves the historian to try and explain it, whether through looking around for the significance of the day (a saint's feast, perhaps), or by considering circumstantial evidence. Hence the speculation that Henry visited Southampton in advance of the army gathering; we have evidence that he went there not long before May 1415, and we have a gap in the evidence for his stay in London in March. It seems logical to suggest the two might be connected. In this way a precise historical form is valuable for it reveals a gap in the data, and accordingly forces us to consider previously unconsidered questions.

The other methodological implication is chronological precision. The rigid date structure forces the historian to be far more exact about dates, plans, orders, logistics, and the time it took to travel or to send a messenger. Although one often reads in history books that two members of Henry's council met in London in early February and then led an embassy into Paris on 9 February, this seems impossible when considered in a strict calendar form. Ambassadors habitually took at least fifteen days to go from London to Paris in winter. Similarly it is not reasonable to assume that all the people who apparently witnessed royal charters in the year 1415 were present at the time of sealing or even at the time of granting these documents, for there is incontrovertible evidence that some of them were at Constance.

We repeatedly find that the evidence is conflicting and misleading, and this sometimes includes contemporary records. We cannot simply ignore such documents where they do not accord with convenient or long-accepted interpretations. In a calendar-based book readers can see for themselves that there are glaring inconsistencies in the records and chronicles. Precision of dating is therefore not only possible in this book but structurally built into it to a greater extent than in other studies.

In some cases, the precise calendar-aligned arrangement of events results in small refinements of detail (the date of the above-mentioned embassy's arrival in Paris is a good example). In others, it reveals significant errors of interpretation that have led to flawed narratives being circulated and widely accepted. For example, in his book *The Medieval Archer*, Jim Bradbury declares that

> Agincourt was far from being a battle that Henry planned and sought . . .
> In the agreements that Henry made before the campaign in order to
> obtain the force he needed, it is clear that an expedition to the south
> figured in Henry's plans. Frequently the agreements specify what wages
> will be paid should the soldiers be called upon to go to Southern France.[7]

On a study of the contemporary evidence in isolation Bradbury is right; many of the indentures for service, which are almost all dated 29 April 1415, give wage rates for fighting in Gascony as well as France. So did the proclamation regarding wages on the third day of the great council of that year (18 April). But as this book shows, this dual wage rate announcement was a smokescreen, created so no French spies would discover where the army was heading. Precise attention to the dating of payments in the Issue Rolls reveals that the decision to head to Harfleur had been made by 16 April at the very latest. Thus we can see that Henry's deliberate ambiguity on the 18 and 29 April has misled Bradbury into thinking that Agincourt was an unplanned and unsought conflict, fought on the back foot. The exact site of battle may have been unplanned, and obviously the ground conditions were beyond Henry's control, but the general policy of fighting a battle between Harfleur and Calais, massacring French men-at-arms with longbows, was very carefully planned.

The above shows that there are a number of advantages in the calendar form, and collectively these go some way to explaining why I have a different reading of the man's character from other writers. The integration of simultaneous aspects of Henry's life, the tendency to be comprehensive with regard to the evidence, and the repetition of personal characteristics in proportion to the historical evidence are all key elements explaining why readers of this book may join me in disagreeing with the post-Agincourt, hero-worshipping verdict on Henry adopted by fifteenth-century chroniclers, Shakespeare, and most historians since the sixteenth century.

Having said this, there are certain disadvantages to the form that should not pass without notice. The key one is the literary challenge, mentioned in the prologue. As stated there, it is impossible to avoid the fact that the calendar is a non-literary structure, so the more details one includes in their correct historical place, the more inflexible the narrative becomes. It reminds me of the often-repeated question, 'How do you stop the facts getting in the way of a good story?' To this question a historian instinctively replies, 'the facts *are* the good story'. However, the facts make for a much better story when the author can deploy them at will, and use them within a looser temporal framework. It may be that the more historians meet the challenges of accuracy, fullness and precision, the more difficult it is for them to create a 'story', or work of literature, out of the characters and events of the past.

A second disadvantage lies in the limited scope of textual criticism. By discussing the battle of Agincourt within an entry for a single day – 25 October 1415 – it is not possible to include all the varying narratives. While modern scholars describe the various stages by stating that 'Chronicler X says this, while Chronicler Y claims the opposite', this style of textual criticism deflates the value of seeing events unfolding. We lose focus on history as a matter of past reality (the goal of historians outside the lecture hall) and become subsumed within history as the analysis of evidence (the prime purpose of history within the lecture hall). Fortunately, given the many detailed contributions from so many academics concerned with Agincourt to date, this is not a problem; those wishing to understand all the various accounts of the battle can make recourse to books by specialists on the battle, especially Anne Curry's *The Battle of Agincourt: Sources and Interpretations*.

A third problem of this detailed chronological form is simply the lack of evidence. While certain aspects of Henry's life are given weight in this book due to their frequent appearance in the contemporary written record, other aspects do not appear at all. We have no chamber accounts for the year 1415, nor any household or great wardrobe accounts (with the exceptions of those concerning military expenditure). One has to ask, therefore, is there a side to Henry that is missing in this book due to the lack of source material for this year? A comparison of the Issue Rolls payments under Henry V with those made under Henry IV does not suggest that there was. Although Henry IV was a similarly serious, religious, dutiful and committed king, he paid for organising jousts, bought hunting birds, enjoyed sword fighting, bought new clothes for his fool, and 'paid a certain woman 20d for undertaking certain affairs for the king', which, even if it was wholly innocent, reminds us that he had an illegitimate son.[8] In the Issue Rolls of the second and third years of the reign of Henry V there is nothing that approximates to such fun – just the one reference to the dining chamber in the lake at Kenilworth Castle. Nevertheless, questions still remain. There are no references to royal hunts taking place in this year; yet we know Henry V enjoyed hunting. There are no references to his reading either – even though we know that he regularly borrowed books from other people. These aspects of his life are therefore probably underrepresented in this book. The same must go for his other interests that are not reflected in the evidence for 1415.

The final problem worth mentioning is a technical one. When were these documents actually drawn up? This question normally presents no significant problem in a less chronologically precise study, but here it matters. Consider the king's orders to close the ports on 3 July: were these delivered before or after he had heard about the way discussions with the French ambassadors were going? Or had he actually given the orders some time before, perhaps days before, and this was simply the date of enrolment? Doubts about the timing of certain documents might lead to certain inaccurate juxtapositions. We know that some documents were dated long after the events to which they relate. This applies to many entries in accounts, which were settled in retrospect, as well as charters that were supposedly witnessed by people who were not even in England on the stated day. For this reason, precision does not always guarantee correctness.

Overall, despite all the problems and challenges, the form of the single year has proved illuminating, stimulating, challenging and worthwhile. I hope that it stands as an example to show that historical discoveries are not just about finding a new piece of evidence or applying post-modern critical techniques to old evidence. Arranging a large number of facts and observations within a new framework can reveal new meanings, raise new questions, offer new insights, and stimulate discussion. Different biographical viewpoints and different chronological layouts – even different conceptual approaches regarding what history is – all help us to see the past differently, and to interact with it more personally, and to understand humanity over long periods of time.

REINTERPRETATION AND THE HISTORICAL CORRELATIVE

To what extent should we judge historical characters? Outside academia, is there any value in such judgments of individuals from the remote past? Are not historians' opinions of people who died several hundred years ago as inconsequential as their opinions on the nameless individuals whose bodies once lay under prehistoric burial mounds?

In the past, a historian's judgment has been seen as an essential part of his or her role. Professor Jack Simmons, reviewing a book on Elizabethan England in 1951, commented that there were four qualities of a great historian: common sense, justice, sympathy and imagination. With regard to justice he declared that this was

> not impartiality – the anaemic, remote detachment of a man looking at the whole story from the superior height of a later age, but some-thing much harder to attain: the true justice of a judge who sets out and weighs the evidence and then pronounces upon the question in dispute. The great historians have never shirked this duty of judgment. Rather they have regarded it as one of the main aims of their work.[9]

I have borne this review in mind ever since reading it, eight years ago; but I have increasingly found myself disagreeing with it. Or, rather, I have found that the point of view of 'the historian' in describing the past is a complicated one. While judgments concerning recent social history are important, because they may affect the way we live our lives today (for example, successes or failures within economic systems, or the National Health Service), the purpose of studying medieval subjects in the public arena is beyond the exercise of judgment; it is an examination of the experiences of the human race over time. It is much more important to understand the past sympathetically – to see why they did what they did, from their own point of view – than to pontificate about those who cannot possibly have known their judge, let alone defend themselves.

Given this suspicion that historical judgment is often unhelpful and unnecessary, this would be the ideal book in which to say that I will leave readers to make their own judgments on Henry V in the year 1415. All the facts that I consider pertinent have been laid out above, and readers may make of them what they will. But in each of my past biographies I have felt obliged to deliver a judgment on the character concerned, and I feel it necessary to do so here. The reason is primarily because reinterpretation has its value, if only as a riposte to what I consider the erroneous judgments of others. Another reason is that, as with the other books, I want to push the understanding of this man a little bit further, to explore the ambiguities and inconsistencies of his behaviour that are so revealing of his character. Finally I want to pursue the reinterpretation in order to say something of the consequences of Henry's decisions in 1415. We cannot say Henry V was good or bad, or right or wrong, without making huge assumptions about moral values across the ages; but we can reinterpret his character and the consequences of his decisions, and that is the purpose of the remainder of this book.

Before addressing the question of what the year 1415 reveals about the character of Henry V, it is necessary to make an observation that is crucial to any historical judgment, reinterpretation or understanding of the past. When discussing any historical fact there is an automatic juxtaposition with its perceived equivalent in our own time, even if we do not realise it. For example, when we read about child-beating in the fourteenth century being seen as a sign of good parental care, and that the medieval father who did not beat his son might be seen as irresponsible, we automatically contrast this with 'good practice' in our own time, and realise that something has changed. Conversely, when we read a medieval poem about unrequited love, or pangs of hunger, or grief following the loss of a child, we automatically compare these emotions and sensations with our own experiences, and suspect that little has changed across the years. Either way, whether we are discussing change or continuity, we compare and contrast the past with our own time; we cannot forget our own norms, our own age.

The inevitable comparisons and contrasts we make when reading historical texts constitute a sort of correlative force that distorts our perception of the past. This is best explained by referring to the literary device of the 'objective correlative', outlined by T. S. Eliot in his essay 'Hamlet and His Problems' (first published in 1922). It is not any single literary image or statement that gives rise to an emotion when reading a piece of literature; it is a set of objects, a series of images. A series of juxtapositions can have far more emotive force than the facts in isolation. To take an example from this book, it is not just that the count of Richemont did not recognise his mother that causes an emotional reaction in the reader. Nor is it that his mother hid from him. Nor is it simply that he had been captured at Agincourt and was in England as a prisoner, or that they had not seen each other for many years, or that she had been forced to give up her children when she married Henry IV. It is the correlation of all these things. The emotional reaction develops from each fact in relation to the others. In Eliot's words, 'it is a set of objects, a situation, a chain of events which shall be the formula of that particular emotion'.

Something similar is operating when we read a history book. We are obtaining a historical sensation from the juxtaposition of behaviour in the past with the norms of our own time. We automatically correlate Richemont's fifteenth-century shame with our own experience of shame. When we read of Henry V ordering women's left arms to be broken, we experience a strong emotion through the contrast of this apparently barbaric act with acceptable behaviour in England today. When we read of the massacre of the prisoners, we contrast this order with our own post-Geneva Convention attitude to war (however many abuses of that convention we might be aware of). When we read of the burning of Jan Hus and John Claydon, we are appalled that these things were done by the Church and the state respectively in God's name. The killing conflicts with the modern paradigm of Christian tolerance and mercy. These are just a few examples of what may be called 'the historical correlative' – the emotions or sensations arising from the automatic correlation of an event in the past with our own time. The fact is that every historical fact or event is subject to this effect, however slight – even the payment of a sum of money (how much or little something costs), or the time it took to travel from London to Paris (different in winter and summer), or the eating of beef for a Christmas feast (no turkeys). Most importantly of all, the historical correlative is a reaction in the reader's mind – and therefore largely beyond the historian's control.

The reason for explaining this point is that any interpretation or reinterpretation of a historical character or event is bound to be affected by the historical correlative. Every fact we may perceive, every suspicion we garner, every piece of knowledge, is automatically correlated, consciously or subconsciously, with the norms of our own time as we personally see them. Even if we make allowances and try to understand that society was far more violent and religious in the fifteenth century than it is now, most of us do not understand exactly how violent or religious it was, and so have no yardstick by which to measure Henry's massacres or religious acts, and so we have no way of obviating the effect of the historical correlative. It demonstrates to us how all historical judgment is inevitably subjective. It is in this light, and only in this light, that we can proceed to make judgments on the past. However accurately all the evidence is laid out, and however precisely it has been examined, historians' judgments are fallible because their experience of life in a later century means their values are different, their understanding of common human behaviour is different, and the expectations of their readers are different.

HENRY V'S CHARACTER

A number of character traits were associated with Henry at the outset of this book. In particular, he was 'circumspect, conscientious, solemn, firm, proud, virtuous and intense'. Through the year many events and facts have served to corroborate these personal traits in particular circumstances. For example, his circumspection is repeatedly evidenced in his reluctance to take any unnecessary risks on the Agincourt campaign: in his choosing a very difficult landing place to avoid encountering French hostility, not risking an all-out attack on the town of Harfleur, refusing to fight at Blanchetaque, and changing direction away from following the French army north from Péronne. In contrast, the risks he did take were all taken for good reasons – the decision to march to Calais was a strategic manoeuvre designed to encourage the French to attack; and the order to advance at Agincourt was given to catch the French off-guard. But while it would be possible to go through the above list of Henry's character traits in this way and find examples to back up each one, this is unnecessary. These traits are the ones that chroniclers noted in him, and are the elements of his character that are not in doubt. A more valuable exercise in this book is to examine what the year 1415 reveals about him – the acts and decisions on which we may base a historical judgment of him in this year.

One element of Henry's character that comes across very strongly in 1415 is his colossal ambition. He wanted to become a great king so desperately that he became one. In his ancestry – particularly in his role model, Edward III – he had an example of what great kingship could be, and he sought to emulate it in every important respect: in war, faith, great buildings, the administration of justice, and even in the way he was seen. For him kingship was itself a crusade. All its facets were part of a spiritual journey in which he saw himself delivering a perfect rule. To achieve any one of his aims would have required a certain determination, but to achieve them all required more than just the determination to *do* something; it required an over-arching ambition to *be* something; and that 'something' was of such a high order that it is fair to rank Henry as one of the most ambitious European monarchs who ever lived.

Ambitious people are rarely humble, and least of all kings. Thus Henry's pride is something we come across time and time again in this book. This is not in itself surprising; but what is interesting is that his pride did not lead to complacency. He was not conceited by his success. He was somewhat sensitive to failure; his own failings were anathema to him, and he was sometimes a harsh critic of himself. When de Gaucourt managed to lead three hundred men into Harfleur after the town had been under siege for three days, exposing Henry's lack of foresight, Henry's response was immediate and swift – to send his brother to cut off the far side of the town. Likewise when there was a sortie from Harfleur on 15 September, Henry's reaction was immediately to order an all-out attack on the *Porte Leure*. His instinct was to defend himself by immediately counter-attacking when he realised he had made a mistake.

Another striking trait that comes across in 1415 is his tenacity. Despite the delays putting back his expedition, he did not give up on his plans. Although the earl of Cambridge's plot and the dangers of a Lollard rising in August led to calls for him to remain in England, he still went ahead with his invasion. Nor did he lose faith in himself when he lost more than 1,330 fighting men at Harfleur, and had to leave behind a further 1,200 men to guard the town. Still he went ahead with his march to Calais, even though he knew the French could summon a far larger army against him. He might have changed his strategy here and there, but he never gave up.

Given this ambition and tenacity, it is not surprising to find that Henry was serious to the point of being humourless, and sometimes bad-tempered. His orders were often issued under pain of the recipient suffering the king's 'grievous wrath' if they were not fully and immediately complied with. One never reads of Henry enjoying himself; he did not hold jousts or any of the celebratory games that we associate with Edward III. He did not encourage any form of indulgence, as far as we can see, and he was deeply hostile to any behaviour that could be considered immoral. He did apparently play cards, chess and tables (a form of backgammon) with his fellow men (as we learn from accounts in other years); and one presumes he drank a lot of wine; but his focus remained on combat, God's work, and contests of will.[10] He was clearly a severe man; and once he had made up his mind on a point, he would not be argued with. One sees this in his actions against Scrope, and also in his refusal to accept the arguments of those trying to dissuade him from marching across France. It is also apparent in his occasional high-handedness – for instance, in the fine he imposed on the earl of March, or the reversal of the terms on which de Gaucourt and the other prisoners from Harfleur had surrendered.

All these traits – ambition, self-criticism, tenacity and a severe, almost puritanical personality – were closely related to his faith. This was extreme. With Edward II, Edward III and Richard II one can question whether they were normally or abnormally religious in comparison with their contemporaries, and make a case that their spirituality was not excessive for the period. However, Henry IV was considerably more serious about religion than his antecedents, and in his eldest son we have a king who was at the very height of religiosity in a deeply religious age. When we describe Edward III as a 'warrior of God' we do so because he was a war leader who was normally religious, and regularly used religious symbols (such as relics, offerings of devotion and pilgrimages) to inspire his army. In contrast, when we describe Henry V as a 'warrior of God' we mean to say that he believed God had made him a warrior, and in fighting he was doing God's work.

There is no doubting Henry's devotion – it is to be discerned in almost every aspect of his life. He did not choose to found normal monasteries, he founded houses for Celestines, Bridgettines and Carthusians: the most zealous orders. His choice of saints was similarly fervent – especially in following St John of Bridlington and the Holy Trinity. The provisions for Masses in his will were excessive, even for the time; and his attribution to God of the cause of victory in battle betokens a religious foundation for even the act of killing fellow Christians. The more one looks, the more one sees the signs of his deep religious conviction. These range from trivialities, such as his higher-than-usual payments to those attending his Maundy Thursday ceremonies, to profound and shocking statements, such as his later declaration that he was 'the scourge of God come to punish God's people for their sins'.[11] No one can doubt that we find a greater degree of spirituality in Henry than among almost any of his contemporaries.

So how do we reconcile Henry's religious devotion with his deliberate breaking of one of the Ten Commandments: *thou shalt not kill*? Moreover, how did he justify to himself breaking that Commandment in God's name?

Various other instances have been noted in the text of acts that seem similarly irreligious. Pawning religious relics to pay for soldiers' wages, dissolving the French monasteries, and failing to give the Englishmen who had died for him at Agincourt a proper Christian burial, are the most obvious. All these, like the massacre of the prisoners, seem ungodly acts. Yet they show that Henry was so convinced that he was a divinely inspired person that he believed he could go beyond the religious expectations of his day. This is most easily explained by referring to Henry IV's killing of Archbishop Scrope in 1405. One might have thought that Henry's father was acting in a godless manner; and many contemporaries thought so. However, it took a great deal of spiritual self-confidence for a king to be sure that he would not suffer divine vengeance for killing an archbishop.

Thus the execution is evidence not of his profanity but of his religious conviction: Henry IV knew where he stood with God. So it was with Henry V. In fact, Henry's spiritual conviction was even more marked because he believed that *everything* he did was a religious act. As he himself put it in explaining his foundation of Syon Abbey: 'he will turn where He wills'. His every deed was moved by God. His will was God's will – as far as his subjects were concerned, the two were inseparable. Thus his war was God's war, and his victories were God's victories, much as the abbot of St Denis had preached in 1414: 'God resolves wars according to His will'.[12] What was different about Henry V was that he was so confident in his belief that God would deliver him victory that he was prepared to put his faith to the ultimate test.

Anyone looking for the source of Henry's courage need look no further than this faith. As made clear in the passages describing Henry on Christmas Day 1414, he was vulnerable – he was aware that at any moment he might lose his crown, his friends' support, his health and his life – but against this he set his faith. Henry really did believe God would protect him and make him victorious. We might say that his courage was the measure of his faith – for it was his faith that placed him in the front line of his army, so close to the enemy that he had a piece of his crown cut off with an axe. One does not need courage when one is unaware of danger, but when one is as open to attack as Henry was when wearing a royal surcoat on the battlefield, facing a larger army, one needs a huge amount of courage. His faith gave him sufficient.

Henry was lucky. Inordinately lucky. Just to take examples from 1415: he was lucky that Ralph Pudsay recaptured Mordach of Fife. He was lucky that the earl of March betrayed the earl of Cambridge and his fellow conspirators. He was lucky that Glendower died when he did. He was enormously lucky that the civil war in France did not end with the confirmation of the Peace of Arras in March, and that the duke of Burgundy repeatedly betrayed the French king. Henry was lucky to be warned by a Gascon about the ambush at Blanchetaque. He was lucky that he found a way across the Somme near Nesle and did not have to march his starving army even further upstream, and even luckier that his army was able to cross the Somme unopposed by the French. He was lucky that the duke of Bourbon decided to fight him without waiting for orders and reinforcements from Rouen, and he was lucky that the French leaders at Agincourt were disorganised and overestimated themselves. Above everything else, he was lucky that it rained so heavily at Agincourt on the night of 24 October. If it had not, the French wings might have been able to charge into the advancing English archers, scattering them before they could shoot enough arrows, thereby winning the battle for France and humiliating Henry and undermining his pretensions to be doing God's work.

From the above it emerges that Henry was one of the most ambitious, lucky and pious kings that England has ever had. But one would not rank him among the kindest. That severity in his demeanour was ruthless, and he was capable of great cruelty. As Waurin said in the passage quoted above, 'he was so feared and dreaded by his princes, knights, captains . . . and the principal reason was that he punished with death without any mercy those who disobeyed or infringed his commands'. The instances to which Waurin was referring mainly date from after 1415; but in the year under study there are three instances that stand out: the massacre of the prisoners at Agincourt, the persecution of Lollards, and the killing of Lord Scrope. Historians have traditionally exonerated Henry on this last point by confusing Scrope's role in the plot and regarding him as guilty. As for the policy of burning Lollards, two methods have been used to exonerate him: firstly, by removing him personally from the position of judge in such matters, and making it a legal process; secondly, by claiming that his attitude was orthodox for the time. Nevertheless, it is worth remarking that no men were burnt for heresy under Edward III or Richard II, and Henry IV's reign saw only two men executed in this way. Henry's reign saw seven burnt alive in the first year alone. That the mayor of London felt the need to write to Henry about burning John Claydon in 1415 directly connects the king with the policy. As for his cruelty in killing the prisoners at Agincourt, it was at best an ungodly decision made in a moment of panic. And such acts paved the way for grosser acts of cruelty in later years. In 1417, at Caen, he gave orders for 1,800 men to be slaughtered in cold blood. The following year at Louviers, he ordered eight gunners to be hanged. Waurin's verdict – that Henry 'punished with death without any mercy those who disobeyed or infringed his commands' – seems borne out in these incidents. In 1422 he had a trumpeter killed merely because the man made him angry.[13] A full biography of Henry V would trace the development of his intoxication with his own power up until his death. Obviously he fell far short of the charming hero of Shakespeare's *Henry V*, and the overseer of such murderous acts hardly deserves to be considered as a candidate for the title 'the greatest man who ruled England'.

Henry's cruelty has been remarked on before by other historians but the near-total exclusion of women from his society, as far as I know, has not previously been remarked upon. The form of this book allows us to use negative evidence in building a picture of his life, and there is a notable absence of any sign of warmth towards any women not intimately connected with his childhood. As mentioned in the prologue, this was partly a result of Henry being an unmarried king. But the complete failure to mention women in his will except two senior members of his family, or to make any grants to any women in their own right who had not looked after him in childhood, or to associate himself with any other women (except in relation to their husbands), cannot be ignored. Even the two women who submitted petitions for him to consider on Good Friday were dismissed and told to pursue their claims in the law courts.

This lack of any closeness towards females other than those 'safe' women from his past or his family, coupled with his separately evidenced lack of indulgence in sexual intercourse, suggests at least a deliberate avoidance of women in 1415, and perhaps even a fear of them. Further evidence for this is to be noted in the homecoming celebrations in London: all the various sets of girls were dressed in virginal white, with signs of chastity and virginity around them. If we also consider the cruelty of the extreme punishment that Henry ordered to be meted out on any women who came within three miles of his army – having their left arms broken – we may read signs of a man who had a difficult relationship with women. Bishop Courtenay's remark to Fusoris – that Henry had not had carnal relations with a woman since becoming king – implies that he had had such relationships before his accession. That Henry turned against that aspect of his life seems beyond doubt. Whether an unfortunate experience left him fearing women as sexual beings, or whether he regretted his pre-accession philandering on moral grounds, is not so clear. Either way, Henry excluded almost all women from his life in this year, with very few exceptions, notably his grandmother and his stepmother; and the latter of these two he later accused of being a witch and treated extremely badly. The outlook for the girl he had decided to take for a bride – the pubescent Katherine of France – was not rosy.

NATURE AND NURTURE

The above description of Henry points to an extraordinary individual: ambitious, tenacious, courageous, ruthless, pious, severe and sometimes cruel. So it is fair to ask, what made him like this? Can we discern any formative influences that will help us understand him?

Henry's innate, serious nature cannot but have been affected by several early developments in his life. Two months short of his eighth birthday, his mother died in childbirth. One indication that this profoundly affected him is his closeness to her mother, his grandmother, Joan Bohun, the dowager countess of Hereford. As noted in the text, she was a very pious woman, to whom Henry gave gifts of land; he also mentioned her in his will. A second indication that his mother's death had an impact on him is his commissioning an effigy to be placed on her tomb at Leicester not long after his accession, twenty years after she died. Her death would have coincided with the beginning of Henry's education in a noble household – so at a time of traumatic changes. He and his brother Thomas were transferred to the household of their grandfather, John of Gaunt. When not with John they stayed with their grandmother, the dowager countess of Hereford, or the even more elderly countess of Norfolk. Thus Henry did not grow up with his sisters or two youngest brothers, and for most of his youth his one constant companion of a similar age was his brother Thomas, whom he did not like very much. In John of Gaunt's household, his companions were mostly knights and grown men-at-arms; and when he was with his grandmother or the countess of Norfolk, his companions were old pious women. On being taken into Richard II's household at the age of twelve, following John of Gaunt's death, he again found himself surrounded exclusively by men, as Richard's ten-year-old wife did not live at court.

Just as much of a loss to Henry was the refusal by Richard II to acknowledge the entail of Edward III. It has been remarked that Henry was so far from the throne at the time of his birth that no one bothered to record the event. This statement is wrong on both accounts. The date and even the time were recorded – 11.22 a.m. on 16 September 1386.[14] Henry would have been brought up by his father to believe that, if Richard II died without an heir, then the line of succession would pass to the Lancastrians, and one day he would inherit. Richard II made his first overt moves to overturn this in 1394, the same year as Henry's mother died. The year was thus a turning point in his life. Not only did he lose his mother, and find himself shuffled between households, but his position in the line of succession also started to slip. At seven this would have meant little to him, but by the time of his father's exile in 1398, when he was twelve, he would have understood only too well that he was no longer seen as a likely future king of England. Before his father returned from France and ousted Richard II, Henry saw his position in the line of succession obliterated. As a boy who had been brought up to believe he was a potential heir to the throne, that had grave implications for his identity. Was he God's chosen sovereign or not?

His sense of vulnerability, and his determination to overcome it, probably dates from this early period of his life. The diminution of his importance must have damaged his esteem. His rivalry with his brother Thomas, who was almost the same age but who was his father's favourite son, must have increased his determination to stand out, to prove himself. His father gave him the opportunity to do just that, when he appointed him to his Welsh command at the age of fourteen. This separated Henry from his brother and gave him a position of respect and independence. His command might at first have been purely nominal, under the tutelage of Henry Percy, but nevertheless he was head of his own household and the only royal person in North Wales.

This start in life does perhaps explain why Henry was as he was in 1415. The ambition and the desire to prove himself in this year correspond with his experiences as a boy: realising that his position in the royal family was being ignored, that he was losing respect from non-family members, and that his father preferred his more martial brother, Thomas. The piety he displayed in 1415 can be traced in the influence of his grandmother, the countess of Hereford, as well as his father. The young Henry may also have felt the need to prove that he deserved to be an anointed king, chosen by God, as his position in the line of succession slipped. In his background, isolated from girls, we might also see why he showed no signs of warmth to any females except those he had known since childhood. As for his other traits of cruelty and the fear of disloyalty, these may be connected with his experiences in Wales (as noted at the start of this book). The disloyalty of those involved in the Epiphany Rising in 1400 and the Percy family's rebellion in 1403 can only have heightened Henry's sense of vulnerability, and made him very sensitive to plots and discussions outside his control.

The last set of formative experiences that needs to be mentioned in an attempt to understand Henry in 1415 is his relationship with his father. As his father's favouritism of Thomas suggests, Henry and his father were never close. They were very alike – determined, headstrong, courageous and tenacious and pious in the extreme – but they disagreed on many issues. There were also some fundamental differences between them. Whereas Henry IV argued the philosophy of rebellion and religion with his enemies, Henry V did not waste words on those who disagreed with him. Whereas Henry IV regarded himself as a king whose piety supported his kingship, Henry V was more fervent, to the point of seeing things the other way around: his kingship supported God's work. Perhaps Henry V saw his father's discussions with his enemies as a sign of weakness. Perhaps he saw his father's long illness as a sign of God's disapproval of his reign. By the time of his regency, Henry V was forming his own ideas about kingship, and his vision so far eclipsed his father's policy of merely steadying the political boat that he can have had little respect for the dying man. In everything he did, he wanted to be seen to eclipse his father's achievements: in spirituality, religious buildings, attention to royal dignity, the suppression of heresy, and leading an army into France.

Such experiences in childhood and youth, and in particular his struggle to maintain self-esteem, royal identity and public respect, gave Henry his declared aim: to win 'the approbation of God and the praise of the world'. It was in the humiliations of his youth, I feel, that his ideas about what it meant to be a divinely anointed king and the advantages of invading France were conceived.

ACCOUNTING FOR 1415: FAILINGS AND SHORTCOMINGS

Henry did not win 'the praise of the world'. There were plenty of men and women in Europe who saw him as a tyrant, and quite a few in England too. Such a view was an inevitable consequence of his kingship, which he saw as being both divinely authorised and justified in its authoritarianism, as indicated by the original Homeric context of his motto *une sanz pluis*:

> . . . As for having several lords, I see no good therein;
> let one and no more be the master, and that one alone be the king

That Henry believed this was his role – and believed that the torrent of good luck he received was confirmation of the sanctity of all his acts – was bound to result in his own power growing too great for him to control. It overwhelmed him. Yet there was a book that justified exactly this all-powerful approach to kingship: the *De Regimine Principum* by Giles of Rome, a text which was well known at the court of Richard II. This exhorted kings to take complete control of their subjects and to demand absolute obedience in all things. The chances of Henry or any other man wielding such enormous power, unchecked, for the benefit of all his subjects, all the time, were non-existent.

Consider the example of Ireland. From Henry's point of view, he had done little there; but what he had done, he had done well. He had appointed a strong soldier-governor to be King's Lieutenant of Ireland, Sir John Talbot. English historians often praise him for this appointment. But from the Irish point of view, the appointment was disastrous. Talbot proved to be utterly ruthless. His method of governing the Irish was to put all the rebels to the sword and to take away their children. Having arrived in November 1414 he had spent almost the whole of 1415 in arms. He attacked Fachtna O'More of Leix, plundered his cattle and horses, and captured his castle. O'More himself was forced to serve in Talbot's army, leaving his son as a hostage with Talbot, and joining him in his relentless pursuit of the native Irish and their English allies. Soon afterwards, O'Reilly of Breifna and O'Farrell of Annaly submitted to Talbot, and another native lord, MacMahon, was forced to surrender. So there was a destructive element to Henry's Irish government. There was also an administrative failure. Talbot was unable to administer or secure the land without money; and in this respect Henry let him down badly. Henry had promised him 4,000 marks per year – and then failed to pay him. In order to keep the loyal

English on his side, Talbot alienated much of the royal income, allowing his people to cream off the revenues at source rather than pay it into the Irish treasury. In addition, he had to plunder continuously, thereby creating no stable relationships with the men he brought back under English command but rather causing lasting grudges. In February 1416 he had to leave Ireland to come to England to ask the king for payment of his own salary – a process which delayed him in England for months, allowing his military achievements in Ireland to be undone. When he left Ireland it was said by an English writer that 'he left with the curses of many, because having run much into debt, he would pay little or nothing at all'. A Gaelic writer went so far as to declare that Talbot was 'the wickedest man to have lived since Herod'. In short, in 1415 Henry V brought terror upon the Irish, and showed no will to try and control it.[15]

Henry placed such a high value on his own authority that he frequently committed acts of high-handedness himself, some of them verging on tyranny, and turned a blind eye to such acts committed in his name. The imprisonment of Italian merchants for not paying towards his expedition to France is one example. His support for his brother's refusal to allow the elected mayor of Lynn to exercise office is another. Restoring the Flemish ships to the men who illegally captured them, in contravention of his own Statute of Truces, is a third. His treatment of the earl of March is a fourth. Indeed, considering Henry placed such a high value on 'justice', it is disquieting how little justice he showed the earl of March – forcing him to seal a recognisance that he would remain loyal, on pain of forfeiting 10,000 marks, and then imposing the full fine on him for simply marrying without permission. Another example of his high-handedness in 1415 is his alteration of the terms of surrender which de Gaucourt and the other knights from Harfleur had to accept. After Agincourt it suited him to insist that they all subject themselves to imprisonment again, regardless of what his officers had previously told them. A sixth example is the baseless charge of conspiring to murder the king and his brothers which he levelled at Scrope, Cambridge and Gray. In fact, a seventh, eighth and ninth are wrapped up in his treatment of Scrope – attempting to try him before a jury (and not before his peers), executing him for a crime he had not committed, and disinheriting his brothers. With regard to this last issue, it is a signal failure that Henry confessed that it troubled him much and yet he never did anything about it.[16]

The complication we have in judging the above high-handed acts is that of the historical correlative, as outlined in a previous section. These acts seem high-handed to us, but did they appear so to contemporaries? And if so, did all contemporaries think alike? Perhaps some people saw Henry's actions against the Italian merchants as justifiable, for it was arguably in the kingdom's interest. Similarly the problems of local government in Lynn had dragged on long enough; a decisive move by the king was perhaps what was needed to bring the men of the town to their senses. The majority considered that the process against Scrope was lawful – even before Henry's post-Agincourt propaganda machine had blackened his name – although Scrope's own household seem to have considered it an act of tyranny. De Gaucourt clearly thought Henry had behaved most unfairly to him. But the fact is that these and almost any other high-handed act could be justified by the majority of contemporaries. High-handedness and even tyranny could be tolerated in a strong king; it was a price worth paying in order to preserve peace among the magnates.

If we have trouble judging Henry for his high-handedness, we have less difficulty when it comes to his outright failures. Stepping away from the propaganda-oriented chronicles has revealed a number of areas where Henry's record falls well short of the glorious, unblemished career we have been led to believe in by traditional historians. He never captured Glendower. Sir John Oldcastle remained at large until Edward Charlton, Lord Powys, captured him in 1417. Henry failed to sort out the mayoral disputes in Lynn. His failure to remedy the state of Berwick Castle, despite the warnings of his council in February 1415, left the north dangerously unprotected.[17] There were more significant failures too. He made mistakes in attacking Harfleur, almost destroying the defensibility of the town; he also made errors on the march to Calais, which resulted in his army becoming weak, hungry and dispirited. The expedition was only saved from complete disaster by a number of strokes of good fortune.

For contemporaries, one of Henry's most obvious failures was a lack of respect for basic chivalric codes. Something of the spirit of chivalry, as well as its shining armour, was sullied by the mud of Agincourt. The massacre of the prisoners is just one of many instances;

another, equally significant at the time, was that so many lords were *killed*; normally codes of honour ensured that great lords were ransomed, not butchered like cattle. From the French point of view, there was also Henry's behaviour at the siege to consider. Henry threatened the people of Harfleur with the law of Deuteronomy, not a chivalric or honourable end to the siege. Like the Black Prince at Limoges, he threatened to massacre women and children. At Agincourt he failed to give a Christian burial even to the fallen Englishmen; only the bones of the two dead lords were taken home for burial. At Calais he failed to live up to the code of honour which de Gaucourt and d'Estouteville expected: they had fulfilled their oaths in turning up to pay their ransom; and they reasonably expected Henry to honour his side of the bargain; but he did not. Henry's refusal to pay his men for the last eight days of the expedition was similarly dishonourable, as was his failure to provide food for the archers when they reached Calais. At the end of the year, we cannot see Henry V in 1415 in a chivalric light. He regarded the common Englishman in his army as little more than a chattel, and the French men-at-arms as enemies of God, to be treated according to God's law, not the laws of chivalry. Only the most important Frenchmen were held in any esteem by him – because they represented the magnitude of his triumph.

Another of Henry's more significant failures was incremental debt. As this book shows, the royal council was aware that he was not financially secure enough to go to war in February 1415; and the budget in June confirmed their impression. And yet he plunged the crown into even greater debt, and even pawned the Crown Henry. Most of the crown in question was not redeemed until 1430.[18] Historians writing in the afterglow of McFarlane's view of Henry have tended to gloss over such failings. One scholar has gone so far as to remark that there was 'no opposition' to Henry's repeated requests for extraordinary taxation from parliament.[19] However, as a closer look reveals, prior to Agincourt there was indeed opposition: in the parliament of November 1414 as well as the York convocation of January 1415; it was rather that the opponents were overruled on both occasions, not that there was 'no opposition'. Similarly it is said that Henry's officers managed to 'mobilise' £131,000 for the Agincourt campaign, with the implication that he should be congratulated for his fiscal resourcefulness. Yet Henry achieved this in the most underhand way. Many items pawned in 1415 were never redeemed in his lifetime. Many debts were never repaid. Many lords were not reimbursed for their troops' wages for several years. All of these effectively constituted short-term loans, repayable when Henry deemed it desirable, but more often than not, he did not deem it desirable in his lifetime. Of the 25,000 marks he undertook to pay for his father's possessions, he only paid 6,000; and he himself 'died almost as insolvent as his late father had been'.[20]

The negative accounting of Henry's year would not be complete without raising the fundamental point of his entire war policy. Just in terms of loss of lives and the heavy ongoing costs, there are good reasons to say that it was a bad strategy as well as a needless one. First, as the mottoes displayed in London on his homecoming reveal, Henry's campaign led to an anti-French rhetoric which was deeply divisive. Whereas in November 1414 some Members of Parliament had argued against war, in November 1415 the French had become 'those who afflict us . . . those who hate us' and Henry was described as England's saviour from such people. This was the result of propaganda. The reality was that the English had not needed saving, and they would have benefited more from peaceful cooperation with France rather than the ensuing hostility that Henry fomented and which lasted decades.

There was a more subtle and damaging implication to this incitement to hate the French, and it is probably the most negative thing one can say about Henry V. The main reason to re-start the war in 1415 was to prove the right of the Lancastrians to occupy the throne of England. However, by making the legitimacy of the Lancastrian dynasty subject to winning victories over the French, Henry mortgaged his future and that of his descendants. They had to be successful – always – for if there was a failure, it would immediately raise the question of whether the Lancastrians still enjoyed God's approval. What Henry had thus started was a war which he could not possibly win, and which would lead to many deaths, including his own and that of his brother, Thomas. It was a fight against fate; and thus a fight against time, for, sooner or later, the French were bound to win a battle or two. And those victories would cast doubt over the legitimacy of the Lancastrians to govern England, as well as France. It is no coincidence that, soon after the war justifying the legitimacy of the Lancastrian dynasty had been lost in France, it shifted on to English soil and became a civil war – the Wars of the Roses.

ACCOUNTING FOR 1415: ACHIEVEMENTS

Professor Curry's assertion that 'for every bad thing one can say about Henry V, there are dozens of good things to say in his defence' is difficult to put into practice for the year 1415. In fact there seem to be relatively few 'good things' one can say about him in this year, especially when trying to defend him against the charges of cruelty, overwhelming pride, high-handedness, incurring crippling debts, ignoring chivalric codes of honour, and mortgaging the future of his entire dynasty. However, the legend of Henry V is not without a basis in reality. What one needs to do is to get away from the day-by-day details of the year, stop criticising him for every niggling failure, and picture the man's vision and achievements in relation to his time. And when we do that, we can say a number of positive things about him.

Many of these positives can be summed up in the word 'unity'. Almost all the domestic rifts which had existed at Christmas 1414 had been healed by the end of the year. Questions over the legitimacy of the Lancastrian dynasty had been emphatically answered at Agincourt – for the time being, at least. Moreover, in the organisation and prosecution of the war, he galvanised the various forces and groups of the kingdom and gave them a common political purpose. At the same time he gave many of them a common spiritual purpose in the eradication of heresy and the defence of the Church. Such unity England had not known in the reigns of Richard II and Henry IV. It thus constitutes a considerable achievement.

The key to the unity of the kingdom was domestic peace between the magnates. Edward II's entire reign had been wrecked by divisions between the great men of the realm. Richard II's had likewise been greatly disturbed, and Henry IV's was one long disturbance from beginning to end. But Henry managed to reconcile most of the disaffected families – the Hollands, the Despensers, the Mortimers, the Percys – and those individuals who refused to accept this reconciliation were forced to keep quiet by the consequences of the earl of Cambridge's plot. At the same time, Henry calmed the possible divisions within his own family by managing his relationship with his brother Thomas in a satisfactory way, and keeping the peace between Thomas and his uncle Henry Beaufort.

Henry's relations with the clergy were similarly enhanced and strengthened. The prelates of both convocations, ever mindful of threats in parliament to remove their temporal income, saw Henry as a strong defender of the Church. In his deeply pious and moral lifestyle – even endowing and building new monasteries – they saw an example of how lords should behave. They also found him willing to continue the campaign against Lollardy for as long as it took to extirpate heresy. In this respect 1415 was particularly important, for the burnings of Claydon and Gurmyn were among the last martyrdoms to take place during this early phase of Lollardy. Inquisitions continued to be held into Lollard practices but increasingly the supposed heretics were absolved of their crimes. Henry was thus seen by the clergy as winning the battle against Lollardy, acting in collaboration with Archbishop Chichele, who issued an order against Lollards in July 1416, and the new pope Martin V, elected in 1417, who similarly issued a bull against followers of Wycliffe. After Oldcastle had been captured, brought to trial and burnt at the stake in 1417, it was many years before anyone else was burnt for Lollardy. The clergy also acknowledged the divine signal in his victory at Agincourt, and Henry's religious propaganda reinforced his image as a man of God. Although there had been opposition to Henry's subsidy in the York convocation of 1415, it did not resurface after he had proved himself as a ruthless oppressor of heretics and a victor on the field of battle.

Parliament likewise was won over by Henry in 1415. Whereas in November 1414 the Speaker, Thomas Chaucer, had had great difficulty in persuading parliament to voice support for the war, and had only elicited the grant in order to defend the realm, the atmosphere in the parliament of November 1415 was euphoric. From this it is evident that Henry pleased the majority of his people. The antagonism which had existed between parliament and the king in the reign of Henry IV was clearly a thing of the past. At the same time Henry's victory pleased the Londoners, who saw themselves in a partnership with the victorious king, claiming that London was 'the city of the king of justice' on his return. This was the very opposite of the suspicion and hostility with which the men of the capital and the king viewed each other in the reign of Richard II.

As the foregoing passages show, Agincourt was the key to his success. Had he lost that battle as originally reported, he would be regarded today as a self-deluded failure. But he did not lose, and the symbolism of that victory was all-important. Agincourt has been described as a 'singularly unproductive victory – from the strategic point of view', but that view is limited in its exclusively secular character. Agincourt delivered the unity of the magnates, clergy, parliament and Londoners in support of the king, and so was of immense strategic value.[21] Symbolic victories demonstrated God's approval, and thus the likelihood of future successes. Agincourt guaranteed Henry's unrivalled tenure of the throne and permitted him to raise more money to send future expeditions to France, culminating in the conquest of Normandy. Had he not won such a decisive victory, his standing in England would have been lower, and his authority to command the kingdom's forces would have been commensurately reduced.

This hints at another of Henry's achievements in 1415: the completion of the restoration of the royal dignity. The previous thirty years had seen the standing of the monarchy in England sink very low – so low that Richard II was deposed in 1399 by overwhelming popular consent. But the new royal family found it almost impossible to recover the dignity of Edward III's time. The rivalry between Henry IV and Richard II continued even after Richard's death, with faked signet letters from him being circulated and a series of rebellions and assassination attempts mounted against Henry IV and his family. The question of Lancastrian legitimacy never went away; and after Henry IV fell ill, the royal dignity sank so low it became a subject for parliamentary discussion. The king was too feeble, too indebted and too vulnerable to reverse the situation. Prince Henry himself directly contributed to the decline of the royal dignity, by trying to arrange his father's abdication. Had that happened, people would have looked on the kings of England as not being kings for life but only for as long as their heirs and parliaments would permit them to occupy the throne. Edward II had been forced to abdicate by parliament in favour of his son; Richard II had been deposed in parliament in favour of his cousin. If Henry IV had also been dethroned, people would have questioned whether his successor was king by the will of God or by the will of parliament.

Henry V's accession did not automatically bring this situation to an end. The pro-Richard II protest in Westminster Abbey at the time of his accession, Sir John Oldcastle's rising, and the earl of Cambridge's plot all served to demonstrate that Henry had to *do* something to restore the royal dignity; he could not just expect it to happen. But he did do what was required. He made good the things his father had left undone, such as reburying Richard II in his rightful place and commissioning the completion of Westminster Abbey. He remedied the shortcomings of royal foundations, such as the collapsing fabric of St Werbergh's church in Chester and the discipline of the Dominican nuns of Dartford. And he set an example of a king who was hard-working, pious, well-read, intelligent, attentive to justice and the public weal, courageous and, most of all, victorious. England could be proud of its king in December 1415.

Henry also raised England's prestige abroad. In fact, he arguably managed to exceed his great-grandfather Edward III in this respect, for his enhancement of English standing was twofold: spiritual as well as military. At Constance he ensured that the English were recognised as a nation in their own right, and maintained a firebrand spokesman there in the bishop of Salisbury. His influence was felt in many aspects of the council's work, from laying down the law on Wycliffe and heresy to the reform of the Church and the papacy. He made Sigismund aware of his desire for there to be close ties between himself and the Holy Roman Empire, and did what he could to demonstrate this affinity to the rest of Christendom. This policy paid off in 1416 when Sigismund came in person to London, was inducted into the Order of the Garter, and agreed a treaty with Henry. All Europe could see the honour bestowed on Henry, and on England.

The military achievement of Agincourt was of even greater significance in enhancing England's international standing. Whether we approve or not, in the fifteenth century success in battle remained *the* benchmark of divine approval and chivalric dignity. Henry could break all the chivalric codes he wanted, but he would still be respected by knights and men-at-arms throughout Europe because he had been successful in battle. He had deliberately set out to emulate Edward III's greatest victories, and he had succeeded; he thus recovered not only the royal dignity in England, but also reinstated English dignity internationally. England was no longer riven by domestic disputes between magnates, or between the king and the Londoners. It was a kingdom that could put forth an army and defeat the French in battle. And if Henry could defeat the French, the greatest military kingdom in Christendom, then he could defeat anyone.

Finally we come to the most lasting and greatest achievement of Henry V in 1415: inspiring a legend. Today his achievements have long been undone or rendered irrelevant. The symbolic value of Agincourt had little practical value after his death, and the war increasingly became a greater liability than an opportunity, until the English were finally thrown out of Gascony in 1453. Henry's policy towards Lollards was temporarily successful; but he could not control people's changing beliefs. In reality he lost the battle against the followers of Wycliffe on 6 July 1415, when Jan Hus became a martyr at Constance and inspired the whole world – including eventually Martin Luther, whose ninety-five theses would trigger the Protestant Reformation 102 years later. But nevertheless, Henry's legend lives on, and he is still considered a great king, even though we live in a world that normally condemns nationalist leaders for starting wars in order to strengthen their domestic political position. Like Jan Hus, Henry V's actual achievements have become less important than his inspirational qualities, which have proved enduring.

In England, of course, Henry's legend has sometimes obscured the real man. Winston Churchill wrote lyrically about him being the founder of the English navy, and being the first English king to use the English language in his letters – forgetting or not realising that Edward III had commanded a considerably larger navy than Henry, and both Edward III and Henry IV had done much more to encourage the use of the English language. Other pseudo-achievements are still pinned on to Henry as a result of contemporary English chroniclers being in such awe of him, and striving to stress his achievements to the point of exaggeration. That they place the numbers of French troops at Agincourt in excess of sixty thousand, and in some cases over a hundred thousand, is a case in point. But we do not need to twist the statistics or invent facts to portray Henry as a single-minded, courageous and inspiring king. His story in 1415 is somewhat like that of Richard I on the Third Crusade. We do not need to believe that crusades were justifiable to appreciate the admirable qualities that the man displayed in the face of adversity. Indeed, we may deplore crusades, and equally disapprove of Henry's recommencement of the war in France; and yet still we may admire the courage and resolution of a man who set out to achieve something, and encouraged men to follow him, and was prepared to risk his life for what he believed was right.

Henry V's claim to greatness today thus lies predominantly in the legend that he inspired. Shakespeare's 'Henry' might have preserved little of the cruelty and 'scourge of God' character of the real Henry, and the playwright certainly imbued his hero with more charm than the real Henry possessed, but we should not forget that Shakespeare was sufficiently inspired by Henry V to create a masterpiece: a sequence of four history plays that culminated in the triumph at Agincourt. Indeed, in that sense, the legend of Henry V really does live on, for Shakespeare's character has developed into a more important cultural figure in the modern world than the real Henry V. There are many biographies of Henry V, and there are many books on Agincourt: but there are even more on the Shakespeare play, *Henry V*. Thus, as a leader of men engaged in a struggle against overwhelming odds, he has come to have meaning for the whole English-speaking world. And although it could be argued that the historical Henry does not deserve the credit for inspiring Shakespeare, it is fair to say that without that seed of greatness, the great work of literature would not have grown.

Let us not pretend, then, that Henry was perfect, nor that he was without blood on his hands. Harfleur, Agincourt, the executioner's block at Southampton, and the fires of Lollardy – his achievements were born out of fear, luck and pride: dirty, bloody. The truth is that in life, as opposed to legend, there are no golden-boy champions; there are only men and women. Some of them achieve great things, some inspire poets to write great works lauding their achievements, but in reality they are all prone to weaknesses and criticism. In this light, the question of whether Henry V was 'the greatest man to rule England' is absurd. Greatness itself is absurd: an undefinable and distorting chimera. We should perhaps think rather in terms of the 'least flawed' ruler. Was Henry the least flawed man ever to rule England? No, he was deeply flawed. But did he achieve something extraordinary despite this, in spite of his weaknesses and his mistakes? Undoubtedly, yes. That is what gives us hope.

Appendix 1

Edward, Duke of York

This book portrays Edward, duke of York, as one of Henry's four closest friends, and thus one of his closest companions, along with his younger brothers and uncles. The relationships between Henry and his three other closest friends – Richard Courtenay, Richard Beauchamp and Thomas Fitzalan – are relatively straightforward and unambiguous. This is not the case with Edward. His entire relationship with the house of Lancaster was complicated to begin with – and grew more so after Henry IV's return to England in 1399. This, for example, is one eighteenth-century verdict on Edward's historical reputation:

> This infamous man . . . had been instrumental in the murder of his uncle the duke of Gloucester, had then deserted [King] Richard by whom he was trusted; had conspired against the life of [King] Henry to whom he had sworn allegiance; had betrayed his associates, whom he had seduced into this enterprise; and now displayed in the face of the world these badges of his multiplied dishonour.[1]

For this reason, he has normally been assigned a more distant position in the post-1399 royal circle. But Henry did not regard Edward with such diffidence. In fact, he almost always included him alongside his own brothers as one of the most trusted members of the royal family. Thus a note explaining his apparent shifts of loyalty prior to 1415, which have led some writers mistakenly to portray him as a disloyal or unreliable man, is necessary.

Edward was born in about 1373. He was the eldest son of Edmund of Langley (d. 1402), duke of York, the fifth son of Edward III. His mother was Isabella of Castile (d. 1393), the daughter of Pedro the Cruel, the ousted king of Castile. Publicly, there were two other children of the union: Constance, who married Thomas Despenser (d. 1400), earl of Gloucester; and Richard of Conisborough (d. 1415), earl of Cambridge. However, as noted in the text, it is possible that Richard of Conisborough was the product of an adulterous liaison between John Holland and the duchess of York in the 1380s.

Edward of York was not born high in the order of succession. According to Edward III's entail of October 1376, ahead of him stood Richard II, John of Gaunt, and Henry of Bolingbroke, as well as his own father.[2] His position was made potentially even lower in 1386 when Richard declared that the earl of March and his younger brother, Roger Mortimer, were next-in-line to the throne (these boys being Edward III's descendants through his second son's only daughter, Philippa).[3] However, by 1393 at the latest, Richard had changed his mind and set the earl of March back on the lowest rung of the royal family.[4] In that year he began to see Edmund of Langley as his heir and, as Edmund was old, his son Edward was the man most likely to be the next king. That Richard was able to overlook John of Gaunt and Henry of Bolingbroke in this reckoning was due to John's age and Richard's personal antipathy to Henry which caused him to plot how to remove Henry from the succession.

Richard II liked Edward. In 1390 he created him earl of Rutland. In 1395 he created him earl of Cork and in 1397 he raised him to a dukedom, creating him duke of Aumale. The following year he went so far as to adopt him as his brother, and suggested to William Bagot that he might resign the throne in Edward's favour. (Richard seems to have imagined a future in which he was the Holy Roman Emperor and Edward of York king of England.) When John of Gaunt died in February 1399 and Henry of Bolingbroke was exiled for life two months later, it looked as if old Edmund of Langley was indeed next in line to the throne, and that Edward would follow him. That same month Richard II drew up a will in which he made it clear that this was the order of succession. It seems likely that he drew up an entailment at the same time settling the throne on Edmund and then his sons Edward and Richard of Conisborough. Edward went to Ireland with the king shortly afterwards, and his father was guardian of the realm when Henry of Bolingbroke landed at Ravenspur at the beginning of July 1399. Also in Ireland with him and the king was the young Henry of Monmouth – the future Henry V – of whom Richard II was fond.

As is well known, Duke Edmund offered no opposition to the return of Henry IV. In so doing he abdicated any right to inherit the throne. In line with his father's acquiescence, Edward also abandoned the king, despite being his adopted brother, and accepted the loss of his title of duke of Aumale in the subsequent parliament. Also in that parliament he defended himself against accusations of complicity in the murder of his uncle, Thomas, duke of Gloucester. As became clear from John Hall's confession in that same parliament, two of Edward of York's valets had been present and one named Francis had helped with the actual killing – but that did not equate to Edward's guilt. The duke of Norfolk had also been present and yet he had clearly tried to stop the murder. It was Richard II's own instructions which were to blame, not the valets who carried them out.[5] Edward may not even have known of the king's order in this regard. He certainly knew he could do nothing to stop him.

It is at this point that traditional readings of Edward tend to go awry. The problem is a general failure to examine the man from a biographical point of view. Edward has always been seen in relation to Richard II or Henry IV – as if the kings' points of view were the only ones which needed to be understood. But Edward's key relationship after Richard II's fall was not with the new king, Henry IV, but with his son, Henry V. The two men were friends. They were closely related and shared a passion for the English language and hunting: Edward wrote a version of Gaston Phoebus's *Book of the Chase* in English and added various chapters of his own composition, and dedicated the whole finished work to Henry. They were also both deeply religious. So when the old duke of York allowed Henry of Bolingbroke to march against Richard II in 1399 on the grounds of justice, Edward was inclined to support this not only out of loyalty to his father, and probably a sense that he was right with regard to the question of justice, but also out of loyalty to his friend, Henry of Monmouth, the future Henry V.

Edward's shift of trust was only a betrayal with respect to Richard II. There were earlier personal ties with the Lancastrians. These he reinforced in January 1400. According to the *Chronicque de la Traïson et Mort de Richart Deux Roy Dengleterre*, Edward was at the meeting on 17 December 1399 in the abbot's lodging at Westminster Abbey, on which occasion five lords, three churchmen, one knight, Richard II's physician and an esquire planned to assassinate Henry IV and his sons in the plot which became known as the Epiphany Rising. However, Edward's role at that meeting was almost certainly nothing more than gathering information. This he divulged to Henry IV, allowing the king to save his own and his sons' lives.[6]

Edward inherited the dukedom of York on the death of his father in 1402. The following year he joined the prince in fighting in Wales against

Glendower, racking up large sums in unpaid wages. He did not fight for the Percy family at Shrewsbury in 1403, even though they too were complaining bitterly about unpaid wages. But despite this loyalty, it is widely accepted that he betrayed the Lancastrians in 1405. In February of that year his sister Constance accused him of being the instigator of the plot to remove the Mortimer heirs from Windsor Castle. Immediately afterwards she declared that he had tried to murder the king at Eltham, either by scaling the walls or attacking him on the road. Far from acknowledging either of these accusations (as his entry in *ODNB* claims), the duke is said to have immediately thrown down his hood in acceptance of the challenge by his sister's champion, to prove his innocence. However, he was arrested on the king's order and locked up in Pevensey Castle while the king decided what to do with him. He petitioned for his release but was not set free until October 1405. After being freed, he remained unswervingly loyal, fighting in Wales again with Henry and doing so much to inspire the troops that Henry made a special mention in parliament of his great service.

Was there any wavering of his loyalty to the Lancastrians in 1399–1400 or in 1405? As neither Henry IV nor Henry V ever held Edward guilty of complicity in the Epiphany Rising, it is likely that he was indeed their agent amidst the plotters, and far from wishing to punish him they owed him their lives. In 1405 his supposed wavering of loyalty was almost entirely the result of his sister's accusations, and there is a high probability that these were groundless.[7] The instigator seems to have been Constance all along. She was the widow of Thomas Despenser, who had been killed for his part in the Epiphany Rising; it would be understandable if she felt a grudge against her brother, especially if we are right in saying that Edward had betrayed that plot and indirectly caused her husband's death.

Henry IV's release of the duke shows that he did not seriously believe that the duke had plotted against his life; he would have had him executed if that was the case. Nor did Edward think he deserved such harsh treatment – he was confident enough to petition for his release after four months. But the king did have personal doubts about Edward for a time. In 1407, after Edward had been released, the council appointed him constable of the Tower, where the king was keeping two of his most valuable prisoners, namely the king of Scotland and Owen Glendower's son. Henry IV decided he should move them. The council over-ruled him, not placing any credibility in his doubts about Edward. That same year, Prince Henry declared in parliament what an inspiring leader Edward had been in Wales. After that Edward became quickly rehabilitated. By early 1409 he was sufficiently restored to Henry IV's favour that he witnessed the king's will.

All this leads us to believe that the reasons for doubting Edward's loyalty were nothing more than the accusations of his undeniably traitorous sister, coupled with the king's lingering doubts about his loyalty (probably due to his earlier closeness to Richard II). Prince Henry, who knew Edward better than his father did, found it easier to see the loyal man he was, and was better placed to appreciate his friendship. Edward had given up a great deal when he had betrayed Richard II. If we lay aside his sister's accusations, his integrity and devotion to the Lancastrian cause were consistent from 1399. He was too close to Richard II through family connections to be a Lancastrian supporter before that time, and after 1399 he was compromised by those same family connections, especially by his sister. But by 1409, he was firmly in favour with both Henry IV and Henry V, and remained one of Henry V's closest friends, having shown he would stick by the Lancastrians in adversity as well as in victory.

Appendix 2

The Great Council, 15–18 April

In the published *Acts of the Privy Council* there are two sets of minutes which relate to the great council of April 1415. The first is dated by the editor to 'March or April 1415'.[1] The second is dated within the text to 16, 17 and 18 April 1415.[2] This appendix is presented to explain why both sets of minutes have been regarded as relating to the same great council, and why the date of the 16th has been regarded as erroneous.

The two sets of minutes appear quite different. The first set begins with the comment that, at the parliament held in late 1414, the king was urged to send negotiators to his adversary and they had now returned with nothing further to report. As a result, the king proposed to go through with his voyage, praying that 'the temporal lords named below' would serve him as far as they had promised in the said parliament. However, although there had been a promise to pay the lords for the second and third quarters at the end of the second quarter, the late collection of the subsidy would not allow this. It was proposed that they be paid for the second and third quarters at the end of each period. Presumably the king withdrew temporarily while they discussed this, for a marginal note records that the earl of Dorset reported to the king that they agreed, subject to receiving sufficient security. Upon hearing this, the king thanked them and asked them to reassemble 'in the same place on the next Wednesday coming' to establish what sort of security they would require. As for the spiritual lords, the king thanked them for their offerings in their convocations and asked them to discuss what other loans they might make for his forthcoming voyage.

The second set of minutes begins with a formal preamble concerning the lords and prelates who attended the council meeting in the Palace of Westminster on the 16th, and notes the king's thanks to them all for responding to the summons. It then lists the lords present. It notes how the king directed the chancellor to remind them all of the matters discussed in the great council at Westminster, when the king had declared his 'firm purpose' to make a voyage to reclaim his inheritance, and how certain sums had been granted by the convocation and by the commonalty of the realm. Nothing more is said about the meeting held on this day. The minutes continue to relate the business of the 17th, in particular the appointment of the duke of Bedford as keeper of the realm in the king's absence, the naming of the royal council, and the provisions for the safekeeping of the kingdom. The minutes for the 18th lay down the rates for wages on the forthcoming expedition.

It is not immediately obvious that these two sets of minutes refer to the same great council. That they do is revealed by the dating of the first set of minutes. As this set refers to the second parliament of 1414 and the return of the subsequent embassy, it must relate to a meeting after 29 March 1415. The decision in principle to accept securities in lieu of unpaid wages indicates that it describes a meeting held before 29 April 1415, for certain indentures dated that day refer to jewels being accepted in lieu of wages for the second and subsequent quarters.[3] The reference to appearing 'in this same place' to agree what securities would be required rules out the meeting in question being held in the week of Wednesday 24 April, as the king and many of the lords would have been at Windsor for the Garter feast the previous day. Thus we may be confident that the first set of minutes relates to a meeting held in one of three weeks in April: that beginning on the 1st, the 8th or the 15th. As the only known great council meeting at this time is the one scheduled for the 15th, for which summons went out in February (see entry under 20 February), there is no doubt that the week starting Monday 15th is correct. This is supported by the minutes of a council meeting held on the 12th which refer to the forthcoming great council on the 15th.[4] Finally, as the text refers to the lords reassembling on 'the next Wednesday coming', it must relate to discussions held on Monday 15th itself – otherwise it would refer to them reassembling 'tomorrow'.

This conclusion seems to contradict the dating of the great council in the second set of minutes to the three days 16-18 April. At first sight it seems possible that the first set of minutes relate to the 15th and the second set to discussions over the three subsequent days. However, the meeting noted as taking place on the 16th cannot have simply been a second day of the great council as the king would not have left it until then to thank the lords for responding to the summons. Furthermore, the first set of minutes – which has many deletions and is clearly a draft – refer to 'the temporal lords named below' but no such list is attached. Instead the list appears in relation to the meeting held on the 16th, which is a neat set with no deletions. Also we should note that the business described as happening on the 16th partly repeats the formal preliminaries described in the first set of minutes, now firmly dated to the 15th. Although the minutes for the 16th refer to a great council in the autumn of 1414, not the parliament (as the first set states), this was in fact a correction. It seems that the minutes dated 16–18 April are a revised set relating to the whole three-day meeting, and that in abstracting data from the first set the reference to 'parliament' had been corrected to 'great council' but the date had been mistakenly copied as the 16th.

Whether this means that the entries for the 17th and 18th have also been misdated is not possible to say for certain. In this book it has been presumed that the request on Monday 15th for the lords to reassemble on Wednesday 17th implies they did not meet on Tuesday 16th. It seems Henry allowed them a day's grace to discuss what form of security they would require. Probably the reason for the misdating of the second set of minutes is the copyist's assumption that all three days were consecutive: he relocated the 15th to the 16th in the neat, final set of minutes to make his document tally with this assumption.

Appendix 3

Casualties at the Siege of Harfleur

As noted in entries for September and early October, a number of important individuals died at Harfleur. It follows that if a number of significant individuals died, then insignificant ones must have died too. Furthermore, many men were sent home. The Burgundian chronicler, Monstrelet, wrote that upwards of two thousand Englishmen died of dysentery at Harfleur.[1] The eye-witness author of the *Gesta* wrote that five thousand men were invalided back to England from Harfleur – this figure does not include those who died at the siege or ran away.[2] If true, this would have had a significant impact on the size of Henry's army, and it would justify the most extreme underestimates of the size of the English army at Agincourt. Therefore the question of how many men died and were incapacitated at Harfleur deserves close attention.

The starting point has to be the number of men who landed with Henry on 14 August. As noted under that date, presuming there were just 247 Cheshire archers, Henry had a minimum of 11,248 fighting men, of whom 2,266 were men-at-arms. In addition there were the servants, pages and other support staff, resulting in at least 15,000 men with the king, excluding mariners.

One way of proceeding is to establish how many men in each company were sick and to apply the average proportion to the whole army. For example, the earl of Arundel sailed with one hundred men-at-arms and three hundred archers. Of these, two men-at-arms and thirteen archers died at Harfleur, and at least fourteen men-at-arms and sixty-eight archers were sent home sick (including the earl himself, with five fit men-at-arms to help him).[3] Thus a quarter of the earl's four hundred fighting men were incapacitated or died at Harfleur. Sir John Harrington's retinue of thirty men-at-arms and ninety archers also saw a quarter incapacitated: ten men-at-arms (including Sir John himself) and twenty archers. The Earl Marshal's company was the worst hit of all. He contracted to provide fifty men-at-arms and 150 archers but in the end served with forty-eight men-at-arms and 171 archers.[4] These totals were reduced by three dead and thirteen sick men-at-arms (including the earl himself), and forty-five sick archers.[5] This amounts to a sick rate of 28% of the company. On the strength of these figures it would be reasonable to speculate that maybe a quarter of the army – a total of 3,750 men, including 2,812 combatants – was either sent home with dysentery or died at Harfleur.[6] This might be said to accord with Monstrelet's figure of 'upwards of two thousand' English dead. If two thousand men died, and 1,700 were shipped home, then the proportions are satisfied.

The problem here is obvious. Not all the companies experienced the same levels of sickness. The ground around Harfleur was uneven: it rose on the western side to Mont Lecomte and Graville, and on the opposite side it rose to Mont Cabert. Between the two hills was a slowly draining, polluted, flooded valley, full of dead animal carcasses and an effluent-producing town. It would be foolish to presume that 15,000 men, spread across this landscape, all used equally dangerous sources of water. Some would have used wells on high ground, some wells on lower ground, some perhaps drew water from the dammed Lézarde; others may have drawn water from the Seine. With a long detour around the flooded area necessary to get from the king's camp to that of the duke of Clarence, we should expect very different levels of contamination, and thus different levels of sickness in the various parts of the camp. As is clear from some of the deaths which had already occurred before this day, the greatest area of infection was around the king's camp. Bishop Courtenay's death is one example of an infected man being in very close proximity to the king for sustained periods – he often shared the king's tent at night. The infection of the earl of Arundel and his men is another sign of the dangerous nature of the water supply used in the area of the king's camp. Another is the heavy losses sustained by the king's own household: a large number of royal servants had to be sent home.[7] The proportion-based methodology used above to ascertain how many people died and suffered from dysentery is thus somewhat misleading. Although the worst-hit areas saw casualty rates around 25%, the camp as a whole was not as badly affected and large sections of it might have gone entirely unscathed. The earl of Oxford had indented to provide forty men-at-arms and one hundred archers; he returned with thirty-nine men-at-arms and eighty-four archers (12% infected). The duke of York's company of four hundred fighting men was even more disease-free: it suffered just twenty-four casualties (6%), presumably having been stationed some way away from those under the king's direct command.

Recognising this problem, Anne Curry sought a different methodology in her 2005 study, *Agincourt: a New History*. Consulting the original accounts, made after the campaign, she observed that Henry kept a good record of those who had been sent back to England with dysentery, for the very good reason that he did not wish to continue paying men who did not serve. Two documents alone record 1,693 names of those sent home sick.[8] Professor Curry noted that not all of those listed were combatants; servants and pages were included. She also pointed out that more troops were arriving all the time, as we have seen from Jean Bordiu's comments in his letter of 3 September. And these reinforcements kept coming, taking the place of their sick counterparts. The earl of Arundel's retinue was almost entirely replenished, all of the sick and deceased archers being replaced by the end of the campaign, and all but six of the men-at-arms.[9]

Professor Curry placed a high degree of confidence in the hypothesis that the list of 1,693 represented practically all those sent home.[10] She found records of fewer than forty deaths at the siege itself and identified 1,330 of the 1,693 named sick as being combatants.[11] She concluded that the English army was depleted by about 1,370 fighting men as a result of the siege, and these were replaced by an unknown number of reinforcements. On this basis she claimed that 'we can prove' the minimum number of men Henry had with him after the siege.[12] Most historians would not agree that her methodology amounts to proof. One of the two lists of the sick is damaged and incomplete. It is also possible that additional, similar lists have disappeared over the centuries. As for her point about reinforcements, it is noticeable that men moved around between companies, so the number of men who fell ill in one company might be 'reinforced' by others from other companies, whose captains had died, without there being any increase in the army's size. But although the evidence does not allow us to say anything is *proven*, Professor Curry's method does allow us to revisit all the evidence – the chronicle sources as well as the lists and accounts – with an open mind.

One thing is certain: there is no evidence supporting Monstrelet's assertion that two thousand Englishmen died at Harfleur. None of the English sources – not even the *Gesta* – supports this figure, for the *Gesta* refers to 'about five thousand men' – a third of the entire force – being shipped back to England, not commenting on the number who died at Harfleur itself. No source on either side describes a death pit, and no other source speaks of such a large number of deaths at Harfleur. Adam Usk states that 'thousands' were sent home or deserted but, like the author of the *Gesta*, he does not mention large numbers of deaths. Le Fèvre and Waurin note that Henry 'lost' five or six hundred men-at-arms during the siege, plus others who had died of dysentery. Also it should be noted that Monstrelet does not mention any English troops being sent home at all, and goes on to state that the number of men remaining included two thousand men-at-arms and 13,000 archers. It therefore seems highly likely that, as he was writing some thirty years later, he was confusing two thousand sick with two thousand dead, and presuming that those 'lost' at Harfleur all died there. If his testimony is set aside as a result, then the question of how many died at Harfleur is answered in a relative way: not enough to draw the attention of the contemporary chroniclers, and not enough to be a significant factor in the surviving campaign accounts. The evidence shows at least thirty-seven did die, but if there were more than this then there were not many more. Probably fewer than fifty Englishmen perished at Harfleur.

Despite the small number of deaths, we can be certain that dysentery was rife in the English camp. The figures of at least 1,693 men sent back to England and thirty-seven dead mean that at least 11% of the entire army was infected, including non-combatants. We can be sure the duke of Clarence's side of the town was also infected, for the duke himself fell ill and so did about two hundred of the 1,044 soldiers in his retinue.[13] On the basis that the companies which experienced the most disease were those around the king's pavilion, the highest casualty rate in this part of the army (25%) must be a maximum. The duke of Clarence's company seems to have suffered losses of about 20%, the duke of York's about 6%. If we assume that the army was divided between these three battles – men commanded by the king, Clarence and York, as Henry had arranged on 17 August – and that the respective maximum casualty rates in each case were 25%, 20% and 6%, then we might conclude that about 17% of the army was incapacitated by sickness. Although this is still a rough estimate, it takes into consideration the possible lacunae in the lists of the sick. Thus we might estimate that the total number of men sent home was between 1,693 and 2,550, of whom between 1,330 and 1,900 were fighting men. This would go some way to explaining why several English chroniclers note that 'thousands' fell ill at Harfleur, and where Monstrelet got his figure of two thousand casualties from. Lastly, the high casualty rate in the area of the king's camp would explain why the eyewitness author of the Gesta stated that five thousand men were sent home. From where he was based – in the royal chapel, close to the worst-affected area – it did seem that very large numbers were sick or dying.

Appendix 4

Numbers at the Battle of Agincourt

As made clear in the main text, there is a serious question hanging over the relative numbers of men who were at the battle of Agincourt. Historians have long since recognised that the *Gesta* is wildly inaccurate in stating that the French had thirty times as many men as the 5,900 fighting men that that chronicle attributes to the English. However, they have been able to reconcile the three-to-one and four-to-one ratios of the monk of St Denis, and even the six-to-one of the Burgundian chroniclers. They have done this by choosing to accept the *Gesta*'s low estimate of the number of Englishmen, and contrasting it with the high estimates of the number of Frenchmen in other chronicles. By arguing that the French fielded between twenty-five and thirty-five thousand men, and the English had just six thousand, the huge discrepancy which forms an important part of the English patriotic story has been maintained. However, to argue this way is to fall into the mistake of accepting a piece of post-Agincourt English propaganda.[1] The author of the *Gesta* was deliberately underestimating the number of Englishmen present because his work was written to stress the 'miracle' that was Agincourt. French chroniclers' claims that the English had ten, twelve, thirteen, fourteen or eighteen thousand archers, and thus as many men as the French, would have resulted in the battle appearing a much smaller 'miracle'.

As we have seen, records of contract and pay exist which allow us to be certain that, when the English army set out from Harfleur, it included 1,500–1,600 men-at-arms, a similar number of pages, 6,600–7,000 archers, and a few dozen chaplains, clerks, surgeons and royal servants, plus any of the reinforcements who had arrived since 15 August. With regard to the numbers of fighting men – men-at-arms and archers – the total was at least 8,100.[2] Depending on the number of reinforcements from England (an indeterminate number), the actual number sent home sick (possibly five hundred fewer, meaning there were five hundred more in the army), and the actual number of Cheshire archers who set out on the campaign (possibly four hundred more), there may have been several hundred more men than this figure of 8,100. Most English chronicles support this, stating that there were between eight and eleven thousand Englishmen at Agincourt.[3] Despite the trials of the march, Henry had lost very few men to illness and death; and we have independent testimony that no more than 160 had been captured on the way.[4] If we conclude that Henry had between eight and nine thousand fighting men with him, we cannot be far wrong. He certainly had considerably more than the 5,900 men that the author of the *Gesta* claims in his hagiographical account of Henry.

The critical question is one of how many French troops there were gathering between Agincourt and Tramecourt, to the south of Ruisseauville. Unfortunately the chronicle of Ruisseauville itself, which accurately states that there were between eight and nine thousand English fighting men, does not give a figure for the French army. The Burgundian writers claim there were eight thousand men-at-arms and four thousand archers, plus 1,500 crossbowmen in the vanguard, and another 1,400 (or 2,400) men-at-arms on the wings.[5] Although we have no pay records, these numbers do correspond roughly with the ten thousand men-at-arms recorded by the duke of Berry's herald, Gilles le Bouvier; and since this was written from the Armagnac perspective it is thus a counterbalance to the Burgundian chroniclers' accounts.[6]

In taking these observations a stage further, Anne Curry assessed the numbers of men in the French companies as indicated in these sources and then compared them to the sizes of companies which were ordered to be mustered, and made allowances for the additional retinues brought to the battle from individual lords with lands in the north of France.[7] This method, which is the most refined yet employed, suggests that there were about eight or nine thousand men-at-arms gathering around the spot where the constable had set his banners. Most companies had been instructed to raise half as many crossbowmen and archers as men-at-arms, so it would be reasonable to assume there were four or five thousand archers and crossbowmen too. Professor Curry suggests this proportion was not achieved, and that the total number of French fighting men was about 12,000.[8] If it *was* achieved – and the presence of many local men and men from the Marches of Boulogne suggests there were other contingents which we should consider – there may have been fourteen or fifteen thousand fighting men, as the Burgundian chronicles suggest.[9] But there were nowhere near the sixty thousand fighting men which the English claim; and this figure is the lowest given for the French army in any English chronicle – some estimates being as high as 160,000.

Professor Curry concluded that the two armies were far more closely matched than most historians assume: twelve thousand fighting Frenchmen against nine thousand fighting Englishmen, a ratio of four-to-three. Although her method minimises French numbers (by limiting her figures to those in the basic army and a few specific additional companies) and maximises English numbers (by assuming the numbers sent home from Harfleur were no greater than the sick lists), her work is a robust challenge to anyone familiar with the old school of Agincourt history (in which six thousand Englishmen defeated twenty-five or thirty thousand Frenchmen). There simply is no evidence that there were that many troops on the French side – except in the pages of chroniclers whose ability to gauge what thirty thousand men looked like must be questioned, even if they were present on the day. It needs to be borne in mind that their main precedent for describing the size of an army in a battle was the Old Testament – which regularly mentions armies of tens or hundreds of thousands of men. The figures preferred in this study incorporate room for error, allowing for more Frenchmen and slightly fewer Englishmen than Professor Curry does, but the most extreme imbalance which is credible is fifteen thousand French troops against 8,100 English: a ratio of about two-to-one.

Notes

Prologue

1. McFarlane, *Lancastrian Kings*, p. 133. It is worth noting that McFarlane did not specify what he meant by 'greatness' or 'the greatest man'. • **2.** McFarlane wrote 'the historian cannot honestly write biographical history: his province is rather the growth of social organisations, of civilisation, of ideas' (quoted in Harriss, *Cardinal Beaufort*, v).

Introduction

1. Vaughan, *John the Fearless*, pp. 44–8. • **2.** Vaughan, *John the Fearless*, pp. 71–2. • **3.** Vaughan, *John the Fearless*, p. 85. The guidebook to *La tour Jean sans Peur*, Paris, suggests that it was not actually the duke's bedchamber. The reasons it gives are that the tower is small, and not of the expected ducal grandeur. The chamber beneath the duke's is described today as the equerry's chamber. However, Vaughan's statement, based on the building accounts, is explicit: the principal room was indeed designed for John's personal safety at night. The fifteenth-century chronicler Monstrelet also states specifically that he built this tower to sleep in at night. The two chambers are supported on huge stone pillars, rising twenty-five feet or so above the first-floor guard chamber, and reached only by an extremely elaborately carved stone staircase, which incorporates several of the duke's heraldic badges. The wonderful staircase ceiling suggests strongly that, although this was a small chamber, it was intended to be seen by the duke. The whole edifice amounted to a lordly stone box supported sixty feet above the walls of Paris. And as the tower was constructed in 1408–9, after the murder of Orléans and John's return to the city, I suspect that the extraordinary design, incorporating so much empty space, was a means of preventing the duke being attacked in his bedchamber by the use of fire. The tower is illustrated in the second plate section of this book. • **4.** Allmand, *Henry V*, p. 48. There had been earlier embassies appointed to negotiate with Burgundian ambassadors – e.g. those of 3 July 1406 and 29 November 1410 (Hardy, *Syllabus*, pp. 556, 566) but these seem to have been for the defence of Calais and the local truce. See Nicolas (ed.), *Privy Council*, ii, pp. 5–6 for the instructions to the ambassadors appointed on 29 November 1410. • **5.** *Fears*, esp. p. 322. • **6.** *Fears*, p. 337; Allmand, *Henry V*, p. 48. • **7.** *Monstrelet*, i, pp. 18–19. Although the then duke of Burgundy (Philip the Bold) was excepted by Louis in this agreement, this was only with regard to Louis' part of the bargain. In other words, Henry would have still been liable to help Louis against John the Fearless's father even though Louis was not bound to help Henry against the duke of Burgundy. • **8.** *Fears*, pp. 114, 134–5, 155. • **9.** Hardy, *Syllabus*, ii, pp. 567–8. An extension of the truce in Flanders was sealed on 27 May 1411. • **10.** In support of this it should be noted that on the same day that Henry appointed the ambassadors to treat with the Burgundians at Calais he granted safe conduct for ambassadors of the king of France to come to England. See *Syllabus*, ii, p. 566. See also p. 567, where redress of injuries with ambassadors from Burgundy and France are simultaneously authorised on 27 March 1411. • **11.** Curry, *Agincourt*, p. 26. • **12.** *Fears*, p. 339; Nicolas (ed.), *Privy Council*, ii, pp. 19–24. • **13.** Given-Wilson (ed.), *PROME*, 1411 November (Introduction) states the fleet sailed in September. Curry, *Agincourt*, p. 27, states that the force was sent to meet the duke of Burgundy at Arras on 3 October. • **14.** Allmand, *Henry V*, pp. 48–9. It is perhaps significant that the name of the duke of Berry was removed from the 1 September instructions to the ambassadors to treat with John the Fearless, removing any requirement for the English to fight Berry on John's behalf. See Nicolas (ed.), *Privy Council*, ii, pp. 21–4. • **15.** *Fears*, p. 338. The consensus view on intervention in France in 1411 is specified in Allmand, *Henry V*, p. 48; Curry, *Agincourt*, p. 27. • **16.** In *Fears*, p. 341, I stated two thousand English archers and eight hundred men-at-arms were at St-Cloud. However, recent research suggests that the expedition consisted of just one thousand men (200 men-at-arms and 800 archers). See Tuck, 'The Earl of Arundel's Expedition', p. 232. See Curry, *Agincourt*, p. 29 for further variations on the number. • **17.** *Fears*, p. 345. • **18.** Hingeston (ed.), *Royal and Historical Letters*, ii, pp. 322–5; Curry, *Agincourt*, p. 31. • **19.** *Fears*, p. 347. They were built at Ratcliffe in the Thames, according to Wylie, *Henry V*, ii, p. 372.

Christmas Day 1414

1. I have presumed that Henry held his Christmas feast in 1415 in Westminster Hall, where the marble seat stood. It is entirely possible that he held it instead on a smaller scale, in the White (or Lesser) Hall, to the south. However, as Christmas was one of the three traditional crown-wearing occasions, and given Henry's attitude to traditional kingship, I suspect that Westminster Hall was the actual venue. • **2.** For Christmas rituals in the medieval royal household, see Hutton, *Rise and Fall*, chapter one. **3.** The problem is dealt with in full in Mortimer, 'Richard II and the Succession'; *Fears*, Appendix Two. A simplified overview appears in Mortimer, 'Who was the rightful king in 1460?' • **4.** *Fears*, pp. 190–1. • **5.** The spice-plate is mentioned in Henry's inventory. See *PROME*, 1423 October, item 31 (the inventory of Henry V), entry no. 8. It is described as 'the great gold spice-plate, set with a balas ruby in the mouth of the eagle on the fruitlet of the said spice-plate'. It had twelve balas rubies and sapphires around the fruitlet, six pearls and four pendant pearls in the beaks of four eagles, and 229 pearls and twenty-four balas rubies and sapphires around the cover. It also had twenty-four clusters, each of four pearls and a diamond, around it, and an eagle with a sapphire in its beak in the bottom of the basin of the spice-plate. Around each of the feet were four large pearls, four balas rubies, four sapphires and 112 pearls. The whole object was worth £602 5s. • **6.** This impression of 'innocence' is not a contemporary description but my own impression, based on studying the English portrait of Henry in the Royal Collections. • **7.** Hutchinson, *Henry V*, p. 72; McFarlane, *Lancastrian Kings*, p. 124. • **8.** Woolgar, *Senses*, p. 138. • **9.** For the slashed sleeves, see the portrait of Henry V in the Royal Collection; for Henry wearing a high-collar gown, see the image of Hoccleve presenting his *The Regement of Princes* to Henry (BL Arundel MS 38, fol. 37); for long sleeves with rich linings see the same image and also the image of Jean de Galopes presenting his translation of Bonaventura's *Life of Christ* to Henry (Corpus Christi College, Cambridge, MS 213 fol. 1r.). For a *hanseline* worth £151 belonging to the king, see Henry's inventory in *PROME*, 1423 October. • **10.** Wylie, *Henry V*, i, p. 191. • **11.** Wylie, *Henry V*, i, p. 190. • **12.** Wylie, *Henry V*, i, pp. 200–1. Both the earl of Ormonde and Bishop Courtenay attested to this separately. • **13.** Wylie, *Henry V*, i, p. 195. • **14.** Wylie, *Henry V*, i, p. 201. • **15.** Wylie, *Henry V*, i, p. 188. • **16.** Barker, *Agincourt*, p. 39. For the exhortation to look the lord directly in the face as a matter of good manners, see Furnival (ed.), *Babees Book*, p. 3. • **17.** Although he did empower negotiators to treat with the king of Aragon and the duke of Burgundy for his marriage to their daughters, these seem not to have been serious offers, as the Aragon negotiators were men of relatively low rank. The marriage to the duke of Burgundy's daughter was negotiated while Henry was still prince; the marriage negotiated when he was king was to Katherine of France. • **18.** His promises to consider no other marriage but to Katherine are in *Foedera*, ix, p. 140 (18 June 1414), p. 166 (18 October 1414), pp. 182–4 (4 December, extending promise to 2 February 1415). • **19.** Writing by the king survives in all three languages. It is not proven that he spoke Latin, but it is probable, given that he chose to write in it. According to Allmand in *ODNB*, Henry V could speak Latin. • **20.** Allmand states in *ODNB* that the fifteenth-century story of his residing at Oxford under Beaufort's care in 1398 is unsupported. • **21.** 'No one expected him to become king', wrote Professor Allmand in his *Henry V* (1992), p. 8. Since that work was written, Edward III's entailment to the throne, made in 1376, has been brought to light by Professor Bennett. This makes clear that Henry IV believed rightly that he was likely to succeed to Richard II's throne if Richard should die without children. By September 1386 Richard had been married for over four years and his wife had not conceived. With regard to Henry V's date of birth on 16 September 1386, see Mortimer, 'Henry IV's date of birth and the royal Maundy', pp. 568–9, n.7. By the time Henry V was six, Richard II had been married for more than ten years without progeny. There was therefore every reason to suspect that Henry IV would indeed inherit the throne, in line with Edward III's entail; and, if not Henry IV, then one of his sons, presumably the eldest, Henry V. Therefore his father and grandfather – at the very least – expected him to inherit. • **22.** For example, Henry IV executed the archbishop of York in 1405 as well as other prelates in later years. Henry V was in opposition to the archbishop of Canterbury in religious and political affairs in the last years of Henry IV's reign. • **23.** For Henry's devotion to the Trinity and to the English saints, see Allmand, *Henry V*, pp. 180–1. For Edward III's devotion to the English saints, see *Perfect King*, p. 60. For Edward III's devotion to the Virgin Mary, see *Perfect King*, pp. 111–12. For Henry IV's devotion to the Trinity, see *Fears*, pp. 196–7. • **24.** Allmand, *Henry V*, p. 33. • **25.** Wylie, *Henry V*, p. 189. • **26.** Curry, *Agincourt*, p. 33; Allmand, *Henry V*, p. 32. • **27.** Harriss, 'The King and his Magnates', quoting Kingsford (ed.), *First English Life*, p. 14. • **28.** For sorcery at the English court, see H. A. Kelly, 'English kings and the fear of sorcery', *Mediaeval Studies*, 39 (1977), 206–38. • **29.** *PROME*, 1423 October, item 31, entries 107 and 700. • **30.** When the archbishop of Canterbury, the bishop of Winchester, and two of the king's brothers flattered the mayor of London by giving him the seat of honour in the Guildhall, the prelates were seated on the mayor's right and the brothers on the mayor's left. See Riley, *Memorials*, pp. 604–5. • **31.** DL 28/1/6 fol. 24r. • **32.** Barker, *Agincourt*, p. 45. • **33.** Barker, *Agincourt*, p. 45. • **34.** This is noted by Waurin, as stated in Jenny Stratford's article on John in *ODNB*. • **35.** This quotation is from G. L. Harriss's article on Humphrey in *ODNB*. • **36.** March witnessed just over half of the royal charters in 1414–16 and, by the reckoning of his own accounts, was in Henry's company in 1414 (*ODNB*), so was very probably there that day. • **37.** Hugh Mortimer, later treasurer of England, had been Henry's chamberlain when prince of Wales (Pugh, *Southampton Plot*, p. 58). He was sufficiently close to Henry for the king to be the supervisor of his will (*Register of Henry*

Chichele, ii, pp. 86–7). He was not related to the main Mortimer family of the earls of March, or any of their collateral branches. He and his brother Thomas were the sons of Thomas and Sarah Mortimer of Helpston, Northants. Hugh held the manor of Great Houghton. His father, Thomas the elder, was the son of Ralph Mortimer and the brother of Joan Sulgrave, who confirmed the manor of Helpston on Hugh and his brother (Northants Record Office F(M) Charter/ 913, 930). The grandfather of Thomas and Hugh, Ralph Mortimer, who was born about 1312, was the son and heir of Ralph Mortimer of Helpston (d. 1325), who was the son of Sir Waleran Mortimer of Exton, Rutland, and Eakley, Bucks (fl. 1295–1317). Sir Waleran was the son of William Mortimer (d. c. 1273) who was in turn the son of Waleran Mortimer, who held part of Eakley in 1242–3 (*Book of Fees*, p. 873). Before that it is not possible to trace the ancestry of this family, but their heraldry shows no connection with the Mortimers of Wigmore. • **38.** Given-Wilson, *Royal Household and the King's Affinity*, p. 60. • **39.** Queen Joan had her own household. For a set of her household accounts, dating from 1419–20, see E 101/406/30. • **40.** McFarlane, *Lancastrian Kings*, p. 124; Wylie, *Henry V*, i, p. 223. • **41.** Wylie, *Henry V*, p. 7. • **42.** Wylie, *Henry V*, pp. 34–5. I mistakenly named him Richard Whytlock , not John, in *Fears*, p. 348. • **43.** Wylie, *Henry V*, p. 8. • **44.** Powell, 'Restoration of Law and Order', p. 63. • **45.** John Fox, *Acts and Monuments* (1641), p. 739. See also John A. F. Thomson, 'Oldcastle, John, Baron Cobham (*d. 1417*)', *ODNB*. • **46.** Fox, *Acts and Monuments*, p. 742; Ruffhead (ed.), *Statutes*, i, p. 493. • **47.** Vale, *English Gascony*, p. 69. • **48.** Wylie, *Henry V*, i, p. 124; Vale, *English Gascony*, p. 72. Some guns were sent to Gascony (see entry for 23 January 1415) but when they were shipped is not clear. • **49.** Vaughan, *John the Fearless*, pp. 99–102. • **50.** On 4 June 1414 Henry authorised his ambassadors to accept the duke of Burgundy's homage at the same time as negotiating an alliance with him. *Foedera*, ix, pp. 137–8. • **51.** Wylie, *Henry V*, i, p. 423. • **52.** Wylie, *Henry V*, i, p. 477. • **53.** Barker, *Agincourt*, p. 92. • **54.** *Foedera*, ix, p. 159. • **55.** *Chronica Maiora*, p. 402. • **56.** Wylie, *Henry V*, i, p. 163. • **57.** *Issues*, p. 336. • **58.** Nicolas (ed.), *Privy Council*, ii, pp. 142–4. • **59.** *PROME*, 1414 November, item 2. • **60.** *CPR*, p. 292. • **61.** *HKW*, pp. 998–1000. • **62.** *Fears*, p. 219; Wylie, *Henry V*, i, pp. 205–8. • **63.** Harriss, 'The King and his Magnates', esp. pp. 35–9. • **64.** Powell, 'Restoration of Law and Order', p. 61.

January

1. See John Russell's *Boke of Nurture*, in Furnivall, *Babees Book*, p. 182 for the lamp. • **2.** Henry V's inventory (*PROME*, 1423 October, item 31) notes many

Arras tapestries. See entries 757–97 in particular. • **3.** This was in the Prince's Palace at Westminster at the time of his death. *PROME*, 1423 October, item 31, entry 773. The following item is no. 768 in the inventory. • **4.** For Henry's clock in the shape of a *nef*, see *PROME*, 1423 October, item 31, entry 247. In *Fears*, p. 92, I noted that his father had a portable clock – or at least a basket to transport a clock – even though the portable clock is supposed not to have been invented until the invention of the spring mechanism in the 1430s. Further research needs to be done in this area to establish whether these references really do relate to portable mechanical timepieces. • **5.** Printed in Furnivall, *Babees Book*, p. 176. • **6.** Hutton, *Rise and Fall*, p. 15. This was normally the duty of the king's chamberlain, Lord Fitzhugh, but he was abroad at this time. • **7.** The royal household accounts for the period are not well preserved. Those for 1415 do not survive at all. The statement here is drawn from the accounts of Henry's father as king, before he was ill, in 1402–3 (E 101/404/23). The amounts spent on the feast for that year, which was held at Windsor Castle, are as follows: Christmas Day £224 18s 5½d; 26th December £76 12s 2d; 27th £81 9s 7d; 28th £81 9s ½d; 29th £64 11s 9d; 30th £67 0s ½d; 31st £87 0s 4½d; 1st January £92 8s 10d; 2nd £70 0s ½d; 3rd £68 18s 2½d; 4th £70 9s 2½d; 5th £64 0s 4½d; 6th (Epiphany) £89 2s 2d; 7th £72 19s 4½d. After that the sums spent each day sunk back well below the £50 mark. • **8.** E 101/406/21 fol. 21r (Thomas More's wardrobe account for 1413). • **9.** Bellaguet (ed.), *Chronique du Religieux*, v, pp. 479–80. • **10.** Allmand, *Society at War*, pp. 25–7; Barker, *Agincourt*, p. 179; Wylie, *Henry V*, i. p.138. • **11.** Loomis (ed.), *Constance*, p. 189. • **12.** Loomis (ed.), *Constance*, p. 87. • **13.** Loomis (ed.), *Constance*, pp. 189–90. For a modern scholar's estimate of how many men were present – 29 cardinals and 600 prelates – see *Chronica Maiora*, p. 400. • **14.** Loomis (ed.), *Constance*, pp. 189–90. • **15.** Loomis (ed.), *Constance*, p. 476. • **16.** Loomis (ed.), *Constance*, p. 98. • **17.** *Chronica Maiora*, p. 399, note 5 cont. on p. 400. • **18.** *Fears*, p. 254. • **19.** Jacob, *Chichele*, pp. 35–8. • **20.** Wylie, *Henry V*, p. 248; *ODNB* (under Oldcastle); Spinka (ed.), *Letters of Jan Hus*, pp. 213–15. • **21.** Most writers state that the English embassy arrived as one, either on 21 January (following Jacob Cerretano's journal) or 31 January (following Richental's chronicle). It was about five weeks' travel from Constance back to London in summer (see *ODNB*, under Catterick). In winter it seems to have been more: Warwick took ten weeks, from 11 November to 21 January (E 101/321/27). Sir Walter Hungerford set out on 27 October (according to his expenses, E 101/321/28), two weeks ahead of Warwick. According to his *ODNB* entry, Robert Hallum preached at Constance on 15 January. Thomas Polton's petition on Henry's behalf was delivered in December 1414, before any prelates arrived, due to his being a protonotary at the curia; this serves as a reminder that not all the English nation arrived as one (Loomis (ed.), *Constance*, p. 471). • **22.** These men had all been present at a meeting of the great council on 29 December. See Wylie, *Henry V*, i, pp. 436–8. John, count of Alençon, had been created a duke the previous day, 1 January (Curry, *Agincourt*, p. 25). • **23.** Vaughan, *John the Fearless*, pp. 193–202; Wylie, *Henry V*, i, p. 401. The council meeting on 2 January can hardly have failed to discuss the civil war. • **24.** *CCR*, p. 165; *Foedera*, ix, p. 188. • **25.** *CCR*, p. 169 (Ireland); *CPR*, p. 288 (man of Calais). • **26.** Johnes (ed.), *Monstrelet*, i, p. 320. • **27.** Hutton, *Rise and Fall*, p. 16. • **28.** *PROME*, 1414 April, item 15. • **29.** *CPR*, p. 294. • **30.** See Mark Ormrod, 'The Rebellion of Archbishop Scrope and the Tradition of Opposition to Royal Taxation', in Dodd and Biggs, *Reign of Henry IV: Rebellion and Survival* (2008), pp. 162–79. • **31.** *Fears*, pp. 286–7. • **32.** Wylie, *Henry V*, i, p. 434. • **33.** Spinka (ed.), *John Hus at the Council of Constance*, p. 30. • **34.** Spinka (ed.), *John Hus at the Council of Constance*, p. 48. • **35.** Fox, *Acts and Monuments*, p. 789. • **36.** Spinka (ed.), *John Hus at the Council of Constance*, pp. 100, 115. • **37.** Spinka (ed.), *John Hus at the Council of Constance*, p. 116. • **38.** He was detained from 28 November. For Lord John de Chlum's petition for him to be released, in line with the emperor's safe-conduct, see Fox, *Acts and Monuments*, p. 823. • **39.** Spinka (ed.), *Letters of John Hus*, p. 148. • **40.** E 403/620. • **41.** For Henry donating 4s per day in 1413, see Thomas More's account E 101/406/21 fol. 5r–17r. This was a regular amount, separate from his oblations. • **42.** *Papal Registers 1404–15*, p. 456. • **43.** *ODNB*; Pugh, *Henry V*, pp. 61–4. They were knighted on the eve of Henry's coronation. • **44.** Spinka (ed.), *Letters of John Hus*, p. 143. • **45.** Spinka (ed.), *Letters of John Hus*, p. 145. • **46.** Barker, *Agincourt*, p. 86 states it was already built; Wylie, *Henry V*, ii, p. 383 is less certain. • **47.** *CPR*, p. 293. • **48.** Barker, *Agincourt*, p. 84. • **49.** *Foedera*, ix, pp. 178–9. Lisle was appointed on 16 November 1414. • **50.** Loomis (ed.), *Constance*, p. 481. • **51.** Loomis (ed.), *Constance*, p. 104. Note that Richental is inaccurate not only with respect to the identities but also the dates of arrival. He declares the English arrived on 31 January. He also stated they arrived on 7 December and that Warwick was accompanied by 'two archbishops and seven bishops' (Loomis (ed.), *Constance*, p. 95). Cerretano's date is to be preferred. • **52.** *Foedera*, ix, pp. 167, 169. • **53.** See Loomis (ed.), *Constance*, p. 481; *Foedera*, ix, p. 162. • **54.** Jacob, *Chichele*, p. 35. • **55.** *Chronica Maiora*, p. 400. • **56.** Wylie, *Henry V*, i, p. 425, n. 3. • **57.** *CPR*, p. 293. • **58.** Dodd, 'Patronage, Petitions and Grace', in Dodd and Biggs, *Reign of Henry IV: Rebellion and Survival*, pp. 105–35, at p. 105. • **59.** Nicolas (ed.), *Privy Council*, ii, pp. 339–41. • **60.** Although there is some doubt about this – Thomas Beaufort's expense account for this journey claims payments from 14 December 1414, and diplomatic expenses were normally reckoned from the day the claimant left London – it is possible that this relates to when his household set out. The documents for the truce, dated 24 January, name all four ambassadors, but Courtenay seems to have travelled ahead without Langley, Beaufort and Grey. Langley and Beaufort were at a council meeting

in London in February in the second year of the reign. See Nicolas (ed.),
Privy Council, ii, pp. 150–1. • **61.** E 403/621 under 18 May. *Issues*, p. 340 correctly
transcribes this. Wylie, i, p. 435 n. 6 has this as 14 December. • **62.** E 101/321/26.
• **63.** E 403/621 records the passage of these three ambassadors under 11 April.
• **64.** *Foedera*, ix, pp. 196–200. It is assumed here that Courtenay agreed the
prolongation. He travelled separately to the other principal ambassadors,
and two of the others were still in England in February, as shown by the
minutes of a council meeting. • **65.** Wylie, *Henry V*, i, p. 436. • **66.** *CPR*, p. 294.
• **67.** *CCR*, p. 169. • **68.** *CCR*, p. 172; *CPR 1413–1416*, p. 280. • **69.** *CPR*, p. 277.
• **70.** *CPR*, p. 275. • **71.** *CPR*, p. 295. • **72.** Barker, *Agincourt*, pp. 94–5. Wylie,
ii, p. 381, states Edward III once owned 150 ships. • **73.** *Foedera*, ix, p. 195.
The petition is dated 21 January, and endorsed by the chamberlain. The
pardon on the Patent Rolls is dated 30 January (*CPR*, p. 275).

February

1. Hutton, *Rise and Fall*, p. 17. • **2.** In 1403, for example, the amount spent on
cooking for the royal household on the eve of Candlemas was £11 15d; on
the last three days of January that year it had been £13 17s 1d, £11 15s 8½d,
£16 5s 4d. Candlemas itself saw £22 10s 1½d spent on cooking. See E 101/404/21.
• **3.** *CPR*, p. 293. • **4.** For other letters issued this day, see the three in *CPR*,
p. 278, among others. None were attested by the king personally. • **5.** Loomis
(ed.), *Constance*, p. 109. • **6.** Loomis (ed.), *Constance*, pp. 210–11. • **7.** Loomis
(ed.), *Constance*, p. 109. • **8.** Loomis (ed.), *Constance*, pp. 109–10. • **9.** Wylie,
Henry V, i, p. 311 n. 2. • **10.** Luke 2: 29–32. • **11.** *CPR*, p. 284. • **12.** Loomis
(ed.), *Constance*, p. 110. • **13.** Vaughan, *John the Fearless*, p. 203; *Monstrelet*, i, p.
324. • **14.** Curry, *Agincourt*, p. 47. • **15.** For the minutes of the meeting see
Nicolas (ed.), *Privy Council*, ii, pp. 150–1. The reference of the original document is now British Library, Cotton Cleopatra F. III fol. 168–9 (formerly foli-
ated 135–6). It reads '*sensuent certains ordennances faites en le moys de ffeurer l'an
du regne du Roy Henri le quint second*'. I am grateful to Julian Harrison, Curator
of Medieval and Earlier Manuscripts at the BL, for checking this detail for
me. The St Denis chronicler states that the English ambassadors rode into
Paris on 9 February. Monstrelet states they entered the city with a company
of six hundred men on the 10th. However, as noted under 9 February, it is
difficult to accept that the whole embassy arrived at that time. Thomas
Beaufort was in Paris by 21 February, as the St Denis chronicler stated. • **16.**
This was in line with the advice of the council of the previous autumn. See
Nicolas (ed.), *Privy Council*, ii, pp. 145–8. • **17.** Nicolas, *Agincourt*, appendix, p.
21. • **18.** Note that it was always described as the nation of *England*, not

Britain. • **19.** Loomis (ed.), *Constance*, p. 483. • **20.** The roll in question is E 403/620. • **21.** Nicolas, *Agincourt*, appendix, pp. 21–3. In February 1417, six great ships are recorded – the *Trinity Royal*, the *Holy Ghost,* the *Nicholas* and three carracks – plus eight barges and ten balingers (24 vessels in all). The list for August 1417 categorises them differently, naming three great ships (including the *Trinity Royal* and the *Holy Ghost*), eight carracks, six ships, one barge, and nine balingers, two of which were associated with the *Trinity Royal* and the *Holy Ghost* (27 vessels). • **22.** *Issues*, p. 338 • **23.** See also Wylie, *Henry V*, i, p. 104. • **24.** Wylie, *Henry V*, i, pp. 101–2. • **25.** Curry, *Agincourt*, p. 48 dates this order to 20 February, citing E 403/619 m. 12. The payment date is clearly under 4 February in E 403/620 as well as under the 20th. • **26.** *CPR*, p. 276. • **27.** *Foedera*, ix, p. 200; *Chronica Maiora*, p. 403; *CPR*, p. 294. • **28.** *CCR*, p. 172. John Clyffe is described as 'master' of the minstrels in E 405/28. • **29.** *CPR*, pp. 278, 281. • **30.** *CCR*, p. 167. • **31.** Loomis (ed.), *Constance*, p. 483. • **32.** *CPR*, p. 280. • **33.** Johnes (ed.), *Monstrelet*, i, p. 322. • **34.** Bellaguet (ed.), *Chronique du Religieux*, v, p. 409. • **35.** Note that the French embassy, which left Paris on 4 June 1415, took thirteen days to reach Calais, and that was later in the year, when the weather was better. One way of tallying the discrepancy noted in the text would be to suggest that the privy council minute is wrongly dated to February but this is unlikely. The account of the embassy delivered the following January in the Tower of London dates the ambassadors' crossing to France in February 1415 (*Foedera*, ix, p. 209). • **36.** For the legal travelling day of twenty miles, see Loomis (ed.), *Constance*, p. 343; for higher travelling speeds see *TTGME*, p. 132. Information about the phases of the moon has been taken from http://eclipse.gsfc.nasa.gov/ phase/ phases1401.html, downloaded 10 September 2008. • **37.** Bishop Langley, the earl of Dorset and Richard Grey travelled together, independent of Courtenay, as the Issue Rolls for 11 April make clear. Richard Redman's chronicle also states that the entry of the embassy was a great spectacle; see Cole (ed.), *Memorials*, p. 31. • **38.** The English embassy as a whole is supposed to have stayed at the *hôtel de Clisson*; but Courtenay was noted as staying at the *hôtel de Navarre* when he received a visit from Fusoris. Although we do not know the exact date of this meeting, Courtenay's different residence suggests he was staying elsewhere prior to the arrival of the other English ambassadors, and that he later joined them at the *hôtel de Clisson*. • **39.** Allmand, *Henry V*, p. 8. The astrological treatises quoted by Professor Allmand (Bodleian Library, Ashmole MS 393, fol. 109–11; MS 192 pt iii, fol. 26–36) state that Henry was born at 11.22 am on 16 September 1386. • **40.** *CPR*, p. 294; Nicolas, *Agincourt*, appendix, pp. 21–3. • **41.** *Monstrelet*, i, p. 322. Waurin's claim that it was eight days' celebration cannot be correct, for Ash Wednesday (the first day of the Lenten fast) fell on the fourth day. • **42.** Hutton, *Rise and Fall*, p. 19. • **43.** Hutton, *Rise and Fall*, p. 19. • **44.** These were favourites of the monks at Westminster in the period. See Harvey, *Living and Dying*, pp. 34–71; also *A Collection of Ordinances and Regulations*, pp. 415–76; *leche Lombard* appears at pp. 458–9. • **45.** Hutton, *Rise and Fall*, pp. 18, 58. • **46.** *Fears*, pp. 211–19. • **47.** Brie (ed.), *Brut*, ii, pp. 494–5. • **48.** Wylie, *Henry V*, i, pp. 211–12. • **49.** *CCR*, p. 167. This letter was issued under the authority of the privy seal; it could have been issued in response to a letter under Henry's signet sent from elsewhere. • **50.** Loomis (ed.), *Constance*, pp. 483–4. • **51.** *CPR*, p. 281. • **52.** Nicolas (ed.), *Privy Council*, ii, pp. x, 341. • **53.** Loomis (ed.), *Constance*, p. 217. • **54.** *Foedera*, ix, pp. 197–200. • **55.** *CPR*, p. 284 (both). • **56.** *CPR*, p. 286. See also the king's order of 28 February to the escheator in Gloucestershire in relation to Richard Beauchamp of Bergavenny and his wife Isabel, she being an heir of the late Thomas, Lord Despenser. *CCR* , pp. 165–6. • **57.** *CCR*, pp. 174–5. The grant to Constance was actually dated 18 February 1415; that to Eleanor 22 February 1415. They have been concatenated here with the other Despenser grant because they clearly relate to the same initiative, which was probably issued in respect of all three parties on the same day, and simply drawn up in separate parts on different days. • **58.** For other acts, see *CCR*, p. 168; *CPR*, pp. 285, 294. • **59.** *CPR*, p. 288. • **60.** *Foedera*, ix, p. 136. • **61.** *Foedera*, ix, p. 141; Wylie, *Henry V*, i, p. 414, n. 6. • **62.** E 405/28. • **63.** *CCR*, p. 173. • **64.** *Foedera*, ix, p. 202; *CPR*, p. 294. • **65.** Curry, *Agincourt*, p. 49. • **66.** Wylie, *Henry V*, i, p. 527. • **67.** Hardy and Hardy (eds), *Waurin*, p. 171. • **68.** Wylie, *Henry V*, i, p. 438 (portrait of Katherine); *Monstrelet*, i, p. 322. • **69.** E 403/620. • **70.** Wylie, *Henry V*, i, p. 415. Vale states that 'in a convention signed by Henry's ambassadors at Ypres on 7 August 1414 John the Fearless agreed to support his [Henry's] claim to the crown [of France] and to furnish him with troops'. Vale, *English Gascony*, p. 70. • **71.** Neither of these payments to Henry Scrope on this roll can relate to his embassy in 1413, for which he was reimbursed in the same year. (See Wylie, *Henry V*, i, pp. 149–50.) The duke of Orléans was in communication with Henry in late 1414, granting safe conducts to Henry's messengers and sending his own chamberlain in November 1414. That November the duke of Burgundy also sent his chamberlain to Henry – it is possible that Scrope's second voyage relates to these further negotiations with Burgundy. See Wylie, *Henry V*, i, pp. 415–16; *Foedera*, ix, p. 179. • **72.** The 'une' does not necessarily relate to a female form of 'one', as spelling of French words, like English, had yet to be standardised. The quotation comes from the *Iliad*, ii, lines 204–5. • **73.** Loomis (ed.), *Constance*, pp. 217–18. • **74.** *Monstrelet*, i, p. 325. • **75.** Wylie, *Henry V*, i, p. 56; *Foedera*, ix, p. 203. • **76.** Wylie, *Henry IV*, iii, p. 395. • **77.** Wylie, *Henry V*, i, p. 221. • **78.** *HKW*, ii, pp. 988–1000. Sutton House followed, in April 1415. See *ibid.*, p. 1004. • **79.** Dugdale, *Monasticon*, vi, p. 29. • **80.** Wylie, *Henry V*, i, pp. 230–1. • **81.** Dugdale, *Monasticon*, vi, pp. 542–3. For the two-storey church, see *ibid.*, p. 541, quoting Weever. • **82.** Dugdale, *Monasticon*, vi, p. 542 (dimensions); *HKW*, i, p. 265

(brickmakers). • **83.** Johnes (ed.), *Monstrelet*, i, pp. 323–5 (where this is dated to the 24th); Vaughan, *John the Fearless*, pp. 203–4; Curry, *Agincourt*, p. 47. See also *de Baye*, ii, p. 210 n. 1, where it is dated to the 23rd. • **84.** Wylie, *Henry V*, i, p. 445. • **85.** Wylie, *Henry V*, i, pp. 90–3. • **86.** *Issues*, p. 339. • **87.** Luard (ed.), *Flores Historiarum*, iii, p. 193; *CCR 1327–30*, p. 4. I am grateful to Kathryn Warner for drawing my attention to these references to *Burgoyne*. • **88.** Markham, *Court of Richard II*, p. 33. This site may also have been used by earlier kings as a retreat. See *CCR 1327–30*, p. 4. • **89.** *HKW*, i, p. 245. • **90.** E 101/620 (last membrane). • **91.** *Issues*, p. 340. This item was on a membrane which is detached from E 101/620. • **92.** *Issues*, p. 340.

March

1. Vaughan, *John the Fearless*, pp. 211–12. • **2.** Loomis, *Constance*, pp. 218–19. • **3.** Dugdale, *Monasticon*, vi, p. 542. This translation has been smoothed somewhat. The exact text is *Haec omnia ad sedulae considerationis examen, inspirante supernam gratiam, in cujus manu sunt regum corda, et testante scriptura, 'ubi voluerit inclinabit'*. • **4.** Fox, *Acts and Monuments*, p. 840; Wylie, *Henry V*, i, p. 286. • **5.** Grime, *Lanterne of Lyght* (1535), fol. ix recto. With regard to the earlier quotations, these have been taken from Fox, *Acts and Monuments*, p. 841 and have not been checked in the 1535 edition. • **6.** Wylie, *Henry V*, i, p. 289. • **7.** Spinka (ed.), *Letters of John Hus*, pp. 148–9. • **8.** *CPR*, p. 288. Temporalities were restored to him on 16 March (*Syllabus*, ii, p. 584). • **9.** E 403/621. See under 1 May. The journey would have entailed three days' travelling each way – the distance to Southampton was 75 miles. Henry may have left in the last week of February and spent several days in Southampton, returning in time to visit the Londoners on the 10th. • **10.** Riley (ed.), *Memorials*, p. 603. • **11.** Loomis (ed.), *Constance*, p. 115. • **12.** Part of this table is preserved on the wall of the undercroft of the hall, in what is now known as the Conciergerie, Paris. • **13.** Wylie, *Henry V*, i, p. 440. • **14.** Curry, *Agincourt*, p. 45; Johnes (ed.), *Monstrelet*, i, pp. 325–6. • **15.** *Foedera*, ix, pp. 210–12. • **16.** *Foedera*, ix, pp. 212–13. • **17.** *Issues*, p. 340. • **18.** E 403/621. • **19.** *Foedera*, ix, pp. 213–14. • **20.** Curry, *Agincourt*, p. 50. • **21.** Loomis (ed.), *Constance*, p. 220. • **22.** Riley (ed.), *Memorials*, pp. 604–5; Wylie, *Henry V*, i, p. 454. • **23.** Hutton, *Rise and Fall*, p. 20. • **24.** Loomis (ed.), *Constance*, p. 490. • **25.** *Foedera*, ix, p. 215. However, it wrongly named Simon Flete as Richard Clitherowe's companion, not Reginald Curteis as it should have done. Curteis and Clitherowe had received the money in February; the commission was correctly issued in their name on 4 April (*Foedera*, ix, pp. 216–17). • **26.** *CCR*, p. 176. • **27.** *CPR*, p. 294. • **28.** *CCR*, p. 162. • **29.** Loomis (ed.), *Constance*, pp. 222,

491. • **30.** Wylie, *Henry V*, i, p. 223. • **31.** Loomis (ed.), *Constance*, pp. 117, 222. • **32.** *Fears*, p. 221. The 'royal predecessors' were named as Edward III, the Black Prince, Richard II or John of Gaunt. • **33.** *CCR*, pp. 268, 270; *Foedera*, ix, p. 216; Wylie, *Henry V*, i, p. 454. • **34.** *CPR*, p. 308. • **35.** Hutton, *Rise and Fall*, pp. 20–1. • **36.** *CPR*, p. 321. • **37.** Loomis (ed.), *Constance*, pp. 223–5. • **38.** This date is an estimate. It took Warwick ten weeks to reach Constance in winter but it took Caterick five weeks to return in summer. Six weeks has been allowed for the most important members of the embassy to return. They were back by 11 May. • **39.** Hutton, *Rise and Fall*, p. 21. • **40.** *CPR*, p. 307. • **41.** *CPR*, p. 321. • **42.** Hutton, *Rise and Fall*, p. 21. • **43.** Mortimer, 'Henry IV's date of birth and the royal Maundy', pp. 567–76, esp. 572; *Fears*, p. 371. This concludes that Maundy Thursday (15 April 1367) was Henry IV's date of birth. Christopher Fletcher, apparently unfamiliar with this work, has subsequently suggested 16 March 1367, which appears in a late-fifteenth-century redaction of the chronicle of John Somer. See Fletcher, *Richard II*, p. 1, n. 4 • **44.** E 101/406/21 fol. 19r. • **45.** The first move towards cramp rings to cure epilepsy occurs in the reign of Edward II, in 1323. See Ormrod, 'Personal Religion of Edward III', p. 864. • **46.** E 101/406/21 fol. 19r. • **47.** Hutton, *Rise and Fall*, pp. 22–3. • **48.** Nicolas (ed.), *Privy Council*, ii, p. 149. • **49.** *English Historical Documents*, p. 208. • **50.** Marx (ed.), *An English Chronicle 1377–1461*, p. 42; Brie (ed.), *Brut*, ii, pp. 374–5. See also *Illustrious Henries*, p. 129. • **51.** Given-Wilson (ed.), *Usk*, p. 253. • **52.** *Chronica Maiora*, p. 399. • **53.** *Sacrosancta* has been described as 'probably the most revolutionary official document in the world'. See Spinka, *John Hus at at the Council of Constance*, p. 64. • **54.** Loomis (ed.), *Constance*, pp. 227–8. • **55.** Hutton, *Rise and Fall*, pp. 23–5. • **56.** E 101/406/21. • **57.** Hutton, *Rise and Fall*, p. 26.

April

1. Hutton, *Rise and Fall*, p. 26. • **2.** *CPR*, p. 327. This was assigned to be paid by the abbot and convent of St Peters Gloucester, receivers of a royal manor worth £48, on 11 June. See *CCR*, p. 219. • **3.** *CPR*, p. 328. • **4.** For example, the meetings of 10 April and 27 May. The only council meeting which Clarence attended in the first half of the year seems to have been the great council of 15–18 April. • **5.** *Issues*, p. 340. • **6.** *Cal. Charter Rolls*, pp. 479–80. Although the terms of the charter had no doubt been established some days or even weeks earlier, it is noticeable that the necessary arrangements for funding the priory were also dated today (e.g. the compensation grants paid to Queen Joan and Sir John Rothenhale), so this was a key date in Henry's religious programme. • **7.** *CPR*, p. 340. These sums had been allocated to her in lieu of her dower. • **8.** *CPR*, p. 372. • **9.** *HKW*, i, p. 266. • **10.** *Cal. Charter Rolls*, pp. 479–80; Dugdale, *Monasticon*, vi, pp. 29–34; Wylie, *Henry V*, i, p. 216. • **11.** *CPR*, pp. 395, 380. The site is not specified as the Celestine one but the measurements and location allow us to compare it to the Syon Abbey site. Both were about thirty-one acres (give or take an acre) and had a common boundary, so seem to have been one site divided in half. Both sites were bordered by the north bank of the Thames and Twickenham field. The grant of several alien priories' estates along with the triangular site described in this grant (and the subsequent identical one of 29 July) is further evidence that this site was that of the planned Celestine foundation. See also *HKW*, p. 266. • **12.** Wylie, *Henry V*, i, pp. 230–1. • **13.** They departed with the French envoys in July. See Wylie, *Henry V*, i, p. 231; *HKW*, p. 266. • **14.** For a description of Jerome see Loomis (ed.), *Constance*, p. 135. • **15.** Loomis (ed.), *Constance*, p. 131. • **16.** *CPR*, p. 296. • **17.** *Foedera*, ix, pp. 216–17. • **18.** Loomis (ed.), *Constance*, pp. 119–20. • **19.** *Foedera*, ix, p. 217; *CPR*, p. 298. • **20.** Nine weeks had passed since John XXIII's confirmation of Patrington's election. This compares with Richard Beauchamp's ten weeks travelling to Constance. In the dark of winter it would appear to have been a hard journey, travelling an average of about sixty miles a week. • **21.** Loomis (ed.), *Constance*, p. 229. • **22.** Bellaguet (ed.), *Chronique du Religieux*, v, p. 503. • **23.** Wylie, *Henry V*, i, p. 452; Bellaguet (ed.), *Chronique du Religieux*, v, pp. 501–5. • **24.** Bellaguet (ed.), *Chronique du Religieux*, v, p. 501. • **25.** *CCR*, p. 268. • **26.** E 101/406/21 fol. 5v. • **27.** Kirby (ed.), *Signet Letters*, p. 161. Kirby suggests the ambassadors who had returned with the cup were Sir John Colvyle and Richard Hals, who had returned in December 1414. A delay of four months before writing to acknowledge a diplomatic gift seems unlikely. It is possible that John Chamberlain returned with it, given his appearance in the February 1415 Issue Rolls. However, that mission too was some months earlier. • **28.** Riley (ed.), *Memorials*, p. 606. • **29.** Rawcliffe, *Medicine and Society*, pp. 120–1. • **30.** *CPR*, p. 342. • **31.** *CCR*, pp. 206–7. These were actually granted on the 8th; they are mentioned here so they may be connected more directly with Henry's instructions. • **32.** *Syllabus*, ii, p. 584; *CPR*, p. 342; Wylie, *Henry V*, i, p. 454. • **33.** These payments appear on the Issue Roll E 403/621 under 27 April. • **34.** Nicolas (ed.), *Privy Council*, ii, pp. 153–4. • **35.** *Foedera*, ix, pp. 225–7; Wylie, i. p. 453. • **36.** *Foedera*, ix, p. 219–20. • **37.** Nicolas (ed.), *Privy Council*, ii, p. 155 (place of meeting); Wylie, *Henry V*, i, p. 496, n. 1 (Star Chamber). • **38.** See Nicolas (ed.), *Privy Council*, ii, p. 156; or *Foedera*, ix, p. 222, for a printed list of those present. Although these minutes locate this meeting to 16 April, the correct date was the 15th. See Appendix 2. • **39.** *Fears*, pp. 368–9. • **40.** *ODNB*. • **41.** 'To Richard of York [Richard of Conisborough], son of the late Edmund, duke of York, to whom Richard II gave 350 marks yearly, on top of the £100 he receives yearly . . .' to be paid until the king can find a means to support 'his young relative'. He received £285 before 5 Dec. 1414 (*Issues*, p. 337). • **42.** *ODNB*, under Richard, earl of Cambridge. • **43.** See Appendix Two. • **44.** Nicolas (ed.), *Privy Council*, ii, p. 151. • **45.** Bellaguet (ed.), *Chronique du Religieux*, v, p. 507. • **46.** Bellaguet (ed.), *Chronique du Religieux*, v, p. 509. • **47.** Bellaguet (ed.), *Chronique du Religieux*, v, p. 511. • **48.** *Gesta*, p. 17. See also Curry, *Agincourt*, p. 55. Curry's comment on this point that 'the truth of this remark is not certain' may be applied to most other chroniclers' remarks throughout history. It is of course possible that this element of the Issue Rolls was only supplied at a later date by a clerk who interpreted the payment in this way, but even so there is plenty of independent evidence of sending ambassadors via Harfleur, the naval base, which does suggest spying. There seems little room for doubt that there was deliberate ambiguity about the destination of the expedition at this juncture. • **49.** *Perfect King*, Appendix Five, pp. 422–6. • **50.** Wylie, *Henry V*, i, p. 138. • **51.** See Barker, *Agincourt*, pp. 175–6 for a neat summary of the strategic advantages. • **52.** Wylie, *Henry V*, i, p. 404. For Bourchier, Phelip and Porter, see above under 24 January and 13 March. • **53.** Nicolas (ed.), *Privy Council*, ii, pp. 157–8. • **54.** *HKW*, ii, p. 1004; *CPR*, p. 346. • **55.** Loomis (ed.), *Constance*, pp. 231–2. • **56.** Loomis (ed.), *Constance*, p. 233. 'Cory' has been corrected to 'Corfe'. • **57.** Nicolas (ed.), *Privy Council*, ii, p. 158. • **58.** *Foedera*, ix, p. 223. The number of archers seems to have been revised to sixty by 23 May. See *ibid.*, p. 250. He was paid for sixty archers, according to the enrolled account E 358/6; by the time of Agincourt he was down to 35. Note: the earldom of Huntingdon had been forfeit by Sir John Holland's father in 1400. Sir John was not formally restored until 1417, when he came of age. However, most contemporary sources – e.g. the *Gesta*, and the May council minutes – refer to him as the earl of Huntingdon. This official indenture for the campaign also names him as an earl. Hence this title has been used in this book. • **59.** *CPR*, p. 329. • **60.** *CPR*, p. 342. • **61.** Oliver, *Monasticon Exonienses*, p. 248. • **62.** Loomis (ed.), *Constance*, p. 131. • **63.** *CPR*, p. 306. • **64.** Henry did not necessarily leave it to the last minute to go to Windsor. The reference to him and the council being at Westminster on 21 April may be an enrolment of a decision made some days earlier. • **65.** For the date of foundation, see *Perfect King*, Appendix Six, pp. 427–9. • **66.** This list is drawn from *CP*, ii, pp. 537–9 and Belz, *Memorials*, pp. 399–400. The order of seating is based on those of 1406, 1408 and 1409, coupled with the order of succession to each seat recorded in *CP*. Where there are discrepancies (the seats of Fitzhugh, Umphraville and Cornwaille) the *CP* order of succession is preferred. For the two tables marked with their names in French see Belz, ix. • **67.** Namely Henry V, Clarence, Gloucester, York, Arundel, Dorset, Salisbury, Talbot, Fitzhugh, Scrope, Morley, Camoys, Felbrigg, Erpingham, Cornwaille, Daubridgecourt. • **68.** Hutton, *Rise and Fall*, p. 27. • **69.** There was no cap at this time. See Belz, *Memorials*, p. lii. • **70.** *PROME* inventory no. 1091. • **71.** *PROME*, 1423 October, item 31, nos 139, 146, 163, 169 and 170. • **72.** *PROME*, 1423 October, item 3, no. 264. • **73.** The ladies who were issued robes in 1413 were the dowager queen of England, the duchesses of Clarence and York, the dowager duchess of York, the countesses of Huntingdon, Westmorland, Dorset, Arundel and Salisbury, the dowager countess of Salisbury, Lady Beauchamp, Lady Ros and Lady Waterton. See Belz, *Memorials*, lv. Most of these had been issued robes in earlier years and were issued them again in later years, so they constituted a group of Ladies of the Garter. See *CP*, ii, pp. 591–6. • **74.** Belz, *Memorials*, ix. In later years these tables were exhibited in the chapel at Windsor – but they were sadly dilapidated by the seventeenth century, and were subsequently destroyed. • **75.** Loomis (ed.), *Constance*, pp. 233–4. • **76.** Loomis (ed.), *Constance*, pp. 234–5. • **77.** *Foedera*, ix, pp. 225–7. • **78.** Petit, *Itinéraires*, pp. 417–8. • **79.** Loomis (ed.), *Constance*, pp. 235–6. • **80.** Wylie, *Henry V*, i, p. 447. • **81.** de Baye, p. 231, n. 1. • **82.** Bellaguet (ed.), *Chronique du Religieux*, v, p. 511. • **83.** Barker, *Agincourt*, p. 98, tries to clarify the total number of ships employed by taking the total paid to Clitherowe and Curteys (£5,050) and dividing it by a 2s per quarterton rate of hire. The result of 631 ships of 'twenty tons' seems to accord with a contemporary report that there were seven hundred ships hired from Holland. However, there are two problems. The first is that not all of the £5,050 was paid for the hire of ships; as this entry in the Issue Rolls makes clear, the £2,166 13s 4d paid on this date was for wages. The second problem is that references to 'ships of twenty/sixty/a hundred tons/tuns' relate not to the tonnage of the ship itself or its displacement but to its carrying capacity of twenty tuns or large barrels. An alternative approach might be to regard the £2,166 13s 4d here mentioned as the total wages of the mariners in going to England, then Harfleur and back again. If there were 700 ships, with 700 masters paid 6d per day, and each ship had an average of 30 mariners at 3d per day (these being the usual rates in England), then this sum would not quite have covered eight days' sailing – hardly enough time, one would have thought to sail from Holland and Zeeland to Southampton, and to load up, sail to Harfleur, unload, and return to Holland and Zeeland. There may have been fewer ships. However, there may have been additional payments for wages (this £2,166 was probably a part-payment), and there may have been different wage rates or numbers of sailors. • **84.** See also the council meeting discussing these, on 15 May. Nicolas (ed.), *Privy Council*, ii, p. 159. • **85.** *CPR*, pp. 306–7. • **86.** These payments are on the Issue Roll for this day: E 403/621. • **87.** Loomis (ed.), *Constance*, pp. 237–8. • **88.** *Foedera*, ix, p. 205. • **89.** *CPR*, p. 302. • **90.** *CPR*, p. 343. • **91.** *Foedera*, ix, p. 228. • **92.** *Foedera*, ix, pp. 235–8. • **93.** Curry, *Agincourt*, p. 67. • **94.** Curry, *Agincourt*, p. 27. There could have been as many as two thousand archers at St-Cloud, but no more. • **95.** Wylie, *Henry V*, i, p. 479.

May

1. From this point, 1 May, certain details noted in the Issue Rolls and other official records have been relegated to the notes. This is because they are worthy of inclusion in order to present as full a record of Henry's activities as possible but in their respective dates they disrupt the flow of the narrative, reducing the readability – and thus the accessibility – of the text. Today, for instance, the Close Rolls note an order to Henry Kays to pay 20 marks annually to the priory of the Virgin and St Thomas the Martyr at Newark, Surrey (*CCR*, p. 211). This was followed on 3 May by a related order to deliver letters patent freeing the same priory from tenths and fifteenths. Today a commission was also issued to arrest Gilbert Hesketh esquire of Chester. Hesketh was to be brought immediately before the king and council in chancery (*CPR*, p. 346). What Hesketh had done to deserve this is unknown, but it is unlikely to have been a serious offence, and possibly was not an offence at all. Hesketh sailed on the forthcoming expedition in the company of Sir William Butler (Nicolas, *Agincourt*, p. 357), and the following year the king granted him and his mother the wardship of his (Hesketh's) under-age cousin (DL 25/1649). • **2.** Hutton, *Rise and Fall*, pp. 28–34. • **3.** These payments all appear under today's date in the Issue Roll, E 403/621. • **4.** Loomis (ed.), *Constance*, p. 238. • **5.** *CPR*, p. 343. • **6.** *CCR*, p. 211. • **7.** *CPR*, p. 320. • **8.** *CPR*, p. 346. • **9.** Hutton, *Rise and Fall*, pp. 35–6. • **10.** *CPR*, p. 321. • **11.** *CPR*, p. 343. For the first case see 22 January. • **12.** *CPR*, p. 343. • **13.** Loomis (ed.), *Constance*, p. 240. • **14.** *Foedera*, ix, p. 239. • **15.** *CPR*, p. 308. • **16.** Wylie, *Henry V*, i, p. 142; *Foedera*, ix, pp. 239–40. • **17.** *CPR*, pp. 344–5. • **18.** Hutton, *Rise and Fall*, pp. 34–5. • **19.** E 101/406/21 fol. 19r. • **20.** *Foedera*, ix, pp. 240–1. • **21.** *Foedera*, ix, p. 241. Barker suggests the recipient was the mayor of London. See Barker, *Agincourt*, p. 109. • **22.** See Wylie, *Henry V*, i, p. 483. Wylie infers the destination was Holywell from the chronicle of Usk, which mentions Henry going on pilgrimages prior to 16 June. Usk was referring only to offerings at London churches immediately before that date (Given-Wilson (ed.), *Usk*, pp. 254–5). The other evidence for the pilgrimage at this time is the account of the Teutonic envoys; but Wylie mistakes the timing of this pilgrimage. As he states on p. 495, it was shortly before the second interview with the envoys – so after they had been in the country for a full month. As they had left Marienburg on 27 March it can hardly be credited that they had been in the country for a full month by 12 May. • **23.** *Foedera*, ix, p. 243 includes a document supposedly attested by the king on the 11th. It is possible that this was in his absence; however the minutes of the council meeting on the 15th specifically state that the king was present. Nicolas (ed.),

Privy Council, ii, p. 159. • **24.** *Gesta*, p. 17, n. 3; Jacob, *Chichele*, p. 35. • **25.** *CPR*, p. 345; Kate Parker, 'Politics and Patronage in Lynn 1399–1416', in Dodd and Biggs (eds), *Rebellion and Survival*, pp. 210–27. • **26.** *Actes Royaux des archives de l'Hérault* . . ., vol 1 (1980), p. 209. • **27.** Warwick had been at Bruges on 1 May (Wylie, *Henry V*, i, p. 455) and returned to London on 11 May (E 101/321/27). Hungerford returned to London on 10 May (E 101/321/28). • **28.** Wylie, *Henry V*, i, p. 495. • **29.** Henry Percy was born on 3 February 1393 (*CP*, ix, p. 715) or 1394 (Wylie, *Henry V*, p. 515, n. 3). Note that Rymer was wrong in placing Percy's petition for his restoration here under 1415. That document is an exemplification, drawn up on 11 May 1416, of Henry's decision on the first day of the parliament of 1416 (16 March), in response to Percy's petition to that parliament. See *Foedera*, ix, pp. 242–3. • **30.** *Foedera*, ix, p. 244. • **31.** Loomis (ed.), *Constance*, pp. 242–4. • **32.** Spinka, *John Hus at the Council of Constance*, pp. 123–7. • **33.** Nicolas (ed.), *Privy Council*, ii, p. 159. It is not clear why Breton ships were classed along with French and Scottish, as the duke of Brittany had a treaty with Henry, as did the duke of Burgundy, who was lord of Flanders. • **34.** *CPR*, p. 327. • **35.** *CPR*, p. 324. It is worth noting that Coventry and Lichfield was still described as *sede vacante* on 8 May. See *Foedera*, ix, p. 256. • **36.** *CP*, viii, p. 451. He was to take one banneret, three knights, fifty-five men-at-arms and 160 mounted archers. • **37.** *CPR*, p. 339. • **38.** Wylie, i, p. 328; Curry, p.67. • **39.** *Foedera*, ix, pp. 248–9. The English calendar entry *CPR*, p. 325 is very brief on this matter, and contracted to the point of being misleading. • **40.** *CPR*, p. 325. • **41.** Wylie, *Henry V*, i, p. 479. • **42.** Nicolas, *Agincourt*, p. 346; when the time came to sail, he had thirty-five men-at-arms and 96 archers. • **43.** Spinka, *John Hus at the Council of Constance*, p. 130. • **44.** All of these payments are from the Issue Roll, E 403/621, under 18 May. • **45.** *Issues*, p. 341; the description of the tabernacle appears in Nicolas, *Agincourt*, appendix, p. 14. • **46.** E 403/621 under 18 May. • **47.** E 101/406/21 fols 7r, 19v. • **48.** Hutton, *Rise and Fall*, p. 36. • **49.** Wylie, *Henry V*, i, p. 222. • **50.** E 403/621 under 20 May. • **51.** Nicolas (ed.), *Privy Council*, ii, pp. 162–4. • **52.** *CPR*, p. 348. • **53.** E 403/621 under 18 May. • **54.** Nicolas (ed.), *Privy Council*, ii, pp. 165–6. • **55.** *CPR*, p. 337. • **56.** *Foedera*, ix, p. 250; *CCR*, p. 212. • **57.** SC 8/332/15714 (petition); *CPR*, p. 361 (grant). A close letter was sent to Henry Kays on 1 June ordering him to deliver the patent letter to Thresk. See *CCR*, p. 217. • **58.** *CPR*, p. 327. • **59.** Also on 26 May Henry relaxed the restrictions on the export of smelted tin. In the parliament of November 1414 the mayor of Calais had written petitioning the king to force all wool, hides, lead and tin to be exported via the Staple at Calais, where it was meant to be weighed and exhibited before being traded further. However, they claimed that smelted tin was being exported directly to the Low Countries. Henry had acknowledged their case and prohibited the exportation of all tin, smelted and unsmelted (*PROME*, 1414 November, item 43). Today he reneged, allowing smelted tin to be exported on payment of the appropriate customs. • **60.** For Henry IV's devotion to the Trinity, see *Fears*, pp. 196–7. • **61.** *CCR*, p. 218. • **62.** Nicolas (ed.), *Privy Council*, ii, pp. 166–7. • **63.** *Foedera*, ix, pp. 251–2. • **64.** *Foedera*, ix, pp. 252–3. • **65.** This is an inference from the Issue Rolls payment dated 24 April 1415. Pugh (*Henry V and the Southampton Plot*, p. 101) states that he had been released on the 24th but this is simply the date of the warrant to deliver him; it was probably not acted upon the same day. As Henry was not keen to waste money the payment for his upkeep is probably a more reliable indicator. • **66.** Nicolas (ed.), *Privy Council*, ii, p. 167. This note has been taken by some historians to mean that Scrope absented himself from the council meeting – for example, Bridgette Vale, in *ODNB*. This is not necessarily the case. The wording suggests only that Scrope had not yet arrived but was expected to arrive soon enough to join in the imminent discussions about relations with the duke of Burgundy. It is therefore evidence that he was late, not that he did not attend. • **67.** Nicolas (ed.), *Privy Council*, ii, p. 168. • **68.** *CPR*, p. 347. • **69.** *CCR*, p. 214; *Foedera*, ix, p. 253. • **70.** *CCR*, p. 213. • **71.** *CPR*, p. 327. • **72.** *CPR*, p. 330. • **73.** *CPR*, p. 330. • **74.** *CCR*, p. 208. • **75.** For her marriage to Robert Chalons, see Smith (ed.), *Expeditions*, p. 294. For her acting as a supervisor of the Lancastrian children, see DL 28/1/6 fol. 35r. • **76.** He had been at Radolfzell since 17 May. • **77.** Loomis (ed.), *Constance*, pp. 246–7. • **78.** Loomis (ed.), *Constance*, p. 452, n. 97. • **79.** *Chronica Maiora*, p. 401. • **80.** Given-Wilson (ed.), *Usk*, p. 255. • **81.** Spinka, *John Hus at the Council of Constance*, pp. 81, 142n. Hus was removed a few days before 3 June, when John XXIII was taken there. • **82.** *Foedera*, ix, p. 253. Of the other nine, one was called Fydeler (Fiddler) and the others had names unrelated to musical instruments. • **83.** *CPR*, pp. 407–8. In each county, one of these men had already contracted to serve on the campaign in person, so there may have been a local recruitment element to this order as well. See Curry, *Agincourt*, p. 67. • **84.** *CPR*, p. 336. • **85.** Hutton, *Rise and Fall*, pp. 58–9. • **86.** This is based on Thomas More's wardrobe book for 1413, E 101/406/21 fol. 7v. Whereas more than £80 was spent on Trinity Sunday 1413, expenses on the following Thursday were just £47. A normal day at this time was between £28 and £31. • **87.** *CPR*, p. 329. • **88.** Wylie, *Henry V*, p. 131. See also *ibid.*, pp. 143–5 for the duplicity of Bergerac and other Gascon towns. • **89.** Spinka, *Jan Hus at the Council of Constance*, p. 139. • **90.** Spinka, *Jan Hus at the Council of Constance*, p. 140.

June

1. Details of the crown jewels have been taken from Nicolas, *Agincourt*, appendices pp. 13–18, and Wylie, *Henry V*, i, pp. 469–76, referring also to Henry's inventory and the image of the crowns in the plate sections of *Fears*. Courtenay probably expected that most items would be redeemed on schedule – by Christmas 1416 or by early 1417 at the latest. Most were not. Many items handed out were still in pawn in 1422, when Henry V died; and although the inventories said that the holders could keep them, the council continued to redeem them. Note that the Pallet of Spain is valued at £200 in Nicolas. As there were so many jewels, this can hardly have been made of anything other than gold; and given its weight, the gold alone should have been worth a considerable proportion of the £200. It is suspected that this assigned value is too low but at this distance in time it is impossible to tell; it might have been broken in some way. Given the similarity with the crown and pallet of Spain described by the earl of Cambridge in his confession, the two have been presumed to be the same. • **2.** In Nicolas, the Pallet of Spain is pledged to John Hende. However, according to the earl of Cambridge's confession, it came to him. See Pugh, *Southampton Plot*, p. 172. • **3.** Wylie, *Henry V*, i, pp. 475–6. • **4.** As some of the indentures of service made clear, today was the day when the jewels would be assigned. See for example the indenture of Lord Scrope in *Foedera*, ix, p. 230. • **5.** *CPR*, p. 346. • **6.** *CCR*, p. 212 (Stone); *CPR*, p. 331 (Hereford). • **7.** For the earlier cases, see 22 January and 6 May. • **8.** *TTGME*, pp. 59, 297. Although Walsingham's account is probably grossly exaggerated, something does seem to have happened at the time, as a writ was issued to enquire into the misdoings. • **9.** *CPR*, p. 337. • **10.** Curry, *Agincourt*, p. 79. • **11.** *Monstrelet*, i, p. 329. • **12.** According to Curry, *Agincourt*, p. 50, the embassy left Paris on 4 June. One would expect Archbishop Boisratier to have been at the council meeting on the 3rd if he had not already left Paris – so it seems reasonable to conclude that he had already left the city. • **13.** For the route taken, see *Monstrelet*, i, p. 329. For the dates of embarkation, see Bellaguet (ed.), *Chronique du Religieux*, v, p. 513. • **14.** *CPR*, p. 325. • **15.** For his campaign in 1341 Edward III ordered 130,000 sheaves of arrows for 7,700 bows. See Bradbury, *Medieval Archer*, p. 94. • **16.** Making and fletching 130,000 sheaves of arrows (excluding making the arrowhead) at 30 mins each arrow would be roughly 1,560,000 man-hours. At 3,000 working hours per man per year, this is 520 man-years – or forty years' work for all thirteen men. • **17.** For the ordinances of 1363, see Bradbury, *Medieval Archer*, p, 93. The original legislation of 1363 had been renewed in the parliaments of 1388 and 1409. • **18.** 7 Henry IV (1406), cap. vii. • **19.** This statement is based on the order of Edward III to gather 130,000 sheaves of arrows, quoted in Bradbury, *Medieval Archer*, p. 94, and mentioned above. As there were twenty-four arrows to a standard sheaf, it equates to 3,120,000 arrows. • **20.** The account of the trial is taken from Spinka, *John Hus at the Council of Constance*, pp. 163–7. • **21.** Spinka (ed.), *Letters of John Hus*, p. 160, n. 2. • **22.** Spinka (ed.), *Letters of John Hus*, pp. 159–60. • **23.** *Foedera*, ix, p. 260

(warrant); p. 262 (prorogation). • **24.** *CPR*, pp. 368–9. • **25.** *CCR*, p. 222; *CPR*, p. 350. These references are methodologically useful in that they reveal the time lapse between a grant and its formal issue. The grant here was specifically made on 5 June; it was drawn up as a close letter on 21 July. It appears on the patent roll dated 5 June, the date of granting. Henry had ratified Dereham's estate the previous day (*CPR*, p. 331). • **26.** *CCR*, p. 223 (Northampton); *CPR*, pp. 338 (Hayne), 386 (Green). • **27.** *CPR*, p. 329. Aristocratic women did not suckle their own infants in the later middle ages. • **28.** *Foedera*, ix, p. 261; *CPR*, p. 346. • **29.** Spinka, *John Hus at the Council of Constance*, p. 167. See also *ibid.*, p. 142. • **30.** *CPR*, p. 330. • **31.** *CPR*, p. 331. • **32.** Pugh, *Southampton Plot*, p. 59. • **33.** S&I, pp. 442–3. • **34.** Wylie, *Henry V*, i, p. 449, n. 3. • **35.** *CCR*, p. 280. • **36.** Pugh, *Southampton Plot*, p. 59. • **37.** The articles are in Spinka, *John Hus at the Council of Constance*, pp. 183–201. • **38.** Spinka, *John Hus at the Council of Constance*, p. 221. • **39.** Spinka, *John Hus at the Council of Constance*, pp. 221–2. • **40.** Loomis (ed.), *Constance*, p. 252. • **41.** Pugh, *Southampton Plot*, p. 101, dates this event to 10 June on the strength of Thomas Gray of Heton's letter of 2 August to Henry, which stated that it took place a week before he met Richard, earl of Cambridge, at Conisborough, which was a week before Midsummer's Day (24 June). Wylie, *Henry V*, i, p. 516 dates this to 31 May. • **42.** *CPR*, p. 331 (Canterbury); *CCR*, p. 221 (Tonge). • **43.** *CCR*, p. 221. • **44.** *CCR*, pp. 279–80. • **45.** *CCR*, p. 277. For a good description about corrodies in practice, see Harvey, *Living and Dying*, chapter six. • **46.** *CPR*, p. 334. • **47.** *CPR*, p. 329. • **48.** *CCR*, p. 214. • **49.** This statement is based on the expenditure of the household in Henry IV's reign. See Given-Wilson, *Royal Household*, appendix one. • **50.** Wylie, *Henry V*, i, p. 476. • **51.** *Issues*, p. 286. • **52.** It is likely that he visited several holy shrines in the last days he was in London – he visited St Paul's and Southwark on the 15th, according to Wylie. • **53.** Wylie, *Henry V*, i, p. 494. Note: the date of all the Teutonic envoys' meetings is approximate. • **54.** Wylie, *Henry V*, i, p. 496. • **55.** *CCR*, p. 220 (Victore); *CPR*, p. 332 (Bury); Wylie, i, p. 482 (Chaucer); *CCR*, p. 221 (Burgh). • **56.** Loomis (ed.), *Constance*, pp. 248–9. • **57.** Fillastre placed it later in his journal, and described the events at Constance of the 15th before those in France of the 8th. See Loomis (ed.), Constance, pp. 249–51. • **58.** Loomis (ed.), *Constance*, p. 251. • **59.** See Gentien's account of the attack in Fillastre's diary, Loomis (ed.), *Constance*, p. 253. For confirmation of John's whereabouts see Petit, *Itinéraires*, p. 419. • **60.** Nicolas (ed.), *Privy Council*, ii, pp. 169–70; *CPR*, p. 333. • **61.** *CPR*, p. 339. The patent letter is dated 'by the king' Westminster, 17 June, but the council meeting was probably the same one as the other case of wrongful dismissal, prior to Henry's departure. • **62.** *CCR*, pp. 220, 222 (Whittington), 221 (Venetians). • **63.** Wylie, *Henry V*, i, pp. 483–5. Most authors, like Wylie, date the king's departure to the 16th. Given-Wilson in *PROME* gives the 15th. Although

Gregory's Chronicle is alone in supplying this date, it is to be preferred since a patent letter 'by the king' is dated at Winchester on the 16th (*CPR*, p. 338). It is unreasonable to suppose that Henry performed these two religious duties and had travelled the 63 miles to Winchester, then dictated a letter which was written up and sealed by a chancery clerk, all on the same day. However, it is possible that Beaufort had taken the king's instructions to draw up this patent letter in advance (see also n. 71 below). Arundel was still in London on the 19th and 24th, according to Nicolas (ed.), *Privy Council*, ii, pp. 170–1. • **64.** Wylie, *Henry V*, i, p. 496. • **65.** Although these are all dated today at Westminster they were dictated 'by the king'. • **66.** These were William Cheyne, Roger Horton (both King's Bench) and John Preston and William Lodyngton (Common Bench). See *CPR*, pp. 332, 335, 338, 340. • **67.** *CPR*, pp. 336, 338. • **68.** *Foedera*, ix, pp. 269–70 (Patrington); *CPR*, p. 347 (Welsh Marches). • **69.** Riley (ed.), *Memorials*, p. 613. • **70.** Wylie, *Henry V*, i, p. 496. • **71.** It was 63 miles along the old road from London to Winchester – normally a two-day journey at least. It is possible Henry took longer but the patent letter to his brother 'by the king' dated there on the 16th suggests otherwise. If Bishop Beaufort had travelled ahead, he may have taken Henry's instructions to write up this letter and sealed it here while staying at Winchester. • **72.** *CPR*, p. 338. • **73.** See the table of towns in *TTGME*, p. 10. • **74.** Wylie, *Henry V*, i, pp. 477–8. The matter was resolved when the men of Salisbury receieved an assignment on the wool customs at Southampton in return for their 100 marks. • **75.** *Chronica Maiora*, p. 402n; Bellaguet (ed.), *Chronique du Religieux*, v, p. 543; Johnes (ed.), *Monstrelet*, p. 329; Pugh, *Southampton Plot*, p. 60. They went to London, and thence to Winchester, where they arrived on 30 June and met Henry on 1 July. Their nervous state is suggested by Wylie, *Henry V*, i, p. 486. Wylie's statement that they were conducted by Sir John Wiltshire is probably an error, based on reading the French *Villequier* for Wiltshire; the Issue Roll in May clearly names Sir John Wilcotes. • **76.** *Foedera*, ix, p. 283. • **77.** Wylie, *Henry V*, i, p. 502. • **78.** For direct reference to Glendower see Thomas Gray's letter in Pugh, *Southampton Plot*, p. 166. David Howel is mentioned on the same page. Percy and March are mentioned throughout the confessions and letters on pp. 160–73. • **79.** Brie (ed.), *Brut*, i, pp. 75–6. • **80.** Pugh, *Southampton Plot*, p. 162. • **81.** For Mordach's recapture being a week after his abduction, see Pugh, *Southampton Plot*, pp. 101, 107, n. 31. For Ralph Pudsay, see *CPR*, p. 339. • **82.** Kirby (ed.), *Signet Letters*, pp. 196–7. • **83.** Wylie, *Henry V*, i, p. 496. • **84.** Nicolas (ed.), *Privy Council*, ii, pp. 170–1. • **85.** Wylie, *Henry V*, i, p. 311. Maidstone is 41 miles from Westminster. It is therefore somewhat unlikely that Archbishop Chichele was at Westminster in the morning and presided at this consecration. But it is difficult to decide which is more likely to be in error – the council minute or the date of the consecration.

Given that it is possible that he did the whole journey in one day, as this was almost the longest day, this has been allowed to stand. • **86.** Curry, *Agincourt*, p. 66. • **87.** Pugh, *Southampton Plot*, p. 168. The purpose of stirring the earl of March has been inferred – the original document is damaged. • **88.** As Lucy declared that part of the plot was to raise the north once Percy was free, it probably took place before it was known in London that Mordach had been recaptured. Cambridge seems to have known on 17 June that Percy was to be delivered to the custody of Robert Umphraville and John Widdrington, so the plot to free Percy probably postdates the instructions regarding his delivery agreed at the council meeting on 21 May. • **89.** The line just preceding this in Pugh, *Southampton Plot*, p. 168, referring to the gathering of Lollards and coats of arms, does not necessarily relate to the Oldcastle rising of 1414 (as Pugh's note suggests); it could be a gathering for a more recent event, such as the sermon on Horsleydown, mentioned under 3 March. • **90.** *Fears*, pp. 206–7. • **91.** *CPR*, p. 356; *ODNB*, under Patrington. Although one might explain this as being due to the hiatus in the papacy, it is noticeable that Henry did not write to Constance or the pope (whichever was in power) asking for his man to be provided, as he did with the new bishop of Norwich in November 1415. Nor did he need to wait for the new bishop to be confirmed by the pope (as Patrington was not provided until December 1417, a week before he died) whereas Henry released the temporalities in August 1416. It is very tempting to see a desire to take the money into royal hands behind this nomination. • **92.** Wylie, *Henry V*, i, p. 472. • **93.** Wylie, *Henry V*, i, p. 496. • **94.** *Foedera*, ix, p. 271. • **95.** *CCR*, p. 218. • **96.** *CCR*, p. 232. • **97.** *CCR*, p. 218. • **98.** Hutton, *Rise and Fall*, p. 38. • **99.** *CCR*, p. 218. • **100.** For the authorship of the will, see Nicolas (ed.), *Privy Council*, ii, p. 182. The will itself is printed in *Foedera*, ix, pp. 272–80. • **101.** For Scrope's statements against the campaign, see Pugh, *Southampton Plot*, p. 164. • **102.** Hutton, *Rise and Fall*, pp. 38–9. • **103.** *CCR*, p. 218. • **104.** *CPR*, pp. 340, 365. Woodhouse's patent letters were dated 25 June and 6 July at Westminster 'by the king'. • **105.** *CPR*, pp. 337–8. • **106.** *CPR*, p. 339. • **107.** Pugh, *Southampton Plot*, p. 162. • **108.** Spinka (ed.), *Letters of Hus*, p. 193. • **109.** *CCR*, p. 210; *CPR*, p. 353. • **110.** *CPR*, p. 355 (both grants). • **111.** *Foedera*, ix, pp. 282–3; Wylie, *Henry V*, i, pp. 486–7. • **112.** *CPR*, p. 342. • **113.** *CPR*, p. 351. This was issued from Westminster 'by the king'. From Winchester today was a grant 'by the king' to the king's servant William Wyghtman of the keeping and governance of a minor, John Harpesfield. See *CPR*, p. 355. • **114.** Wylie, *Henry V*, i, p. 487 has mistranslated *le roi baisa la lettre* as 'the king put down the letter'. It clearly means 'kissed' as the Latin version *rex osculatus est litteras* says (albeit referring to more than one letter). • **115.** Bellaguet (ed.), *Chronique du Religieux*, v, pp. 513–14.

July

• **1.** For times of meals see Harvey, *Living and Dying*, p. 43. • **2.** *CPR*, p. 339. Other letters dated at Winchester today include an order for the justices of the peace and the royal justices not to hold any sessions in Hampshire while the king was lodged there (*CCR*, p. 216) and the presentation of William Croydon, a royal chaplain, to the vicarage of Amberly in the diocese of Chichester (*CPR*, p. 339). • **3.** According to the chronicler Monstrelet the archbishop ended his speech with an offer of French lands and the hand in marriage of the king's daughter, Katherine, stating that this was conditional on Henry disbanding the army he was mustering at Southampton and refraining from invading France. However, Monstrelet seems to be less reliable and more prone to later prejudice than the official St Denis chronicler, from whose account details of the French embassy in early July is taken. See Johnes (ed.), *Monstrelet*, i, p. 329. • **4.** Bellaguet (ed.), *Chronique du Religieux*, v, p. 517. • **5.** Nicolas (ed.), *Testamenta Vetusta*, i, pp. 189–90. • **6.** Spinka (ed.), *Letters*, p. 206. • **7.** Bellaguet (ed.), *Chronique du Religieux*, v, pp. 517–19. Also today Henry renewed his licence for the chapter of Chichester Cathedral to elect a new bishop. He probably suggested they elect his humble nominee, Stephen Patrington, at the same time. See *CPR*, p. 338. • **8.** Wylie, *Henry V*, i, p. 489. • **9.** Bellaguet (ed.), *Chronique du Religieux*, v, p. 519. • **10.** *CCR*, p. 215 (dated Winchester). The ports were Sandwich, Lynn, Melcombe, Southampton, Great Yarmouth, Chichester, Plymouth, Fowey, Bristol, Bridgewater, St Botolph's town (Boston), Kingston upon Hull, Newcastle upon Tyne, Dover and Dartmouth. • **11.** Loomis (ed.), *Constance*, pp. 253–5. • **12.** The other lords named were the bishops of Norwich and Chester, the duke of York and the earls of Huntingdon and March. Note that there was no bishop of Chester in 1415; however, Langley was almost certainly there, as he had led previous embassies to France, and had greeted the ambassadors on their arrival. • **13.** Bellaguet (ed.), *Chronique du Religieux*, v, pp. 519–21. The French text, which I have otherwise used here, states that the archbishop referred to 'your two kingdoms' which seems most unlikely; the Latin 'both kingdoms' is original and to be preferred. • **14.** Wylie, *Henry V*, i, pp. 502–3. • **15.** Wylie, *Henry V*, i, p. 416. • **16.** Wylie, *Henry V*, i, pp. 503–4. • **17.** *CPR*, pp. 301–2 (York), 341 (murder), 407 (shipbuilding). The ship was probably not the famous *Grace Dieu*, the largest ship of the middle ages, as this was commissioned the following year from William Soper. • **18.** *CPR*, p. 342. This commision was actually dated Portchester; but given the distance from Winchester to Portchester (18 miles), it is unlikely that Henry himself rode to and from the castle before the morning. • **19.** Spinka, *John Hus at the Council of Constance*, pp. 224–5. • **20.** Hus's last letters appear in Spinka (ed.), *Letters of John Hus*, pp. 207–11. • **21.** The account of Hus's death is taken from Spinka, *John Hus at the Council of Constance*, pp. 225–34, and Loomis (ed.), *Constance*, pp. 133–4. • **22.** Wylie, *Henry V*, i, pp. 504–5. Note the claim made by two others of the embassy that this was not Fusoris's first meeting with the king, he having spent two hours with him the previous afternoon. Fusoris denied this. See p. 505, n. 6. • **23.** Most of this passage comes from Wylie but this specific point is in Bellaguet (ed.), *Chronique du Religieux*, v, p. 525. • **24.** Wylie, *Henry V*, i, pp. 505–6. • **25.** Bellaguet (ed.), *Chronique du Religieux*, v, pp. 522–5. • **26.** Johnes (ed.), *Monstrelet*, i, pp. 329–30. • **27.** Pugh, *Southampton Plot*, p. 60. • **28.** Loomis (ed.), *Constance*, pp. 256–7. • **29.** Kirby (ed.), *Signet Letters*, p. 197 (Bordeaux); *CPR*, p. 348 (Fife). • **30.** Wylie, *Henry V*, i, p. 511. • **31.** Wylie, *Henry V*, i, p. 507. • **32.** *Gesta*, p. 17; Wylie, *Henry V*, i p. 512. • **33.** *CCR*, pp. 206 (Calais), 216 (*Trinity Royal*), 219 (Venetians). • **34.** *CCR*, pp. 216 (sergeants), 223 (Wakeryng), 225 (Bordiu), 232 (Rochford). • **35.** *CPR*, p. 351 (both Loddyngton and crown). • **36.** Kirby, *Signet Letters*, p. 161. • **37.** Nicolas, *Agincourt*, appendix, p. 66. • **38.** Wylie, *Henry V*, i, p. 498. • **39.** Curry, *Agincourt*, p. 126. • **40.** *CCR*, pp. 277–8. • **41.** Loomis (ed.), *Constance*, pp. 55, 258. • **42.** See Gray's letter of confession in Pugh, *Southampton Plot*, pp. 161–3, and Scrope's letter, *ibid*. p. 169. For the relationship between Lucy and Gray, see *ibid*. p. 187. Gray later claimed that Scrope and Arundel had both agreed to support the earl of March three years earlier; but this was probably an attempt to spite Arundel when Gray was facing trial, as Arundel was one of the king's closest friends and his loyalty was never in doubt. • **43.** *Foedera*, ix, p. 287. • **44.** *Perfect King*, p. 283. The petition is SC 8/332/15711. • **45.** *CPR*, p. 359. • **46.** This is Hamulton as transcribed by Pugh, *Southampton Plot*, p. 163. The confession states that Gray came there that day. But he woke up at Southampton, so had reached Southampton on the night of the 20th and it was at Southampton that Cambridge and Gray plotted together (*ibid*., p. 182). • **47.** *Testamenta Vetusta*, i, p. 192. • **48.** Their commissions were drawn up on the 25th, and their instructions on the 28th. See *Foedera*, ix, pp. 293–7. • **49.** Wylie, *Henry V*, i, p. 94. • **50.** Pugh, *Southampton Plot*, p. 164. • **51.** Pugh, *Southampton Plot*, p. 169. • **52.** John Wakeryng, keeper of the privy seal, was probably at Waltham with the chancellor (*CPR*, p. 350). • **53.** *CCR*, p. 224. Thomas was Henry Beaufort's stepfather and guardian as well as his cousin. • **54.** *CPR*, p. 350. As with many of the other similar grants being made at this time, Henry stated that if the money was not repaid within the year, the recipients might dispose of the tabernacle as they saw fit, provided they give the king a month's notice. • **55.** *CPR*, p. 356. • **56.** Barker, *Agincourt*, p. 77; Wylie, *Henry V*, i, pp. 520–1. • **57.** *Monstrelet*, i, p. 331. • **58.** Curry, *Agincourt*, p. 77. • **59.** *CCR*, p. 278 dates this to 24 June. *Foedera*, ix, p. 289 dates it to 24 July, not 24 June; Curry in *Agincourt*, p. 74, follows the July dating. I presume the July date is more likely to be correct, as men were not mustering in June and so were not likely to have need to complain of molestation. • **60.** *Foedera*, ix, p. 288. • **61.** *CPR*, p. 358. Also today Henry dictated a signet letter to the keeper of the privy seal telling him to draw up a licence for the convent of St John the Baptist, Godstow, to elect a new abbess. See Kirby, *Signet Letters*, p. 161. • **62.** *CPR*, p. 328. • **63.** Otway-Ruthven, *Medieval Ireland*, pp. 348–9. • **64.** Henry's first will, in Latin, appears in *Foedera*, ix, pp. 289–93. His second, in English, is in Nichols (ed.), *Royal Wills*, pp. 236–43. The apparent antipathy to Thomas is strengthened in this second will, of 1417, in which he bequeathed the duchy of Lancaster to be divided between his two younger brothers, missing out Thomas entirely. For Henry's third will, see P. and F. Strong, 'The Last Will and Codicils of Henry V', *EHR*, xcvi, pp. 79–102. • **65.** Pugh, *Southampton Plot*, pp. 164–5. • **66.** Pugh, *Southampton Plot*, pp. 169–70. • **67.** *Fears*, pp. 206–7. • **68.** See Pugh, *Southampton Plot*, pp. 172–3. Cambridge admitted Scrope knew nothing of the cry of usurper, nor of the plan to give battle with men of the north. • **69.** Wylie, *Henry V*, i, p. 493. • **70.** Curry, *Agincourt*, p. 80. Other royal business conducted today includes Henry's grant of permission for Janico Dartasso to reside in England for life and to continue to receive the annuities granted him there by the king and his father and Richard II, regardless of any laws requiring him to live in Ireland if he enjoyed an income from those parts. A similar grant was made on Henry's orders to the Irishman, Philip Natervyle. See *CPR*, p. 356. Today also Henry waived any royal rights in the advowson of a Norfolk church so that Thomas Beaufort could grant it in its entirety to the priory of St Cross and St Mary, Wormingay, to endow a vicar to pray for his soul (*CPR*, p. 349). • **71.** Vaughan, *John the Fearless*, p. 212. • **72.** *CPR*, p. 344; Curry, *Agincourt*, p. 76. • **73.** *S&I*, p. 443. • **74.** Curry, *Agincourt*, p. 80. • **75.** The original is printed in Bellaguet (ed.), *Chronique du Religieux*, v, pp. 526–30. See also Wylie, *Henry V*, i, p. 493; Curry, *Agincourt*, p. 51; Nicolas, *Agincourt*, appendix pp. 5. The last is a very erratic translation. The same letter appears dated 5 August in Waurin, pp. 179–80 and Monstrelet, i, pp. 331–2. • **76.** *CPR*, p. 353. • **77.** *Foedera*, ix, p. 297. • **78.** *Foedera*, ix, p. 298. • **79.** Kirby, *Signet Letters*, p. 161; *CPR*, pp. 356–7. • **80.** *CPR*, p. 358. The trustees were Thomas Beaufort, Lord Fitzhugh, Sir John Rothenhale, and Robert Morton. • **81.** *CCR*, p. 223. The names were John Yate corviser, John Snowhite corviser, and Christopher Horylade of Derby, all of whom had been arrested in the Southampton area. • **82.** Pugh, *Southampton Plot*, p. 165. • **83.** Wylie, *Henry V*, ii, pp. 97–8. • **84.** Vaughan, *John the Fearless*, p. 204; Barker, *Agincourt*, p. 59; Curry, *Agincourt*, p. 109; Wylie, *Henry V*, ii, pp. 99–100. • **85.** Johnes (ed.), *Monstrelet*, i, p. 332. • **86.** *EHD*, p. 210; Pugh, *Southampton Plot*, p. 157; *Chronica Maiora*, pp. 404–5. • **87.** Pugh, *Southampton Plot*, p. 170 • **88.** *Issues*, p. 342. • **89.** Wylie, *Henry V*, i, p. 530. • **90.** *PROME*, 1415 November, item 9; *CPR*, p. 409. The lords were the Earl Marshal and the earls of

Salisbury, Suffolk and Oxford, Lord Zouche, Lord Camoys, Lord Fitzhugh and Sir Thomas Erpingham. The justices were William Lasingby and Robert Hull.

August

1. Hutton, *Rise and Fall*, p. 44. • **2.** Mortimer, 'Richard II and the Succession to the Throne', pp. 333–4. • **3.** Pugh, *Southampton Plot*, pp. 167–71. • **4.** The first version appears in Pugh, *Southampton Plot*, pp. 166–7; the second on pp. 172–3. • **5.** Pugh, *Southampton Plot*, pp. 166–7, 172–3. • **6.** *CPR*, p. 331 (Grawe); *CPR*, p. 365 (More); C 53/185, nos 10 & 11 (Joan). Those mentioned as witnesses were 'Henry, archbishop of Canterbury; our very dear uncle, the bishop of Winchester, our chancellor; Thomas bishop of Durham; Richard bishop of Norwich; Thomas duke of Clarence, John duke of Bedford, and Humphrey duke of Gloucester our very dear brothers; Edward our very dear kinsman, duke of York; Edmund earl of March; Thomas earl of Arundel our treasurer; and Richard earl of Warwick our very dear kinsman, Sir Henry Fitzhugh our chamberlain; Sir Thomas Erpingham, our steward of the household; and John Wakeryng keeper of the privy seal'. Note, Erpingham had been replaced as steward on 24 July, so this grant must have originally been made and witnessed before then, and was simply engrossed or sealed today. • **7.** Pugh, *Southampton Plot*, p. 182. • **8.** Pugh, *Southampton Plot*, p. 129. • **9.** Pugh, *Southampton Plot*, pp. 182–3. • **10.** Pugh, *Southampton Plot*, p. 183. • **11.** *CCR*, pp. 278–9. • **12.** Johnes (ed.), *Monstrelet*, i, p. 331; Waurin, p. 178; Curry, *Agincourt*, p. 80. • **13.** Taylor, Roskell (eds), *Gesta*, p. 21. • **14.** Wylie, *Henry V*, i, p. 530. • **15.** Walsingham, *Chronica Maiora*, p. 405. • **16.** Walsingham, *Chronica Maiora*, p. 406; Wylie, *Henry V*, i, p. 528. • **17.** Pugh, *Southampton Plot*, p. 173. • **18.** *CPR*, p. 409. • **19.** Pugh, *Southampton Plot*, pp. 184–5. • **20.** Pugh, 'The Southampton Plot of 1415', pp. 67–8, 129. • **21.** *CCR*, p. 225. • **22.** Pugh, 'The Southampton Plot of 1415', p. 64. • **23.** *CPR*, pp. 349–50. • **24.** *Foedera*, ix, pp. 302–3. • **25.** *CPR*, p. 360. • **26.** *CPR*, pp. 328, 361. • **27.** *CPR*, p. 378. • **28.** *CPR*, pp. 360; 361–2. • **29.** *Testamenta Vetusta*, i, pp. 190–1 (West, dated 1 August), 192–3 (Oxford); Nicolas, *Agincourt*, pp. 339–40; 352 (for the retinues). • **30.** *CPR*, p. 349. • **31.** See Archer, Walker (eds), *Rulers and Ruled*, p. 91 for Sir John Mortimer's comments on March. • **32.** *CCR*, p. 278. • **33.** *Foedera*, ix, p. 254. The earlier order had been issued on 28 May. • **34.** Curry, *Agincourt*, p. 76. • **35.** Wylie, *Henry V*, ii, pp. 2–3; Willett, 'Memoir on British Naval Architecture', *Archaeologia*, 11, pp. 154–9 at p. 155 for the colour of the sails. • **36.** *CCR*, p. 208. • **37.** *CCR*, pp. 210–11, 225; *Foedera*, ix, pp. 304–5; Curry, *Agincourt*, p. 49. • **38.** *CPR*, p. 352. • **39.** *CCR*, p. 227; Wylie, *Henry V*, i, p. 535.

• **40.** *CPR*, p. 349. • **41.** Henry acknowledged later that it much troubled him that he had given away the Scrope lands. However, despite this confession, he never took steps to reverse the distribution. Wylie, *Henry V*, i, p. 537; *PROME*, 1423 October, item 29; *CPR*, p. 361. • **42.** *CPR*, p. 353. • **43.** *Gesta*, p. 21; Wylie, *Henry V*, ii, p. 5. • **44.** Curry, *Agincourt*, pp. 73, 284. Thirty-five pages accompanied thirty-nine men-at-arms on the return journey. • **45.** For Curry's estimates of the numbers, see Curry, *Agincourt*, pp. 75–7. Curry discounts the pages, and so assumes the total number of men was in the region of 12,000. There is no reason to suppose the earl of Oxford's retinue was not representative of the whole army; therefore any assessment of the total number of men must include a number of pages more or less equivalent to the number of men-at-arms. • **46.** *Perfect King*, p. 247. • **47.** *Gesta*, p. 23; Curry, *Agincourt*, p. 81. • **48.** *Gesta*, p. 23. Note: 'Steward' is spelled 'Stewart' herein. • **49.** *Gesta*, p. 25. • **50.** *Gesta*, p. 23. There were several ways of reckoning time. The oldest was to divide the daylight into twelve hours, so this could mean around midday. However the same chronicler uses the timing of 'the fifth hour after noon' (*horam quintam post nonam*), so if he had meant between 12 and 1 p.m. he would not have used the older system. Hence the sixth hour here is likely to relate to the sixth hour after midnight, which chimes with Henry's proclamation of the previous day that he would land in the morning. • **51.** Wylie, *Henry V*, ii, p. 19; Curry, *Agincourt*, p. 82. For Edward III's knighting his son, see *Perfect King*, p. 226. • **52.** Wylie, *Henry V*, ii, p. 52. Curry, quoting the Berry Herald, suggests they were both at Caudebec and that the numbers of men with them were exaggerated. Curry, *Agincourt*, p. 87. • **53.** *Gesta*, p. 33; Curry, *Agincourt*, p. 84. • **54.** Curry notes in 'Military Ordinances', p. 244, that Upton's ordinances do not include the clause regarding wearing the cross of St George; all the other ordinances, including those of Richard II, do include it. However, it is highly probable that the cross of St George was worn on the 1415 campaign. The French were noted to have worn the white cross in response. In 1415 it was probably thought unnecessary at the outset to spell out the need to wear the red cross; but a few infractions of this rule may have led to it being stipulated in later ordinances. • **55.** Wylie, *Henry V*, i, p. 404. • **56.** *Gesta*, pp. 29–31; Wylie, *Henry V*, ii, p. 7; Curry, *Agincourt* pp. 84, 335. • **57.** *Monstrelet*, i, p. 333. • **58.** *Gesta*, pp. 33–5. • **59.** The great gun is named in Brie (ed.), *Brut*, ii, p. 553. • **60.** Wylie, *Henry V*, ii, p. 25; Curry, *Agincourt*, pp. 90–1. • **61.** Curry, 'Military Ordinances', p. 229. The earliest surviving set of military ordinances are the twenty-six clauses governing the behaviour of men on Richard II's expedition to Scotland in 1385, See Maurice Keen, 'Richard II's Ordinances of War of 1385', in Rowena Archer and Simon Walker (eds), *Rulers and Ruled*, pp. 33–48. • **62.** Curry, 'Military Ordinances', pp. 221–3. Although Curry is very circumspect in choosing the set which relates to 1415 – she considers it possible also that the St John's College set could also relates to 1415 – the set known as Upton's ordinances seems most likely. The order to captains to proclaim them and receive copies, which appears only in the preamble to Upton's set, became enshrined in the main text of the other sets. There are fewer clauses, suggesting the later sets were amplifications of these fourteen. Unlike the later sets of ordinances, the first two clauses of Upton's set tally with the description of the first part of the proclamation as recorded in the *Gesta*. The six clauses in Upton which are not in the St John's College set seem more theoretical and possibly based on general experience of warfare (in Wales, for example); the three in the St John's set which are not in Upton seem closely based on the experience of fighting in France. All the St John's College ordinances are in the later Mantes set, so if the Mantes ordinances were based on one or the other, it was far more likely to have been the St John's College set, which was thus probably more recent. • **63.** The military ordinances of Upton have been published in their Latin form in Upton, *De Studio Militari*, pp. 133–45. The ordinances of Mantes (1419 or more probably 1421) have often been used as those governing the army in 1415. A calendar of all of Henry V's ordinances appears as an appendix to Curry, 'The Military Ordinances of Henry V', pp. 240–9. According to the French chronicle of the abbey of St Denis, the English deemed it 'an almost unpardonable crime to have women of easy virtue in the camp' (*S&I*, p. 105). This is supported by the last of Upton's ordinances. For prostitutes in the English royal household, see Given-Wilson, *Royal Household*, p. 60. • **64.** Nichols (ed.), *Collection of all the Wills*, pp. 217–23 (in French, but dated under 22 August); *Testamenta Vetusta*, i, p. 186 (English calendar, following Nichols and dated 22 August); *Foedera*, ix, pp. 307–9 (French, correctly dated). • **65.** For the identification of the baker as Gurmyn, see Wylie, *Henry V*, i, p. 289. • **66.** Wylie, *Henry V*, i, p. 290; Fox, *Acts and Monuments*, pp. 840–1. • **67.** Barker, *Agincourt*, p. 180. • **68.** *Gesta*, p. 35. • **69.** *Gesta*, p. 37. • **70.** Raoul le Gay was given exaggerated figures concerning Henry's army – including 50,000 men and 12 cannon. The latter would have been easier to count than the former, so perhaps are not quite as exaggerated. But le Gay would not have been given this number if there had been more. See Wylie, *Henry V*, ii, p. 27. • **71.** *Fears*, pp. 303–4. • **72.** *Gesta*, p. 37. • **73.** For the number of gunners, see Nicolas, *Agincourt*, p. 386. • **74.** Curry, *Agincourt*, p. 113. • **75.** *CCR*, pp. 280–1; Wylie, *Henry V*, p. 104. For Hovingham and Flete remaining at the duke's court, see the entry for 7 December. • **76.** Wylie, *Henry V*, ii, p. 52. • **77.** Curry, *Agincourt*, p. 85. • **78.** Riley (ed.), *Memorials*, pp. 617–18. • **79.** Curry, *Agincourt*, p. 87; Wylie, *Henry V*, ii, p. 96. The latter states two galleys, not one. • **80.** Nicolas, *Agincourt*, appendix, pp. 6–7. • **81.** Johnes (ed.), *Monstrelet*, i, p. 334. • **82.** *Gesta*, p. 39. • **83.** *Gesta*, p. 41. • **84.** Wylie, *Henry V*, ii, pp. 25–6. • **85.** Curry, *Agincourt*, p. 103; Wylie, *Henry V*, ii, p. 53. • **86.** Curry, *Agincourt*, p. 94; *Gesta*, pp. 41–3.

• **87.** Johnes (ed.), *Monstrelet*, i, p. 334. • **88.** Wylie, *Henry V*, ii, p. 27. The question of Henry's ill-health was one previous example of Courtenay misinforming Fusoris. • **89.** Petit, *Itinéraires*, p. 420. • **90.** Wylie, *Henry V*, ii, p. 29. • **91.** Bellaguet (ed.), *Chronique du Religieux*, v, p. 535. • **92.** Curry, *Agincourt*, pp. 104–5. • **93.** Wylie, *Henry V*, ii, p. 100. • **94.** Rawcliffe, *Medicine and Society*, p. 4; *S&I*, p. 435. • **95.** For Henry's nightly inspections of his lines, see Curry, *Agincourt*, p. 93.

September

1. *Chronica Maiora*, p. 408. • **2.** Wylie, *Henry V*, ii, pp. 41–2; *Chronica Maiora*, pp. 408–9. For the heat, see Curry, *Agincourt*, p. 92. • **3.** *CP*, v, p. 482; Curry, 'Agincourt', in *ODNB*. • **4.** *Foedera*, ix, pp. 310–11; Wylie, ii, p. 40, n. 5. • **5.** Curry, *Agincourt*, p. 96. • **6.** This letter is much misquoted in many sources. For instance it is often said that the king requested cannon be sent to him; that in fact was a separate request, made in June. A full text of the letter appears in *S&I*, pp. 444–5. • **7.** Curry, *Agincourt*, pp. 122–3 (Arundel's company). • **8.** *S&I*, p. 445. • **9.** *Issues*, p. 342. This payment was made on 4 October in respect of the messenger carrying the order to Dover. It must have been about a month earlier that Henry summoned the fishermen. • **10.** Wylie, *Henry V*, ii, p. 53; Curry, *Agincourt*, p. 105. • **11.** Bellaguet (ed.), *Chronique du Religieux*, v, p. 541. • **12.** Wylie, *Henry V*, ii, p. 29. • **13.** Wylie, *Henry V*, i, p. 292. • **14.** Bellaguet (ed.), *Chronique du Religieux*, v, pp. 539–41; Curry, *Agincourt*, p. 105. • **15.** Wylie, *Henry V*, i, 291–2. • **16.** Wylie, *Henry V*, ii, p. 42; Curry, *Agincourt*, p. 92. • **17.** Loomis (ed.), *Constance*, pp. 259, 283. • **18.** Loomis (ed.), *Constance*, p. 135. • **19.** Curry, *Agincourt*, pp. 96–105. • **20.** *Gesta*, p. 45. • **21.** Curry, *Agincourt*, p. 91. • **22.** Curry, *Agincourt*, p. 95. • **23.** *Gesta*, p. 47 • **24.** *Gesta*, p. 49. • **25.** *Chronica Maiora*, pp. 406–7. • **26.** Nicolas, *Agincourt*, appendix, p. 25. • **27.** Curry, *Agincourt*, p. 107. • **28.** Walsingham actually says the Sunday after Michaelmas; the *Gesta* does not mention any of this bargaining about the date but states the Sunday before Michaelmas. See *Gesta*, p. 51; *Chronica Maiora*, p. 407. • **29.** Wylie, *Henry V*, ii, p. 100. • **30.** *Gesta*, p. 51; *Chronica Maiora*, pp. 407–8. • **31.** Bellaguet (ed.), *Chronique du Religieux*, v, pp. 535–7. • **32.** Curry, *Agincourt*, p. 107. • **33.** Johnes (ed.), *Monstrelet*, i, p. 336. • **34.** Johnes (ed.), *Monstrelet*, i, p. 336; Barker, *Agincourt*, p. 239. • **35.** The dating of this event comes from a single fifteenth-century manuscript, and so is open to question. See *ODNB*, under Glendower. • **36.** *Gesta*, p. 53. *Chronica Maiora*, p. 408 states at this juncture there were sixty-four hostages. • **37.** *Gesta*, p. 52. • **38.** Wylie, *Henry V*, ii, p. 56. • **39.** Froissart, quoted in Gilbert, 'A Medieval Rosie the Riveter', p. 350. • **40.** Riley (ed.), *Memorials*, pp. 619–20; *S&I*, pp. 441–2. • **41.** Curry, *Agincourt*, pp. 97–8. • **42.** *Chronique de Ruisseauville*, quoted in Curry, *Agincourt*, p. 162; *S&I*, p. 124. • **43.** Johnes (ed.), *Monstrelet*, i, p. 337; *Gesta*, p. 55. • **44.** Wylie, *Henry V*, ii, pp. 63–5, 331. • **45.** Wylie, *Henry V*, ii, p. 58. • **46.** Curry, *Agincourt*, pp. 109–10; Wylie, *Henry V*, ii, pp. 102–3. • **47.** *CP*, v, p. 458. • **48.** *Perfect King*, p. 172. • **49.** It is stated that Bruges was accompanied by Raoul de Gaucourt in *Gesta*, p. 57. It is worth noting that de Gaucourt does not mention this in his statement but rather stresses how ill he was at the time. See Nicolas, *Agincourt*, appendix, p. 25; Curry, *Agincourt*, p. 117. See under 29 September for a strategic reason why de Gaucourt might have been sent to the dauphin. • **50.** *Foedera*, ix, p. 313 (Latin); Nicolas, *Agincourt*, appendix, pp. 29–30 (English). • **51.** Wylie, *Henry V*, ii, p. 46. • **52.** His four men-at-arms are named in Nicolas, *Agincourt*, p. 357. • **53.** *Gesta*, pp. 55–7; Nicolas, *Agincourt*, appendix, p. 25. • **54.** Wylie, *Henry V*, ii, p. 101. • **55.** Fox, *Acts and Monuments*, pp. 838–9. • **56.** See the *ODNB* entry for Richard Beauchamp, earl of Warwick. • **57.** *PROME*, 1415 Nov., introduction; *CCR*, pp. 287–8. • **58.** See the *ODNB* entry for Warwick. He was at Harfleur but not at Agincourt, 'having been sent to Calais with prisoners'. • **59.** On this parallel with Edward III, see C.J. Rogers, 'Henry V's Military Strategy in 1415', pp. 399–422. • **60.** Barker, *Agincourt*, pp. 220–1; Curry, *Agincourt*, p. 118. Curry is sceptical about the veracity of this report, which was put forward by Titus Livius Frulovisi, who was employed by Humphrey. The implication of this account would be that Humphrey had supported Henry V when even Thomas's courage had failed him. Thomas and Henry V were both dead by the time this account was written, so they could not dispute it. • **61.** *S&I*, p. 65. • **62.** *Gesta*, p. 61. • **63.** *S&I*, p. 65.

October

1. Wylie, *Henry V*, ii, p. 47. • **2.** Wylie, *Henry V*, ii, p. 101; Curry, *Agincourt*, pp. 112–13. • **3.** Vaughan, *John the Fearless*, p. 212. • **4.** Loomis (ed.), *Constance*, p. 60. • **5.** Henry had originally set sail with at least 11,248 fighting men: 2,266 men-at-arms and 8,982 archers. About forty or fifty fighting men had died at Harfleur, and he had sent home between 1,330 and 1,900 more. If the losses were in the standard 3:1 proportion of archers to men-at-arms, then he had at least 1,781 men-at-arms and 7,527 archers remaining. It is unlikely that he had more than 1,926 men-at-arms and 7,952 archers. • **6.** For Botreaux, see Curry, *Agincourt*, p. 121. According to *S&I*, p. 430, in 1416 the deputies were four barons: Hastings, Grey, Clinton and Bourchier. Technically there was no Lord Hastings in 1415, and no Lord Bourchier either; so these 'barons' must have been Sir Edward Hastings and Sir William Bourchier. These four men were not necessarily those deputed to defend Harfleur in 1415, but the companies of Sir Edward Hastings and Lord Clinton were amalgamated in the garrison (according to Curry, 'Agincourt', in *ODNB*). Wylie states that the captains were Sir John Fastolf, John Blount and Thomas Carew; Fastolf was certainly there as he led the sortie in November (Wylie, *Henry V*, ii, p. 332). • **7.** This total of 10,000 is backed up by a newsletter issued after the battle (see *S&I*, p. 264). It is in excess of the 5,000 archers and 900 men-at-arms given in the *Gesta* (and other chronicles based on it) as the *Gesta* allows for 5,000 men being sent home. This was almost certainly an exaggeration, to enhance the 'miracle' aspect of Agincourt. Adam Usk and the London Chronicles state there were 10,000 men on the march; Thomas Walsingham, *Brut* and John Strecche all say 8,000. The latter could relate to just fighting men, not including the pages; this section of the army creates a substantial ambiguity. One English source – Benet's chronicle – gives the figure of 11,000 men. French sources claim many more; but the smallest figures given by the French roughly correspond with the largest figures given by the English writers, which in turn tally with the record sources at about ten thousand men. See the comparison table in Curry, *Agincourt*, pp. 326–8. • **8.** For a licence to return to England from Harfleur dated today, see Curry, *S&I*, p. 447. • **9.** Wylie, *Henry V*, ii, p. 74; *S&I*, p. 124. • **10.** Curry, *Agincourt*, p. 120. • **11.** *Foedera*, ix, p. 314. • **12.** Curry, *Agincourt*, p. 126. • **13.** Barker, *Agincourt*, p. 224. • **14.** *Foedera*, ix, pp. 314–15. A translation appears in *S&I*, pp. 446–7. • **15.** Barker, *Agincourt*, p. 229. • **16.** The new agreement with John the Fearless, negotiated by Morgan, was delivered to Westminster on the 10th; a messenger from Morgan carrying this had probably passed through Calais on the 6th, 7th or 8th. • **17.** Curry, *Agincourt*, p. 107. • **18.** *S&I*, p. 67. • **19.** Curry, *Agincourt*, p. 157; Hardy (ed.), *Waurin*, p. 190; Wylie, *Henry V*, ii, pp. 75–6, 88. • **20.** *Gesta*, pp. 60–1; Johnes (ed.), *Monstrelet*, i, p. 337; Wylie, *Henry V*, ii, p. 88; *S&I*, p. 6; Curry, *Agincourt*, pp. 126, 324. • **21.** *Gesta*, p. 61; Wylie, *Henry V*, ii, p. 114. • **22.** Wylie, *Henry V*, ii, p. 90; Curry, *Agincourt*, pp. 126, 154, 156. • **23.** Curry, *Agincourt*, p. 126. • **24.** Wylie, *Henry V*, ii, p. 92. • **25.** Rawcliffe, *Medicine and Society*, p. 182. • **26.** *Testamenta Vetusta*, i, p. 186. • **27.** Vaughan, *John the Fearless*, p. 207. • **28.** Barker, *Agincourt*, p. 238. • **29.** Curry, *Agincourt*, p. 160. • **30.** *Gesta*, p. 63; Wylie, *Henry V*, ii, pp. 92–3; Curry, *Agincourt*, p. 127. • **31.** Curry, *Agincourt*, p. 128. • **32.** Curry, in *Agincourt*, p. 127, points out that it is 35km from Arques to Eu, and the English army was travelling at an average of about 22km per day if they ended their fourth day's march at Arques. But the English clearly did not stay at Arques; they marched through. Thus it would appear that by the end of the fourth day they had covered more than the 88km from Harfleur – perhaps nearer 98km. This would leave them with a much more manageable 25km to Eu. This would in turn be in line with an average • 24.5km per day since leaving Harfleur. • **33.** *S&I*, p. 57. • **34.** Curry, *Agincourt*, p. 128; Barker, *Agincourt*, p. 234. • **35.** Petit, *Itinéraires*,

p. 421. • **36.** Vaughan, *John the Fearless*, p. 208. • **37.** Curry, *Agincourt*, p. 106. • **38.** Wylie, *Henry V*, ii, p. 63, n. 7. • **39.** Curry, *Agincourt*, pp. 134–5. • **40.** Curry, *Agincourt*, pp. 141–2. • **41.** *Gesta*, p. 63. • **42.** *S&I*, p. 147. • **43.** Curry, *Agincourt*, pp. 131–2, 135. • **44.** Barker, *Agincourt*, p. 229. • **45.** *Gesta*, p. 65. • **46.** Johnes (ed.), *Monstrelet*, i, p. 337; Wylie, *Henry V*, ii, p. 111. • **47.** Riley (ed.), *Memorials*, pp. 620–1. • **48.** *CP*, i, p. 246; Wylie, *Henry V*, p. 68; *ODNB* (under 'Thomas Fitzalan'). • **49.** *S&I*, p. 88. In the hope of pre-empting enquiries about the identity of the John Mortimer here mentioned, he was not the Sir John Mortimer executed in 1424 as supposed by Edward Powell in 'The Strange Death of Sir John Mortimer: Politics and the Law of Treason in Lancastrian England', in Archer and Walker (eds), *Rulers and Ruled*, p. 86. The John Mortimer knighted on the Agincourt campaign died at Agincourt (Kirby (ed.), *IPM*, xx, p. 109). This identifies him as John Mortimer (1392–1415) of Martley, the great-great-grandson of Roger, Lord Mortimer of Chirk (1256–1326), and thus the fourth cousin twice removed of Edmund Mortimer (1391–1425), earl of March. • **50.** *Gesta*, p. 67. • **51.** Johnes (ed.), *Monstrelet*, i, p. 337. • **52.** *Issues*, p. 342. • **53.** Curry, *Agincourt*, p. 132; Wylie, *Henry V*, ii, p. 112. • **54.** Curry, *Agincourt*, p. 163; *S&I*, p. 124. • **55.** *S&I*, pp. 43, 148; Curry, *Agincourt*, p. 139; Wylie, *Henry V*, ii, p. 114. • **56.** *S&I*, p. 148. • **57.** *CPR*, p. 379. The grant was finally made on 28 November. • **58.** *S&I*, pp. 30, 77. • **59.** *Gesta*, p. 69; Curry, *Agincourt*, p. 140 notes that some French sources place the order for the stakes to be made on the 20th. • **60.** *Gesta*, p. 69; Wylie, *Henry V*, ii, p. 117; *S&I*, pp. 57, 66. • **61.** Curry, *Agincourt*, pp. 108–9; Wylie, *Henry V*, ii, pp. 104, 122. • **62.** Petit, *Itinéraires*, p. 421. • **63.** Curry, *Agincourt*, pp. 139, 324. • **64.** *S&I*, p. 44; *Gesta*, p. 71; Curry, *Agincourt*, p. 143. • **65.** *S&I*, p. 57. • **66.** Curry, *Agincourt*, pp. 145–6. • **67.** *Gesta*, p. 71 notes the order to burn the villages. *S&I*, p. 103 states that they were indeed burnt. • **68.** *Gesta*, pp. 73–5. • **69.** *S&I*, pp. 148–9. • **70.** *Gesta*, p. 75. • **71.** Curry, *Agincourt*, p. 148. • **72.** Curry, *Agincourt*, pp. 141, 150; *S&I*, p. 172. • **73.** *S&I*, p. 111. • **74.** Curry, *Agincourt*, p. 121. • **75.** *S&I*, pp. 45, 77. For a discussion as to which lords sent the heralds, see Curry, *Agincourt*, pp. 149–52. I suspect that some chroniclers' addition of the name of the duke of Orléans was in light of his command at the battle, and that the duke of Bourbon issued the challenge. • **76.** *S&I*, p. 180. • **77.** *Gesta*, p. 75. • **78.** *S&I*, p. 132; Wylie, *Henry V*, ii, pp. 121–2. • **79.** Johnes (ed.), *Monstrelet*, i, p. 338; Curry, *Agincourt*, pp. 218–9; *S&I*, p. 180. • **80.** Curry, *Agincourt*, p. 221. • **81.** *S&I*, p. 132. • **82.** Curry, *Agincourt*, p. 153. • **83.** *Gesta*, pp. 76–7. • **84.** Curry, *Agincourt*, p. 156. • **85.** *S&I*, p. 172. • **86.** Wylie suggests it in *Henry V*, ii, p. 127. See Curry, *Agincourt*, pp. 152–3 for a supporting view. • **87.** *S&I*, p. 117. • **88.** Curry, *Agincourt*, p. 156. • **89.** Curry, *Agincourt*, p. 160; *S&I*, p.152. • **90.** *S&I*, p. 58. • **91.** *S&I*, p. 68. • **92.** *Gesta*, p. 77. • **93.** *S&I*, p. 173. • **94.** Curry, *Agincourt*, p. 218. • **95.** *Gesta*, p. 79; *S&I*, p. 59 (for Henry riding ahead). • **96.** *Gesta*, p. 79. • **97.** *S&I*, p. 45. • **98.** *Perfect King*, p. 393; *Fears*, pp. 197, 265. • **99.** For example, the chronicle of Ruisseauville, *S&I*, p. 124. • **100.** *S&I*, p. 153. • **101.** *S&I*, pp. 50, 63. • **102.** See Curry, *Agincourt*, pp. 215, 218. Curry supposes that the duke of Orléans was not with the army during the day of the 24th but did send out the count of Richemont during the night. This would suggest he arrived late on the evening of the 24th or during the night. Gilles le Bouvier (the Berry Herald) states that he arrived on the day of battle itself, as Henry was drawing up his troops. *S&I*, p. 181. • **103.** *S&I*, p. 59; Curry, *Agincourt*, p. 168. • **104.** Curry, *Agincourt*, p. 215; *S&I*, p. 155. • **105.** *S&I*, pp. 59, 69, 92, 154. • **106.** *S&I*, p. 154. • **107.** *S&I*, p. 163. Although note that one of the commanders named is the count of Marle, who is named by the Berry Herald as taking his place in the main battle (*S&I*, p. 181). • **108.** The placing of the French crossbowmen is noted in both English and French sources: *S&I*, pp. 36 (crossbowmen at the back of the men-at-arms and on the wings), 106 (crossbowmen not at their post, having been given permission to depart), 125 (archers not used), 159 (archers ordered not to shoot for fear of hitting the men-at-arms) and 173 (the archers, crossbowmen and infantry at the rear). Pierre Cochon notes that all those of lower status were pushed to the rear (*S&I*, p. 113). • **109.** *S&I*, pp. 34, 36, 106, 161, 181; Curry, *Agincourt*, pp. 222–5. See also *S&I*, p. 61 for the wings of the French army being forward, like horns. • **110.** *S&I*, p. 111. • **111.** *S&I*, p. 172. • **112.** *S&I*, pp. 34, 46, 59. • **113.** *Gesta*, p. 83. It is worth noting that the two men whom Henry had appointed to lead the vanguard and rear-guard embodied what he had to lose. The duke of York's brother had been the traitorous earl of Cambridge who had sought to put the earl of March on the throne. Sir Thomas Camoys was similarly connected to the supposed conspirators. His wife was Elizabeth Mortimer – the widow of Hotspur, the mother of Henry Percy, and the aunt of the earl of March. If God were to be seen to favour Henry's enemies, then the verdict of an English defeat would not just stand for France but also for Henry's enemies in England, for it could be seen to vindicate the earl of Cambridge's cause and the earl of March's claim. • **114.** *S&I*, pp. 132–3, 154, 157. • **115.** *S&I*, p. 184. The follow-up statement that both of the men dressed like the king were killed may reflect a deliberate attempt to detract from Henry's posthumous heroic reputation by associating Henry with this somewhat unchivalrous tactic, which the count would have learnt about during his time as a prisoner in England. At least one if not both of the men dressed as Henry IV at Shrewsbury were killed. See *Fears*, pp. 268–9, 272–3. The fact that no other French source mentions two men dressed as Henry probably indicates it is a malicious assertion. • **116.** *S&I*, pp. 46, 52, 95, 154–5. • **117.** *S&I*, p. 134. • **118.** *S&I*, p. 70. • **119.** *S&I*, pp. 60, 71. • **120.** *S&I*, pp. 104, 118, 124, 129–30, 125, 132, 153, 189. Note the French writers themselves are divided on whether such negotiations took place the previous evening or this morning. It is exceedingly doubtful that Henry ever made an offer of any sort. The only reason for supposing he

might have done so are the moments when he chose to avoid conflict, firstly
at Blanchetaque and secondly after leaving Péronne. But both those decisions
had been taken to avoid fighting on ground which the French had chosen.
Henry did not try to avoid battle at Agincourt. If he did send heralds to the
French, then they were most probably sent the previous day, to request a
truce overnight. • **121.** *S&I*, pp. 124, 130. • **122.** This is the Burgundian view. See
S&I, p. 159. • **123.** *S&I*, p. 181. • **124.** *S&I*, pp. 61, 71. The latter does not name
the lords. • **125.** *S&I*, pp. 153, 164. • **126.** *S&I*, p. 157. • **127.** *S&I*, pp. 72–3 (Pseudo-
Elmham). • **128.** Most chronicles which mention the stakes say the archers
took them. Some do not mention them in the fight, however; and one specifically says the archers did not carry them (*S&I*, p. 72). Probably some did
take them and some left them. • **129.** *Gesta*, pp. 85–7; *S&I*, pp. 72 (mouthfuls
of earth), 159–60 (Erpingham). • **130.** *S&I*, pp. 181–2. • **131.** For Clignet de
Brabant leading this charge, see *S&I*, p. 173. For only 120 men being able to
respond and charge with him, see *S&I*, p. 160 (p. 186 states 300). For Guillaume
de Saveuses and his 300, see *S&I*, p. 161. • **132.** For the rain overnight and the
muddiness of the field, see *S&I*, pp. 34 (*Gesta*: rain the whole night through),
51 (*Walsingham*: softness of the ground), 106 (*monk of St Denis*: torrents of
rain . . . quagmire), 113 (*Pierre Cochon*: so much rain, ground soft), 115 (*French
Chronicle*: newly worked land), 124 (rain all night), 125 (*ibid*: feet often sank
deep into the ground), 130 (*des Ursins*: raining a long time, soft ground, feet
sank into the ground), 133 (*des Ursins*: rain, soft ground, progress difficult),
154 (*Burgundians: Monstrelet, le Fèvre, Waurin*: rain all night; churned up ground),
159 (*Burgundians*: many horses churn up the ground . . . a quagmire). • **133.**
For the disrupting of the French vanguard, see *S&I*, pp. 125, 161. For the three
columns, see *Gesta*, p. 89. • **134.** For the piles of dead, see *S&I*, pp. 37, 47, 92
(two spears' height). For the tightly packed third rank, and Guichard Dauphin
and Vendôme, p. 107. • **135.** *S&I*, p. 107. • **136.** Curry, *Agincourt*, p. 253. • **137.**
S&I, p. 168. The French assigned the honour of killing him to the duke of
Alençon, although whether Alençon was fighting against the vanguard or the
main battle is uncertain. In the Burgundian chronicles, Alençon is supposed
to have attacked the king after killing the duke of York – but the king was
in the main battle, and some distance away from York. • **138.** Given-Wilson (ed.),
Usk, pp. 256–7. No source mentions Sir John Mortimer of Martley; his death
on 25th or 28th October is noted in Kirby (ed.), *IPM*, xx, p. 109 (writ issued 5
December). He was certainly on the campaign, as he was knighted at Pont
Rémy. *The Visitation of Kent*, p. 209, quoting BL Harleian MS 6138 fol. 125,
calls him Hugh Mortimer and states he was slain at Agincourt. For Dafydd
Gam's attempt on Glendower's life, see *Fears*, pp. 291, 430 (n. 27). • **139.** *S&I*,
p. 62. • **140.** *S&I*, pp. 52, 125, 131, 134, 162, 168. For Henry fighting with a
battle axe see *ibid*, p. 52. For Humphrey wounded in the groin and Henry
defending him, *ibid*, pp. 47, 62, 73, 184. For the cutting of Henry's crown, *ibid*,

pp. 47, 94, 157 (where it was cut by one of the eighteen). • **141.** S&I, pp. 60, 115, 162, 174–5. • **142.** S&I, p. 115 (point of defeat). Des Ursins states he had just a dozen men (S&I, p. 134). • **143.** S&I, p. 134. • **144.** S&I, p. 163. • **145.** S&I, p. 163. • **146.** For orders concerning the baggage, see S&I, pp. 35, 59, 69, 154. For the attack on the baggage train, see S&I, pp. 53, 118, 125, 163. For the jewels found, see S&I, p. 125; Nicolas, Agincourt, appendix, p. 26. • **147.** Riley (ed.), Memorials, p. 621. • **148.** Ambühl, 'Fair share of the profits', pp. 137–9; Barker, Agincourt, p. 302. That the dukes of Orléans and Bourbon were taken at this time, and not at a later point, is suggested by the author of the Gesta, which notes that these two men were kept alive during the massacre. The Burgundians seem to suggest Orléans was found at a later time. See S&I, p. 165. • **149.** Ambühl, 'Fair share of the profits', p. 135. • **150.** S&I, p. 127. • **151.** S&I, pp. 37, 62, 88, 125, 131, 190. It is possible that the two accounts which refer to the new army being led by the duke of Brabant have confused this with the regrouped army under Clignet de Brabant. Alternatively, the Ruisseauville writer might have attributed to Clignet command of a force which should have been connected with the duke of Brabant. • **152.** For instance, see the article by Jerome Taylor, 'The Battle of Agincourt: Once more unto the breach', in The Independent, Saturday 1 November 2008. • **153.** S&I, p. 118; Johnes (ed.), Monstrelet, i, p. 342. • **154.** Wylie, Henry V, ii, p. 172. • **155.** S&I, p. 47. • **156.** S&I, p. 62. • **157.** For example, the duke of Brabant's body was found some way away from the battlefield (S&I, p. 174). Ghillebert de Lannoy's companions were burnt alive in a house in Maisoncelles – out of sight of the French lines. • **158.** S&I, pp. 37, 108, 125, 163. • **159.** Tuck, 'The Earl of Arundel's Expedition', p. 233. • **160.** Wylie, Henry V, ii, p. 172. The chronicle of St Denis supports this, stating that the order was executed quickly. See S&I, p. 108. • **161.** S&I, p. 62. Frulovisi had information from Humphrey, duke of Gloucester, which may underpin this point. However, he claims that Henry threatened that he would kill the prisoners unless they withdrew. It is difficult to see how this was true, given that the French did not advance and yet he killed the prisoners anyway. • **162.** S&I, pp. 125, 184. • **163.** S&I, p. 37. • **164.** S&I, p. 165. • **165.** This suggestion is based on le Fèvre's statement that he kept his army arrayed and no French showed despite his being in the field for four hours. The 'four hours' cannot relate to the battle itself, as Henry had actually been in the field since dawn; so it is assumed that it relates to the period of time he was waiting after the end of the battle. English chronicles also state that it was not until evening that Henry left the battlefield; see S&I, pp. 63, 74. • **166.** S&I, pp. 108–9. • **167.** S&I, p. 165. • **168.** S&I, p. 94; Curry, Agincourt, p. 290. • **169.** For numbers of the French dead, see S&I, pp. 11, 53, 93, 110, 118, 127, 134, 168, 182; Barker, Agincourt, pp. 324–5. The last is Gilles le Bouvier's account, which states that 4,000 French knights and esquires were killed, and 500–600 other 'men of war', supporting the notion that infantry and archers were sent to the back. • **170.** *S&I*, p. 126. • **171.** *S&I*, p. 133. • **172.** *S&I*, p. 126. • **173.** *S&I*, p. 165. • **174.** *S&I*, p. 48. • **175.** *S&I*, p. 52. • **176.** *S&I*, p. 74. • **177.** *S&I*, p. 166. • **178.** *S&I*, p. 175. • **179.** *S&I*, pp. 109–10. • **180.** *CPR*, p. 381; Wylie, *Henry V*, ii, p. 63. • **181.** *S&I*, pp. 74–5. • **182.** Riley (ed.), *Memorials*, pp. 621–2; *ODNB*. • **183.** Curry, *Agincourt*, pp. 282–3; *S&I* , p. 167; Ambühl, 'Fair share of the profits', pp. 140–1. • **184.** *S&I*, p. 444. Wylie, *Henry V*, ii, p. 41 states that the decision was in response to Henry's letter of 3 September; but this does not mention war engines, and the June letter does. • **185.** Vale, *Gascony*, p. 75. • **186.** *Issues*, p. 342. This payment is dated 15 October. • **187.** Nicolas (ed.), *Privy Council*, ii, pp. 182–4. • **188.** *CCR*, p. 237. • **189.** *CPR*, p. 378. • **190.** Wylie, *Henry V*, i, p. 537, n. 9. • **191.** *S&I*, p. 131.

November

1. Hutton, *Rise and Fall*, p. 45. • **2.** A particularly good description of the plights of some of the Agincourt widows is given in Barker, *Agincourt*, pp. 324–9. • **3.** Wylie, *Henry V*, iii, p. 1. • **4.** Loomis (ed.), *Constance*, pp. 267–9. • **5.** *CPR*, p. 380 (Norwich); *CCR*, p. 240 (March). The entry for Edmund in *ODNB* states that the full fine of 10,000 marks was due. The *CCR* entry does not overtly state that this was an instalment. • **6.** Belz, *Garter*, lvi–lvii; *Gesta*, p. 133; *CP*, ii, p. 539. • **7.** *PROME*, 1415 November. • **8.** *CCR*, p. 236. • **9.** *CCR*, p. 245; *HKW*, i, p. 266. • **10.** Nicolas, *Agincourt*, appendix, pp. 25–6. • **11.** *CPR*, p. 382. • **12.** *CCR*, p. 287. • **13.** *CPR*, p. 380. • **14.** *PROME*, 1415, appendix; *CPR*, p. 371. • **15.** de Baye, pp. 222–3. • **16.** *Chronica Maiora*, p. 413; *Gesta*, pp. 100–1; Bellaguet (ed.), *Chronique du Religieux*, v, p. 583. • **17.** Nicolas, *Agincourt*, appendix, p. 52. • **18.** *Foedera*, ix, pp. 319–20; Ambühl, 'Fair share of the profits', pp. 136–7. • **19.** Nicolas, *Agincourt*, appendix, p. 27. • **20.** *Gesta*, p. 100, n. 3 (stayed two days); Jacob, *Chichele*, p. 113. • **21.** Jacob, *Chichele*, p. 113; Allmand, *Henry V*, p. 97; *Gesta*, p. 100. • **22.** Given-Wilson (ed.), *Usk*, p. 259. • **23.** *CCR*, p. 256. • **24.** *CPR*, p. 382. • **25.** *CPR*, p. 381. • **26.** *Foedera*, ix, p. 320. The grant is dated as being dictated at Westminster – but as yet Henry was still somewhere between Rochester and Eltham Palace. See Allmand, *Henry V*, p. 97. Presumably Rippon had returned with Warwick earlier in the year, as he was mentioned by Cerretano as being part of the initial English delegation. • **27.** Loomis (ed.), *Constance*, p. 137. • **28.** Loomis (ed.), *Constance*, p. 264, where the date is 22 November (corrected to 21st on p. 540). • **29.** *CCR*, p. 237. • **30.** Wylie, *Henry V*, i, pp. 536–7, n. 10. • **31.** *CPR*, p. 411. • **32.** *Gesta*, p. 102 (quotation); Given-Wilson (ed.), *Usk*, p. 261 (four miles). • **33.** *Gesta*, p. 107. • **34.** *Gesta*, pp. 107–9. • **35.** *Gesta*, p. 113. • **36.** Given-Wilson (ed.), *Usk*, p. 263; Capgrave, *Illustrious Henries*, p. 134; *Chronica Maiora*, p. 413. Usk states this funeral Mass was held the next day; Walsingham on 1 December. Other

chroniclers state there were more than twelve bishops – sixteen or eighteen.
• **37.** Curry, *Agincourt*, p. 284. • **38.** Vale, *English Gascony*, p. 75. • **39.** Petit, *Itinéraires*, p. 422. • **40.** *S&I*, p. 178; Vaughan, *John the Fearless*, p. 209. • **41.** Johnes (ed.), *Monstrelet*, i, p. 348. • **42.** Given-Wilson (ed.), *Usk*, p. 263. • **43.** *Foedera*, ix, pp. 320–1. • **44.** *Foedera*, ix, p. 321. • **45.** *CCR*, p. 242. • **46.** *CPR*, pp. 379, 380. The letters to the pope and the council were dated 25 November. • **47.** Nicolas (ed.), *Privy Council*, ii, pp. 184–5. • **48.** Wylie, *Henry V*, ii, p. 332. • **49.** *ODNB*, under Thomas Beaufort. • **50.** *CPR*, p. 380. • **51.** *CPR*, p. 381. • **52.** Wylie, *Henry V*, ii, p. 69; *Foedera*, ix, pp. 321–2. • **53.** *Foedera*, ix, p. 324. • **54.** *CPR*, p. 379. The order was given for the patent letter to be drawn up on 3 December. *CCR*, p. 236. • **55.** *CCR*, p. 297; *Foedera*, ix, p. 322. • **56.** The messenger had arived in Henry's absence, before 30 October. See *Issues*, p. 343, where he was rewarded with gilt-silver cups which had belonged to Henry Scrope. • **57.** Wylie, *Henry V*, p. 314. Hingman returned to England in or before 1425, when he became deputy to Bishop Wakeryng of Norwich, who was then at Constance. The last known Greenland-generated Norse documents date from 1408; so presumably Hingman returned to Europe when the Greenland community was given up. • **58.** Petit, *Itinéraires*, p. 422 • **59.** Vaughan, *John the Fearless*, p. 209. • **60.** *Cal. Charter Rolls*, v, p. 482. • **61.** *S&I*, p.185.

December

1. *Chronica Maiora*, p. 413; Wylie, *Henry V*, ii, p. 270. • **2.** *CPR*, pp. 374 and 379 (Arundel), 377 (Robesart), 378 (Clitherowe and Cawardyn), 383 (Dominicans), 402 (Bedford). • **3.** Petit, *Itinéraires*, p. 423; *S&I*, p. 178. • **4.** Bellaguet (ed.), *Chronique du Religieux*, v, pp. 583, 587; Johnes (ed.), *Monstrelet*, i, p. 350. • **5.** Nicolas (ed.), *Privy Council*, ii, pp. 186–7. • **6.** Bellaguet (ed.), *Chronique du Religieux*, v, p. 585; Johnes (ed.), *Monstrelet*, i, p. 350. • **7.** Parker, 'Politics and Patronage in Lynn', p. 224. • **8.** *CPR*, p. 411. • **9.** *CCR*, p. 287 (French); *CPR*, pp. 374 (Kent), 405 (Wales). • **10.** Vaughan, *John the Fearless*, p. 209; Bellaguet (ed.), *Chronique du Religieux*, v, p. 226. • **11.** Wylie, *Henry V*, i, pp. 96–7. • **12.** *CCR*, pp. 230 (Somercotes), 236 (Wyrom and Sherman). *CPR*, pp. 379 (coal, abbot of Canterbury), 384 (Charterhouse). • **13.** Bellaguet (ed.), *Chronique du Religieux*, v, p. 227, quoting *Juvénal des Ursins*, p. 525; Johnes (ed.), *Monstrelet*, i, p. 349. • **14.** For the names of the ambassadors, see Johnes (ed.), *Monstrelet*, i, p. 349. For the date of sending them, see *de Baye*, p. 228, n. 2. • **15.** *Foedera*, ix, p. 323; Ambühl, 'Fair share of the profits', p. 138, n. 41. • **16.** *CPR*, p. 378. • **17.** *CPR*, p. 380. • **18.** Wylie, *Henry V*, i, p. 537, n. 8. • **19.** *CPR*, p. 384; Wylie, *Henry V*, i, pp. 536–7. • **20.** *Issues*, p. 343. • **21.** *de Baye*, p. 227, n. 1, quoting *Juvénal des Ursins*, p. 525; Johnes (ed.), *Monstrelet*, i, p. 348. • **22.** Johnes (ed.), *Monstrelet*, i, p. 348; Petit, *Itinéraires*, p. 423. • **23.** *CPR*,

p. 405. • **24.** Wylie, *Henry V*, i, p. 104. • **25.** *CPR*, p. 385. The reversion was after the death of Thomas Erpingham. • **26.** *CPR*, p. 383. • **27.** *CPR*, pp. 398–9. • **28.** Nicolas (ed.), *Privy Council*, ii, pp. xv, 188–91; *Foedera*, ix, pp. 324–5. • **29.** Johnes (ed.), *Monstrelet*, i, p. 349; *de Baye*, p. 228, n. 2; Petit, *Itinéraires*, p. 423; Bellaguet (ed.), *Chronique du Religieux*, v, p. 585. • **30.** *de Baye*, p. 229. • **31.** *De Baye*, p. 229, n. 1, quoting *Juvénal des Ursins*, p. 525. • **32.** *CPR*, p. 397. • **33.** Bellaguet (ed.), *Chronique du Religieux*, v, p. 585; *de Baye*, pp. 228–9, n. 2. • **34.** *Foedera*, ix, pp. 325–6. • **35.** *CPR*, p. 381. • **36.** Loomis (ed.), *Constance*, p. 504. • **37.** The terms of 13 December appear in Loomis (ed.), *Constance*, pp. 269–79. Benedict XIII was finally deposed on 26 July 1417. • **38.** Loomis (ed.), *Constance*, p. 138. • **39.** E 403/623; *Issues*, pp. 343–4. • **40.** Bellaguet (ed.), *Chronique du Religieux*, v, p. 585. • **41.** *Foedera*, ix, p. 327. • **42.** Bellaguet (ed.), *Chronique du Religieux*, v, p. 583. • **43.** Wylie, *Henry V*, ii, p. 332. Wylie claims this sortie was led by Beaufort, but he seems to have been back in England by the end of November and to have remained there until early 1416. • **44.** Wylie, *Henry V*, ii, p. 106; Barker, *Agincourt*, p. 238. • **45.** *Issues*, p. 344. • **46.** *Issues*, pp. 344–5 • **47.** Bellaguet (ed.), *Chronique du Religieux*, v, p. 589; *de Baye*, p. 233. • **48.** For the feast being at Lambeth, see *Chronica Maiora*, p. 413. The date given is 1416 but Christmas 1415 is obviously intended, from the positioning of the reference. See also *Gesta*, pp. 113–14. • **49.** Dockray, *Warrior King*, p. 222.

Conclusion

1. McFarlane, *Lancastrian Kings and Lollard Knights*, p. 133. The line was actually written in 1954 according to Curry, *Agincourt . . . Erpingham*, p. 9. • **2.** Allmand, *Henry V*, p. 3. • **3.** Allmand, *Henry V*, p. 443. • **4.** Curry, *Agincourt . . . Erpingham*, p. 9. • **5.** Pugh, *Southampton Plot*, p. 145. • **6.** Hardy (ed.), *Waurin*, p. 391. • **7.** Bradbury, *Medieval Archer*, p. 117. • **8.** *Issues*, pp. 278 (joust), 280 (sparrowhawk), 284 (swordfight, and king's fool), 285 ('to a certain woman'). • **9.** J. Simmons, 'Mr Rowse's Masterpiece', *National & English Review* (January 1951), pp. 44–5. • **10.** For chess, cards and tables, see Dockray, *Warrior King*, p. 214. • **11.** Dockray, *Warrior King*, p. 222. He said this at Caen, in 1419, when asked how he justified killing so many innocent people. • **12.** Allmand, *Society and War*, p. 42. • **13.** Dockray, *Warrior King*, p. 214. • **14.** Allmand, *Henry V*, p. 8. The ambiguity in Allmand's text is clarified in Mortimer, 'Henry IV's date of birth and the royal Maundy', pp. 568–9, n. 7. • **15.** Otway-Ruthven, *Medieval Ireland*, pp. 165, 334, 348–50; *ODNB*, under John Talbot. • **16.** Wylie, *Henry V*, i, p. 537; *PROME*, iv, p. 213 (1423); *CPR*, p. 361. • **17.** *HKW*, ii, pp. 569–70. • **18.** Nicolas, *Agincourt*, appendix, p. 15. • **19.** Harriss, *Shaping the Nation*, p. 592. • **20.** Pugh, *Southampton Plot*, p. 138. • **21.** Vale, *English Gascony*, p. 76.

Appendix 1

1. *Testamenta Vetusta*, i, p. 189, quoting Hume, vol. iii, p. 64. • 2. Bennett, 'Edward III's Entail', p. 608. • 3. For the declaration being in 1386 not 1385, see Mortimer, 'Richard II and the Succession', pp. 325–8. • 4. Mortimer, 'Richard II and the Succession', pp. 331–3. • 5. For the murder of the duke of Gloucester, see *Fears*, pp. 142–6; James Tait, 'Did Richard II Murder the Duke of Gloucester?', in T. F. Tout and James Tait (eds), *Historical Essays by Members of the Owens College Manchester* (1902); A. E. Stamp, 'Richard II and the Death of the Duke of Gloucester', *EHR*, 38 (1923), pp. 249–51; R. L. Atkinson, 'Richard II and the Death of the Duke of Gloucester', *EHR*, 38 (1923), pp. 563–4; A. E. Stamp, 'Richard II and the Death of the Duke of Gloucester', *EHR*, 47 (1932), p. 453. • 6. *Fears*, pp. 205–9. • 7. Riley (ed.), *Annales*, p. 399 refers to Thomas Mowbray, Earl Marshal, confessing that he was aware of the duke's plot to rescue the boys. This has been seen as corroboration of Constance's accusations. However, the chronicler may just have been describing the plot as 'news of the duke's intentions' as a shorthand for the plan. The duke offered to defend himself in a duel to protest his innocence. The *ODNB* states that he confessed he knew of the plot after an initial denial; I do not know of the source for this, but, even if correct, it does not mean that he was complicit in his sister's designs.

Appendix 2

1. Nicolas (ed.), *Privy Council*, ii, pp. 150–1. • 2. Nicolas (ed.), *Privy Council*, ii, pp. 154–5. • 3. See for example that of Lord Scrope of Masham, printed in *Foedera*, ix, pp. 230–2. • 4. Nicolas (ed.), *Privy Council*, ii, p. 154.

Appendix 3

1. Johnes (ed.), *Monstrelet*, i, p. 334. • 2. *Gesta*, pp. 58–9. • 3. Curry, *Agincourt*, pp. 122–3. • 4. *S&I*, p. 436. • 5. *S&I*, p. 434. Barker, *Agincourt*, p. 215 states that 47 archers were sent back to England. • 6. This is the method used in Barker, *Agincourt*, pp. 215–16. • 7. Curry, *Agincourt*, p. 123. • 8. *Gesta*, p. 59, n. 5; Wylie, *Henry V*, ii, p. 67. • 9. Wylie, *Henry V*, ii, p. 67. In addition, it is worth noting that some men seem to have returned with more men in their company than they had at the outset, presumably due to reorganisation of companies during the campaign. This would mean our understanding that these were all 'reinforcements' would be wrong. • 10. Curry, *Agincourt*, p. 123. • 11. The ratio of

combatants to non-combatants in the lists of the sick sent home, 1,330 out of 1,693 (79%), compares closely with the ratio of combatants to non-combatants in the army as a whole (between 75% and 78%, depending on the number of Cheshire archers); so we can be confident that these lists describe men of all status groups, occupations and ranks, not just the combatants. • **12.** The 'we can prove . . .' statement is to be found in Curry, *Agincourt*, p. 123. • **13.** *S&I*, pp. 429–30, 433. For the number in his retinue, see Wylie, *Henry V*, ii, p. 63. He had contracted to provide 960, which is the figure Curry uses, but according to Wylie he actually mustered 798 archers and 246 men-at-arms. Of these a total of 742 men made it back to England; it is not clear how many were invalided home from Harfleur and how many died at the battle.

Appendix 4

1. The *Gesta* is normally regarded as a work of propaganda, written to bolster Henry's reputation. Anne Curry writes that 'the purpose of the *Gesta* was likely to extol to a European audience at the council of Constance the king's virtues as a Christian prince' (*Agincourt*, p. 260). Chris Given-Wilson questioned the assumption that it was a propaganda-related piece in a talk delivered at the University of Exeter in November 2007, pointing out that it was written in Latin, which relatively few contemporaries would have been able to understand. However, as Curry suggests, and as this book shows, Henry's ambition in 1415 was coupled with his need for divine approbation. It was as clerically orientated propaganda that the *Gesta* was written, by a priest. One might say that propaganda concerning military miracles – divine intervention in military affairs – *had* to be written by a priest, in Latin. The language of this book does not invalidate its propaganda purposes. • **2.** In Curry, *Agincourt*, p. 228, the 'minimum figure' for the English army is 8,732 fighting men: 1,593 men-at-arms and 7,139 archers. This incorporates her assumption that the lists of those sent back to England with dysentery are complete. It also seems not to account for the 160 Englishmen who had fallen into French hands since leaving Harfleur. • **3.** Curry, *Agincourt*, pp. 326–7; *S&I*, p. 12. • **4.** Nicolas, *Agincourt*, appendix, pp. 25–6. • **5.** *S&I*, p. 156. • **6.** *S&I*, p. 181. • **7.** Curry, *Agincourt*, pp. 222–8, esp. 226. • **8.** Curry, *Agincourt*, p. 228. • **9.** *S&I*, p. 156. With regard to other retinues, the duke of Alençon seems to have no retinue in Curry's reckoning, unlike all the other dukes. There may be other hidden retinues within the army. The men from the Marches of Boulogne are mentioned in the Burgundian chronicles (*S&I*, p. 157).

Select Bibliography and List of Abbreviations

Works which are abbreviated in the notes are here given under both the abbreviation and the editor's or author's name. All places of publication are London unless otherwise stated.

Unpublished Manuscripts in the National Archives

DL 25/1649
DL 28/1/6
C53/184–5
E 101/47/11
E 101/321/26–29
E 101/404/21.
E 101/404/23
E 101/406/21–30
E 358/6
E 361/7
E 403/620–623
E 405/28
E 407/11

A Collection of Ordinances and Regulations for the Government of the Royal Household (1790)

Christopher Allmand, *Henry V* (1992)

Christopher Allmand (ed.), *Society at War* (Woodbridge, 1998)

Rémy Ambühl, 'A Fair Share of the Profits? The Ransoms of Agincourt (1415)', *Nottingham Medieval Studies*, 50 (2006), pp. 129–50

Rowena Archer and Simon Walker (eds), *Rulers and Ruled in Late Medieval England: Essays presented to Gerald Harriss* (1995)

Archives départmentales de l'Hérault, *Actes Royaux des archives de l'Hérault ...* vol. 1 (Montpellier, 1980)

R. L. Atkinson, 'Richard II and the Death of the Duke of Gloucester', *EHR*, 38 (1923), pp. 563–4

Gérard Bacquet, *Azincourt* (Bellegarde, 1977)

J. F. Baldwin, *The King's Council in England During the Middle Ages* (Oxford, 1913, reprinted 1969)

Juliet Barker, *Agincourt: the King, the Campaign, the Battle* (2005)

M. L. Bellaguet (ed.), *Chronique du Religieux de Saint-Denys contenant le Règne de Charles VI, de 1380 à 1422*, vol. 5 (Paris, 1844)

George Frederick Beltz, *Memorials of the Order of the Garter From its Foundation to the Present Time* (1841)

Michael Bennett, 'Edward III's Entail and the Succession to the Crown, 1376–1471', *EHR*, 113 (1998), pp. 580–609

Douglas Biggs, '"A wrong whom conscience and kindred bid me to right": a reassessment of Edmund Langley, duke of York, and the usurpation of Henry IV', *Albion*, 26 (1994), pp. 253–72

The Book of Fees Commonly Called Testa de Nevill (3 vols, 1920–31)

BL: British Library

Jim Bradbury, *The Medieval Archer* (Woodbridge 1985, rep. 1998)

F. W. D. Brie (ed.) *The Brut* (2 vols, Oxford, 1906–8)

R. A. Brown, H. M. Colvin and A. J. Taylor, *History of the King's Works: the Middle Ages* (2 vols, 1963)

Cal. Charter Rolls: Calendar of the Charter Rolls Preserved in the Public Record Office, 1226–1516 (6 vols, 1903–1927)

Calendar of State Papers and Manuscripts Relating to English Affairs Existing in the Archives and Collections of Venice and in Other Libraries of Northern Italy, vol. 1: 1202–1509 (1864, reprinted 1970)

CCR: Calendar of the Close Rolls 1413–1419 (1929)

Chronica Maiora: David Preest and James G. Clark (eds), *The Chronica Maiora of Thomas Walsingham, 1376–1422* (Woodbridge, 2005)

C. A. Cole (ed.), *Memorials of Henry the Fifth, King of England*, Rolls Series, 11 (1858)

CP: G. E. Cokayne, revised by V. Gibbs, H. A. Doubleday, D. Warrand, Lord Howard de Walden and Peter Hammond (eds), *The Complete Peerage of England, Scotland, Ireland, Great Britain and the United Kingdom extant, extinct or dormant* (14 vols, 1910–1998)

CPR: Calendar of the Patent Rolls 1413–1416 (1910)

Anne Curry, *Agincourt: a New History* (Stroud, 2006)

Anne Curry, 'The Military Ordinances of Henry V: Texts and Contexts', in Given-Wilson, Kettle and Scales (eds), *War, Government and Aristocracy*, pp. 214–49

Anne Curry (ed.), *Agincourt 1415: Henry V, Sir Thomas Erpingham and the Triumph of the English Archers* (Stroud, 2000)

Anne Curry (ed.), *The Battle of Agincourt: Sources and Interpretations* (Woodbridge, 2000)

de Baye: Alexandre Tuetey (ed.), *Journal de Nicolas de Baye, Greffier du Parlement de Paris 1400–1417*, vol. 2 (Paris, 1888)

Frederick Devon (ed.), *Issues of the Exchequer* (1837)

Keith Dockray, *Warrior King: the Life of Henry V* (Stroud, 2007)

Gwilym Dodd and Douglas Biggs (eds), *Henry IV: the Establishment of the Regime* (Woodbridge, 2003)

Gwilym Dodd and Douglas Biggs (eds), *The Reign of Henry IV: Rebellion and Survival* (Woodbridge, 2008)

Gwilym Dodd, 'Patronage, Petitions and Grace', in Dodd and Biggs (eds), *Rebellion and Survival*, pp. 105–35

Mark Duffy, *Royal Tombs of Medieval England* (Stroud, 2003)

Sir William Dugdale, *Monasticon Anglicanum: a New Edition . . . by John Caley Esq., Henry Ellis . . . and the Reverend Bulkeley Bandinel* (6 vols, 1817–30)

Christopher Dyer, *Standards of Living in the Later Middle Ages* (Cambridge, revised edn, 1998)

EHD: A. R. Myres (ed.), *English Historical Documents vol. 4: 1327–1485* (1969)

EHR: *English Historical Review*

Fears: Ian Mortimer, *The Fears of Henry IV: the Life of England's Self-Made King* (2007)

Christopher Fletcher, *Richard II: Manhood, Youth and Politics, 1377–1399* (Oxford, 2008)

Foedera: Thomas Rymer (ed.), *Foedera, conventiones, literae, et cujuscunque generis acta publica* (20 vols, 1704–35)

John Fox, *Acts and Monuments of Matters Most Special and Memorable Happening in the Church, with an Universall Historie of the Same*, vol. 1 (1641)

Frederick J. Furnivall (ed.), *The Babees Book*, Early English Text Society (1868; reprint, Woodbridge, 1997)

Gesta: Frank Taylor and John S. Roskell (eds), *Gesta Henrici Quinti: the Deeds of Henry the Fifth* (Oxford, 1975)

James E. Gilbert, 'A Medieval "Rosie the Riveter"? Women in France and Southern England during the Hundred Years War', in Villalon and Kagay (eds), *The Hundred Years War*, pp. 333–64

Chris Given-Wilson, *The Royal Household and the King's Affinity: Service, Politics and Finance in England 1360–1413* (1986)

Chris Given-Wilson (ed.), *The Chronicle of Adam Usk* (Oxford, 1997)

Chris Given-Wilson (ed.), *Parliamentary Rolls of Medieval England* (CD ROM ed., Woodbridge, 2005)

Chris Given-Wilson, Ann Kettle and Len Scales (eds), *War, Government and Aristocracy in the British Isles c. 1150–1500: Essays in Honour of Michael Prestwich* (Woodbridge, 2008)

John Grime, *The Lanterne of Lyght* (1535)

T. D. Hardy (ed.), *Syllabus . . . of Rymer's Foedera* (3 vols, 1869–85)

Sir William Hardy and Edward L. C. P. Hardy (eds), *A Collection of the Chronicles and Ancient Histories . . . by John de Waurin, Lord of Forestel . . . 1399–1422* (1887)

G. L. Harriss, 'The King and his Magnates', in Harriss (ed.), *Henry V: the Practice of Kingship*, pp. 53–74

G. L. Harriss (ed.), *Henry V: the Practice of Kingship* (Stroud, 1993)

Gerald Harriss, *Cardinal Beaufort: a Study of Lancastrian Ascendancy and Decline* (Oxford, 1988)

Gerald Harriss, *Shaping the Nation: England 1360–1461* (Oxford, 2005)

Barbara Harvey, *Living and Dying in England 1100–1540: the Monastic Experience* (Oxford, 1993; reprinted 1995)

F. S. Haydon (ed.), *Eulogium (Historiarum sive Temporis): Chronicon ab Orbe Condito usque ad Annum Domini MCCCLXVI* (3 vols, 1858–63)

F. C. Hingeston (ed.), *The Book of the Illustrious Henries by John Capgrave* (1858)

F. C. Hingeston (ed.), *The Chronicle of England by John Capgrave* (1858)

F. C. Hingeston (ed.), *Royal and Historical Letters During the Reign of Henry IV, King of England and France and Lord of Ireland* (2 vols, 1860, 1964)

HKW: R. A. Brown, H. M. Colvin and A. J. Taylor, *History of the King's Works: the Middle Ages* (2 vols, 1963)

Harold F. Hutchinson, *Henry V: a Biography* (1967)

Ronald Hutton, *The Rise and Fall of Merry England: the Ritual Year 1400–1700* (Oxford, 1994)

Issues: Frederick Devon (ed.), *Issues of the Exchequer* (1837)

E. F. Jacob, *Archbishop Henry Chichele* (1967)

E. F. Jacob, *Henry V and the Invasion of France* (1947)

E. F. Jacob, *The Register of Henry Chichele, Archbishop of Canterbury, 1414–1443*, Canterbury and York Series, vols 42, 45–7 (4 vols, 1937–47)

Thomas Johnes (ed.), *The Chronicles of Enguerrand de Monstrelet* (2 vols, 1853)

H. A. Kelly, 'English Kings and the Fear of Sorcery', *Mediaeval Studies*, 39 (1977), pp. 206–38

C. L. Kingsford (ed.), *The First English Life of Henry V* (Oxford, 1911), pp. 11–12

J. L. Kirby (ed.), *Calendar of Signet Letters of Henry IV and Henry V* (1978)

J. L. Kirby (ed.), *Calendar of Inquisitions Post Mortem . . . vol. 20: 1–5 Henry V* (1995)

Louise Ropes Loomis (trans.), *The Council of Constance: the Unification of the Church* (New York, 1961)

H. R. Luard (ed.), *Flores Historiarum* (3 vols, 1890)

William Marx (ed.), *An English Chronicle 1377–1461: a New Edition* (Woodbridge, 2003)

Gervase Mathew, *The Court of Richard II* (1968)

K. B. McFarlane, 'England: the Lancastrian Kings, 1399–1461', in C. W. Previté-Orton and Z. N. Brooke (eds), *The Cambridge History of Medieval Europe, vol 8: the Close of the Middle Ages* (Cambridge, 1936), pp. 362–93

K. B. McFarlane, *Lancastrian Kings and Lollard Knights* (Oxford, 1972)

Peter McNiven, *Heresy and Politics in the Reign of Henry IV: the Burning of John Badby* (Woodbridge, 1987)

Monstrelet: Thomas Johnes (ed.), *The Chronicles of Enguerrand de Monstrelet* (2 vols, 1853)

D. A. L. Morgan, 'The political after-life of Edward III: the apotheosis of a Warmonger', *EHR*, 112 (1997), pp. 856–81

Philip Morgan, 'Memories of the Battle of Shrewsbury' (paper delivered at Nottingham 2006)

Ian Mortimer, 'Henry IV's Date of Birth and the Royal Maundy', *Historical Research*, 80 (2007), pp. 567–76

Ian Mortimer, 'Richard II and the Succession to the Crown', *History*, 91, 303 (2006), pp. 320–36

Ian Mortimer, *The Fears of Henry IV: the Life of England's Self-Made King* (2007)

Ian Mortimer, *The Perfect King: the Life of Edward III, Father of the English Nation* (2006)

Ian Mortimer, *The Time Traveller's Guide to Medieval England* (2008)

Ian Mortimer, 'York or Lancaster? Who was the Rightful Heir to the Throne in 1460?', *Richard III Society Bulletin* (Autumn 2008), pp. 20–4

A. R. Myres (ed.), *English Historical Documents vol. 4: 1327–1485* (1969)

J. Nichols (ed.), *A Collection of All the Wills Now Known to be Extant of the Kings and Queens of England . . .* (1780, reprinted New York, 1969)

Donald M. Nicol, 'A Byzantine Emperor in England: Manuel II's visit to London in 1400–1401', *University of Birmingham Historical Journal*, 12, 2 (1970), pp. 204–25

Sir Nicholas Harris Nicolas, *History of the Battle of Agincourt and of the Expedition of Henry the Fifth into France in 1415* (2nd ed., 1832)

Sir Nicholas Harris Nicolas (ed.), *Proceedings and Ordinances of the Privy Council of England* (7 vols, 1834–37)

Sir Nicholas Harris Nicolas (ed.), *Testamenta Vetusta: Illustrations from Wills of Manners, Customs, etc. from the Reign of Henry the Second to the Accession of Elizabeth I*, vol. 1 (1826)

ODNB: *Oxford Dictionary of National Biography from the earliest times to the year 2000* (on-line edition, Oxford, 2004, with corrections and additions)

George Oliver, *Monasticon Diocesis Exonienses* (Exeter, 1846)

Mark Ormrod, 'The Rebellion of Archbishop Scrope and the Tradition of Opposition to Royal Taxation', in Dodd and Biggs (eds), *Rebellion and Survival*, pp. 162–79

W. M. Ormrod, 'The Personal Religion of Edward III', *Speculum*, 64 (1989), pp. 849–911

A. J. Otway-Ruthven, *A History of Medieval Ireland* (1968, reprinted 1993)

Papal Registers: J. A. Twemlow (ed.), *Calendar of Entries in the Papal Registers relating to Great Britain and Ireland: Papal Letters vol. 6: 1404–1415* (1904)

Kate Parker, 'Politics and Patronage in Lynn 1399–1416', in Dodd and Biggs (eds), *Rebellion and Survival*, pp. 210–27

Perfect King: Ian Mortimer, *The Perfect King: the Life of Edward III, Father of the English Nation* (2006)

Ernest Petit, *Itinéraires de Philippe le Hardi et de Jean Sans Peur, ducs de Bourgogne* (Paris, 1888)

Edward Powell, 'The Strange Death of Sir John Mortimer: Politics and the Law of Treason in Lancastrian England', in Archer and Walker (eds), *Rulers and Ruled in Late Medieval England*, pp. 83–98

Edward Powell, 'The Restoration of Law and Order', in Harriss (ed.), *Henry V: the Practice of Kingship*, pp. 53–74

David Preest and James G. Clark (eds), *The Chronica Maiora of Thomas Walsingham, 1376–1422* (Woodbridge, 2005)

PROME: Chris Given-Wilson (ed.), *Parliamentary Rolls of Medieval England* (CD ROM ed., Woodbridge, 2005).

T. B. Pugh, *Henry V and the Southampton Plot of 1415*, Southampton Record Series (1988)

T. B. Pugh, 'The Southampton Plot of 1415', in R. A. Griffiths and J. W. Sherborne (eds), *Kings and Nobles in the Later Middle Ages: a Tribute to Charles Ross* (Gloucester, 1986), pp. 62–89

Carole Rawcliffe, *Medicine and Society in Later Medieval England* (1999)

Henry Thomas Riley (ed.), *Johannis de Trokelowe et Henrici de Blaneforde . . . chronica et annales*, Rolls Series, 28 (1866)

Henry Thomas Riley (ed.), *Memorials of London and London Life in the XIIIth, XIVth and XVth Centuries* (1888)

Henry Thomas Riley (ed.), *Thomae Walsingham Quondam Monachi S. Albani Historia Anglicana* (2 vols, 1863–4)

Clifford J. Rogers, 'Henry V's Military Strategy in 1415', in Villalon and Kagay (eds), *The Hundred Years War*, pp. 399–428

Paul Roubiczek and Joseph Kalmer, *Warrior of God: the Life and Death of John Hus* (1947)

Owen Ruffhead (ed.), *Statutes at Large, from Magna Charta to the End of the Last Parliament in Eight Volumes*, vol. 1 (1763)

Thomas Rymer (ed.), *Foedera, conventiones, literae, et cujuscunque generis acta publica* (20 vols, 1704–35)

S&I: Anne Curry (ed.), *The Battle of Agincourt: Sources and Interpretations* (Woodbridge, 2000)

V. J. Scattergood and J. W. Sherborne, *English Court Culture in the Later Middle Ages* (1983)

J. Simmons, 'Mr Rowse's Masterpiece', *National and English Review* (January 1951), pp. 44–5

Lucy Toulmin Smith (ed.), *Expeditions to Prussia and the Holy Land made by Henry Earl of Derby . . . in the Years 1390–1 and 1392–3*, Camden Society, New Series 52 (1894)

Matthew Spinka, *John Hus at the Council of Constance* (New York, 1965)

Matthew Spinka (ed.), *The Letters of John Hus* (Manchester, 1972)

A. E. Stamp, 'Richard II and the Death of the Duke of Gloucester', *EHR*, 38 (1923), pp. 249–51

A. E. Stamp, 'Richard II and the Death of the Duke of Gloucester', *EHR*, 47 (1932), p. 453.

Jenny Stratford, 'The Royal Library in England Before the Reign of Edward IV', in Nicholas John Rogers (ed.), *England in the Fifteenth Century: Proceedings of the 1992 Harlaxton Symposium* (Stamford, 1994), pp. 187–197

Jenny Stratford (ed.), *The Lancastrian Court: Proceedings of the 2001 Harlaxton Symposium* (Donington, 2003)

Paul Strohm, *England's Empty Throne: Usurpation and the Language of Legitimation 1399–1422* (1998)

P. and F. Strong, 'The Last Will and Codicils of Henry V', *EHR*, 96, pp. 79–102

James Tait, 'Did Richard II Murder the Duke of Gloucester?', in T. F. Tout and James Tait (eds), *Historical Essays by Members of the Owens College Manchester* (1902)

Frank Taylor, 'The Chronicle of John Strecche for the Reign of Henry V, 1414–1422', *Bulletin of the John Rylands Library, Manchester*, 16 (1932), pp. 137–87

Frank Taylor and John S. Roskell (eds), *Gesta Henrici Quinti: the Deeds of Henry the Fifth* (Oxford, 1975)

Testamenta Vetusta: Sir Nicholas Harris Nicolas (ed.), *Testamenta Vetusta: Illustrations from Wills of Manners, Customs, etc. from the Reign of Henry the Second to the Accession of Elizabeth I*, vol. 1 (1826)

TNA: The National Archives, Kew

TTGME: Ian Mortimer, *The Time Traveller's Guide to Medieval England* (2008)

Alexandre Tuetey (ed.), *Journal de Nicolas de Baye, Greffier du Parlement de Paris 1400–1417*, vol. 2 (Paris, 1888)

J. A. Twemlow (ed.), *Calendar of Entries in the Papal Registers relating to Great Britain and Ireland: Papal Letters vol. 6: 1404–1415* (1904)

Anthony Tuck, 'The Earl of Arundel's Expedition to France, 1411', in Dodd and Biggs (eds), *Rebellion and Survival*, pp. 228–39

Nicholas Upton, *De Studio Militari* (1654)

M. G. A. Vale, *English Gascony 1399–1453* (Oxford, 1970)

Richard Vaughan, *John the Fearless: the Growth of Burgundian Power* (1966)

Andrew L. J. Villalon and Donald J. Kagay (eds), *The Hundred Years War* (Leiden, 2004)

J. Webb (ed.), 'A Translation of a French Metrical History', *Archaeologia*, 20 (1824), pp. 13–239

Ralph Willett, 'Memoir on British Naval Architecture', *Archaeologia*, 11, pp. 154–99

C. M. Woolgar, *The Senses in Medieval England* (2006)

James Hamilton Wylie, *A History of England under Henry the Fourth* (4 vols, 1884–98)

James Hamilton Wylie and William Templeton Waugh, *The Reign of Henry the Fifth* (Cambridge, 3 vols, 1914–29)

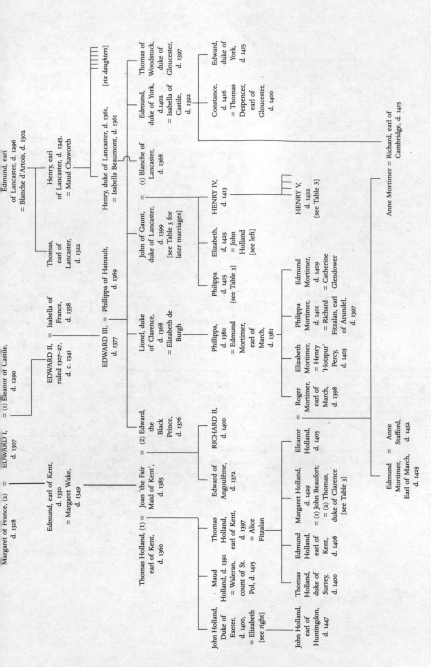

Table 1: THE ENGLISH ROYAL FAMILY BEFORE 1399

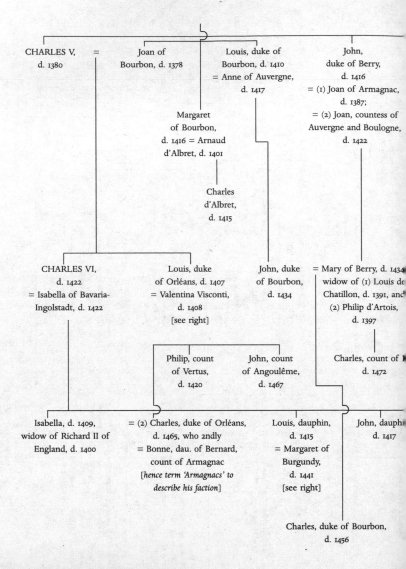

Table 2: THE FRENCH ROYAL FAMILY

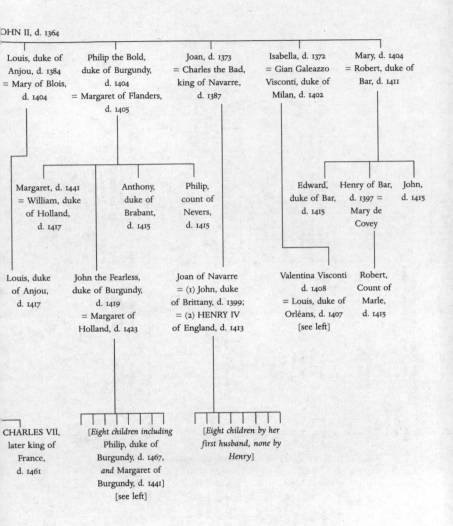

JOHN II, d. 1364

Louis, duke of Anjou, d. 1384 = Mary of Blois, d. 1404

Philip the Bold, duke of Burgundy, d. 1404 = Margaret of Flanders, d. 1405

Joan, d. 1373 = Charles the Bad, king of Navarre, d. 1387

Isabella, d. 1372 = Gian Galeazzo Visconti, duke of Milan, d. 1402

Mary, d. 1404 = Robert, duke of Bar, d. 1411

Margaret, d. 1441 = William, duke of Holland, d. 1417

Anthony, duke of Brabant, d. 1415

Philip, count of Nevers, d. 1415

Edward, duke of Bar, d. 1415

Henry of Bar, d. 1397 = Mary de Covey

John, d. 1415

Louis, duke of Anjou, d. 1417

John the Fearless, duke of Burgundy, d. 1419 = Margaret of Holland, d. 1423

Joan of Navarre = (1) John, duke of Brittany, d. 1399; = (2) HENRY IV of England, d. 1413

Valentina Visconti d. 1408 = Louis, duke of Orléans, d. 1407 [see left]

Robert, Count of Marle, d. 1415

CHARLES VII, later king of France, d. 1461

[*Eight children including* Philip, duke of Burgundy, d. 1467, *and* Margaret of Burgundy, d. 1441] [see left]

[*Eight children by her first husband, none by Henry*]

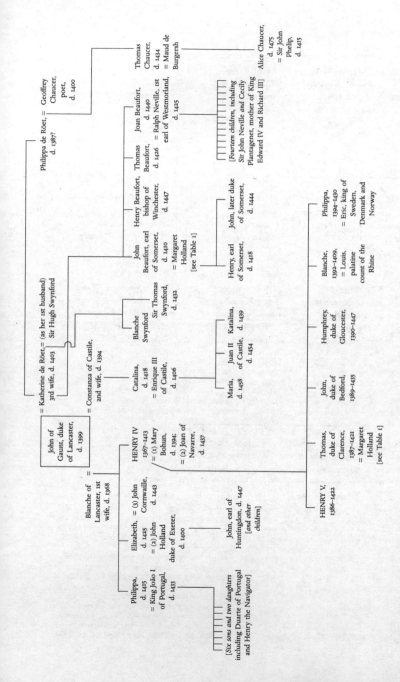

Table 3: THE ENGLISH ROYAL FAMILY AFTER 1399

Index